Future of Business and Fin

More information about this series at http://www.springer.com/series/16360

Satinder Dhiman • Ramanie Samaratunge
Editors

New Horizons in Management, Leadership and Sustainability

Innovative Case Studies and Solutions for Emerging Economies

 Springer

Editors
Satinder Dhiman
School of Business
Woodbury University
Burbank, CA, USA

Ramanie Samaratunge
Department of Management
Monash University
Clayton, VIC, Australia

ISSN 2662-2467   ISSN 2662-2475   (electronic)
Future of Business and Finance
ISBN 978-3-030-62173-5   ISBN 978-3-030-62171-1   (eBook)
https://doi.org/10.1007/978-3-030-62171-1

This Springer imprint is published by the registered company Springer Nature Switzerland AG
The registered company address is: Gewerbestrasse 11, 6330 Cham, Switzerland

This volume is humbly dedicated to our sisters and brothers serving in the Emerging Economies, in particular those working together to transform knowledge into action to achieve a humane, healthy and inclusive world.

Introduction

"No one ever makes a billion dollars. You take a billion dollars."
~Alexandria Ocasio-Cortez to the author Ta-Nehisi Coates[1]

This edited volume had its genesis in the 16th International Conference on Business Management (ICBM) held during December, 12–14, 2019 at Monash University (Caulfield campus) in Melbourne, Australia—hosted by Monash Business School, in partnership with the Faculty of Management Studies and Commerce, University of Sri Jayewardenepura (USJ), and the Sri Lanka Institute of Development Administration (SLIDA). The resonant theme of the conference was: *'Transforming knowledge into action: Towards sustainable development in emerging economies.'*

The conference touched on some key elements of knowledge creation and dissemination. Knowledge is undoubtedly a critical force in economic development. Knowledge is all the more important today as we live in an increasingly knowledge-rich world where new ideas, new modes of thinking and new discoveries push the boundaries of our understanding on a daily basis. Yet knowledge by itself adds little value to development efforts. The emphasis is on *transforming* knowledge into action so that novel projects are implemented, products and services are created, and tangible outcomes achieved. To do so, new knowledge must be created as well as existing knowledge be disseminated and shared. This knowledge must then be transformed into relevant action. Thus, to drive economic growth and competitiveness, countries must not only promote reliable and useful knowledge creation and assimilation but also harness and transform this knowledge effectively into policy and practices. United Nation's Sustainable Development Goals (SDGs) emphasize creating shared prosperity across countries by ending extreme poverty and achieving sustainable development. We believe that the creation of knowledge and effective transformation of knowledge into action are essential antecedents for achieving SDGs.

---

[1] US Congresswoman Rep. Alexandria Ocasio-Cortez told author Ta-Nehisi Coates at a Martin Luther King Jr. Day event during the week of January 20, 2020. See: AOC Calls Out Billionaires at MLK Day Event | NowThis. Retrieved August 8, 2020: https://www.youtube.com/watch?v=lAnRUepeb_U

Yet many countries in the world still struggle to harness the power of knowledge for achieving sustainable development. Emerging economies in particular with their weak institutions and low resource base, often lag behind in relevant and useful knowledge production as well as in transforming such knowledge into wealth and development. This conference aims to explore the many pathways that enable emerging countries to transform knowledge into action to achieve economic and sustainable development. We take a holistic approach to 'transforming knowledge' that goes beyond the mere 'application of knowledge' i.e., knowledge created in one context applied as it is to another context. Instead our definition of transformation includes the assimilation, adaptation, and contextualization of knowledge to suit the unique contexts, needs and conditions existing in emerging countries.

Truly global in scope and strength, this volume highlights the concerted efforts of more than 60 scholar-practitioners to understand and share their findings regarding the broader themes of management, entrepreneurship, macroeconomic policy, health care policy, leadership, and sustainability.

The following pages provide a synoptic overview of the various sections and chapters in this volume.

Part I, comprising five chapters, focuses on *Organization Studies*.
- In Chapter 1, authors opine that perceived quality is the single most important determinant of brand value for a given brand. Through secondary data analysis on fourteen countries, they identified the brand value gap that exists between Sri Lanka and other nations within and outside the region. For this, an aggregate measure was defined as the mean per capita brand value (MPCBV). It was found that Sri Lanka does not perform badly in MPCBV at regional level, but compared to developed nations, Sri Lanka lags way behind, in part because developed countries are branded highly as nations. The chapter proposed a conceptual framework to suggest avenues to increase the competitiveness of Sri Lankan products and services globally. Its conceptual framework demonstrates that the role of quality can be analytically generalized to any developing nation.
- In Chapter 2, the authors identify the impact of CSP on firm financial performance of listed companies in Colombo Stock Exchange. Further the study investigated the moderating effect of ownership structure on the above relationship. Data for the study was collected from 30 companies which are listed under Chemical & Pharmaceutical sector, Beverage Foods and Tobacco, Hotel and Manufacturing sector for the six-year period from 2013 to 2018. Return on Equity (ROE) and Return on Assets (ROA) were used to measure the firm financial performance. Results of the study revealed that there is a significant positive impact of corporate social performance on financial performance of listed companies. Moreover, the study revealed that the ownership concentration negatively moderates the relationship between corporate social performance and firm's financial performance. Findings of the study can help policy makers and regulators to better identify how the ownership concentration is associated with firm incentives to engage in social performance which leads towards better financial performance.

- Chapter 3 explores the moderating role of firm size on the relationship between capital structure and performance of Pakistani textile sector. The study extracted statistics from the annual reports of the textile firms listed at Pakistan Stock Exchange (PSE) from 2010 to 2017. The study applies several panel data diagnostic tests and then projected a Feasible Generalized Least Squares (FGLS) regression model for testing primary and moderated effects of firm size on capital structure-performance relation by taking asset tangibility as a control variable. The study outcomes depict that 65% assets of Pakistani textile companies are financed by debt, suggesting that textile companies are functioning with high levels of financial leverage. The total debt ratio of firms is moderately highly leveraged, as the average value is around 65%. The research has important practical consequences that will help textile industry financial managers adopt the optimal mix of capital structure when debt borrowing could enhance performance.

- Chapter 4 aims to investigate the influence of innovative marketing strategy on the development of MSMEs in Sri Lanka. Primary data collection was adopted to collect data from owners of MSMEs by using questionnaires. Stratified proportionate random sampling method was utilized to select samples. A total of 686 valid questionnaires were collected from respondents. The researcher used exploratory factor analysis to identify the dimensions of factors and structural equation modeling to investigate the strength of the relationship among variables. The result of study proved that MSMEs enhance their performance through innovative marketing strategy. In particular, application of the innovative marketing strategy for MSMEs caused an increase in the internal process performance, customer performance, learning and growth performance and financial performance. This research indicates that owners of MSMEs need to apply the innovative marketing strategy to develop their firms and to upgrade micro firms towards small and medium level.

- Chapter 5 investigates how organizational culture influenced successful and unsuccessful operationalization of the Balanced Scorecard (BSC) in a clustered apparel firm in Sri Lanka, illuminating the influence of human and non-human actors. Actor-Network Theory (ANT) was adopted as the theoretical lens, incorporating a qualitative, case-study approach; data were gathered from interviews and documentary evidence. Findings revealed that the cluster which possessed a hierarchical culture failed in operationalization of BSC, while the cluster which possessed a clan culture (friendly, team-oriented and innovative culture) succeeded in operationalization of the BSC. The divisional leaders of the clusters were key actors who shaped their divisional controls. Middle-level managers and lower-level employees also influenced operationalization of the management controls from the grass roots level. Non-human actors such as ERP systems and training on the BSC influenced operationalization of the BSC. Our study also revealed the existence of a subculture within a cluster (Cluster X) that led it to fail BSC operationalization while illuminating that the other cluster, which did not have any subcultures, succeeded in operationalization of BSC.

Part II, comprising four chapters, focuses on *Entrepreneurship Studies*.

- Chapter 6 examines the direct and indirect effects of informal-sector micro-entrepreneurs' political and business connections on their self-efficacy and firm performance via the mediating role of perceived-support from the institutional environment in an emerging economy, Sri Lanka. Findings using matched survey data from 635 entrepreneurs and their case officers reveal that micro-entrepreneurs' utilization of business ties and political ties impact firm performance through the mediated role of the perceived support from the regulatory and cognitive environments and self-efficacy. We argue that, for informal-sector micro-entrepreneurs, their business and political connections provide a crucial link to the formal institutional environment thereby increasing their self-efficacy and performance.

- In Chapter 7, authors observe that current understanding of women entrepreneurs in emerging economies remains limited despite the fact that women entrepreneurs are rapidly growing across the globe. In particular, there are few empirical findings on how women entrepreneurs identify opportunities, access resources and develop business networks. Floriculture is a booming agribusiness in Sri Lanka, especially for women growers. This research identifies the social reality of respondents and examines it objectively. The research used a mixed design, with questionnaire surveys. The interview sample was of floriculturists in Western Province. Variables of influence included support from family and supports from institutes. The study found that 76% of the women sampled received support from their family and 16% support from other institutes. The results revealed that both strong ties and weak ties play a significant role in determining business growth for Sri Lankan women entrepreneurs.

- Chapter 8 examines how weak and strong network ties of micro-entrepreneurs influence their entrepreneurial self-efficacy, and thereby micro-enterprise performance, in the informal sector of Sri Lanka. Using matched data from 635 micro-entrepreneurs and case officers employed by government, structural equation modelling is employed to test the hypothesized relationships. In line with social cognitive theory, findings confirm that, whereas weak ties lead to enhanced entrepreneurial self-efficacy, strong ties do not. Furthermore, weak ties predicted micro-enterprise performance through enhancing entrepreneurial self-efficacy. These findings provide new insights into an emerging yet under-researched area.

- Chapter 9 explores the micro and small-scale ventures that are known as vital vectors for eradication of poverty and uplifting the livelihood of the community. Entrepreneurial orientation (EO) in three dimensions – proactiveness, innovativeness and risk-taking ability – provides insights into entrepreneurial behaviour of business holders. The present research is focused on the EO of business holders in turbulent environments towards business performance. The quantitative research was carried out with 92 business holders in an industrialised zone in Sri Lanka. The findings revealed that in a changing environment the most vigilant EO dimension is risk-taking ability. In-depth analysis of risk-taking ability showcased that micro and small entrepreneurs in high competitive platforms do not tend to go for high-risk projects. Thus it can be concluded that entrepreneurs in turbulent environments take calculated risks to thrive in the businesses.

Part III, comprising four chapters, focuses on *Environment Management*.

- Chapter 10 aims to explore motivation for listed companies to engage in businesses with varying potential for environmental sensitivity and the types of measures they take towards managing environmental concerns in Sri Lanka. This study applies a Mixed Method Research (MMR) approach, focusing on its one paradigm: QUAL + quan. Using a multi-stage purposeful sampling method, 34 companies were selected from four industry sectors. Data were collected mainly through in-depth interviews and discussion with environmental officers of companies and government authorities (Central Environment Authority – CEA, and Sri Lanka Standard Institution – SLSI) together with a questionnaire survey. Thematic analysis and content analysis were used for qualitative data and frequency tables for quantitative data. Findings reveal that all responding companies typically take measures for environmental protection to comply with environmental legislation, the National Environmental Act, and with SLS ISO EMS standards. This suggests that businesses must improve awareness among all personnel on legal compliance and standards observance.

- In Chapter 11, authors explore the importance of sustainability as vital for manufacturing organizations to address major environmental issues. In response to addressing environmental issues firms need to adopt Green human resource management (GHRM) practices to improve sustainable performance (SP). The purpose of this mixed-method study was to examine the relationship between GHRM practices (Green selection and recruitment, Green training, and development, Green assessment, and rewards) and SP. This study employed an explanatory, sequential, mixed-method design, using both quantitative and qualitative data. The results showed that GHRM practices have a positive relationship with SP, and major themes of green HRM practices emerged to explain SP. This chapter makes novel contributions to green HRM and sustainability performance but also adheres to inherent limitations and outlines directions for future research.

- Chapter 12 provides an empirical analysis to discover significant determinants of environmental management (waste treatment, energy reduction, recycling, remanufacturing, environmental design and environmental management systems) that managers may need in order to achieve environmental sustainability within their organization. The hypothesized relationships of this model are tested with data collected from 30 rubber manufacturing firms in Sri Lanka, using panel models during the period 2012–2016. The study found that, in general, environmental management does not significantly impact on business performance. It also found that environmental investment weakened the relationship between environmental management and business performance. Analysis revealed that only two specific determinants of environmental management, furnace oil usage and environmental design, have a significant impact on performance of a firm.

- Chapter 13 states that the present-day value of a business is judged through multiple dimensions, paying attention to economic, social and environmental concerns. Global megatrends (demographic transitions, urbanization, climate and resources, commodity cycles, technological disruptions, fragility and violence, shifts in the global economy, debate about globalization and many other forces operating in the environment) and challenges are expected because any risk in macro circumstances leads to extreme disruptive challenges and gradual modification of risk in businesses, which will affect the change in equilibrium of businesses and this will manifest in manufacturing processes. A better understanding of the linkages between these trends and the associated changes in economic, social and environmental conditions is needed for long-run survival in businesses.

Part IV, comprising three chapters, focuses on *Macroeconomic Policy*.

- Chapter 14 aims to explore the determinants of economic growth using different methodologies. In the context of developing countries, political shocks and instabilities are found to be a major determinant of economic growth. Thus the main objective of this study is to examine determinants of Real Gross Domestic Product (RGDP) with a special reference to political instability, which is a less examined phenomenon in the local and international literature. The study employed secondary data from 1971 to 2016. RGDP was considered as the dependent variable and foreign direct investment, inflation, population growth, fixed domestic capital formation, trade openness, political instability and the introduction of the open economy concept have been considered as explanatory variables. Population growth rate, inflation and political instability were found to have no significant impact on Sri Lanka's RGDP. These findings have significant policy implications.

- Chapter 15 examines the association between budget deficit and selected macroeconomic variables in Sri Lanka, Malaysia and South Korea, 2000–2016. The Sri Lankan finding was that there was uni-directional causality between the variables. In the Malaysian study, there was no causality between budget deficit and the variables. In South Korea, the study identified uni-directional causality between the variables. The panel analysis suggested that debt and real GDP growth rate are significant variables in controlling a budget deficit. A country's debt level is a significant variable in controlling the size of the deficit. In Sri Lanka, it is important to consider economic policy strategies implemented by Malaysia and South Korea to mitigate prevailing economic issues of a sustained sizable budget deficit, significant debt maturities, weaker public finances, and higher domestic and foreign currency debt, all of which disrupt achievement of sustained economic growth.

- Chapter 16 aims to describe the behavior of the All Share Price index (ASPI), which is the broader market price index of the Colombo Stock Exchange (CSE). The behavior of the ASPI was simultaneously analyzed under three different perspectives: macro-economic variables, elections, and the civil war. Monthly ASPI data collected from the Colombo Stock Exchange was utilized in this study as the dependent variable, along with the monthly data collected from the data library of the Central Bank of Sri Lanka from 1994 to 2017 as independent variables. The results revealed that during the post-war period the conditional heteroscedastic nature of the ASPI cannot be found. The study concluded that even the termination of the civil war created a sudden rise in the ASPI and a positive condition where investors can come and invest in Sri Lanka, along with that the economical status of the country and the political status and the events of the country have their influences on the stock market.

Part V, comprising three chapters, focuses on *Higher Education Management.*

- Chapter 17 studies the use of social media in student learning and its effect on academic performance. Social media in higher education has researched by many, but the impact on students' academic performance has not been addressed sufficiently, particularly in Sri Lanka. Hence, the objective of this study is to examine the impact of social media on students' academic performance. A comprehensive model has been formulated and validated using data collected from 320 undergraduates. The measurement model analysis provides adequate construct validity and reliability and the structural model provides a good model fit. Of ten hypotheses, nine are supported. The findings reveal that integrating social media in teaching and learning can assist in enhancing students' academic performance.

- Chapter 18 aims to explore how the entrepreneurial leader builds an Entrepreneurial University through assessing the role of a Vice Chancellor in the implementation of this concept in a Sri Lankan state university. Qualitative approach (a case study) is adopted using interviews with current and former Vice Chancellors of the University of Delta which was supported by documentary evidence. The Triple Helix Model is applied to illuminate the leaders' role in building an EU. Accordingly, it was revealed that Vice Chancellors contributed in building an EU through acting as the key collaborating agents that link the university, government and industry while integrating these sectors into a single platform; being creative and innovative; strengthening staff; providing leadership for projects to raise quality of higher education. Finally, all these actions link together in building an EU which ensures production of graduates possessing entrepreneurial behavior, convergence of academic entrepreneurship while securing quality and sustainability of the higher education institution.

- Chapter 19 explains the imperative of linking with micro small medium enterprises (MSMEs) as vital contributors to the process of commercialization of new knowledge discovered in the higher education sector. Higher Education in management has the greatest challenge to equalize graduates' knowledge and skills with existing employment opportunities. MSMEs are job creators in the economy and contributors to sustainable development. If the education system of higher education in management does not withstand future needs, this will impair the social, economic and environment conditions of the country. To sustain the balance in these three pillars of sustainability, management graduates who will be future managers should be educated well with the needed skills and knowledge through a sustainable curriculum, which can be enriched with the linkage with the MSMEs during study, a milestone for business startup, employment opportunities and industry intakes.

Part VI, comprising two chapters, focuses on *Human Resource Management*.

- Chapter 20 examines envy, one of the rampant negative emotions in the workplace, and its impact on job engagement. The study was conducted on a sample of 162 academic staff members working as full-time academics in private higher educational institutes in the Colombo District. Data were collected through a standard and validated questionnaire survey. The results of the study found that there is a significant impact of feeling envied by others and feeling envious of others on emotional and cognitive engagement. However, there is no impact of feeling envied by others and feeling envious of others on physical engagement. The study illustrated that feeling envied by others and feeling envious of others are negatively associated with emotional engagement, whereas feeling envied by others and feeling envious of others are positively associated with cognitive engagement. The study proposes that managing employee envy is worthwhile because it leads them to better engage themselves in their work role physically, emotionally and cognitively.

- Chapter 21 presents a model for successful implementation of HR analytics. New technologies, digitization and artificial intelligence create demand within organizations for different skill sets as well as new ways of working. On the world stage, the Asian region is expected to grow fastest in HR analytics due to rapid digital transformation. HR analytics enables organizations to make evidence-based strategic business decisions that lead to achieving a sustained competitive advantage. Hence, HR analytics will be an innovative addition for effective talent management of organizations. Although some organizations practice HR analytics, it is observed that the adoption and diffusion of HR analytics are still sluggish in emerging markets. In this chapter, we apply the diffusion of innovation theory to examine the factors that affect the adoption and diffusion of HR analytics in Sri Lanka as an empirical context. The objectives are to understand the current state of HR analytics, identify the challenges and barriers to implement HR analytics and build a model for the successful implementation of HR analytics.

Part VII, comprising two chapters, focuses on *Corporate Governance*.

- Chapter 22 explores corporate social responsibility (CSR) reporting practices of Chinese MNCs. It studies how EMNCs manage sustainability reporting in the outward foreign direct investment (FDI), helping both practitioners and researchers to address challenges these EMNCs may face. This paper addresses this research gap by selecting China, a leading emerging economy. We review the key strands within the field of CSR reporting and the status quo of the CSR research in China. In developing new significant areas of enquiry, we draw on a specific context, the Australian Mining Industry, to further highlight differences in, for instance, legitimizing strategies between Australia and China. We illuminate challenges facing Chinese MNCs in managing CSR reporting when conducting outward FDI. We propose areas where CSR research could be developed in the context of Chinese MNCs.

- Chapter 23 examines the nature and the level of compliance with corporate governance best practices in Sri Lankan listed companies using a constructed Corporate Governance Index (CGI). It aims to examine the relationship between corporate governance and corporate performance. This study was conducted as a quantitative study based on the annual reports of 133 public listed companies in Sri Lanka in 18 different sectors for the period 2009–2016. The constructed CGI covered five corporate governance categories: Board of Directors, Shareholders, Chief Executive Officer (CEO) and Management, Communication and Disclosure, and Stakeholders. The results indicated a significant positive relationship between financial performance in terms of Return on Equity (ROE) and Return on Assets (ROA) with the level of compliance with corporate governance principles and a negative relationship with market performance in terms of Tobin's Q with such principles. The analysis further revealed a positive relationship between the stakeholder sub-index, the CEO and Management sub-index and the Communication and Disclosure sub-index and corporate financial and market performance indicators. The findings of this study are expected to have significant policy implications.

Part VIII, comprising one chapter, focuses on *Health Policy and Healthcare Management*.

- Chapter 24 presents some lessons from Sri Lanka regarding behavior change to improve dietary diversity of pregnant mothers through counselling. Sri Lanka being a middle-income country performs outstandingly in health-related indicators at par with the developed world. Despite continuous political commitment, together with the dedication of health professionals, it still has been unable to reach the desired level in nutritional indicators. The opportunity of improving maternal nutrition without being an economic burden to the country is worthy of studying. The objective of the study was to improve dietary diversity of pregnant mothers through nutritional counselling, in the Kalutara district. The study was a cluster-randomized community trial (n = 270 per arm) conducted in two phases. The 1st phase was a nutritional counselling training to intervention group PHMM, and the 2nd phase was intervening to change the diet of the pregnant mother through PHMM. Pregnant mothers were recruited to the study before 12 weeks of gestation and followed up until the delivery to assess the birth outcome. During the pregnancy, PHMM were intervening strike through the pregnant mother and her family with nutritional counselling.

Part IX, comprising one chapter, focuses on *Democratic Governance*.

- Chapter 25 explores the phenomena of perplexing coexistence of democracy, transparency and development in the contemporary era. Though both democracy and development are two conventional words in the modern world, but the interrelation between them is crucial. Democracy is one of the state principles that can act as an important catalyst to make development more viable. We can consider democracy as the process where development is the output. Economist Amartya Sen defined development as a process of expanding the real freedoms that people enjoy. And democracy is the process of institutionalization of that freedom. So the correlation between democratization and development is quite inherent. Sen's view is now widely accepted: development must be judged by its impact on people, not only by changes in their income but more generally in terms of their choices, capabilities and freedoms. We should be concerned about the distribution of these improvements, not just the simple average for a society. However, recently diverse winds of democracy are blowing that are affecting the trend of development. This chapter explores the current state of interrelation between democracy and development based on secondary data and empirical knowledge. It develops a compact understanding about the contemporary interrelation between democracy and development.

Part X, comprising one chapter, focuses on *Disaster Management*.
- Chapter 26 investigates Jeddah city, rapidly expanding in the number of buildings and population, to address the rapid evaluation of residential buildings using the Rapid Evaluation Method (REM) to assess building stock to determine hazard and evaluating vulnerability with scoring method from FEMA 155. Two districts were selected based on cluster analysis of population and building data. One is a developing urbanized area, and the other is a traditional area. This offers a possibility to compare the vulnerability of buildings built according to different seismic codes and to make assumptions about the rest of the city based on typical structures. The basic structural score was determined considering the building structure and moderate seismicity of the region using score modifiers, e.g., vertical irregularity and soil score modifier, assuming sabkhas. The result of the investigation shows different levels of vulnerability and areas where intervention is needed.

Part XI, comprising one chapter, focuses on *Spirituality and Management*.
- Chapter 27 explores the influence of Buddhist philosophy, as a motivator for sustainability reporting (SR) by companies, in a developing country setting. The data was collected through semi-structured interviews with managers of listed and non-listed companies in Sri Lanka, a country ingrained in Buddhist philosophy for over two and a half millennia. The findings indicate that corporate social responsibility has been practiced in Sri Lankan society from ancient times. The beliefs, thinking patterns and mindset of listed and non-listed company managers, born and raised under Buddhist background, is heavily influenced by Buddhist teachings of 'kamma', rebirth, conservation, empathy and social sustainability. Evidenced in the study is the translation of personal values to corporate values as the motivation for sustainability projects and SR. Contrary behavior demonstrated by a large conglomerate and a subsidiary of a multinational company indicated these companies did not appreciate the local values and beliefs inspired by Buddhist philosophy.

The last chapter pertaining to the Buddhist philosophy is a fitting coda to this volume. We, all educators, are little Bodhisattvas who have avowed to work ceaselessly toward the twin goals of wisdom and compassion, and to share our knowledge until every single human being on this planet is liberated from the economic grind.

Satinder Dhiman
Ramanie Samaratunge

Contents

The original version of this book was revised. The correction is available at
https://doi.org/10.1007/978-3-030-62171-1_28

About the Editors

Satinder Dhiman Recognized as a lead thinker for his pioneer contributions to the field of transformational leadership, workplace spirituality, workplace wellbeing, sustainability, and fulfillment in personal and professional arena, Professor Dhiman is a sought after Keynote speaker at regional, national and international conferences. In 2013, Dr. Dhiman was invited to be the opening speaker at the prestigious TEDx Conference @ College of the Canyons in Santa Clarita, California. Since then, he has led several major national and international conferences as co-organizer and/or as track chair.

With an instructional and research focus on leadership and organizational behavior—and with specific concentration on sustainability, workplace spirituality and wellbeing—Professor Dhiman holds a PhD in Social Sciences from Tilburg University, Netherlands, an EdD in Organizational Leadership from Pepperdine University, Los Angeles, an MBA from West Coast University, Los Angeles, and a Master's degree in Commerce from Panjab University, Chandigarh, India, having earned the Gold Medal. *He has also completed advanced Executive Leadership Programs at Harvard, Stanford, and Wharton.*

Recipient of several prominent national and international academic and professional honors, Dr. Dhiman won the Woodbury University Ambassador of the Year Award in 2015 and 2017 and MBA Professor of the Year Award in 2015; Scholarly and Creative Writing Award, 2019; Most Valuable MBA Professor Award, 2018; Most Inspirational and Most Charismatic MBA Teacher Award 2012, 2013/2014/2018; the Steve Allen Excellence in Education Award in 2006, and *the prestigious ACBSP International Teacher of the Year Award in 2004.* Most recently, Professor Dhiman chaired an all-academy symposium at the Academy of Management that received 2019 Best Symposium Proposal Award. He was also invited by Monash University, Australia, to lead a track in Spirituality in Management in the 16th International Conference in Business Management, held during Dec. 12–15, 2019.

Professor Dhiman has done over 50 Conference Presentations and more than 50 Invited Keynotes, Plenary Sessions, Distinguished Key Guest Lectures and Creative Workshops—*nationally and internationally* and have published over 60 peer-reviewed journal articles and book chapters. Author, translator, editor, co-author, co-editor of over 35 management, leadership, spirituality, sustainability and accounting-related books and research monographs, his recent books include: *Bhagavad Gītā and Leadership: A Catalyst for Organizational Transformation* (2019—Palgrave Macmillan); *Managing by the Bhagavad Gītā: Timeless Lessons for Today's Managers* (2018—Springer; with Amar); *Holistic Leadership* (Palgrave 2017), *Gandhi and Leadership* (Palgrave 2015), *Seven Habits of Highly Fulfilled People* (2012); and co-editing and co-authoring, with Marques, *Spirituality and Sustainability* (Springer 2016), *Leadership Today* (Springer, 2016), *Engaged Leadership* (Springer, 2018), *New Horizons in Positive Leadership and Change* (Springer, 2020), and *Social Entrepreneurship and Corporate Social Responsibility* (Springer, 2020). He has also translated several Indian spiritual classics into English, including the *Sahaja Gītā*.

He is the *Editor-in-Chief* of six multi-author *Major Reference Works*, including: *Springer Handbook of Engaged Sustainability* (2018—Springer International, Switzerland) and *Palgrave Handbook of Workplace Spirituality and Fulfillment* (2018—Palgrave Macmillan, USA); Routledge Companion to Mindfulness at Work (2020); *Palgrave Handbook of Workplace Wellbeing—A* (2021—Palgrave Macmillan); *Editor-in-Chief* of *Palgrave Studies in Workplace Spirituality and Fulfillment; Routledge Frontiers in Sustainable Business;* and co-editor of *Springer Series in Management, Change, Strategy and Positive Leadership.*

Some of his forthcoming titles include *Leading without Power: A Model of Highly Fulfilled Leaders* (2021—Palgrave Macmillan); *Conscious Consumption: Healthy, Humane and Sustainable Living* (2021—Routledge, UK); *Wise Leadership for Turbulent Times* (2021—Routledge, UK); *Creative Leadershift: Discover. Innovate. Enact.* (2022—Routledge, with Chandra Handa); and Editor-in-Chief: *Palgrave Handbook of Servant Leadership* (2022) and *Springer Handbook of Global Leadership and Followership* (2022).

Currently, Professor Dhiman serves as the Associate Dean, Chair and Director of the MBA Program; and as the Professor of Management at Woodbury University, Burbank, California.

He has served as the Chair for a special MBA Program for the Mercedes-Benz executives, China. He was invited as Distinguished Visiting Professor at the Tecnológico de Monterrey, Guadalajara campus, Mexico; and has served as E-Commerce curriculum lead advisor, Universidad Francisco Gavidia, El Salvador, and coordinator for LA Fieldtrip for MBA students for the Berlin University for Professional Studies (DUW). He has served as the President (2016–2018) and now serves as a distinguished *Patron*, International Chamber for Service Industry (ICSI).

Dr. Dhiman has served as Accreditation Consultant, Evaluator, and Site Visit Team Leader for the Accreditation Council for Business Schools and Programs (ACBSP) for more than 25 universities in America, Canada, Europe, and Asia. He has published research with his colleagues in *Journal of Values-Based Leadership*,

Organization Development Journal, Journal of Management Development, Journal of Social Change, Journal of Applied Business and Economics, and *Performance Improvement*.

Professor Dhiman is the Founder-Director of Forever Fulfilled, a Los Angeles-based Wellbeing Consultancy that focuses on workplace wellness, workplace spirituality, and self-leadership.

Ramanie Samaratunge is an Associate Professor in the Department of Management, Monash Business School, Monash University, Australia. Appointed to the University in 1997, she has been an Associate Professor since 2013 and has played a key role in the Department's creation and implementation of 'Flagship Programs' for public sector training in the South Asian Region.

Associate Professor Samaratunge is a highly successful supervisor of honours, master's and PhD research, with an outstanding record in guiding and mentoring her students to successful completion and subsequent careers. Within in the University and in the Department of Management she has served as a Department Representative on the Faculty Board, deputy Director – Education, and as a member of the Human Ethics Committee. She is also acknowledged as a committed, caring teacher at all levels in her areas of expertise, and she has been a significant contributor to the development and review of policy and management programs in a number of graduate and undergraduate courses in the Department of Management.

Her extensive community engagement, with particular emphasis on Sri Lanka, where she was born, has included a foundational role in establishing the Past Pupils' Association of Anula Vidyalaya, Victoria, to foster continuing association with alumnae of the School now resident in Australia, and a valuable scholarship program to promote the education of young women at secondary and tertiary level in Sri Lanka. She is also an Executive Member of the Alumni Association of Sri Jayewardenepura University.

She is an internationally renowned management scholar with 30 years' experience working in the public and private sector, including consultancies in Australia and Asia. She was previously at the University of Sri Jayewardenepura, from which she also graduated with first class honours in Public Administration (Bachelor of Science (Honour) and where she subsequently completed a Diploma I Applied Statistics (First Class). She completed her MA in Carleton University, Canada. She holds a PhD from Monash University, Australia. She has served on international and local advisory bodies and is a member of many international professional bodies.

She has been a Visiting Fellow at the Institute for Development Policy and Management, University of Manchester (United Kingdom), at the Institute for Human Development, India, at the Sri Lanka Institute of Development Administration, Colombo, Sri Lanka, and at the University of Sri Jayewardenepura

Associate Professor Samaratunge has published a number of book chapters, several government and industry reports, and journal articles in leading international management journals such as International Journal of Intercultural Relations, Australian Journal of Management, Journal of Business Ethics and Human Relations. She is represented in conference proceedings and invited keynote speeches. She also reviews for many top-ranking journals. Her co-authored book (2015), *Skilled Migration, Expectation and Reality: Chinese Professionals and the Global Labour Market*, has marked a very significant contribution to the understanding of workplace integration challenges for Asian-region skilled immigrants, whose role in Australia's migration program is pivotal to the national economy and a key linkage with countries in the region – notably Australia's largest trading partner.

Since 2010, she has been instrumental in establishing and leading Monash University programs in partnership with the Sri Lanka Institute of Development Administration and with funding from the (Commonwealth) Department of Foreign Affairs and Trade in Australia. These programs have significantly enhanced the operational and research capacity of public officials in Sri Lanka and become model programs for a number of other developing countries including Bangladesh and Nepal. From 2010 to 2015 she was formally an Advisor to SLIDA, and the close partnership between SLIDA and Monash University continues with her close involvement in the ongoing development of training programs. The programs have underpinned capability building and service delivery at the grassroots level as essential pathways to transitioning developing or emerging economies to become successful global representatives of countries that have been able to address endemic poverty and disadvantage. A key feature of the programs, in addition to the rich balance of industry, government and expert workshops offered within Australia, and balanced by in-country programs, has been the close mentoring for participants to develop projects of immediate value to their own home districts and country, and to which they themselves have a deep personal and professional commitment. Participants propose what is needed, and the mentoring continues during the program to the point where the participants return and implement their plans in their home country, and then the implementation is evaluated and used to inform future work and training – and program development. At every stage, expert mentoring is provided through Dr. Samaratunge's efforts and the enthusiastic engagement of her colleagues at Monash University and at SLIDA.

Between 2014 and 2019 she received, with colleagues, no fewer than 16 grants for research and training projects, and has initiated further applications to extend Monash University's regional engagement to Japan. In the same period she co-authored 22 refereed journal articles, with a further 11 in train. In addition to her 2015 book, she has co-authored a further four books. In 2012 she was instrumental in mounting the highly successful NAPSIPAG Conference in Colombo, a first for Sri Lanka.

Associate Professor Samaratunge has received numerous awards, including a Dean's commendation for research impact in 2014, and a Dean's commendation for Innovation and External Collaboration in 2013 for research in collaboration at

Monash University. These have acknowledged the substantial impact that her research on her own behalf and in collaboration have had on the wider community, both academic and professional and both national and international.

Her research interests include international public policy and management, cross-cultural management, CSR, entrepreneurship and immigrants in Australia, and her supervision of students also includes interests in international management, change management, international human resource management and international public policy. She has also demonstrated an enviable capacity to extend these interests to the very specific, sometimes parallel but quite different projects of her students in domestic (Australian) and international areas of research.

About the Contributors

W. A. Menaka Imashi Abeyratna is a lecturer of the Faculty of Management of Horizon Campus, Sri Lanka. She has been teaching core subjects of human resource management and organizational behaviour at postgraduate and undergraduate levels. She has also been teaching marketing management, strategic management and international business courses to undergraduate students following local and foreign-affiliated degree programmes. Her research interests span the business management spectrum, focusing on the areas of organizational behavior, organizational psychology, human resource management and marketing management. She completed her Master of Science degree in Management from the University of Sri Jayewardenepura, and her Bachelor of Science degree in Management with a First Class Honours from the University College Dublin-National University of Ireland.

Lakmal Abeysekera is a Lecturer in the Department of Management in the Monash Business School, Monash University, Australia. He conducts research in the areas of work- family conflict, flipped classrooms, culture and work values. His research has been published in leading international journals such as International Journal of Human Resource Management, Asia Pacific Journal of Management, and Higher Education Research and Development.

Thanuksha Abeywardana is an officer in Sri Lanka Administrative Service. She is currently serving as Senior Consultant at Sri Lanka Institute of Development Administration (SLIDA), Colombo 07. Previously she held executive positions at Ministry of Home Affairs. She read for her B.Sc. (Special) degree in Zoology, Master in Environment Science, Master in Business Administration from the University of Peradeniya in Sri Lanka. She obtained Post Graduate Diploma in e-Governance from Postgraduate Institute of Management, University of Sri Jayewardenepura, Sri Lanka. Later she studied at International Christian University, Tokyo, Japan and obtained Master of Art in International Relations.

Anas Ahmed is affiliated with the College of Engineering, University of Jeddah, Saudi Arabia, with a 2010 PhD in Industrial Engineering, University of Miami, Florida. Positions held include in 2017 Vice Dean, College of Engineering, University of Jeddah, and 2014 Chairman, Department of Industrial Engineering, University of Jeddah.

A. R. Ajward is a senior lecturer and researcher attached to the Department of Accounting, Faculty of Management Studies and Commerce, University of Sri Jayewardenepura, and has a service of almost 15 years. He is also a Fellow of the Institute of Chartered Accountants of Sri Lanka and Fellow of the Institute of Certified Management Accountants of Sri Lanka. He serves as the General Secretary of the Research Council of University of Sri Jayewardenepura, and the Editor of Chief in journals including the Journal of Applied Research of CA Sri Lanka. His research interests span areas of corporate governance, professional ethics, auditing and assurance, accounting education and financial reporting. He has more than 50 refereed publications in these areas. He has recently ventured into exploring data analytics in accounting with special emphasis on accounting fraud.

V. I. Amaratunge is an independent researcher and a postgraduate candidate reading for a Master's in International Business at the Melbourne Business School, the University of Melbourne. He obtained his bachelor's degree, B.Com (Special) Degree with a class-standing from the Faculty of Management Studies and Commerce, University of Sri Jayewardenepura, Sri Lanka in 2019. He is also a passed-finalist of the Chartered Institute of Management Accountants (CIMA), United Kingdom. Visitha has a service history of almost four years in the fields of accounting, finance and consultancy. His research interests span the areas of corporate governance, professional ethics, auditing and assurance, accounting education and financial reporting and business and development economics.

Bhadra J. H. Arachchige is a Senior Lecturer in HRM at the Department of HRM, Faculty of Management Studies and Commerce, University of Sri Jayewardenepura. She was the former coordinator of the MBA program and the first head of the Department of Human Resources Management. She has been teaching core subjects of human resource management and research methodology in the MBA program and undergraduate level. She has published widely across a range of fields and has presented papers at various international conferences. Her research interests are in organizational psychology, and contemporary issues HRM.

Uzma Bashir is currently a Lecturer in the School of Commerce & Accountancy and an Assistant Director QEC (Quality Assurance Cell) at Minhaj University, responsible for completing the Self-Assessment process for over 100 degree programs and providing administrative support to all the teaching faculty. Qualifications include an MBA from the well-reputed business school of Lahore city and two publications in both national and international journals.

S. Buvanendra is a senior lecturer attached to the Department of Finance at University of Colombo, Sri Lanka. She holds BBA (Hons.) degree with finance specialization from University of Jaffna; MBA in General Management with Merit pass from University of Colombo; PhD with finance specialization from the Pondicherry Central University, India. She is a recipient of the Indian Commonwealth Scholarship in 2012. In addition, she is a recipient of prestigious Australian Award

Fellowship (AAF) in 2017. Her research interests are in the areas of capital structure, corporate governance, behavioral finance and entrepreneurship. She has published a number of articles in reputed international and local journals.

G. D. T. D. Chandrasiri is a lecturer (Probationary) in the Department of IT, Faculty of Management Studies and Commerce, University of Sri Jayewardenepura. She is graduated in B.Sc. in Information Systems (Special) degree with a first class from the same university. Her research interests focus mainly on e-Learning, blended learning, and technology acceptance. Her work has been presented in international conferences and has been published in international journals.

N. W. K. D. K. Dayarathna is a senior lecturer at the University of Sri Jayewardenepura, Sri Lanka. He has served as a visiting lecturer and a tutor at La Trobe University, Swinburne University, Ballarat University and Melbourne Institute of Technology in Australia. He received a BMgt in HRM from the University of Kelaniya and his Masters degree in HRM from the University of Sri Jayewardenepura, Sri Lanka. He received his PhD in HRM from La Trobe University. His areas of expertise include HRM, High Performance Work Systems and Case Study Method in Research. Dr. Dayarathna is an active researcher and author. He completed his PhD in 2016 and continues to be a researcher with publications in reputed international journals such as Review of International Business and Strategy and Thunderbird International Business Review.

Pathmani Mangalika de Silva is a locally and globally recognised leader in international management systems, namely quality, food safety, environment and occupational health and safety in the capacity of system auditor, trainer, and consultant. Currently Mangalika is the President for Asia Pacific Quality Organization (APQO) headquartered in New Zealand, and the President for Sri Lanka Association for Quality. Previously she worked at Sri Lanka Standards Institution in various capacities and as National Quality Award Examiner. Mangalika received her first quality related training in Japan, on TQM and certification systems. Mangalika is the recipient of a number of international awards, including APQO's MMG Medal for Professional Women in Global Quality Leadership 2010 in Nepal, and APQO Award for Woman in Quality Leadership 2016 in New Zealand, in recognition of her contribution in promoting quality management in the region. Currently, Mangalika is a doctoral candidate at the University of Sri Jayewardenepura.

S. H. P. de Silva is a medical doctor graduated from University of Colombo with both Master's degree and Doctorate degree in Community Medicine. He became the head of the department in the Department of Research and Evaluation, National Institute of Health Sciences, Kalutara, Sri Lanka immediately after his post-graduate training. From there, he contributed to the massive development of the institute until it becomes the first collaborative public health training institute to the World Health Organization from the South East Asian Region. He takes the leadership in Research and Evaluation training to public health staff in Sri Lanka. He is a pioneer researcher in incorporating GIS technology into health system research in the country.

K. S. Dilhani is an officer of Sri Lanka Administrative Service from 2006. Currently she is serving as the Divisional Secretary, Seethawaka, Sri Lanka. Previously she also held several government executive positions in the Ministry of home affairs, labor and indigenous medicine. She obtained her bachelor degree in Economics from University of Peradeniya. Sri Lanka and M. A. in Applied Economics from the same University. Further she received Diploma in Public Administration from Sri Lanka Institute of Development Administration (SLIDA).

D. B. P. H. Dissabandara is a Senior Professor of Finance and Corporate Governance and the immediate past Head of the Department of Finance of the University of Sri Jayewardenepura. At present he is also the Vice Chancellor and CEO of the Saegis Campus. He is the former Deputy Secretary General of the National Economic Council of Sri Lanka and the Director General of SEC of Sri Lanka. He was the first Professor of Finance and Governance in Sri Lanka. His major areas of specialization are Corporate Finance and Corporate Governance; and his main areas of teaching include Corporate Finance, Corporate Governance, Auditing and Strategic Management. He has also held chairmanships and director-ships in several companies and some voluntary positions such as Member of the University Council, Board of Management of the Postgraduate Institute of Management, and Chairman – Strategic Planning and Faculty Accreditation Committee. He is also a member of Chartered Institute for Securities & Investment, UK.

D. M. S. B. Dissanayake has more than 11 years' experience in lecturing, with a career starting as a Computer Instructor. After completing them first degree, the author started a career as a Visiting Lecturer, followed by a Post Graduate Diploma in Economic Development, Masters of Financial Economics and Masters in Economics at the University of Colombo. While reading for a PhD degree, the author conducts visiting Lectures for the MFE Degree at the University and has also joined the Aquinas College of Higher Studies as a Senior Lecturer, and is currently Head of the Research Centre at the ACHS.

D. H. S. W. Dissanayake is a Senior Lecturer and Researcher at the Department of Accountancy, Faculty of Business Studies and Finance, Wayamba University of Sri Lanka. She is currently studying for a PhD in Management at University of Sri Jayewardenepura, and has completed her MSc in Applied Finance there. She has almost eight years' experience in teaching and research. She is passed finalist of the Institute of Chartered Management Accountants (UK). She served as head of the Department of Accountancy and Reviewer of the Journal of Accountancy and Finance and participated in conferences. Her main research areas are Corporate Governance, Corporate Sustainability and Environmental Management Accounting.

Kumudinei Dissanayake is a Professor attached to the Department of Management and Organization Studies, Faculty of Management and Finance, University of Colombo, Sri Lanka. She earned her Doctoral Degree from Meiji University, Japan. Her research interests are in evolving forms of organizations, new modes of working, individual career, women entrepreneurs, and green practices in organizations. She has authored several books and published research papers in local and international journals.

Ummara Fatima is currently working as an Assistant Professor in the School of Commerce & Accountancy (Minhaj University), with an MBA from the well-reputed business school of Lahore city, nine publications in national and international journals, eleven conference presentations, work as a Research Assistant with the office of deputy chairman BOG Minhaj University on national and international projects.

K. R. Gangadhara is currently serving as a Senior Assistant Secretary to the President. He was a Senior Consultant at Sri Lanka Institute of Development Administration (SLIDA) which is the national institute for professional development of executive level officers in the public sector of Sri Lanka. Mr Gangadara is a member of the Sri Lanka Administrative Service. Having joined the public service in 2006 he has worked in several government ministries and departments. He obtained his B. Sc. (Special) degree in Geology from University of Peradeniya and he received the Diploma in Public Administration awarded by Sri Lanka Institute of Development Administration. In 2012, he entered to the prestigious Crawford School of Public Policy of the Australian National University and obtained Master of International & Development Economics.

Lanumodara Fattrishiya Dedunu Zoysa Gunathilaka holds a PhD in Environmental Management & Sustainability, and MSc in Management, University of Sri Jayewardenepura. She graduated from the University of Moratuwa in Sri Lanka specializing in Rubber and Plastic Technology (Polymer Science). She also holds a Diploma, in Quality Management, Sri Lanka Standard Institute (SLSI) and the Engineering Council Exam-Charted Engineering (CEI)-Part 1. Dr. Gunathilaka is currently the Head of Sustainability and Green Manufacturing in Latexco NV, in Belgium. She is a researcher, and author of many academic and professional publications in Management, Environmental Science, Climate Change, Sustainability and Banking & Finance etc., in academic and professional journals. Dr, Dedunu has more than 15 years of extensive national and international experience in Research & Development.

Kennedy D. Gunawardana is a Senior Professor of Accounting Information Systems at the Department of Accounting, University of Sri Jayewardenepura, Sri Lanka. His teaching and research areas are Cost and Management Accounting, Accounting Information Systems, Artificial Neural Networks for Accounting and Research Methodology in Accounting and Finance. Kennedy is the first Sri Lankan link Artificial Intelligence to the field of accounting and finance for corporate sector predictions – he developed a new course unit called Artificial Neural Network for Accounting. Kennedy served as Chairman of the Board of Study in Management from 2010 to 2016, and as the first coordinator of the PhD in Management Program of the Faculty of Management Studies & Commerce, from 2014 to 2020. Kennedy worked as chairman of several public sector and private sector organizations, and is currently a board member of many academic institutions, and a visiting faculty member for many state universities.

R. Navodya Gurusinghe is a PhD student in Human Resource Management at the University of Sri Jayewardenepura, Sri Lanka. She earned her Master of Business Administration from Buckinghamshire New University and her Bachelor of Arts (Hons) in Business Management from the University of Sunderland. She has eight years of work experience in the field of higher education in both public and private institutions. She currently works as a Senior Assistant Registrar at General Sir John Kotelawala Defence University, Sri Lanka. Her research interests include HR analytics and talent management.

N. L. Harmer graduated from Wayamba University of Sri Lanka with BSc Special Degree in Accountancy and Business Finance. Currently she is working at Allianz Insurance Lanka limited, under the tax and regulatory reporting unit. Her research interest includes corporate reporting and accounting practices.

N. Hemachandra is a medical doctor graduated from University of Colombo Sri Lanka with both Master's degree and Doctorate degree in Community Medicine. After completing her Doctorate, she was appointed as the National Programme Officer to Maternal Care at the Family Health Bureau of Sri Lanka. During her career in the Family Health Bureau, she revised the pregnancy record of the country to include risk factors and detail history on past pregnancies. Furthermore, she developed a new care package for pregnant mothers in the country and trained all health staff in the country on the new package establishing the sustainable maternal care addressing current health issues in the field. She is continuing her work towards the betterment of the maternal care in the country. E-mail nilmini0822@gmail.com

Miskat Jahan currently has joined as a Lecturer at Comilla University, Bangladesh, in the Public Administration Department. She has completed BSS and MSS from Dhaka University in Public Administration with outstanding academic results, obtaining double gold medals. She has more than three years' solid experience in the development sector working in various rigorous, evidence-based research projects. Her areas of interest include local governance, public policy, global politics and development issues.

Nihal P. Jayamaha is a senior lecturer attached to Massey University. Nihal received his PhD in 2008 from the same university, with an endorsement in Technology Management. Nihal's teaching and research interests cover quality engineering, quality improvement, sustainability, quality management models and systems, and latent variable modelling techniques (e.g. structural equation modelling). Prior to becoming an academic, Nihal worked in the utility industry in the UAE, and in Sri Lanka for around 20 years in various capacities, including as an electrical engineer, senior technical auditor, and a project manager. Nihal has published in prestigious academic journals such as the International Journal of Production Research, Journal of Industrial Ecology, Environmental Science & Technology, Total Quality Management & Business Excellence, International Journal of Lean Six Sigma, International Journal of Quality and Reliability Management, Benchmarking: An International Journal, The TQM Journal, and Measuring Business Excellence.

K. K. Kapiyangoda is a senior lecturer attached to the Department of Management and Organization Studies, Faculty of Management and Finance of University of Colombo, Sri Lanka. She holds Bachelor of Business Administration (Accounting) Special Degree from University of Colombo. She also holds MBA from University of Colombo with a gold medal for Financial Reporting and Management Controls. She is also a CIMA passed finalist and currently serves as the coordinator for the Higher Diploma in Entrepreneurship and Small Business Management programme conducted by University of Colombo. Her research interests are in the areas of management control systems, entrepreneurship, small businesses management and family business management.

Orsolya K. Kegyes-Brassai is affiliated to the Faculty of Architecture, Civil Engineering and Transport Sciences, Szechenyi Istvan University, Hungary, where positions held include Associate Professor (from 2015), and Senior Lecturer, after earlier work as a Cultural Heritage Manager and Sustainable Development Officer.

Noor Ullah Khan is currently working as Assistant Professor at the Department of Human Resource Management, NUST Business School (NBS). He teaches courses in the areas of Human Resource Management, Organizational Behaviour, and Research Methods at both undergraduate and graduate levels. He is well-equipped with both quantitative and qualitative research methods. He has published research articles in ISI and Scopus indexed journals. He also published a book chapter in Emerald Publisher. He worked on a start-up research grant program (SRGP) and participated at several international conferences. His Ph.D. thesis model focused on key areas including green HRM, sustainable, and sustainable performance using a mixed-method approach. Hence, this current book chapter is one of the outcomes of his PhD thesis submitted to Universiti Teknologi Malaysia (UTM).

Thilakshi Kodagoda is a Professor in Human Resources Management Department at the Faculty of Management and Finance, University of Colombo, Sri Lanka. Her research focuses on a variety of labour market issues, including the combination of paid and unpaid work, work-life balance policies, gender at workplace, women in small business and Millennials' behaviour at work. She is also interested in qualitative methods. She has published in journals such as Gender in Management, Asia-Pacific Journal of HR, Journal of Education and Work and Journal of Management and Enterprise Development.

Ajantha Sisira Kumara is currently attached to the Department of Public Administration, University of Sri Jayewardenepura as a Senior Lecturer. He has supervised postgraduate research in the fields of health policy and administration, health economics, demography, and welfare policy evaluation. He has been involved in many collaborative research projects funded by the Australian Government. In 2014, he was awarded the Australia Award Fellowship (AAF) to conduct research on patterns, determinants, and consequences of out-of-pocket healthcare expenditure of Sri Lankan households. He was awarded the "Endeavour Postdoctoral Research Fellowship" by the Australian Government in 2018. He has widely published in policy, social science and health journals.

M. Naidoo has over 34 years' academic teaching experience globally, having held permanent faculty positions in Australia and South Africa. He has been an adjunct lecturer in China, Singapore, Malaysia, India, Denmark and Myanmar. His research interests include environmental management accounting, cost and cost control, decision making systems, ERP systems, and accounting education. He has published widely. He was the first recipient of the prestigious Nelson Mandela AusAid Scholarship in 1999–2000. He is a Chartered Accountant with CAANZ and currently a Senior lecturer at the VU Business School.

Alexander Newman is a Professor of Management in the Department of Management in Deakin Business School, and the Associate Dean (International) for the Faculty of Business and Law. Prior to joining Deakin, Alex worked at Monash University. He has also worked in both China and Japan, and previously taught at Nottingham University Business School in Ningbo China. He conducts research in the areas of organizational behaviour, leadership and entrepreneurship. His research has been published in leading international journals such as the Journal of Organizational Behavior, Journal of Vocational Behavior, Journal of Applied Psychology, the Leadership Quarterly, Human Resource Management and Entrepreneurship, Theory and Practice.

Asfia Obaid has experience of over 20 years with NUST Business School (NBS) and currently Heads the Management and HR Department which includes the sub-specialized areas of Strategy and Entrepreneurship. She teaches courses in the areas of Human Resource Management and Organizational Behaviour and Design. She has a diverse experience of teaching in taught and research-based programs at various levels including undergraduate, graduate, postgraduate, and executive education. Her interests in research include HRM System Strength, Strategic HRM, and Compensation and her approach to research is largely qualitative. In the last five years, she has worked on various consultancy projects, has won research grants, and has presented at numerous international conferences. Additionally, she has supervised over 65 Research Projects and theses of graduating students.

S. M. P. C. Padmini is Senior Scientist at Sri Lanka Council for Agricultural Research Policy. She is the Convener of National Committee of Floriculture Research and Development and National Committee on Natural Resources Management, Sustainable Agriculture and Climate Change. She has conducted researches on Development of Floricultural Supporting Networks for Women Growers in Sri Lanka and published research papers related to floriculture sector in Sri Lanka.

P. M. D. S. Pathiraja obtained his first degree in BSc Accountancy & Business Finance from Wayamba University of Sri Lanka. Currently he is working as an Assistant Lecturer at Rajarata University of Sri Lanka while following Master of Science in Applied Finance at University of Sri Jayewardenepura. He is lecturing in the field of Business Valuation, Investment and Portfolio Management, Management Science and Financial Accounting. His research interests include Integrated Reporting, Forensic Accounting, Risk Management and Behavioural Finance.

D. P. P. N. Peiris (Nilanka Peiris) is a graduate from the University of Colombo with a Bachelor of Science Special Degree in Statistics with Computer Science offered by the Department of Statistics, Faculty of Science. He has presented his article titled "Predicting All Share Price Index (ASPI) of Colombo Stock Exchange on Macro-Economic Variables and Exogenous Factors" at the 12th International Research Conference "Challenges to Humankind in the Face of New Technologies" of General Sir John Kotelawala Defence University, Sri Lanka. Currently, he is working as a Data Analyst at Microimage (Pvt.) Ltd. He is also a freelance researcher who has worked with several postgraduate and undergraduate research sharing his knowledge of statistical analysis and conducting surveys. He is a Microsoft Certified Azure Data Scientist Associate.

W. A. N. Priyadarshanie is a senior lecturer at Department of Accountancy, Wayamba University of Sri Lanka. She obtained her first degree and master's degree from University of Sri Jayewardenepura in Accounting & Finance. She is lecturing in the field of corporate reporting, financial reporting and forensic accounting. She is also an associate member of Chartered Accountants of Sri Lanka. Her research interests include corporate disclosures, integrated reporting, IFRS adoption and forensic accounting.

S. Rajumesh PhD, MBA, PGD, BBA, is a Senior Lecturer and researcher at the Department of Marketing, Faculty of Management Studies and Commerce, University of Jaffna. He served as Coordinator for Master of Business Administration, Senior Student Counsellor, Director for Career Guidance Unit, Coordinator for Diploma in Marketing, and Alumni Officer of the University of Jaffna. He served as Convener of the International Conference on Contemporary Management (ICCM) organized by the Faculty of Management Studies and Commerce, University of

Jaffna. Further He contributed as Chief Editor to the ICCM to publish the blind reviewed research papers in the proceeding. He blind reviewed research papers for different journals and conference proceedings. He has published research papers in the area of marketing in the blind reviewed indexed journals.

R. B. B. S. Ramachandra is a medical doctor by profession currently working as the Director to District General Hospital Embilipitiya which is a tertiary care hospital in Sri Lanka. She is qualified with a Master's Degree and a Doctorate Degree in Public Health from University of Colombo, Sri Lanka. She has more than 14 years' experience in public health during her carrier before moving into medical administration. She was mainly involved in public health teaching focusing epidemiological researches. She was a renounced lecturer in public health and a leading character in many new developments in her work place such as establishing an ethics review committee, revising training curriculum of Public health midwives, Public Health Inspectors and developing new training curriculums for medical officer/non-communicable diseases. She is continuing her professional development in a new angle with the current opportunity of becoming an administrator.

R. M. A. K. Rathnayake is a senior lecturer and researcher attached to the Department of Business Economics, Faculty of Management Studies and Commerce, University of Sri Jayewardenepura, with tenure of approximately 14 years. He obtained his B.A in Business Statistics (Special) Degree from the University of Sri Jayewardenepura, with a first class standing, and Master's in Economics from the University of Colombo. He is in the final stages of his PhD studies in Economics from the University of Colombo. His research interests span agriculture economics, banking and financial markets, development economics. He has a number of conference and refereed publications in these areas.

Chao Ren (Joe) is a PhD candidate at the Department of Management, Monash University, Australia. His research concentrates on management controls, accounting and accountability, public management, people management, corporate social responsibility, and Chinese management studies. His publications have appeared in leading international journals such as Journal of Accounting, Accountability, and Auditing.

Ramanie Samaratunge is an Associate Professor at Monash Business School, Monash University, Australia. She is an internationally renowned management scholar with 30 years' experience working in the public and private sector, including consultancies in Australia and Asia. She was previously at the University of Sri Jayewardenepura, from which she also graduated with first-class honors in Public Administration. She holds a PhD from Monash University, Australia. Her research focuses on humor in management, governance, entrepreneurship and Asian immigrants. Associate Professor Samaratunge has published several book chapters, several government and industry reports, and journal articles in leading international management journals such as International Journal of Intercultural Relations, Australian Journal of Management, Journal of Business Ethics and Human Relations.

S. M. Samarasinghe is a senior lecturer in the Department of IT, University of Sri Jayewardenepura, Sri Lanka. She holds a B.Com. (Special) and an M.Sc. (Management) from the University of Sri Jayewardenepura and a Ph.D. from Massey University, New Zealand. Her research interests focus mainly on e-Learning/m-Learning, technology acceptance, and e-commerce/m-commerce. Her work has been published in international journals and has been also presented in international conferences.

V. Sathana is a Senior Lecturer at the University of Jaffna. Her work focuses on Marketing strategy, Development of Micro, Small and Medium Enterprises (MSMEs), Entrepreneurial orientation and Market orientation. She earned her MBA from University of Kelaniya and MA in Public Administration and BBA from the University of Jaffna. She has submitted her PhD research on "Marketing strategies and development of MSMEs of Northern Province, Sri Lanka". She is currently contributing for the Incubation cell of Faculty of Management Studies and Commerce, University of Jaffna. She received two research grants focused on development of MSMEs. She presently works on a research project on a network relationship marketing strategy for MSMEs. She has been voluntarily working on the "Kuviyam" Project, created by the Sri Lankan diaspora.

Roselina Binti Ahmad Saufi is a Professor in Business and Management and the Dean for Faculty of Entrepreneurship and Business, Universiti Malaysia Kelantan. Roselina's works focus on capacity building, human resource development, and rural entrepreneurs' development. She has rendered her services to several agencies including governments and NGOs in Malaysia, Indonesia, Vietnam, Laos, Thailand, China, Finland, Japan, and the Maldives. Has been a Visiting Professor to Syarif Hidayatullah State Islamic University Jakarta, Indonesia; Anhui Xinhua University, P.R. China; Xiamen University (Malaysia); DRB HICOM University of Automotive, a Fellow at the Putra Business School, and an honorary guest at the International School of Media & Management, Kolkata, India. She obtained her PhD and Master of Business Administration in 1995 and 1991, respectively, from the University of Sheffield, United Kingdom. She has received several awards at both the national and international levels in the field of human resources and leadership.

L. D. J. U. Senarath is a professor in public Health attached to the Department of Community Medicine, Faculty of Medicine, University of Colombo. He also serves as a lecturer to the Post Graduate Institute of Medicine, Colombo, Sri Lanka and has held the post of Secretary to the Board of Study in Community Medicine, Post Graduate Institute of Medicine, Colombo. Professor Senerath is a renowned researcher with most of his contribution towards improving nutritional status of Sri

Lankans, and a leading researcher in Infants and Young Children's Feeding (IYCF). His involvement in child nutrition has added multiple developments to Sri Lankan health system. He is a supervisor to many professionals during both master's degree and doctorate degrees.

R. Senathiraja is a former Dean of the Faculty of Management and Finance at University of Colombo (UOC), Sri Lanka, and currently serves as the Director of the Centre for Contemporary Indian Studies at UOC. She received her PhD in Corporate Entrepreneurship with specialization in management studies from the Madras University, India; MSc in Small and Medium Entrepreneurship from the University of Sri Jayawardenapura; BCom (First Class) from Jaffna University, Sri Lanka. Her research primarily examines the role of entrepreneurship, innovation, and organizational behavior in both government and private sectors. Her work has been published in several journals, including the International Journal of Marketing Study and American Journal of Industrial and Business Management. She has been a recipient of prestigious scholarships and programmes such as the Indian Commonwealth Scholarship (2005), American Fellowship of South Asian Women Leadership in University Administration (2016), and the United States Educational Leadership Programme (2017).

Md Faiz Shah is a researcher in the School of Business and Law, Central Queensland University, Melbourne. He holds a PhD (2012) in Policy and Planning Sciences majoring in Risk Engineering, from University of Tsukuba, Japan, where he has also been a postdoctoral researcher. From 2013 to 2019 he was Assistant Professor, College of Engineering, University of Jeddah, Saudi Arabia. Prior to that he had experience as Deputy Program Manager, Emergencies, Save the Children USA, in Dhaka, and worked there is earthquake responses and disaster management.

S. Shivany is a Senior Lecturer in Marketing, Department of Marketing, Faculty of Management Studies and Commerce, University of Jaffna. She Completed her Bachelor Degree in Marketing at University of Jaffna, and her MBA In Marketing at Colombo University. She completed Her PhD at the Post Graduate Faculty of University of Jaffna. She has published more than 50 Research Papers and three books. She has presented many research papers at National and International Conferences. Dr. Shivany is a Fellow Member of CIM (UK), and Member of SLIM (Sri Lanka). She is interested in the areas of MSME sector development, University-business Linkages, Women development via micro businesses, and entrepreneurial marketing.

R. H. Surangi Lewis, MBA, ACMA, CGMA is a practitioner in the corporate world, who is striving to apply principles to the real business world to discover novel management and leadership styles. She is presently engaged by one of the largest apparels manufactures in Sri Lanka as Divisional Finance Manager. She has an MBA from the University of Colombo, with a special award for Business

Statistics, and she has excelled in research on practical applications and cultural impacts of one of contemporary management's accounting practices, the Balanced Scorecard. She has earned her professional qualification in CIMA-UK (Chartered Institute of Management Accountants). Presently she is a CIMA member and a young experienced leader with a demonstrated history of working in the apparel and fashion industry, including hands-on experience in leading and mentoring a dynamic team using strong interpersonal skills and advances in business intelligence skills.

Parves Sultan is at the School of Business and Law, CQUniversity, Melbourne campus, Australia. He has a PhD in Marketing, CQUniversity, Australia, is a Senior Lecturer there. In 2011 he Assistant Professor, University of Canberra. His broad research interests include communication, brand performance and image, and behavior.

Prabanga Thoradeniya joined the Monash Business School's Department of Accounting in July 2005. Prior to this, she worked at the Australian National University. Prabanga has also worked overseas, in industry as an accountant and a lecturer in Accounting at the University of Colombo. Prabanga's main research interests are in the areas of environmental, social and sustainability accounting and management accounting. Prabanga has a PhD from the Australian National University. Currently, she teaches and researches in the areas of Management Accounting and Sustainability Accounting. She is a member of CIMA (UK), CPA (Australia) and CMA (Australia).

Heng Hee Ting is a research analyst in the banking industry.

T. Velnampy obtained his Bachelor of Commerce Degree and Master of Philosophy (M Phil). He proceeded to a PhD in Madras University under the Indian Council for Cultural Relations (ICCR) Scholarship and then obtained MA in Tamil with Distinction. He has number of publications in indexed and non-indexed journals and 12 books published to his credit. He served as Senior Students' Counselor, Head of Department of Accounting, and the Dean. His teaching and research are in the fields of Accounting and Finance, and Human Resource Management.

G. Wickremasinghe is currently a Senior Lecturer attached to Victoria University Business School. He holds a PhD in Finance from Monash University and is a full member of CA (ANZ), CPA Australia and the Institute of Public Accountants Australia. He is currently the Associate Editor of Qualitative Research in Financial markets and holds memberships of editorial boards a number of journals. Dr Wickremasinghe has held a number of leadership positions at Victoria University, including those of the Acting Head of School of Accounting and Finance, post-graduate research coordinator, and the discipline leader for finance and statistics. His teaching and research interests are mainly in accounting and finance. His publication record to date includes 40 research papers in refereed journals. In addition, he has presented 16 research papers at local and international conferences.

Nilupama Wijewardena is a lecturer in the School of Management at RMIT University in Australia. She has a first-class honors degree in Public Administration from the University of Sri Jayewardenepura, Sri Lanka. She completed her PhD specializing in Organizational Behavior at Monash University, Australia. Her research interests are varied and include humor at work, emotions in work life, creating positive work environments, entrepreneurship and public management. She has published in top tier journals such as Human Relations, Personnel Review, Australian Journal of Management and International Journal of Public Administration and has also contributed to edited books. She also acted as a columnist for the Sri Lankan Daily Mirror from February to September 2011. Her book (co-authored with Ramanie Samaratunge & Charmine Härtel) titled "Managing with humor: A novel approach to building positive employee emotions and psychological capital" was published by Springer Singapore in 2019.

I. M. Withanawasam is a Senior Lecturer and Head of the Department of Accounting and Finance in the Faculty of Management and Finance, University of Ruhuna, Sri Lanka. She won VU International Postgraduate Research Scholarship under which she completed her PhD (Accounting) at Victoria University, Melbourne. She is a former Dean and a Head of the Department, and a former Coordinator of NUFU Project. She has served the national and international community through several statutory bodies and other committees in the university system. She has 28 years' experience as a University lecturer. Her research interests include Efficiency and Accountability in Higher Education; Management Control Systems; Management Accounting practices; and Role of Accounting in Environmental Management, some of which are predominantly qualitative and published in recognized indexed Journals.

Part I

Organization Studies

Position of Sri Lankan Products in the Global Market: A Comparison of Brand Values

Pathmani Mangalika de Silva, Kennedy D. Gunawardana, and Nihal P. Jayamaha

1.1 Introduction

The brand is the primary point of differentiation that provides a competitive edge to a business (Keller 2016). Therefore, the brand is an important weapon in a company's arsenal when it comes to competing and growing in the marketplace. With a few exceptions, Sri Lankan brands do not have the same standing as international brands, even after normalizing for the scale of operation. Although a few Sri Lankan companies perform exceptionally well internationally as contract manufacturers, they do not have a specific brand name associated with them. To the best of our knowledge, Sri Lankan brands have not been compared with foreign brands for brand value on a common footing. To address this gap, we compared top Sri Lankan brands against top brands in foreign countries, to examine the existing gap, with a view to proposing how the gap between Sri Lanka and developed countries can be narrowed.

As an emerging economy, a key challenge Sri Lanka faces in achieving sustainable development is developing business models that can effectively respond to external environmental forces characterized by volatility, uncertainty, complexity, and ambiguity (VUCA) (Bennett and Lemoine 2014; Johansen and Euchner 2013). In particular, rapid technological development and global economic changes have made strategic planning a challenge (Autry et al. 2010; Guo and Chen 2018;

P. M. de Silva (✉) · K. D. Gunawardana
Faculty of Management Studies and Commerce, University of Sri Jayewardenepura, Nugegoda, Sri Lanka
e-mail: kennedy@sjp.ac.lk

N. P. Jayamaha
School of Food and Advanced Technology, Massey University, Palmerston North, New Zealand
e-mail: N.P.Jayamaha@massey.ac.nz

© The Author(s), under exclusive license to Springer Nature Switzerland AG 2021
S. Dhiman, R. Samaratunge (eds.), *New Horizons in Management, Leadership and Sustainability*, Future of Business and Finance,
https://doi.org/10.1007/978-3-030-62171-1_1

Kumarasinghe and Hoshino 2010). Therefore, developing appropriate and strong strategies to face new challenges and threats created by a changing environment is one of the important concerns in today's business world (Bennett and Lemoine 2014; Kumarasinghe and Hoshino 2003). Sri Lanka is a recently graduated upper middle-income country with a GDP per capita of USD 4102 (2018), and social indicators rank among the highest in South Asia and compare favorably with those in middle-income countries (World Bank 2019). While product quality is a complex, multifaceted concept, very few would disagree that product quality is a key determinant of competitive advantage and brand equity (Elmadag and Peneklioglu 2018; Garvin 1984). Although many Sri Lankan organizations have been implementing quality practices to stay competitive in both domestic and international markets, irrespective of their business, only a few are successful in achieving high levels of brand recognition (Kaluarachchi 2010; Perera and Chaminda 2013). For example, a Sri Lankan public sector hospital won several national quality awards for being more responsive to public demands (Kaluarachchi 2010).

Employee engagement is a factor that contributes positively to employee productivity and thus to organizational effectiveness (Gruman and Saks 2011; Iddagoda et al. 2016). A high-performance workforce tends to boost workplace productivity, which in turn helps to improve the business performance of companies (Gunawardana 2009). Articles in the business press and practitioner-oriented journals suggest that many manufacturing firms operating in the country do the right things, such as obtaining quality certifications, introducing high-involvement work practices (HIWPs) to workplaces, and creating a continuous improvement culture. However, the effectiveness of these interventions, particularly in a global context, remains unclear, except in the case of a few selected commodities and services (Wickramasinghe and Gamage 2011). Arguably, a good starting point for setting a benchmark is to limit the comparison to the best Sri Lankan and foreign organizations, putting them on a common footing. In the present study, we use brand value as the criterion variable for comparison.

The research questions that underpin our study are:

RQ1:   What is the gap between top-performing Sri Lankan brands and top-performing brands in other parts of the world?

RQ2:   What seems to be the association between (a) national culture and brand value and (b) economic development and brand value?

RQ3:   What short-, medium- and long-term avenues are available to increase the brand value of Sri Lankan brands?

The rest of the paper is structured as follows. Section 1.2 provides the literature leading to the three research questions. Section 1.3 describes the methodology adopted to answer the research questions. Section 1.4 provides the key findings. Section 1.5 concludes the paper outlining limitations of the study, takeaways from the study, and scope for further research through reflection questions.

1.2   Literature Review

1.2.1   Brand Value and Brand Equity

One of the best indicators of the performance of a particular brand is brand value. Put simply, *brand value* is the worth of a brand to a focal company of a supply chain (Aaker 1992; Raggio and Leone 2007). Thus, brand value is a financial calculation based on the net present value of a particular brand to the focal company. The immediate determinant of brand value is the market share of the brand stemming from sales figures, attributing to customer-level outcomes (Aaker 1992; Nadanyiova and Kliestikova 2018; Winzar et al. 2018). A construct closely associated with brand value is *brand equity*, which is sometimes used interchangeably with brand value in marketing and consumer research (Winzar et al. 2018). Aaker (1992, p. 28) defines brand equity as a "set of brand assets and liabilities linked to the brand's name and symbol." Thus, as a financial and marketing concept, the brand equity of a firm is defined as the "incremental cash flows which accrue to branded products over unbranded products" (Simon and Sullivan 1993, p. 28).

Four determinants of brand equity (brand assets) are identified in the literature: brand loyalty, brand awareness, perceived quality, and brand associations (Aaker 1992; Atilgan et al. 2005; Hosseini et al. 2013; Nguetsop et al. 2016). For the sake of completion, Aaker (1992) identifies "other proprietary brand assets," such as patents, as the fifth category of brand assets. Figure 1.1 depicts Aaker's model, which explains how brand equity creates brand value through customer-level outcomes. Through analysis of empirical studies, Aaker (1992) highlights that perceived quality is the most significant determinant of brand equity, as that leads to return on investment, market share, brand value, and shareholder value. In addition, Aaker also highlights the significance of brand loyalty, because loyalty directly translates to profit (e.g., cost reduction in promotion).

Nguetsop et al. (2016) developed and tested a model that explains brand equity via its four determinants: brand awareness, perceived quality, brand trust, and brand loyalty. They posited brand awareness and perceived quality as key drivers of brand equity (Fig. 1.2). In keeping with the manufacturing viewpoint of Garvin (1984), service viewpoint of Zeithaml (1988), and marketing viewpoint of Aaker (1992), we define perceived quality as the *end customer's judgment of the superiority of a product or a service.*

1.2.2   The Role of Perceived Quality in Building Market Share

The fundamental purpose of any business organization is to make a profit and increase market share. Organizations can make a profit if the price charged for its output is greater than its production costs and overheads and if the product is valued by the customers. The price that customers are prepared to pay for a product is a measure of the value of the product to customers (Hill 2011). Profit can be increased by adding value to a product (then, customers are willing to pay more) and by

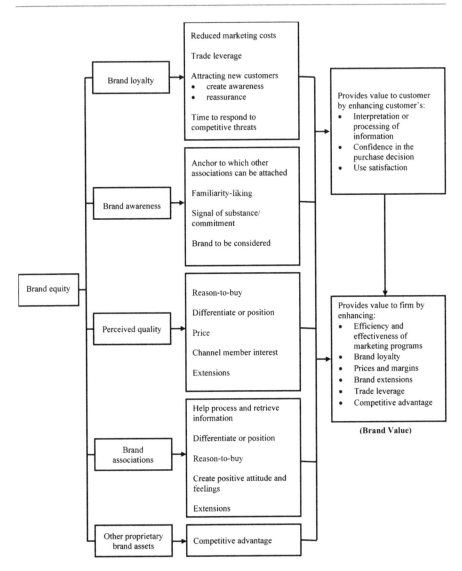

Fig. 1.1 Aaker's model for explaining brand value creation. (Source: Aaker 1992, p. 29)

lowering the costs of creating the value to increase the margin (Maury 2018; Porter 1985). Value is added to a product when an organization improves the product's quality, provides a service to the customer, or customizes the product to meet customer needs in such a way that the customer will pay more for it, that is, when the organization differentiates their product from that offered by competitor's (Hill 2011; Porter 1985). For example, customers perceive Mercedes to be a superior brand to Hyundai. Therefore, the customer will pay more for a Mercedes Benz car than a comparable Hyundai car. The costs of value creation are lowered when an

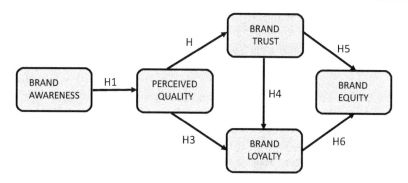

Fig. 1.2 Explaining brand equity via its four determinants. (Source: Nguetsop et al. 2016, p. 157)

organization finds ways to perform value creation activities more efficiently which, in the modern era, is achieved through *lean management* strategies (Hines et al. 2004; van Assen 2018).

Although Porter (1985) suggested differentiation and low cost as the two generic strategies for gaining competitive advantage (Hill 2011), it can be argued that lean management strategies do create both differentiation (focusing on product/service dimensions that customers value) and low cost (Anderson 2020; Hines et al. 2004). Lean methodologies achieve continuous improvement by reducing waste and non-value-adding activities, which can be passed on to the customer (the cost aspect of competitive advantage), and by using time productively to focus on quality attributes that are valued by the customer (the differentiation aspect of competitive advantage) (Gamage et al. 2017; Hines et al. 2004; Womack and Jones 2003). Consequently, customer perception about service quality, product quality, and price competitiveness is almost equally important in building up their satisfaction as objective or actual quality, such as actual functionality of a product or service. Customer satisfaction is a good predictor of purchase behavior (repurchase, purchase intention, brand choice, and switching behavior) and therefore plays a key role in marketing and increasing market share (Hallak et al. 2018; Tsiotsou 2006).

Perceived quality has been defined as the customer's judgment about a product's overall excellence or superiority. Perceived quality differs from objective or actual quality. Perceived product quality is a global assessment characterized by a high abstraction level (Zeithaml 1988). Jacoby et al. (1971) have emphasized the difference between objective and perceived quality. Objective quality refers to the actual technical excellence of the product, which can be verified and measured (Monroe and Krishnan 1985, as cited in Zeithaml 1988). Perceived quality, which is one of the main elements of brand equity, is the overall perception of customers with regard to the excellence and quality of a product or service compared to rival offerings (Severi and Ling 2013). Perceived quality lends value to a brand in several ways: high quality gives customers a good reason to buy the brand and allows the brand to differentiate itself from its competitors; a premium price can be charged, and it allows a strong basis for the brand extension (Alhaddad 2015). Perceived quality is understood as an antecedent of satisfaction (Bou-Llusar et al. 2001).

Customer involvement, overall satisfaction, and perceived product quality can be used as predictors of purchase intentions (Tsiotsou 2006). Customers with high perceived quality of brands would show higher purchase intention, while customers with a low perceived quality would tend to dismiss their purchase intention (Calvo-Porral and Lévy-Mangin 2017). Customers will evaluate the perceived quality of a product from their purchase experience. As a result, brand loyalty and brand preference will increase, as well as purchase intention (Chi et al. 2009). Customers' purchase decisions can be influenced by brand awareness; therefore a brand name can come to mind as soon as a customer is considering buying a product. This is why products with higher brand awareness have higher market share and better-quality evaluation. Perceived quality can help customers to make a subjective judgment on overall product quality, leading to that product having a salient differentiation and becoming a preferred brand in customers' minds (Aaker 1991; Chi et al. 2009).

Expanding globally allows companies to increase their profitability on a scale that isn't available to purely domestic businesses. However, local companies in developing countries should critically evaluate their brands' potential before starting to compete in foreign markets. This potential may be related to product and brand factors. Only if product factors are conducive to meeting the needs, wants, and taste of global customers should a company develop a product or service offering that has the potential to succeed as a global brand. Otherwise, companies must concentrate on the local market. Gaining global brand recognition is a challenging proposition for developing countries, due to several interrelated factors such as the brand of the country itself; culture, education, access to technology, and access to capital. However, our present study focuses on country-specific factors that affect quality, which is purported to be a significant determinant of the values of the brands associated with each country.

1.2.3   Country-Specific Factors Affecting Quality

In quality management literature, culture is often hypothesized as a factor affecting the quality of products associated with a focal company (Dastmalchian et al. 2000; Fischer et al. 2005; Kull and Wacker 2010). Culture can be assessed as having two components: the culture of the organization, and the culture of the wider group to which people belong—typically, national culture (Dastmalchian et al. 2000; Kattman 2014; Tallaki and Bracci 2017). The second factor often hypothesized as affecting quality is the level of industrialization (economic development) of a country (Manders 2015; Naor et al. 2010; Ralston et al. 1993). We discuss these factors in turn.

1.2.3.1 National Culture

Culture can be defined as the way a group of people act, feel, and think (Hofstede et al. 2010). Consequently, organizations, as well as the wider societies in which those organizations operate, such as countries and nations, have unique cultures.

Anthropologists argue that the culture of a country (national culture) has an effect on work practices, because certain work practices are viewed more favorably by some national cultures than the others, irrespective of the influence of an organization's leaders and its own culture (Kull and Wacker 2010; Newman and Nollen 1996). Others argue that national culture does not play a significant role in shaping the way people act, feel, and think in an organization. They argue that this can be shaped by the organization and its leaders (Kattman 2014; Naor et al. 2010; Netland et al. 2013).

National culture is a multidimensional concept, no matter which measurement framework is used, for example, Hofstede's original framework (Hofstede 1980), Hofstede's augmented framework (Hofstede 2019), the GLOBE framework (House et al. 2004), and so on. As ours is a preliminary study, we used Hofstede's original framework for the present study (the original framework contains only four dimensions of national culture). The four dimensions of this framework—power distance (PD), individualism-collectivism (IDV), uncertainty avoidance (UA), and masculinity/femininity (MAS)—are described as follows.

PD is the extent to which members of a society accept and are comfortable with the fact that power is unequally distributed in the society (Hofstede et al. 2010). A high PD is viewed as being suitable for procedural tasks such as continuous improvement, but not for big-step improvements or innovations (Bockstedt et al. 2015; Flynn and Saladin 2006). *IDV* refers to the extent to which members of a society are integrated into groups. A collectivist culture (a low IDV score) would treat attaining group goals as being important over personal goals; an individualist culture (a high IDV score) would treat attaining personal goals as being more important than group goals (Hofstede et al. 2010). A collectivist culture is viewed as being suitable for procedural tasks such as continuous improvement, but not for big-step improvements or innovations (Bockstedt et al. 2015; Flynn and Saladin 2006). *UA* refers to the extent to which members of a society tolerate uncertainties and ambiguities (Hofstede et al. 2010). A UA culture (a high UA score) is less inclined to embrace innovation. Rather, they would be more comfortable with procedural tasks such as continuous improvement (Flynn and Saladin 2006; Reimann et al. 2008; Zhang and Wu 2014). *MAS* refers to the extent to which members of a society accept emotional gender roles. Masculine cultures are expected to be assertive and task/achievement oriented, while feminine cultures are expected to be gentle and quality of work life oriented (Hofstede et al. 2010). Contrary to popular belief, empirical research shows that feminine cultures tend to outperform masculine cultures, in innovation (Kaasa and Vadi 2010; Khan and Cox 2017).

1.2.3.2 Industrialization/Economic Development

A theory that is often used to compare industrialized countries (the traditional western block) with less industrialized countries is the convergence versus divergence theory. The convergence theory argues that high levels of industrialization generate economic and technological preconditions and common organizational structures and practices to achieve high performance (Naor et al. 2010; Ralston et al. 1993). The convergence theory goes on to argue that as nations become industrialized (transitioning from socialist/developing economies to free market economies), people in transitioning economies begin to embrace values, attitudes, and behaviors of people in free economies, and consequently, the businesses in transitioning economies will remain culture free (Naor et al. 2010; Ralston et al. 1993). The divergence theory, on the other hand, argues that organizations are "culture bound" in that business structures and practices vary across national cultures (Naor et al. 2010). Studies that have taken the economy (typically GDP per capita) as a factor affecting the effectiveness of business practices include the work of Franke and Nadler (2008); Manders (2015); and Naor et al. (2010).

The propositions that drive the data collection and data analysis of our study are as follows:

P1:   There is a significant gap between Sri Lankan brands and foreign brands, both at the regional level and global level.

P2:   A significant portion of the brand value gap between Sri Lankan brands and foreign brands is attributable to the culture and economy of Sri Lanka.

1.3   Methodology

We used publicly available data on brand values, as well as brand ratings of top brands (ranked 1–10) of different countries published by the UK-based firm Brand Finance® (Brand Finance®, 2018). The data were sourced from the URL https://brandirectory.com/. Unfortunately, we had to limit the sample size of each country to the top 10 brands, as the brand values (US$ amounts) of brands ranked below 10 were generally unavailable.

We selected 14 countries across the world for our study: Australia, Canada, China, Germany, India, Indonesia, Japan, Malaysia, Singapore, Sri Lanka, Sweden, Switzerland, the United Kingdom, and the United States. They were selected, as far as possible, in a random manner to reflect different culture clusters. Sri Lanka, India, and Indonesia represent South Asia (Indonesia was drafted to South Asia because only Sri Lanka and India are featured in the brand directory as South Asian countries). Japan, Singapore, China, and Malaysia represent East and South East Asia. Germany, Switzerland, and Sweden represent Germanic and Nordic Europe. The United States, the United Kingdom, Australia, and Canada represent the Anglo cluster.

We compared the mean normalized brand value (brand value divided by the size of the population of the country) and the brand rating of top-performing businesses across the globe. The publisher of the database that we used adopted the *royalty relief methodology* to estimate the brand value of a particular asset (Rubio et al. 2016). More specifically, we compared country averages based on the 95% confidence interval (CI) of normalized mean brand values (the average brand value per capita) and brand ratings; we also conducted a one-way analysis of variance and Tukey's range test for additional rigor (Keselman and Rogan 1977).

As regards brand ratings, we used the following heuristic to convert a rating into a numeric figure (Table 1.1). Since we were dealing with the top 10 brands, the

Table 1.1 Value assigned against brand ratings

Brand rating	Assigned value
AAA	100
AA+	97
AA	94
AA-	91
AAA-	88
A+	85
A	82
A-	79
BBB+	75

brand ratings of none of the brands in our sample went below the A- mark. The scales were fixed by taking AAA as 100 and BBB+ as 75, in keeping with scores assigned in business studies on credit ratings (we considered brand ratings and credit ratings to be complementary). It is important to note that while brand values are absolute, brand ratings are relative (i.e., comparing a brand relative to its competitors within a country).

The top 10 brands of each country were treated as samples of the best performers of each country, and the comparison of means (95% confidence intervals) was treated as being equivalent to comparing financial and market performance of top performers in each country, because brand values and market share are strongly positively correlated (Aaker 1992; Nadanyiova and Kliestikova 2018; Winzar et al. 2018).

In keeping with our theorizations (Sect. 1.2.3.1), we studied the association between national cultural dimensions and normalized brand values. We obtained national cultural dimensions from publicly available data published by Hofstede and his associates (Hofstede 2019). We also studied the associations between per capita income and normalized brand values, as an attempt to compare the relationship between brand value and industrialization (Sect. 1.2.3.2). We used the per capita income of countries published by the World Bank (2019) as a proxy for the industrialization (economic development) of the respective countries.

1.4   Key Findings

1.4.1   Country Comparison

The results shown in Fig. 1.3 clearly suggest that the top brands of Sri Lanka and the two comparable regional nations India and Indonesia (underlined in Fig. 1.3) are way behind the brands of East Asian, South East Asian, and European origin, in terms of per capita brand value (e.g., the mean value of $8.29 for Sri Lanka versus the mean value of $475.32 for Singapore). However, Fig. 1.3 suggests that at the regional level, Sri Lankan brands perform as well as Indian and Indonesian brands. Thus, the above finding only partially supports the proposition P1. However, this finding provides some congruence with our assertion that "gaining global brand

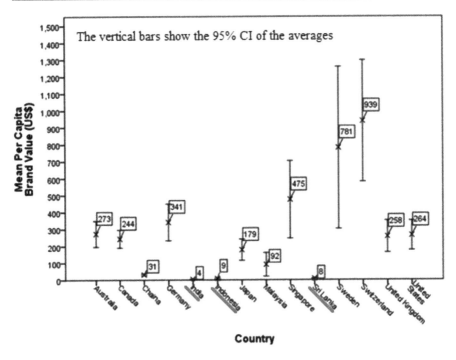

Fig. 1.3 Per capita brand value of top-performing brands in selected countries

recognition is a challenging proposition for developing countries, due to several interrelated factors such as the brand of the country itself, culture, education, access to technology and access to capital" (see Sect. 1.2.2). However, the results shown in Fig. 1.4 suggest that brand ratings across countries are on an even keel, which in turn suggests that the top brands of each country are equally competitive within the markets in which they operate.

To analyze the country's effect on per capita brand value, we conducted a one-way analysis of variance (ANOVA). The results are shown in Table 1.2. They show that approximately 57% of the variability of data is explained by the factor "Country." As expected, the factor "Country" becomes statistically significant ($p < 0.001$).

Table 1.3 depicts data that we collected to analyze the correlations between national culture dimensions and mean per capita brand value and the correlations between per capita incomes and mean per capita brand value. Table 1.4 depicts these correlations.

The analysis of correlations in Table 1.4 suggests that the mean per capita brand value (MPCBV) is strongly positively correlated with the per capita income (PCI) of the country. This association is graphically shown in Fig. 1.5. An interesting finding is that countries within the Anglo and South Asian clusters show a remarkable within-cluster similarity of mean per capita brand value. The apparent outliers in the linear association include Sweden and Switzerland. It is interesting to know why the

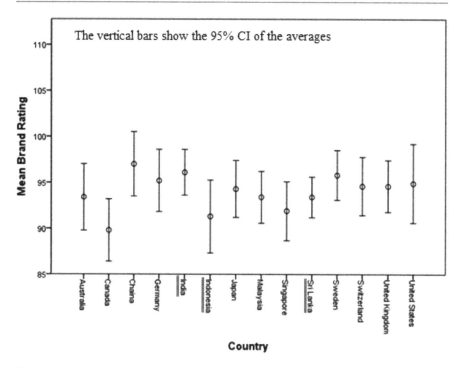

Fig. 1.4 Mean brand rating of top-performing brands in selected countries

Table 1.2 Results of one-way analysis of variance of per capita brand value

Source	DF	Adj SS	Adj MS	F-value	P-value
Country	13	10,607,589	815,968	12.88	0.000
Error	126	7,982,373	63,352		
Total	139	18,589,962			

$R^2 = 57.06\%$; adjusted $R^2 = 52.63\%$; predicted $R^2 = 47.00\%$

top brands of these two countries are able to command high brand values, although part of it is because these countries have been branded as top nations—due to favorable value systems, quality of life, business potential, heritage and culture, tourist attractions, and the "made in ..." image—based on branding research (e.g., see FutureBrand 2020). However, the answer cannot be this simple, because Japan is branded as the top-ranked nation (Japan just beats Norway, Sweden, and Switzerland to emerge on top) in the nation brand rankings, yet we find Japan in the "moderate spectrum" of MPCBV (Fig. 1.5). The same can be said of Germany (second only to Japan, Norway, Switzerland, Sweden, and Finland in nation-branding ranking), which does not return high a MPCBV as Singapore (ranked eighteenth in the nation-branding scale).

Of the antecedents of brand value (see Fig. 1.1), finding out which component/s of brand equity is/are responsible most for brand value, keeping in mind that brand value is a function of market share in dollar terms (not percentage terms), is

Table 1.3 Cultural dimension scores, per capita income, and mean per capita brand values by country

Country	Hofstede cultural dimension scores[a]				Per capita income (US $) in 2017[b]	Mean per capita brand value (US $)
	PD	UA	IDV	MAS		
Australia	38	51	90	61	53,831	273.10
Canada	39	48	80	52	44,841	243.60
China	80	30	20	66	8612	31.16
Germany	35	65	67	66	44,680	341.10
India	77	40	48	56	1980	4.34
Indonesia	78	48	14	46	3837	8.94
Japan	54	92	46	95	38,214	179.20
Malaysia	100	36	26	50	10,118	91.60
Singapore	74	8	20	48	56,746	475.00
Sri Lanka	80	45	35	10	4135	8.29
Sweden	31	29	71	5	54,075	781.00
Switzerland	34	58	68	70	80,296	939.00
United Kingdom	35	35	89	66	39,532	257.50
United States	40	46	91	62	59,939	264.50

[a]From https://www.hofstede-insights.com/product/compare-countries/
[b]From https://data.worldbank.org/indicator/NY.GDP.PCAP.CD

Table 1.4 Correlations between national cultural dimensions and MPCBV

Variable	PD	UA	IDV	MAS	PCI
PD					
UA	−0.308				
IDV	−0.873***	0.239			
MAS	−0.158	0.537*	0.140		
PCI	−0.791***	0.099	0.637**	0.209	
MPCBV	−0.637**	−0.057	0.396	−0.089	0.849***

$***p < 0.001; **p < 0.015; p < 0.05$

important in increasing the brand value of a product/service. We argue that while the net present value of future returns of a brand (hence brand value) is highly dependent on the branding of the nation itself, since branding a nation as high is difficult to achieve in the short to medium term, the focus should be more on enhancing perceived quality, which is intricately linked to the "made in ..." dimension of country branding.

The analysis of correlations in Table 1.4 also suggests that MPCBV is strongly negatively correlated with the PD dimension of the national culture of the country ($r = -0.637$). This association is graphically shown in Fig. 1.6. Sweden, Switzerland, and Singapore appear way above the trend. Singapore's case is particularly relevant to Sri Lanka, because Sri Lanka and Singapore have similar PD scores. It could possibly be that there is a great deal of value addition in the goods and services produced in Singapore, which is a wealthy nation.

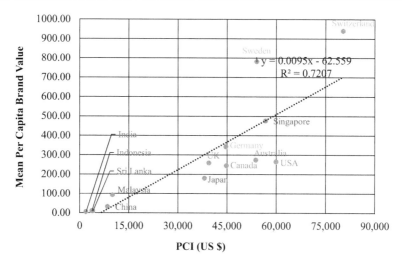

Fig. 1.5 The association between MPCBV and PCI

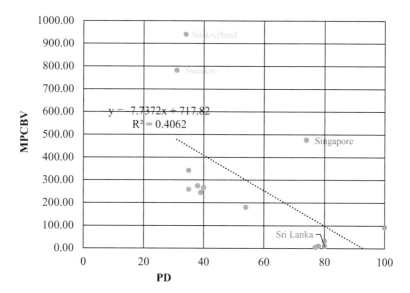

Fig. 1.6 The association between MPCBV and PD

The scatter plots shown in Figs. 1.7, 1.8, and 1.9 suggest that national culture dimensions IDV, UA, and MAS are not strongly associated with mean per capita brand value, although Sweden, Singapore, and Switzerland continue to appear above the trend lines (consequently, they are better performers). Needless to say, per capita income (the economic prosperity of a nation) is an obvious factor that increases brand value. For example, Sweden's # 1 brand in brand value (IKEA)

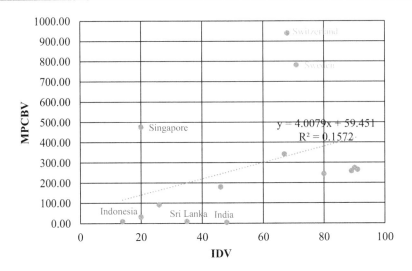

Fig. 1.7 The association between MPCBV and IDV

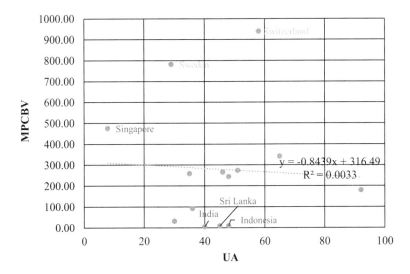

Fig. 1.8 The association between MCBV and UA

commands the best brand name for furniture in Sri Lanka because of IKEA's superior brand equity. IKEA customers are able and willing to pay more money than customers who buy furniture made in Sri Lanka, even though from a narrow product focus, both products are similar, except in the perceived quality dimension.

The conclusion is that, if Sri Lankan companies are to become globally competitive, there is much they can learn from developed nations who are branded highly as nations. Moreover, a country such as Sri Lanka has to move away from the

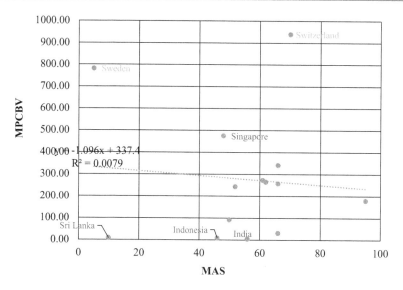

Fig. 1.9 The association between MPCBV and MAS

middle-income trap, and as the country transitions towards a strong market economy, the businesses in Sri Lanka will embrace the structures, systems, and practices that are prevalent in free market economies in the west (e.g., ease of operating a business, high quality of life for its people, increasing productivity, and value addition to products). Singapore, which was on equal footing with Sri Lanka in the early 1960s, became a wealthy nation by rapidly moving towards a strong market economy, by establishing western-style structures and good governance (Mahizhnan 1999). Productivity and innovation have been the forte in Singaporean businesses. The Standards, Productivity and Innovation Board (SPRING), Singapore (now known as Enterprise Singapore), acts as a gatekeeper of industry efficiency by providing guidance and structures to continually improve businesses in that country. In this regard, SPRING-Singapore embraces total quality management (TQM) and related approaches.

Total quality management (TQM) is an attractive proposition for businesses on three counts. Firstly, businesses that pursue TQM are customer-focused; secondly, improving quality and customer satisfaction is a journey that businesses need to undertake—businesses in Sri Lanka (or in South Asia in general) cannot become globally competitive overnight, and one must appreciate that there are factors beyond their control, at least in the short term, standing in the way of their journey towards excellence (e.g., changing the value system, creating many different value-added solutions). Thirdly, and more importantly, TQM recognizes that a focus on human resources is the key to success because it the creation of a "human resource focus" (e.g., creating high-performance teams) that leads to efficient and effective processes that deliver results (Mai et al. 2018; Porter and Tanner 2012). In addition, TQM theory acknowledges that it is these soft skills that bring competitive advantage to firms, and not hard skills such as measurement, data analysis, and benchmarking, which are easy for competitors to imitate (Laker and Powell 2011; Dubey and Gunasekaran 2015).

1.4.2 Regional Comparison of Brand Values

To analyze the regional effect on per capita brand value, we conducted a one-way analysis of variance (ANOVA). As mentioned earlier, the four regional culture clusters that our study covered are Anglo (United States, United Kingdom, Australia, and Canada); Eastern (Japan, Singapore, China, and Malaysia); Germanic (Germany, Switzerland, and Sweden); and South Asian (Sri Lanka, India, and Indonesia). Readers may note that Sweden is a Nordic European country, which has been drafted into the Germanic cluster, in much the same way as Indonesia has been drafted into the South Asian cluster to accompany India and Sri Lanka. The ANOVA results are shown in Table 1.5. They show that approximately 40% of the variability of data is explained by the factor "Region" (the remaining 60% coming from country-to-country variation within each culture profile/group). As expected, the regional factor emerges as statistically significant ($p < 0.001$) in the one-way ANOVA. Cleaner results could have been obtained if secondary data had been available from many different countries to create clean culture clusters. The only clean culture cluster in this study is the Anglo culture and to some extent the South Asian culture. The results shown in Fig. 1.5 clearly indicate that for these cleaner culture clusters, there is hardly any difference in MPCBV between the countries within the culture clusters.

Since there are only four regions (as opposed to fourteen countries), it is easier to show a pairwise comparison of the difference of regional means for per capita brand value. Figure 1.10 shows Tukey's simultaneous 95% confidence intervals for regions (pairwise comparisons). The bars closing the vertical hash line indicates no mean differences. Figure 1.10 shows that the South Asian cluster lags behind the other three culture clusters and the largest discrepancy is between South Asian and Germanic clusters.

1.4.3 TQM and Sustainability Leading to Country Brand

TQM can become more compelling if it expands to embrace the triple bottom-line dimensions of *sustainable development*. The concept of sustainable development is the overall outcome of the growing awareness of the global integrations between environmental and socioeconomic challenges to achieve a healthy and wealthy future for humanity (WCED 1987). Businesses should therefore focus on how quality-oriented approaches such as TQM can be deployed as a tool to achieve a

Table 1.5 Results of one-way analysis of variance of per capita brand value

Source	DF	Adj SS	Adj MS	F-value	P-value
Region	3	7,517,483	2,505,828	30.78	0.000
Error	136	11,072,479	81,415		
Total	139	18,589,962			

$R^2 = 40.44\%$; adjusted $R^2 = 39.12\%$; predicted $R^2 = 36.52\%$.

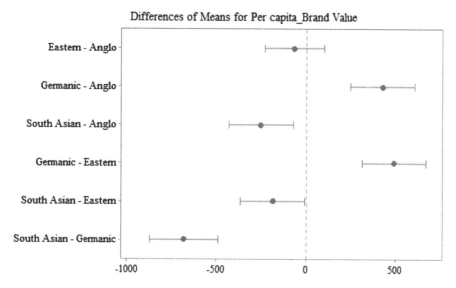

Fig. 1.10 Tukey's simultaneous 95% confidence intervals for regions

balance (or integration) within the competing dimensions of sustainable development (Isaksson 2006; Nyirenda and Ngwakwe 2014; Zink 2007). Consequently, researchers have investigated the synergies between TQM and sustainable development. For example, Isaksson (2006) investigated how process management in TQM can be used as a tool, for improving not only the economic performance of a company but also its environmental and social performance. TQM, on the other hand, could play a critical role in transforming a company towards corporate sustainability through underpinning the development of congruent goals, by resolving the conflicts between the triple bottom-line dimensions of sustainable development (Zink 2007).

According to Todorut (2012), a TQM-based complex management system has the potential to produce a learning organization which often adapts to environmental and social changes (i.e., continuous improvement). The positive attitude of managing change with quality leads to improved customer satisfaction (a TQM principle), which also enhances the brand value (Mehra et al. 2001).

Although these potential benefits have been known for the past two decades, only a few businesses (mainly multinational companies and large-scale industries) have committed to sustainable development in the past, particularly due to the fact that many have focused only on economic growth (Chandrakumar and McLaren 2018). However, an emerging interest is currently being observed in all businesses, from single-proprietor enterprises to large corporations with thousands of employees across the world. This is demonstrated by the increasing number of businesses committing to achieve the Sustainable Development Goals proposed by the United Nations in 2015 (UN 2015, p. 41).

1.5   Conclusion

This exploratory study benchmarked countries and regions based on the business performance criterion variable "brand value," after normalizing for the size of the population (i.e., MPCBV). The purpose was to examine the MPCBV gap between Sri Lanka and the rest of the world, within and outside the region (South Asia). As an aggregate country measure, MPCBV increases when a country can produce many products/services carrying high brand values. The *takeaways of our study*, based on our data analysis and literature synthesis, are as follows:

1. Sri Lanka does not do a bad job in MPCBV at the regional level, but it lags behind developed nations, as these nations are branded highly.
2. To improve MPCBV, Sri Lanka will have to improve its own brand as a nation, but Sri Lanka also should select products/services that it can leverage, in the short term.
3. Quality management initiatives such as lean and TQM have a vital role to play in improving the brand value of products and services.
4. It is becoming clear that the journey towards high MPCBV as a nation cannot be undertaken by the quality fraternity and business leaders in Sri Lanka alone; policy makers have a big role to play in nation branding. However, there are things the quality fraternity and business leaders can do in the short term to increase MPCBV, such as a strategic selection of products/services to pursue.
5. It is useful to identify what short-, medium-, and long-term measures are at the disposal of policy makers, business leaders, and the quality fraternity, in order that a multitude of Sri Lankan brands—not just tea, apparel, tourism, and cricket—can compete successfully with foreign brands in the global markets.

Figure 1.11 summarizes these takeaways as a conceptual framework.

We pose the following *reflective questions* as avenues for future research:

1. How reliable and valid is MPCBV as a construct that measures the overall competitiveness of products and services that a nation produces?
2. If a country excels at a regional level in product/service branding (e.g., Singapore compared to its neighbors), what lessons can be learned from that?
3. What are the short-term measures that quality fraternity and business leaders can take to increase the overall competitiveness of Sri Lankan products and services in the global market?
4. Related to (3) above, what specific quality management strategies and best practices should be promoted by the quality fraternity to increase the overall competitiveness of Sri Lankan products and services in the global market?
5. What short-, medium-, and long-term measures can the policy makers take to increase the overall competitiveness of Sri Lankan products and services in the global market?

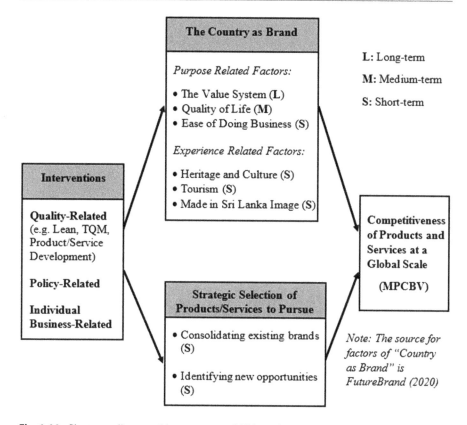

Fig. 1.11 Short-, medium-, and long-term possibilities to improve MPCBV of Sri Lanka

Generalization of our study findings needs to be done with caution, as we dealt with nonprobability samples, although we selected countries for our study randomly. A more comprehensive study is required to calibrate Sri Lanka against other nations within and outside the region on brand competitiveness. A challenge developing countries face today is achieving development in a sustainable manner to improve the branding of the nation itself (see Fig. 1.11). Sustainable development was not a concern when industrialized countries developed their economies to their current positions. Achieving quality, productivity, and industrial development, while meeting sustainability goals, will be a challenging proposition for countries such as Sri Lanka. The conceptual model that we developed (Fig. 1.11) shows the complexity of the task at hand very clearly.

Acknowledgment   The authors are indebted to research scientist Dr. Chanjief Chandrakumar of Massey University, New Zealand, for providing insights on sustainability.

References

Aaker, D. A. (1991). *Managing brand equity*. New York: The Free Press.

Aaker, D. A. (1992). The value of brand equity. *Journal of Business Strategy, 13*(4), 27–32. https://doi.org/10.1108/eb039503.

Alhaddad, A. (2015). Perceived quality, brand image and brand trust as determinants of brand loyalty. *Journal of Research in Business and Management, 3*(4), 1–8. http://www.questjournals.org/jrbm/v3-i4.html.

Anderson, D. M. (2020). *Design for manufacturability: How to use concurrent engineering to rapidly develop low-cost, high-quality products for lean production*. New York: Routledge.

Atilgan, E., Aksoy, Ş., & Akinci, S. (2005). Determinants of the brand equity: A verification approach in the beverage industry in Turkey. *Marketing Intelligence Planning, 23*(3), 237–248. https://doi.org/10.1108/02634500510597283.

Autry, C. W., Grawe, S. J., Daugherty, P. J., & Richey, R. G. (2010). The effects of technological turbulence and breadth on supply chain technology acceptance and adoption. *Journal of Operations Management, 28*(6), 522–536. https://doi.org/10.1016/j.jom.2010.03.001.

Bennett, N., & Lemoine, G. J. (2014). What a difference a word makes: Understanding threats to performance in a VUCA world. *Business Horizons, 57*(3), 311–317. https://doi.org/10.1016/j.bushor.2014.01.001.

Bockstedt, J., Druehl, C., & Mishra, A. (2015). Problem-solving effort and success in innovation contests: The role of national wealth and national culture. *Journal of Operations Management, 36*(1), 187–200. https://doi.org/10.1016/j.jom.2014.12.002.

Bou-Llusar, J. C., Camisón-Zornoza, C., & Escrig-Tena, A. B. (2001). Measuring the relationship between firm perceived quality and customer satisfaction and its influence on purchase intentions. *Total Quality Management, 12*(6), 719–734. https://doi.org/10.1080/09544120120075334.

Brand Finance. (2018). *Global rankings*. Retrieved August 28, 2019, from https://brandirectory.com/rankings

Calvo-Porral, C., & Lévy-Mangin, J.-P. (2017). Store brands' purchase intention: Examining the role of perceived quality. *European Research on Management and Business Economics, 23*(2), 90–95. https://doi.org/10.1016/j.iedeen.2016.10.001.

Chandrakumar, C., & McLaren, S. J. (2018). Towards a comprehensive absolute sustainability assessment method for effective Earth system governance: Defining key environmental indicators using an enhanced-DPSIR framework. *Ecological Indicators, 90*, 577–583. https://doi.org/10.1016/j.ecolind.2018.03.063.

Chi, H. K., Yeh, H. R., & Yang, Y. T. (2009). The impact of brand awareness on consumer purchase intention: The mediating effect of perceived quality and brand loyalty. *The Journal of International Management Studies, 4*(1), 135–144. http://www.jimsjournal.org/17%20Ya%20Ting%20Yang.pdf.

Dastmalchian, A., Lee, S., & Ng, I. (2000). The interplay between organizational and national cultures: A comparison of organizational practices in Canada and South Korea using the Competing Values Framework. *International Journal of Human Resource Management, 11*(2), 388–412. https://doi.org/10.1080/095851900339927.

Dubey, R., & Gunasekaran, A. (2015). Exploring soft TQM dimensions and their impact on firm performance: Some exploratory empirical results. *International Journal of Production Research, 53*(2), 371–382. https://doi.org/10.1080/00207543.2014.933909.

Elmadag, A. B., & Peneklioglu, O. (2018). Developing brand loyalty among SMEs: Is communication the key? *Small Enterprise Research, 25*(3), 239–256. https://doi.org/10.1080/13215906.2018.1522271.

Fischer, R., Ferreira, M. C., Assmar, E. M. L., Redford, P., & Harb, C. (2005). Organizational behaviour across cultures: Theoretical and methodological issues for developing multi-level frameworks involving culture. *International Journal for Cross-Cultural Management, 5*(1), 27–48. https://doi.org/10.1177/1470595805050823.

Flynn, B. B., & Saladin, B. (2006). Relevance of Baldrige constructs in an international context: A study of national culture. *Journal of Operations Management, 24*(5), 583–603. https://doi.org/10.1016/j.jom.2005.09.002.

Franke, G. R., & Nadler, S. S. (2008). Culture, economic development, and national ethical attitudes. *Journal of Business Research, 61*(3), 254–264. https://doi.org/10.1016/j.jbusres.2007.06.005.

FutureBrand. (2020). FutureBrand Country Index 2019. Retrieved June 1, 2020, from futurebrand-country-index/download.

Gamage, P., Jayamaha, N. P., & Grigg, N. P. (2017). Acceptance of Taguchi's quality philosophy and practice by lean practitioners in apparel manufacturing. *Total Quality Management & Business Excellence, 28*(11–12), 1322–1338. https://doi.org/10.1080/14783363.2015.1135729.

Garvin, D. A. (1984). Product quality: An important strategic weapon. *Business Horizons, 27*(3), 40–43. https://doi.org/10.1016/0007-6813(84)90024-7.

Gruman, J. A., & Saks, A. M. (2011). Performance management and employee engagement. *Human Resource Management Review, 21*(2), 123–136. https://doi.org/10.1016/j.hrmr.2010.09.004.

Gunawardana, K. D. (2009). An analysis of the critical factors of ISO 9001:2000 management practices and customer satisfaction of the selected listed manufacturing companies in Sri Lanka, *Vidyodaya Golden Jubilee Issue*, 129–148.

Guo, Z., & Chen, J. (2018). Multigeneration product diffusion in the presence of strategic consumers. *Information Systems Research, 29*(1), 206–224. https://doi.org/10.1287/isre.2017.0720.

Hallak, R., Assaker, G., & El-Haddad, R. (2018). Re-examining the relationships among perceived quality, value, satisfaction, and destination loyalty: A higher-order structural model. *Journal of Vacation Marketing, 24*(2), 118–135. https://doi.org/10.1177/1356766717690572.

Hill, C. W. L. (2011). *Global Business Today* (7th ed.). New York: McGraw-Hill.

Hines, P., Holweg, M., & Rich, N. (2004). Learning to evolve: A review of contemporary Lean thinking. *International Journal of Operations & Production Management, 24*(10), 994–1011. https://doi.org/10.1108/01443570410558049.

Hofstede, G. (1980). *Culture's consequences: International differences in work-related values.* Beverly Hills: Sage.

Hofstede, G. H. (2019). *Country comparison.* Retrieved February 20, 2019, from https://geert-hofstede.com/countries.html

Hofstede, G., Hofstede, G. J., & Minkov, M. (2010). *Cultures and organizations: Software of the mind* (3rd ed.). New York: McGraw-Hill.

Hosseini, S. E., Jafari, M., & Jafari, E. (2013). The effects of advertising and price promotion on brand equity dimensions of Samsung Company. *Advances in Environmental Biology, 7*(13), 4344–4348. http://www.aensiweb.com/old/aeb/2013/4344-4348.pdf.

House, R. J., Hanges, P. J., Javidan, M., Dorfman, P. W., & Gupta, V. (2004). *Culture, leadership, and organizations: The GLOBE study of 62 societies.* Thousand Oaks: Sage.

Iddagoda, Y. A., Opatha, H. H. D. N. P., & Gunawardana, K. D. (2016). Towards a conceptualization and an operationalization of the construct of employee engagement. *International Business Research, 9*(2), 85–98. https://doi.org/10.5539/ibr.v9n2p85.

Isaksson, R. (2006). Total quality management for sustainable development: Process based system models. *Business Process Management Journal, 12*(5), 632–645. https://doi.org/10.1108/14637150610691046.

Jacoby, J., Olson, J. C., & Haddock, R. A. (1971). Price, brand name, and product composition characteristics as determinants of perceived quality. *Journal of Applied Psychology, 55*(6), 570–579. https://doi.org/10.1037/h0032045.

Johansen, B., & Euchner, J. (2013). Navigating the VUCA world. *Research-Technology Management, 56*(1), 10–15. https://doi.org/10.5437/08956308x5601003.

Kaasa, A., & Vadi, M. (2010). How does culture contribute to innovation? Evidence from European countries. *Economics of Innovation and New Technology, 19*(7), 583–604. https://doi.org/10.1080/10438590902987222.

Kaluarachchi, K. A. S. P. (2010). Organizational culture and total quality management practices: A Sri Lankan case. *The TQM Journal, 22*(1), 41–55. https://doi.org/10.1108/17542731011009612.

Kattman, B. (2014). In today's global environment organizational culture dominates national culture! *Benchmarking: An International Journal, 21*(4), 651–664. https://doi.org/10.1108/bij-06-2012-0044.

Keller, K. L. (2016). Reflections on customer-based brand equity: Perspectives, progress, and priorities. *AMS Review, 6*(1–2), 1–16. https://doi.org/10.1007/s13162-016-0078-z.

Keselman, H. J., & Rogan, J. C. (1977). The Tukey multiple comparison test: 1953–1976. *Psychological Bulletin, 84*(5), 1050–1056. https://doi.org/10.1037/0033-2909.84.5.1050.

Khan, R., & Cox, P. (2017). Country culture and national innovation. *Archives of Business Research, 5*(2), 85–101. https://doi.org/10.14738/abr.52.2768.

Kull, T. J., & Wacker, J. (2010). Quality management effectiveness in Asia: The influence of culture. *Journal of Operations Management, 28*(3), 223–239. https://doi.org/10.1016/j.jom.2009.11.003.

Kumarasinghe, S., & Hoshino, Y. (2003). Influence of corporate culture, structure and strategy on organizational performance: An empirical study of business organizations in Sri Lanka. *Japanese Journal of Administrative Science, 16*(3), 227–242. https://doi.org/10.5651/jaas.16.227.

Kumarasinghe, S., & Hoshino, Y. (2010). The role and perceptions of middle managers and their influence on business performance: The Case of Sri Lanka. *International Business Research, 3*(4), 3–16. https://doi.org/10.5539/ibr.v3n4p3.

Laker, D. R., & Powell, J. L. (2011). The differences between hard and soft skills and their relative impact on training transfer. *Human Resource Development Quarterly, 22*(1), 111–122. https://doi.org/10.1002/hrdq.20063.

Mahizhnan, A. (1999). Smart cities: The Singapore case. *Cities, 16*(1), 13–18. https://doi.org/10.1016/S0264-2751(98)00050-X.

Mai, F., Ford, M. W., & Evans, J. R. (2018). An empirical investigation of the Baldrige framework using applicant scoring data. *International Journal of Quality & Reliability Management, 35*(8), 1599–1616. https://doi.org/10.1108/ijqrm-12-2016-0215.

Manders, B. (2015). *Implementation and Impact of ISO 9001*. Rotterdam: Erasmus Research Institute and Management.

Maury, B. (2018). Sustainable competitive advantage and profitability persistence: Sources versus outcomes for assessing advantage. *Journal of Business Research, 84*, 100–113. https://doi.org/10.1016/j.jbusres.2017.10.051.

Mehra, S., Hoffman, J. M., & Sirias, D. (2001). TQM as a management strategy for the next millennia. *International Journal of Production and Operations Management, 21*(5–6), 855–876. https://doi.org/10.1108/01443570110390534.

Monroe, K.B., & Krishnan, R. (1985). The effect of price on subjective product evaluations. In J. Jacoby & J. Olson (Eds), *Perceived quality* (pp. 209–232). Lexington, MA: Lexington Books.

Nadanyiova, M., & Kliestikova, J. (2018). Brand value and the factors affecting it. In N. Tsounis & A. Vlachvei (Eds.), *Advances in panel data analysis in applied economic research: 2017 International conference on applied economics (ICOAE)* (pp. 391–402). Cham: Springer. https://doi.org/10.1007/978-3-319-70055-7.

Naor, M., Linderman, K., & Schroeder, R. (2010). The globalization of operations in Eastern and Western countries: Unpacking the relationship between national and organizational culture and its impact on manufacturing performance. *Journal of Operations Management, 28*(3), 194–205. https://doi.org/10.1016/j.jom.2009.11.001.

Netland, T. H., Mediavilla, M., & Errasti, A. (2013). The insignificant role of national culture in global lean programmes. In C. Emmanouilidis, M. Taisch, & D. Kiritsis (Eds.), *Advances in production management systems: Competitive manufacturing for innovative products and services* (pp. 454–462). Heidelberg: Springer. https://doi.org/10.1007/978-3-642-40361-3.

Newman, K. L., & Nollen, S. D. (1996). Culture and congruence: The fit between management practices and national culture. *Journal of International Business Studies, 27*(4), 753–779. https://doi.org/10.1057/palgrave.jibs.8490152.

Nguetsop, M. L., Amoro, G., Wang, Z., Gondje-Dack, Igor-Mathieu, & Management. (2016). An applied study on brand equity: Factors affecting brand equity case study of Mtn Telecom

Cameroon. *European Journal of Business, 8*(9), 151–170. https://iiste.org/Journals/index.php/EJBM/article/view/29575/30368

Nyirenda, G., & Ngwakwe, C. C. (2014). Environmental management practices for sustainable development: Agenda for harmonization. *Environmental Economics, 5*(1), 76–85.   https://businessperspectives.org/journals/environmental-economics/issue-222/environmental-management-practices-for-sustainable-development-agenda-for-harmonization.

Perera, L. C. R., & Chaminda, J. W. D. (2013). Corporate social responsibility and product evaluation: The moderating role of brand familiarity. *Corporate Social Responsibility and Environmental Management, 20*(4), 245–256. https://doi.org/10.1002/csr.1297.

Porter, M. (1985). *Competitive advantage.* New York: Free Press.

Porter, L., & Tanner, S. (2012). *Assessing business excellence.* London: Routledge.

Raggio, R. D., & Leone, R. P. (2007). The theoretical separation of brand equity and brand value: Managerial implications for strategic planning. *Journal of Brand Management, 14*(5), 380–395. https://doi.org/10.1057/palgrave.bm.2550078.

Ralston, D. A., Gustafson, D. J., Cheung, F. M., & Terpstra, R. H. (1993). Differences in managerial values: A study of US, Hong Kong and PRC managers. *Journal of International Business Studies, 24*(2), 249–275. https://doi.org/10.1057/palgrave.jibs.8490232.

Reimann, M., Lünemann, U. F., & Chase, R. B. (2008). Uncertainty avoidance as a moderator of the relationship between perceived service quality and customer satisfaction. *Journal of Service Research, 11*(1), 63–73. https://doi.org/10.1177/1094670508319093.

Rubio, G., Manuel, C. M., & Pérez-Hernández, F. (2016). Valuing brands under royalty relief methodology according to international accounting and valuation standards. *European Journal of Management and Business Economics, 25*(2), 76–87. https://doi.org/10.1016/j.redeen.2016.03.001.

Severi, E., & Ling, K. C. (2013). The mediating effects of brand association, brand loyalty, brand image and perceived quality on brand equity. *Asian Social Science, 9*(3), 125.137. https://doi.org/10.5539/ass.v9n3p125.

Simon, C. J., & Sullivan, M. W. (1993). The measurement and determinants of brand equity: A financial approach. *Marketing Science, 12*(1), 28–52. https://doi.org/10.1287/mksc.12.1.28.

Tallaki, M., & Bracci, E. (2017). International manufacturing strategy: The impact of misalignment between national culture and organizational structure. In L. Brennan & A. Vecchi (Eds.), *International manufacturing strategy in a time of great flux, measuring operations performance* (pp. 43–61). doi:https://doi.org/10.1007/978-3-319-25351-0_3.

Todorut, A. V. (2012). Sustainable development of organizations through total quality management. *Procedia- Social and Behavioral Sciences, 62,* 927–931. https://doi.org/10.1016/j.sbspro.2012.09.157.

Tsiotsou, R. (2006). The role of perceived product quality and overall satisfaction on purchase intentions. *International Journal of Consumer Studies, 30*(2), 207–217. https://doi.org/10.1111/j.1470-6431.2005.00477.x.

UN (United Nations). (2015). *Transforming our world: The 2030 agenda for sustainable development.* New York: United Nations.

van Assen, M. F. (2018). Exploring the impact of higher management's leadership styles on lean management. *Total Quality Management & Business Excellence, 29*(11–12), 1312–1341. https://doi.org/10.1080/14783363.2016.1254543.

WCED (World Commission on Environment and Development). (1987). *Our Common Future: The Brundtland Report* (Australian ed.). Melbourne: Oxford University Press.

Wickramasinghe, V., & Gamage, A. (2011). High-involvement work practices, quality results, and the role of HR function: An exploratory study of manufacturing firms in Sri Lanka. *The TQM Journal, 23*(5), 516–530. https://doi.org/10.1108/17542731111157626.

Winzar, H., Baumann, C., & Chu, W. (2018). Brand competitiveness: Introducing the customer-based brand value (CBBV)–competitiveness chain. *International Journal of Contemporary Hospitality Management, 30*(1), 637–660. https://doi.org/10.1108/ijchm-11-2016-0619.

Womack, J. P., & Jones, D. T. (2003). *Lean thinking: Banish waste and create wealth in your corporation.* New York: Free Press.

World Bank. (2019). *The World Bank in Sri Lanka*. Retrieved August 28, 2019, from https://www.worldbank.org/en/country/srilanka

Zeithaml, V. A. (1988). Consumer perceptions of price, quality, and value: a means-end model and synthesis of evidence. *Journal of Marketing, 52*(3), 2–22. https://doi.org/10.2307/1251446.

Zhang, D., & Wu, S. J. (2014). The focus of quality management practices: A national culture perspective. *International Journal of Business and Management, 9*(2), 91–102. https://doi.org/10.5539/ijbm.v9n2p91.

Zink, K. J. (2007). From total quality management to corporate sustainability based on a stakeholder management. *Journal of Management History, 13*(4), 394–401. https://doi.org/10.1108/17511340710819615.

The Effect of Corporate Social Performance on Firm Financial Performance: The Moderating Effect of Ownership Concentration

2

N. L. Harmer, P. M. D. S. Pathiraja,
and W. A. N. Priyadarshanie

2.1 Introduction

Corporate social responsibility (CSR) has become an issue of emergent interest in the business world. CSR is an instrument which firms used to show their corporate social performance (CSP) (Williams and Siegel 2001). CSP is indicative of an agency problem, a clash among the interest of CEOs and stockholders. Corporations are practicing different categories of CSP such as environmental effort, philanthropy, ethical labor practices, and volunteering. Social performance becomes essential to develop a competitive advantage in today's environment. Moreover, a number of scholars and practitioners are paying more attention to corporate social performance (Griffin and Mahon 1997). An effort to increase the environmental and social performance is done to maintain the image and corporate reputation which increased the legitimacy of the corporation. According to Fisman et al. (2005), the effect of CSR on profit is stronger in competitive industries. Further they revealed that CSR is used as a means of differentiation in competitive environments. Most of these studies have been concerned about the direct relationship between corporate social performance and a firm's financial performance (FP). The findings of these studies showed mixed results of the relation between corporate social responsibility and financial performance.

This motivates us to find whether there is any factor that makes this relationship weak or strong. Further, Grewatsch and Kleindienst (2017) emphasized the need for more studies on the mediators and moderators of corporate social relationship and financial performance relationship. The role of corporate governance factors for the CSR–FP relationship is especially limited within the context of developing

N. L. Harmer · P. M. D. S. Pathiraja (✉) · W. A. N. Priyadarshanie
Wayamba University of Sri Lanka, Kuliyapitiya, Sri Lanka
e-mail: nadeesha@wyb.ac.lk

© The Author(s), under exclusive license to Springer Nature
Switzerland AG 2021
S. Dhiman, R. Samaratunge (eds.), *New Horizons in Management, Leadership and Sustainability*, Future of Business and Finance,
https://doi.org/10.1007/978-3-030-62171-1_2

countries (Selcuk 2019). According to Peng and Yang (2014), ownership concentration is common in emerging markets. The theory which relates to ownership concentration is the agency theory. Agency theory argues that concentrated ownership can be an incentive for shareholders to direct the managers to improve performance and shareholder value. Thereby the purpose of this study is to investigate the moderating effect of the ownership concentration on the relationship between CSP and a firm's FP. The findings of the study will fill the knowledge gap in the moderating effect of ownership concentration.

2.2   Literature Review

Previous studies have found various empirical results of relations between CSP and a firm's FP. Abeysinghe and Basnayake (2015) found that there is a negative relationship between CSR disclosures and the financial performance of selected Sri Lankan commercial banks. Further findings revealed that financial performance will not be totally dependent on CSR disclosures.

The same results were found by Tyagi and Sharma (2013) who addressed the question of whether corporate social performance is linked to corporate financial performance using empirical methods. Data covering a 7-year period from 2005 to 2011 was used for the study. This study also confirmed a negative relationship between CSP and corporate financial performance. In contrast to the above results, Javeed and Lefen (2019) revealed a significant positive association between CSR and firm performance using a sample of manufacturing companies in Pakistan.

The studies which found the negative relationship between CSP and a firm's FP argue that the funds that are used for CSP could have been used for firm effective investments (Gollop and Roberts 1983; Smith and Sims 1985). Researchers who found a positive relationship suggest that despite the extra cost of engaging in CSR activities, firms benefit from CSR through improved relationships with stakeholders in line with the stakeholder theory. Firms benefit from CSR via improved reputation.

Since there are contradictory empirical findings in the studies to find the relationship between CSP and firm financial performance, Grewatsch and Kleindienst (2017) emphasized the need for more studies on the mediators and moderators for that relationship. Accordingly, Mahoney and Roberts (2007) examined the relationship of corporate social performance to financial performance and institutional ownership. Peng and Yang (2014) examined the role of the ownership concentration on the link between CSP and FP from five highly polluting industries in Taiwan. According to the findings of this study, the relationship between CSP and short-run FP is negatively moderated by a high degree of control–cash flow divergence, and also there is a negative relationship between CSP and long-run FB among firms with a high degree of control–cash flow divergence. The study concluded that ownership concentration plays a critical monitoring role in the association between CSP and FB in emerging markets.

This study found no significant relationship between a composite measure of firms' CSP and FP. Further the results revealed that there is a significant relationship between firms' composite CSP measure and the number of institutions investing in firms' stock. Fisman et al. (2005) found that the profit effects of CSR are more positive when large external shareholders are on the board.

Wang et al. (2013) found that CSR disclosure is certainly positively accompanying with ownership concentration. Utomo et al. (2017) found ownership concentration positively related to firm performance. But there is no relationship between ownership concentration and environmental performance. Ishtiaq et al. (2017) concluded that ownership structure controls the organizations' success. Therefore many studies have used ownership structure as a moderating variable to the relationship between corporate social performance and firm performance. Selcuk (2019) investigated the impact of CSR engagement on firm financial performance in a developing country and analyzed the moderating role of ownership concentration in the CSR financial performance relationship. There is a positive relationship between CSR and FP while ownership concentration negatively moderates that relationship. In contrast to the above results, Ishtiaq et al. (2017) discovered that the ownership concentration significantly positively moderates the relationship between CSR and FP in non-financial companies of Pakistan stock exchange. Since there are contradictory results in the studies on testing the moderating effect of ownership concentration in the relationship between corporate social performance and firm performance, this study is focused to examine the impact of CSP on firm performance and the moderation effect of ownership structure in the Sri Lankan context.

2.2.1   Research Questions

1. Is there any relationship between CSP and firm performance?
2. Is there any moderating effect of ownership structure on the relationship between CSP and financial performance?

2.2.2   Research Hypotheses

H1 – There is a significant relationship between CSP and firm performance.
H2 – Ownership concentration has a significant influence on the relationship between CSP and financial performance.

2.3   Methodology

2.3.1   Data Collection Method

Secondary data were obtained from the annual reports. Data was collected from 30 companies which are listed under chemical and pharmaceutical; beverage, food, and tobacco; hotel and travel; and manufacturing sectors for the 6-year period from

2013 to 2018. Companies were selected proportionately from each sector. Most environment-related sectors were selected for the study.

2.3.2 Operationalization of the Variables

The dependent variable of the study was the firm performance which is measured by return on equity (ROE) and return on assets (ROA). ROE and ROA indicate the firms' efficiency of utilizing and managing their assets to maximize profitability (Table 2.1).

2.4 Research Model

This study considered secondary data of 30 companies listed in the Colombo Stock Exchange for 6 years which represent panel data series. Panel data consist of both time series and cross-sectional data.

To select the best-suited model for panel data analysis, the Hausman test was carried out. Based on the result of the Hausman test, the random effect model and fixed effect model were used to run the regression equation. There are two main objectives of this study: to examine the direct relationship between the firm's CSP and FP and the moderating effect of the ownership concentration on the relationship between CSP and FP. Thereby, there are two steps in the study.

Step 1 tested the direct relationship between CSP and FP. The estimated regression equation is

$$FP = \alpha 0 + \alpha 1 PCI + \alpha 2 OWC + \alpha 3 MTB + \alpha 4 SIZE + \alpha 5 DBT + \alpha 6 GDPGR + \varepsilon_{it}$$

Step 2 tested the moderating effect of Ownership Concentration on the above relationship. The estimated regression equation is

$$FP = \alpha 0 + \alpha 1 PCI + \alpha 2 OWC + \alpha 3 MTB + \alpha 4 SIZE$$
$$+ \alpha 5 DBT + \alpha 6 GDPGR + \alpha 7 PCI * OWC + \varepsilon_{it}$$

Financial performance was measured by using two performance variables return on equity (ROE) and return on assets (ROA).
Model 1

$$FP = \alpha 0 + \alpha 1 CSP + \alpha 2 OWC + \alpha 3 MTB + \alpha 4 SIZE + \alpha 5 DBT + \alpha 6 GDPGR + \varepsilon_{it}$$

Model 2

$$FP = \alpha 0 + \alpha 1 CSP + \alpha 2 OWC + \alpha 3 MTB + \alpha 4 SIZE$$
$$+ \alpha 5 DBT + \alpha 6 GDPGR + \alpha 7 PCI * OWC + \varepsilon_{it}$$

FP = Financial performance
CSP = Corporate social performance
OWC = Ownership concentration

Table 2.1 Operationalization of variables

Dependent variables	Financial performance	Return on equity (ROE) = profit for the year/shareholders' average equity	Ishtiaq et al. (2017)
		Return on assets (ROA) = net income/total assets	Peng and Yang (2014)
Independent variable	Corporate social performance	Measured by setting a numerical value 1 for the firms with pollution control investment and 0 otherwise	Al-Jaifi (2017)
Moderate variable	Ownership concentration	Sum of ownership percentage of five largest investors	Chien and Peng (2012)
Control variables	Market to book value	(market value of equity/book value of equity)*100	Ishtiaq et al. (2017) and Chien and Peng (2012)
	Firm size	Natural logarithm of a firm's total assets	
	Leverage	Total debts/total assets	Ishtiaq et al. (2017) and Chien and Peng (2012)
	GDP growth	Annual growth rate of Sri Lanka gross domestic production	Chien and Peng (2012)

Source: Author-constructed

MTB = Ratio of the market value of equity to its book value of equity
SIZE = Natural logarithm of a firm's total assets
DBT = Ratio of debt to assets
GDPGR = Annual growth rate of Sri Lanka gross domestic production

2.4.1   Hypotheses of the Study

H1 – There is a significant relationship between corporate social performance and
    financial performance.
H2 – Ownership concentration moderates the relationship between corporate social
    performance and financial performance.

2.4.2   Conceptual Framework (Fig. 2.1)

Fig. 2.1 Conceptual
framework

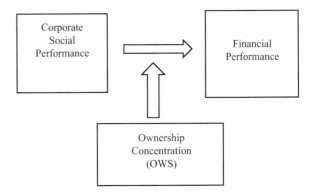

2.4.3   Descriptive Statistics (Table 2.2)

According to the descriptive statistics, the average return on equity of sampled companies is 11%. But it can be spread out from the average value by 18%. And also
ROE range between a maximum of 95% to a minimum of −46%. According to the
statistics, it can be summarized that the average value of the return on assets is 7%
with a minimum value of −18% and a maximum value of 44%. The standard deviation of ROA is 8%. It indicates that an average value of 7% can be spread by 8%.
The spread of the observations of the return on assets is relatively low.

The average value of the ownership concentration is 80%. It means that there is
a high ownership concentration in Sri Lankan listed companies with a minimum
value of 55% and a maximum value of 100%. The standard deviation of this variable is 10%. The mean value of the market to book value of equity is 94%. This

Table 2.2 Descriptive statistics

	ROE	ROA	PCI	OWC	MTB	NLT	DTA	GDPGR
Mean	0.11	0.07	0.69	0.80	0.94	21.72	0.25	0.04
Median	0.10	0.06	1.00	0.81	0.83	21.65	0.22	0.04
Maximum	0.95	0.44	1.00	1	3.77	23.47	0.77	0.05
Minimum	−0.46	−0.18	0.00	0.55	0.03	19.03	0.00	0.03
Std. dev.	0.18	0.08	0.46	0.10	0.62	1.06	0.19	0.01

Source: Research data

average value can be spread by 62%. The minimum value of the market to book value of equity is 3.07%, and the maximum value is 377%.

The average value of debt to total assets ratio is 25%. It indicates that averagely companies have financed their 25% of assets by debt. The standard deviation of this variable is 19%. The minimum value of debt to total assets ratio is 0%, and the maximum value is 77%. The ordinary value of the growth rate of the gross domestic product is 4.16% for the time period of 2013 to 2018. The minimum value of the growth rate of the gross domestic product is 3.3% (2016/2017), and the maximum value of the growth rate of the gross domestic product is 5% (2013/2014).

2.4.4 Correlation Analysis (Table 2.3)

According to the correlation analysis, there is a positive correlation between financial performance (measured by ROA and ROE) and corporate social responsibility. Ownership concentration is also positively concentrated with both ROE and ROA. It indicates that powerful shareholders are able to influence on the financial performance of companies.

2.4.5 Regression Analysis

Multiple regression was applied to analyze the panel data. The dependent variable of this study was the firm's financial performance which was measured by ROE and ROA. The analysis consisted of two steps. First, the direct relationship between corporate social performance and financial performance was tested. Second, the moderating effect of ownership concentration on the relationship between corporate social performance and financial performance was verified.

The Hausman test was used to select the most appropriate regression model (fixed effect model or the random effect model) to analyze the panel data. The hypotheses tested under the Hausman test are as follows:

H_0 – Random effect model is appropriate.

H_1 – Fixed effect model is appropriate.

2.4.6 Return on Equity (ROE)

Result of the Hausman Test (Table 2.4)

The probability value of the chi-square statistic is not significant at 5% significance level. As per the Hausman test, the null hypothesis was accepted and the alternative hypothesis rejected. Thereby the Hausman test concluded that the random effect model is more appropriate to analyze the panel data (Table 2.5).

$$ROE = -0.544 + 0.0809CSP + 0.166OWC - 0.026MTB$$
$$+0.025NLT - 0.155DBT - 0.232GDPGR + \varepsilon_{it}$$

Table 2.3 Correlation statistics

	ROE	ROA	CSP	OWC	MTB	LNTA	DEBT	GDPGR
ROE	1.000	0.870	0.252	0.341	-0.256	0.133	0.062	-0.007
ROA	0.870	1.000	0.272	0.472	-0.349	0.170	-0.110	-0.039
PCI	0.252	0.272	1.000	0.098	0.063	0.206	-0.147	0.003
OWC	0.341	0.472	0.098	1.000	-0.415	0.169	-0.127	-0.015
MTB	-0.256	-0.349	0.063	-0.415	1.000	0.035	0.015	-0.030
LNTA	0.133	0.170	0.206	0.169	0.035	1.000	0.005	-0.022
DEBT	0.062	-0.110	-0.147	-0.127	0.015	0.005	1.000	-0.008
GDPGR	-0.007	-0.039	0.003	-0.015	-0.030	-0.022	-0.008	1.000

Source: Research data

Table 2.4 Hausman test statistics (ROE)

Correlated random effects – Hausman test			
Test cross-sectional random effects			
Test summary	Chi-sq. statistic	Chi-sq. d.f.	Prob.
Cross-sectional random	11.063639	6	0.0864

Source: Research data

Table 2.5 Regression analysis ROE (Model 01)

Variable	Coefficient	t statistic	Prob.
C	−0.544	−1.129	0.260
CSP	0.0809	3.141	0.002
OWC	0.166	1.723	0.086
MTB	−0.026	−1.570	0.118
NLT	0.025	1.138	0.256
DTA	−0.155	−1.982	0.049
GDPGR	−0.232	−0.238	0.812

Source: Research data

Corporate social performance positively influenced on the firm's financial performance. The coefficient value is 0.0809. The probability value is 0.0020 which is significant at 5% confidence level. Therefore, H1 can be accepted. It is concluded that there is a positive and statistically significant relationship between corporate social performance and a firm's financial performance. The debt-to-asset ratio has also a significant effect on the firm's performance. There is a negative impact of debt level on the firm's financial performance (Table 2.6).

$$ROE = -0.710704 + 0.654739CSP + 0.557695OWC$$
$$-0.036372MTB + 0.018031NLT$$
$$-0.170736DBT - 0.196268GDPGR$$
$$-0.708687CSP*OWC + \varepsilon_{it}$$

Table 2.6 Regression analysis ROE (Model 02)

Variable	Coefficient	t-statistic	Prob.
C	−0.710704	−1.490900	0.1378
CSP	0.654739	4.546270	0.0000
OWC	0.557695	4.178473	0.0000
MTB	−0.036372	−2.23814	0.0265
NLT	0.018031	0.825666	0.4101
DTA8	−0.170736	−2.25779	0.0252
GDPGR	−0.196268	−0.21121	0.8330
CSP*OWC	−0.708687	−4.04794	0.0001

Source: Research data

Table 2.7 Hausman test statistics (ROA)

Correlated random effects – Hausman test			
Test cross-sectional random effects			
Test summary	Chi-sq. statistic	Chi-sq. d.f.	Prob.
Cross-sectional random	15.407298	6	0.0173

Source: Research data

The interaction between the independent variable and moderate variable measures the moderation effect. So according to the results, the interaction between PCI and OWC (PCI*OWC) is −0.708687. And also the probability value of the coefficient is 0.0001 which is significant at 5% significance level. Accordingly, H2 is accepted. It is concluded that there is a significant moderating effect of ownership concentration on the relationship between financial performance and corporate social performance. Ownership concentration negatively moderates that relationship.

By comparing with Model 01, the adjusted R-squared increases by 4.33% from 9.26% to 13.74%. The change in the adjusted R-squared is significant. ($P < 5\%$), which indicates that the interaction between pollution control investment and ownership concentration contributes significantly to the model.

2.4.7 Return on Asset

2.4.7.1 Result of the Hausman Test (Table 2.7)

The probability value of the chi-square statistic is significant at 5% significance level. The alternative hypothesis was accepted and the null hypothesis rejected. Results of the Hausman test indicated that the fixed effect model is the most appropriate model to analyze the data set which explains the return on assets as the dependent variable (Table 2.8).

Based on the results of fixed effect regression model, the following equation can be identified:

Table 2.8 Regression analysis ROA (Model 01)

Variable	Coefficient	t-statistic	Prob.
C	−0.848	−1.603	0.110
CSP	0.049	3.016	0.003
OWC	0.075	1.266	0.207
MTB	−0.017	−1.588	0.114
NLT	0.042	1.723	0.086
DTA	−0.182	−3.305	0.001
GDPGR	−0.450	−0.768	0.443

Source: Research data

$$\text{ROA} = -0.848 + 0.049\text{CSP} + 0.075\text{OWC} - 0.017\text{MTB} + 0.042\text{NLT} - 0.182\text{DBT}$$
$$-0.450\text{GDPGR} + \varepsilon_{it}$$

The coefficient value of pollution control investments is 0.049. It specifies that there is a positive impact of investments in pollution control on return on investment. The probability value of the coefficient is 0.0030 which is significant at 5% confidence level. Therefore, H_1 can be accepted. Based on the above result, it can be concluded that there is a positive and statistically significant impact of corporate social performance on financial performance at 5% confidence level.

The coefficient value of ownership concentration is 0.075 which explains that when the sum of the ownership percentage of the five largest investors is increased by 1 unit, the return on assets will increase by 0.075 units. The probability value of the coefficient is 0.2073 which is not significant at 5% confidence level. Then it can be concluded that, though ownership concentration positively influenced on financial performance, it is not significant (Table 2.9).

Based on the results of the regression analysis, the following equation can be identified:

$$\text{ROA} = -0.955 + 0.255\text{PCI} + 0.214\text{OWC}$$
$$- 0.021\text{MTB} + 0.041\text{NLT} - 0.188\text{DTA} - 0.432$$
$$\text{GDPGR} - 0.254\text{PCI} * \text{OWC} + \varepsilon_{it}$$

Model 2 tested the moderating effect of the ownership concentration on the relationship between financial performance and corporate social performance. By comparing with Step 01, the adjusted R-squared increases by 1.07% from 63.04% to 64.11%. The change in the adjusted R-squared is significant. ($P < 5\%$), which indicates that the interaction between pollution control investment and ownership concentration contributes significantly to the model.

The coefficient value of the PCI*OWC is -0.254441. And also the probability value of the coefficient is 0.0229 which is significant at 5% significance level. According to that H2 is accepted. And it is concluded that there is a significant moderating effect of ownership concentration on the relationship between financial performance and corporate social performance.

Table 2.9 Regression analysis ROA (Model 02)

Variable	Coefficient	t-statistic	Prob.
C	−0.955	−1.824	0.0701
CSP	0.255	2.809	0.0057
OWC	0.214	2.545	0.0120
MTB	−0.021	−2.008	0.0465
NLT	0.0417	1.737	0.0845
DTA	−0.188	−3.460	0.0007
GDPGR	−0.432	−0.748	0.4553
CSP*OWC	−0.254	−2.300	0.0229

Source: Research data

2.5   Conclusion

The aim of the study was to examine the impact of corporate social performance on the firms' financial performance and to study the role of ownership concentration on the relationship between corporate social performance and a firm's financial performance. Corporate social performance can be considered as a principal–agent problem due to managers overinvesting in social activities to improve the company's reputation as a good social citizen. The study was focused on the selected environment-related industries in the Colombo Stock Exchange. The findings of this study concluded that there is a significant positive impact of investment in pollution control on the financial performance of the listed companies. Further it revealed that the relationship between corporate social performance and a firm's financial performance is negatively moderated by ownership concentration. The results are in line with the findings of Peng and Yang (2014) and Selcuk (2019) who found the same argument. It is claimed that the financial performance of companies can be improved by increasing attention to the firm's corporate social performance. Moreover, this relationship exists when the ownership percentage of the largest owners is low which leads to more shared ownership. Controlling shareholder affects the link between corporate social performance and financial performance negatively. The findings of the study will help policy makers and regulators better identify how the ownership concentration is associated with firm incentives to engage in social performance.

Chapter Takeaways
- Corporate social performance (CSP) refers to the principles, practices, and outcomes of businesses' relationships with people, organizations, institutions, communities, societies, and the earth in terms of the deliberate actions of businesses towards these stakeholders as well as the unintended externalities of business activity.
- Ownership concentration was measured by taking the sum of ownership percentage of the five largest investors.
- Ownership concentration in Sri Lankan listed companies is high.
- Corporate social performance positively influenced on the firm's financial performance.
- The relationship between corporate social performance and a firm's financial performance is negatively moderated by ownership concentration.

Reflection Questions
- What is meant by corporate social performance?
- What is meant by ownership concentration?
- What is the use of the Hausman test?
- How does corporate social performance influence on firm performance?
- How does ownership structure moderate the relationship between corporate social responsibility and firm performance?

References

Abeysinghe, A., & Basnayake, W. (2015). *Relationship between corporate social responsibility disclosure and financial performance in Sri Lankan domestic banking industry*. In 6th international conference on Business & Information ICBI Sri Lanka: Faculty of Commerce and Management Studies, University of Kelaniya, pp. 111–128.

Al-Jaifi, H. A. (2017). Ownership concentration, earnings management and stock market liquidity: Evidence from Malaysia. *Corporate Governance, 17*(3), 490–510.

Chien, C. C., & Peng, C. W. (2012). Does going green pay off in the long-run? *Journal of Business Research, 65*(11), 1636–1642.

Fisman, R., Heal, G., & Nair, V. (2005). *Corporate social responsibility: Doing well by doing good?* (Working Paper). https://pdfs.semanticscholar.org/389a/e50f1d85a6d6941762a5d90ef-fcfd4f7471b.pdf

Gollop, F., & Roberts, M. J. (1983). Environmental regulation and productivity growth: The case of fossil-fuel electric power generation. *Journal of Political Economy, 91*(4), 654–674.

Grewatsch, S., & Kleindienst, I. (2017). When does it pay to be good? Moderators and mediators in the corporate sustainability–corporate financial performance relationship: A critical review. *Journal of Business Ethics, 145*(2), 383–416.

Griffin, J. J., & Mahon, J. F. (1997). The corporate social performance and corporate financial performance debate: Twenty-five years of incomparable research. *Business and Society, 36*, 5–31.

Ishtiaq, M., Latif, K., Khan, A. N., & Noreen, R. (2017). Corporate social responsibility and firm performance: The moderating effect of ownership concentration. *Journal of Managerial Sciences, 11*(3), 354–386.

Javeed, S. A., & Lefen, L. (2019). An analysis of corporate social responsibility and firm performance with moderating effects of CEO power and ownership structure: A case study of the manufacturing sector of Pakistan. *Sustainability, 11*, 248. https://doi.org/10.3390/su11010248.

Mahoney, L., & Roberts, R. W. (2007). Corporate social performance, financial performance and institutional ownership in Canadian firms. *Accounting Forum, 31*(3), 233–253.

Peng, C. W., & Yang, M. L. (2014). The effect of corporate social performance on financial performance: The moderating effect of ownership concentration. *Journal of Business Ethics, 123*(1), 171–182.

Selcuk, E. A. (2019). Corporate social responsibility and financial performance: The moderating role of ownership concentration in Turkey. *Sustainability, 11*(13), 1–10.

Smith, J. B., & Sims, W. A. (1985). The impact of pollution charges on productivity growth in Canadian brewing. *RAND Journal of Economics, 16*(3), 410–423.

Tyagi, R., & Sharma, A. K. (2013). Corporate social performance and corporate financial performance: A link for the Indian firms. *Issues in Social and Environmental Accounting, 1*, 4–29.

Utomo, M. N., Wahyudi, S., & Muharam, H. (2017). *The relationship between ownership concentration, environmental performance and firm performance: Evidence from Indonesia*. In Proceedings of the international conference on Management Sciences Indonesia, pp. 24–34.

Wang, J., Song, L., & Yao, S. (2013). The determinants of corporate social responsibility disclosure: Evidence from China. *The Journal of Applied Business Research, 29*(6), 1833–1848.

Williams, A., & Siegel, D. (2001). Corporate social responsibility: A theory of the firm perspective. *Academy of Management Review, 26*, 117–127.

The Moderating Role of Firm Size to Capital Structure-Financial Performance Relationship: A Panel Data Approach

3

Ummara Fatima and Uzma Bashir

3.1 Introduction

The primary goal of an organization is to augment its profitability and minimize cost: when organizations search for assets to fund investments, they take this as an important objective (Nassar 2016). In an era of intense competition, designing the capital structure for an organization is the most important decision and a perplexing task (Pouraghajan et al. 2012). Capital structure is a "firm's financing through a mixture of debt and equity" (Mujahid and Akhtar 2014). Capital structure decision defines the cost of capital and changes the market value of a company. In short, capital structure affects other features of a company, such as performance and productivity.

Financing decisions allude to major corporate choices, because an optimal capital structure, describing the corporate financing mix, can augment the stock price and value of an organization (Vătavu 2015). There has been a perplexing issue in accounting and corporate finance literature, the theory of capital structure, and its link with firm value, since Modigliani and Miller's pivotal work (Modigliani and Miller 1958). Nevertheless, in the real world, the limiting assumptions of Modigliani and Miller do not exist. This has impelled numerous academics to present a further explanation for this proposition, particularly after the pivotal work of Jensen and Meckling (1976), which shows that the leverage portion in capital structure impacts the performance of a firm (Harris and Raviv 1990; Graham and Harvey 2001; Brav et al. 2005). Numerous researchers have followed the Jensen and Meckling debate to examine the link involving capital structure-performance over recent decades. Yet empirical evidence shows inconsistent and mixed results.

U. Fatima (✉) · U. Bashir
School of Commerce & Accountancy, Minhaj University, Lahore, Pakistan
e-mail: uzmabashir@mul.edu.pk

© The Author(s), under exclusive license to Springer Nature
Switzerland AG 2021
S. Dhiman, R. Samaratunge (eds.), *New Horizons in Management, Leadership and Sustainability*, Future of Business and Finance,
https://doi.org/10.1007/978-3-030-62171-1_3

41

In developed countries such as the United States of America and Europe, the performance effects of capital structure choices are vast. Empirically little has been identified about such implications in developing countries such as Pakistan. In Pakistan, the capital market is not effective and suffers a high level of information asymmetry compared to developed countries. The financing decisions in the market environment are subject to a significant degree of irregularity. When considering Pakistan as a sample of developing economies, it is imperative to inspect the strength of capital structure decisions on the performance of the firm.

Section 3.2 provides a review of the literature. Section 3.3 defines the research methodology. The next section explains the empirical analysis, and the last explains presents the conclusion and recommendations.

3.1.1   Objectives of the Study

The study is conducted to achieve the following objectives:
- To explore the relationship between capital structure and firm performance of the textile sector of Pakistan
- To explore the moderating impact of firm size on capital structure-performance relation of the textile sector of Pakistan

The research work has important practical consequences that will let financial managers of the textile industry identify and adopt the optimal mix of capital structure, which could enhance firm performance.

3.2   Review of Literature

Modigliani and Miller's "MM propositions" are criticized due to the absence of a perfect market, and, consequently, relevancy theories have been developed. In this respect, trade-off theory, agency theory, and the pecking order are important theories. Trade-off theory emphasizes a proper trade-off between tax saving from debt, financial distress costs, and a decrease in agent cost and bankruptcy. Thus a firm can enhance its performance by using an optimum debt ratio where the tax advantage is maximum at minimum cost (Masulis 1988).

Agency theory states that, as the probability of bankruptcy rises, high debt confirms the improved performance of the management (Jensen and Meckling 1976). This also incorporates good corporate governance mechanisms to ensure shareholders' interests (Bokhari et al. 2019). The pecking order theory relates to "firms' inclination to internal finance over external finance and debt over equity" (Myers and Majluf 1984). Different theories on capital structure have been developed by numerous researchers over time, affecting, or affected by, performance. Researchers of developed and developing economies have discovered the leverage-performance relationship by considering these theories. Yet the relation between leverage and performance turns to be more critical due to the less productive capital markets of the developing countries (Ebaid 2009). In developing countries, hostile features are the reason for an inverse leverage-performance relationship (Hailu 2015; Alipour and Pejman 2015; Boadi and Li 2015).

The traditional theory assumes that the ideal blend of capital guarantees a low weighted cost of capital that amplifies the stock market price. The leverage and equity ratios are not adequate for deciding about performance, because there are other factors meddling in these connections (Vătavu 2015). Currently, several researchers have been exploring the capital structure effect on firm performance. Different disciplines cover the area of research: e.g., in the financial sector (Skopljak and Luo 2012) or in the nonfinancial sector (Banerjee and De 2014; Mujahid and Akhtar 2014) and both financial and nonfinancial sectors (Gabrijelčič et al. 2013). Under different situations, a certain financial ratio has both the same or diverse relationship with capital structures. For instance, Saeedi and Mahmoodi (2011) explored an inverse effect of capital structure on ROE (return on equity) and insignificant relationship between capital structure and ROA, whereas Ebrati et al. (2013) discovered a parallel effect for assets but a positive relation for ROE. Dewi et al. (2018) found that size and capital structure together had no significant effect on firm value. Yet empirical evidence shows inconsistent and mixed results. Some studies have explored the positive relationship between leverage and firm performance (Detthamrong et al. 2017; Roden and Lewellen 1995; Ghosh and Jain 2000). However, numerous others have explored an inverse relationship between leverage and firm performance (Nguyen et al. 2017; Fama and French 1998; Graham et al. 2000; Simerly and Li 2000). Singh and Batra (2018) found a mixed and weak correlation between capital structure and various financial parameters.

In the present age, firm size is very significant because of the positive impact of economies of scale. Big firms can enjoy low cost-benefit ratios in contrast to small firms. Firms on the cutting-edge hope to expand their size to get a competitive edge on their rivals by bringing down costs and expanding their market worth. Big firms are in a situation to avail themselves of both finance sources (internal and external). They have the choice to decrease their debt level, which could enhance market credibility, firm worth, and stock price. The use of debt provides leverage and enhances productivity (Shaheen and Malik 2012). The size of the firm has an impact on the capital structure and performance relationship of a firm. As Muritala (2018) found, size and asset tangibility have a positive relationship with firm performance. Shaheen and Malik (2012) have argued that firm profitability has a positive relationship with firm size and an inverse association with leverage. In Thailand 493 nonfinancial firms were examined by Haidar (2019) during 2001–2014, and he found that financial leverage has a positive relationship with performance. The study divided firms into big and small subsamples and observed that leverage mediates the impact of audit committee size on the performance of big firms. In Kenya, the moderating effect of firm size on the relationship between capital structure and financial distress of nonfinancial firms has been examined. The outcomes are that size has a significant moderating influence on the relation between capital structure and financial distress. In brief, the literature states that debt has an inverse impact on financial distress (Muigai and Muriithi 2017).

The capital structure literature has developed gradually, and researchers have discovered numerous factors that can impact the decisions about finance and performance. Previous researchers have explored the factors that impact the level of leverage or the variables that impact the firm decision on capital structure such as the level of profit, size, age, etc., as these components impact the firm decision of capital structure (Memon et al. 2018). Numerous researchers have explored the relationship between capital structure and firm performance while considering numerous moderating variables. For example, Iqbal and Javed (2017) explored the moderating impact of corporate governance on the capital structure-performance relationship. Mohammad and Bujang (2019) also argued that size was a contingency approach between intellectual capital, capital structure, and performance relationship. This describes that the capital structure has a distinct impact on performance, and the primary motivation behind this investigation is to discover the impact of capital structure on the performance of the textile sector of Pakistan. This study developed hypotheses to test the relation between size, capital structure, and firm performance. The study applies various econometric techniques and panel data diagnostic tests while expanding the time span of the study compared to the previous literature.

3.3   Hypothesis

H_1: Capital structure positively enhances the financial performance of the textile firms in Pakistan.

H_2: Firm size moderates the relationship between capital structure and financial performance of the textile sector of Pakistan.

The main purpose of developing the hypotheses is to explore the relationship between firm size, capital structure, and financial performance of the textile sector of Pakistan.

3.4   Research Method

3.4.1   Data and Sample

To realize the goals of the study, 155 textile firms listed on the PSE were selected using total population sampling (a type of purposive sampling technique). Listed firms with zero sales and having no data available were deleted from the sample, and remaining firms were tested for the availability of financial data from 2010–2017. This yielded a sample of 98 firms.

3.4.2   Measurement of Study Variables

Table 3.1 describes the variables of the study and how they are operationalized:

Table 3.1 Measurement of the study variables

Variables	Measurements	Notation
Independent variables		
Short-term debt	"Short-term debt/total assets"	SDR
Long-term debt	"Long-term debt/total assets"	LDR
Total debt	"Total debt/total assets"	TDR
Moderating variable		
Firm size	"Natural logarithm of sales"	SZ
Dependent variable		
Return on assets	"Profit before taxes/total assets"	ROA
Control variable		
Asset tangibility	"Tangible assets/total assets"	AT

3.4.3 Conceptual Framework (Fig. 3.1)

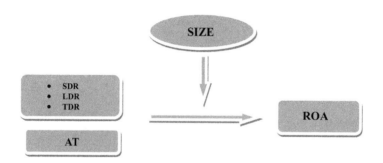

Fig. 3.1 Relationship between size, capital structure, and performance

3.4.4 Analysis Tools

Several panel data diagnostic tests were applied to check the normality of data. The fixed effect or LSDV (least square dummy variables) model and random effect model are employed, respectively, to check the primary and moderated relationship between firm size, capital structure, and performance of the textile sector of Pakistan. A feasible generalized least square (FGLS) regression model is used for testing primary and moderated effects of firm size, capital structure, and performance. To check the likelihood of such effect, SDR, LDR, TDR (predictor), and firm size (moderator) are multiplied to create an interaction variable, (SDR*SZ), (LDR*SZ), and (TDR*SZ), to predict performance (ROA). The equation for the moderated regression model is specified in the section below.

3.4.5 Empirical Model Specification

Following are the study models:

$$\text{ROA}_{it} = \beta_0 + \sum_{i=1}^{3} \beta_i X_i + \mu_{it} \tag{3.1}$$

$$\text{ROA}_{it} = \beta_0 + \sum_{i=1}^{3} \beta_i X_{it} + \sum_{i=1}^{3} \varnothing_i \left(X_{it} * SZ_{it} \right) + \mu_{it} \tag{3.2}$$

where
ROA_{it} = return on assets
β_0 = intercept term
β_i = negative or positive coefficients of the independent variables
$\varnothing_i$ = moderating variable's coefficients
X_{it} = vector of the independent variables
μ_{it} = error term

3.4.5.1 Sub-models for Empirical Testing
1. $\text{ROA}_{it} = \alpha + \beta_1 \text{LDR}_{it} + \beta_2 \text{TDR}_{it} + \beta_3 \text{SZ}_{it} + + \beta_4 \text{AT}_{it} + \varepsilon_{it}$
2. $\text{ROA}_{it} = \alpha + \beta_1 \text{SDR}_{it} + \beta_2 \text{TDR}_{it} + \beta_3 \text{SZ}_{it} + + \beta_4 \text{AT}_{it} + \varepsilon_{it}$
3. $\text{ROA}_{it} = \alpha + \beta_1 \text{SDR} + \beta_2 \text{SDR}^*\text{SZ} + \beta_3 \text{TDR} + \beta_4 \text{TDR}^*\text{SZ} + \beta_5 \text{SZ} + \beta_6 \text{AT} + \varepsilon_{it}$
4. $\text{ROA}_{it} = \alpha + \beta_1 \text{LDR} + \beta_2 \text{LDR}^*\text{SZ} + \beta_3 \text{TDR} + \beta_4 \text{TDR}^*\text{SZ} + \beta_5 \text{SZ} + \beta_6 \text{AT} + \varepsilon_{it}$

3.5 Results

3.5.1 Descriptive Analysis

Table 3.2 demonstrates the summary of descriptive statistics of moderating, independent, dependent, and control variables. The table expresses the directions of variables of the model. It depicts that the sampled firms received a 322% return if they financed their assets by a total debt of 65% (Afza and Ahmed 2017). The results show that approximately 65% of the total assets of textile companies of Pakistan are financed by debt, suggesting that the Pakistani textile firms function with a high level of financial leverage (Ebrati et al. 2013). This may be due to the capital-intensive nature of the Pakistani textile industry (Shah and Khan 2007). The total debt ratio of the textile firms of Pakistan is moderately highly leveraged, as the average value is around 65%. On average, 22% of the selected sample firms finance their assets through long-term debt, whereas financing through short-term debt is relatively high at 44%. This shows that the textile firms are financing more from short-term debt than long-term debt, which reveals that the textile sector of Pakistan lacks an established public debt market. The results endorse the outcomes of Demirgüç-Kunt and Maksimovic (1999), signifying that the firms in emerging states utilize

Table 3.2 Descriptive statistics

	ROA	SDR	LDR	TDR	AT	SZ
Mean	3.222471	0.440641	0.225534	0.657033	0.811970	14.80997
Median	3.140000	0.426000	0.172730	0.638900	0.811750	14.87825
Maximum	32.50000	1.888800	1.167800	2.151300	9.587000	17.81268
Minimum	−74.47000	0.017419	0.001900	0.030700	0.078020	5.921578
Skewness	−1.593017	1.441554	1.754410	1.215767	17.79447	−1.110767
Kurtosis	13.76381	8.998238	6.557560	6.681639	387.0272	7.575390
Observation	784	784	784	784	784	784

Source: Author's calculations

considerably less long-term debt. Thus, direct borrowing from banks is the only enduring supply of financing accessible to the textile industry of Pakistan.

3.5.2 Panel Data Diagnostic Tests

3.5.2.1 Panel Unit Root Test

The study applies the panel unit root test to decide about the panel data stationarity. This includes elucidating for the ρ value in the general equation:

$$Y_{it} = \propto + \rho Y_{it-1} \pm \mu_{it}$$

where $t = 8$ years and $i = 98$ textile firms.

To avoid invalid results of regression, this diagnostic testing is important (Granger et al. 1974). The study applies the Levin, Lin, and Chu test, which uses a common unit root process (Levin et al. 2002). The remaining set of tests was Im, Pesaran, and Shin's W-stat (Im et al. 2003), ADF-Fisher chi-square, and PP-Fisher chi-square assumed individual unit root process. Grounded on the outcomes shown in Table 3.5, the study rejects the null hypothesis. In effect, the majority of the test results concludes that all the study variables are stationary and therefore can be used in levels instead of their first difference (Table 3.3).

3.5.2.2 Panel-Level Heteroscedasticity Test

When the variance of the residuals does not remain constant, there is an issue of heteroscedasticity. The Breusch-Pagan test is adopted to test for panel-level heteroscedasticity. The LM-critical value was 7.814 with a corresponding LM-Statistical value 14.4. The conclusion was drawn from the comparison of LM-critical and LM-statistical. The comparison results signify the issue of heteroscedasticity. This classical linear regression assumption violation is corrected by employing the FGLS estimation method despite the ordinary least square (OLS).

3.5.2.3 Autocorrelation Test

The study uses the Durbin-Watson test to identify autocorrelation. The test statistics is as follows:

$$d = \frac{\sum_{i=2}^{n} (e_i - e_{i-1})^2}{\sum_{i=1}^{n} e_i^2}$$

The test result shows that there is no issue of autocorrelation.

3.5.2.4 Cross-Sectional Dependence Test

To check the cross-sectional dependence, three tests were used, respectively: Breusch-Pagan LM, Pesaran-scaled LM, and Pesaran CD. The results of these tests indicate the presence of cross-sectional dependence in residuals. The issue is resolved by employing the FGLS estimation technique (Table 3.4).

Table 3.3 Panel unit root test

Variable	Levin, Lin, and Chu test		Im, Pesaran, and Shin W-stat		ADF-Fisher chi-square		PP-Fisher chi-square	
	Statistic	P-value	Statistic	P-value	Statistic	P-value	Statistic	P-value
LDR	−97.402	0.0000	−64.012	0.0000	545.108	0.0000	408.544	0.0000
SDR	−135.47	0.0000	−51.312	0.0000	435.203	0.0000	297.456	0.0000
TDR	−15.191	0.0000	−12.717	0.0000	396.045	0.0000	275.275	0.0002
AT	8.8021	1.0000	−5.5437	0.0000	344.577	0.0000	327.870	0.0000
SZ	−164.40	0.0000	−56.151	0.0000	357.779	0.0000	655.874	0.0000
ROA	−10.546	0.0000	−7.0281	0.0000	348.898	0.0000	237.834	0.0221

Source: Author's calculations

Table 3.4 Cross-sectional dependence test

Breusch-Pagan LM		Pesaran-scaled LM		Pesaran CD	
Statistic	P-value	Statistic	P-value	Statistic	P-value
9660.291	0.0000	50.33186	0.0000	53.23220	0.0000

Source: Author's own calculations

3.5.3 Correlation Analysis

Table 3.5 describes the correlations between study variables. The correlations specify that all three debt ratios SDR, LDR, and TDR have a negative correlation with ROA. Moreover, asset tangibility also has a negative correlation with ROA. Size has a positive correlation with ROA. The overall results reveal that the study variables have a positive correlation with each other. High correlation cannot be seen between study variables.

3.5.4 Panel Model Regression Results

For testing the primary impact of capital structure on firm performance, the FGLS is applied. To detect proper methodology, the study executed a statistical test called the Hausman test (Hausman 1978). The results supported the fixed effect model in identifying the effect of capital structure on firm performance (see Table 3.6). Accordingly, the panel regression model for fixed effects is estimated as suggested by Torres-Reyna (2007).

Table 3.6 illustrates the outcomes of Model 1 estimation under Equations 1a and 1b. The panel regression for fixed effects estimates ROA as the dependent variable and short-term debt, long-term debt, total debt, and firm size as the independent variables. Asset tangibility is used as the control variable. The study results show

Table 3.6 FGLS fixed effect panel regression results (for primary effects)

Dependent variable: financial performance		
Variable	Equation 1a	Equation 1b
Constant	−1.9145 (0.3764)	−1.9326 (0.3985)
SDR		−6.1101*** (0.0000)
LDR	3.2367** (0.0476)	
TDR	−4.9529** (0.0016)	−1.6301** (0.0427)
SZ	0.5566** (0.0040)	0.5687** (0.0048)
AT	−0.7167** (0.0137)	0.6097*** (0.0000)
Statistics		
R-squared	0.7072	0.7024
Adjusted R-squared	0.6464	0.6406
Durbin-Watson stat	2.1156	2.1236
Observations	784	784

Source: Author's own calculations
Significance level $*p < 0.10$, $**p < 0.05$, and $***p < 0.01$

Table 3.5 Pearson correlation matrix

	ROA	SDR	LDR	TDR	SZ	AT	SDRSZ	LDRSZ	TDRSZ
ROA	1.0000	-0.328	-0.201	-0.395	0.2614	-0.015	-0.269	-0.168	-0.341
SDR		1.000	-0.025	0.596	0.006	0.215	0.968	-0.044	0.597
LDR			1.000	0.543	-0.296	0.128	-0.094	0.978	0.459
TDR				1.000	-0.201	-0.001	0.521	0.500	0.954
SZ					1.000	-0.017	0.188	-0.193	0.021
AT						1.000	0.225	0.139	-0.000
SDRSZ							1.000	-0.075	0.594
LDRSZ								1.000	0.471
TDRSZ									1.000

Source: Author's calculations

that the model has a "coefficient of determination" (R-squared) of 0.7072 and demonstrates that the independent variables described up to 70.72% of the variations in the dependent variable. The Durbin-Watson statistic of 2.12 shows no autocorrelation among residuals. The effects exhibited in Table 3.6 further demonstrate that the coefficients of TDR and SDR are negative and significant, suggesting that highly indebted firms generally rely more on short-term debt but show less performance. Borrowing incurred financial cost which decreases the net income and causes a negative effect on performance. The results support the findings of Ahmed Sheikh and Wang (2013) and Zeitun and Tian (2007).

The results further show that the coefficient of LDR is positive and significant, which illustrates that more long-term debt in capital structure positively enhances the performance of the textile sector of Pakistan. Here the results contradicted the finding of Ahmed Sheikh and Wang (2013). An important performance determinant is firm size. Size has an unclear impact on firm performance. There is more diversification in larger firms because these firms acquire advantages from the economy of scale while having more capital and resources (Frank and Goyal 2003). For a large firm manager, it is difficult to control the operations and the efficacy of the activities related to firm development. Further, in small firms there is no conflict of interest, as these firms are more likely to be led by proprietors. The study shows *a* positive and significant relationship between firm size with performance. The results are consistent with the findings of Ahmed Sheikh and Wang (2013) and Zeitun and Tian (2007). This implies that firm size plays an important part in regulating the financial performance of the textile sector of Pakistan. AT has both a positive and negative (Ahmed Sheikh and Wang 2013) relationship with firm performance.

The interaction terms of capital structure and firm size presents interesting results. Table 3.7 shows that the coefficient of TDR*SZ illustrates both a negative significant and insignificant relationship. This means that increasing the total debt capital of Pakistani textile companies does not improve performance. Therefore, financially it makes them lesser sound. The results imply that firm size has both significant and insignificant moderating impact on capital structure and performance relation. These study results contradict Ozgulbas et al. (2006). They are consistent with Mule et al. (2015) in Equation 1b, while inconsistent in Equation 1a. The results depict accurately that the high level of TDR is both disturbing and favorable for financial performance status. The results are inconsistent with Jonsson (2007) in Equation 1a, who found that large firms negotiate fewer interest rates on LDR and thus can augment performance.

3.6   Conclusion and Recommendations

The study concludes that the forms of capital structure (SDR, LDR, and TDR) generally decrease financial performance among listed textile firms of Pakistan. However, firm size has both significant and insignificant moderating effects on the abovementioned relationship. The implication is that large-scale firms, unlike small firms, are proficient in engaging huge debt, but this still has a negative effect on

Table 3.7 FGLS fixed effect panel regression results (for moderated effects)

Dependent variable: financial performance		
Variable	Equation 1a	Equation 1b
Constant	5.707388(0.2900)	4.6076 (0.3363)
SDR		−1.8169 (0.7578)
LDR	−44.56804*** (0.0000)	
TDR	−0.778254 (0.8416)	−11.132*** (0.0000)
LDR*SZ	3.162378*** (0.0000)	
TDR*SZ	−0.041038 (0.9049)	0.6567** (0.0012)
SDR*SZ		−0.3019 (0.4778)
SZ	−0.085198 (0.8443)	0.1224 (0.7515)
AT	−0.663480** (0.0002)	0.6856*** (0.0000)
Statistics		
R-squared	0.7316	0.7120
Adjusted R-squared	0.6745	0.6507
Durbin-Watson stat	2.0951	2.1702
Observations	784	784

Source: Author's calculations
Significance level $*p < 0.10$, $**p < 0.05$, and $***p < 0.01$

performance. Based on the observed results, the study establishes that firm size exerts both significant and insignificant moderating effects on the capital structure-performance relationship of textile companies of Pakistan. The study recommended some suggestions. Firstly, generally in making leverage choices, the finance managers of nonfinancial firms should attentively consider the size of their companies. Secondly, in the selection of debt maturation, firms of large size should prefer long-term debt rather than short-term debt, as long-term debt is observed to positively impact on the performance of large firms.

This study was conducted in an emerging market of Pakistan. For developed countries a similar study could be undertaken in the future. Future researchers can expand the variables of the study and with longer time periods. Data from multiple countries could also be a good dimension to expand the current study.

Chapter Takeaways/Lessons
- The decision about the capital structure of a firm is an important decision in the study of financial management. This study helps financial managers to opt the optimal level of capital structure by a mix of both debt and equity.
- The study helps management to understand the importance of firm size that could positively or negatively impact the relationship between capital structure and financial performance.
- The performance effects of capital structure choices are vast in developed countries. Empirically little is identified about such implications in developing countries such as Pakistan. In Pakistan, the capital market is not effective and suffers from a high level of information asymmetry. Thus, the work could facilitate the financial managers of developing countries.

- Capital structure is composed of debt and equity. The study elaborates three dimensions, SDR, LDR, and TDR, which could help industry experts to put more focus on each dimension that could maximize the value of the firms.
- Last but not least, the study helps researchers to understand the relationship between firm size, capital structure, and financial performance.

Reflection Questions
- The firm-specific factors are recognized as the main determinants of leverage ratios. Do the performance effects of capital structure choices differ in developed and developing countries?
- What is capital structure irrelevance as described in the Modigliani-Miller model? Elaborate other relevance theories.
- How different forms of capital structure (SDR, LDR, and TDR) increase and decrease financial performance?
- What sort of moderating effect firm size has on the relationship between capital structure and firm performance in Pakistani textile firms?
- How important is firm size for the finance managers of nonfinancial firms in generally making leverage choices?

References

Afza, T., & Ahmed, N. (2017). Capital structure, business strategy and firm's performance: Evidence from Pakistan. *European Online Journal of Natural and Social Sciences, 6*(2), 302–328.

Ahmed Sheikh, N., & Wang, Z. (2013). The impact of capital structure on performance: An empirical study of non-financial listed firms in Pakistan. *International Journal of Commerce and Management, 23*(4), 354–368.

Alipour, M., & Pejman, M. E. (2015). The impact of performance measures, leverage and efficiency on market value added: Evidence from Iran. *Global Economics and Management Review, 120*, 6–14.

Banerjee, A., & De, A. (2014). Determinants of corporate financial performance relating to capital structure decisions in Indian iron and steel industry: An empirical study. *Paradigm, 18*(1), 35–50.

Boadi, E. K., & Li, Y. (2015). An empirical analysis of leverage and financial performance of listed non-financial firms in Ghana. *International Journal of Economics and Finance, 7*(9), 120.

Bokhari, I. H., Areeba, S., & Ghumman, I. J. (2019). Corporate governance, dividend policy, capital structure and firm financial performance with moderating role of political instability. *Pakistan Journal of Social Sciences (PJSS)*, 109–126.

Brav, A., Graham, J. R., Harvey, C. R., & Michaely, R. (2005). Payout policy in the 21st century. *Journal of Financial Economics, 77*(3), 483–527.

Demirgüç-Kunt, A., & Maksimovic, V. (1999). *Institutions, financial markets, and firms' choice of debt maturity*. Washington, DC: The World Bank.

Detthamrong, U., Chancharat, N., & Vithessonthi, C. (2017). Corporate governance, capital structure and firm performance: Evidence from Thailand. *Research in International Business and Finance, 42*, 689–709.

Dewi, D. K., Amboningtyas, D., & Paramita, P. D. (2018). The optimize influence of firm size, capital structure, and financial ratio to company value is moderated by dividend policies on sector a varety of industry companies listed in Indonesia stock exchange period of 2012–2016. *Journal of Management, 4*(4).

Ebaid, I. E. (2009). The impact of capital-structure choice on firm performance: Empirical evidence from Egypt. *The Journal of Risk Insurance, 10*(5), 477–487.

Ebrati, M., Ebrati, M., Bakhshi, M., & Emadi, F. (2013). Studying the effect of financial leverage and ownership structure on investment growth opportunities. *Journal of Basic and Applied Scientific Research, 3*(6), 380–385.

Fama, E. F., & French, K. R. (1998). Taxes, financing decisions, and firm value. *The Journal of Finance, 53*(3), 819–843.

Frank, M. Z., & Goyal, V. K. (2003). Testing the pecking order theory of capital structure. *Journal of Financial Economics, 67*(2), 217–248.

Gabrijelčič, M., Herman, U. & Lenarcic, A. (2013). Debt financing and firm performance before and during the crisis: Micro-financial evidence from Slovenia.

Ghosh, A., & Jain, P. C. (2000). Financial leverage changes associated with corporate mergers. *Journal of Corporate Finance, 6*(4), 377–402.

Graham, J. R., & Harvey, C. R. (2001). The theory and practice of corporate finance: Evidence from the field. *Journal of Financial Economics, 60*(2), 187–243.

Graham, K. C., Mathur, L. K., & Mathur, I. (2000). The interrelationship between culture, capital structure, and performance: Evidence from European retailers. *Journal of Business Research, 50*(2), 185–191.

Granger, C. W., Newbold, P., & Econom, J. (1974). Spurious regressions in econometrics. In B. H. Baltagi (Ed.), *A companion of theoretical econometrics* (pp. 557–561).

Haidar, M. (2019). *Does corporate governance moderate the relationship between capital structure and firm performance?: Evidence from the Netherlands.* Master's thesis, University of Twente.

Hailu, A. (2015). The impact of capital structure on profitability of commercial banks in Ethiopia.

Harris, M., & Raviv, A. (1990). Capital structure and the informational role of debt. *The Journal of Finance, 45*(2), 321–349.

Hausman, J. A. (1978). Specification tests in econometrics. *Econometrica, 46*(6), 1251–1271.

Im, K. S., Pesaran, M. H., & Shin, Y. (2003). Testing for unit roots in heterogeneous panels. *Journal of Econometrics, 115*(1), 53–74.

Iqbal, M., & Javed, F. (2017). The moderating role of corporate governance on the relationship between capital structure and financial performance. *International Journal of Research in Business and Social Science (2147–4478), 6*(1), 89–105.

Jensen, M. C., & Meckling, W. H. (1976). Theory of the firm: Managerial behavior, agency costs and ownership structure. *Journal of Financial Economics, 3*(4), 305–360.

Jonsson, B. (2007). Does the size matter? The relationship between size and profitability of Icelandic firms. *International Journal of Business and Management, 9*(4), 43–55.

Levin, A., Lin, C. F., & Chu, C. S. J. (2002). Unit root tests in panel data: Asymptotic and finite-sample properties. *Journal of Econometrics, 108*(1), 1–24.

Masulis, R. W. (1988). *The debt equity choice.* Cambridge, MA: Ballinger.

Memon, F., Bhutto, N. A., & Abbas, G. (2018). Capital structure and firm performance: A case of textile sector of Pakistan. *Asian Journal of Business and Management Sciences*, 9–15.

Modigliani, F., & Miller, M. H. (1958). The cost of capital, corporation finance and the theory of investment. *The American Economic Review, 48*(3), 261–297.

Mohammad, H. S., & Bujang, I. (2019). Firms' size as a contingency approach in the relationships of intellectual capital, capital structure and financial performance. *International Journal of Academic Research in Business and Social Sciences, 9*(3).

Muigai, R. G., & Muriithi, J. G. (2017). The moderating effect of firm size on the relationship between capital structure and financial distress of non-financial companies listed in Kenya. *Journal of Finance and Accounting, 5*(4), 151–158.

Mujahid, M., & Akhtar, K. (2014). Impact of capital structure on firms financial performance and shareholders wealth: Textile sector of Pakistan. *International Journal of Learning and Development, 4*(2), 27.

Mule, R. K., Mukras, M. S., & Nzioka, O. M. (2015). Corporate size, profitability and market value: An econometric panel analysis of listed firms in Kenya. *European Scientific Journal, 11*(13).

Muritala, T. A. (2018). An empirical analysis of capital structure on firms' performance in Nigeria. *IJAME, 0*(0).

Myers, S. C., & Majluf, N. S. (1984). Corporate financing and investment decisions when firms have information that investors do not have. *Journal of Financial Economics, 13*(2), 187–221.

Nassar, S. (2016). The impact of capital structure on financial performance of the firms: Evidence from Borsa Istanbul. *Journal of Business & Financial Affairs, 5*(2).

Nguyen, T. T., Camacho, D., & Jung, J. E. (2017). Identifying and ranking cultural heritage resources on geotagged social media for smart cultural tourism services. *Personal and Ubiquitous Computing, 21*(2), 267–279.

Ozgulbas, N., Koyuncugil, A. S., & Yilmaz, F. (2006). Identifying the effect of firm size on financial performance of SMEs. *The Business Review, 6*(1), 162–167.

Pouraghajan, A., Malekian, E., Emamgholipour, M., Lotfollahpour, V., & Bagheri, M. M. (2012). The relationship between capital structure and firm performance evaluation measures: Evidence from the Tehran Stock Exchange. *International Journal of Business and Commerce, 1*(9), 166–181.

Roden, D. M., & Lewellen, W. G. (1995). Corporate capital structure decisions: Evidence from leveraged buyouts. *Financial Management, 24*(2), 76–87.

Saeedi, A., & Mahmoodi, I. (2011). Capital structure and firm performance: Evidence from Iranian companies. *International Research Journal of Finance and Economics, 70*, 21–28.

Shah, A. & Khan, S. (2007). Determinants of capital structure: Evidence from Pakistani panel data.

Shaheen, S., & Malik, Q. A. (2012). The impact of capital intensity, size of firm and profitability on debt financing in textile industry of Pakistan. *Interdisciplinary Journal of Contemporary Research in Business*.

Simerly, R. L., & Li, M. (2000). Environmental dynamism, capital structure and performance: A theoretical integration and an empirical test. *Strategic Management Journal*, 31–49.

Singh, S., & Batra, G. S. (2018). The relationship between firm performance and capital structure: Evidence from Taiwan. *Iranian Journal of Accounting, Auditing & Finance, 2*(1).

Skopljak, V., & Luo, R. (2012). Capital structure and firm performance in the financial sector: Evidence from Australia. *Asian Journal of Finance & Accounting, 4*(1).

Torres-Reyna, O. (2007). *Panel data analysis fixed and random effects using Stata. v. 4.2. Data & statistical services*. Princeton: Princeton University.

Vătavu, S. (2015). The impact of capital structure on financial performance in Romanian listed companies. *Procedia Economics and Finance, 32*, 1314–1322.

Zeitun, R. & Tian, G. G. (2007). Capital structure and corporate performance: Evidence from Jordan.

Role of Innovative Marketing Strategy for Success of Micro, Small, and Medium Enterprises (MSMEs)

4

V. Sathana ⓘ, T. Velnampy ⓘ, and S. Rajumesh ⓘ

4.1 Introduction

Large firms are a threat to small businesses in all countries (Wanninayake and Chovancova 2013). "The Government of Sri Lanka recognizes MSMEs as the backbone of the economy" (Gunawardana 2016, p. 3). MSMEs in Sri Lanka have been struggling to compete with other firms (Vijayakumar 2013; Gajanayake 2010). In addition, the postwar environment of Sri Lanka contains huge problems and challenges (Shivany et al. 2015). "In 1983, 98% of MSMEs accounted for 48.6% of total employment and 31.1% of value added. In 2008, 93% of MSMEs accounted for 29.6% total employment and 20.3% of value added, this evidence clearly shows clearly the poor development of MSMEs" (Vijayakumar 2013, p. 41). Even though MSMEs have accounted for a vast percentage of establishments in Sri Lanka, their contribution to the economy is very low (Vijayakumar 2013). Earlier studies emphasized that MSMEs in Sri Lanka have been struggling to compete with nationally and internationally branded products (Vijayakumar 2013; Gajanayake 2010; Pushpakumari and Watanabe 2009). "Soon after the war, local productions were subjected to a market shock as road connectivity resumed to the wider market with far more advanced production" (Sivatheepan et al. 2018, p. 9). Most of the MSMEs were collapsed and destroyed by internal war while the remaining enterprises in Sri Lanka were vulnerable (Sivatheepan et al. 2018). MSMEs in the Northern Province have not been well developed and have thus diminished over 10 years. MSMEs make a vital contribution to GDP in Sri Lanka. In the Northern Province, more than 99% of enterprises are MSMEs. The growth rates of GDP contribution from the Northern Province were 9% in 2011, 0% in 2012, −8% in 2013, 15% in 2014, 5%

V. Sathana (✉) · T. Velnampy · S. Rajumesh
University of Jaffna, Jaffna, Sri Lanka
e-mail: vsathana@univ.jfn.ac.lk; tvnampy@univ.jfn.ac.lk; rajumesh@univ.jfn.ac.lk

© The Author(s), under exclusive license to Springer Nature
Switzerland AG 2021
S. Dhiman, R. Samaratunge (eds.), *New Horizons in Management, Leadership and Sustainability*, Future of Business and Finance,
https://doi.org/10.1007/978-3-030-62171-1_4

57

in 2015, 10% in 2016, and 0% in 2017 (Central Bank Report 2015, 2018). These numbers display the fluctuating trend of GDP contribution from the NP. This trend also indicates the poor condition of MSMEs in the Northern Province.

The marketing strategy plays an important role in every organization. The marketing of goods or services is the ultimate objective and goal of all types of organizations (Baker and Hart 2008; Kotler et al. 1999). Marketing strategy has been becoming a popular concept among institutions to improve their organization performances (Baker and Hart 2008; Hunt 2017). The application of a marketing strategy allows for the better management of environmental challenges and result in superior performance, sustainable growth, and the development of the organizations themselves (Baker and Hart 2008; Kotler et al. 1999; Hunt 2017). Resource advantage theory of competition explains that marketing strategy is an intangible resource to firms and superior financial performance is achieved by the application of superior marketing strategy (Hunt and Morgan 1995; Hunt 2013; Hunt et al. 2006). MSMEs have limited finance, human, information, and organizational resources (Baker and Hart 2008; O'Dwyer et al. 2009a, b, c). Due to these characteristics, MSMEs cannot apply the common and conventional strategies used by most other firms (Gilmore et al. 2001; Quaye and Mensah 2019). Innovative marketing strategy is the effective specific marketing strategy which was suggested for MSMEs (Carson and Gilmore 2000; Haddad et al. 2019). Even though the literature suggested innovative marketing strategy and variables for MSMEs, they were not empirically tested for any MSMEs. Furthermore, these suggested variables were not tested for any MSMEs in the Sri Lankan context. As such, this research was initiated to study the current value of innovative marketing strategy to the MSMEs in Sri Lanka and to discover the extent to which innovative marketing strategy contributes to the success of MSMEs in the country.

4.2   Literature Review

4.2.1   Micro, Small, and Medium Enterprises

In the Sri Lankan context, the national policy framework for SME development categorized MSMEs as being a part of the "manufacturing sector and service sector and defined micro, small and medium enterprises, as made up of an enterprise which employ less than 300 employees and which has an annual turnover not exceeding Rs.750 Mn" (National Policy Framework for SME Development, p. 3; Gunawardana 2016, p. 18) (Appendix 4.1). The Department of Census and Statistics (2013/2014) categorized MSMEs as belonging to industry and construction as well as trade and services. Moreover, MSMEs were defined based on the "person engaged" for industry and construction, trade, and services which are less than 200, 35, and 75, respectively (Appendix 4.2). MSMEs have limited resources such as finance, human resource, time, lack of expertise, and limited impact in the marketplace (Gilmore et al. 2001). MSMEs have small budgets, but smaller budgets are less complex because there is less room in the budgets. MSMEs have a simpler structure and less restriction on access to internal financial resources (Loucks et al. 2010). MSMEs have limited employee resources such as a lack of knowledge and skills (Loucks et al. 2010). MSMEs do not have any corporate strategy and mission. MSMEs fail to use formal strategic tools, but they use informal and dynamic strategies (Meers and Robertson 2007; Hudson et al. 2001). The haphazard, informal, and unstructured environment of MSMEs leads to short-term focus and irrational decision-making (Blankson and Stokes 2002).

4.2.2   Innovative Marketing Theory

Innovative marketing means creating products or services using new ideas to capture the market opportunity in a new way (O'Dwyer et al. 2009a). The elements of innovative marketing are categorized in terms of marketing variables, modification, customer focus, integrated marketing, unique proposition, and market focus.

Marketing variables: MSMEs engage in innovative marketing in response to market requirements by altering their marketing activities and development of new products. Moreover, marketing adaptations are related to continuous supplemental changes or alterations to products and marketing mix distribution channels which enable them to differentiate their product or service in a niche market from the standardized offerings of large firms (Cummins et al. 2000).

Modification: Within this context, the marketing behaviors of MSMEs fit with the action-oriented activities required to identify change opportunities and nurture continual change in the MSMEs and their markets. The marketing activities of MSMEs can extend from innovative to highly innovative, while sticking to the basic concept of existing features, and it is not essential to adopt products' originality (Cummins et al. 2000). Such adaptations form a central element of MSME innovative marketing may it be proactive or reactive, by initially focusing on the innovations of products and services (Stokes 2000).

Customer focus: Customization is highly possible for micro and small businesses; they can be successful by developing strongly personal relationships (O'Donnell and Cummins 1999). One of the key aspects of MSME marketing strategies is to be innovative in their customer orientation. Stokes (2000) demonstrated that it is essential to identify potential customer groups by process of elimination based on common customer traits. This innovative approach to customers is critical in establishing a competitive advantage for MSMEs (O'Dwyer et al. 2009a).

Integrated marketing: Innovation is pervasive throughout marketing. MSMEs involve continuously small alternatives and change these practices and activities. They make niche customers differentiated the products that are different from the standardized offerings of larger firms (Cummins et al. 2000). This differentiation can be possible due to the prompt marketing of information using formal or informal strategies, which are indicative of the interactive and integrated marketing methods favored by MSMEs (O'Dwyer et al. 2009a).

Market focus: Firms should focus on market-related positioning factors and the adoption of a more flexible structural design for the management of marketing. MSMEs concentrate on financial success as marketing objectives, and they also include the vision for the SME. This, in turn, focuses on the competitive differentiation achieved through innovation, enabling the formation and maintenance of the material competitive advantage which is required of innovative marketing (O'Dwyer et al. 2009a).

Unique proposition: The characteristics of innovation within enterprises have been identified as the search for creative, novel, or unusual solutions to problems and needs. This includes the development of new products and services and new processes for performing organizational functions. In addition, O'Dwyer et al. (2009a) suggest that the purpose of market innovation is "to identify better (new) potential markets, and satisfy those target customers." Hence the dimensions of innovative marketing are uniqueness, newness, and unconventionality.

4.2.2.1 Characteristics of Innovation in Business

In facing the challenges posed by limited growth conditions and larger resource-rich competitors, MSMEs compete using a combination of invention and pioneering products or services and by adopting flexible business structures, strategies, and culture. Innovation is the most significant factor that can be used by MSMEs to compensate for any disadvantages experienced because of their size. Innovativeness can be defined in terms of its nature, continuity, and attributes of innovation (O'Dwyer et al. 2009b).

Nature of innovation: "Innovation takes the form of either radical or incremental innovations where radical innovations produce fundamental changes in the activities of organizations and large departures from existing practices while incremental innovations are the improvement of existing process, product, service or market approach and involve a lesser degree of departure from existing practices" (O'Dwyer et al. 2009a, p. 50).

Continuity of innovation: Continuous incremental innovation concentrated on existing market conditions, and discontinuous innovation focuses on altering market conditions to achieve competitive advantage. The vast majority of MSMEs successfully engage in a process of incremental innovations, which has a cumulative and positive effect on their business (O'Dwyer et al. 2009b).

Degree of innovations: Johannessen et al. (2001) illustrated the three degrees of the innovation process within a company. The first degree is innovation, which involves changes within the model of existing production methods and management philosophy. The second focuses on changes from one production method and management philosophy to a new type. Meanwhile, the third concentrates on changes within the model of the new productions and management philosophy.

4.2.3 Development of MSME

Yang and Xu (2006) and Lavric (2010) described that the MSME development presupposes their growth in the efficiency and efficacy of their organization. Yang and Xu (2006) identified four elements of MSME development: changes in the number of MSMEs, production value, profits, and number of employees in each region, in order to analyze regional differences of entrepreneurship. Lavric (2010) discovered six elements in the MSMEs: the number of enterprises, the number of persons employed, the gross value added, the apparent labor productivity, the rate of profitability, and the propensity to invest.

Number of enterprises: It represents one of the most often used indicators in the studies. It is considered to be a proper proxy to illustrate the level of the entrepreneurship spirit from a country, especially when it's divided by the population number (the density), making therefore possible the comparison between different states, regions, and even localities. At the same time for single MSMEs, it is the base for the qualitative expansion. For a single MSME, an increase in branches, outlets, or enterprises is considered to measure the development of MSME.

Number of persons employed: It is also a very popular indicator which is taken into account, and this is because of the social implications it brings along. MSMEs should be treated with priority because they are the only ones that still create jobs; the number of persons employed gives us a clue over these development tendencies and also over the employment structure of MSMEs and large enterprises. For single MSMEs, a number of persons are employed in a MSME.

Gross value added: "In comparison with the first two, it is an indicator of results, representing actually the amount of actual salaries and other elements related to labor by factoring in cost, profit, exploitation subsidies and fixed capital amortization, after subtracting production taxes. The total value of raw materials consumed, cost of industrial and non-industrial services provided by others and fuel, electricity and water consumption, have all been defined as the value of inputs (intermediate consumptions)" (Lavric 2010, p. 934). Gross value added is calculated as the difference between the value of output and the value of intermediate consumptions. For a single SME, gross value added is the difference between the gross value of product and expenses (intermediate consumption).

Apparent labor productivity: "It is defined as gross value added (at factors cost) per person employed. The word 'apparent' refers to the fact that this is a broad evaluation of what happens physically at the production level. This measure will be analyzed from two perspectives concerning the rate of growth (determined using the growth rates of gross value added and persons employed and the ratio between the MSMEs labor productivity" (Lavric 2010, p. 934). Labor productivity of a single SME is a gross value added (at factors cost) per person employed in a MSME.

Profitability rate: "It is calculated as the ratio between the gross profit and the gross value added at factors cost and represents pretty well the performances of the enterprise" (Lavric 2010, p. 934). In other words, this measure reveals the MSME's capacity to accomplish its primary reason of existence, as it is being one of the variables that illustrate the enterprise's efficiency. The net profitability rate is considered for a single MSME.

Propensity to invest: "It is determined as the ratio between the gross investments and the gross value added at factors cost and aims to emphasize the future development perspective of the MSMEs sector" (Lavric 2010, p. 934). The specificity of this measure consists actually of the fact that it is a present allocation of resources for future results and therefore it catches the mentality, vision, and risk tolerance that entrepreneurs and managers manifest in real life. This is the future investment in the gross profit for single SME.

4.2.4   Balanced Scorecard Performance

Karabulut (2015) explained a model of the balanced scorecard approach for the performance of a manufacturing firm in Turkey. The balanced scorecard approach is used to measure the performance of firms. It links an organizational strategy to firm performance. It reveals financial performance, customer performance, internal business process performance and learning, and growth performance. The financial dimension focuses on financial objectives which reflect the firm's success in reaching its goals. The customer dimension determines a firm's goals based on customer evaluation criteria. The dimensions of internal business process force managers to keep a smooth process in firms. The learning and growth perspective defines the structure, critical factors, internal business processes, and customer processes to improve the growth of the firm in the long term.

4.3   Hypothesis Development

The previous marketing literatures, theories, and models regarding MSME marketing and development are touted as the foundations required to design the appropriateness of a marketing strategy for MSMEs. In this context, the theory of resource advantage is mainly underpinned to produce an appropriate model. Furthermore, MSME marketing characteristics are also underpinned to produce and construct this model of MSMEs in a strong way. Resource advantage theory explains that superior resources lead to superior financial performance (Hunt and Morgan 1995; Hunt 2013, 2017, 2018). The resources can be tangible and intangible; a marketing strategy is an intangible resource to firms (Hunt et al. 2006). The managers or owners are the responsible ones and adopt suitable strategies to achieve superior performance, and resource characteristics are heterogeneous and imperfectly mobile (Hunt 2013, 2017, 2018). The firm's resources are financial, physical, legal, human, organizational, informational, and relational (Hunt 2018). MSMEs have limited resources (Baker and Hart 2008; O'Dwyer et al. 2009a, b, c). Gilmore et al. (2001) acknowledged that managers of MSMEs understand the limited resource capacity and follow innovative marketing rather than the conventional marketing and then practices used in large companies. Innovative marketing strategy was suggested for MSMEs by Baker and Hart (2008); O'Dwyer, Gilmore, and Carson (2009a, b, c); Carson and Gilmore (2000); Quaye and Mensah (2019); and Finoti et al. (2017). This strategy is suggested as a valuable, unique, and superior intangible resource that can be used by MSMEs to achieve superior performance under resource advantage theory (Hunt 2013, 2017, 2018).

The objective of the organization is to earn superior financial performance (Hunt 2018). Shareholder benefits are considered as major objectives of any organization, and marketing understands this strategic role (Lukas et al. 2005). This resource advantage theory focuses only on the shareholders as a financial success (Hunt 2018); in contrast this research underpinned balance scorecard performance measurement considering the benefit to all stakeholders as a customer, internal process, and employees (Freeman 1984). Moreover, measurement regarding the development of SMEs was examined and adopted as an indicator of performance development in this research. Hence the balanced scorecard performance measurement with the SME development indicators is utilized to measure the development of SMEs; it is a special aspect in this research. Overall, the new insights of this research found that marketing strategy as intangible resources was linked with performance development.

In facing the challenges posed by limited growth conditions, innovation is the most significant factor that can be used by MSMEs to compensate for any disadvantages that arise experienced because of their size or their internal and external environments (O'Dwyer et al. 2009b; Ferreira and Coelho 2020). The success of MSME innovation is determined by its newness, the extent of its adoption, and its translation into an exploitable opportunity for the MSME. "Marketing's role in innovation is to provide the concepts, tools and infrastructure to close the gap between innovation and market positioning to achieve a sustainable competitive advantage" (Gardner 1991, p. 49). Small firms can compete using the development of innovative products or processes, which is reliant on the accurate market and customer information (Haddad et al. 2019; Low and MacMillan 1988). Creative, alternative, and instinctive marketing practices may flourish even under financial resource constraints. "The innovative behaviour is illustrated as exploitation of an opportunity by the owner/managers" (O'Dwyer et al. 2009a, p. 51). Innovative marketing is a significant, unique, and valuable intangible resource that can contribute to the success of MSMEs (O'Dwyer et al. 2009a). Innovative marketing strategy is a superior resource which leads to the superior performance of MSMEs (O'Regan and Ghobadian 2005; O'Dwyer et al. 2009c; Karabulut 2015).

Small firm owners/managers can achieve a sustainable competitive advantage by encouraging strong market orientation which stems from engaging in innovative practices. The key factors of MSME are profitability, long-term growth, and survival (O'Dwyer et al. 2009c; Ferreira and Coelho 2020). When innovative marketing is integrated fully into the organization and used on a proactive/reactive basis to support MSMEs operating in a dynamic environment, it can successfully be used to successfully achieve organizational goals (Finoti et al. 2017; O'Dwyer et al. 2009c).

In addition, innovation can exist within MSME marketing and contribute to organizational success (O'Dwyer et al. 2009b). It depends upon the application of the perceived value of a marketing throughout the organization, and the integration of marketing helps achieve organizational goals. Innovation is essential in order to guarantee the growth of the business within a highly competitive environment (O'Dwyer et al. 2009b). Innovative marketing objectives concentrate on the level at which new products or services meet their commercial objectives and the vision for the MSME. The perception of innovation encompasses customer satisfaction, a competitive advantage, creativity, and profit (O'Dwyer et al. 2009a).

Drucker (1954) linked innovation with marketing, and the purpose of innovation is to create a customer base, because customers determine what the business is. "Dynamically continuous innovations use new technology to serve an established function where consumers often adapt their behaviour; this adaptation may be resisted if the change in behaviour is substantial and if the costs are too high" (O'Dwyer 2009, p. 32). Amendment to its distribution channel helps gain a competitive advantage and increase cost efficiency as well as customer satisfaction. The attributes of IMS reflect the response of customers to the proposed innovation from their perception of the strength of the advantages posed by the innovation (relative advantage) (Karabulut 2015). Kleindl et al. (1996) found that one of the key aspects of MSME marketing strategies is their aim to be innovative in their customer orientation. Stokes (2000) revealed that segmentation, targeting, and positioning processes are traditional approaches to eliminate unsuitable groups and select potential customer groups. This innovative approach to customers is critical in establishing a competitive advantage for MSMEs and has significance for MSMEs in positively impacting customer satisfaction and, in turn, company performance (Kandampully 2002; Stokes 2000).

While a few MSMEs may experience rapid growth as a result of innovation, the majority of MSMEs successfully engage in a process of incremental innovation, which creates more customer demand and long-term sustainability (Carroll 2002; Stokes 2000). Innovation is evidenced through the production of a unique concept pieced together from existing ideas and concepts and including the involvement of employees, development of new intelligence and ideas, and employee satisfaction (Cummins et al. 2000). Incremental innovation is a smaller change from existing practices; it induces the internal process related to product or services (Ettlie and Subramaniam 2004). Continuous incremental innovations result from the ongoing improvement of techniques in the internal process. Small firms have been found to have higher rates of innovation compared to their share of sales or number of employees (Das and He 2006). The MSMEs utilize market intelligence to maximize their market focus for the benefit of the business. With regard to these facts and evidences, the researcher hypothesized that:

H1: Innovative marketing strategy influences on the development of MSMEs.

H1a: Innovative marketing strategy influences on the financial performance of MSMEs.

H1b: Innovative marketing strategy influences on the customer performance of MSMEs.

H1c: Innovative marketing strategy influences on the internal process performance of MSMEs.

H1d: Innovative marketing strategy influences on the learning and growth performance of MSMEs.

4.4   Methodology

This study formulated the research hypothesis and framework, which was validated using a questionnaire survey followed by structural equation modeling (SEM) analysis. The study adopted innovative marketing strategy as an independent variable and MSME development as the dependent variable (business performance). The study also explored the effect of IMS on the development of MSMEs.

This study designed a questionnaire based on current theories and literature. Measures for innovative marketing strategy were derived from a review of the innovative marketing literature (Rajapathirana and Hui 2018; O'Dwyer et al. 2009a, b, c; Baker and Hart 2008). To measure the development of MSMEs, variable items and scales were designed on the basis of literature regarding MSME development (Yang and Xu 2006; Lavric 2010) balance scorecard performance measurement (Wu and Lin 2016; Karabulut 2015; Hubbard 2009; Tsai and Chou 2009) and the feedback obtained in the interview and focus group discussion.

Based on the literature, variables of innovative marketing strategy were identified. Further, we conducted both a pretest and a pilot test prior to the formal survey. In the pretest, convenience sampling was used to select 10 owners of SMEs. Furthermore, two group discussions and interviews with four academic experts on marketing and entrepreneurship research were adopted for this study. The findings revealed that a number of question items were unclear. These sentences were subsequently modified, and one item from IMS and one inappropriate aspect of MSME development were deleted. Finally, this questionnaire employed questions drawn from relevant research that underwent semantic modification by scholars and experts as well as adjustments proposed by MSME owners. In addition to that, convenience sampling was then employed to select 48 MSMEs for the pilot test. Reliability and validity analyses were conducted on the data, the results of which presented a Cronbach's exceeding 0.7 for each aspect with eigenvalues over 1 and cumulative explained variance exceeding 0.5. Moreover, the factor loadings were greater than or close to 0.5, and the item-to-total correlation coefficients exceeded or were close to 0.5, indicating strong reliability and convergent validity (Kerlinger 1978). In its final form, the test passed reliability and validity testing in a pilot test, indicating good content validity. The final questionnaire was divided into three parts as profile information of MSMEs, IMS, and MSME development. Innovative marketing strategy comprised 3 aspects which included 17 items and MSME performance, comprising 4 aspects with 26 items. All question items were assessed using a five-point Likert scale with higher scores indicating a higher level of satisfaction.

The target population in MSMEs in the Northern Province included 3203 owners of MSMEs. The proportionate stratified random sampling method was used to select samples for this study. A total of 1038 samples were selected to issue the questionnaire; 686 of them were considered valid which represent a response rate of 66%. According to Bentler and Chou (1987), samples should be at least five times the number of estimated parameters, and Boomsma and Hoogland (2001) claimed that a sample size in the 200–400 range is the most appropriate for SEM analysis. Thus, the sample size in this study was deemed acceptable.

4.5   Key Findings

The innovative marketing strategy included 17 items. Initially the insignificant values of intercorrelation between items were excluded; they were three items, viz., "Vision (VIS), Profit focus (PF) and Image (IMA)." All other values of the commonalities of 14 items from innovative marketing strategy were above 0.5, excluding "customer focus (IM13)" which had a value of 0.405. Development of MSME included 26 items. Initially the insignificant values of intercorrelation between items were excluded; they were six items, viz., "Return on asset(ROA), Gearing (GEAR), Gross value added (GVA), Number of enterprises (NEN), Ratio of Number of new products to total (RNP) and Duration to launch a new product (DLNP)." All values of the commonalities of 20 items from the development of MSME were above 0.5. Further, the factor of a component was decided based on an eigenvalue greater than 1. Four factors were identified from the exploratory factor analysis (Table 4.1). In summary, exploratory factor analysis identified three factors that could be extracted from the items related to innovative marketing strategy and four factors from MSME development. Our results presented a Cronbach's value between 0.773 and 0.929 for each aspect (factors), thereby demonstrating the acceptable overall reliability of the questionnaire (as shown in Table 4.1). The eigenvalue of each factor was above 1, the cumulative explained variance exceeded 0.6, and the factor loadings of each item were all higher than 0.5.

The study also used AMOS software to conduct confirmatory factor analysis (CFA) in order to further determine the efficiency and construct validity of the measurement scale models. CFA showed that x^2/df is 3.5, root mean square residual (RMR) is 0.048, goodness-of-fit index (GFI) is 0.871, normed fit index (NFI) is 0.899, adjust goodness-of-fit index (AGFI) is 0.847, comparative fit index (CFI) is 0.92, and root mean square of approximation (RMSEA) is 0.060. All indexes of this model met or came close to the acceptable standards (Bentler 1990). Lower factor loading of all items should be deleted for latent construct due to the unidimensionality problem. For newly developed items, the factor loading for every item should exceed 0.5. For an established item, the factor loading for every item should be 0.6 or higher (Hair et al. 2014). Construct validity is made up of four components, viz., convergent validity, discriminant validity, nomological validity, and face validity (Hair et al. 2014). Convergent validity can be estimated by factor loadings, average variance extracted (AVE), and reliability (Table 4.2).

Table 4.1 EFA result with factor loading and reliability of innovative marketing strategy and development of MSMEs

Aspects and items	Code	Factor loading	% of explained variance	Cumulative explained variance (%)	Cronbach's alpha
Marketing variable (MI)			48.622	48.622	0.902
Product enhancement	PE	0.83			
Use different marketing communications	DMC	0.82			
Adopt pricing system	PS	0.85			
Alteration of the distribution channel	DC	0.91			
Market centered	MC	0.90			
Customer focus	CF	0.61			
Unique proposition (UP)			15.336	63.958	0.888
New	NEW	0.84			
Unique	UNI	0.88			
Unconventional	UNC	0.77			
Product quality	PQ	0.94			
Integrated marketing (IM)			9.358	73.315	0.886
Proaction	PRO	0.85			
Change	CHA	0.76			
Marketing integration	MI	0.89			
Permeation of marketing throughout	PMT	0.89			
Financial performance (FP)			42.969	42.969	0.889
ROI	ROI	0.855			
Sales revenue	SR	0.878			
Cash flow	CAF	0.768			
Profitability rate	PIT	0.795			
Capital growth	CGR	0.550			
Labor productivity	LAP	0.753			
Number of employees	NOE	0.749			
Customer performance (CP)			14.850	57.820	0.929
Number of new customers	NNC	0.941			
Sales to new customers	SNC	0.890			
Sales to current customers	SCC	0.851			
Customer retention rate	CRR	0.820			
Internal process performance (IPP)			6.864	64.684	0.915

(continued)

Table 4.1 (continued)

Aspects and items	Code	Factor loading	% of explained variance	Cumulative explained variance (%)	Cronbach's alpha
Technology for new process and new product development	NPD	0.923			
Production cost	PC	0.912			
Duration of productions	DP	0.759			
Defective production rate	DPR	0.715			
Ratio of on time delivery	ROTD	0.707			
Learning and growth performance (LGP)			5.230	69.914	0.773
Employee happiness	EH	0.956			
Gathering information about new product and customers	IAPC	0.715			
Employee turnover	ET	0.624			
Number of employee suggestion and implementation	ESI	0.593			

The standardized regression weight of all items is above 0.6 of the standardized regression weight except the customer focus (CF) with 0.524 and the number of employee suggestions and implementation of 0.546. AVEs of learning and growth performance are 0.461 which is close to 0.5 (Table 4.3). All other AVE values of constructs are above or close to 0.5. The values of the construct reliability of all factors are above 0.7 (Table 4.3). These measures ensured the validity of the factors which were adopted for the model. The diagonal value should be higher than the square root of AVE to prove the discriminant validity (Hair et al. 2014). All the factors have high discriminant validity and are given in Table 4.3.

4.5.1 Structural Model Validity

AMOS 20.0 software was used to conduct SEM, following the criteria of the good model (Hu and Bentler 1999), to ensure consistency with the following criteria: x^2/df should be less than 3 (Hair et al. 2014), the RMSEA value should be less than 0.05, and the GFI, AGFI, RFI, NFI, and CFI indicators should be greater than 0.9 (Joreskog and Sorbom 1989). The findings indicated that the relevance of the overall model was close to, or met, the ideal standard, thereby demonstrating that the proposed model was acceptable, as shown in Table 4.4.

Table 4.2 Factor loading of the measurement model

Items	Item no.	Factor loading
Innovative marketing strategy		
Marketing variable (MV)		
Product enhancement	PE	0.860
Use different marketing communications	DMC	0.825
Adopt pricing system	PS	0.865
Alteration of the distribution channel	DC	0.820
Market centered	MC	0.812
Customer focus	CF	0.524
Unique proposition		
New	NEW	0.830
Unique	UNI	0.796
Unconventional	UNC	0.804
Product quality	PQ	0.851
Integrated marketing		
Proaction	PRO	0.829
Change	CHA	0.836
Marketing integration	MI	0.804
Permeation of marketing throughout	PMT	0.783
Financial performance		
ROI	ROI	0.777
Sales revenue	SR	0.792
Cash flow	CAF	0.737
Profitability rate	PIT	0.744
Capital growth	CGR	0.731
Labor productivity	LAP	0.680
Number of employees	NOE	0.673
Customer performance		
Number of new customers	NNC	0.845
Sales to new customers	SNC	0.909
Sales to current customers	SCC	0.878
Customer retention rate	CRR	0.881
Internal process performance		
Technology for new process and new product development	NPD	0.801
Production cost	PC	0.856
Duration of productions	DP	0.867
Defective production rate	DPR	0.797
Ratio of on time delivery	ROTD	0.805
Learning and growth performance		
Employee happiness	EH	0.679
Gathering information about new product and customers	IAPC	0.776
Employee turnover	ET	0.693
Number of employee suggestions and implementations	ESI	0.546

Table 4.3 Average variance extracted (AVE), construct reliability (CR), and discriminant validity of construct

	CR	AVE	IM	IPP	CP	FP	MV	UP	LGP
IM	0.887	0.662	**0.814**						
IPP	0.915	0.684	0.562	**0.827**					
CP	0.932	0.774	0.520	0.791	**0.880**				
FP	0.891	0.540	0.185	0.428	0.412	**0.735**			
MV	0.913	0.640	0.687	0.725	0.765	0.371	**0.800**		
UP	0.893	0.675	0.477	0.324	0.317	0.143	0.420	**0.822**	
LGP	0.771	0.461	0.339	0.564	0.512	0.677	0.489	0.204	**0.679**

4.5.2 Hypothesis Testing

According to the Path analysis, innovative marketing strategy (IMS) has a positive influence on the development of MSMEs (SRW = 0.88) as shown in Fig. 4.1, thereby supporting H1. IMS has a positive effect on financial performance (SRW = 0.46, Fig. 4.2), which supports H1a. IMS has an effect on customer performance (SRW = 0.85, Fig. 4.2), thus supporting H1b. IMS has a positive effect on the IPP (SRW = 0.91, Fig. 4.2), hence supporting H1c. IMS has an effect on the LGP (SRW = 0.60, Fig. 4.2), thereby supporting H1d. In summary, IMS enhances MSME development directly. Our results show (Table 4.5) that innovative marketing strategy has the greatest effect on SME development. However, with regard to the effect of innovative marketing strategies, the greatest influence appears to be the effect of innovative marketing strategy on IPP, followed by customer performance, then LGP, and ultimately financial performance.

4.6   Conclusion and Discussion

Despite IMS having been suggested for MSMEs, no studies have not sought the effect on the business performance in Sri Lanka. This study selected owners of MSMEs as respondents to investigate the influence of IMS with an effective measurement scale. The findings provide a valuable intangible resource for MSMEs. This study has developed an influencing model to illustrate the effectiveness of IMS implemented by MSMEs. From the findings of the study, three dimensions were diagnosed for the MSMEs in the Sri Lankan context. These included marketing variables, integrated marketing, and unique proposition.

This research indicated that "marketing variables" contribute highly to MSMEs. Hence, MSMEs need to apply the marketing variables (0.92) of IMS on a weekly basis. Under the marketing variables, product enhancement, pricing system, and marketing communications are the most important factors for MSMEs. Moreover, distribution channel, market centered, and customer focus are the other important factors for marketing variables. The second important variable for IMS is "integrated marketing" which includes change, proaction, marketing integration, and the permeation of marketing throughout. Among these factors, change and proaction

Table 4.4 Structural model validity

x^2	df	x^2/df	p-value	RMR	GFI	AGFI	NFI	CFI	RMSEA
2551.607	1022	2.497	0.00	0.088	0.865	0.854	0.861	0.911	0.047

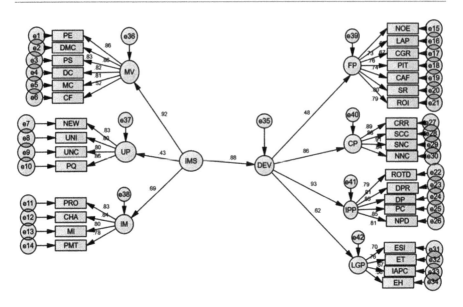

Fig. 4.1 Path model of IMS and development of SMEs

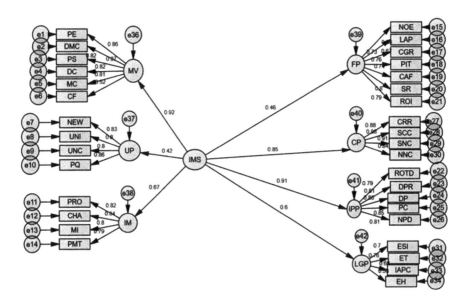

Fig. 4.2 Path model of IMS and dimension of the development of SMEs

are the effective factors for the integrated marketing of IMS. MSMEs need to apply the integrated marketing of IMS (0.67) for every month. The third vital variable of IMS is "unique proposition" which includes product quality and can be new, unconventional, and unique. Product quality needs to be a highly considered factor for unique proposition. The newness and unconventional aspects of products or

Table 4.5 Hypotheses of IMS and development of SMEs

Hypotheses	Standardized regression weights (SRW)	Significant level	Conclusion
Innovative marketing strategy – development	0.88	0.000	H1: accepted
Innovative marketing strategy – financial performance	0.46	0.000	H1a: accepted
Innovative marketing strategy – customer performance	0.85	0.000	H1b: accepted
Innovative marketing strategy – internal process performance	0.91	0.000	H1c: accepted
Innovative marketing strategy – learning and growth performance	0.60	0.000	H1d: accepted

services are also significant factors for a unique proposition. This research indicated that MSMEs need to apply the unique proposition of IMS (0.42) on a yearly basis.

Our results identified one key path, through which IMS highly induces the development of MSMEs. The second most important path is the enhancement of internal process performance by applying the IMS. This research proved that innovative marketing strategy also has a high influence on the internal process performance, particularly a firm admits short duration to produce products/services with a low cost of production. Firms adopted advanced technology for new process and product/service development. It also caused a low defective production rate. The third path is that IMS enhances customer performance. This result demonstrates the vigorous customer development of MSMEs through the IMS application in the Northern Province. This result indicated that MSMEs obtain new customers, increase sales to new and existing customers, and continuously retained customers by applying IMS. Next, the findings ensured that IMS induces the learning and growth performance of MSMEs. This result explains the need for IMS to foster positive learning and growth performance of MSMEs. By applying this strategy, the most important benefit is that the firm gathered information about new products/services as well as its customers. Meanwhile the second benefit is that it was possible to have a low employee turnover. Further employees of MSMEs are willing and happy to learn and grow in their work, and employees are highly open to giving suggestions and implementations. Finally, this result revealed that IMS influences on the financial performance of MSMEs. According to the result, by applying IMS, MSMEs are possible to earn high sales revenue and ROI, then earn an adequate profit, and have sufficient cash flow. Another important benefit is that it increases the capital investment of the business. At last this strategy helps to sustain high labor productivity and increase the number of employees for MSMEs' work.

Our findings suggest that MSMEs should persist with IMS in order to develop their performances of MSMEs, which is consistent with the findings of Finoti et al. (2017) and Haddad et al. (2019). MSMEs are able to use innovative marketing strategies on a weekly basis and continue to implement IMS in order to develop themselves which was previously described by Baker and Hart (2008). Our result indicates that IMS enhances the internal process performance which is consistent with Carroll (2002) and Stokes (2000). Furthermore, IMS induces the customer performance of MSMEs, which is consistent with the literature of Karabulut (2015), Kandampully (2002), and Stokes (2000). The innovative marketing strategy has a positive effect on learning and growth performance of SMEs. This is an important finding that is related to Carroll (2002) and Ettlie and Subramaniam (2004). Innovative marketing strategy had a positive effect on the financial performance of SMEs, which is consistent with the O'Dwyer, Gilmore, and Carson, (2009a, b) and Cummins et al. (2000). These results indicate that MSMEs should apply innovative marketing strategies to develop performance.

4.6.1 Limitations and Suggestions

This study examined MSMEs in the Northern Province. Most of the enterprises are on a micro level. These results are not generalized to medium enterprises. Further research can take MSMEs from other provinces, thus allowing for comparison among the two sets of data. MSMEs have certain characteristics such as size and age of the firm, which may exercise an influence over the result and may be considered as the moderating variable of the cause-effect relationship between innovative marketing strategy and performance. Regarding research methodology, 15 categories of MSMEs were adopted for this study. Future researchers can accommodate more categories of MSMEs. This research applied variables which existed in the literature and concepts and did not explore new variables. Future researchers could explore variables of innovative marketing strategy with a qualitative study relating to the context of MSMEs in Sri Lanka.

4.6.2 Implications

The current study integrates the resource advantage theory with the innovative marketing theory and balance scorecard theory of performance in driving the theoretical framework. Meanwhile, the framework addresses the specific nature of MSMEs in Sri Lanka. Therefore, the framework of the study is new for the area and deviates from the conventional frameworks applied in the various other areas. This empirical investigation has confirmed the value of a marketing strategy to develop the MSMEs. This study attempts to answer an unproved aspect of previous studies. Accordingly, the effect of innovative marketing strategy on the development of MSMEs has been tested. This study ensured the essential each factor of innovative marketing strategy for MSMEs. Further to this, the study found that financial, customer, learning and growth, and internal process performance are the vital dimensions of the performance development of MSMEs in Sri Lanka. Moreover, this indicated that the MSMEs prefer to apply innovative marketing strategy to achieve more financial success, increase customers, increase internal process, and increase learning and growth in this postwar market. Altogether this study indicated that innovative marketing strategy boosts the development of MSMEs. As far as MSMEs are concerned, the most critical challenge is to develop a MSME in a developing country. Marketing strategy helps to manage the aforementioned challenges. In addition to that, the developed framework can be used as a strategic plan for the development process of the MSME sector. This can be done by determining the appropriate level of a marketing strategy for the development of MSMEs. The value of this research is to use this model as an instrument to improve the MSME sector. In particular, innovative marketing strategies can be instrumental in bringing about improvement in financial success, customer performance, internal process performance, and learning and growth performance. Moreover, owners of MSMEs can understand each innovative marketing features and the level of each factor that must be maintained in the Sri Lankan context. MSMEs implement innovative marketing programs to enhance their performance.

Takeaways: Marketing Strategy Lesson for MSMEs

Lesson 1: Understand the need and value of IMS for MSMEs. This study has developed an influencing model which illustrated the effectiveness of IMS to MSMEs. Findings produced a valuable intangible resource for MSMEs. MSMEs need to apply IMS when facing challenging and competitive environments. This research also explains the value of IMS for the stakeholders of MSMEs.

Lesson 2: Diagnose the readiness of the MSMEs to adopt IMS. MSMEs suffer from limited resources pertaining to finance, human, organizational, and relational resources. This research diagnosed the unique capabilities of MSMEs when using IMS. MSMEs need to devote their time to apply the IMS to overcome their barriers. This research suggested three dimensions of IMS, namely, marketing variables, integrated marketing, and unique proposition. MSMEs need to apply the marketing variables of IMS for every week, the integrated marketing of IMS for every month, and the unique proposition of IMS for every year.

Lesson 3: Understand the characteristics of MSMEs' marketing. MSMEs have the features of resource scarcity, while at the same time they have flexible structure and decision-making characteristics. This research considered the features of MSMEs in a developing country and postwar market features which contain huge problems and challenges as opposed to MSMEs in developed countries.

Lesson 4: Identify the broad scope of performance development of MSMEs. In this research, the stakeholder-based balanced scorecard performance and the MSME's development indicators were applied when producing the *performance development of MSMEs*. This broad scope includes financial performance, customer performance, internal process performance, and learning and growth performance.

Lesson 5: Evaluate the influence of IMS on the development of MSMEs. This research proved that there is a significant influence of IMS on the development of MSMEs. In particular, the results indicated that the implementation of innovative marketing strategies by MSMEs can help to boost internal process performance and assist with vigorous customer development of MSMEs through the IMS in Northern Province. Moreover, the findings ensured that IMS induces the learning and growth performance as well as the financial performance of MSMEs.

Reflection Questions

1. What is the current value of the innovative marketing strategy for the MSMEs in Sri Lanka?
2. What are the important dimensions and indicators of IMS in relation to MSMEs in Sri Lanka?
3. What are the current problems and challenges of MSMEs in Sri Lanka?
4. What types of performance are expected to develop for MSMEs in Sri Lanka?
5. To what extent does innovative marketing strategy contribute to the success of MSMEs in Sri Lanka?

Appendices

Appendix 4.1

Sector	Criteria	Medium	Small	Micro
Manufacturing sector	Annual turnover	Rs. Mn. 251–750	Rs. Mn.16–250	Less than Rs. Mn. 15
	No. of employees	51–300	11–50	Less than 10
Service sector	Annual turnover	Rs. Mn. 251–750	Rs. Mn.16–250	Less than Rs. Mn. 15
	No. of employees	51–200	11–50	Less than 10

Appendix 4.2

	SME groups	Criteria (number of persons engaged)
Industry and construction	Micro	1–4
	Small	5–24
	Medium	25–199
	Large	200 and above
Trade	Micro	1–3
	Small	4–14
	Medium	15–34
	Large	35 and above
Services	Micro	1–4
	Small	5–15
	Medium	16–74
	Large	75 and above

References

Baker, M., & Hart, S. (2008). *The marketing book*. London: Routledge.

Bentler, P. M. (1990). Comparative fit indexes in structural models. *Psychological Bulletin, 107*(2), 238.

Bentler, P. M., & Chou, C. P. (1987). Practical issues in structural modeling. *Sociological Methods & Research, 16*(1), 78–117.

Blankson, C., & Stokes, D. (2002). Marketing practices in the UK small business sector. *Marketing Intelligence & Planning, 20*(1), 49–61.

Boomsma, A., & Hoogland, J. J. (2001). The robustness of LISREL modeling revisited. Structural equation models: Present and future. *A Festschrift in honor of Karl Jöreskog, 2*(3), 139–168.

Carroll, D. (2002). Releasing trapped thinking in colleges. Part 2: Managing innovation and building innovation into ordinary work. *Quality Assurance in Education, 10*(1), 5–16.

Carson, D., & Gilmore, A. (2000). SME marketing management competencies. *International Business Review, 9*(3), 363–382.

Central Bank Report. (2015). *Statistical appendix*, Sri Lanka. www.cbsl.gov.lk › files › annual_report › 14_Appendix.

Central Bank Report. (2018). *Statistical appendix*, Sri Lanka. www.cbsl.gov.lk › annual_report › 2018 › 14_Appendix.

Cummins, D., Gilmore, A., Carson, D., & O'Donnell, A. (2000). Innovative marketing in SMEs: A conceptual and descriptive framework. *International Journal of New Product Development and Innovation Management, 2*(3), 231–248.

Das, T. K., & He, I. Y. (2006). Entrepreneurial firms in search of established partners: Review and recommendations. *International Journal of Entrepreneurial Behavior & Research, 12*(3), 114–143.

Department of Census and Statistic. (2013/2014). *Atlas of economic activities of Sri Lanka*. Ministry of National Policies and Economic Affairs. http://www.statistics.gov.lk/EconomicCensus/DCS_IndCondTtradeService_Atlas_2014_Final.pdf

Drucker, P. F. (1954). *The practice of management*. New York: Harper & Row.

Ettlie, J. E., & Subramaniam, M. (2004). Changing strategies and tactics for new product development. *Journal of Product Innovation Management, 21*(2), 95–109.

Ferreira, J., & Coelho, A. (2020). Dynamic capabilities, innovation and branding capabilities and their impact on competitive advantage and SME's performance in Portugal: The moderating effects of entrepreneurial orientation. *International Journal of Innovation Science, 12*, 255. https://doi.org/10.1108/IJIS-10-2018-0108.

Finoti, L., Didonet, S. R., Toaldo, A. M., & Martins, T. S. (2017). The role of the marketing strategy process in the innovativeness-performance relationship of SMEs. *Marketing Intelligence & Planning, 35*(3), 298–315.

Freeman, R. E. (1984). *Strategic management: A stakeholder perspective*. Boston: Pitman.

Gajanayake, R. (2010). *The impact of marketing strategies and behavior of small and medium enterprises on their business growth*. In International conference on Business and Information (ICBI), University of Kelaniya.

Gardner, D. M. (1991). Exploring the marketing/entrepreneurship interface. In G. E. Hills (Ed.), *Research at the marketing/entrepreneurship interface* (pp. 3–21). Chicago: University of Illinois.

Gilmore, A., Carson, D., & Grant, K. (2001). SME marketing in practice. *Marketing Intelligence & Planning, 19*(1), 6–11.

Gunawardana, D. P. (2016). *National Policy Framework for SME Development*. http://www.industry.gov.lk/web/images/pdf/gg.pdf

Haddad, M. I., Williams, I. A., Hammoud, M. S., & Dwyer, R. J. (2019). Strategies for implementing innovation in small and medium-sized enterprises. *World Journal of Entrepreneurship, Management and Sustainable Development, 16*(1), 12–29.

Hair, J. F., Black, W. C., Babin, B. J., & Anderson, R. E. (2014). *Multivariate data analysis*. Global Edition.

Hu, L. T., & Bentler, P. M. (1999). Cutoff criteria for fit indexes in covariance structure analysis: Conventional criteria versus new alternatives. *Structural Equation Modeling: A Multidisciplinary Journal, 6*(1), 1–55.

Hubbard, G. (2009). Measuring organizational performance: Beyond the triple bottom line. *Business Strategy and the Environment, 18*(3), 177–191.

Hudson, M., Smart, A., & Bourne, M. (2001). Theory and practice in SME performance measurement systems. *International Journal of Operations & Production Management, 21*(8), 1096–1115.

Hunt, S. D. (2013). A general theory of business marketing: RA theory, Alderson, the ISBM framework, and the IMP theoretical structure. *Industrial Marketing Management, 42*(3), 283–293.

Hunt, S. D. (2017). Strategic marketing, sustainability, the triple bottom line, and resource-advantage (RA) theory: Securing the foundations of strategic marketing theory and research. *Academy of Marketing Science (AMS) Review, 7*(1–2), 52–66.

Hunt, S. D. (2018). Advancing marketing strategy in the marketing discipline and beyond: From promise, to neglect, to prominence, to fragment (to promise?). *Journal of Marketing Management, 34*(1–2), 16–51.

Hunt, S. D., & Morgan, R. M. (1995). The comparative advantage theory of competition. *Journal of Marketing, 59*(2), 1–15.

Hunt, S. D., Arnett, B. D., & Madhavaram, S. (2006). The explanatory foundations of relationship marketing theory. *Journal of Business & Industrial Marketing, 21*(2), 72–87.

Johannessen, J. A., Olsen, B., & Lumpkin, G. T. (2001). Innovation as newness: What is new, how new, and new to whom? *European Journal of Innovation Management, 4*(1), 20–31.

Joreskog, K. G., & Sorbom, D. (1989). *LISREL 7: A guide to the program and applications*. Chicago: SPSS.

Kandampully, J. (2002). Innovation as the core competency of a service organization: The role of technology, knowledge and networks. *European Journal of Innovation Management, 5*(1), 18–26.

Karabulut, A. T. (2015). Effects of innovation types on performance of manufacturing firms in Turkey. *Procedia-Social and Behavioral Sciences, 195*, 1355–1364. https://doi.org/10.1016/j.sbspro.2015.06.322.

Kerlinger, F. N. (1978). Similarities and differences in social attitudes in four Western countries. *International Journal of Psychology, 13*(1), 25–37.

Kleindl, B., Mowen, J., & Chakraborty, G. (1996). *Innovative market orientation an alternative strategic orientation in marketing research at the marketing/entrepreneurship interface*. In Research at the Marketing/Entrepreneurship interface, University of Illinois at Chicago, conference proceedings, pp. 211–288.

Kotler, P., Armstrong, G., Saunders, J., & Wong, V. (1999). *Principles of Marketing* (2nd European Ed.). Prentice Hall Europe.

Lavric, V. (2010). The development of the SMEs sector in Romania. An approach regarding the dynamics and the perspectives. *Revista de Management Comparat International, 11*(5), 931–939.

Loucks, E. S., Martens, M. L., & Cho, C. H. (2010). Engaging small-and medium-sized businesses in sustainability. *Sustainability Accounting, Management and Policy Journal, 1*(2), 178–200.

Low, M. B., & MacMillan, I. C. (1988). Entrepreneurship: Past research and future challenges. *Journal of Management, 14*(2), 139–161.

Lukas, B. A., Whitwell, G. J., & Doyle, P. (2005). How can a shareholder value approach improve marketing's strategic influence? *Journal of Business Research, 58*(4), 414–422.

Meers, K. A., & Robertson, C. (2007). Strategic planning practices in profitable small firms in the United States. *The Business Review, 7*(1), 302–307.

National Policy Framework for SME Development. http://www.industry.gov.lk/web/images/pdf/framew_eng.pdf

O'Donnell, A., & Cummins, D. (1999). The use of qualitative methods to research networking in SMEs. *Qualitative Market Research: An International Journal, 2*(2), 82–91.

O'Dwyer, M. (2009). *Marketing the SME: Innovation and approach*. Cambridge Scholars Publishing.

O'Dwyer, M., Gilmore, A., & Carson, D. (2009a). Innovative marketing in SMEs. *European Journal of Marketing, 43*(1/2), 46–61.

O'Dwyer, M., Gilmore, A., & Carson, D. (2009b). Innovative marketing in SMEs: An empirical study. *Journal of Strategic Marketing, 17*(5), 383–396.

O'Dwyer, M., Gilmore, A., & Carson, D. (2009c). Innovative marketing in SMEs: A theoretical framework. *European Business Review, 21*(6), 504–515.

O'Regan, N., & Ghobadian, A. (2005). Innovation in SMEs: The impact of strategic orientation and environmental perceptions. *International Journal of Productivity and Performance Management, 54*(2), 81–97.

Pushpakumari, M. D., & Watanabe, T. (2009). Do strategies improve SME performance? An empirical analysis of Japan and Sri Lanka. *Meijo Asian Research Journal, 1*(1), 61–75.

Quaye, D., & Mensah, I. (2019). Marketing innovation and sustainable competitive advantage of manufacturing SMEs in Ghana. *Management Decision, 57*(7), 1535–1553.

Rajapathirana, R. J., & Hui, Y. (2018). Relationship between innovation capability, innovation type and firm performance. *Journal of Innovation & Knowledge, 3*(1), 44–55.

Shivany, S., Thirunavukkarasu, V., & Kajendra, K., (2015). *Consumer responses towards the 4PS marketing strategies in the conflict affected areas of Sri Lanka: A grounded theory approach*. In 12th International Conference on Business Management (ICBM), University of Jaffna.

Sivatheepan, B., Kadirgamar, A., Kandiah, A., Krishnananthan, S., Navaratnam, S., Sooriasegaram, M., & Surenthirakumaran, R. (2018). *Economic development framework for a Northern Province Master Plan*. https://www.cbsl.gov.lk/sites/default/files/cbslwebdocumentsEconomic%20Development%20Framework%20NP-English.pdf

Stokes, D. (2000). Entrepreneurial marketing: A conceptualization from qualitative research. *Qualitative Market Research: An International Journal, 3*(1), 47–54.

Tsai, W. H., & Chou, W. C. (2009). Selecting management systems for sustainable development in SMEs: A novel hybrid model based on DEMATEL, ANP, and ZOGP. *Expert Systems with Applications, 36*(2), 1444–1458.

Vijayakumar, S. (2013). The trend and impact of small and medium enterprises on economic growth in Sri Lanka. *International Journal on Global Business Management & Research, 2*(1), 39.

Wanninayake, M. C. B., & Chovancova, M. (2013). *Exploring the impact of consumer ethnocentrism on impulsive buying decisions: With evidence from Sri Lanka*. In Proceedings of WSEAS international conference on Economic, Political and Law Science, 2012a, Tomas Bata University in Zlin, Czech Republic, pp. 247–252.

Wu, S. I., & Lin, S. R. (2016). The effect of green marketing strategy on business performance: A study of organic farms in Taiwan. *Total Quality Management & Business Excellence, 27*(1–2), 141–156.

Yang, K., & Xu, Y. (2006). Regional differences in the development of Chinese small and medium-sized enterprises. *Journal of Small Business and Enterprise Development, 13*(2), 174–184.

Role of Organizational Culture and Actors on Success and Failure of Balanced Scorecard Operationalization: A Case Study of a Clustered Firm

5

K. K. Kapiyangoda and R. H. Surangi Lewis

5.1 Introduction

5.1.1 Background of the Study and Research Issue

Management control systems (MCS) include decision supportive practices such as budgeting, activity-based costing (ABC), balanced scorecard (BSC), etc., which aid management in decision-making. These controls are shaped by various considerations, ranging from technology, competition, and management ideologies (Cobb et al. 1995; Innes and Mitchell 1990). Among these considerations, culture plays a vital role in shaping the MCS (Reginato and Guerreiro 2013; Jackson et al. 2012; Kapiyangoda and Gooneratne 2018). However, there is a limited number of studies in the area of culture focusing on how actors influenced operationalization of these controls (Zawawi 2018; Quattrone and Hopper 2005; Gamage and Goonerathne 2017).

Although there are studies on the BSC and its application under different phenomena (Chavan 2009; Kasurinen 2002; Olve et al. 2003), there is a dearth of research knowledge in the application of the BSC in a clustered firm (ABC Company Ltd.) in which BSC operates smoothly in one cluster (Cluster Y) and its operationalization is a failure in the other (Cluster X). Different influences of organizational actors forming diversified cultures within the organization have affected this success and failure of BSC operationalization. Hence this study explores how the

K. K. Kapiyangoda (✉)
Department of Management and Organization Studies, Faculty of Management and Finance, University of Colombo, Colombo, Sri Lanka
e-mail: kumudukapiyangoda@mos.cmb.ac.lk

R. H. Surangi Lewis
Faculty of Management and Finance, University of Colombo, Colombo, Sri Lanka

© The Author(s), under exclusive license to Springer Nature Switzerland AG 2021
S. Dhiman, R. Samaratunge (eds.), *New Horizons in Management, Leadership and Sustainability*, Future of Business and Finance,
https://doi.org/10.1007/978-3-030-62171-1_5

subculture which existed within a cluster (Cluster X) influenced operationalization of the BSC. Our study examined how the actors (human and non-human) influenced a clustered firm in the Sri Lankan apparel manufacturing industry to result in success (Cluster Y) and failure (Cluster X) of BSC implementation by incorporating ANT and exploring how the subculture within a cluster (Cluster X) influenced its operationalization. This paper seeks to capture the diversity of culture which prevailed within ABC Company Ltd. and identify how this diversity influenced the operationalization of BSC.

5.2 Literature Review

5.2.1 Organizational Culture

Drawing on Schein (1985), organizational culture can be defined as the pattern of basic assumptions and shared meaning among members within an organization. There are different types of organizations, and accordingly the values pertaining to these organizations vary significantly (Sheridan 1992; Dhingra and Pathak 1972). According to Cameron and Quinn (2006) and Denison and Spreitzer (1991), types of organizational culture can be classified as hierarchy culture, clan culture, adhocracy culture, and market culture. Hierarchical culture (Corley 2004) creates a structured work environment; procedures decide what people do; leaders are driven by their efficiency-based coordination; keeping the organization functioning smoothly is most crucial; and formal rules and policy keep the organization together (Meyer and Rowan 1977). Trustful delivery and smooth planning define success, and the personnel management has to guarantee work and predictability. In a clan culture, the working environment is friendly (Sugita and Takahashi 2015), and the leaders or the executives are seen as mentors. The organization is held together by loyalty and tradition which emphasize long-term human resource development; such organizations promote teamwork, participation, and consensus. In an adhocracy culture, employees take risks, and leaders are seen as innovators and risk takers; experiments and innovation are the bonding materials within the organization, and the long-term goal is to grow. Market culture-based organizations are result-based, emphasizing finishing work and getting things done; people are competitive and focused on goals, reputation and success are the most important, and the organizational style is based on competition (Cameron and Quinn 2006).

5.2.2 Organizational Subcultures

An organization is best interpreted as interactions of subcultures in a macro context driving towards forming the organizational culture. Subcultures of an organization are essentially based on the education level, shared tasks, and similarity of organizational experiences (Schein 2010), which is based on distinctive patterns of shared ideologies and sets of cultural forms (Trice and Beyer 1993) that deviate subcultures from the core ideology of the organization (Trice 1993). Hence subcultures are more likely to be seen in complex, large, bureaucratic organizations because these have a variety of functions and technologies (Rose 1988; Trice and Beyer 1993; Van Maanen and Barley 1985), which are reflected in diversified management practices (Jones 1983).

Studies have shown how organizational subcultures have influenced shaping controls (Ahrens and Mollona 2007; Goddard 1999). Ahrens and Mollona (2007) demonstrated how the subcultures of different shop floors (hot and cold) of a steel mill constituted practices of controls which enabled organizational members to pursue diverse objectives related to their various wider cultural aspirations. Goddard's (1999) study of three governmental organizations in the UK and Canada's Ontario and Quebec showed a departmental culture and how department heads significantly influenced departmental culture and the financial control systems.

5.2.3 Organizational Culture and MCS

Studies have explored the direct relationship between organizational culture and MCS (Reginato and Guerreiro 2013; Jackson et al. 2012; Hofstede et al. 1990; Kapiyangoda and Gooneratne 2018) and have confirmed that corporate culture directly affects the success of management tools (Rigby and Bilodeau 2007). As a result of observing such relationships, Herath (2007) included organizational culture as a component when designing a framework to study MCS. Baird et al.'s (2007) study, which was based on O'Reilly III et al. 1991, revealed that organizational culture-related factors (i.e. outcome orientation, respect for people, team orientation, innovation, attention to detail, and stability) affected successful operation of ABC (Baird et al. 2004).

5.2.4 Cultural Influences on BSC Implementation

As studies reveal, the BSC should match the existing organizational mission, strategy, technology (Kaplan and Norton 1993; Chavan 2009), and culture in order to make its implementation a success (Markus and Pfeffer 1983; Kasurinen 2002; Chavan 2009; Kaplan and Norton 1993; Olve et al. 2003). Kaplan and Norton (2004) report that companies that successfully implemented the BSC had a culture in which "people were deeply aware of and internalized the mission, vision, and core values needed to execute the company's strategy" (Kaplan and Norton 2006; Lipe and Salterio 2000). Studies have confirmed that there is a direct relationship between organizational culture and successful implementation of the BSC (Assiri et al. 2006; Deem et al. 2010) because the BSC is part of the belief system unique to a particular organization (Gibbons and Kaplan 2015; Kaplan and Norton 1993).

Chavan (2009) has revealed that the BSC requires understanding, commitment, and support from the very top of the business, and this encourages a risk-taking culture to facilitate smooth operationalization of the BSC (Rhodes et al. 2008).

When focusing on the leadership styles that are appealing for the BSC, a collaborative leadership style stimulates empowerment and aligns goals and decisions with corporate objectives while facilitating the BSC operation (Rhodes et al. 2008).

5.3 Theoretical Framework

5.3.1 Actor-Network Theory (ANT)

ANT (Latour 1987, 1999, 2005; Law 1992) originated in the field of science and technology-related studies. It is a framework to examine the infrastructure surrounding technological achievements through assigning agency (Law 1992) to both human and non-human actors (Bijker et al. 1987), while treating social relations, including power and organization, as network effects (Law 1992). According to Law (1997) as cited in Quattrone and Hopper (2005), organizations are viewed as interconnected networks:

> We have… different organizations. A series of them. Alongside one another. So to speak a multiple reality, not one that is singular. [However] these different organizations do not inhabit entirely separate worlds. They do not happily co-exist in parallel universes. Instead they support, undermine, and in general interfere with one another in complex and uncertain ways […] they are partially connected. (p. 761)

ANT is distinctive because it shows that networks are materially heterogeneous and it argues that society and organizations would not exist if they were simply social. Agents, texts, devices, and architectures are all generated by, form part of, and are essential to networks of the social. Therefore all humans and non-humans should be analyzed equally (Law 1992). This concept is known as a *principle of symmetry*; that is, humans and non-humans (e.g., artifacts, organization structures) should be integrated into the same conceptual framework and assigned equal amounts of agency (Law 1992).

5.3.2 ANT in Management Control Research

The ANT has been widely used in MCS related research in order to understand interorganizational (Chua and Mahama 2007) and intraorganizational relationships (Cuganesan and Lee 2006; Sandhu et al. 2008; Quattrone and Hopper 2005).

Lowe (2001) highlighted that ANT has been widely incorporated in the area of management accounting, especially in studies focused on the implementation of accounting tools such as ABC (Briers and Chua 2001; Alcouffe et al. 2008). Similarly, ANT has been incorporated in the area of budgeting of a state-owned commercial bank in Sri Lanka (Gooneratne and Hoque 2013) which explains how MCS is exercised while integrating ANT and new institutional sociology and illustrates the influence of human actors and non-human actors in the process of budget implementation and continuation. Incorporating ANT, Quattrone and Hopper (2005) identified that the information systems which support the MCS of a multinational company should be aligned with the culture of the operating country in order to make the operationalization of MCS a success. Adding to this literature, Sandhu et al. (2008) showed how interorganizational and intraorganizational relationships impact long and short ties that affected localization of the BSC of a security company in Singapore incorporating ANT. However, they did not reveal the specific cultural dimensions (i.e., hierarchy culture, clan culture) related to organizational culture which affected this BSC implementation.

Under the theoretical backdrop above, it is clear that there is a lacuna in research in identifying how organizational culture influenced successful and unsuccessful operationalization of BSC in a clustered firm. Therefore, in order to fill this gap, ANT was incorporated to illuminate the actors (human and non-human) who shaped the cultures unique to Cluster X and Cluster Y of ABC Company Ltd., and this also facilitated understanding the existence of subcultures within Cluster X and how these unique and complex cultural considerations determined the success and failure of BSC operationalization of the two clusters.

5.4 Research Design

5.4.1 Qualitative Methodology

The socially constructed nature of reality, the intimate relationship between the researcher and what is studied, and the situational constraints that shape inquiry are acknowledged in qualitative research. The way that social experience is created and meaning is given is answered through such research (Vaivio 2008), while capturing the actor's perspective by detailed interviews and observations (Denzin and Lincoln 2000). Therefore it was decided to incorporate qualitative methodology in order to capture how the actors and organizational culture influenced BSC implementation in the focused clustered firm.

5.4.2 Case Study Approach

A case study is an empirical inquiry that investigates contemporary phenomenon, within its real-life context, when the boundaries between the phenomenon and context are not clearly evident and in which multiple sources of evidence are used (Yin 2009). The researchers had direct contact with organizational participants, particularly through interviews and direct observations that provide primary research data for an in-depth analysis of organizational conditions that is essential for understanding organizational and cluster-specific culture (Ferreira and Merchant 1992). Accounting and other controls cannot be fully understood in isolation, and a more contextual approach is required to comprehend the BSC (Otley and Berry 1994). Thus, in order to analyze and understand how organizational culture and its actors influenced BSC operationalization, a case study methodology was most suitable for our research.

5.4.3 Data Collection Methods

In-depth interviews were the mode of primary data collection. Through this method different views of the key actors of the organization were captured. Probing questions were raised in order to facilitate gathering rich data (Qu and Dumay 2011). A documentary analysis was also conducted on management reports in order to compare and contrast the present level of operationalization of the BSC within the two clusters. Documentary evidence was utilized as a part of data triangulation. Managerial reports, training manuals, performance reports, financial indicators, and regulatory documents were analyzed to gather supportive information.

5.4.4 Stages of Data Collection

Data were collected in two stages: a pilot study and the main study. General interviews were held in the pilot study which were designed to obtain an overview of the culture and the BSC implementation in ABC Company Ltd. The head of finance and head of planning and risk management from each cluster were interviewed. During the pilot phase, the culture of the organization was explained by the interviewees as structured and hierarchical, with each cluster having a different board of directors. It was evident from the pilot study that the BSC operation within each cluster was influenced by its unique culture.

During the main study, the interviewees were selected based on purposive sampling, selecting the most appropriate people to provide the most relevant, rich data. Fourteen top and middle-level managerial employees were interviewed from each cluster. Table 5.1 shows the designations of those interviewed in each cluster. The interviews were based on an interview guide which contained open-ended questions for rich, in-depth data.

5.4.5 Data Analysis

Special attention was given to the thematic analysis of Braun and Clarke (2013), which was followed in the analysis of data. As the initial step, the data collected through interviews were transcribed, then all the transcribed data were read and familiarized while taking note of the items of potential interest. Next the data set was coded, giving words or phrases for groups of ideas expressed by interviewees (Miles et al. 1994). Then the themes were searched and identified. Similar ideas expressed by different interviewees were easily identified and categorized through the identification of themes. The themes were reviewed to identify and understand similar themes while analyzing relationships among different themes. After review, each theme was defined and named, ensuring that similar themes were not repeated, and then these were related to the ANT. Finally, discovered themes were written, elaborating on each and finalizing the analysis.

	Designation of the interviewee	Cluster
Table 5.1 Details of interviewees	Chief financial officer (CFO)	X
	General manager – risk (GM-Risk)	
	General manager IT (GM-IT)	
	Chief marketing officer (CMO)	
	Chief operations officer (COO)	
	Chief planning officer (CPO)	
	General manager – supply chain (GM-SC)	
	Chief financial officer (CFO)	Y
	General manager – risk (GM-Risk)	
	General manager IT (GM-IT)	
	Chief marketing officer (CMO)	
	Chief operations officer (COO)	
	Chief planning officer (CPO)	
	General manager – supply chain (GM-SC)	

5.5   Findings: Influence of Culture and Actors on Operationalization of the BSC in Cluster X and Cluster Y

5.5.1   Case Study and Its Organizational Culture

ABC Company Ltd. is one of the leading mass-scale apparel companies in Sri Lanka, producing a range of garments for the local and foreign markets. It includes the main hub (head office), 14 local factories, and 2 foreign factories operated in Bangladesh and Vietnam under its central control. Altogether, the company possesses more than 20,000 employees of whom 12,000 belong to Cluster X and 8000 to Cluster Y.

The prevailing culture within the organization was expressed by key informants, elaborating its cultural aspects. The organizational culture is hierarchical, as the organizational rules and regulations determine the task assigned and duties to be performed by each employee within a formal environment. Figure 5.1 shows the hierarchy, with four directors assigned to Cluster X and three to Cluster Y. The cross-communication between these directors governing each cluster has been identified as poor and inadequate, because they independently govern each cluster, which causes differences between the two clusters in terms of culture, performance, and operationalization of the BSC.

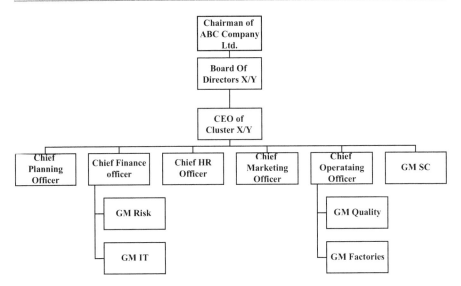

Fig. 5.1 The organizational hierarchy of Cluster X and Cluster Y

5.5.2 Prevailing Culture of Cluster X

Cluster X includes eight manufacturing units. The CFO of this cluster (young and a recently joined member in charge of 18 employees) expressed that Cluster X consisted of a hierarchical and less democratic culture run under formal and stringent rules and regulations:

> Currently the cluster has a more hierarchical culture where authority determines everything. Work environment is more formalized, rules determine what people need to do. Always leaders or the top management try to follow the rules which exist within the organization. Cost is one of the main driving forces and everybody had to work to reduce cost as it has a direct relationship with the financial KPI achievement.

The GM-Risk observed how management and employees within the cluster were reluctant to change and adapt innovations:

> They do not like to change or accept new things easily and they want to keep on doing same practices which have been implemented by previous generations of management. I believe this is mainly because there are a lot of executives who have being working at this cluster for more than five years and their knowledge about the changing world has not been upgraded.

This view on the prevailing culture within Cluster X was shared by several employees, including the GM-IT, who has more than 8 years' experience in the organization: in her view, the culture is "friendly," but pressure from the top management acts as a driver for target achievement.

5.5.2.1 Subculture Within Cluster X

Key informants explained that the culture of the finance department could be viewed as a subculture when compared to the overall culture of the cluster. According to the CFO, the prevailing culture within the finance department was different to the hierarchical culture and was influenced by himself. As the CFO he initiated an open culture in order to promote innovative practices within the department:

> When it comes to the finance department, I always try to create an open culture in order to encourage innovation with the control in my hands. I always go into details when we review performance in order to determine reasons and to locate what went wrong. However, I have given freedom for the employees to work independently, but I hardly see this culture in any of the other departments of the cluster.

In contrast, the COO believed that the best mechanism to manage the operations team was to follow a bureaucratic, top-down management style rather providing democracy:

> I believe there are subcultures within the organization based on the nature of the job, performance targets and employee background and the expected job role. When it comes to the operations team, it is mandatory to monitor them and follow up for day–to-day targets, otherwise we won't be able to track them nor their work. Therefore, I always try to monitor them very closely.

The CPO observed that the formation of the subculture within a cluster was enforced by the leader of the division and his way of managing employees. These ideas were confirmed by the GM-IT and CMO.

5.5.3 Prevailing Culture Within Cluster Y

The culture within Cluster Y is result-oriented but more flexible and less autocratic in nature compared with Cluster X. The COO perceived the existing culture in Cluster Y was more participatory and encouraged suggestions of employees when decisions were made:

> The culture is very welcoming and encourage the participation of every employee within the organization in decision making. Everyone is willing to help each other to meet their objectives thereby ensuring a very collaborative culture.

Similarly, the CPO, with more than 3 years' experience in the division, regarded the culture as decentralized; suggestions, innovations, and novel practices were acknowledged. Cultural aspects made employees more supportive towards tasks and responsibilities of the department.

5.5.3.1 Nonexistence of Subcultures Within Cluster Y

Data revealed that subcultures did not exist within Cluster Y, and confirming this idea the CFO elaborated:

As far as the finance department is concerned, there is no major differences between cluster-specific culture and departmental culture. As the head of the finance department of Cluster Y, I facilitate more open, flexible and empowering and participative culture in order to improve innovation and business skills. So that people can think differently and act correctly in different market situations and competitive environments.

The COO, CPO, and GM-SC also affirmed that subcultures were not evident in Cluster Y. Supporting these claims the CMO said:

There is no major variance in the cultures among the departments in our Cluster, everyone is focused on customers and their satisfaction. I will also not allow to have subcultures within the merchandising department where I always try to keep whole team as a one unit and move forward.

5.5.4 Prevailing Culture of the Clusters and BSC Implementation

The interview data unraveled the differences of culture in the two clusters, where Cluster X consists of an authoritarian rule-driven culture (hierarchical culture) and Cluster Y consists of a more flexible, democratic, team-oriented culture (clan culture). The influence of these diversified cultures on BSC implementation was investigated in order to identify how it made BSC implementation a success in Cluster Y and a failure in Cluster X.

The CFO of Cluster X recognized that the hierarchical culture, intention to maximize profits, and lack of knowledge among employees on the BSC have made it unsuccessful in Cluster X:

I feel that the existing culture of Cluster X is having some negative impact towards the practice of BSC as there is lack of congruence and support from the employees extended towards the operationalization of BSC. Employees are dictated to do what they should do. There is no thinking out of the box. As the hierarchical culture demands, their major orientation is profit maximization, the other aspects of the BSC seems to be less focused. Less exposure and training on BSC implementation is provided. People are busy obeying rules.

He recognized that BSC implementation within the cluster was a failure because of manual computation of KPIs and lesser usage of the ERP system. The other interviewees in the cluster confirmed the same viewpoints as reasons for the failure of the operationalization of the BSC.

Officials from Cluster Y conveyed a rather different message: BSC implementation had yielded successful results. The CFO of Cluster Y commented that the supportive nature of the open and flexible culture of the cluster had facilitated the operationalization of its BSC:

Obviously the friendly culture of Cluster Y supports having an effective BSC. Mainly having an open culture provokes learning avenues and opportunities for the entire staff to be trained on BSC.

The CPO of Cluster Y elaborated that the management information system which was facilitated by the ERP system also affected the successful operationalization of its BSC. As he explained, a clan culture facilitated adaptation of novelties while triggering cluster-wide incorporation of the ERP system, which produced KPIs easily in order to facilitate BSC operation.

5.5.5   Influence of Subcultures on BSC Implementation

The interviewees revealed that there were subcultures operating within Cluster X whereas in Cluster Y there were no subcultures observed. The GM-Risk of Cluster X recognized the prevailing subculture of the finance division was an obstacle to BSC implementation in Cluster X:

> I feel the subculture of the finance department in Cluster X works as an obstacle in BSC operationalization because they are working in isolation to achieve their own objectives which doesn't support to drive as one cluster to achieve common objectives. This creates competition among departments within the same cluster in which they try to work to highlight their own department.

However, the subculture that prevailed in Cluster X (the finance department) demonstrated a clan culture, in which ERP implementation was encouraged and provision of training and exposure set the correct environment to operationalize the BSC within their subculture.

The CPO of Cluster Y reported that they did not encourage subcultures within the cluster, which was one of the reasons for successful BSC operationalization:

> I believe subcultures can deviate an organization from its common goal if they are principally different. Therefore, we don't encourage sub-cultures and make sure everyone is in the right path and to ensure goal congruence, likewise, we have managed successful BSC implementation.

The CFO and CMO of Cluster Y also believed that subcultures should not be encouraged within clusters to ensure that divisions did not vary from the organization's common goal, which led to successful BSC operationalization.

5.5.6   Data in Light of ANT

This section shows how the data collected were illuminated through the ANT. The information was placed in the network context, identifying the human and non-human actors that formulated the culture that was unique to each cluster (hierarchical culture in Cluster X and clan culture in Cluster Y), while identifying the formation of subculture (X1 – a clan culture) within the finance department of Cluster X. Within the context of ABC Company Ltd., the BSC was identified as an element which draws together human and non-human actors (Sandhu et al. 2008), and therefore it was recognized as a boundary object in relation to the ANT. Figure 5.2 shows this interplay between human and non-human actors within Cluster X and Cluster Y which influenced the operationalization of BSC.

5.5.6.1 Human Actors

The senior management (leaders of divisions) of Cluster X and Cluster Y, which includes the CFO, CMO, COO, CPO, CHRO, GM-IT, and GM-SC, was identified as the key human actors who influenced BSC operationalization. They could be identified as the actors who defined the culture of the cluster and drove the BSC. More importantly, the CFO (leader) of the finance division of Cluster X took prominence in establishing a clan culture which facilitated the successful adaptation of the BSC. The middle and lower-level employees also had a considerable role when accepting and following the MCS (i.e., BSC), as they had a responsibility to operationalize the BSC within the cluster from the grassroots level.

5.5.6.2 Non-human Actors

Non-human actors include the nonliving entities of the network which perform vital functions in the network. These are often identified as the facilitators or intermediaries between human actors. In ABC Company Ltd., ERP system and training on the BSC have been identified as the non-human actors of the two clusters.

ERP Systems

Both of the clusters incorporated ERP systems as a means of gathering data, but the level of incorporation in each cluster to process data differed. Cluster Y, which inculcates an open and an innovative culture, seemed to embrace ERP systems to a greater extent when generating and processing data in order to operationalize the BSC.

In Cluster X, where a hierarchical and traditional culture is embedded, managerial information was processed manually, maintaining the traditional top-down information processing system in which ERP system is less used. The COO of Cluster X confirmed this:

> Most of the reports that we currently use are not taken from ERP system. As a result, these reports have the problem of duplication of data and include errors, which has a negative impact on the decision-making ability and BSC operation of the cluster.

It was evident that the culture of the cluster had influenced the level of incorporation of technology to process data, which in turn influenced BSC operationalization.

Training and Exposure on the BSC

Training and exposure on the BSC influenced successful or unsuccessful operationalization. As the GM-SC of Cluster X explained, in a hierarchical culture in which opportunity for learning was limited and employees were expected to follow the guidelines and rules, knowledge transfer or training was less a focus, leading to

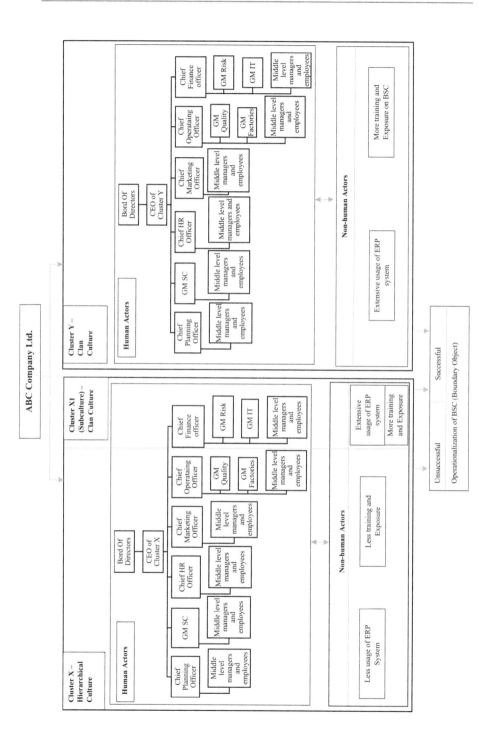

Fig. 5.2 Operationalization of the BSC in Cluster X and Cluster Y in light of ANT

BSC failure. Cluster Y encouraged knowledge transfer mechanisms, backed by the friendly and open culture, and adequate training on the BSC was provided for newly recruited employees, maximizing their exposure to BSC operationalization and aided the smooth functioning of BSC within the cluster.

5.6   Data Analysis and Conclusion

5.6.1   Data Analysis

5.6.1.1 Organizational Culture and MCS

Organizational culture affects implementation (Rigby and Bilodeau 2007), improvement and removal of controls (Tessier and Otley 2012; Schäffer et al. 2015). Our study based on ABC Company Ltd. also revealed similar findings, while further extending the literature through elaborating that, in addition to the organizational culture, a cluster-specific culture had an impact in successful MCS operationalization. As the respondents revealed, the cluster which consisted of a hierarchical culture failed in BSC operationalization due to its rigid operations, but Cluster Y, which had a friendly, team-oriented culture operated the BSC well. Hence the organizational or divisional culture should match with the operationalization of BSC in order to make it a success (Markus and Pfeffer 1983; Kasurinen 2002; Chavan 2009; Kaplan and Norton 1993; Olve et al. 2003; Assiri et al. 2006; Deem et al. 2010).

5.6.1.2 Analysis in Light of ANT

ANT has been incorporated as a theoretical lens in many management control-related studies exploring implementation of ABC (Briers and Chua 2001; Alcouffe et al. 2008) and budgeting (Gooneratne and Hoque 2013), showing how human and non-human actors are involved in shaping of controls. Similarly, our study also reveals how BSC has been operationalized in a clustered firm in the apparel industry through identifying how the various actors which constitute organizational and divisional culture contribute in BSC operationalization within a cluster.

The literature has highlighted how organizational members are involved in selecting, continuing, and changing the MCS (Schäffer et al. 2015; Bhimani 2003; Reginato and Guerreiro 2013; Tessier and Otley 2012; Gamage and Goonerathne 2017). Some studies have also explained how these changes in MCS and their implementation were driven by the diverse objectives of organizational actors, which includes managers, workers (Ahrens and Mollona 2007), and especially leaders who are connected with financial operations and strategic functions (Kapiyangoda and Goonerathne 2014; Gamage and Goonerathne 2017; Tessier and Otley 2012). Corporate culture and departmental leaders or heads significantly influence departmental culture and respective financial control systems (Ahrens and Mollona 2007). Similarly, our study also reveals that the divisional leaders, such as CFO, CMO, COO, CPO, CHRO, GM-IT, GM-SC, and GM-Risk, play a key role in shaping the divisional culture and influence operationalization of MCS (i.e., BSC). The CFO of Cluster X embedded an open and friendly culture which facilitated the smooth operation of BSC; in Cluster Y, less support was extended by the CFO backed by the rule-driven hierarchical culture, and failure ensued.

Similar to Quattrone and Hopper (2005) and Lowe (2001), our study has also revealed that non-human actors such as the information system (i.e., ERP systems) play a crucial role in operationalization of MCS. Cluster X, which depended on the manual system of record keeping failed in BSC operationalization, whereas the finance department of Cluster X and Cluster Y, which utilized the ERP system across their divisions, operated BSC successfully. Lack of knowledge of employees on the BSC, reflected in a lack of training in Cluster X, led the cluster to fail in BSC operation. Similar findings have been shown by Kapiyangoda and Goonerathne (2014) in discussing how a BSC failed in a commercial bank in Sri Lanka due to lack of BSC-related knowledge among organizational members.

5.6.2 Conclusion

5.6.2.1 Objective 1: How Has Organizational Culture Influenced Successful or Unsuccessful Operationalization of the BSC in the Two Clusters of ABC Company Ltd.?

ABC Company Ltd. is a clustered firm which operates BSC successfully in one cluster and unsuccessfully in another, which is mainly influenced by diversity or difference of culture prevalent within the two clusters. This study also showed how successful BSC operationalization was influenced by the nonexistence of subcultures within the Cluster Y, whereas in Cluster X where subcultures existed, BSC operationalization failed, because the cluster could not move in one direction.

5.6.2.2 Objective 2: How Does the Involvement of Human and Non-human Actors Which Form Part of Organizational Culture Contribute to the BSC Operationalization in the Two Clusters of ABC Company Ltd.?

Application of ANT has illuminated the key human and non-human actors who influenced operationalizing BSC. The senior management and leaders of the divisions could be identified as the key human actors who influenced the BSC operationalization through their leadership. Middle and lower-level employees also played a considerable role as they had the responsibility to understand and operationalize the BSC. In addition, the incorporation of ERP systems and training on and exposure to the BSC were identified as the non-human actors which closely linked the human actors within the network of the clustered firm and triggered the operationalization of BSC.

Chapter Takeaways

1. An organization which inculcates an open, friendly, and a flexible culture is more likely to succeed in operationalization of BSC.

2. An organization which possess a hierarchical and a less democratic culture which is run under formal rules and regulations is more likely to fail in operationalization of BSC.
3. The successful operationalization of BSC is influenced by the nonexistence of subcultures, whereas in the cluster where subcultures existed, hindered operationalization of the BSC, as it deviated the cluster from moving towards achieving one goal.
4. ANT could be used as theoretical lens to illuminate the key human and nonhuman actors that influenced operationalizing BSC within the two clusters leading it to be successful in one cluster while unsuccessful in the other. The senior management/leaders of the divisions were identified as the key human actors who influenced BSC operationalization through leadership. Middle and lower-level employees also played a considerable role as they had the responsibility to understand and operationalize the BSC.
5. ANT illuminates that non-human actors such as ERP systems and training and exposure on the BSC closely link the human actors within the network of the clustered firm, and this drives the operationalization of BSC towards success.

Reflection Questions

1. What type of an organizational culture facilitates operationalization of BSC?
2. What type of an organizational culture hinders/disturbs the operationalization of BSC?
3. How does the existence of subcultures within a cluster of an organization affect operationalization BSC?
4. Incorporating ANT, briefly explain how the human actors influence operationalization of BSC in an organization.
5. Incorporating ANT, briefly explain how the non-human actors influence operationalization of BSC in an organization.

References

Ahrens, T., & Mollona, M. (2007). Organisational control as cultural practice – A shop floor ethnography of a Sheffield steel mill. *Accounting, Organizations and Society, 32*(4–5), 305–331.

Alcouffe, S., Berland, N., & Levant, Y. (2008). Actor-networks and the diffusion of management accounting innovations: A comparative study. *Management Accounting Research, 19*(1), 1–17.

Assiri, A., Zairi, M., & Eid, R. (2006). How to profit from the balanced scorecard: An implementation roadmap. *Industrial Management & Data Systems, 106*(7), 937–952.

Baird, K. M., Harrison, G. L., & Reeve, R. C. (2004). Adoption of activity management practices: A note on the extent of adoption and the influence of organizational and cultural factors. *Management Accounting Research, 15*(4), 383–399.

Baird, K., Harrison, G., & Reeve, R. (2007). Success of activity management practices: The influence of organizational and cultural factors. *Accounting & Finance, 47*(1), 47–67.

Bhimani, A. (2003). A study of the emergence of management accounting system ethos and its influence on perceived system success. *Accounting, Organizations and Society, 28*(6), 523–548.

Bijker, W. E., Hughes, T. P., & Pinch, T. (1987). *The social construction of technological systems: New directions in the sociology and history of technology.* London: MIT Press.

Braun, V., & Clarke, V. (2013). *Successful qualitative research: A practical guide for beginners.* London: Sage.

Briers, M., & Chua, W. F. (2001). The role of actor-networks and boundary objects in management accounting change: A field study of an implementation of activity-based costing. *Accounting, Organizations and Society, 26*(3), 237–269.

Cameron, K. M., & Quinn, R. E. (2006). *Diagnosing and changing culture: Based on the competing values framework.* San Francisco: Jossey-Bass.

Chavan, M. (2009). The balanced scorecard: A new challenge. *Journal of Management Development, 28*(5), 393–406.

Chua, W. F., & Mahama, H. (2007). The effect of network ties on accounting controls in a supply alliance: Field study evidence. *Contemporary Accounting Research, 24*(1), 47–86.

Cobb, I., Helliar, C., & Innes, J. (1995). Management accounting change in a bank. *Management Accounting Research, 6*(2), 155–175.

Corley, K. G. (2004). Defined by our strategy or our culture? Hierarchical differences in perceptions of organizational identity and change. *Human Relations, 57*(9), 1145–1177.

Cuganesan, S., & Lee, R. (2006). Intra-organisational influences in procurement networks controls: The impacts of information technology. *Management Accounting Research, 17*(2), 141–170.

Deem, J. W., Barnes, B., Segal, S., & Preziosi, R. (2010). The relationship of organizational culture to balanced scoreboard effectiveness. *SAM Advanced Management Journal, 75*(4), 31–39.

Denison, D. R., & Spreitzer, G. M. (1991). Organizational culture and organizational development: A competing values approach. *Research in Organizational Change and Development, 5*(1), 1–21.

Denzin, N. K., & Lincoln, Y. S. (2000). *The Sage handbook of qualitative research* (2nd ed.). Thousand Oaks: Sage.

Dhingra, O. P., & Pathak, V. K. (1972). Organizational culture and managers. *Indian Journal of Industrial Relations*, 387–405.

Ferreira, L. D., & Merchant, K. A. (1992). Field research in management accounting and control: A review and evaluation. *Accounting, Auditing & Accountability Journal, 5*(4).

Gamage, S. D. D., & Goonerathne, T. N. (2017). Management controls in an apparel group: An institutional theory perspective. *Journal of Applied Accounting Research, 18*(2), 222–241.

Gibbons, R., & Kaplan, R. S. (2015). Formal measures in informal management: Can a balanced scorecard change a culture? *American Economic Review, 105*(5), 447–451.

Goddard, A. (1999). Culture and Drama: The role of financial control systems in the organisational process in three local government organisations. *International Journal of Public Sector Management, 12*(6), 516–532.

Gooneratne, T. N., & Hoque, Z. (2013). *Actor-network, external institutionalism and management control systems in a state-owned commercial bank.* Paper presented at the seventh Asia Pacific Interdisciplinary Research in Accounting (APIRA) conference, Kobe, Japan.

Herath, S. (2007). A framework for management control research. *Journal of Management Development, 26*(9), 895–915.

Hofstede, G., Neuijen, B., Ohayv, D., & Sanders, G. (1990). Measuring organizational cultures: A qualitative and quantitative study across twenty cases. *Administrative Science Quarterly, 35*, 285–316.

Innes, J., & Mitchell, F. (1990). *Activity based costing: A review with case studies.* London: Chartered Institute of Management Accountants.

Jackson, W. J., Paterson, A. S., Pong, C. K., & Scarparo, S. (2012). "How easy can the barley brie" Drinking culture and accounting failure at the end of the nineteenth century in Britain. *Accounting, Auditing & Accountability Journal, 25*(4), 635–658.

Jones, G. R. (1983). Transaction costs, property rights, and organizational culture: An exchange perspective. *Administrative Science Quarterly, 28*, 454–467.

Kapiyangoda, K. K., & Goonerathne, T. N. (2014). Change of management control from the balance scorecard to budgeting: Case-study evidence from a commercial bank. *Colombo Business Journal, 4*(2), 52–66.

Kapiyangoda, K., & Gooneratne, T. (2018). Institutions, agency, culture and control: A case study of a multinational operating company. *Journal of Accounting & Organizational Change, 14*(4), 402–428.

Kaplan, R. S., & Norton, D. P. (1993). Implementing the balanced scorecard at FMC corporation: An interview with Larry D. Brady. *Harvard Business Review, 71*(5), 143–147.

Kaplan, R. S., & Norton, D. P. (2004). Measuring the strategic readiness of intangible assets. *Harvard Business Review, 82*(2), 52–63.

Kaplan, R. S., & Norton, D. P. (2006). How to implement a new strategy without disrupting your organization. *Harvard Business Review, 84*(3), 100.

Kasurinen, T. (2002). Exploring management accounting change: The case of balanced scorecard implementation. *Management Accounting Research, 13*(3), 323–343.

Latour, B. (1987). *Science in action: How to follow scientists and engineers through society.* Cambridge, MA: Harvard University Press.

Latour, B. (1999). On recalling ANT. *The Sociological Review, 47*(1, suppl), 15–25.

Latour, B. (2005). *Reassembling the social: An introduction to social life.* Oxford: OUP/ Blackwell's.

Law, J. (1992). Notes on the theory of the actor-network: Ordering, strategy, and heterogeneity. *Systems Practice, 5*(4), 379–393.

Law, J. (1997). *Heterogeneities.* Lancaster, Centre for Science Studies, Lancaster University.

Lipe, M. G., & Salterio, S. E. (2000). The balanced scorecard: Judgmental effects of common and unique performance measures. *The Accounting Review, 75*(3), 283–298.

Lowe, A. (2001). Casemix accounting systems and medical coding: Organisational actors balanced on "leaky black boxes". *Journal of Organizational Change Management, 14*(1), 79–100.

Markus, M. L., & Pfeffer, J. (1983). Power and the design and implementation of accounting and control systems. *Accounting, Organizations and Society, 8*(2–3), 205–218.

Meyer, J. W., & Rowan, B. (1977). Institutionalized organizations: Formal structure as myth and ceremony. *American Journal of Sociology, 83*(2), 340–363.

Miles, M. B., Huberman, A. M., Huberman, M. A., & Huberman, M. (1994). *Qualitative data analysis: An expanded sourcebook.* Thousand Oaks: Sage.

O'Reilly III, C. A., Chatman, J., & Caldwell, D. F. (1991). People and organizational culture: A profile comparison approach to assessing person-organization fit. *Academy of Management Journal, 34*(3), 487–516.

Olve, N. G., Petri, C. J., Roy, J., & Roy, S. (2003). *Making scorecards actionable: Balancing strategy and control.* Hoboken: Wiley.

Otley, D. T., & Berry, A. J. (1994). Case study research in management accounting and control. *Management Accounting Research, 5*(1), 45–65.

Qu, S. Q., & Dumay, J. (2011). The qualitative research interview. *Qualitative Research in Accounting & Management, 8*(3), 238–264.

Quattrone, P., & Hopper, T. (2005). A time-space odyssey: Management control systems in two multi-national organisations. *Accounting, Organizations and Society, 30*(7–8), 735–764.

Reginato, L., & Guerreiro, R. (2013). Relationships between environment, culture, and management control systems. *International Journal of Organizational Analysis, 21*(2), 219–240.

Rhodes, J., Walsh, P., & Lok, P. (2008). Convergence and divergence issues in strategic management–Indonesia's experience with the Balanced Scorecard in HR management. *The International Journal of Human Resource Management, 19*(6), 1170–1185.

Rigby, D., & Bilodeau, B. (2007). Bain's global 2007 management tools and trends survey. *Strategy & Leadership, 35*(5), 9–16.

Rose, R. A. (1988). Organizations as multiple cultures: A rules theory analysis. *Human Relations, 41*(2), 139–170.

Sandhu, R., Baxter, J., & Emsley, D. (2008). The balanced scorecard and its possibilities: The initial experiences of a Singaporean firm. *Australian Accounting Review, 18*(1), 16–24.

Schäffer, U., Burns, J., Nixon, B., Strauss, E., & Zecher, C. (2015). The role of management control systems in situations of institutional complexity. *Qualitative Research in Accounting & Management, 12*, 395.

Schein, E. H. (1985). Defining organizational culture. *Classics of Organization Theory, 3*(1), 490–502.

Schein, E. H. (2010). *Organizational culture and leadership* (Vol. 2). Hoboken: Wiley.

Sheridan, J. E. (1992). Organizational culture and employee retention. *Academy of Management Journal, 35*(5), 1036–1056.

Sugita, M., & Takahashi, T. (2015). Influence of corporate culture on environmental management performance: An empirical study of Japanese firms. *Corporate Social Responsibility and Environmental Management, 22*(3), 182–192.

Tessier, S., & Otley, D. (2012). From management controls to the management of controls. *Accounting, Auditing & Accountability Journal, 25*(5), 776–805.

Trice, H. M. (1993). *Occupational subcultures in the workplace* (No. 26). Ithaca: Cornell University Press.

Trice, H. M., & Beyer, J. M. (1993). *The cultures of work organizations*. Upper Saddle River: Prentice-Hall.

Vaivio, J. (2008). Qualitative management accounting research: Rationale, pitfalls and potential. *Qualitative Research in Accounting & Management, 5*(1), 64–86.

Van Maanen, J., & Barley, S. R. (1985). Cultural organization: Fragments of a theory. In *Organizational culture*. Beverly Hills: Sage.

Yin, R. K. (2009). *Case study research: Design and methods* (4th ed.). Thousand Oaks: Sage.

Zawawi, N. H. M. (2018). Actor-network theory and inter-organizational management control. *International Journal of Business & Society, 19*.

Part II

Entrepreneurship Studies

Do Entrepreneurial Business and Political Connections Lead to Greater Firm Performance? Exploring Informal-Sector Micro-enterprises in Sri Lanka

Nilupama Wijewardena, Ramanie Samaratunge, Ajantha Sisira Kumara, and Kumudinei Dissanayake

6.1 Introduction

In the special issue of *Strategic Entrepreneurship Journal* devoted to 'Entrepreneurship and Strategy in the Informal Economy', Ketchen Jr. et al. (2014) list institutional theory and network theory as the two theories most 'valuable to the investigation of informal economy-related phenomena' (p. 96). They acknowledge that, although the informal economy comprises 'business activities that occur outside of formal institutional boundaries but within the boundaries of informal institutions' (Webb et al. 2014, p. 1), informal entrepreneurs nevertheless depend on, navigate and manipulate both these formal and informal institutional environments for survival. At the same time, informal entrepreneurs look to their personal and occupational networks to survive and thrive in an environment characterized by the

N. Wijewardena (✉)
Department of Management, International Business and Entrepreneurship, School of Management, College of Business & Law, RMIT University, Melbourne, VIC, Australia
e-mail: nilu.wijewardena@rmit.edu.au

R. Samaratunge
Department of Management, Monash Business School, Monash University, Clayton, VIC, Australia
e-mail: ramanie.samaratunge@monash.edu

A. S. Kumara
Department of Public Administration, Faculty of Management Studies and Commerce, University of Sri Jayewardenepura, Nugegoda, Sri Lanka
e-mail: mhasisira@sjp.ac.lk

K. Dissanayake
Department of Management & Organization Studies, Faculty of Management and Finance, University of Colombo, Colombo, Sri Lanka
e-mail: kumudisa@mos.cmb.ac.lk

© The Author(s), under exclusive license to Springer Nature Switzerland AG 2021
S. Dhiman, R. Samaratunge (eds.), *New Horizons in Management, Leadership and Sustainability*, Future of Business and Finance, https://doi.org/10.1007/978-3-030-62171-1_6

lack of formal governance and structure to economic activity (Ketchen Jr. et al. 2014). Thus, institutional theory and network theory provide appropriate theoretical lenses to conduct further research on informal economic activities.

Accordingly, this study examines the impact of Sri Lankan informal-sector micro-entrepreneurs' business and political connections on their perception of support extended by the regulatory, cognitive and normative environments and how this in turn predicts their self-efficacy and firm performance using matched survey data from 635 micro-entrepreneurs and their case officers. We focus on micro-entrepreneurs' business and political connections as although the impact of social networks on entrepreneurship within emerging economies has received much attention, the role of business and political ties has not (Sheng et al. 2011). Micro-entrepreneurs utilize both types of connections as strategic resources for business (Webb et al. 2014; Chen et al. 2009; Muttakin et al. 2015; Zhou 2013). Business connections refer to social network ties to other entrepreneurs in and outside their localities (Sheng et al. 2011) while political connections refer to social network ties to the state and its agents (Zhou 2013).

The institutional theory states that the 'behaviour of individuals as well as organizations is embedded in and influenced by a broader environment, which is comprised of other organizations and governed by rules and norms' (Sambharya and Musteen 2014, p. 317). The institutional theory provides a useful theoretical lens on how external factors such as culture, traditions, regulatory environments and history help to shape entrepreneurial activities and success (Bruton et al. 2010). Generally, an efficient and well-functioning institutional environment exerts a positive influence on new entrepreneurial entrants and their subsequent life trajectories (Manolova et al. 2008). Yet the quality of the institutional framework within a country can lead to the spread of either productive, unproductive, or even destructive entrepreneurial initiatives (Baumol 1990). Research shows that in contexts where formal institutions operate imperfectly and fail to support economic activities, particularly as in emerging countries, entrepreneurs tend to look towards and rely more on informal mechanisms and key social ties (Light and Dana 2013; Webb et al. 2014). These entrepreneurs generally stay 'hidden' and receive little formal support from the institutional environment compared to their counterparts in the formal sector (Bruton et al. 2011; Bruton et al. 2008; Khavul et al. 2009; Spence 2016) and the limited benefits associated with compliance greatly discourage them to become formal. Yet without linking to the formal institutional environment, they cannot escape vulnerability and Bottom of the Pyramid (BOP) status (Thai and Turkina 2014). Research shows that firm performance and long-term survival are two chronic issues faced by many informal entrepreneurs (Schoar 2010) compared to their counterparts in the formal sector. Hence we argue that compared to close family and kinship ties, micro-entrepreneurs' business and political ties offer greater opportunities for gaining support and linking to the formal institutional environment. It is timely to identify when and how informal-sector micro-entrepreneurs' business and political ties can lead them to better affiliate and explore opportunities for gaining support from the formal institutional environment, thereby increasing their firm performance.

The study makes the following contributions. As per Ketchen Jr. et al. (2014), the study uses institutional theory and network theory to explore the effects that micro-entrepreneurs' business ties and political ties have on their perceived support from the institutional environment and their resultant self-efficacy and firm performance. While research has demonstrated the entrepreneurial effects of network ties in the forms of weak and strong ties (Khayesi et al. 2014), and bonding and bridging ties (Putnam 2000), business and political ties have received limited attention (Sheng et al. 2011; Muttakin et al. 2015; Zhou 2013). We argue that for these entrepreneurs who operate outside the boundary of the formal institutional environment, business and political connections comparatively offer greater avenues for crossing this boundary and linking to the formal institutional environment.

Second, while the importance of the institutional environment on entrepreneurship has been well-documented (Amato et al. 2017; Autio and Fu 2015; Zhou 2013), no study has, to the best of our knowledge, examined how each component of the institutional environment in an emerging country context is perceived by micro-business entrepreneurs in the informal sector. Our findings reveal the relative importance of environmental components for deriving greater self-efficacy and firm performance from micro-entrepreneurs' occupational ties, paving the way for strategically linking micro-entrepreneurs to the institutional environment for their sustainability and development.

Third, following Shane and Venkataraman's (2000) call to investigate entrepreneurial cognitions in the entrepreneurial process, there is an important theoretical contribution in examining a key mechanism linking social network ties to entrepreneurial self-efficacy (Chen et al. 2009; Yamakawa et al. 2015). While the effects of self-efficacy on entrepreneurial outcomes are well-documented (Hopp and Stephan 2012), research has not examined what factors lead entrepreneurs running micro-enterprises to have higher levels of self-efficacy. We argue that self-efficacy beliefs can be developed by linking informal-sector micro-entrepreneurs to the formal institutional environment and that such beliefs in turn predict their firm performance.

6.2 Literature Review and Hypothesis Development

6.2.1 Informal Entrepreneurship

Informal entrepreneurship, particularly in emerging economy contexts, is gaining increasing scholarly attention as a potential driving force for economic development, employment creation and wealth formation (ILO 2011a, b). Autio and Fu (2015) highlight that the informal-sector accounts for 'close to half of all non-agricultural employment in Sub-Saharan Africa, 51% in Latin America and Caribbean region, and the highest rates, 58% are observed in South and East Asia' (p. 4). More than 50% of micro-enterprises within the informal economy in emerging countries are unregistered (Acs et al. 2013; Williams et al. 2016) and operate in the informal sector (Williams 2014), engaging in such legitimate business as selling fruit, clothing and household goods, mainly on streets (Siqueira et al. 2016). They are not primarily opportunity-driven but necessity-driven to entrepreneurship for survival (Light and Dana 2013; Schoar 2010; Viswanathan et al. 2014; Welter et al. 2015). Large numbers of informal-sector micro-entrepreneurs might be explained by either too much or too little government intervention (Williams and Martinez-Perez 2014), but their contribution to the formal economy certainly remains too vital to be left unnoticed (Castro et al. 2014; Lee and Hung 2014).

Informal entrepreneurship drives employment generation, a critical factor in determining the dynamics of emerging economies. It also assists poverty eradication: nearly 1.3 billion people remain in extreme poverty (on a daily income of less than US$1.25). It enables poor people to generate family income (Bruton et al. 2013) and employment for their family members and friends, providing a critical springboard for escaping poverty (Williams and Shahid 2016), in contexts where social security payments have been severely challenged or have vanished due to market liberalization (Samaratunge and Nyland 2007). Thus, understanding different means to increase firm performance is of the utmost importance to eradicate poverty and boost the economic growth of emerging economies (Muttakin et al. 2015; Siqueira et al. 2016).

6.2.2 Informal Entrepreneurship and Institutional Environment

There is a growing recognition that entrepreneurial behaviour is context-dependent and needs to be interpreted in the environment in which it occurs (Williams and Vorley 2014) as institutional arrangements, such as how contracts are enforced, businesses are registered and new businesses can be started, naturally predict the growth of entrepreneurship and entrepreneurial activities. The regulatory, cognitive and normative dimensions of the institutional environment have been widely used to explain this influence on businesses (Roxas and Coetzer 2012; Zhu et al. 2012). The regulatory dimension represents formal, codified and explicit guidelines for business decisions, enforced through regulations. The cognitive dimension consists of the knowledge base adopted in the business community and the normative dimension comprises of informal systems of values (Busenitz et al. 2000; Roxas and Coetzer 2012; Welter and Smallbone 2011). Hence, business enterprises, irrespective of scale and level of economic development, function in a synthesis of environments. However, the level of fusion is weak in emerging economies. Many micro-entrepreneurs confront difficulties in coping with weak property rights (La Porta et al. 1999), weak rule of law (Azmat and Samaratunge 2013), inadequate investor protection (La Porta et al. 2000), low-quality government (Samaratunge et al. 2008), restricted press freedom (Kaufmann et al. 2009) and lack of transparency (Fan et al. 2011), which compel them to run their businesses informally (Sutter et al. 2017). In contexts where a large number of informal businesses exist, an alternative institutional environment, based on social networks and taken-for-granted social behaviour, becomes critical to facilitating entrepreneurship before undertaking necessary governance and economic reforms (Luo and Junkunc 2008; Bruton et al. 2011; Thai and Turkina 2014). Yet interestingly, 'being excluded from these things [formal institutional environment] did not make them [micro-entrepreneurs] feel helpless; rather, they use available resources to create alternatives for the objects and systems they lacked' (Viswanathan et al. 2014, p. 170). As Peng and Luo (2000, p. 486) point out, 'armed with useful ties and contacts', and using them strategically, a person can become an entrepreneur 'by brokering the connection between others'.

Yet micro-entrepreneurs do not wholly operate outside the formal institutional environment. Business and political connections provide crucial linkages to the formal environment. In the case of micro-entrepreneurs operating outside the formal institutional environment, their business connections may comprise of other business owners, wholesale buyers and suppliers of material both within their localities and within the formal environment. At the same time, although they remain unregistered and hidden from the regulatory environment, they have ties with political agents at different levels of government. Entrepreneurs well-connected to their business community receive valuable business information, suppliers and customers, leading to better firm performance (Burt 2001; Moran 2005). Entrepreneurs' business connections can further provide them with knowledge and understanding on ways of conducting business, values and norms pertaining to business conduct and the rules and regulations that govern the operations of a business. Political institutions can also extensively impact entrepreneurial choice (Autio and Fu 2015) and wealth creation (Acemoglu and Robinson 2012), particularly in emerging economies (Zhou 2013). Additionally, entrepreneurs can draw on their political connections to understand the regulatory environment governing business conduct and gain insights into how businesses operate in general and the informal value system followed by them. Such insights and understanding gained through their business and political connections can render informal-sector micro-entrepreneurs to feel that they too are, at least to a certain extent, part of the formal institutional environment. Their business and political connections may provide the crucial link that prompts them to associate with the formal institutional environment and perceive that they gain support and security from the three components of the environment. The following hypotheses are therefore proposed:

H1a: There is a significantly positive relationship between informal-sector micro-entrepreneurs' level of utilization of *connections with the business community* and their perceived support from the *regulatory environment*.

H1b: There is a significantly positive relationship between informal-sector micro-entrepreneurs' level of utilization of *connections with the business community* and their perceived support from the *cognitive environment*.

H1c: There is a significantly positive relationship between informal-sector micro-entrepreneurs' level of utilization of *connections with the business community* and their perceived support from the *normative environment*.

H2a: There is a significantly positive relationship between informal-sector micro-entrepreneurs' level of utilization of *connections with political authorities* and their perceived support from the *regulatory environment*.

H2b: There is a significantly positive relationship between informal-sector
        micro-entrepreneurs' level of utilization of *connections with political authorities*
        and their perceived support from the *cognitive environment*.

H2c: There is a significantly positive relationship between informal-sector
        micro-entrepreneurs' level of utilization of *connections with political authorities*
        and their perceived support from the *normative environment*.

6.2.3   Informal Entrepreneurship, Institutional Environment, Self-Efficacy and Firm Performance

Much of the literature examines the determinants of small firm performance to help entrepreneurs enhance business growth (Blackburn et al, 2013). Entrepreneurs' self-efficacy (Forbes 2005), which relates to the assessment of capacity to achieve performance (Bandura 1986, p. 391), is a factor that predicts firm performance. Bandura (1977) states that self-efficacy beliefs are contingent on 'performance accomplishments, vicarious experience, verbal persuasion, and physiological states' (p. 195). We posit in our paper that the informal-sector micro-entrepreneurs' perceived support from the institutional environment leads to increases in these four antecedents, thereby leading to higher self-efficacy beliefs. Performance accomplishments are built up through repeated successful personal mastery experiences (Bandura 1977). Informal-sector micro-entrepreneurs network ties to the business and political sector can provide them with the resources and information needed to successfully engage in their business activities. Thus, over time as these successes become frequent, the support that they perceive from the institutional environment can increase their personal mastery in their entrepreneurial activities. Vicarious experiences relate to gaining experience and learning by observing others (Bandura 1977). Informal-sector micro-entrepreneurs through the ties they maintain with the business and political sector can observe how political agents behave, how rules and regulations are implemented, how their business connections behave in specific situations and face challenges and what cultural norms govern these situations. Such vicarious learning can increase their level of self-efficacy. The ties that they maintain can also persuade them with verbal suggestions as to their ability to successfully complete a given task. As Bandura (1977, p. 198) observes, 'people who are socially persuaded that they possess the capabilities to master difficult situations and are provided with provisional aids for effective action are likely to mobilize greater effort than those who receive only the performance aids'. Physiological states relate to the arousal of emotions and physiology to stress and challenging situations. High emotional states and physiological arousal can impede performance, and hence effective coping mechanisms help to reduce high emotional and physiological arousal in individuals, thereby increasing their self-efficacy beliefs. We posit that informal-sector micro-entrepreneurs can draw on their business and political ties in times of trouble and challenges, thereby using them as a source of coping.

In summary, self-efficacy explains how entrepreneurs feel about their capacity to run their businesses successfully. With high levels of self-efficacy, it is more likely that entrepreneurs utilize more energy in their work and are committed to succeed. Given the low socioeconomic status of micro-entrepreneurs, their perceived support from the regulatory, cognitive and normative environments provides them with a lifeline to access resources, information and support which boosts their self-confidence and in turn their own perceptions of their ability to face given situations. This leads to the following hypotheses:

H3 (a): There is a significantly positive relationship between informal-sector micro-entrepreneurs' *self-efficacy* and their perceived support from *the regulatory environment*.

H3(b): There is a significantly positive relationship between informal-sector micro-entrepreneurs' *self-efficacy* and their perceived support from the *cognitive environment*.

H3(c): There is a significantly positive relationship between informal-sector micro-entrepreneurs' *self-efficacy* and their perceived support from the *normative environment*.

H4: Informal-sector micro-entrepreneurs' *firm performance* is positively and significantly related to their *self-efficacy*.

Additionally, we want to examine whether informal-sector micro-entrepreneurs' network ties have a direct link to increased firm performance. Network theory states that entrepreneurs utilize their social networks for resource mobilization, accessing sources of finance and gathering information on market opportunities and trends. Such support has a positive impact on entrepreneurs' firm performance. We posit in our paper that the informal-sector micro-entrepreneurs' business connections can provide them with the resources and information to help them attain higher firm performance. Likewise, their political connections too can provide them with the necessary regulatory information, introductions to key government agents, permission to set up business ventures, etc. that can collectively lead to higher firm performance. Therefore, we present the following hypotheses:

H5a: Informal-sector micro-entrepreneurs' connections with the business community are positively and significantly related to their firm performance.

H5b: Informal-sector micro-entrepreneurs' connections with political authority are positively and significantly related to their firm performance.

Figure 6.1 shows the conceptual model of the study along with associated relationships between the key variables and the hypotheses developed in the above sections.

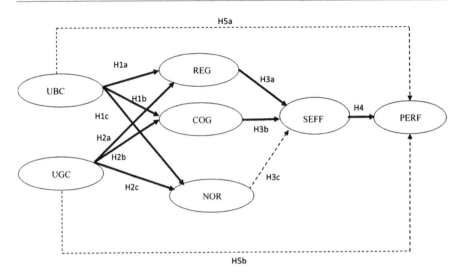

Fig. 6.1 The conceptual model

6.3   Setting the Scene: Sri Lanka

Sri Lanka is a lower-middle-income country with a relatively high level of economic growth compared to most of its neighbours (World Bank 2014, 2015). While
it stands out in the region in key social indicators (Asian Development Bank 2015),
a significant percentage of the labour force still works in the informal-sector
(Monteith and Giesbert 2017), and of these most start their own business as micro-
entrepreneurs (Central Bank of Sri Lanka 2014). Most informal entrepreneurs
(75%) reside in rural Sri Lanka, and entrepreneurs who are relatively young find
informal entrepreneurship to be more attractive (Williams and Shahid 2016).
According to the Sri Lanka Labour Force Survey (2019), informal-sector employment accounts for more than 57% of total employment. A weak institutional environment, political instability (until 2009) and lack of good governance have
significantly contributed to this situation (Asian Development Bank 2015). The
degree of asymmetry between formal and informal institutions determines the tendency of entrepreneurs to operate in the informal sector (Williams and Shahid
2016). Accordingly, greater alignment between these institutions encourages for-
mality among entrepreneurs, while lesser alignment encourages informality. Sri
Lanka provides a classic example for the latter in an emerging country. Reduction
of welfarism has been politically sensitive since independence in 1948, and therefore, the government has welcomed micro-entrepreneurship as a strategic move to
reduce social security payments with the introduction of economic liberalization
(Sanderatne 2002; Samaratunge and Nyland 2007). The government facilitates
micro-entrepreneurs as a part of its poverty eradication strategy and acknowledges
their existence, despite sector informality. Therefore, micro-entrepreneurship in the
informal sector in Sri Lanka is being identified as a legitimate and necessary activity.

6.4   Methodology and Data

6.4.1   Data Collection

Two questionnaires were used to collect data. The main questionnaire sought data on entrepreneurs' level of utilization of connections with the business community and government authorities, three dimensions of perceived institutional support, entrepreneurial self-efficacy and demographic information. The questionnaire for officials mainly sought data on entrepreneurs' performance. Hence, data on entrepreneurial performance are other-rated data; all other data are self-rated. This is a novel element in surveys of this nature, and it helps to gather more objective information, particularly on variables like entrepreneurial performance: officials are better able to provide a relative evaluation on entrepreneurs' performance because an official supervises more than one micro-entrepreneur.

Primary data were collected from 15 divisions covering northern, eastern, southern and western parts of Sri Lanka. A total of 750 (50 entrepreneurs per division) micro-entrepreneurs were invited to attend their respective divisional secretariat on a prearranged date to complete the survey. From those invited, 635 participated. After removing 9 questionnaires with erroneous completion, there were 626 complete cases for analysis – a response rate of 83.5%.

6.5   Analysis and Results

6.5.1   Measurement of Variables

1. Utilization of Connections with the Business Community

As suggested by Welter and Smallbone (2011) in line with Busenitz et al. (2000) and Urban (2013), the scale considers domestic buyers, domestic suppliers and domestic competitors as the major parties of the business community with whom micro-entrepreneurs often maintain contact. The micro-entrepreneurs' degree of utilization of connections with these parties is measured using a 7-point Likert scale ranging from 1 (very little) to 7 (very much). The internal consistency of the scale is satisfactory, as shown by the composite reliability of 0.83.

2. Utilization of Connections with Government Authorities

This scale takes into account central government, provincial government, local government and other public sector authorities, including the divisional secretariat office, banks, line ministries and departments (etc.), as the elements of the set of government authorities. A 7-point Likert scale ranging from 1 (very little) to 7 (very much) measures the level of utilization of connections with government authorities. This scale is also found to be reliable for measuring the construct (composite reliability = 0.83).

3. Perceived Support from the Regulatory Environment

Perceived support from the regulatory environment was measured by asking micro-entrepreneurs to evaluate the degree of assistance they perceived as receiving from government and ministries and grassroots-level authorities (Busenitz et al. 2000; Manolova et al. 2008; Roxas and Coetzer 2012; Urban 2013). Also measured was the extent to which regulations and procedures followed when starting, continuing and expanding microenterprises are supportive and protective. This measure was evaluated using a 7-point Likert scale (1 = very little support, to 7 = very much support). The internal consistency of the measure is found to be satisfactory with a composite reliability of 0.79.

4. Perceived Support from the Cognitive Environment

This examines the perceived support extended when acquiring knowledge with regard to the operations of micro-businesses. Perceived support in relation to how and where to acquire knowledge of the legal environment, risk management, marketing and business consultation facilities is evaluated using a 7-point Likert scale (1 = very little support, to 7 = very much support). The variable is proven reliable, with a composite reliability of 0.87.

5. Perceived Support from the Normative Environment

The normative environment of micro-entrepreneurs is defined as the environment in which they are psychologically motivated via recognizing them, valuing their creative thinking and admiring the ownership of businesses (Busenitz et al., 2000). A 7-point Likert scale (1 = very little support, to 7 = very much support) measured micro-entrepreneurs' perceived support from the normative environment in starting, continuing and expanding microenterprises. The scale is also found to be internally consistent with a composite reliability of 0.85.

6. Entrepreneurial Self-Efficacy

Entrepreneurial self-efficacy is measured using the scale in Forbes (2005). This captures self-efficacy in terms of domains such as innovation, financial, marketing, management and risk-taking. Each item represents a particular task, and micro-entrepreneurs were asked to indicate their level of certainty in their ability to perform it. Each item is measured along a 5-point Likert scale (1 = completely unsure to 5 = completely sure). The internal consistency of the scale is satisfactory, with composite reliability of 0.92.

7. Performance

To measure performance, the scale developed by Wiklund and Shepherd (2005), a five-item scale, is used by supervisors to evaluate and compare the performance of entrepreneurs working under their supervision. The scale includes these items such as higher net profit, sales revenue, sales growth, greater capacity to succeed in the long run and greater innovation. The supervisors were asked to indicate their evaluation of performance using a Likert scale (1 = strongly disagree to 5 = strongly agree). The internal consistency of the measure is also found to be satisfactory, with a composite reliability of 0.82.

6.5.2 Sample Profile

The majority of the sample is female (75.2%), married (79.1%) and aged 31–50 years (68.2%). The majority (71.8%) of the sample has passed the General Certificate of Education (Ordinary Level) or General Certificate of Education (Advanced Level) examination, while a few (2.5%) have higher levels of education. In self-reported income earned from entrepreneurial activities, 82.9% reported a monthly income less than or equal to LKR 30,000; less than 1% reported that they earned a monthly income greater than LKR 100,000.

With regard to ownership of businesses, 72.4% operate their businesses as sole owners and 23.3% as family businesses. The third ownership type is 'partnerships', accounting for 4.3%. Finally, 94.4% operate their businesses with fewer than 5 paid employees; 2.1% have employed more than 10 employees (Appendix 6.1).

6.5.3 Measurement Model

All standardized factor loadings are greater than 0.42 (the minimum loading is 0.43). This can be considered satisfactory, following the rule of thumb that variables with loadings larger than 0.4 should be considered adequate in defining a factor (Kline 2005). All loadings are statistically significant at $p < 0.001$. There are 26 items of the total of 36 with a loading greater than or equal to 0.7: the majority of items have high factor loadings. The composite reliability (CR) of all the latent constructs is greater than 0.7, which indicates good internal consistency (Appendix 6.2).

To examine the convergent validity of the constructs, the average variance extracted (AVE) for each is calculated. If AVE for a construct is greater than 0.5, it achieves convergent validity (Fornell and Larcker 1981). The initial CFA shows that the constructs of 'entrepreneurial self-efficacy' and 'entrepreneurial performance' do not reach a satisfactory level of convergent validity: they initially reported AVE of less than 0.5. Thus, initially, this indicated that the original set of items does not correlate well with each other within their latent variables, and therefore, the latent variable is not well explained by its observed items. As suggested by Tellis et al. (2009), exploratory factor analysis (EFA) was conducted to identify cross-loading items: they are prime candidates for the issue of having low AVE. Accordingly, items 1, 12 and 14 were removed from the list for the construct 'entrepreneurial self-efficacy', and item 5 was removed from the list for 'entrepreneurial

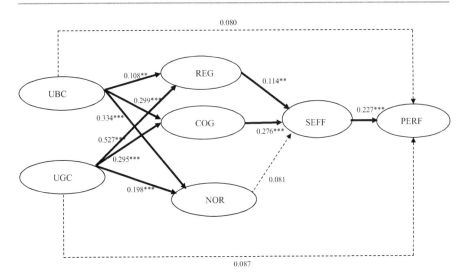

Fig. 6.2 The model with SEM results

performance'. CFA was then undertaken, and AVE for all the items had values greater than 0.5, confirming convergent validity.

The model provides a good fit to the data, as demonstrated by model fit indices. The relative chi-square (χ^2/df) reaches an acceptable ratio with 2.816: according to Kline (2005), a ratio 3:1 or less is considered acceptable for a good fit. The model's root mean square error of approximation (RMSEA) of 0.054 indicates that the model fits well to the covariance matrix of the population; models with RMSEA less than 0.07 are considered to be a better fit (Steiger 2007). The model's SRMR of 0.046 indicates a good fit, as it is below the generally accepted cut-off point of 0.05 (Byrne 1998; Diamantopoulos and Siguaw 2000; Kline 2005). The comparative fit index (CFI), a popular measure of overall model fit (Sorenson et al. 2009), varies from zero (completely not fit) to one (perfect fit). This model's CFI of 0.91 indicates a good overall fit, because it is beyond the threshold value of 0.9 (Kline, 2005). Also, weak correlations among main study variables are evident (Appendix A3).

6.5.4   Structural Model (Hypothesis Testing)

After estimating a common measurement model, a structural model was estimated to test hypotheses (Fig. 6.2).

First, the structural model also provides a good fit to the data, with relative chi-square = 2.696, RMSEA = 0.052, SRMR = 0.055, CFI = 0.91 and CD = 0.983. The standardized path coefficients are calculated using the maximum likelihood method (Table 6.1 with their t-values and the indices for the model's goodness of fit).

The results are controlled for micro-entrepreneurs' level of education, age, gender and whether they are based in Colombo or not.

Table 6.1 SEM results of hypothesis testing

Hypotheses	Path analysis and model fit	Standardized coefficient	t-value	Result
H1a	UBC REG —→	0.108**	2.33	Supported
H1b	UBC COG —→	0.299***	6.59	Supported
H1c	UBC NOR —→	0.334***	7.09	Supported
H2a	UGC REG —→	0.527***	12.75	Supported
H2b	UGC COG —→	0.295***	6.47	Supported
H2c	UGC NOR —→	0.198***	4.16	Supported
H3a	REG SEFF —→	0.114**	2.13	Supported
H3b	COG SEFF —→	0.276***	4.66	Supported
H3c	NOR SEFF —→	0.081	1.44	Not supported
H4	SEFF PERF —→	0.227***	4.97	Supported
H5a	UBC PERF —→	0.080	0.122	Not supported
H5b	UGC PERF —→	0.087	0.084	Not supported
Model fit indices				
	Index	Value		
	Chi2(df)	1841.52 (683)		
	Chi2/df	2.696		
	RMSEA	0.052		
	CFI	0.91		
	SRMR	0.055		
	CD	0.983		

Note: ***$p < 0.01$, **$p < 0.05$, N = 626

Results show that micro-entrepreneurs' utilization of connections with the business community has a significantly positive impact on perceived support from a regulatory environment, cognitive environment and normative environments, separately. The standardized path coefficients are 0.11 ($p < 0.05$), 0.29 ($p < 0.001$) and 0.33 ($p < 0.001$), respectively. Therefore, the higher the level of utilization of connections with the business community (local buyers, suppliers and competitors), the higher the level of perception towards the support received from the regulatory, cognitive and normative environments. Accordingly, H1 (a), H1(b) and H1(c) are supported.

The direct influence of micro-entrepreneurs' level of utilization of connections with political authorities on their perception towards support received from the institutional environment was tested using H2(a) to H2(c). The results show that utilization of such connections has a significantly positive influence on their perception towards support received from the institutional environment. In particular, micro-entrepreneurs' perceived support from the regulatory, cognitive and normative environments is significantly and positively impacted by their level of utilization of connections with political authorities (path coefficients are 0.53 ($p < 0.001$), 0.30 ($p < 0.001$) and 0.20 ($p < 0.001$), respectively). This supports H2(a), H2(b) and H2(c).

In presenting hypothesis H3(a) to H3(c), we are particularly interested in examining whether micro-entrepreneurs' degree of self-efficacy is influenced by their perceived support from the institutional environment. Results of the hypotheses testing show that micro-entrepreneurs' self-efficacy is positively and significantly influenced by their level of perceived support from the regulatory and cognitive environments (path coefficients are 0.114 ($p < 0.005$) and 0.276 ($p < 0.001$), respectively). Thus, the results support H3(a) and H3(b), with a higher degree of micro-entrepreneurs' perceived support from the regulatory and cognitive environments associated with higher levels of self-efficacy. However, the results show that there is no significant association between self-efficacy and perceived support from the normative environment (path coefficient = 0.081 ($p > 0.1$)), and therefore, H3(c) is not supported.

Furthermore, our results support H4, demonstrating that micro-entrepreneurs' business performance is positively and significantly impacted by their degree of self-efficacy (path coefficient = 0.227, $p < 0.001$). Thus, after controlling for micro-entrepreneurs' level of education, age, gender and living area, micro-entrepreneurs with higher levels of self-efficacy demonstrated higher levels of business performance. Finally, in order to determine whether self-efficacy and institutional support fully or partially mediate the link between micro-entrepreneurs' business/government connections and their business performance, we tested H5(a) and H5(b) to examine whether there is a direct association between business/government connections and their business performance. However, the results do not support both hypotheses, concluding that business performance of micro-entrepreneurs is not directly associated with their connections with other business organizations and government organizations (path coefficients = 0.080 ($p > 0.1$) and 0.087 ($p > 0.1$), respectively). Hence, we can conclude that the relationship between micro-entrepreneurs' firm performance and utilization of their business/government connections is fully mediated by perceived support from regulatory and cognitive institutional environment and their level of self-efficacy.

In order to check the robustness of our results, we further calculated the direct, indirect and total effect of main variables of interest on self-efficacy and business performance (Table 6.2).

Accordingly, utilization of business connections and political connections separately creates significantly positive indirect effects on entrepreneurial performance via perceived support from the institutional environment and self-efficacy. Also, utilization of business and political connections does not create significant direct effects on entrepreneurial performance. Hence, the results in Table 6.2 further indicate that the link between the utilization of business and political connections and firm performance is fully mediated by the perceived support from the institutional environment and self-efficacy.

6.6   Discussion

The focus of this study has particular significance for Sri Lanka (and may interest other emerging economies), because of the nature of its economy and business and because of explicit government recognition that the informal sector plays an

Table 6.2 Effects on entrepreneurial self-efficacy and performance

	Direct effect	Indirect effect	Total effect
Impact on entrepreneurial self-efficacy			
Utilization of connections with the business community	No path	0.041*** (5.06)	0.041*** (5.06)
Utilization of connections with government authorities	No path	0.061*** (5.35)	0.061*** (5.35)
Perceived support from the regulatory environment	0.0416** (2.10)	No path	0.0416** (2.10)
Perceived support from the cognitive environment	0.103*** (4.43)	No path	0.103*** (4.43)
Perceived support from the normative environment	0.036 (1.44)	No path	0.036 (1.44)
Impact on entrepreneurial performance			
Utilization of connections with the business community	0.028 (1.54)	0.009*** (3.53)	0.037** (2.09)
Utilization of connections with government authorities	0.036 (0.021)	0.015*** (3.61)	0.051** (2.40)
Perceived support from the regulatory environment	No path	0.009 (1.93)	0.009 (1.93)
Perceived support from the cognitive environment	No path	0.024*** (3.29)	0.024*** (3.29)
Perceived support from the normative environment	No path	0.008 (1.38)	0.008 (1.38)
Entrepreneurial self-efficacy	0.238*** (4.67)	No path	0.238*** (4.67)

Note: ***$p < 0.01$, **$p < 0.05$, N = 626
t-values are in parentheses

important role in national development. Given the time required to develop and extend structures that support a formal economy (apposite regulation, government – positive – attention, access to formal financing, etc.), and the inevitable remediation that follows emergence from civil conflict and re-establishment of a more cohesive, robust civil society, the informal sector plays an important part in establishing and expanding small, family-supporting businesses.

Findings support the notion that the informal sector's connections to the business community and politicians or public servants positively impacted perceived support from the regulatory, cognitive and normative environments. This is interesting, given the lack of empirical evidence to better understand how informal-sector entrepreneurs' business and political connections lead to their sense of support they receive from the institutional environment in which they operate (Sheng et al. 2011). Micro-business entrepreneurs who use business ties with other entrepreneurs can easily extend their activities (Zhou 2013). They have informal and BOP status so that business and political connections form an essential platform for their business development (Sheng et al. 2011). They may see the close connections with the business community and politicians as a pathway to access the services of the regulatory, cognitive and normative environments. Such connections can provide entrepreneurs with vital information on navigating the regulatory environment, offer accumulated knowledge of common business practices (cognitive) and connect them to values, norms, beliefs and traditions (normative). Under the Sri Lankan government's strategic initiative to develop micro-entrepreneurship to eradicate poverty, micro-business owners who utilize political connections are better positioned to gain greater support from the institutional environment.

The findings also show that micro-entrepreneurs' utilization of business connections and political authority led to higher increases in their self-efficacy via perceived support from the regulatory and cognitive environments and that this in turn led to higher firm performance. Thus, the regulatory and cognitive dimensions of the institutional environment and self-efficacy fully mediated the relationship between micro-entrepreneurs' business/political connections and firm performance. The reason for this may be that these entrepreneurs mostly draw on their business and political connections to understand and link to the rules and regulations governing business conduct (regulatory environment) and ways of doing business (cognitive environment) such that they gain a high level of confidence and worth in regard to their abilities to engage in entrepreneurial activities through associations with these dimensions leading to increased self-efficacy and then firm performance. For micro-business owners, this may be of paramount importance, because they operate in a harsh, unpredictable environment, where resources are scarce. Thus, existing business/political connections may negate such hardships to a greater extent and help owners gain a sense of entrepreneurial capability. This implies a role for government authorities in boosting self-efficacy and thereby improving firm performance. Government authorities at the grassroots level need to create avenues such as business clusters where informal-sector micro-entrepreneurs can interact with each other and share their experiences.

Perceived support from the regulatory and the cognitive environments has positive impacts on entrepreneurial self-efficacy, while the perceived support from the normative environment does not. These results indicate that the three components of the institutional environment differently impact informal-sector entrepreneurial self-efficacy.

The taken-for-granted individual perception of institutional support can be negative in emerging economies, due to the underdeveloped nature of their institutional environments (Welter and Smallbone 2011). This has been proven in developing economy contexts in general (Setty and Moorthy 2010) and in Sri Lanka (Attygalle et al. 2014). However, it is noted that (social) networking affects individual perceptions (Brown et al. 2014). Thus, micro-entrepreneurs may hold negative perceptions towards institutional support in terms of difficulty in obtaining financial support, complexity of documentation, bureaucratic government offices (Amine and Staub 2009), education, prior experience and knowledge on technology and cultural and social impression on their business – all three dimensions (Gupta et al. 2013). However, this negativity might diminish in light of information shared and consultation through business and political connections.

These results suggest the possibility that business and political connections of micro-entrepreneurs are strong enough to 'create a new perception' or 'change a pre-occupied perception' on the existing institutional support. This can be related to action learning, too, which happens at small-scale enterprises (Clarke et al. 2006).

These findings do not neatly fit with the literature reported in other South Asian countries like Nepal and India, because most such findings deny the fact that rural informal-sector women micro-entrepreneurs benefit from business connections (Gupta et al. 2013). This particular finding could be bound to the very nature of the majority of respondents covered in the present study – women surviving in civil war-affected areas.

6.7   Conclusion

The study has revealed interrelationships between utilization of business and political connections, perceived institutional support, self-efficacy and firm performance of micro-entrepreneurs in the Sri Lankan informal sector. Utilization of business and political connections directly leads to enriched perception on the support from micro-entrepreneurs' institutional environments. Of the sub-elements of the institutional environment, perceived support from the regulatory and cognitive environments positively influenced entrepreneurs' self-efficacy, which then resulted in higher firm performance. The study concludes, too, that firm performance is not *directly* influenced by the utilization of business and political connections but only via perceived support from the regulatory and cognitive environments and self-efficacy.

However, these findings are based only on cross-sectional data (albeit substantial and nation representative), and therefore, the study has not considered the dynamics of these inter-linkages. This invites future studies that use panel data to account for structural changes of the links between utilization of business and government connections, perceived institutional support, self-efficacy and firm performance. There is also an avenue for a study considering other emerging market countries simultaneously, enabling an international comparison of such links. Finally, this study is limited to Sri Lanka; the findings may therefore not be representative of other emerging market economies.

Chapter Takeaways

1. The informal sector in developing countries is characterised by micro-entrepreneurs who engage in precarious and subsistence entrepreneurial activities, often hidden from the formal institutional environment and lacking access to financial and other resources necessary for entrepreneurial success. Hence, low firm performance and long-term survival are key issues facing these informal entrepreneurs.
2. Yet the informal sector provides crucial income-generating and employment opportunities for the majority of the rural poor in developing countries which

ultimately contribute to economic development in these countries. Thus, the informal sector is very important and warrants further research.

3. The formal institutional environment is characterised by three components, viz. regulatory, cognitive and normative environments. The quality of the institutional environment in a country determines the emergence and strength of its formal sector and its performance and growth.

4. Self-efficacy, which relates to a person's belief in his/her own capacity to achieve performance, is very important for entrepreneurs as it can determine success in entrepreneurial activities.

5. The current research shows that although informal-sector entrepreneurs stay hidden from the formal institutional environment, their business and political ties help them link with the formal institutional environment and gain higher self-efficacy.

Reflection Questions

1. Do some background research on the informal sector in your country, and find out how prevalent it is, who the main entrepreneurs are, what they do and what they contribute to the economy.

2. What are the characteristics of the three components of the institutional environment, and how do each of these components help entrepreneurship?

3. Why do you think informal entrepreneurs stay 'hidden' from the formal Institutional environment?

4. Although lacking in other resources, informal-sector entrepreneurs are embedded in their social networks. What are the components of these social networks, and in the absence of other resources, how do such social networks help informal entrepreneurs?

5. Why is self-efficacy important for entrepreneurs? How can self-efficacy be developed in entrepreneurs?

Appendixes

Appendix 6.1: Sample Profile

	N	Frequency (%)
Gender		
Male	155	24.8
Female	471	75.2
Age (in years)		
<30	46	7.4

	N	Frequency (%)
31–40	199	31.8
41–50	228	36.4
>50	153	24.4
Marital status		
Single	56	8.9
Married	495	79.1
Widowed	41	6.6
Other	34	5.4
Highest educational attainment		
Primary	161	25.7
Ordinary level	294	47.0
Advanced level	155	24.8
Above advanced level	16	2.5
Self-reported income (in LKR; 1 USD = 145.77 LKR on average in July and August 2016 when the survey was conducted)		
<10,000	246	39.3
10,001–30,000	273	43.6
30,001–50,000	77	12.3
50,001–100,000	25	4.0
>100,000	5	0.8
Ownership of the business		
Sole	453	72.4
Family	146	23.3
Partnership	27	4.3
Number of paid employees		
<5	591	94.4
5–10	22	3.5
>10	13	2.1

Appendix 6.2: Results of the Measurement Model

Variable and item	Source	Factor loading (standardized)	t-value	CR	AVE
Utilization of connections with the business community (UBC)	Smallbone and Welter (2011)			0.83	0.63
UBC 01		0.84	45.07		
UBC 02		0.90	51.87		
UBC 03		0.60	20.73		
Utilization of connections with government authorities (UGC)	Smallbone and Welter (2011)			0.83	0.51

Variable and item	Source	Factor loading (standardized)	t-value	CR	AVE
UGC 01		0.77	38.51		
UGC 02		0.86	54.43		
UGC 03		0.78	39.05		
UGC 04		0.61	21.46		
UGC 05		0.49	14.49		
Perceived support from a regulatory environment (REG)	Busenitz et al. (2000)			0.79	0.51
REG 01		0.78	37.64		
REG 02		0.86	46.30		
REG 03		0.69	25.74		
REG 04		0.43	11.64		
Perceived support from the cognitive environment (COG)	Roxas and Coetzer (2012), Urban (2013)			0.87	0.63
COG 01		0.79	42.02		
COG 02		0.84	51.78		
COG 03		0.80	43.84		
COG 04		0.75	34.58		
Perceived support from the normative environment (NOR)	Roxas and Coetzer (2012), Urban (2013)			0.85	0.59
NOR 01		0.68	26.05		
NOR 02		0.73	30.86		
NOR 03		0.85	48.90		
NOR 04		0.81	43.29		
Entrepreneurial self-efficacy (SEFF)	Forbes (2005)			0.92	0.51
SEFF 02		0.67	27.96		
SEFF 03		0.66	26.77		
SEFF 04		0.70	31.04		
SEFF 05		0.72	34.52		
SEFF 06		0.71	32.17		
SEFF 07		0.67	28.04		
SEFF 08		0.77	42.45		
SEFF 09		0.77	42.86		
SEFF 10		0.71	32.48		
SEFF 11		0.71	33.29		
SEFF 13		0.72	33.73		
SEFF 15		0.70	32.16		

Variable and item	Source	Factor loading (standardized)	t-value	CR	AVE
Entrepreneurial performance (PERF)	Wicklund and Shepherd (2005)			0.82	0.54
PERF 01		0.72	29.00		
PERF 02		0.84	40.96		
PERF 03		0.77	32.88		
PERF 04		0.59	18.50		

Model fit indices
$\chi^2(df) = 1613.802(573)$, $\chi^2/df = 2.816$, RMSEA $= 0.054$, CFI $= 0.91$, SRMR $= 0.046$, CD $= 0.99$

Note: all of the items are significant at $p < 0.001$ error level, $N = 626$ after list-wise deletion, *AVE* average variance extracted, *CR* composite reliability, *RMSEA* root mean square error of approximation, *SRMR* standardized root mean square residual, *CFI* comparative fit index, *CD* coefficient of determination

References

Acemoglu, D., & Robinson, J. A. (2012). *Why nations fail: The origins of power, prosperity and poverty*. New York: Crown Business.

Acs, Z., Desai, S., Stenholm, P., & Wuebker, R. (2013). Institutions and the rate of formal and informal entrepreneurship across countries (interactive article). *Frontiers of Entrepreneurship Research, 35*, 1–24.

Amato, C., Baron, R. A., Barbieri, B., Belanger, J. J., & Pierro, A. (2017). Regulatory modes and entrepreneurship: The mediational role of alertness in small business success. *Journal of Small Business Management, 55*(S1), 27–42. https://doi.org/10.1111/jsbm.12255.

Amine, L. S., & Staub, K. M. (2009). Women entrepreneurs in sub-Saharan Africa: An institutional theory analysis from a social marketing point of view. *Entrepreneurship & Regional Development: An International Journal, 21*(2), 183–211.

Asian Development Bank. (2015). *Sri Lanka's growth to development in 2015, rebound in 2016*. Geneva: ADB.

Attygalle, K., Edirisinghe, C., Hirimuthugodage, D., Madurawala, S., Senaratne, A., & Wijesingha, A. (2014). *Female entrepreneurship and the role of business development services in promoting small and medium women entrepreneurship in Sri Lanka*. http://www.ips.lk/research/highlights/highlight_archive/2014/entrepreneurs.pdf.

Autio, E., & Fu, K. (2015). Economic and political institutions and entry into formal and informal entrepreneurship. *Asia Pacific Journal of Management, 32*(1), 67–94.

Azmat, F., & Samaratunge, R. (2013). Exploring customer loyalty at bottom of the pyramid in South Asia. *Social Responsibility Journal, 9*(3), 379–394.

Bandura, A. (1977). Self-efficacy: Toward a unifying theory of behavioral change. *Psychological Review, 84*(2), 191–215.

Bandura, A. (1986). *Social foundations of thought and action: A social cognitive theory*. Englewood Cliffs: Prentice-Hall.

Baumol, W. J. (1990). Entrepreneurship: Productive, unproductive and destructive. *Journal of Business Venturing, 11*, 3–22.

Blackburn, R. A., Hart, M., & Wainwright, T. (2013). Small business performance: Business, strategy and owner-manager characteristics. *Journal of Small Business and Enterprise Development, 20*(1), 8–27.

Brown, M. A., Alkadry, M. G., & Resnick-Luetke, S. (2014). Social networking and individual perceptions: Examining predictors of participation. *Public Organization Review, 14*(3), 285–304.

Bruton, G. D., Ahlstrom, D., & Obloj, K. (2008). Entrepreneurship in emerging economies: Where are we today and where should the research go in the future. *Entrepreneurship Theory and Practice, 32*(1), 1–14.

Bruton, G. D., Ahlstrom, D., & Li, H. (2010). Institutional theory and entrepreneurship: Where we are now and where do we need to move in the future? *Entrepreneurship Theory and Practice, 34*(3), 421–440.

Bruton, G. D., Khavul, S., & Chavez, H. (2011). Micro lending in emerging economies: Building a new line of inquiry from the ground up. *Journal of International Business Studies, 42*, 718–739.

Bruton, G. D., Ketchen, D. J., & Ireland, R. D. (2013). Entrepreneurship as a solution to poverty. *Journal of Business Venturing, 28*(6), 683–689.

Burt, R. S. (2001). Structural holes versus network closure as social capital. In N. Lin, K. Cook, & R. S. Burt (Eds.), *Social capital: Theory and research* (pp. 31–56). New York: Transaction Publishers.

Busenitz, L., Gomez, C., & Spencer, J. (2000). Country institutional profiles: Unlocking entrepreneurial phenomena. *Academy of Management Journal, 43*(5), 994–1003.

Byrne, B. M. (1998). *Structural equation modeling with LISREL, PRELIS and SIMPLIS: Basic concepts, applications and programming.* Mahwah: Lawrence Erlbaum Associates.

Castro, J. O. D., Khavul, S., & Bruton, G. D. (2014). Shades of Grey: How do informal firms navigate between macro and meso institutional environments? *Strategic Entrepreneurship Journal, 8*, 75–94.

Central Bank of Sri Lanka. (2014). *Annual report.* Colombo: Central Bank of Sri Lanka.

Chen, X., Yao, X., & Kotha, S. (2009). Entrepreneur passion and preparedness in business plan presentations: A persuasion analysis of venture capitalists' funding decisions. *Academy of Management Journal, 52*(1), 199–214.

Clarke, J., Thorpe, R., Anderson, L., & Gold, J. (2006). It's all action, it's all learning: Action learning in SMEs. *Journal of European Industrial Training, 30*(6), 441–455.

Department of Census and Statistics of Sri Lanka (2019). *Sri Lanka Labour Force Survey - Annual Report 2019*, Department of Census and Statistics of Sri Lanka accessed on 20th November 2020.

Diamantopoulos, A., & Siguaw, J. (2000). *Introducing LISREL.* London: Sage.

Fan, J. P. H., Wei, K. C. J., & Xu, X. Z. (2011). Corporate finance and governance in emerging markets: A selective review and an agenda for future research. *Journal of Corporate Finance, 17*(2), 207–214.

Forbes, D. P. (2005). The effects of strategic decision making on entrepreneurial self efficacy. *Entrepreneurship Theory and Practice, 29*(5), 599–626.

Fornell, C., & Larcker, D. F. (1981). Evaluating structural equation models with unobservable variables and measurement error. *Journal of Marketing Research, 18*(1), 39–50.

Gupta, P. D., Guha, S., & Krishnaswami, S. S. (2013). Firm growth and its determinants. *Journal of Innovation and Entrepreneurship, 2*(1), 1–14.

Hopp, C., & Stephan, U. (2012). The influence of socio-cultural environments on the performance of nascent entrepreneurs: Community culture, motivation, self-efficacy and start-up success. *Entrepreneurship and Regional Development, 24*(9–10), 917–945.

ILO (Ed.). (2011a). *Employment in the informal economy, key indicators of the labour market (KILM)* (7th ed.). Geneva: ILO.

ILO. (2011b). *Statistical updates on employment in the informal economy.* Geneva: ILO.

Kaufmann, D., Kraay, A., & Mastruzzi, M. (2009). *Governance matters VIII: Aggregate and individual governance indicators 1996-2008.* Policy research working paper 4978. New York: World Bank.

Khavul, S., Bruton, G. D., & Wood, E. (2009). Informal family business in Africa. *Entrepreneurship Theory and Practice, 33*(6), 1219–1238.

Khayesi, J., George, G., & Antonakis, J. (2014). Kinship in entrepreneur networks: Performance effects of resource assembly in Africa. *Entrepreneurship Theory and Practice, 38*(6), 1323–1342.

Kline, R. B. (2005). *Principles and practice of structural equation modeling* (2nd ed.). New York: Guilford.

Ketchen, D. J., Ireland, R. D., & Webb, J. W. (2014). Toward a research agenda for the informal economy: A survey of the strategic entrepreneurship journal's editorial board. *Strategic Entrepreneurship Journal, 8*(1), 95–100.

La Porta, R., López-de-Silanes, F., & Shleifer, A. (1999). Corporate ownership around the world. *Journal of Finance, 54*(2), 471–517.

La Porta, R., López-de-Silanes, F., Shleifer, A., & Vishny, R. W. (2000). Investor protection and corporate governance. *Journal of Financial Economics, 58*(1–2), 3–27.

Lee, C., & Hung, S. (2014). Institutional entrepreneurship in the formal economy: China's Shan-Zhai mobile phones. *Strategic Entrepreneurship Journal, 8*, 16–36.

Light, I., & Dana, L. (2013). Boundaries of social capital in entrepreneurship. *Entrepreneurship Theory and Practice, 37*(3), 603–624.

Luo, Y., & Junkunc, M. (2008). How private enterprises respond to government bureaucracy in emerging economies: The effects of entrepreneurial type and governance. *Strategic Management Journal, 2*, 133–153.

Manolova, T. S., Eunni, R. V., & Gyoshev, B. S. (2008). Institutional environments for entrepreneurship: Evidence from emerging economies in Eastern Europe. *Entrepreneurship Theory and Practice, 32*(1), 203–218.

Monteith, W., & Giesbert, L. (2017). 'When the stomach is full we look for respect': Perceptions of 'good work' in the urban informal sectors of three developing countries. *Work Employment and Society, 31*(5), 816–833.

Moran, P. (2005). Structural vs relational Embeddedness: Social capital and managerial performance. *Strategic Management Journal, 26*(12), 1129–1151.

Muttakin, M. B., Monem, R. M., Khan, A., & Subramaniam, N. (2015). Family firms, firm performance and political connections: Evidence from Bangladesh. *Journal of Contemporary Accounting & Economics, 11*(3), 215–230.

Peng, M., & Luo, Y. (2000). Managerial ties and firm performance in a transition economy: The nature of a micro-macro link. *Academy of Management Journal, 43*(3), 486–501.

Putnam, R. D. (2000). *Bowling alone: The collapse and revival of American Community*. New York; London: Simon & Schuster.

Roxas, B., & Coetzer, A. (2012). Institutional environment, managerial attitudes and environmental sustainability orientation of small firms. *Journal of Business Ethics, 111*(4), 461–476.

Samaratunge, R., & Nyland, C. (2007). The management of social protection in Sri Lanka. *Journal of Contemporary Asia, 37*, 346–363.

Samaratunge, R., Alam, Q., & Teicher, J. (2008). The new public management reforms in Asia: A comparison of south and southeast Asian countries. *International Review of Administrative Sciences, 74*(1), 25–46.

Sambharya, R., & Musteen, M. (2014). Institutional environment and entrepreneurship: An empirical study across countries. *Journal of International Entrepreneurship, 12*(4), 14–330.

Sanderatne, N. (2002). *The informal sector in Sri Lanka: Its nature and extent and the impact of globalization*. Colombo: ILO Office.

Schoar, A. (2010). The divide between subsistence and transformational entrepreneurship. *Innovation Policy and the Economy, 10*(1), 57–81.

Setty, E. D., & Moorthy, P. K. (2010). *Strategies for developing women entrepreneurs*. New Delhi: Akansha Publishing House.

Shane, S., & Venkataraman, S. (2000). The promise of entrepreneurship: A field of research. *Academy of Management Review, 25*(1), 217–226.

Sheng, S., Zhou, K. Z., & Li, J. J. (2011). The effects of business and political ties on firm performance: Evidence from China. *Journal of Marketing, 75*(1), 1–15.

Siqueira, A. O., Webb, J. W., & Bruton, G. D. (2016). Informal entrepreneurship and industry conditions. *Entrepreneurship Theory and Practice, 40*(1), 177–200.

Sorenson, R. L., Goodpaster, K. E., Hedberg, P. R., & Yu, A. (2009). The family point of view, family social capital, and firm performance: An exploratory test. *Family Business Review, 22*(3), 239–253.

Spence, L. J. (2016). Small business social responsibility: Expanding core CSR theory. *Business & Society, 55*(1), 23–55.

Steiger, J. H. (2007). Understanding the limitations of global fit assessment in structural equation modeling. *Personality and Individual Differences, 42*(5), 893–898.

Sutter, C., Webb, J., Kistruck, G., Ketchen, D. J., Jr., & Ireland, R. D. (2017). Transitioning entrepreneurs from informal to formal markets. *Journal of Business Venturing, 32*(4), 420–442.

Tellis, G. J., Prabhu, J. C., & Chandy, R. K. (2009). Radical innovation across nations: The preeminence of corporate culture. *Journal of Marketing, 73*(1), 3–23.

Thai, M. T. T., & Turkina, T. (2014). Macro-level determinants of formal entrepreneurship versus informal entrepreneurship. *Journal of Business Venturing, 29*(3), 490–510.

Urban, B. (2013). Social entrepreneurship in an emerging economy: A focus on the institutional environment and social entrepreneurial self-efficacy. *Managing Global Transitions, 11*(1), 3–25.

Viswanathan, M., Echambadi, R., Venugopal, S., & Sridharan, S. (2014). Subsistence entrepreneurship, value creation, and community exchange systems: A social capital explanation. *Journal of Macro Marketing, 34*(2), 213–226.

Webb, J. W., Ireland, R. D., & Ketchen, D. J., Jr. (2014). Toward a greater understanding of entrepreneurship and strategy in the informal economy. *Strategic Management Journal, 8*, 1–15.

Welter, F., & Smallbone, D. (2011). Institutional perspectives on entrepreneurial behavior in challenging environments. *Journal of Small Business Management, 49*(1), 107–125.

Welter, F., Smallbone, D., & Pobol, A. (2015). Entrepreneurial activity in the informal economy: A missing piece of the jigsaw puzzle. *Entrepreneurship and Regional Development, 27*(5–6), 292–306.

Wiklund, J., & Shepherd, D. (2005). Entrepreneurial orientation and small business performance. *Journal of Business Venturing, 20*(1), 71–91.

Williams, C. C. (2014). Out of the shadows: A classification of economies by the size and character of their informal sector. *Work Employment and Society, 28*(5), 735–753.

Williams, C. C., & Martinez-Perez, A. (2014). Entrepreneurship in the informal economy: A product of too much or too little state intervention? *International Journal of Entrepreneurship and Innovation, 15*(4), 227–237.

Williams, C. C., & Shahid, M. S. (2016). Informal entrepreneurship and institutional theory: Explaining the varying degrees of (in)formalization of entrepreneurs in Pakistan. *Entrepreneurship & Regional Development, 28*(1–2), 1–25.

Williams, N., & Vorley, T. (2014). Institutional asymmetry: How formal and informal institutions affect entrepreneurship in Bulgaria. *International Small Business Journal, 33*(8), 840–861.

Williams, C. C., Martinez-Perez, A., & Kedir, A. M. (2016). Informal entrepreneurship in developing economies: The impacts of starting up unregistered on firm performance. *Journal of Entrepreneurship, Theory and Practice, 41*(5), 773–799.

World Bank. (2014). *Sustaining development success in Sri Lanka.* http://www.worldbank.org/en/news/opinion/2014/01/30/sustaining-development-success-sri-lanka

World Bank. (2015). *Sri Lanka: A systematic country diagnostic* [Press release]. http://www.worldbank.org/en/news/feature/2016/02/15/sri-lanka-a-systematic-country-diagnostic

Yamakawa, Y., Peng, M. W., & Deeds, D. (2015). Rising from the ashes: Cognitive determinants of venture growth after entrepreneurial failure. *Entrepreneurship Theory and Practice, 39*(2), 209–236.

Zhou, W. (2013). Political connections and entrepreneurial investment: Evidence from China's transition economy. *Journal of Business Venturing, 28*(2), 299–315.

Zhu, Y., Wittmann, X., & Peng, M. K. (2012). Institution-based barriers to innovation in SMEs in China. *Asia Pacific Journal of Management, 29*(4), 1131–1142.

A Question of Ties: The Impact of Social Ties on Resource Mobilization of Women Entrepreneurs in the Sri Lankan Floriculture Industry

7

S. M. P. C. Padmini, Thilakshi Kodagoda, and Ramanie Samaratunge

7.1 Introduction

Many unemployed women and housewives start small floriculture nurseries as a means of self-employment without formal support. The Sri Lankan government has sought to boost the floriculture sector: the national policy framework (Department of National Planning 2010) aims to develop it as an income-generating pathway for unemployed women. But the main barrier for developing the sector is the unavailability of sufficient data. Floriculture is a high-income-generating agricultural business that can be used for socio-economic development in Sri Lanka. Great opportunities exist, especially for women growers and their networks. However, this potential has not been used properly (Export Development Board of Sri Lanka 2008). This research identifies the social reality of respondents and examines it objectively.

Women-led businesses are, globally, a rapidly growing entrepreneurial population (Brush and Cooper 2012), generating considerable recent scholarly attention (Duberley and Carrigan 2012; Lamine et al. 2015). Another important area is networks in entrepreneurship. Access to, and interaction with, social networks is critical for small entrepreneurs in procuring resources, information, and opportunities through strong or weak ties (Arregle et al. 2015; Bhagavatula et al. 2010; Kotha and George 2012; Macpherson et al. 2015). Better developed networks representing

S. M. P. C. Padmini (✉)
Sri Lanka Council for Agricultural Research Policy, Colombo, Sri Lanka

T. Kodagoda
Faculty of Management and Finance, University of Colombo, Colombo, Sri Lanka

R. Samaratunge
Department of Management, Monash University, Clayton, VIC, Australia
e-mail: ramanie.samaratunge@monash.edu

© The Author(s), under exclusive license to Springer Nature
Switzerland AG 2021
S. Dhiman, R. Samaratunge (eds.), *New Horizons in Management, Leadership and Sustainability*, Future of Business and Finance,
https://doi.org/10.1007/978-3-030-62171-1_7

greater, higher-quality ties are certainly highly beneficial for entrepreneurs, especially at the start-up stage (Elfring and Hulsink 2003). Yet research into how the specific dimensions and configuration of these social ties impact entrepreneurial outcomes remains (Elfring and Hulsink 2003): strong and weak ties contribute differently to an enterprise's outcomes.

7.2   Literature Review

Given the leading role of women entrepreneurs in developing countries for generating employment, achieving gender equality, and reducing poverty, an analysis of their main characteristics and unique contextual factors provide a valuable foundation for 'developing successful entrepreneurship-related policies and for understanding a country's competitiveness and growth potential' (De Vita et al. 2014). We still know little about how women entrepreneurs identify opportunities, access resources, and build legitimacy for their firms despite the fact that researchers increasingly highlight that 'entrepreneurial activity is embedded in network relationships that direct resource flows to entrepreneurs who are somehow better connected' (Stam et al. 2014). The peculiarities of the country-specific sociocultural and institutional environment in each individual country create complexities for women entrepreneurs in determining their business success, where the creation and usefulness of business networks are guided by unique cultural norms. Therefore, country-specific studies provide us the opportunity to investigate how certain contextual factors may differently influence women entrepreneurs' ability to mobilize critical resources. By doing so, these studies make a significant contribution to advancing our understanding of this multifaceted entrepreneurial phenomenon.

The positive impact of networks on entrepreneurial activities is well established, especially in emerging country contexts (Haugh and Talwar 2016; Newman et al. 2014). Although early research on entrepreneurship focused primarily on entrepreneurs isolated from their social environments, later scholars questioned this view, and thus the notion of entrepreneurship embedded in dynamic social networks was born (Qureshi et al. 2016). Networks provide crucial social capital, defined as the sum of actual and potential resources derived from an individual's network of social relationships with others (Adler and Kwon 2002), and thus access to 'critical resources such as knowledge, power, trust, reciprocity (Patel and Terjesen 2011).

Network scholars have examined entrepreneurship in terms of understanding the various relationships and resource access in networks (network content), coordination of these relationships and resources (governance), and patterns of relationships taking prominence. With regard to network content, researchers have primarily focused on the types of network ties (e.g. strong and weak ties, bonding, and bridging ties) and the characteristics of the network (e.g. density, centrality: Qureshi et al. 2016). This study utilizes theory and empirical evidence pertaining to strong and weak ties to examine women entrepreneurs' ability to mobilize resources and gain opportunities. The next section of the paper examines in depth the nature of strong and weak ties and their implications for entrepreneurs' opportunity and resource mobilization.

7.3   Strong vs Weak Ties

Granovetter's (1973) seminal work on social ties portrayed social networks as a tool linking the micro and macro levels of sociological theory and argued that 'the degree of overlap of two individuals' friendship networks varies directly with the strength of their tie to one another. Granovetter (1973) believed social ties to lead to the dissemination of influence and information, mobility opportunity, and community organization. The strength of a tie was defined as the 'combination of the amount of time, the emotional intensity, the intimacy (mutual confiding), and the reciprocal services which characterize the tie' (Granovetter 1973). By this definition, stronger ties would involve greater time commitment, the similarity in between the persons involved, and reciprocity of services (Arregle et al. 2015; Granovetter 1973) and trust (McEvily et al. 2003). Strong ties typically consist of family or close friendship connections, while weak ties include casual friends, acquaintances, and business affiliates (Patel and Terjesen 2011).

The literature provides ample discussion on the importance of strong and weak ties for entrepreneurships (Lamine et al. 2015) and how entrepreneurs' embeddedness in social relations determines the outcomes gained (Arregle et al. 2015). While some studies conclude the necessity of strong ties over weak ones (Steier and Greenwood 2005), others point to the importance of having a mix of strong and weak ties for entrepreneurial success (Elfring and Hulsink 2003). Jack (2005) demonstrates that strong ties are 'instrumental for business activity and used extensively to provide knowledge and information but also to maintain, extend and enhance business and personal reputations'. Such benefits have the following attributes: 'It is cheap; it is more trustworthy because it is richer, more detailed and accurate; it is usually from a continuing relationship and so in economic terms it is more reliable' (Jack 2005). Strong ties lead to the exchange of 'tacit knowledge, trust-based governance, and resource cooptation' (Elfring and Hulsink 2003).

However, one criticism of strong ties is that information tends to become redundant over time and the ties themselves do not let novel information and opportunities to filter through (Arregle et al. 2015). Weak ties, on the other hand, provide access to novel information, diverse knowledge, and opportunities (Arregle et al. 2015). From an embeddedness perspective, it befits entrepreneurs to strive for an intermediate level of embeddedness in social ties characterized by lack of greater or lesser embeddedness in strong ties. This is likely to bring about the optimal results.

Baddegamage (2012) states that 5000 direct employment opportunities and over 15,000 indirect employment opportunities have been borne through floriculture supplies and exports in Sri Lanka. Exports of floriculture have demonstrated a growth of 9% from 2002 to 2007. The European market remains the major export destination for Sri Lankan exporters; however deviations in targeted export markets are visible. Focus on South Asian and Middle Eastern nations are observed with a 26.5% increase to South Korea and 19.8% to the Middle East. Both the Export Development Board of Sri Lanka (2008) and International Labor Organization recognize the possible existence of a large domestic market for floriculture products in Sri Lanka and indicate a close relation with other industries on the growth of the domestic market.

The Sri Lankan government has made attempts to boost the floriculture sector. The national policy framework (Department of National Planning 2010) aimed to develop the floriculture sector as a source of income-generating pathway to unemployed women in the country. One impediment to developing the sector is the dearth of data on the Sri Lankan floriculture sector. The 2006 survey on small- and medium-sized floriculture entrepreneurs in Sri Lanka, carried out by Sri Lanka Council for Agricultural Research Policy, mainly focused on the status of the floriculture sector in Sri Lanka (Niranjan and Gunasena 2006), but did not consider specifically the growers or their support systems such as network capacity. Given the lack of studies on this sector, little is known about how woman growers in developing countries can benefit more from this sector.

Sri Lankans use flowers in numerous events in daily life such as during weddings and funerals and also in places of worship (in Buddhists temples and Hindu Kovils). In addition, the development of the tourism industry and service sectors in the country has increased demand for floriculture products especially for indoor decorations. Floriculture creations are available in e-markets in Sri Lanka, the best example being the 'Lassana Flora' website. Many beauty culture therapists and health spas in the country use flowers for many therapeutic techniques. Thus there is considerable internal demand for floriculture products in Sri Lanka, although this demand is not being met at the moment in some areas. Sudhagar (2013) noted that Sri Lanka imports Indian floriculture products from India notably the Jasmine flowers which are used in religious ceremonies in Anuradhapura Buddhist temples. Presently, the Department of National Botanic Garden and Department of Agriculture have established a joint program to cultivate jasmine flowers in Sri Lanka to fulfil this demand.

The community-based and cooperative developments are mainly due to the increasing trust between community members and collective actions, known as social capital (Janssens 2010). Social capital refers to the trust and shared norms of behaviour that arise within informal social networks, and it influences the resources that an individual can mobilize through a social network (Janssens 2010; Ju and Fu 2012). Janssens (2010) highlighted that women empowerment and social capital enhanced the development of roads, schools, and bridges in Bihar in India. Bihar is one of poorest Indian states where lower caste people live. Ju and Fu (2012) analyzed many social capital theories and found that social capital is team strength. The best example of the use of social capital is jasmine growers in Karnataka state in India. Cnaan et al. (2014) reported that several lessons could be learned from this successful community enterprise, and it has provided thousands of households in the region with a guaranteed income from jasmine production.

Ju and Fu (2012) reviewed theories of social capital and found that there is no general definition of it, but three different theories were noted, as follows. First, social capital contains three components: the resources embedded in the social structure, the person's capacity to use those resources, and the objective ability to use or mobilize these resources. Second, social capital is the sum of the potential and real resources embedded in the network and owned by individuals or organizations. Third, social capital is the contact between the main social unit and the society and the capability to access resources through that contact. Munasib and Jordan (2011) viewed social capital as community involvement – farmers used it as a part of sustainable agricultural practices. This study evaluated the linkages of growers with supporters to improve the income of rural women and reduce the poverty of rural families. Rao and Ibanez (2005) found a causal and positive impact of social funds on trust as well as on collective action and that better educated and better networked individuals gained more benefits from social funds. Wetterberg (2007) illustrated the importance of the social capital concept and incorporated constellations of social ties for antipoverty operations. Those social ties are networks, organizations, and government-mandated organizations.

Social capital is defined as the informal forms of relationships with organizations, networks, and associations; it helps share knowledge, mutual trust, social norms, and unwritten rules (Shoji et al. 2012). Social capital plays a vital role in reducing poverty and facilitating rural development (Shoji et al. 2012). Fafchamps and Minten (2002) convincingly described how social capital helps earn high profits in trade by reducing transaction costs and also helps solve the problem of poverty in rural areas. Shoji et al. (2012) studied social capital investment in Sri Lankan farmer societies and noted the expenditure on community ceremonies, participation in community work (*Shramadana*), and participation in communal irrigation maintenance. However, they reported that, when the farmers faced credit constraints, they reduced their investment in social capital and reduced their general trust, thereby exposing themselves to potential poverty traps. Tripp et al. (2005) also noted low investment in social capital in the dissemination of information in farmer field schools in Sri Lanka. Farmer field schools train farmers to practice integrated pest management (IPM) and to produce insecticide-free rice for the market; the farmers could not secure a good market for their products. Because of poor support from society, farmers who had been trained abandoned their IPM practices, and with that knowledge sharing also disappeared. Accordingly social capital development varies as a result of many factors (Tripp et al. 2005).

Zell et al. (2014) argued that support networks are a type of social network with a unique collection of people but they rely on help with finance, information, technology, and other facilities. Interaction with each other is essential to the success of the business, and some studies have indicated that those network links assisted with the emergence of organizations (Newbert and Tornikoski 2012). In their survival and growth, humans rely on the interaction with one another, and this collaboration is enforced by social, religious, legal, and political institutions. Such cooperation has helped develop cooperatives societies in the past (Matthew et al. 2014). Empowerment of women is very important in developing countries, because their participation is very important to the socio-economic development of a country (Noreen 2011). Moreover, the networking ability of women is very high, and they are considered self-help groups (Rani 2014).

Women define family (i.e. children, parents, and partner) as a key unit in their life; empirical evidence illustrates the influence of family capital and its effect on women entrepreneurs. Family capital is the social, human, and financial resources available from family sources (Danes et al. 2009) and defines human, social, psychological, and financial capital as attributes of the family contribution to business (i.e. family capital). Further, Danes et al. (2009) emphasize that this includes the 'knowledge, experience, ability and energy' of family members that are at the disposal of the business. However, family capital cannot be purchased or hired; its existence is based on continuing relationships within a family.

The term 'family mastery' (Imig 2003) defines the collective nature within a family to successfully accomplish a task utilizing their collaborative human capital. Danes et al. (2002) imply that family firms create an environment of 'collaborative dialogue' (Sorenson et al. 2009), which leads to broader access to extensive understanding, especially when family firms face problems. However, a conflict of expectations within a family unit or a reverse method of 'family mastery' will generate a collective sense of negativity and failure, thereby impacting individual confidence and human capital (Imig 2003).

The perspective of family capital from a societal viewpoint influences access to a broader variation of resources. Access and availability to social capital or support are bounded by reciprocal links between education, employment, and culture within a family and the image presented to the external environment (Edwards et al. 2003). Social capital is defined as access to resources that are unavailable within a family unit via societal networks (Gofen 2009). According to the World Bank Report (1994), their societal environment is a condition that may restrict women from initiating entrepreneurship.

Emotional support, social networking, and financial support (Friedemann-Sánchez 2008) appear as key dimensions of support presented to women through family capital. As discussed by Friedemann-Sánchez (2008), Sorenson et al. (2009) unpack the network relationship as a key attribute of family social capital. Research suggests that strong social networking family environments offer access to financial resources, extra support, expertise, encouragement, and a strong customer base and build a strong social status, thus fostering a better business image. Dyer (2006) argues that these attributes contribute to the business, ultimately influencing its performance.

A contextual study on businesswomen in China and Nigeria showed that 85% women received business support from partners or family. Women who were divorced or single had received most support from their family. Family support is a predominantly influential attribute for businesswomen in both Nigeria and China. Ten per cent of the women surveyed received support from other businesswomen and 5% from their colleagues; however, the research also notes one respondent who stated that support from and reliance on women cause difficulties when it comes to long-term success (Kitching and Woldie 2004).

Hence the impact of financial support and the inability to meet business needs are highly constraining factors for women entrepreneurs, and this disparity of financial support is due to gender-based stereotypical ideologies that disregard women's capability to lead, manage, and sustain a sole business (Brush et al. 2004). A contrasting study which suggests that women do not face gender barriers, however, also shows that they rely more strongly upon 'person-equity' (i.e. family resources) for finance than do men (Birley 1986). A survey focused on New York women entrepreneurs demonstrated that 78.6% had never tried to obtain funding from external investors.

Research suggests that women in the agriculture industry are able to provide for their children and household food needs. Compared to men, women are much more likely to invest in the needs of their children and the household, whereas men spend on personal items (Gautam et al. 2012). However, the same woman is branded as 'unskilled' in the majority of flowers and cutting production organizations (Elson and Pearson 1981).

It is a common observation that the voices of women are not heard in the agriculture industry as well as they are within the family (Gautam et al. 2012). Research suggests that this is due to women's lack of knowledge on new technologies, because women are largely restricted by cultural constraints on their pursuit of education. Gautam et al. (2012) go further to suggest that even women conversant with technology have their opinions ignored, because men occupy a higher position. Similarly, research conducted in Papua New Guinea indicates that women have the ability to distinguish problems, but it has uncovered barriers in the labour market, the lack of training programs focused on business skills and deficits in finance knowledge for women in horticulture. Family social capital supports family firms through knowledge transfer (Carr et al. 2013), which, according to the preceding study, most women in floriculture lack to a greater extent.

Sorenson et al. (2009) present a model depicting collaborative dialogue and its direct effect on ethical norms that directly impact family social capital and where family social capital directly influences firm performance. However, families with limited dialogue may only be outcome-oriented and hence they disregard 'moral intuitions'. Hence family firms do not necessarily create collaborative dialogue.

7.3.1 Research Questions and Hypotheses

The main research question was to examine the influence of social ties on women growers and to identify the main barriers they faced in developing their businesses. The questionnaire was developed for a mixed-method approach, using a World Bank-developed questionnaire for social capital development. Reliability tests were conducted for the questionnaire.

7.4 Methodology

The research used a mixed (qualitative and quantitative) design, with questionnaire surveys aligned with the study's objectives and segmented research focus attributes. The interview sample was 300 floriculturists in the Western Province. Questionnaires sought general characteristics and personal information and family social capital fragment by spouse, children, parents and siblings, and relatives. Variables of influence included moral support, financial support, physical/labour support, transport and assisting with household chores, and supports from institutes such as for training. The core research method comprises questionnaire surveys derived from the research objective and segmented research focus attributes. The questionnaire was translated into Sinhala and Tamil to enable farmers to understand the question and answer options. The qualitative approach involved interviews with 1% of floriculturist sample.

The research sought a national sample, as most previous floriculture research information on Sri Lanka only focused on particular districts. Data collected embrace an overall sample size of 320 floriculturists from 03 districts of Western Province. Due to communication and accessibility limitations, this research was not able to focus on a large number of participants from the districts compared to others.

The questionnaire is divided into two distinctive segments: (a) general characteristics and personal information and (b) family social capital broken down by spouse, children, parents and siblings, and relatives. Variables of influences focused on include support of spouse/relatives/children (through moral support, financial support, physical/labour support, transport, and assisting with household chores) and government support/nongovernment support/social networking initiatives.

7.5   Key Findings

The study found that 76% of the women sampled received moral support from their spouse – a highly influential factor for developing and expanding the social network and support chains. Such moral support was mostly in the form of motivation (96%) to continue and develop the business and in guidance (83%). Family social capital supports family firms through knowledge transfer (Carr et al. 2013). The woman sample strongly relied on it and received most support from their spouse, indicating a strong tie. Of the women growers, 89% were members of a growers' club. A surprisingly large proportion of women enrolled with a club (87%) cited Suwahas Mala society as their main floricultural support society – the primary government-established programme to support floriculture farmers. A smaller segment (16%) indicated support from other floriculture support societies. Almost 60% of the sample stated that they received professional training from a vocational training centre, with 34% citing structured training courses. The results revealed that both strong ties and weak ties play a significant role in determining business growth for Sri Lankan women entrepreneurs and suggested further research to study the available and absent ties to improve the floriculture sector.

The sample obtained for this research indicates that a majority of women in floriculture are married and more than half of the sample is above the age of 50 years. Most women have pursued their education to advanced or ordinary level education, while less than one fifth of the sample has only reached a below-ordinary-level qualification. Around 40% of women have established their floriculture venture in the industry for 1–3 years, and 26% of women have operated for more than 6 years (Table 7.1).

Even though a majority of the enterprises have only been established within a 5-year time frame, a considerable proportion of the sample employs support.

Table 7.1 Sample demographics

Characteristic	Percentage (%)
Age	
Under 30	2
30–40	15
41–50	33
50+	51
Marital status	
Married	90
Single	6
Widowed	4
Educational level	
Below O/L	20
O/L	29
A/L	41
Higher education	10
Years in the industry	
<1	19
1–3	40
4–5	15
>6	26

Women growers in the sample indicated their current monthly income as LKR10,000, and this had fallen by 23% (Fig. 7.1). Other growers indicated that they earned more than LKR 10,000 monthly, and details are illustrated in Fig. 7.1.

Study of the literature revealed that support networks among growers link to the improved income of rural women and reduced poverty levels of those families (Munasib and Jordan 2011). Wetterberg (2007) illustrated the importance of the social capital concept and incorporated constellations of social ties for antipoverty operations. Those social ties are networks (friends and neighbours), organizations, and government-mandated organizations (Fig. 7.2).

The implementation of national policies in Sri Lanka has initiated a more supportive culture for establishing small-scale businesses. As a consequence, many support networks were developed by government organizations and NGOs for the sector to provide training, plant materials, and infrastructure facilities to empower women in rural and suburban areas.

Similar to results obtained for floriculture support societies, female floriculture growers identified the main benefit of government support as skills and knowledge transfer, followed by moral support and marketing/promotion. A large proportion also said that government establishments provided their businesses with employees. However, compared to the percentages attained by benefits of floriculture support societies, government establishments received fewer citations from those sampled. Inability to access financial support is a highly constraining factor for women entrepreneurs, and, as discussed, this disparity of financial support is due to gender-based stereotypical views of women's capacity to lead, manage, and sustain a sole business (Brush et al. 2004).

Fig. 7.1 Monthly income distribution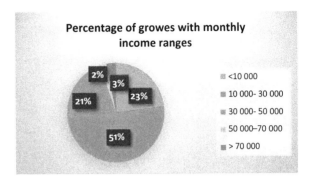

Percentage of growes with monthly income ranges

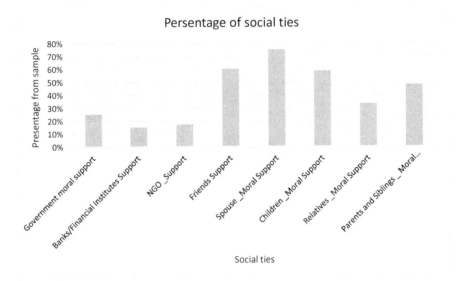

Fig. 7.2 Percentage of social ties

Woman floriculture growers were asked if and how their friends helped the business. Bearing in mind that the literature does not touch upon the help of friends, a comparatively large proportion or 56.2% of the sample cited their friends' help (Fig. 7.3).

Compared to all other forms of support, where skills and knowledge transfer lead, in this segment of support of friends, moral support takes the centre stage but closely followed by skills and knowledge transfer. Friends also assist with marketing and promotion, provide employees, and help improve social relationships. The addition of another individual to the social network expands the existing network multiple times, and therefore with the help of a friend, these women are able to gain a wide range of advantages and information.

Emotional support, social networking, and financial support (Friedemann-Sánchez 2008) are key dimensions of support for women through family capital.

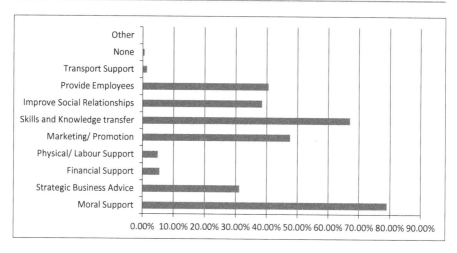

Fig. 7.3 Dimensions of friends' support to the floriculture venture

Strong social networking family environments offer access to financial resources, extra support, expertise, encouragement, and a strong customer base and build a strong social status, producing a better business image (Fig. 7.4).

As indicated by the graph, female farmers received most support from their spouse, followed by their children, parents, and finally other relatives.

In results from this research, a majority (76.06%) of the sampled women stated that they have received moral support from their spouse. Moral support is, according to the literature, a highly influential factor for developing and expanding the social network and support chains. Moral support has been offered to these women by their spouse mostly in the form of motivation (95.78%) to continue and develop the business and in guidance (82.92%). Family social capital supports family firms through knowledge transfer (Carr et al. 2013), but only around half of the sample revealed that they received advice (57.58%) or emotional support (20.73%) from their spouse (Figs. 7.5 and 7.6).

Over half of the women (64.38%) stated they received financial support from their spouse. This form of financial support includes mostly the investment of the spouses' salary to the business (70.75%), while some invested their savings (44.90%). Only a minor proportion gave financial support in terms of a loan (8.39%). This demonstrates that the spouse believes in the floriculture business strongly enough to invest their salary and savings in it.

Women also greatly rely on their spouse for physical or labour support. Around 70% of the sample noted that they received such labour or physical support. This mostly included watering (87%) and planting (81%), but they also assist women to participate at exhibitions (40%) and in finding markets (37%) (Fig. 7.7).

Women also experience the negativity of family capital, lack of physiological support, and inability to balance work and life. Here 72.41% of the women received support from their spouse with household chores, mainly cleaning (86.9%) and grocery shopping (68.55%), as well as cooking (56.85%) and childcare (51.21%) (Fig. 7.8).

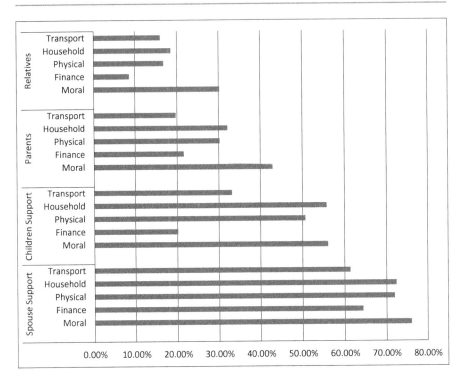

Fig. 7.4 Support received by family social capital

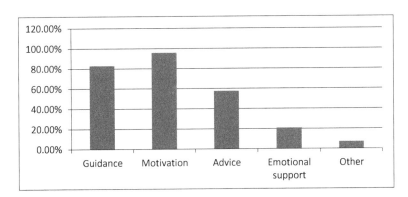

Fig. 7.5 Dimensions of spouses' moral support

Women received least help from their spouse for transport (61.31%). Of the sample that claimed they received transport support, this was mainly to provide transport to shows or exhibitions (91.67%) (Fig. 7.9).

The impact of small-scale firms is increasingly contributing to the development of a country, especially in developing counties (Bhagavatula et al. 2010). Demand for floriculture as a product and a career is continuously growing (Export

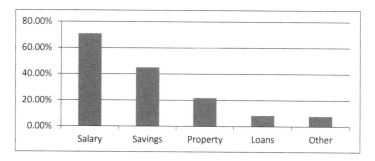

Fig. 7.6 Dimensions of spouses' financial support

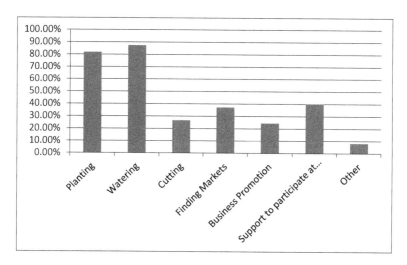

Fig. 7.7 Dimensions of spouses' physical/labour support

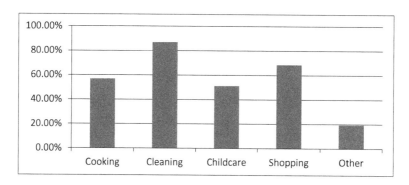

Fig. 7.8 Dimensions of spouses' household chore support

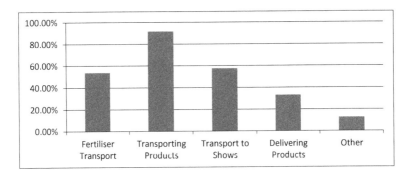

Fig. 7.9 Dimensions of spouses' transport support

Development Board of Sri Lanka 2008; Garcia 2013), as is shown by the increasing number of individuals attempting to enter the industry through floriculture growth and trade markets. Sri Lanka has improved from a developing country to a middle-income ranked nation with its increase in income levels and ability for people to spend on leisure activities (World Bank 2011). Such individuals are attracted by the perceived richness, subtlety, and beauty signified by floral products. However, Sri Lankan floriculture growth is unable to meet existing demand. National exhibitions, such as wedding shows at BMICH or flower stalls at the Diyatha Uyana in Battaramulla, attract large numbers of international growers, indicating the incapacity of national production to meet growing demand. As in the Philippines (Garcia 2013), to ensure that demand is met, Sri Lanka imports large quantities of orchids, jasmine, roses, and other popular types of flora (Sudhagar 2013). This has supplemented the advance of substitute products, such as the growing import market segment for various ranges of artificial flowers, ranging from cheap plastic to expensive quasi-realistic flowers.

Most importantly, the floriculture industry has allowed rural communities to improve their societal standing and livelihood, especially in developing countries in Asia and Africa (Agoramoorthy and Hsu 2012; Dolan and Sorby 2003). Similarly, as we found, the Sri Lankan floriculture industry has particularly targeted suburban communities, and it has enabled those societies to venture into entrepreneurial businesses, providing international market prospects, from the space of their own home and land. The characteristics identified in the industry continue to encourage rural women to enter the floriculture industry.

Empirical studies demonstrate the impact of small-scale floricultural enterprises on female entrepreneurs. The initial factors influencing entry to the industry are particularly advantageous for Sri Lankan women. Firstly, it is simply a start-up from home. Secondly, small-scale floriculture farms have few expenses and a low need for expensive resources (although they need water, which is a scarce resource). In fact, the most expensive input is fertilizer; most Sri Lankan farmers have access to slow-release fertilizer, so that a small quantity is sufficient for substantial production of flowers. In addition, unlike other forms of agriculture, floriculture does not harm the environment; its production is low in carbon release as well as environmental pollution.

Female floriculture growers do not experience difficulty in initiating a floriculture production, but to ensure business survival, they do require funds. Customers expect and admire a wider variety of flowers; hence finance is needed to purchase seed, pots, nets, and the like. This research identified that some women have taken on loans while others have successfully reinvested the income generated from the floriculture business to improve production. Women have resorted to loans if they have either invested money generated from the business to their family or for their personal needs.

Money saved from the business before expenses may not be sufficient to support significant investment. With an adequate loan, women are able to invest a larger sum in the business, resulting in a business surge and noticeable outcome. Research also identified that women who have resorted to loan facilities are successfully paying back the debt.

Most Sri Lankan women are stay-at-home mothers, as tradition and custom require a woman to look after children while the man works. Statistics indicate that, of the economically inactive population in Sri Lanka, 74% are females and, comparing employment in agriculture, the majority in that sector are female. Therefore, this scenario is perfect for women to pursue floricultural enterprises, because, once household duties have been completed, women are free to busy themselves with floriculture production. Unlike the clash between work and family that women entrepreneurs struggle through (Stoner et al. 1991), home-based floriculture production does not require the woman to leave home nor does it influence her ability to delay family responsibilities. In fact, the woman has an opportunity to provide the household with more capital, which in turn influences the family's livelihood of the family and reduces female dependence on males for family income.

Women entrepreneurs dedicate their time and energy to the wellbeing of the family. The earnings obtained from floriculture is invested in children and family needs. While a woman is satisfied with the ability to provide financially for her family, she is also personally satisfied to be investing her time in a venture that can be viewed as a recreational activity as well as an enterprise with high growth opportunities.

Research identified some women who are highly successful and have ventured into mass production. These women noted that floriculture companies and organizations (e.g. hotels, export agencies, etc.) come to their homes to purchase products. In some instances, these women earn over Rs. 100,000 per month. However, such organizations only focus on large-scale farmers.

This research identified that majority of women ventured into floriculture as a recreational activity, because it was especially inviting due to its low costs and ability to reduce stress. Later these women developed their production into a business. Having taken a business perspective, most women joined floricultural societies or botanical gardens to expand their skills and knowledge and pursue the business. According to Bhagavatula et al. (2010), a successful entrepreneur requires more than a good network; they should know how to utilize the network for their benefit, the ability to scan the information gained, and how to identify opportunities; this is when human capital (experience, skills, and intelligence) is employed. Sri

Lankan floriculture growers, the focus of this present research, have managed to successfully utilize their existing human capital and networks to further expand on those aspects through access to a wider society.

Development in technology, education, and medicine has influenced global life expectancy, such that Sri Lanka now has an expectancy of 78 years. However, the age of retirement is still to be revised to balance that life expectancy, and it stands at 60 years of age. Many of those who retire at 60 spend a large part portion of their remaining years unproductively. Introduction of small-scale floriculture farms has changed the wastage inherent in underutilization of labour. Most women identified in this research are retired; they have decided to plant flowers as an escape from the isolated lifestyle they led after retirement. According to the women approached, this helps them relax and enjoy their remaining days.

Floriculture draws on underutilized labour. Culturally, women stay home to care for children, and, once the children are grown up, these women are left without occupation. The literature has identified the barriers women face in business (Gautam et al. 2012). This research also recognized that women lack knowledge, skills, and experience of the working environment, in addition to their age. Therefore, women are unable to pursue a career. Programs initiating women into start-up ventures from home are able to make use of such underutilized labour, which will otherwise be wasted.

Since a large proportion of the Sri Lankan population is women, most of whom are unemployed, able working capacity remains unexploited. Friedemann-Sánchez (2008) has recognized that women prefer the flexibility of home-based businesses, because this allows for a balance of work and life. Research shows that floriculture presents new horizons for Sri Lankan stay-at-home mothers: the ability to earn income and improve individual and family livelihoods and personal satisfaction.

Carr et al. (2013) assert that family social capital supports firms through knowledge transfer. According to results in the present research, family capital has impacted the development of enterprises, from planting flowers for recreation to an income-generating business. Most women who have achieved business development have received more family support, especially moral support from the spouse. An empirical study by Birley (1986) comments on the expectations that women place on family resources for finances. Similarly, this research found that young married women enjoy rewards from their husbands' savings and salary since parts of these have been invested in their business. These women cited their husbands' help during the weekends and support with childcare and household duties if they are busy with floricultural activities. In some instances, for women who are around the age of 30 years, their parents also help with the business.

As most women in this study are retired, their children are already working; these children assist their mother with finance to help expand the business.

The study found that 76% of the women sampled received moral support from their spouse – a highly influential factor for developing and expanding the social network and support chains. Such moral support was mostly in the form of motivation (96%) to continue and develop the business and in guidance (83%). Of the women growers, 89% were members of a growers' club. A surprisingly large proportion of women enrolled with a club (87%) cited Suwahas Mala society as their main floricultural support society – the primary government-established programme to support floriculture farmers.

7.6   Conclusion and Recommendations

The results revealed that both strong ties and weak ties play a significant role in determining business growth for Sri Lankan women entrepreneurs and suggested further research to study the available and absent ties to improve the floriculture sector.

Acknowledgements The authors gratefully acknowledge the National Science Foundation (NSF), Sri Lanka, for the financial support extended to complete this research (RG/2015/SS/01 – July 2015 – July 2016).

References

Adler, P. S., & Kwon, S. W. (2002). Social capital: Prospects for a new concept. *Academy of Management Review, 27*, 17–40.

Agoramoorthy, G., & Hsu, M. J. (2012). Impact of floriculture development enhances livelihood of India's rural women. *Journal of Agriculture and Rural Development in the Tropics and Subtropics (JARTS), 113*(1), 69–76.

Arregle, J., Batjargal, B., Hitt, M. A., Webb, J. W., Miller, T., & Tsui, A. S. (2015). Entrepreneurs' social networks and new venture growth. *Entrepreneurship: Theory and Practise, 39*, 313–344.

Baddegamage, M. (2012). *Industry capability report: Sri Lankan floriculture sector*. Colombo: Export Development Board, Sri Lanka.

Bhagavatula, S., Elfring, T., van Tilburg, A., & van de Bunt, G. G. (2010). How social and human capital influence opportunity recognition and resource mobilization in India's handloom industry. *Journal of Business Venturing, 25*, 245–260.

Birley, S. (1986). Succession in the family firm: The inheritor's view. *Journal of Small Business Management, 24*, 36–43.

Brush, C. G., & Cooper, S. Y. (2012). Female entrepreneurship and economic development: An international perspective. *Entrepreneurship & Regional Development: An International Journal, 24*(1–2), 1–6.

Brush, C., Carter, N., Gatewood, E., Greene, P., & Hart, M. (2004). *Clearing the hurdles: Women building high-growth businesses*. Upper Saddle River: FT Press.

Carr, R., Parker, C. M., Castleman, T., & Mason, C. (2013). Factors affecting SME owner-managers' willingness to share knowledge online in rural local business networks. *Journal of Internet Commerce, 12*(4), 307–331.

Cnaan, R. A., Ganesh Bhat, G., Meijs, L. C. P. M., & Handy, F. (2014). You reap what you pick. *Journal of Enterprising Communities: People and Places in the Global Economy, 8*(2), 86–102.

Danes, S., Rueter, M. A., & Doherty, W. (2002). Family FRO model: An application to family business. *Family Business Review, 15*(1), 31–43.

Danes, S. M., Stafford, K., Haynes, G., & Amarapurkar, S. S. (2009). Family capital of family firms: Bridging human, social, and financial capital. *Family Business Review, 22*, 199–216.

De Vita, L., Mari, M., & Poggesi, S. (2014). Women entrepreneurs in and from developing countries: Evidences from the literature. *European Management Journal, 32*, 451–460.

Department of National Planning. (2010). *Mahinda Chintana: Vision for the future'. The development policy framework*. Colombo: Ministry of Finance and Planning, Government of Sri Lanka.

Dolan, C., & Sorby, K. (2003). Gender and employment in high-value agriculture industries. In *Agriculture and rural development working paper* (pp. 7–10). Rome: FAO.

Duberley, J., & Carrigan, M. (2012). The career identities of 'mumpreneurs': Women's experiences of combining enterprise and motherhood. *International Small Business Journal, 29*(1), 1–21.

Dyer, W. G. (2006). Examining the 'family effect' on firm performance. *Family Business Review, 19*(4), 253–273.

Edwards, R., Franklin, J., & Holland, J. (2003). *Families and social capital: Exploring the issues.* London: ESRC Research Group.

Elfring, T., & Hulsink, W. (2003). Networks in entrepreneurship: The case of high-technology firms. *Small Business Economics, 21*, 409–422.

Elson, D., & Pearson, R. (1981). 'Nimble fingers make cheap workers': An analysis of women's employment in third world export manufacturing. *Feminist Review, 7*(1), 87–107.

Export Development Board of Sri Lanka. (2008). *Developing the floriculture sector in North Western and North-Central Provinces* (pp. 4–48). Colombo: Export Development Board of Sri Lanka.

Fafchamps, M., & Minten, B. (2002). Returns to social network capital among traders. *Oxford Economic Papers, 54*(2), 173–206.

Friedemann-Sánchez, G. (2008). Assets in intra-household bargaining among women workers in Colombia's flower industry. *Feminist Economics, 12*(1), 247–269.

Garcia, A. L. P. (2013). Market structure, conduct and performance of cut-flower growers in selected cities in Mindanao, Philippines. *Asian Journal of Business and Governance, 3*(1), 83–102.

Gautam, U. S., Singh, A., & Singh, S. R. K. (2012). Participatory approach of women in agriculture: Vision 2025. *Indian Research Journal of Extension Education, 1*, 38–42.

Gofen, A. (2009). Family capital: How first-generation higher education students break the intergenerational cycle. *Family Relations, 58*(1), 104–120.

Granovetter, M. S. (1973). The strength of weak ties. *American Journal of Sociology, 78*(6), 1360–1380.

Haugh, H., & Talwar, A. (2016). Linking social entrepreneurship and social change: The mediating role of empowerment. *Journal of Business Ethics, 133*(4), 643–658.

Imig, D. R. (2003). Family capital versus family social capital: Different boundaries, different processes involvement in entrepreneurship. *Entrepreneurship and Regional Development, 21*(3), 1.

Jack, S. L. (2005). The role, use and activation of strong and weak network ties: A qualitative analysis. *Journal of Management Studies, 42*(6), 1233–1259.

Janssens, W. (2010). Women's empowerment and the creations of Social Capital in Indian villages. *World Development, 38*(7), 974–988.

Ju, L., & Fu, X. (2012). The development of scaling table about inner social capital in technology innovation team and the test of its reliability and validity – Based on empirical analysis of technology innovation teams in agriculture industry of Sichuan Province. *Journal of Agricultural Science, 4*(8), 124–135.

Kitching, B., & Woldie, A. (2004). *Female entrepreneurs in transitional economies: A comparative study of businesswomen in Nigeria and China.* Honolulu: Hawaii International Conference on Business.

Kotha, R., & George, G. (2012). Friends, family or fools: Entrepreneur experience and its implications for equity distribution and resource mobilization. *Journal of Business Venturing, 27*, 525–543.

Lamine, W., Jack, S., Fayolle, A., & Chabaud, D. (2015). One step beyond? Towards a process view of social networks in entrepreneurship. *Entrepreneurship & Regional Development, 27*(7–8), 413–429.

Macpherson, A., Herbane, B., & Jones, O. (2015). Developing dynamic capabilities through resource accretion: Expanding the entrepreneurial solution space. *Entrepreneurship & Regional Development: An International Journal, 30*, 1–34.

Matthew, M., Naude, W., & Viviers, W. (2014). Challenges for the floriculture industry in a developing country: A South African perspective. *Development Southern Africa, 23*(4), 511–528.

McEvily, B., Perrone, V., & Zaheer, A. (2003). Trust as an organizing principle. *Organization Science, 14*(1), 91–103.

Munasib, A. B. A., & Jordan, J. L. (2011). The effect of social capital on the choice to use sustainable agricultural practices. *Journal of Agricultural and Applied Economics, 43*(2), 213–227.

Newbert, S. L., & Tornikoski, E. T. (2012). Supporter networks and network growth: A contingency model of organizational emergence. *Small Business Economics, 39*, 141–159.

Newman, A., Schwartz, S., & Borgia, D. (2014). How does microfinance enhance entrepreneurial outcomes in emerging economies? The mediating mechanisms of psychological and social capital. *International Small Business Journal, 32*, 158–179.

Niranjan, S. K. D. F., & Gunasena, H. P. M. (2006). Floriculture sector development programm: Small and medium scale entrepreneurs in Sri Lanka. *Sri Lanka Council for Agricultural Research Policy, 40*, 1–49.

Noreen, S. (2011). Role of microfinance in empowerment of female population of Bahawalpur district. *International Conference on Economics and Finance Research, IPEDR, 4*, 1.

Patel, P. C., & Terjesen, S. (2011). Complimentary effects of network range and tie strength in enhancing transnational venture performance. *Strategic Entrepreneurship Journal, 5*, 58–80.

Qureshi, I., Kistruck, G. M., & Bhatt, B. (2016). The enabling and constraining effects of social ties in the process of institutional entrepreneurship. *Organization Studies, 37*(3), 425–447.

Rani, S. (2014). Entrepreneurial empowerment of women through self-help group. *International Journal of Research in IT & Management, 4*(2), 27–35.

Rao, V., & Ibanez, A. M. (2005). The social impact of social funds in Jamaica: A 'participatoy econometric' analysis of targeting, collectiveaction, and participation in community-driven development. *Journal of Development Studies, 41*(5), 788–838.

Shoji, M., Aoyagi, K., Kasahara, R., Sawada, Y., & Ueyama, M. (2012). Social capital formation and credit access: Evidence from Sri Lanka. *World Development, 40*(12), 2522–2536.

Sorenson, K. L., Goodpaster, K. E., Hedberg, P. R., & Yu, A. (2009). The family point of view, family social capital, and firm performance: An exploratory test. *Family Business Review, 22*(3), 239–253.

Stam, W., Arzlanian, S., & Elfring, T. (2014). Social capital of entrepreneurs and small firm performance: A meta-analysis of contextual and methodological moderators. *Journal of Business Venturing, 29*(1), 152–173.

Steier, L., & Greenwood, R. (2005). Entrepreneurship and the evolution of Angel Financial Networks. *Organization Studies, 21*(1), 163–192.

Stoner, C. R., Hartman, R. I., & Arora, R. (1991). Work/family conflict: A study of women in management. *Journal of Applied Business Research (JABR), 7*(1), 67–74.

Sudhagar, S. (2013). Production and marketing of cut flowers (rose and gerbera) in Hosur Taluk. *International Journal of Business and Management Invention, 2*(5), 15–25.

Tripp, R., Wijeratne, M., & Piyadasa, V. H. (2005). What should we expect from farmer field schools? A Sri Lanka case study. *World Development, 33*(10), 1705–1720.

Wetterberg, A. (2007). Crisis, connections, and class: How social ties affect household welfare. *World Development, 35*(4), 585–606.

World Bank. (2011). *Gender equality and development, World Bank Report 2012*. Washington, DC: World Bank.

Zell, D., McGrath, C., & Vance, C. M. (2014). Examining the interaction of extroversion and network structure in the formation of effective informal support networks. Institute of Behavioral and Applied Management. *Journal of Behavioral and Applied Management, 15*(2), 59–81.

Examining the Influence of Network Ties on Self-Efficacy and Entrepreneurial Performance in the Informal Sector in Sri Lanka

8

Ajantha Sisira Kumara, Ramanie Samaratunge, Alexander Newman, and Lakmal Abeysekera

8.1 Introduction

Scholarly attention to entrepreneurship occurring in the informal sector has produced a considerable amount of research (De Castro et al. 2014; Light and Dana 2013; Siqueira et al. 2016; Sutter et al. 2017; Williams and Shahid 2016; Webb et al. 2013). This is not surprising given the critical role informal sector activity plays in increasing economic and social benefits (Viswanathan et al. 2014), particularly for those in poverty at the "bottom of the pyramid." The informal sector, characterized by activities occurring outside of formal regulations and infrastructures (Sutter et al. 2017), accounts for 40–60% of the world's GDP (Schneider and Williams 2013). In particular, in emerging economies, around 70% of all entrepreneurs run sole-trading enterprises (ILO 2014), half of which are unregistered (Acs et al. 2013; Williams et al. 2017), and largely operate at subsistence levels, being "hidden" from formal institutional structures and ignored by government (Muñoz and Dimov 2014). Yet these businesses represent legitimate economic activities such as small-scale household manufacturing and trading (Siqueira et al. 2016), with micro-entrepreneurs often pushed into entrepreneurship in order to provide a survival income for their families. Thus entrepreneurship in the informal sector is an important resource for

A. S. Kumara (✉)
Department of Public Administration, Faculty of Management Studies and Commerce, University of Sri Jayewardenepura, Nugegoda, Sri Lanka
e-mail: mhasisira@sjp.ac.lk

R. Samaratunge · L. Abeysekera
Department of Management, Monash University, Clayton, VIC, Australia
e-mail: ramanie.samaratunge@monash.edu; lakmal.abeysekera@monash.edu

A. Newman
Faculty of Business and Law, Deakin University, Melbourne, VIC, Australia
e-mail: a.newman@deakin.edu.au

emerging countries to attain socioeconomic development (Schneider and Enste 2013; Siqueira et al. 2016). However, despite the significant contribution made by the informal sector to economic activity in emerging economies, limited research has examined the factors which contribute to micro-enterprise performance.

In light of growing evidence of the importance of network ties to micro-entrepreneurship in the informal sector (Assudani 2009; Light and Dana 2013; Viswanathan et al. 2014), given the difficulties they face in acquiring resources necessary to operate their firms (Khayesi et al. 2014), the present study posits that network ties can foster micro-enterprise performance through enhancing the entrepreneurial self-efficacy (ESE) of microentrepreneurs. More specifically, we examine whether, contrary to research findings on larger small- and medium-sized enterprises in the formal sector of emerging economies (Stam et al. 2014), micro-entrepreneurs' weak network ties (contacts with individuals outside their immediate network of friends and family) have a stronger influence on the performance of their micro-enterprises than strong ties (their close family and friendship networks) through the mediating mechanism of ESE. In doing so we draw on prior research which shows that although micro-entrepreneurs in the informal sector tend to depend heavily on their close family and friends (i.e., strong ties) for support, such ties may not always have a positive influence on the performance of their businesses as "the obligations to extended families run deep" which commonly includes having to pay back the support received (Khavul et al. 2009, p. 1223). In particular, we draw on research which suggests the cost of maintaining strong ties may sometimes outweigh the benefits it brings in the informal context where dependence on strong ties for firm survival and performance is high (Khavul et al. 2009; Khayesi et al. 2014; Stewart 2003). In contrast to findings on small- and medium-sized enterprises, we argue that weak ties are likely to have a stronger influence on the performance of micro-enterprises as they provide access to alternative sources of vicarious learning, support, and encouragement that can aid micro-entrepreneurs, and are not as burdensome in nature as strong ties (Santarelli and Tran 2013).

In explaining the effects of network ties on micro-enterprise performance, we focus on ESE as a key "entrepreneurial cognition" or "psychological resource" which helps micro-entrepreneurs maintain high levels of performance. We argue that ESE is especially important to business success in the informal sector as micro-entrepreneurs typically lack the human, financial, and social capital needed to succeed in business and are driven to entrepreneurship through necessity rather than opportunity, given limited opportunity to access higher education or formal employment (McMullen et al. 2008; Bradley et al. 2012). Due to these factors, micro-entrepreneurs in the informal sector are typically less confident to overcome challenges in their working lives and deal with those operating in the formal sector and are therefore less likely to seek out entrepreneurial opportunities and ways of exploiting such opportunities (Bullough et al. 2014). ESE therefore acts as an important psychological resource from which micro-entrepreneurs can draw upon when operating in an informal sector characterized by high levels of risk and uncertainty (Welter and Smallbone 2011). In examining ESE as the underlying psychological mechanism linking network ties to firm performance, we follow the calls of researchers (Shane and Venkataraman 2000) to examine the role of entrepreneurial cognitions in the entrepreneurial process. ESE is a key entrepreneurial cognition which has been found to explain significant variance in the performance of entrepreneurial firms above and beyond more material resources such as adequate financing and human resources (Baum et al. 2001; Baum and Locke 2004; Bullough et al. 2014; Chen et al. 2009; Hmieleski and Baron 2008; Hmieleski and Corbett 2008; McGee and Peterson 2017; Miao et al. 2017), especially in collectivistic cultures such as Sri Lanka (Miao et al. 2017). Despite this there has been limited investigation as to the sources of micro-entrepreneurs' ESE. Drawing on the key tenets of Bandura's (1986) social learning theory, we therefore highlight how network ties, through providing micro-entrepreneurs opportunities for vicarious learning and access to sources of support and encouragement (social persuasion), enhance micro-enterprise performance through the mediating mechanism of ESE (Prodan and Drnovsek 2010). In examining these issues, we draw on data from "the 2016 Survey on Informal Sector Micro Entrepreneurs in Sri Lanka," conducted by the researchers as part of a larger study on micro-enterprises in the informal sector. This yielded a database of 635 micro-entrepreneurs in the informal sector which was matched with performance data provided by their case officers. Data from this survey were analyzed to test the hypothesized relationships between micro-entrepreneurs' network ties, ESE, and firm performance.

In examining the effects of network ties on micro-enterprise performance, we seek to make the following contributions to the literature. First, we make an important empirical contribution by examining the relative influence of weak and strong network ties on the performance of micro-enterprises, in an under-researched context, the informal sector of an emerging economy. While a growing body of work has examined the influence of weak and strong ties on the performance of small- and medium-sized enterprises operating in the formal sector in developed and emerging economies (Stam et al. 2014), little attention has been paid to examining the relative effects of such ties on micro-enterprise performance in the informal sector of emerging economies. As such, our understanding of how network ties influence the performance of micro-enterprises operating in the highly unregulated and volatile informal sector in emerging economies is limited. This is a great concern as more than a billion entrepreneurs worldwide operate within this context (Venugopal et al. 2015). In order to address such concerns, the conceptual model built and tested in this study enhances our empirical knowledge about this largely under-researched, yet highly important cohort, of the world's entrepreneurs. It allows us to determine whether there are differences in the effects of strong and weak ties on micro-enterprise performance in the informal sector compared to small- and medium-sized enterprises operating in more formal contexts.

Second, as well as examining the relative importance of strong and weak ties to the performance of micro-enterprises in the informal sector, we make an important theoretical contribution by highlighting a key psychological mechanism which may explain the effects of network ties on micro-enterprise performance. In particular, we examine whether strong and weak network ties influence micro-enterprise performance through fostering the ESE of micro-entrepreneurs in line with the vicarious learning and social persuasion pathways alluded to by Bandura's social cognitive theory (Bandura 1986).

Third, we make an important contribution to policy development. Understanding whether and how network ties influence ESE can assist policy makers to develop appropriate support mechanisms to enhance micro-enterprise performance through the development of ESE. This is especially important in light of previous work which shows how weak profitability resulting from low levels of performance creates barriers for micro-enterprises to grow in scale (Azmat and Samaratunge 2013), thereby trapping them at the "bottom of the pyramid" within the informal sector (Viswanathan et al. 2014).

Overall, we believe our study lays the initial foundation for a larger, evidence-based approach to assisting micro-entrepreneurs in the informal sector of emerging countries. The remainder of the paper is organized as follows. First, we provide an overview of research on micro-enterprises in developing countries and outline the research context: the informal sector in Sri Lanka. We then review the literature on network ties, ESE, and firm performance and develop hypotheses for relationships between these constructs. The methods used to test the hypotheses and the results of the empirical analyses are then presented. Following this, the findings and their implications for entrepreneurship theory are then discussed and policy implications highlighted. We conclude by highlighting some limitations of the study and directions for future research.

8.2   Theoretical Background and Hypothesis Development

8.2.1   Micro-Entrepreneurs in the Informal Sector of Developing Countries

The informal sector, defined as an economic activity that is unregistered yet produces legal products (Hart 1973; Nichter and Goldmark 2009), contributes a significant proportion of GDP in both developed and emerging economies (Schneider et al. 2010). More than half of the world's population, and the overwhelming majority of the poor, are part of the informal economy or are dependent on it (Jütting and Laiglesia 2009). Individuals operating in the informal sector are typically micro-entrepreneurs (Carree and Thurik 2010), and their entrepreneurial activities provide a significant complement to the GDP of the formal economy. Micro-entrepreneurship in the informal sector accounts for "39.8% of the GDP in Brazil, 46.1% in Russia, 23.1% in India, and 57.9% in Nigeria" (Webb et al. 2013, p. 599), and the majority of employment across emerging economies. Despite the importance of their economic contribution, there is a dearth of data on micro-enterprises especially in countries such as Sri Lanka (Arunatilake and Jayawardena 2010).

There is also a lack of agreement between countries on what constitutes a micro-enterprise operating in the informal sector (Arunatilake and Jayawardena 2010). However, there is a general agreement that micro-enterprises have few formal procedures, do not engage in bookkeeping and maintenance of accounts, recruit employees on noncontractual arrangements terminable at will, and are not registered with the government (ILO 2013; 2014). They are predominantly small (Prahalad 2005; Weidner et al. 2010), either run by a sole-trader without employing others or employ up to a maximum of five employees (Azmat and Samaratunge 2009; IPS and Oxfam 2014; Moore and Spence 2006; OECD 2014) and generally engage in agriculture, fishing, livestock rearing, and petty trading (Rodrigo 2001). They typically work without any brand capital and experience low public visibility. Having highlighted the key characteristics of micro-enterprises in the informal sector, we now highlight the context in which the present study is conducted.

8.2.2 Research Context: Sri Lanka

Sri Lanka, with a population of 21.2 million and an annual economic growth rate of 4.4% in 2016, has met most of its Millennium Development Goal targets in health, education, and gender equality, outperforming other South Asian countries (Abeygunawardana and Van Doorn 2017). Despite its 30-year long ethnic conflict which consumed significant human and physical resources (Pradhan 2001), Sri Lanka has been able to maintain an adult literacy rate of nearly 91% and life expectancy above 70 years (Central Bank of Sri Lanka 2014). In spite of these remarkable achievements for an emerging country, serious socioeconomic disparities across different regions prevail in Sri Lanka (IPS 2012).

A spectacular expansion of the informal sector was evident in Sri Lanka after its economic liberalization in 1977, creating a challenging even volatile environment for micro-entrepreneurs (see Sanderatne 2002). According to the government's estimation, more than 63% of the labor force in Sri Lanka is employed in the informal sector, the majority being women (ILO 2012), and as such is vulnerable to economic shocks that may cause individuals to fall back into extreme poverty (Department of Census and Statistics 2013).

While unregistered enterprises may be deemed unlawful in developed countries, unregistered micro-enterprises in Sri Lanka are sanctioned and supported by the government. This is partly due to the large proportion of entrepreneurial activity accounted for by micro-enterprises in the informal sector of the economy (Sanderatne 2014) and partly because such enterprises support the formal economy by being suppliers and customers to larger regulated businesses. The general consensus is that developing the informal economy fosters regional development and employment creation in Sri Lanka (Sanderatne 2001). Despite the direct linkage between these sectors, the data on micro-entrepreneurial activity in the informal sector are limited (Senanayake et al. 2012; Sanderatne 2002, 2014), and the characteristics and contribution of micro-entrepreneurs in the informal sector have yet to be explored (Sanderatne 2014). Therefore, under the Sri Lankan post-conflict agenda, there is a pressing need to explore the factors which determine the performance of micro-enterprises in the informal sector. In light of the fact that the Sri Lankan government has recently begun to focus on the promotion of micro-enterprises as a key development strategy to address regional disparities, eradicate poverty, and foster inclusive growth (De Alwis 2009; Government of Sri Lanka 2014; IPS 2012; NEDA 2013), the findings of the present study will be useful in informing policy development aimed at fostering entrepreneurship in the informal sector in Sri Lanka.

8.2.3   Micro-Entrepreneurs' Network Ties and Firm Performance

Granovetter's (1973) seminal work on network ties portrays social networks as a tool linking the micro and macro levels of sociological theory and postulates that "the degree of overlap of two individuals' friendship networks varies directly with the strength of their tie to one another" (p. 1360). Granovetter argued that social ties lead to the dissemination of influence and information, mobility opportunity, and community organization. He defined the strength of a tie as the "combination of the amount of time, the emotional intensity, the intimacy (mutual confiding), and the reciprocal services which characterize the tie" (Granovetter 1973, p. 1361). Under this definition, strong ties involve greater time commitment, a similarity between the persons involved and reciprocity of services (Arregle et al. 2015; Granovetter 1973), and trust (McEvily et al. 2003). Strong ties typically refer to relationships with family or close friends, while weak ties include those with acquaintances and business affiliates (Patel and Terjesen 2011).

The extant literature has extensively debated the relative importance of entrepreneurs' strong and weak ties (Lamine et al. 2015), and entrepreneurs' embeddedness in social networks (Arregle et al. 2015), to entrepreneurial outcomes. While some studies conclude that strong ties are more beneficial than weak ones as tie strength increases the willingness of network contacts to furnish support and resources (e.g., Jack 2005; Steier and Greenwood 2000) and reduce the cost of exchange as they are built on "repeat interactions with known individuals" (Khavul et al. 2009, p. 1223), others point to the importance of having a mix of strong and weak ties for entrepreneurial success (e.g., Elfring and Hulsink 2003), as weak ties provide access to novel information, diverse knowledge, and experiences from which entrepreneurs can learn from and obtain support (Arregle et al. 2015). In addition, it has also been shown that strong ties may not be as useful as weak ties as the information from them becomes redundant over time and that the ties do not let novel information and opportunities filter through (Arregle et al. 2015; Santarelli and Tran 2013). This suggests that entrepreneurs should not become overreliant on strong ties and should cultivate weak ties, especially when they are looking to grow their business and innovate (Santarelli and Tran 2013).

Extant research on entrepreneurial firms has established that both strong and weak network ties have a significant influence on firm performance (Gronum et al. 2012). For example, in a meta-analysis of 59 primary studies on the relationship between network ties and small- and medium-sized enterprise performance, Stam et al. (2014) found both strong and weak network ties to have a positive and significant relationship on performance outcomes. On average, they found weak ties had a significantly stronger influence on firm performance than strong ties. However, they also found that in the case of emerging economies, strong ties had a significantly stronger influence on the performance of small- and medium-sized enterprises than weak ties. This finding was put down to the fact that in emerging economies, the absence of a reliable government and established rule of law makes market transactions relatively difficult, fostering a reliance on personal relationships with known individuals to obtain resources, and protects one's business from exploitation. As such they argue that strong ties act as a mechanism through which entrepreneurs in emerging economies navigate weak institutional environments with poor information availability.

Although Stam et al. (2014) found that strong ties exert a stronger influence on enterprise performance in emerging economies, most studies included in their meta-analytical work focused on more established small- and medium-sized enterprises operating in the formal sector of such economies, bringing into question the generalizability of their findings to micro-enterprises in the informal sector. We argue that although we might expect both strong and weak ties to exert a significant influence on the performance of micro-enterprises in the informal sector of emerging economies, as both sets of ties provide access to sources of vicarious learning, encouragement, and support, weak ties are more likely to have stronger effects on performance, given the costs associated for micro-entrepreneurs in maintaining strong ties in the informal sector of emerging economies are significant and in some cases might neutralize or outweigh the benefits that they bring. There is growing evidence that although micro-entrepreneurs in the informal context can obtain material resources at relatively low-cost from their strong network ties, such ties may also result in "excessive expectations of obligatory behavior and possibly result in problems of free riding and unwillingness to experiment beyond the network" (Inkpen and Tsang 2005, p. 153). This is especially the case for micro-enterprises headed by women, whose strong ties are primarily limited to their immediate family members and close relatives who are predominantly male (Darley and Blankson 2008). For example, in examining the importance of network ties to entrepreneurial performance in the informal sector in Africa, Khayesi et al. (2014) found that entrepreneurs are often faced with demands for money, resources, and business assets by kin relations, enhancing costs to the firm, and negatively influencing their performance. Based on their findings, they argue that entrepreneurs should include weaker nonfamily ties in their social networks in order to reduce the costs of raising resources. Similarly, Khavul et al. (2009) find that strong network ties also constrain the performance of micro-enterprises in the informal sector. They argued that although strong ties with family members create an opportunity to mobilize resources, such an opportunity is subject to the costs of opportunism and agency that result from obligation to family members. Such ties, they argue, play a constraining role on the performance of enterprises operating in the informal sector.

In contrast, weak ties provide micro-entrepreneurs access to resources that cannot be obtained from strong ties with family and close friends (Khavul et al. 2009; Khayesi et al. 2014). For example, weak ties provide access to role models from outside their immediate network with dissimilar experiences and knowledge. Such role models act as important sources of vicarious learning for the micro-entrepreneur and also act as an important source of encouragement and emotional support. As we explain later, the new knowledge and emotional support (vicarious learning and social persuasion pathways as specified in social cognitive theory) provided by weak ties should enhance micro-enterprise performance. In support of such assertions, there is growing evidence that highlights strong effects of weak network ties on the performance of enterprises in emerging economies with large informal sectors such as Africa and South Asia (where the present study is located) that have predominantly collectivistic values (Acquaah 2007; Boso et al. 2013; Viswanathan et al. 2010), where reciprocity of goodwill within community members is promoted and valued (Williams and Shahid 2016). This leads us to the following hypotheses:

Hypothesis 1(a).   Strong ties of micro-entrepreneurs in the informal sector are positively related to micro-enterprise performance.

Hypothesis 1(b).   Weak ties of micro-entrepreneurs in the informal sector are positively related to micro-enterprise performance.

Hypothesis 1(c).   The weak ties of micro-entrepreneurs in the informal sector are more strongly related to firm performance than their strong ties.

8.2.4   Micro-Entrepreneurs' Network Ties and Entrepreneurial Self-Efficacy

Shane and Venkataraman (2000) highlight two main factors which explain why some entrepreneurs are better able to identify and exploit entrepreneurial opportunities than others. The first relates to the ability of the entrepreneur to obtain the necessary information to identify business opportunities and scarce resources, an outcome influenced by his/her network ties. Second, it is necessary for an entrepreneur to possess the appropriate cognitions to exploit such opportunities. Therefore, when examining phenomena related to entrepreneurship, it is critical to not only identify sources from which information is acquired by an entrepreneur but also factors which influence entrepreneurial cognitions (Mitchell et al. 2002). In the present study, we draw on Bandura's social cognitive theory (SCT) (Bandura 1986, 2006), to highlight the role played by micro-entrepreneurs' network ties in the development of their ESE. Central to SCT is the idea that human functioning is influenced by "people's judgments of their capabilities to organize and execute courses of action required to attain designated types of performances" (Bandura 1986, p. 391). Bandura (1986) termed such cognitive judgments "self-efficacy." In the entrepreneurship literature, the concept of ESE has been the subject of much attention from scholars (Bullough et al. 2014; Chen et al. 1998; Wennberg et al. 2013). It captures the degree to which the entrepreneur feels they are capable of performing the tasks associated with running an entrepreneurial venture (Chen et al. 1998). When an entrepreneur has high levels of ESE, i.e., is confident in his/her entrepreneurial abilities, he/she will be more likely to attempt entrepreneurial tasks and persist when faced with challenges in the entrepreneurial process.

Prior research suggests that self-efficacy beliefs develop as the individual interprets information from four specific sources: previous performance outcomes (mastery experiences), witnessing the behavior and performance outcomes of others (vicarious learning), obtaining feedback from others on one's behavior and performance outcomes (social persuasion), and emotional arousal experienced while carrying out a certain task (affective states) (Bandura 1997). Building on SCT we argue that network ties, especially weak ties with those from outside the micro-entrepreneur's immediate network, will cultivate ESE through providing the micro-entrepreneur with opportunities for vicarious learning and social persuasion. For example, by interacting with others from outside their immediate social network, especially with business contacts from the wider community, who have different experiences from themselves, micro-entrepreneurs will be able to observe how others navigate challenges they face in the entrepreneurial process and role model their own behaviors on such individuals (i.e., act as a source of vicarious learning) (Shane 2000). In addition, weak ties act as a source of emotional support and encouragement from individuals who have faced and overcome difficulties in the entrepreneurial process and understand how the micro-entrepreneur is feeling (i.e., act as an effective source of social persuasion) (Davidsson and Honig 2003). As such weak ties enhance the micro-entrepreneur's self-efficacy in generating and implementing new courses of action in their business, especially when the other person being observed is from a similar background to the observer (i.e., is also an entrepreneur) and has a track record of success, because such individuals will be perceived as being credible and legitimate role models (Bandura 1997). In line with the tenets of SCT, a growing number of studies have confirmed a significant relationship between the network ties possessed by an entrepreneur, especially their weak ties and their ESE (Baron et al. 2005; Ozgen and Baron 2007). Although some work has shown that strong network ties with family members also exert significant effects on the ESE of entrepreneurs (Chen and He 2011), we argue that in the informal context, strong ties with close friends and family are often a weaker source of vicarious learning and social persuasion as they bring fewer unique insights from those already possessed by the micro-entrepreneur and impose significant emotional burdens through excessive expectations of obligatory behavior (Khavul et al. 2009; Khayesi et al. 2014). Such burdens we argue lessen the benefits that strong ties bring as sources of vicarious learning and social persuasion.

There is growing evidence which suggests that network ties, especially weak ties, exert a significant influence on the self-efficacy of micro-entrepreneurs operating in the informal sector of developing economies (Viswanathan et al. 2010). For example, Venugopal et al. (2015) found educational interventions aimed at enhancing self-efficacy to positively influence entrepreneurial intentions of those living under subsistence conditions (i.e., similar to our study's sample). In particular, they found a positive relationship between the weak ties of micro-entrepreneurs' in the informal sector (e.g., those with government agencies, nonprofit organizations, and other businesses) and ESE. Similarly, in a study of micro-enterprises in India, Viswanathan et al. (2010) found that micro-entrepreneurs reported higher levels of self-efficacy when they actively sought market information beneficial to their firm from sources close (i.e., strong ties) as well as distant (i.e., weak ties). In conclusion, although we expect both weak and strong ties to influence micro-entrepreneurs' ESE in the informal sector, we expect the relationship between weak ties and ESE to be more significant than the relationship between strong ties and ESE, because weak ties are more likely to provide entrepreneurs with greater access to opportunities for vicarious learning and social persuasion, which in turn will enhance their self-belief that they will be able to succeed in their entrepreneurial endeavors (Davidsson and Honig 2003). This leads us to:

Hypothesis 2(a).   Strong ties of micro-entrepreneurs in the informal sector are positively related to their entrepreneurial self-efficacy.

Hypothesis 2(b).   Weak ties of micro-entrepreneurs in the informal sector are positively related to their entrepreneurial self-efficacy.

Hypothesis 2(c).   The weak ties of micro-entrepreneurs in the informal sector are more strongly related to their entrepreneurial self-efficacy than their strong ties.

8.2.5   Mediating Impact of Entrepreneurial Self-Efficacy on Firm Performance

As well as explaining the effects of network ties on ESE, SCT also provides an explanation as to why entrepreneurs high in ESE are able to maintain higher levels of firm performance than those low in ESE (Drnovšek et al. 2010). Scholars have argued this may result from the fact that those high in ESE exert greater effort over a longer length of time, persist through setbacks in the entrepreneurial process, and view failure as an opportunity to learn (Krueger and Brazeal 1994). In this study we argue that ESE enables informal sector micro-entrepreneurs to combine and process seemingly unconnected information to improve the performance of their enterprises (Mitchell et al. 2002). In line with SCT theory, there is growing evidence of a positive link between ESE and the performance of entrepreneurial ventures (Anna et al. 2000; Baum et al. 2001; Baum and Locke 2004; Forbes 2005; Hmieleski and Corbett 2008; Miao et al. 2017). For example, meta-analytical work by Miao et al. (2017) demonstrated a strong relationship between ESE and firm performance, especially in collectivistic cultures such as Sri Lanka. Similarly, Hmieleski and Corbett (2008) found that improvisational behavior had a positive influence on the performance of new ventures for entrepreneurs with high levels of entrepreneurial self-efficacy and a negative relationship for entrepreneurs low in self-efficacy. This pattern is likely to be even more pronounced in micro-enterprises operating in the informal sector of developing economies as those with confidence in their skills and abilities as entrepreneurs (i.e., ESE) would be in a better position to overcome the constant instability and volatility that characterize the marketplace of micro-enterprises in the informal sector (Viswanathan et al. 2010). This leads us to:

Hypothesis 3.   Entrepreneurial self-efficacy of micro-entrepreneurs in the informal sector is positively related to micro-enterprise performance.

In line with the above hypotheses, we also expect ESE to partially mediate the effects of network ties on micro-enterprise performance. This is consistent with prior research which has found a positive relationship between network ties and ESE (Ozgen and Baron 2007) and between ESE and firm performance (Hmieleski

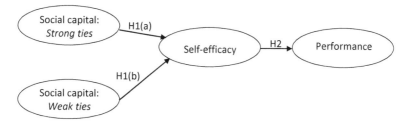

Fig. 8.1 Conceptual model to examine direct and indirect effects

and Corbett 2008; Miao et al. 2017). Although network ties might theoretically enhance micro-enterprise performance through providing micro-entrepreneurs with other benefits (e.g., access to material resources) meta-analytical work suggests that ESE is a key "psychological resource" which explains variance in entrepreneurial success, above and beyond other key materials and psychological resources (Rauch and Frese 2007). In other words, we argue that the relationship between the network ties of micro-entrepreneurs in the informal sector and micro-enterprise performance will be partially explained by the mediating mechanism of ESE. This leads us to:

Hypothesis 4(a).   Entrepreneurial self-efficacy of micro-entrepreneurs in the informal sector partially mediates the relationship between their strong ties and micro-enterprise performance.

Hypothesis 4(b).   Entrepreneurial self-efficacy of micro-entrepreneurs in the informal sector partially mediates the relationship between their weak ties and micro-enterprise performance.

As depicted in Fig. 8.1, hypotheses 1(a), 1(b), 2(a), 2(b), and 3 are directly tested using structural equation modelling, while comparative [i.e., hypotheses 1(c) and 2(c)] and mediational hypotheses [i.e., hypotheses 4(a), and 4(b)] are tested using the results of the main hypotheses from hypotheses 1(a) to 3. For example, comparative hypothesis 1(c) is tested by the results of hypotheses 1(a) and 1(b).

8.3   Methodology and Data Collection

8.3.1   Survey Design and Administration

Data were collected from multiple sources, using two sets of survey questionnaires, one for entrepreneurs operating micro-enterprises in the informal sector and another for government officials in charge of supporting micro-enterprise development (i.e., case officers from the divisional secretariat). Both surveys were initially written in English and subsequently translated into Sinhala and Tamil, two regional languages in Sri Lanka. An experienced translator registered with the Department of Official Languages Sri Lanka was used to translate both surveys. Next, following the recommendations made by Hui and Triandis (1985), the Sinhala and Tamil versions of both surveys were back-translated into English to ensure that items used carried the same meaning in all three languages. This procedure is consistent with previous research utilizing survey questionnaires initially designed in English and subsequently translated into other languages prior to administration (Kautonen et al. 2015).

While researchers in developed countries can often rely on formal business registries to build a representative sample, the lack of business registries of micro-enterprises means such an approach was impossible for the present study conducted in the informal sector of an emerging economy (Bullough et al. 2014). Instead, we sourced a list of entrepreneurs from 15 divisional secretariats (i.e., divisional-level government agents in Sri Lanka), covering the northern, eastern, southern, and western parts of Sri Lanka who acted as a liaison between the entrepreneurs and the research team. The divisional secretariats possess significant inside knowledge about micro-entrepreneurs residing within the divisions given that entrepreneurs were reliant on the divisional secretariat to help them obtain financing and other forms of support. They were thus able to act as a liaison between the researchers and micro-entrepreneurs. We asked each divisional secretariat to randomly select 50 entrepreneurs from the list they provided (a total of 750 across the 15 divisions). The entrepreneurs were then invited to attend their respective divisional secretariat on a nominated day to complete the survey. Of those invited, 635 entrepreneurs participated. Although the literacy rate of our participants was consistent with the high literacy rate found in Sri Lanka (Central Bank of Sri Lanka 2014), to reduce errors associated with respondent comprehension of items, we trained local graduates employed within each divisional secretariat to assist entrepreneurs in completing the survey. Furthermore, two experienced researchers from the research team supervised the administration of surveys in each divisional secretariat. This approach is consistent with previous research undertaken on informal entrepreneurship in a developing country context (Bullough et al. 2014). After eliminating participants with missing responses on our key variables, we used 615 complete cases for this study, amounting to a response rate of 82.4%.

Each divisional secretariat assisted the researchers to locate case officers who oversaw the activities of each entrepreneur surveyed. The case officer questionnaire was sent to them by post for completion. In total, surveys were distributed to 321 case officers, as some officials oversaw the business activities of more than one entrepreneur in their division. These surveys were then matched with the surveys completed by the corresponding entrepreneurs. Both entrepreneurs and case officers who participated in the study were assured anonymity and guaranteed that their responses to the survey questionnaires would be kept confidential.

8.3.2   Method of Data Analysis

We applied structural equation modeling (SEM) to test our hypotheses. When applying SEM as the technique for data analysis, a two-step approach is generally used (see Anderson and Gerbing 1988; Yieh et al. 2007). In the first step, confirmatory factor analysis (CFA) was conducted to assess the measurement model through assessing the goodness of fit of the variables in our study. In line with recent work, we also used composite reliability estimates to determine the reliability of the variables (Peterson and Kim 2013). After estimating the measurement model, in the second step of the analysis, the structural model was estimated to test the proposed hypotheses.

8.3.3 Measures

Table 8.1 presents the standardized factor loadings of all variables in the CFA and their respective t-values.

Strong and weak ties were measured using the scales developed by Perry-Smith (2006), which capture the strength of such ties by assessing the closeness, duration of the relationship, and frequency of contact. We asked entrepreneurs to list the people who acted as sources of support and advice for their business. In doing so, we asked them to consider a fixed number of possible contact persons, including spouses, children, parents, grandparents, other family members, very close friends, good friends, acquaintances, members of community development organizations, and members of business associations. We separated these contacts into strong and weak ties, depending on the relationship between the two parties. Strong ties included those with one's spouse, children, parents, grandparents, other family members, and very close friends, whereas weak ties refer to those with acquaintances, members of community development organizations, and members of business associations (Sullivan and Ford 2014). We then proceeded to measure the social capital generated from both sets of ties by measuring both the duration of the ties as a source of business support and advice (not the actual length they had had a relationship as that person) in period of years (1 = less than 2 years; 2 = 2 to 5 years; 3 = 5 to 10 years; 4 = more than 10 years) and the frequency of contact (1 = not often, 2 = several times a year, 3 = once a month, 4 = several times a month, 5 = several times a week, 6 = daily). We then created a composite measure of both strong and weak ties by combining the number, frequency, closeness, and duration of ties possessed by each entrepreneur. As shown in Table 8.1, standardized factor loadings were greater than 0.70 and composite reliability greater than 0.79 for both strong and weak ties. Consequently we combined closeness, frequency, and duration of network relationship to generate two separate composite factors representing strong and weak ties. The empirical data was consistent with our conceptualization of strong and weak ties, in that strong ties as a source of business advice were longer in duration, closer, and more frequently consulted than weak ties.

Entrepreneurial self-efficacy was measured using the 15-item scale developed by Forbes (2005). Each item represents a particular entrepreneurial task, and entrepreneurs were asked to indicate their level of confidence in their ability to perform the task described, e.g., "develop new ideas," "develop new markets," "develop new products and services," and "develop new methods of production, marketing, and management." Each item was measured using a five-point Likert scale ranging from 1 (completely unsure) to 5 (completely sure). The scale had a composite reliability of 0.93.

Table 8.1 Results of the measurement model

Variable and item	Source	Factor loading (standardized)	t-value	CR
Social capital: strong ties (SCSTP)	Perry-Smith (2006)			0.79
Strong ties closeness		0.81	29.86	
Strong ties frequency		0.72	25.16	
Strong ties duration		0.71	24.97	
Social capital: weak ties (SCWT)	Perry-Smith (2006)			0.95
Weak ties closeness		0.94	135.29	
Weak ties frequency		0.93	129.40	
Weak ties duration		0.91	106.57	
Entrepreneurial self-efficacy (SEFF)	Forbes (2005)			0.93
SEFF 01		0.61	22.64	
SEFF 02		0.66	26.65	
SEFF 03		0.66	26.64	
SEFF 04		0.70	30.43	
SEFF 05		0.73	34.24	
SEFF 06		0.71	32.44	
SEFF 07		0.67	27.62	
SEFF 08		0.77	39.99	
SEFF 09		0.78	41.82	
SEFF 10		0.71	33.26	
SEFF 11		0.72	34.00	
SEFF 12		0.58	20.73	
SEFF 13		0.71	33.47	
SEFF 14		0.59	21.62	
SEFF 15		0.70	31.15	
Entrepreneurial performance (PERF)	Subjective measure			0.83
PERF 01		0.68	24.58	
PERF 02		0.77	33.94	
PERF 03		0.82	41.77	
PERF 04		0.65	23.43	
PERF 05		0.57	17.80	

Model fit indices
$\chi^2(df) = 1302.621, \chi^2/df = 2.77$ RMSEA = 0.053, CFI = 0.924, SRMR = 0.041, CD = 1.00

Note: All of the items are significant at $p < 0.001$ error level, N = 615 after listwise deletion, *AVE*: average-variance extracted, *CR*: composite reliability, *RMSEA*: root mean square error of approximation, *SRMR*: standardized root mean square residual, *CFI*: comparative fit index, *CD*: coefficient of determination

Following the approach of recent research, we used a subjective measure of micro-enterprise performance (e.g., Wiklund and Shepherd 2005), comprising five items (Model 1). Case officers were asked to compare the performance of the focal enterprise with that of similar enterprises in terms of net profit, sales revenue, sales growth, capacity to succeed in the long run, and innovativeness. A sample item included "In comparison to similar businesses this business has higher net profits." Items were measured on a Likert scale ranging from 1 (strongly disagree) to 5 (strongly agree). The composite reliability of this scale was 0.83. In order to check the robustness of our findings, we estimated a second model (Model 2) by including self-reported income as an alternative measure of micro-enterprise performance.

In line with previous research, we controlled for variables that may influence entrepreneurial outcomes: age, gender, level of education, and the location of the microbusiness (Ahlin et al. 2014; Davidsson and Honig 2003; Fedderke et al. 1999; Khedhaouria et al. 2015; Ottósson and Klyver 2010; Perry-Smith 2006). Also, we controlled for firm age, length of the link with case officers (to rule out the fact that case officers who had longer relationships with entrepreneurs might rate their performance more positively), ownership type, and number of paid employees when estimating Model 1. In Model 2, we controlled for all the aforementioned variables except for the variable of length of the link with case officers as self-reported income was taken as the dependent variable in that model.

8.4 Analysis and Results

8.4.1 Sample Profile

The majority of entrepreneurs in our sample were between 31 and 50 years (68%). The sample comprised predominantly of entrepreneurs who were women (75%) and married (79%) and had completed at least 11 years of education (73%). Seventy percent of the participants resided outside Colombo, the main commercial city of Sri Lanka, and 73% operated a sole proprietorship. These characteristics are representative of micro-entrepreneurs in Sri Lanka more generally (Table 8.2).

The significantly greater number of female than male entrepreneurs can be attributed to cultural norms in Sri Lanka (Gunawardana 2013), where females are encouraged to become entrepreneurs in the informal sector to earn supplementary income for their families. Female entrepreneurs have been designated by the Sri Lankan government as the "new engines of growth" that are vital to increase economic prosperity (OECD 2014; IPS and Oxfam 2014). Combining the financial responsibilities of the family with rigid household work can impose greater stress on women but can nonetheless provide women with opportunities for being independent and supporting their family income (UN 2011). Promoting entrepreneurship amongst women is a top priority for the Sri Lankan government to reduce poverty (IPS and Oxfam 2014) and increase women's empowerment (Government of Sri Lanka 2014). This has resulted in female-owned enterprises becoming the fastest-growing segment of small-to-medium enterprises (SMEs) in Sri Lanka (Government of Sri Lanka 2014).

Table 8.2 Sample profile

	N	Frequency (%)
Gender		
Male	152	24.8
Female	463	75.2
Age (in years)		
< 30	46	7.4
31–40	194	31.4
41–50	225	36.7
> 50	150	24.5
Marital status		
Single	55	8.9
Married	485	79.2
Widowed	40	6.6
Other	35	5.3
Highest educational attainment		
Primary	156	25.4
Ordinary level	292	47.4
Advanced level	151	24.6
Above advanced level	16	2.6
Self-reported income (in LKR; 1 USD = 145.77 LKR on average in July and August 2016 during which the survey was conducted)		
< 10,000	241	39.2
10,001–30,000	270	43.9
30,001–50,000	76	12.4
50,001–100,000	24	3.8
> 100,000	4	0.7
Ownership of the business		
Sole	446	72.5
Family	142	23.1
Partnership	27	4.4
Location of the business		
Colombo	182	29.6
Outside Colombo	433	70.4
Number of paid employees		
< 5	581	94.5
5–10	21	3.4
> 10	13	2.1

The case officers who participated in the study consisted primarily of women (76%), aged between 30 and 50 years (88%), who had completed a minimum of an undergraduate degree (63%), and on average had close contact with the entrepreneur to whom their responses were matched for at least 4 years (SD = 4.1). The means, standard deviations, and correlation coefficients of study variables are reported in Table 8.3.

Table 8.3 Descriptive statistics and correlation coefficients

Variables	Mean	S.D.	Min	Max	1	2	3	4	5	6	7	8	9	10	11	12	13	14
1. Age	2.78	0.90	1	4	1													
2. Gender	0.25	0.43	0	1	0.01	1												
3. Education	0.27	0.44	0	1	−0.16**	0.05	1											
4. Living in Colombo	0.29	0.45	0	1	0.07	−0.13**	−0.04	1										
5. Firm age (in years)	8.04	8.40	<1	48	0.35**	0.14**	−0.12**	0.01	1									
6. Case officer's link (duration)	3.95	3.99	<1	40	0.04	−0.03	−0.06	0.18**	0.06	1								
7. Sole owner	0.71	0.46	0	1	0.03	0.05	−0.01	0.15**	0.05	0.01	1							
8. Family-own	0.23	0.42	0	1	−0.04	−0.01	−0.01	−0.14**	−0.02	−0.02	−0.85***	1						
9. Number of paid employees	1.08	0.33	1	3	−0.02	0.11**	−0.01	0.01	0.05	0.09*	−0.03	−0.06	1					
10. Social capital: strong ties	1.24	1.90	0	5.33	−0.22**	0.08	0.12**	−0.02	−0.45**	−0.04	0.01	−0.03	−0.02	1				
11. Social capital: weak ties	0.34	0.91	0	4.67	−0.15**	0.02	0.09*	0.08*	−0.25**	−0.06	−0.03	−0.04	0.02	−0.04	1			
12. Self-efficacy	3.85	0.64	1	5	−0.09*	0.16***	0.20***	−0.12**	−0.04	−0.04	0.01	−0.03	0.07	0.04	0.17***	1		
13. Performance	3.59	0.66	1	5	−0.09	0.12**	0.14**	−0.18***	0.03	−0.03	−0.03	0.02	0.09**	0.07	0.02	0.30***	1	
14. Income strata	1.84	0.84	1	5	−0.03	0.25**	0.22**	0.15**	0.06	0.09**	0.04	−0.01	0.12**	−0.09**	−0.03	0.18**	0.27**	1

Note: ***$p < 0.001$, **$p < 0.01$, *$p < 0.05$

8.4.2   Measurement Model

The standardized factor loading obtained from the confirmatory factor analysis (CFA) for each item under their respective latent constructs is presented in Table 8.1. Each of the standardized factor loadings for items is greater than 0.56, which is above the recommended minimum value for standardized factor loading of 0.50. The composite reliability (CR) of all latent constructs is greater than 0.7, indicating good internal consistency (Hair et al. 2010).

The proposed measurement model provides a good fit to the data with relative chi-square (χ^2/df) = 2.77, comparative fit index (CFI) = 0.924, standard root mean square error of approximation (RMSEA) = 0.053, standard root mean square residual (SRMR) = 0.041, and coefficient of determination (CD) = 1.00. These statistics are better than the recommended cutoffs of a relative chi-square less than 3 (Kline 2011), a CFI beyond 0.9 (Kline 2011), an RMSEA less than 0.07 (Steiger 2007), an SRMR less than 0.05 (Byrne 1998; Diamantopoulos and Siguaw 2000; Kline 2011), and a CD closer to one (1.00).

8.4.3   Structural Model (Hypothesis Testing)

After analyzing the measurement model, we estimated the structural models (Model 1 and Model 2) to test the hypotheses. Model 1 exhibited a good fit to the data with a relative chi-square of 2.52, RMSEA of 0.050, SRMR of 0. 052, CFI of 0.91, and a CD of 0.991. Model 2 also demonstrated a good fit with approximately similar statistics (relative chi-square = 2.66, RMSEA = 0.050, CFI = 0.910, SRMR = 0.054, CD = 0.992). The standardized path coefficients were calculated using the maximum likelihood method and reported in Table 8.4 along with their t-values and the indices for the model's goodness of fit for Models 1 and 2.

As can be seen in Table 8.4, Model 1, micro-entrepreneurs' strong ties and weak ties were not directly related to micro-enterprise performance as reported by the case officers [path coefficients = 0.05($p > 0.05$) and − 0.02 ($p > 0.05$), respectively]. However, the results of Model 2, which used an alternative measure of performance (self-reported income), highlight a positive relationship between micro-entrepreneurs' weak ties and micro-enterprise performance (path coefficient = 0.05 ($P < 0.05$) Therefore, although the results across both models do not support hypothesis 1(a), hypotheses 1(b) and 1(c) were supported by the results of Model 2 suggesting that weak ties are more strongly related to micro-enterprise performance than strong ties.

For hypotheses 2(a), 2(b), and 2(c), we examined the direct relationship between entrepreneurs' network ties and their ESE. The results in Table 8.4 show that entrepreneurs' weak ties are positively related to their ESE [in Model 1: path coefficient = 0.17 ($p < 0.001$)], supporting hypothesis 2(b). However, contrary to hypothesis 2(a) strong ties were not positively related to their ESE [path coefficient = 0.06 ($p > 0.05$)]. Collectively the findings for hypotheses 2(a) and 2(b) provide support for hypothesis 2(c).

Table 8.4 SEM results of hypotheses testing

Hypotheses	Path analysis and model fit	Model 01 (other-rated performance)			Model 02 (self-rated performance proxied by firm income)		
		Standardized coefficient	t-value	Result	Standardized coefficient	t-value	Result
Relationships							
H1(a)	SCWT → PERF	−0.02	−0.50	Not supported	0.08*	2.08	Supported
H1(b)	SCST → PERF	0.05	1.08	Not supported	0.08	1.80	Not supported
H2(a)	SCWT → SEFF	0.17***	4.01	Supported	0.17***	4.01	Supported
H2(b)	SCST → SEFF	0.06	1.22	Not supported	0.06	1.22	Not supported
H3	SEFF → PERF	0.26***	5.90	Supported	0.13***	3.33	Supported
Comparative hypotheses							
H1(c)	Collectively from H1(a) and H1(b)			Not supported			Supported
H2(c)	Collectively from H2(a) and H2(b)			Supported			Supported
H4(a)	Collectively from H2(a) and H3			Supported			Supported
H4(b)	Collectively from H2(b) and H3			Not supported			Not supported
Indices of goodness of fit							
	$\chi^2(df)$	1303.89 (518)			1048.32 (394)		
	χ^2/df	2.52			2.66		
	RMSEA	0.050			0.050		
	CFI	0.910			0.910		
	SRMR	0.052			0.054		
	CD	0.991			0.992		

Note: $***p < 0.001$, $**p < 0.01$, $*p < 0.05$, N = 615
The impact on entrepreneurial self-efficacy is controlled for age, gender, education, and living area. The impact on firm performance is additionally controlled for firm age, nature of ownership, the length of the entrepreneurs' official link with the case officer, and number of paid employees in Model 1. In Model 2, we use the same controls except the entrepreneurs' official link with the case officer

We next tested the direct influence of ESE on micro-enterprise performance in line with hypothesis 3. The results in Table 8.4 show that ESE is positively related to micro-enterprise performance as reported by case officers [Model 1: path coefficient = 0.26 ($p < 0.001$)], supporting hypothesis 3. Our findings were also robust across an alternative measure of micro-enterprise performance (self-reported income) [Model 2: path coefficient = 0.13 ($p < 0.001$)].

We computed the direct effects, indirect effects, and total effects of the independent, mediator, and control variables on micro-enterprise performance (presented in Table 8.5). The delta method is applied to compute t-values and standard errors of direct, indirect, and total effects of each covariate (Sobel 1987). Also, when computing those effects in Model 2 where we need to deal with an observed endogenous variable (self-reported performance), normalization constraints are imposed automatically by the *teffects* command in STATA. Accordingly, the direct effect of weak ties (a latent construct) on self-reported performance (an observed endogenous variable) and the direct effect of ESE (a latent construct) on self-reported performance were normalized to unity (1) to avoid routine iteration of the model without reaching to a solution (Acock 2013).

The results in Table 8.5 provide further confirmation of the previous results in Table 8.4 with regard to hypotheses testing. For instance, the results of Model 1 indicate that micro-enterprise performance is not directly affected by either strong or weak ties. It also confirms that only weak ties exert a significant indirect influence on micro-enterprise performance via ESE. Together these results provide support for the mediated hypothesis 4(b) but not hypothesis 4(a). In Model 2, subject to the constraints imposed on the direct effects of weak ties and ESE, a significant positive total effect was found between weak ties and micro-enterprise performance. However, the direct, indirect, and total effects of strong ties on micro-enterprise performance were statistically insignificant even after imposing normalizations. This also confirms that hypothesis 4(a) is not supported whereas hypothesis 4(b) is supported.

Collectively these results indicate that micro-entrepreneurs' weak ties positively influence their level of ESE, which subsequently leads to enhanced micro-enterprise performance. Therefore, in the case of micro-entrepreneurship, ESE plays a significant and pivotal role as a mediating factor between entrepreneurs' weak ties and the performance of the micro-enterprises they operate. The significant paths are presented in Fig. 8.2.

Regarding control variables, we found some similarities and some differences across Models 1 and 2. In both models micro-enterprises based in Colombo (the commercial capital of Sri Lanka) were rated as having lower levels of performance than those based outside Colombo. In addition, those micro-enterprises with more paid employees had significantly higher levels of performance across both models. Finally, firm age and ownership type did not predict micro-enterprise performance across both models. In Model 1, the length of a micro-entrepreneurs relationship with case officers (not entered as control in Model 2) also did not predict case officers' performance ratings.

Table 8.5 Effects on firm performance

	Model 01			Model 02		
	Direct effect	Indirect effect	Total effect	Direct effect	Indirect effect	Total effect
Variables of interest						
Social capital: strong ties	0.02 (1.07)	0.006 (1.19)	0.026 (1.34)	0.04 (1.80)	0.004 (1.14)	0.044 (1.96)
Social capital: weak ties	−0.01 (−0.48)	0.02*** (3.21)	0.01 (0.51)	1.00 (constrained)	0.27 (1.52)	1.27*** (7.04)
Self-efficacy	0.32*** (5.28)	No path	0.32*** (5.28)	1.00 (constrained)	No path	1.00 (constrained)
Control variables						
Age	−0.07* (−2.30)	No path	−0.07* (−2.30)	−0.03 (−0.84)	No path	−0.03 (−0.84)
Gender (male = 1, female = 0)	0.07 (1.23)	No path	0.07 (1.23)	0.51*** (7.02)	No path	0.51*** (7.02)
Education	0.09 (1.58)	No path	0.09 (1.58)	0.31*** (4.40)	No path	0.31*** (4.40)
Living in Colombo	−0.19*** (−3.35)	No path	−0.19*** (−3.35)	−0.35*** (−5.11)	No path	−0.35*** (−5.11)
Firm age	−0.0001 (−0.05)	No path	−0.0001 (−0.05)	−0.003 (−0.85)	No path	−0.003 (−0.85)
Case officer's link (duration)	0.01 (1.52)	No path	0.01 (1.52)	Not controlled		
Sole owner	−0.04 (−0.32)	No path	−0.04 (−0.32)	0.18 (1.16)	No path	0.18 (1.16)
Family-own	−0.06 (−0.49)	No path	−0.06 (−0.49)	0.23 (1.43)	No path	0.23 (1.43)
Number of paid employees	0.19** (2.50)	No path	0.19** (2.50)	0.18* (1.92)	No path	0.18* (1.92)

Note: ***$p < 0.001$, **$p < 0.01$, *$p < 0.05$, t-values are in parentheses, N = 615

Regarding differences across models, we found that micro-entrepreneurs self-reported performance was significantly higher for male than female employees (Model 2), whereas case officers' ratings of performance were not different between male or female entrepreneurs. In Model 2 entrepreneurs with greater levels of formal education also reported higher levels of performance. In contrast, in Model 1, there was no significant difference in the performance ratings provided by case officers between less and more educated micro-entrepreneurs.

8.5 Discussion

Despite growing work examining the effects of network ties on entrepreneurial outcomes, limited work has been done on the relative importance of strong and weak ties in predicting the performance of micro-enterprises operating in the informal

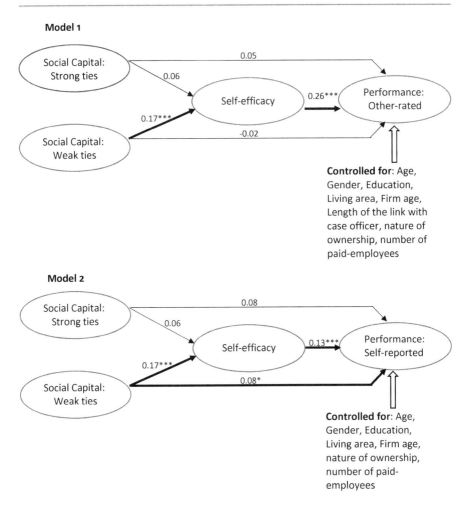

Fig. 8.2 Empirical results of the full model

sector and how this influences their performance. To help address such issues, the present study examined whether the strong and weak network ties of micro-entrepreneurs in the informal sector of a developing economy positively influenced micro-enterprise performance and whether ESE acted as a mediating mechanism linking network ties to micro-enterprise performance. In contrast to the findings of previous work on small- and medium-sized enterprises in developing economies (Stam et al. 2014), we found that weak ties had stronger effects on micro-enterprise performance than strong ties. More specifically, we found that while strong ties did not influence micro-enterprise performance, weak ties positively influenced micro-enterprise performance through enhancing the ESE of micro-entrepreneurs.

In examining these issues, the present study makes a number of key contributions. First, our findings make an important contribution to the entrepreneurship literature by showing that in the informal sector, weak ties rather than strong positively impact micro-enterprise performance through enhancing the entrepreneurial self-efficacy of micro-entrepreneurs. More specifically, in line with SCT (Bandura 1986, 2006), our findings suggest that the weak ties of entrepreneurs act as an important source of ESE. As highlighted earlier, weak ties provide entrepreneurs with access to vicarious learning opportunities, support, and encouragement, which in turn lead entrepreneurs to feel more confident in developing new ideas and persevere in the entrepreneurial process when faced with challenges (Ozgen and Baron 2007). Ties with business people outside their immediate network (as opposed to family or close friends) are likely to be a stronger source of vicarious learning and social persuasion for the entrepreneur, as such individuals are more likely to be seen by the entrepreneur as credible and legitimate role models due to their having a track record of success in business. Weak ties are also likely to have more diverse experiences and sources of information than strong ties and therefore act as a more important source of vicarious learning. Past research undertaken in developed economies (Ozgen and Baron 2007) has found that the entrepreneur's weak ties outside their family and close friends not only provide access to material resources but also foster an entrepreneur's psychological resources such as their self-efficacy. The findings from our study both confirm and extend this knowledge by empirically validating the positive relationship found between weak ties and ESE of micro-entrepreneurs operating in the informal context of a developing economy.

Second, by providing evidence that weak ties are more strongly associated to micro-enterprise performance than strong ties (albeit indirectly) for micro-enterprises in the informal sector of a developing economy, our study challenges the widely held notion that social network ties universally facilitate entrepreneurship (Light and Dana 2013). The findings from the present study are also interesting in that they contradict the findings of recent meta-analytical work, which suggests that while weak ties are generally more important to entrepreneurial performance in established economies, strong ties are more important in developing economies (Stam et al. 2014). Our findings may reflect the context in which the present study was conducted, the informal sector of a developing country, where entrepreneurs are overly dependent on strong ties with their immediate circle of friends and family (Arregle et al. 2015). Prior research also suggests that there are significant costs associated with maintaining strong ties in the informal context which may neutralize or outweigh the benefits that they bring (Khavul et al. 2009; Khayesi et al. 2014), such as expectations of obligatory behavior from the entrepreneur (Khavul et al. 2009). For example, Khayesi et al. (2014) found that the performance of enterprises is constrained in the informal sector, as entrepreneurs are faced with demands for money, resources, and business assets from close friends and family.

The findings from the present study lead to a number of implications for both entrepreneurs and policy makers. As we found that weak ties were indirectly related to the performance of micro-enterprises, entrepreneurs operating in informal sectors of developing economies should seek opportunities to build connections with those outside their immediate circle of family and friends. To do this, they may consider joining business or community development associations where they can learn from other entrepreneurs with greater experience and knowledge. This will assist them to build their confidence to experiment with new ideas and persevere in the entrepreneurial process (Arregle et al. 2015; Ozgen and Baron 2007). In contrast, because we found that strong ties do not lead to improved micro-enterprise performance, entrepreneurs should be careful not to spend too much time seeking business advice from those in their immediate network, such as family members and close friends, since such ties do not act as strong sources of vicarious learning and social persuasion that foster entrepreneurial self-efficacy. Although we did not find that an entrepreneur's strong network ties negatively influenced micro-enterprise performance, past research (Baker and Nelson 2005; Khavul et al. 2009) has found strong network ties to constrain an entrepreneur's ability to grow their business. This is especially true for female entrepreneurs operating micro-enterprises in the informal sector of developing economies (Khavul et al. 2009) – the majority of our study's sample. Therefore, to increase the performance and growth of their enterprises, micro-entrepreneurs, in particular female micro-entrepreneurs, should seek to obtain and utilize information sourced from those outside their immediate family and close friends (i.e., from weak ties).

Our findings also provide important implications for policy makers. In order to foster higher levels of performance amongst micro-entrepreneurs operating in the informal sector, case officers in government tasked with supporting entrepreneurship should consider building forums with which entrepreneurs can build weak ties with one another. For instance, they may support the establishment of local business associations and community development organizations and encourage entrepreneurs to seek membership of such entities. They might also organize regular networking events where entrepreneurs interact with others or develop formal mentoring schemes where experienced entrepreneurs are paired with novice entrepreneurs.

8.6   Limitations and Future Research

This study should be viewed in the context of its limitations. First, as the study utilized data from Sri Lanka, the findings may not be generalizable to other developing economies or to the developed world. To gain a deeper understanding and confirm the generalizability of the findings, future research should extend the present research to other developing economies and developed economies. Second, the study examined only the role played by ESE in mediating the relationship between network ties and firm performance. Future work should examine the relative importance of ESE vis-a-vis other possible mechanisms (e.g., entrepreneurial alertness and resilience) that may explain the effects of network ties on firm performance, as well as control for the access to material resources that network ties provide. Finally, the use of cross-sectional data is a major weakness of our study, as it does not allow us to measure causal relationships between our variables. Researchers should consider adopting a longitudinal study design to capture the dynamic process by which network ties influence firm performance over time.

8.7   Conclusion

The present study found a positive relationship between an entrepreneur's weak ties and the performance of the micro-enterprises they operate through the mediating mechanism of ESE in the informal sector of an emerging economy, Sri Lanka. In contrast, the relationship between the entrepreneur's strong ties and micro-enterprise performance was not significant. Our findings are consistent with SCT, in that they suggest that weak ties act as an important source of vicarious learning and social persuasion for micro-entrepreneurs, which fosters their ESE, leading them to perform at a higher level. We hope the present study will serve as a basis for additional research to provide greater clarity around the cognitive mechanisms by which social networks foster improved performance for entrepreneurs operating in the informal sector of developing economies.

Chapter Takeaways

1. Social cognitive theory provides an accurate framework to examine the influence of network ties on entrepreneurial self-efficacy and performance of micro-entrepreneurs operating in the informal sector of an emerging economy.
2. The findings of this study challenge the popularly held notion that network ties, both strong and weak, universally facilitate self-efficacy and firm performance with only weak ties found to be influential.
3. The weak network ties of micro-entrepreneurs act as an important source in developing their self-efficacy, an important psychological resource for all entrepreneurs, in particular, those operating in an unstable subsistence marketplace.
4. Given the importance of weak network ties in positively influencing self-efficacy and, through it, firm performance, it is important for micro-entrepreneurs operating in the informal sector of emerging economies to actively seek to establish connections with those outside their immediate family and friends.
5. From a policy development point of view, it is important for government agents tasked with facilitating entrepreneurship in the informal sector to develop community-based forums such as local business associations and community development organizations which encourage and provide a platform for micro-entrepreneurs to expand their weak network ties.

Questions for Reflection

1. Why do strong ties not influence micro-entrepreneurs' self-efficacy or firm performance?
2. Is the dominant influence of weak ties on self-efficacy and firm performance unique to micro-entrepreneurs?
3. Is self-efficacy of greater importance to micro-entrepreneurs operating in the informal sector of emerging economies compared to opportunity-driven entrepreneurs operating small or medium enterprises in the formal sector of developed economies? Why?

4. What mechanisms are used by micro-entrepreneurs to expand their network, especially in establishing and maintaining connections with those other than close family and friends?
5. How can government agents charged with the facilitation of micro-entrepreneurship in the informal sector of emerging economies positively influence a micro-entrepreneur's network (i.e., weak ties), self-efficacy, and firm performance?

References

Abeygunawardana, K. W. N., & Van Doorn, R. (2017). *Sri Lanka Development Update.* Washington, DC: World Bank Group.

Acock, A. C. (2013). *Discovering structural equation modelling using Stata.* College Station: Stata Press.

Acquaah, M. (2007). Managerial social capital, strategic orientation, and organizational performance in an emerging economy. *Strategic Management Journal, 28*(12), 1235–1255.

Acs, Z., Desai, S., Stenholm, P., & Wuebker, R. (2013). Institutions and the rate of formal and informal entrepreneurship across countries. *Frontiers of Entrepreneurship Research, 35*(15), 1–24.

Ahlin, B., Drnovšek, M., & Hisrich, R. (2014). Entrepreneurs' creativity and firm innovation: The moderating role of entrepreneurial self-efficacy. *Small Business Economics, 43*(1), 101–117.

Anderson, J. C., & Gerbing, D. W. (1988). Equation modelling in practice: A review and recommended two-step approach. *Psychological Bulletin, 103*(3), 411–423.

Anna, A. L., Chandler, G. N., & Jansen, E. D. (2000). Women business owners in traditional and non-traditional industries. *Journal of Business Venturing, 15*(3), 279–303.

Arregle, J. L., Batjargal, B., & Hitt, M. A. (2015). Family ties in entrepreneurs' social networks and new venture growth. *Entrepreneurship Theory and Practice, 39*(2), 313–344.

Arunatilake, N., & Jayawardena, P. (2010). Why people choose to participate in the informal sector in Sri Lanka. *Indian Journal of Labour Economics, 53*(2), 225–249.

Assudani, R. H. (2009). Ethnic entrepreneurship: The distinct role of ties. *Journal of Small Business and Entrepreneurship, 22*(2), 197–206.

Azmat, F., & Samaratunge, R. (2009). Responsible entrepreneurship in developing countries: Understanding the realities and complexities. *Journal of Business Ethics, 90*(3), 437–452.

Azmat, F., & Samaratunge, R. (2013). Exploring customer loyalty at the bottom of the pyramid in South Asia. *Social Responsibility Journal, 9*(3), 379–394.

Baker, T., & Nelson, R. E. (2005). Creating something from nothing: Resource construction through entrepreneurial bricolage. *Administrative Science Quarterly, 50*(3), 329–366.

Bandura, A. (1986). *Social foundations of thought and action: A social cognitive theory.* Englewood Cliffs: Prentice-Hall.

Bandura, A. (1997). *Self-efficacy: The exercise of control.* New York: Freeman.

Bandura, A. (2006). Toward a psychology of human agency. *Perspectives on Psychological Science, 1*(2), 164–180.

Baron, R., Byrne, D., & Branscombe, N. R. (2005). *Social psychology* (11th ed.). Boston: Pearson Allyn and Bacon.

Baum, J. R., & Locke, E. A. (2004). The relationship of entrepreneurial traits, skill, and motivation to subsequent venture growth. *Journal of Applied Psychology, 89*(4), 587–598.

Baum, J. R., Locke, E. A., & Smith, K. G. (2001). A multidimensional model of venture growth. *Academy of Management Journal, 44*(2), 292–303.

Boso, N., Story, V. M., & Cadogan, J. W. (2013). Entrepreneurial orientation, market orientation, network ties, and performance: Study of entrepreneurial firms in a developing economy. *Journal of Business Venturing, 28*(6), 708–727.

Bradley, S. W., McMullen, J. S., & Artz, K. (2012). Capital is not enough: Innovation in developing economies. *Journal of Management Studies, 49*(4), 684–717.

Bullough, A., Renko, M., & Myatt, T. (2014). Danger zone entrepreneurs: The importance of resilience and self-efficacy for entrepreneurial intentions. *Entrepreneurship Theory and Practice, 38*(3), 473–499.

Byrne, B. M. (1998). *Structural equation modelling with LISREL, PRELIS and SIMPLIS: Basic concepts, applications and programming*. Mahwah: Lawrence Erlbaum Associates.

Carree, M. A., & Thurik, A. R. (2010). The impact of entrepreneurship on economic growth. In Z. J. Acs & D. B. Audretsch (Eds.), *Handbook of entrepreneurship research* (pp. 557–594). New York: Springer.

Central Bank of Sri Lanka. (2014). *Annual Report*. Colombo.

Chen, C. C., Greene, P. G., & Crick, A. (1998). Does entrepreneurial self-efficacy distinguish entrepreneurs from managers? *Journal of Business Venturing, 13*(4), 295–316.

Chen, Y., & He, Y. (2011). The impact of strong ties on entrepreneurial intention: An empirical study based on the mediating role of self-efficacy. *Journal of Chinese Entrepreneurship, 3*(2), 147–158.

Chen, X., Yao, X., & Kotha, S. (2009). Entrepreneur passion and preparedness in business plan presentations: A persuasion analysis of venture capitalists' funding decisions. *Academy of Management, 52*(1), 199–214.

Darley, W. K., & Blankson, C. (2008). African culture and business markets: Implications for marketing practices. *Journal of Business and Industrial Marketing, 23*(6), 374–383.

Davidsson, P., & Honig, B. (2003). The role of social and human capital among nascent entrepreneurs. *Journal of Business Venturing, 18*(3), 301–331.

De Alwis, A. S. (2009). *A regional analysis of credit needs and unmet demand for microfinance*. Colombo: Central Bank of Sri Lanka.

De Castro, J. O., Khavul, S., & Bruton, G. D. (2014). Shades of grey: How do informal firms navigate between macro and meso institutional environments? *Strategic Entrepreneurship Journal, 8*(1), 75–94.

Department of Census and Statistics. (2013). *Status of statistics in informal sector using Sri Lanka labour force survey*. Colombo.

Diamantopoulos, A., & Siguaw, J. (2000). *Introducing LISREL*. London: Sage Publications.

Drnovšek, M., Wincent, J., & Cardon, M. S. (2010). Entrepreneurial self-efficacy and business start-up: Developing a multi-dimensional definition. *International Journal of Entrepreneurial Behavior and Research, 16*(4), 329–348.

Elfring, T., & Hulsink, W. (2003). Networks in entrepreneurship: The case of high-technology firms. *Small Business Economics, 21*(4), 409–422.

Fedderke, J., De Kadt, R., & Luiz, J. (1999). Economic growth and social capital: A critical reflection. *Theory and Society, 28*(5), 709–745.

Forbes, D. P. (2005). The effects of strategic decision making on entrepreneurial self-efficacy. *Entrepreneurship Theory and Practice, 29*(5), 599–626.

Government of Sri Lanka. (2014, September 24). Sri Lanka implements loan schemes to benefit women entrepreneurs in North and East, *Colombo Page*.

Granovetter, M. (1973). The strength of weak ties. *American Journal of Sociology, 78*(6), 1360–1380.

Gronum, S., Verreynne, M., & Kastelle, T. (2012). The role of networks in small and medium-sized enterprise innovation and firm performance. *Journal of Small Business Management, 50*(2), 257–282.

Gunawardana, S. J. (2013). Rural Sinhalese women, nationalism and narratives of development in Sri Lanka's post-war economy. In J. Elias & S. Gunawardana (Eds.), *Global political economy of the household in Asia* (pp. 27–42). London: Palgrave Macmillan.

Hair, J. F., Black, W. C., & Babin, B. J. (2010). *Multivariate data analysis* (7th ed.). London: Prentice-Hall.

Hart, K. (1973). Informal income opportunities and urban employment in Ghana. *The Journal of Modern African Studies, 11*(1), 61–89.

Hmieleski, K. M., & Baron, R. A. (2008). When does entrepreneurial self-efficacy enhance versus reduce firm performance? *Strategic Entrepreneurship Journal, 2*(1), 57–72.

Hmieleski, K. M., & Corbett, A. C. (2008). The contrasting interaction effects of improvisational behavior with entrepreneurial self-efficacy on new venture performance and entrepreneur work satisfaction. *Journal of Business Venturing, 23*(4), 482–496.

Hui, C. H., & Triandis, H. C. (1985). Measurement in cross-cultural psychology: A review and comparison of strategies. *Journal of Cross-Cultural Psychology, 16*(2), 131–152.

Inkpen, A. C., & Tsang, E. W. K. (2005). Social capital, networks, and knowledge transfer. *Academy of Management Review, 30*(1), 146–165.

Institute of Policy Studies (IPS). (2012). *Sri Lanka: The state of economy – post-conflict growth: Making it inclusive.* Colombo: Institute of Policy Studies.

Institute of Policy Studies (IPS), Oxfam. (2014). *Female entrepreneurship and the role of business development services in promoting small and medium women entrepreneurship in Sri Lanka.* Colombo: Institute of Policy Studies and Oxfam.

International Labour Organisation (ILO). (2012). *Statistical updates on employment in the informal economy.* Geneva.

International Labour Organisation (ILO). (2013). *Measuring informality: A statistical manual on the informal sector and informal employment.* Geneva.

International Labour Organisation (ILO). (2014). *Transitioning from the informal to the formal economy.* Geneva.

Jack, S. L. (2005). The role, use and activation of strong and weak network ties: A qualitative analysis. *Journal of Management Studies, 42*(6), 1233–1259.

Jütting, J. P., & Laiglesia, J. R. (2009). Employment, poverty reduction and development: What's new? In J. P. Jütting & J. R. Laiglesia (Eds.), *Is informal normal? Towards more and better jobs in developing countries* (pp. 1–20). Paris: OECD.

Kautonen, T., Gelderen, M., & Fink, M. (2015). Robustness of the theory of planned behavior in predicting entrepreneurial intentions and actions. *Entrepreneurship Theory and Practice, 39*(3), 655–674.

Khavul, S., Bruton, G. D., & Wood, E. (2009). Informal family business in Africa. *Entrepreneurship Theory and Practice, 33*(6), 1219–1238.

Khayesi, J., George, G., & Antonakis, J. (2014). Kinship in entrepreneur networks: Performance effects of resource assembly in Africa. *Entrepreneurship Theory and Practice, 38*(6), 1323–1342.

Khedhaouria, A., Gurău, C., & Torrès, O. (2015). Creativity, self-efficacy, and small-firm performance: The mediating role of entrepreneurial orientation. *Small Business Economics, 44*(3), 485–504.

Kline, R. (2011). *Principles and practice of structural equation modelling* (3rd ed.). Paris: Guilford Press.

Krueger, N. F., & Brazeal, D. (1994). Entrepreneurial potentiel and potentiel entrepreneurs. *Entrepreneurship Theory and Practice, 18*(3), 91–104.

Lamine, W., Jack, S., & Fayolle, A. (2015). One step beyond? Towards a process view of social networks in entrepreneurship. *Entrepreneurship and Regional Development, 27*(7–8), 413–429.

Light, I., & Dana, L. (2013). Boundaries of social capital in entrepreneurship. *Entrepreneurship Theory and Practice, 37*(3), 603–624.

McEvily, B., Perrone, V., & Zaheer, A. (2003). Trust as an organizing principle. *Organization Science, 14*(1), 91–103.

McGee, J. E., & Peterson, M. (2017). The long-term impact of entrepreneurial self-efficacy and entrepreneurial orientation on venture performance. *Journal of Small Business Management, 57*(3), 720–737.

McMullen, J. S., Bagby, D. R., & Palich, L. E. (2008). Economic freedom and the motivation to engage in entrepreneurial action. *Entrepreneurship Theory and Practice, 32*(5), 875–895.

Miao, C., Qian, S., & Ma, D. (2017). The relationship between entrepreneurial self-efficacy and firm performance: A meta-analysis of main and moderator effects. *Journal of Small Business Management, 55*(1), 87–107.

Mitchell, R. K., Busenitz, L., & Lant, T. (2002). Toward a theory of entrepreneurial cognition: Rethinking the people side of entrepreneurship research. *Entrepreneurship Theory and Practice, 27*(2), 93–104.

Moore, G., & Spence, L. (2006). Editorial: Responsibility and small business. *Journal of Business Ethics, 67*(3), 219–226.

Muñoz, P., & Dimov, D. (2014). The call of the whole in understanding the development of sustainable ventures. *Journal of Business Venturing, 30*(4), 632–654.

National Enterprise Development Authority (NEDA). (2013). *Micro-enterprise policy paper*, National Enterprise Development Authority. Available at http://neda.lk/pdf/policy/micro_enterprise_policy%2003.pdf. Accessed 5 Feb 2019.

Nichter, S., & Goldmark, L. (2009). Small firm growth in developing countries. *World Development, 37*(9), 1453–1464.

OECD. (2014). *Women in business 2014: Accelerating entrepreneurship in the Middle East and North Africa region.* London: OECD.

Ottósson, H., & Klyver, K. I. M. (2010). The effect of human capital on social capital among entrepreneurs. *Journal of Enterprising Culture, 18*(4), 399–417.

Ozgen, E., & Baron, R. A. (2007). Social sources of information in opportunity recognition: Effects of mentors, industry networks, and professional forums. *Journal of Business Venturing, 22*(2), 174–192.

Patel, P. C., & Terjesen, S. (2011). Complementary effects of network range and tie strength in enhancing transnational venture performance. *Strategic Entrepreneurship Journal, 5*(1), 58–80.

Perry-Smith, J. E. (2006). Social yet creative: The role of social relationships in facilitating individual creativity. *Academy of Management Journal, 49*(1), 85–101.

Peterson, R. A., & Kim, Y. (2013). On the relationship between coefficient alpha and composite reliability. *Journal of Applied Psychology, 98*(1), 194–198.

Pradhan, G. (2001). Economic cost of Sri Lanka's ethnic conflict. *Journal of Contemporary Asia, 31*(3), 375–384.

Prahalad, C. K. (2005). *The fortune at the bottom of the pyramid: Eradicating poverty through profits.* New Delhi: Wharton School.

Prodan, I., & Drnovsek, M. (2010). Conceptualizing academic-entrepreneurial intentions: An empirical test. *Technovation, 30*(5–6), 332–347.

Rauch, A., & Frese, M. (2007). Let's put the person back into entrepreneurship research: A meta-analysis on the relationship between business owners' personality traits, business creation, and success. *European Journal of Work and Organizational Psychology, 16*(4), 353–385.

Rodrigo, C. (2001). *Labour market developments: Sri Lanka country profile in the 1990s*, unpublished mimeo. Colombo: ILO.

Sanderatne, N. (2001). *The informal sector in Sri Lanka: Its nature and extent and the impact of globalisation.* ILO Issues Paper, Colombo.

Sanderatne, N. (2002). *The informal sector in Sri Lanka: Its nature and extent and the impact of globalization.* Colombo: ILO.

Sanderatne, N. (2014). *Exploring the Complexity of the Informal Economy, Book Review.* Available at http://www.sundaytimes.lk/140406/business-times/exploring-the-complexity-of-the-informal-economy-91223.html. Accessed 3 Aug 2019.

Santarelli, E., & Tran, H. T. (2013). The interplay of human and social capital in shaping entrepreneurial performance: The case of Vietnam. *Small Business Economics, 40*(2), 435–458.

Schneider, F., Buehn, A., & Montenegro, C. E. (2010). New estimates for the shadow economies all over the world. *International Economic Journal, 24*(4), 443–461.

Schneider, F., & Enste, D. (2013). *The shadow economy: An international survey* (2nd ed.). Cambridge: Cambridge University Press.

Schneider, F., & Williams, C. C. (2013). *The shadow economy.* London: Institute of Economic Affairs.

Senanayake, S. M. P., Wimalaratana, W., & Premaratne, S. P. (2012). Informal sector and the economy in Sri Lanka. *Sri Lanka Economic Journal, 12*(2), 1–20.

Shane, S. (2000). Prior knowledge and the discovery of entrepreneurial opportunities. *Organization Science, 11*(4), 448–469.

Shane, S., & Venkataraman, S. (2000). The promise of entrepreneurship as a field of research. *Academy of Management Review, 25*(1), 217–226.

Siqueira, A. O., Webb, J. W., & Bruton, G. D. (2016). Informal entrepreneurship and industry conditions. *Entrepreneurship Theory and Practice, 40*(1), 177–200.

Sobel, M. E. (1987). Direct and indirect effects in linear structural equation models. *Sociological Methods and Research, 16*(1), 155–176.

Stam, W., Arzlanian, S., & Elfring, T. (2014). Social capital of entrepreneurs and small firm performance: A meta-analysis of contextual and methodological moderators. *Journal of Business Venturing, 29*(1), 152–173.

Steiger, J. H. (2007). Understanding the limitations of global fit assessment in structural equation modelling. *Personality and Individual Differences, 42*(5), 893–898.

Steier, L., & Greenwood, R. (2000). Entrepreneurship and the evolution of angel financial networks. *Organization Studies, 21*(1), 163–192.

Stewart, A. (2003). Help one another, use one another: Toward an anthropology of family business. *Entrepreneurship Theory and Practice, 27*(4), 383–396.

Sullivan, D. M., & Ford, C. M. (2014). How entrepreneurs use networks to address changing resource requirements during early venture development. *Entrepreneurship Theory and Practice, 38*(3), 551–574.

Sutter, C., Webb, J. W., Kistruck, G., & Ireland, R. D. (2017). Transitioning entrepreneurs from informal to formal markets. *Journal of Business Venturing, 32*(4), 420–442.

United Nations (UN). (2011). *Food crises and gender inequality*. Geneva: Department of Economics and Social Affairs.

Venugopal, S., Viswanathan, M., & Jung, K. (2015). Consumption constraints and entrepreneurial intentions in subsistence marketplaces. *Journal of Public Policy and Marketing, 34*(2), 235–251.

Viswanathan, M., Echambadi, R., & Venugopal, S. (2014). Subsistence entrepreneurship, value creation, and community exchange systems: A social capital explanation. *Journal of Macro Marketing, 34*(2), 213–226.

Viswanathan, M., Sridharan, S., & Ritchie, R. (2010). Understanding consumption and entrepreneurship in subsistence marketplaces. *Journal of Business Research, 63*(6), 570–581.

Webb, J. W., Bruton, G. D., & Tihanyi, L. (2013). Research on entrepreneurship in the informal economy: Framing a research agenda. *Journal of Business Venturing, 28*(5), 598–614.

Weidner, K. L., Rosa, J. A., & Viswanathan, M. (2010). Marketing to subsistence consumers: Lessons from practice. *Journal of Business Research, 63*(6), 559–569.

Welter, F., & Smallbone, D. (2011). Institutional perspectives on entrepreneurial behavior in challenging environments. *Journal of Small Business Management, 49*(1), 107–125.

Wennberg, K., Pathak, S., & Autio, E. (2013). How culture moulds the effects of self-efficacy and fear of failure on entrepreneurship. *Entrepreneurship and Regional Development, 25*(9–10), 756–780.

Wiklund, J., & Shepherd, D. (2005). Entrepreneurial orientation and small business performance. *Journal of Business Venturing, 20*(1), 71–91.

Williams, C. C., & Shahid, M. (2016). Informal entrepreneurship and institutional theory: Explaining the varying degrees of (in)formalization of entrepreneurs in Pakistan. *Journal Entrepreneurship and Regional Development, 28*(1–2), 1–25.

Williams, C. C., Martinez-Perez, A., & Kedir, A. M. (2017). Informal entrepreneurship in developing economies: The impacts of starting up unregistered on firm performance. *Entrepreneurship Theory and Practice, 41*(5), 773–799.

Yieh, K., Chiao, Y. C., & Chiu, Y. K. (2007). Understanding the antecedents to customer loyalty by applying structural equation modelling. *Total Quality Management and Business Excellence, 18*(3), 267–284.

Entrepreneurial Orientation of Rural Business Holders (Micro and Small): Evidence from Industrialized Suburbs of an Emerging Economy

9

Thanuksha Abeywardana, K. R. Gangadhara, and K. S. Dilhani

9.1   Introduction

Micro and small businesses are considered the growth engine (Lumpkin and Dess 1996) of emerging economies like Sri Lanka. Styles et al. (2006) point out that micro and small businesses engage strongly in global economic development. Thus, promoting micro- or small-scale business in the state economy is vital for economic sustainability. With the concept of an open economy, establishment of industrial zones in developing countries is a key strategy for economic development. In a vibrant environment, Okpara (2009) further elaborates that micro and small enterprises are popular for dynamic, innovative, efficient, flexible, and quick decision-making. International market-oriented industrial zones assist in the surge of micro and small businesses for domestic market. However, stabilization of macro-scale business in industrial zones creates a challenging environment for survival of micro- and small-scale ventures. Micro and small businesses are vital for local communities where such communities experience shopping with acquaintances and relations (Brown 2018). Brown (2018) observes that small businesses in cities offer more diverse and personalized customer experiences.

Open economic trends amalgamated with globalization enhance the enterprises' (SMEs) growth and development. Thus the government of Sri Lanka considers SMEs a thriving sector in economic development, where the government intervention is to provide the platform for gaining national and international competitiveness for local businesses. SMEs are considered a driving force for local economic

T. Abeywardana (✉) · K. R. Gangadhara
Sri Lanka Institute of Development Administration, Colombo, Sri Lanka
e-mail: thanuksha@slida.lk

K. S. Dilhani
Divisional Secretariat, Seethawaka, Sri Lanka

© The Author(s), under exclusive license to Springer Nature
Switzerland AG 2021
S. Dhiman, R. Samaratunge (eds.), *New Horizons in Management, Leadership and Sustainability*, Future of Business and Finance,
https://doi.org/10.1007/978-3-030-62171-1_9

growth, regional development, employment generation, and thereby poverty eradication. The national policy framework for small and medium enterprise (SME) development has determined that the SME sector is a strategic sector in policy formulation in Sri Lanka (Ministry of Industry and Commerce n.d.): more than 75% of enterprises come under the SME sector; it provides around 45% of employment opportunities and contributes to 52% of gross domestic production.

Even though the large-scale businesses in industrial zones contribute to the national economy significantly (in 2018, the Census and Statistics Department indicated that industrial contribution for the employed population was 28.4%), micro and small business contribution to raising the livelihood of community is yet to be counted. High-success firms with high standards of entrepreneurial orientation (EO) have faced the uncertainties and thrived (Rauch et al. 2009; Zahra and Covin 1995). Thus the hardship taken to survive by micro and small businesses in the industrial zone in relation to medium and export market-oriented ventures needs to be recognized. According to Advocata (2020), the main hindrances for micro and small businesses are financial constraints or funding limitations and business registration processes. However, Okpara (2009) highlights that successful establishment and performance by the firm or business solely depends on EO attributes. This is further supported by Keh et al. (2007): EO directly and indirectly influences firm performance. Adomako et al. (2016) emphasize that EO directs the firm to behave strategically.

EO research is highly organized and carried out by countries in the Western hemisphere. Thus Asia-centered entrepreneurial orientation-based research is very limited. Hence, this research bridges the gap of non-Western preference for entrepreneurial orientation. It evaluates how micro and small businesses successfully orient towards entrepreneurship within an industrialized zone. The objective is to understand the nature of entrepreneurial orientation of micro and small business holders towards establishing in an economic zone.

9.2 Literature Review

9.2.1 Entrepreneurial Orientation

Entrepreneurial orientation refers to processes, practices, and decision-making activities that are accomplished by entering new or existing markets with new or existing goods or services (Lumpkin and Dess 1996). Lumpkin and Dess (1996) put forward five dimensions of firm EO: autonomy, innovativeness, risk-taking, proactiveness, and competitive aggressiveness. They suggest that these attributes can be varied independently in accordance with environmental and organizational contexts. Miller (1983) argues that proactiveness, risk-taking, and innovativeness are the basic and unidimensional strategic orientation of individual-based business performance. Covin and Slevin further emphasize that in a competitive environment, innovativeness and proactiveness are dominant dimensions for the survival of a firm.

From 1973 to 2010, the periodic study of the definitions of EO showed the fundamental changes of the concept (Covin and Wales 2011). Thus, predominantly used attributes of EO descriptions were innovativeness, proactiveness, and risk-taking. Of the 13 definitions, 4 solely described the abovementioned dimensions, i.e. innovativeness, proactiveness, and risk-taking. Dess and Lumpking (2005) point out that entrepreneurial orientation is viewed as planning patterns of decision-making strategies and entrepreneurial process. According to Dess and Lumpking (2005), Miller and Friesen put forward 11 dimensions of strategy making process (adaptiveness, integration, innovation, etc.), and Fredrickson shows a few others, such as comprehensiveness, proactiveness, assertiveness, risk-taking, and rationality. Avlonitis and Salavou (2007) cited product innovativeness and performance measurement of EO, using proactiveness and risk-taking. Moreno and Casillas (2008) point out that innovative, proactive and risk-taking dimensions of EO influence the growth of the organization. Recent studies such as Adomako et al. (2016) used three dimensions of EO to measure EO that consists of innovativeness, risk-taking, and proactiveness. According to Naldi et al. (2007), in EO risk-taking is generally associated with innovative and proactive strategies. Hence, this research is examining EO in a competitive environment for rural micro and small businesses, utilizing three dimensions, proactiveness, risk-taking, and innovativeness for the business performance.

9.2.1.1 Proactiveness

Dess and Lumpkin (2005: 148) posit that proactiveness is "a forward-looking perspective characteristic of a marketplace leader that has the foresight to seize opportunities in anticipation of future demand". According to Keh et al. (2007), proactiveness explains the entrepreneurs' ability to dominate competitors. Okpara (2009) shows that in an international business platform, business owners showed a more proactive approach in export market identification. The same paper discussed previous research on proactiveness, which is considered as opportunity-seeking, forward-looking (Styles et al. 2006); identifying opportunities and market trends, assessing the strengths and weaknesses of opportunities, and forming teams capable of exploiting them (Styles et al. 2006); and seeking attractive niches and creating the necessary resources to facilitate new entry (Lumpkin and Dess 2001).

9.2.1.2 Innovativeness

The research of Okpara (2009) puts forward that innovation capacity of business owners assists in increasing profitability, sales, and growth of the venture. Okpara further asserts that innovativeness is essential to overcome barriers and challenges in export markets. In 1954 Schumpeter defined innovativeness as a creative spirit, supportive to research and development, introductive new products, services, and technologies (Lumpkin and Dess, 2001). Timmons et al. (2004) observe that entrepreneurial thinking is novel and shows adaptation in changing environments. Kropp and Zolin (2005) emphasize that innovativeness is applied creativity in the business context. Dess and Lumpkin (2005: 148) remark that innovativeness is "A willingness to introduce newness and novelty through experimentation and creative processes aimed at developing new products and services, as well as new processes".

9.2.1.3 Risk-Taking

Risk-taking and the business performance have a positive relationship (Okpara 2009). Previous studies such as Leko-Simi and Horvat state that high-performing firms have a higher possibility of risk-taking and that the risk-taking characteristics include taking risk or avoiding risk, which can be developed with the experience. "Making decisions and taking action without certain knowledge of probable outcomes; some undertakings may also involve making substantial resource commitments in the process of venturing forward" (Dess and Lumpkin 2005, 148).

9.2.2 Entrepreneurial Performance

Adomako et al. (2016) put forward that in a changing environment, firms give priority to establishing within the uncertain environment and get competitive advantage by exploiting niche markets and geographically different markets. Rauch et al. (2009) emphasize the positive relationship between EO and business performance. Okpara (2009) comments that reliance on one or a few indicators in determining performance may result in false interpretation, e.g. performance in growth in sales, growth in profit, growth in employment, overall performance, and additional facilities. However, these criteria were furnished in previous studies such as Zou et al. (1998). Davidsson et al. (2002) observe the contradiction between profitability and growth of the organization in measuring organizational performance. Thus it is important to explore in detail the growth and the profitability of the organization. Moreno and Casillas (2008) determine that the business can grow exponentially when introducing product or technology development and market or product diversification.

9.3   Methodology

9.3.1   Population and Sample

The research was carried out with micro and small business holders in a quantitative research design. The research defines a micro and small-size business as a firm with fewer than 50 employees. MSMEs are defined in Sri Lanka in terms of annual turnover and number of employees. Micro businesses are composed of less than LKR 15 million and fewer than 10 employees. Small enterprises comprise 11–50 employees with annual turnover of LKR 16 to 250 million; medium firms consist of 51–300 employees with LKR 251–750 million turnover (Ministry of Industry and Commerce n.d.). Thus the population of the study was selected from the business holders who commenced their businesses by 2015, which was 16 years after the establishment of industrial zone. Of the 105 business holders in a nearby industrial zone, 92 were randomly selected for the research. Out of the sample, only one business was small-scale; all other businesses were micro-scale.

9.3.2 Research Context

The Seethawaka Divisional Secretariat, which is 150 km² in extent, has a total population of 113,807 (Census and Statistics, 2012) in 68 Grama Niladhari Divisions (village-level administrative unit). The total population of the research is within five village-level administration units (Grama Niladhari Divisions, i.e. Ukwattha, Kudagama, Agra Pedesa, Seethagama, and Weralupitiya) which are adjacent to the industrial zone of Seethawaka Divisional Secretariat. The industrial zone is 57 km away from the commercial city of Colombo. It is the industrial zone that is located within Colombo District. In 1999 the industrial zone in Seethawaka was established to raise the national economy of the country.

Secondary data were collected through the website of the Seethawaka Divisional Secretariat. The secondary resource materials were in the Sinhala language. In addition, the Seethawaka Divisional Secretariat's resource profile, which was in the Sinhala language, was also used. Primary data were collected from July to August of 2019, using surveys and questionnaires.

9.3.3 Variables

9.3.3.1 Firm Performance
The performance of the business was determined by subjective measures. The measures of the growth of the business were determined by the perception of the business owner. The scale developed and tested for reliability by Okpara (2009) was localized and utilized to measure the performance of the business. The performance of the firm was measured using a five-item, five-point Likert scale. Statements of prior research such as "our export market has been very profitable" were transformed to "our local market has been very profitable" to match research dealing with local businesses.

9.3.3.2 Entrepreneurial Orientation
Based on prior research into EO attributes, the questionnaire was developed for innovativeness, proactiveness, and risk-taking. Okpara (2009) carried out a research study on export performance of SMEs in Nigeria; that study's questionnaire was adopted in the present research with modifications that align with the local context. A four item, five-point Likert scale was utilized to measure proactiveness, risk-taking, and innovativeness. All the materials of primary and secondary resources and data were translated into English later.

9.3.4 Data Analysis

The data were analysed descriptively and quantitatively.

9.4 Results and Discussion

9.4.1 Descriptive Data Analysis

The descriptive analysis of demographic factors and business factors with business performance is discussed in this section.

Almost all businesses adjacent to the industrialized zone are single-owner ventures. Out of 92 business holders, 27.3% engaged in commercial activities such as managing boutiques, guest houses, communication centers, and dress-making centers (Fig. 9.1). The next largest group of 25.3% consists of businesses engaged in private tuition, maintaining cab services, gem businesses, music and sound suppliers, astrological activities, computer centers, construction material suppliers, garment fashion centers, welding, vehicle painting and services, plant production, beauty culture activities, and so on. These businesses directly and indirectly connect with the industrial zone where they cater to the workforce and the infrastructure development in the area. As expected, the sectors where the least number of business people is engaged are agricultural businesses (0.6%) and the tourism industry (1.3%).

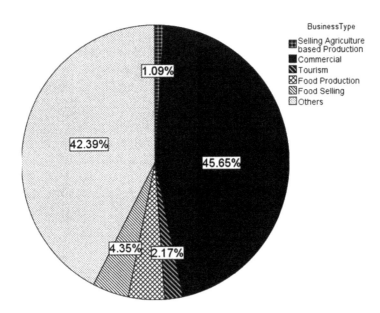

Fig. 9.1 Micro and small business categories

Business holders who are less than 32 years of age and more than 58 years of age did not show high performance (Fig. 9.2). Ages between 32 and 59 are the most productive age cluster for the EO of the business holders.

The age of business holders behaves differently with the three attributes of entrepreneurial orientation. Between the age clusters of 35 years and 59 years, the business holders show high proactiveness than do other age groups. However, the lower limit of age cluster business holders who showed high innovativeness is up to 40 years. A similar pattern is observed with the risk-taking ability of business holders.

Considering overall performance of business holders with regard to gender, females showed less satisfaction with business performance. Gender and the three attributes of EO showed varied outcomes. Both innovativeness and risk-taking ability of females showed moderate competency compared to males. Except in innovativeness, in the other two attributes, proactiveness and risk-taking ability, males showed higher competency than females. However, the innovativeness of both genders of business holders adjacent to the industrial zone showed less competence.

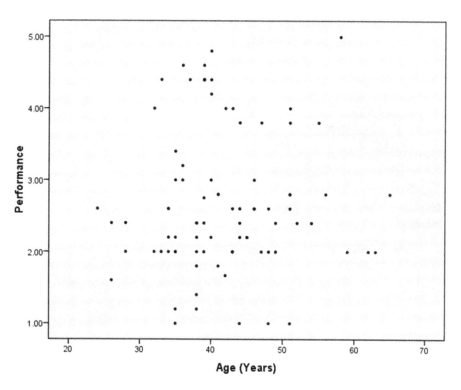

Fig. 9.2 Age distribution of business holders and their performance

9.4.2 Quantitative Data Analysis

The results were analysed quantitatively and discussed for the relationship between EO attributes and entrepreneurial performance of the micro and small business holders in challenging environment.

The relationship between business nature and demographic factors of business owner were analysed using correlation analysis (Table 9.1).

The findings of Table 9.1 show that, with total performance, only business type and gender were statistically significant. There is a relationship with the total

Table 9.1 Correlation for firm performance and business owner demography

		Business type	Nature of business	Age	Gender	Number of employees	Educational qualification
Our local market has been very profitable	Pearson correlation	−.297[a]	−.077	.098	−.267[b]	−.113	.110
	Sig. (2-tailed)	.006	.475	.364	.012	.354	.307
We have generated a high volume of sales from our local market	Pearson correlation	−.222[b]	−.146	.036	−.298[a]	−.169	.156
	Sig. (2-tailed)	.046	.187	.751	.006	.171	.158
We have achieved a rapid growth in local activities in the last 3 years	Pearson correlation	−.215	−.004	−.058	−.179	−.167	.172
	Sig. (2-tailed)	.053	.972	.602	.102	.173	.115
We have expanded our operations in the last 3 years	Pearson correlation	−.247[b]	−.184	−.033	−.126	−.299[b]	−.027
	Sig. (2-tailed)	.025	.091	.765	.251	.013	.804
Overall performance of our business has been very satisfactory	Pearson correlation	−.019	−.040	−.050	−.192	−.112	.010
	Sig. (2-tailed)	.866	.714	.648	.074	.355	.928
Total performance	Pearson correlation	−.244[b]	−.104	.016	−.238[b]	−.211	.049
	Sig. (2-tailed)	.026	.337	.887	.026	.080	.647

[a]Correlation is significant at the 0.01 level (2-tailed)
[b]Correlation is significant at the 0.05 level (2-tailed)

performance of the firm and business type and gender ($p < 0.05$). The business types showed a wide range from agriculture, commercial, services, tourism, food and beverages to ornamental fish markets. A significant point is that these two variables (business type and gender) show weak negative relationship with performance. Other variables such as nature of business, age, number of employees and educational qualifications did not show any statistically significant relationship with business performance. Adomako et al. (2016) say that firm performance has a negative relationship with age, market scope, and industry type. Further, firm size and higher educational qualification of managers have influenced achievement of greater performance of the firm.

When analysing the single performance attributes separately with business and owner demography, rapid growth in local activities and owner satisfaction of business performance did not show any statistically significant relationship with business and owner demography ($p > 0.05$). However, business type showed a negative, weak relationship with profitability in the local market, generating high volume sales from local markets and expansion of the business. The negativity of the relationship may be due to the attraction of more small- and medium-scale businesses to the industrial zone.

When interpreting Table 9.2, it is observed that EO attributes show different levels of relationship with business performance.

Risk-taking and all business performance dimensions have statistically significant relationships (Table 9.2). For instance, risk-taking capacity of business holder showed a 53.7% strong relationship with the profitable local market. Okpara (2009) comments that turbulence in export markets makes business owners take more risk than in the domestic business environment. However, challenging environments in

Table 9.2 Correlation for firm performance and entrepreneurial orientation

Performance dimensions		Proactiveness	Innovativeness	Risk-taking
Our local market has been very profitable	Pearson correlation	.149	.075	.537[a]
	Sig. (2-tailed)	.167	.486	.000
We have generated a high volume of sales from our local market	Pearson correlation	.163	.060	.446[a]
	Sig. (2-tailed)	.142	.591	.000
We have achieved a rapid growth in local activities in the last 3 years	Pearson correlation	.169	.116	.400[a]
	Sig. (2-tailed)	.123	.292	.000
We have expanded our operations in the last 3 years	Pearson correlation	.116	.102	.314[a]
	Sig. (2-tailed)	.290	.355	.003
Overall the performance of our business has been very satisfactory	Pearson correlation	.313[a]	.317[a]	.239[b]
	Sig. (2-tailed)	.003	.003	.026

[a]Correlation is significant at the 0.01 level (2-tailed)
[b]Correlation is significant at the 0.05 level (2-tailed)

domestic business fields also create a turbulent environment for domestic business holders into taking a risk to establish ventures. Thus the statement is evident in the present study.

Proactiveness and innovativeness did not show any statistically significant relationship with performance attributes except overall satisfaction of business success. However, Lumpkin and Dess (2001) point out that proactiveness is more important for the improvement of the business in the initial stage than at the mature stage. Avlonitis and Salavou (2007) argue that active entrepreneurs are more active in product innovation introduction and assets exploitation.

Many domestic-oriented entrepreneurs fear to enter the global market by taking risks, and they encounter problems of completion, market growth, and other challenges to success (Okpara 2009). The present research findings show the notable behaviour of entrepreneurs with risk-taking ability, which was analysed in depth in Table 9.3.

Table 9.3 Correlation with risk-taking attributes and business performance dimensions

		Local market profitable	Generated high volume of sales	Rapid growth in local activities	Expanded operations	Overall performance very satisfactory
We have a strong tendency toward projects with low risk	Pearson	.649[a]	.512[a]	.415[a]	.345[a]	.080
	Sig. (2-tailed)	.000	.000	.000	.001	.462
We have a strong tendency towards projects with high risk	Pearson	−.019	−.072	−.021	−.058	−.020
	Sig. (2-tailed)	.862	.521	.852	.603	.852
In our business fearless measures are needed to be successful	Pearson	.308[a]	.340[a]	.283[a]	.202	.289[a]
	Sig. (2-tailed)	.004	.002	.009	.064	.007
In our business it is better to explore it gradually to be successful	Pearson	.163	.184	.187	.192	.345[a]
	Sig. (2-tailed)	.130	.097	.086	.078	.001
Total risk	Pearson	.537[a]	.446[a]	.400[a]	.314[a]	.239[b]
	Sig. (2-tailed)	.000	.000	.000	.003	.026

[a]Correlation is significant at the 0.01 level (2-tailed)
[b]Correlation is significant at the 0.05 level (2-tailed)

Table 9.3 shows the noteworthy pattern of the dimensions of risk-taking ability with business performance. Having a strong tendency towards low-risk projects shows a statistically significant moderate relationship with generating high volume sales, achieving rapid growth in local activities and expansion of operations and a strong relationship with local market profitability. However, it does not show any relationship with the business owner's perception on satisfaction with the performance of the business.

Tendency towards high-risk projects and all dimensions of business performance do not show any statistically significant relationship. The reason behind this attitude may be the unwillingness of micro-level entrepreneurs to thrive in the local business with high risk. The entrepreneurs try to get calculated risk rather than high risk. Leko-Simi and Horvat argue that risk-taking ability includes both ends of risk-taking and risk avoiding when it is necessary.

However, practising fearless measures in order to be successful shows a statistically significant but weak positive relationship with the five dimensions of business performance.

Gradual exploration in order to be successful and four dimensions of business performance do not assist any statistically significant relationship, except for owner perception on overall successful business performance. However, total risk shows a moderately weak statistically significant relationship with the five dimensions of business performance.

9.5   Conclusion

The research focused on business performance and entrepreneurial orientation. The present research revealed that risk-taking ability of entrepreneurs has a higher contribution than the other two attributes, proactiveness, and innovativeness. Thus, in turbulent and highly completive environments, entrepreneurs who are thriving are calculated risk-takers compared to other, more passive entrepreneurs. A low tendency towards high-risk entrepreneurial actions implies that fast-moving risky actions are not favoured by local micro-scale entrepreneurs.

The policy potential of Sri Lanka is more towards an orientation aspect where entrepreneurs are willingly taking risks for their business success. Also, with the industrialized zone opportunities, government intervention is necessary for diversification of value-added products or location of the businesses. Moreover, there is a need to amend the enterprise policy to attract entrepreneurs who perform at a much higher level.

Contribution and Implication

There have been many studies on entrepreneurship. The studies on EO are limited. The EO of micro and small businesses in challenging environments like an industrialized zone is rarely explored by researchers. Thus, this study makes a significant contribution to the theory and application of the entrepreneurial orientation aspect. Furthermore, entrepreneurial orientation dimensions have significant effect on performance of micro and small business holders. Thus, the paper focuses on entrepreneurial orientation towards entrepreneurial performance in challenging environments such as giant industries in industrial zones where both opportunities and challenges exist for small ventures. Therefore, this study provides a platform for both business holders and policy makers to think strategically about entrepreneurial orientation in rural and dynamic environments.

Lessons

Among many attributes of entrepreneurial orientation, most researchers have focused on proactiveness, innovativeness, and risk-taking ability.

The present research shows that the business holders who are younger than 32 years and older than 58 years do not perform well in the sub-industrialized zone.

In a turbulent environment, risk-taking ability shows the significant importance for business holders to succeed.

In the uncertain and competitive environments, entrepreneurs take calculated risks.

Local micro-scale entrepreneurs who perform well in their businesses avoid fast-moving high-risk activities.

Reflective Questions

Why micro and small businesses are important in the economy?

What do you understand by entrepreneurial orientation?

What are the different entrepreneurial performance measurements?

What is the significance of the study, in relation to the demographic factors such as age and gender?

Why do you think that the risk-taking ability is important in an uncertain environment?

References

Adomako, S., Narteh, B., Danquah, J. K., & Analoui, F. (2016). Entrepreneurial orientation in dynamic environments: The moderating role of extra-organizational advice. *International Journal of Entrepreneurial Behavior & Research, 22*(5), 616–642.

Advocata. (2020). *Executive summary. Barriers to micro and small enterprises in Sri Lanka.* Retrieved from https://static1.squarespace.com

Avlonitis, G. J., & Salavou, H. E. (2007). Entrepreneurial orientation of SMEs, product innovativeness, and performance. *Journal of Business Research, 60*(5), 566–575.

Brown, J. M. (2018, October 15). How important are small businesses to local economies? *Chron.* Retrieved from https://smallbusiness.chron.com/important-small-businesses-local-economies-5251.html

Covin, J. G., & Wales, W. J. (2011). The measurement of entrepreneurial orientation. *Journal of Entrepreneurship Theory and Practice, 1*(1), 1–26.

Davidsson, P., Delmar, F., & Wiklund, J. (2002). Entrepreneurship as growth; growth as entrepreneurship. Strategic entrepreneurship: Creating a new mindset, *6*(1), 328–342.

Department of Census and Statistics. (2018). *Economic statistics of Sri Lanka 2018.* Colombo: Department of Census and Statistics.

Dess, G. G., & Lumpkin, G. T. (2005). The role of entrepreneurial orientation in stimulating effective corporate entrepreneurship. *Academy of Management Perspectives, 19*(1), 147–156.

Keh, H. T., Nguyen, T. T. M., & Ng, H. P. (2007). The effects of entrepreneurial orientation and marketing information on the performance of SMEs. *Journal of Business Venturing, 22*(4), 592–611.

Kropp, F., & Zolin, R. (2005). *Technological entrepreneurship: The role of small business innovation research.* Programs Academy of Marketing Science Review. Via https://www.researchgate.net/publication/27470897_Technological_entrepreneurship_and_small_business_innovation_research_programs

Lumpkin, G. T., & Dess, G. G. (1996). Clarifying the entrepreneurial orientation construct and linking it to performance. *Academy of Management Review, 21*(1), 135–172.

Lumpkin, G. T., & Dess, G. G. (2001). Linking two dimensions of entrepreneurial orientation to firm performance: The moderating role of environment and industry life cycle. *Journal of Business Venturing, 16*(5), 429–451.

Miller, D. (1983). The correlates of entrepreneurship in three types of firms. *Management Science, 29*(7), 770–791.

Ministry of Industry and Commerce. (n.d.). *National policy framework for SME development.* http://www.industry.gov.lk/web/images/pdf/framew_eng.pdf

Moreno, A. M., & Casillas, J. C. (2008). Entrepreneurial orientation and growth of SMEs: A causal model. *Entrepreneurship Theory and Practice, 32*(3), 507–528.

Naldi, L., Nordqvist, M., Sjöberg, K., & Wiklund, J. (2007). Entrepreneurial orientation, risk taking, and performance in family firms. *Family Business Review, 20*(1), 33–47.

Okpara, J. O. (2009). Strategic choices, export orientation and export performance of SMEs in Nigeria. *Management Decision, 47*(8), 1281–1299.

Owoseni, O. O., & Adeyeye, T. C. (2012). The role of entrepreneurial orientations on the perceived performance of small and medium-scale enterprises (SMEs) in Nigeria. *International Business and Management, 5*(2), 148–154.

Rauch, A., Wiklund, J., Lumpkin, G. T., & Frese, M. (2009). Entrepreneurial orientation and business performance: An assessment of past research and suggestions for the future. *Entrepreneurship Theory and Practice, 33*(3), 761–787.

Styles, C., Kropp, F., Lindsay, N. J., & Shoham, A. (2006). Entrepreneurial, market, and learning orientations and international entrepreneurial business venture performance in South African firms. International marketing review.

Timmons, J. A., Spinelli, S., & Tan, Y. (2004). *New venture creation: Entrepreneurship for the 21st century* (Vol. 6). New York: McGraw-Hill/Irwin.

Zahra, S. A., & Covin, J. G. (1995). Contextual influences on the corporate entrepreneurship-performance relationship: A longitudinal analysis. *Journal of Business Venturing, 10*(1), 43–58.

Zou, S., Taylor, C. R., & Osland, G. E. (1998). The EXPERF scale: A cross-national generalized export performance measure. *Journal of International Marketing, 6*(3), 37–58.

Part III

Environment Management

Exploring Motivation for Listed Companies and Measures Taken Towards Managing Environmental Collision: Evidence from Sri Lanka

10

I. M. Withanawasam, G. Wickremasinghe, and M. Naidoo

10.1 Introduction

Global and national pressures often motivate 'development' to take place in ways that are unsustainable environmentally and economically. The ultimate consequence of such practices has been environmental degradation and pollution (Environmental Foundation Limited-EFL, 2006). Even though Sri Lanka has a uniquely rich and valuable natural environment, this has being speedily degraded as a result of development with short-term goals that ignore environmental sustainability. Therefore, besides global pressure, Sri Lanka itself has realized the importance of protecting the environment while development projects are going on. Sri Lanka has also recognized the necessity of initiating and complying with laws, regulations, norms and standards in order to minimize pollution ensuring environmental protection (EFL, 2006).

Environmental costs lead to societal and economic issues that affect the internal and external surroundings of organizations. Economic issues arise through high wastage and high costs of environmental protection and management, which ultimately result in increased costs of production and associated price levels. Societal

---

The original version of this chapter was revised. The correction to this chapter is available at https://doi.org/10.1007/978-3-030-62171-1_28

I. M. Withanawasam (✉)
Department of Accounting and Finance, Faculty of Management and Finance, University of Ruhuna, Matara, Sri Lanka
e-mail: induwithana@badm.ruh.ac.lk

G. Wickremasinghe · M. Naidoo
Victoria University Business School, Victoria University, Melbourne, Australia
e-mail: guneratne.wickremasinghe@vu.edu.au; jayce.naidoo@vu.edu.au

© The Author(s), under exclusive license to Springer Nature Switzerland AG 2021, Corrected Publication 2021
S. Dhiman, R. Samaratunge (eds.), *New Horizons in Management, Leadership and Sustainability*, Future of Business and Finance, https://doi.org/10.1007/978-3-030-62171-1_10

issues mostly arise through wastewater; fuel and material; emissions; landfill of used goods; extraction of natural resources such as forest, natural gas, coal, oil, gold and other minerals; human activities; and machine operations. Societies are apprehensive about pollution of the air, water, marine environment and land used for life and growth and about increasing noise or vibration. All these may have a greater impact on human lives (health problems) and working and living conditions (quality of life) (Indrani, Wickremasinghe & Naidoo, 2019).

Many internal and external stakeholders, particularly in private sector companies, have turned increasing attention to the environmental performance of organizations (International Federation of Accountants–IFAC, 2005). According to Bennett et al. (2011), the environment and sustainability are relatively new issues for business but are now recognized as pressing and urgent issues for humanity generally and perhaps the single most important issue for this generation. This can affect business in a number of ways – in particular, through government policies and stakeholder pressures. In that sense, it is clear that taking care of the environment has become an enormous preoccupation worldwide (Savage & Jasch, 2005).

As sustainability is being recognized as a source of competitive advantage, organizations move into achieving sustainable economic, social and environmental performance, although economic growth remains at the core of business (Hart & Milstein 2003; Porter & Kramer, 2006). Thus, business sustainability efforts are mainly directed towards expanding markets and maintaining business as usual. According to Hart and Milstein (2003), a sustainable enterprise is one that contributes to sustainable development by delivering simultaneously economic, social and environmental benefits.

As illustrated by IFAC (2005), the types and strengths of environmental pressures may differ extensively from country to country and across different industry sectors. However, such environmental pressures force many organizations to search for new, creative and cost-effective ways to manage and minimize environmental impacts (IFAC, 2005). It is apparent that different motives affect measures taken by business. Empirical research, however, is scarce on this, particularly in the Sri Lankan context. Contributing to this research gap, this study mainly focuses on exploring motivation for listed companies and types of measures taken in the Sri Lankan context towards managing environmental impacts.

10.2   Literature Review

This section analyses relevant literature under four main categories.

10.2.1 Environment and Sustainability

Environment and sustainability are now recognized as persuasive and crucial issues for societies generally, conceivably the single most important issue of this generation, yet they seem to be rather new issues for business (Bennett, Schaltegger &

Zvezdov, 2011). This can affect businesses in different ways, in particular through government policies and stakeholder pressure.

Staniskis and Stasiskiene (2006) state that environmental policy must move from a reactive stance to a more proactive, sustainable development approach. Supporting this view, Koontz et al. (2010) demonstrate the importance and popularity of collaborative approaches to environmental policy planning and management, stressing that government has left a heavy imprint on each of these. Babiak and Trendafilova (2011), observing social and environmental challenges facing society that are so complex and multidimensional, indicate that the only solution is for government, non-profits and businesses to work together.

Pajula and Vatanen (2017) also illustrate that, motivated by public awareness and international regulations and standards, sustainability and environmental impacts have become increasingly important factors to distinguish between competing products and services. Introducing methods and tools to assess and reduce environmental impacts, and improve resource efficiency and sustainability management, they suggest that 'life cycle thinking' forms one of the basic principles of sustainable development, and they present 'life cycle assessment' as the leading method for assessing the potential environmental impacts of a product, process or service throughout its life cycle (ISO 14040-44).

10.2.2 Motives for EM Measures

Relating to motives behind EM measures, Tilt (1997) states that environmental law appears to be a major influence on companies' policy development and environmental activities. Schaltegger and Burritt (2010) recognize legislation as one of the six main factors that influence management to consider sustainability. Babiak and Trendafilova (2011) find that strategic motives are the primary reason for adopting environmental corporate responsibilities (CSR), whereas motives to address institutional pressures are a factor to a lesser extent.

In view of motives, Schaltegger and Burritt (2010, p. 378) present six factors that may encourage managers to establish an accounting system that provides information for assessing corporate actions on sustainability issues: (i) 'green washing'; (ii) mimicry and industry pressure; (iii) legislative pressure, stakeholder pressure and ensuring the 'license to operate'; (iv) self-regulation; (v) corporate responsibility and ethical reasons; and (vi) managing the business case for sustainability. However, they recognize legislation as one of the main factors that influence management to consider sustainability issues. They further state that, apart from the ethical arguments of corporate responsibility, all six points are concerned with either corporate benefit or avoidance of detriment.

10.2.3 Environmental Management Systems (EMSs): Conceptions and Considerations

10.2.3.1 EMS and the European Eco-Management and Audit Scheme (EMAS)

The EMAS is a voluntary management tool available for any kind of organization aiming to improve its environmental and financial performance and communicate its environmental achievements to stakeholders and society in general. Examining the value of an EMAS to an organization, Albelda (2011) states that the EMAS is not only regarded as a system to reduce the organization's environmental impacts, it is also perceived as a scheme that signals environmental friendliness to internal and external stakeholders and can become a means of integrating environmental concerns into an organization's collective values. Similarly, Staniskis and Stasiskiene (2006) point out that many companies are increasingly interested in the application of economic incentives, at least as it supplements or reinforces environmental standards.

The views of Tilt (1997), Staniskis and Stasiskiene (2006), and Bracke, Verbeke and Dejonckheere (2008) reveal that responding proactively to growing environmental pressure is a widespread trend among companies. They emphasize that the EMAS is a voluntary scheme, and thus participation decisions will follow a comparison of the monetary and non-monetary costs and benefits. Kollman and Prakash (2002) and Watson and Emery (2004) also state that EMAS is considered the standard of environmental excellence and is more stringent and demanding than ISO 14001. As a result, it can be expected that implementing the EMAS is more costly than ISO 14001, and consequently the number of EMAS-registered companies is rather small compared to the number of ISO 14001-certified ones.

Expressing somewhat similar ideas, Watzold (2009) indicates that the EMAS is slightly more demanding than ISO 14001 in terms of requirements for improving legal compliance. The EMAS requires, in addition to an EMS, a valid environmental statement to inform the public. However, legal compliance is not a necessary condition for ISO 14001 certification, and thus less costly than EMAS, because it does not require an environmental statement, which generates on average only a few benefits. Companies derive higher net benefits from ISO 14001, as its participation cost is lower and because it is an international standard. Also, ISO 14001 is an internationally recognized standard, whereas the EMAS is only for European firms. Giving the EMAS preferential treatment, therefore, leads to higher costs and foregone benefits for EMAS participants (Watzold, 2009).

On the other hand, highlighting similarities, Watzold also indicates that ISO 14001 and the EMAS are based on the same principles, and both are EMS standards that define certain requirements that ought to be met by a company through its EMS. Also, ISO 14001 provides for companies an alternative to the EMAS. Although it is expected there will be a minimum level of environmental performance by organizations implementing an EMS according to ISO 14001 or the EMAS, there are no commitments setting specified levels of environmental performance to be attained, and these are treated in essence as procedural requirements. Thus, once meeting these requirements, the particular company may apply to external bodies for certification of ISO 14001 or registration of the EMAS, and then, with this certification or registration, the company can use this recognition for its external and internal communication (Watzold, 2009).

10.2.3.2 EMS and Organizational Performance

Melnyk, Sroufe and Calantone (2003), supporting these views, indicate that the ISO 14001-EMS standards are a process, not performance standards: these standards do not mandate a particular organization's optimum environmental performance level but describe a system to help an organization achieve its own environmental objectives. Melnyk et al. (2003), in a survey of North American managers (plant-level experts) and their attitudes towards EMS and ISO 14001, reveal that, with the introduction of ISO 14001, attention has turned to corporate EMS, assuming that such a system is critical to a firm's ability to reduce or eliminate waste and pollution created by the fabrication, use and disposal of a product while improving overall performance (environmental and operations) at the same time.

Melnyk et al. (2003) reveal that, basically, a formal EMS does play a critical role in improving overall performance (environmental and operations) and it also affects the frequency with which various environmentally related options are used. EMS certification does have a more significant incremental impact on performance with which various environmentally-related options are used. EMS certification does have a more significant incremental impact on performance and on the reactive options the plants involved in the firm than the situation not having EMS certification. Further, with this experience, it has a greater impact on the selection and use of environmental options. They conclude that the EMS is important, because it is not only at the heart of the ISO 14001 certification process but is also integrated within operations management, and, further, the certification, as embodied within the ISO 14001 environmental standards, brings with it real benefits.

Nawrocka and Parker (2009), through a meta-study involving a pool of 23 research articles which connected environmental performance to EMS, find that, although the number of studies regarding this connection is increasing, the results of these appear to be inconclusive: some authors claim that EMS leads to improving environmental performance, while others show that there is no such connection, at least not in the areas selected for investigation. They notice that those evaluations are dealing with different industrial sectors, companies of different sizes and, last but most importantly, different preconceptions of what environmental performance are, and firms apply different approaches to discuss the environmental performance of EMS. Two main reasons are identified behind such mixed conclusions: (i) there is no agreement as to what environmental performance is or how to measure it; and (ii) there is neither clarity nor agreement on how or why EMS are expected to aid performance.

Therefore, Nawrocka and Parker (2009) suggest that definition of performance must be clearly stated in any study, albeit varied or subjective, and that it has to be recognized that all research methods have their own strengths and limitations. Also, they suggest that it is more fruitful to research how EMS affect performance, rather than whether they do so or not, because if someone asks whether EMS lead to improve performance, the answer will quite likely be 'it depends', whereas if someone asks how EMS affect performance, this will at least generate useful insight into improving the systems. Finally, these various results support a hypothesis that the effects of EMS are not general but dependent on other factors, such as the management style and goals of the particular company, its operating environment, culture and stakeholders.

10.2.3.3   EMS as a Part of a Management System

These interpretations provide evidence that an EMS is considered part of a management system. As indicated in the literature on business and the environment, Tilt (1997) identifies the development of corporate environmental policies as an important step in becoming environmentally aware, and through a survey the author reveals that Australian companies appear to be continuing interest in the environment, developing corporate environmental policies. Thus, investigating some of the major influences on developing corporate environmental policies by those companies, the author finds that environmental law (or the threat of environmental law) appears to be a major influence on companies' policy development and environmental activities. Linked to these views, Kokubu and Nishioka (2005) state that the Ministry of Environment guidelines that stress the need for environmental accounting reporting in Japan strongly influence Japanese companies.

According to Tilt (1997), this emphasis on reporting internally to the organization, rather than external disclosure, indicates that companies are taking a proactive stance in striving to prevent external pressures by implementing a corporate environment policy and using it to improve their environmental performance. Kokubu and Nishioka (2005), however, reveal that Japanese corporate environmental accounting was oriented to external reporting rather than internal management functions.

10.2.4 Environmental Legislation and Standards in the Sri Lankan Context

Sri Lanka has about 80 laws and other regulatory measures relating to environmental protection (Ministry of Environmental – MoE, 2012). This trend is undoubtedly due to its understanding, apart from global pressure, of the importance of protecting the environment and the necessity of initiating and complying with laws, regulations, norms and standards to ensure environmental protection and minimize pollution. The National Environmental Act No. 47 of 1980 is the most important of these, with extensive provisions on pollution control, regulation of development and preparation of management plans for protecting the environment. The National Environmental Act (NEA) is enacted as an umbrella law in addressing a variety of environmental matters, while other environmentally related laws, such as the Coast Conservation Act No. 57 of 1981, Marine Pollution Prevention Act No. 35 of 2008,

Plant Protection Act No. 35 of 1999 and Soil Conservation Act No. 25 of 1951, deal with specific aspects.

The Central Environmental Authority (CEA), which was established in 1981 under the provision of the NEA, is the key central body to regulate under the purview of the MoE the preservation of the environment and minimization of pollution. The CEA meets its responsibilities particularly through the Initial Environmental Examination (IEE), Environmental Impact Assessment (EIA), Environmental Protection Licence (EPL) and other regulatory measures (www.cea.lk).

IEE and EIA: The NEA has identified two levels in the EIA process which project proponents may be asked to do. The IEE applies if the environmental impacts of a project are not very significant, which is a relatively short and simple study; the EIA applies if the potential impacts of a project appear to be more significant, which is a more detailed and comprehensive study of environmental impacts compared to an IEE (NEA, 1980). The EIA is in effect in Sri Lanka as an effective tool for integrating environmental considerations into development planning (NEA, 1980).

EPL: As prescribed in the NEA, the EPL is a regulatory/legal tool controlled by the CEA for all industries. Lists of industries and activities needing an EPL are announced in the gazette from time to time. The main objectives of the EPL are to prevent or minimize the release of discharges and emissions into the environment from industrial activities; to develop an approach to pollution control; to contain the burden on industry and to ensure waste minimization through pollution abatement technology and new knowledge such as cleaner production.

Renewal of EPL: After ensuring conformity of all conditions stipulated by the previous EPL relating to the industry, renewal of the EPL is considered by the CEA. For this purpose, monitoring is carried out by relevant authorities under the control of the CEA by inspecting industries at regular intervals and reviewing reports (www.cea.lk).

Initiating legal proceedings against industries: If industrialists violate any terms, conditions and standards stipulated in the licence, undertake prescribed activities without obtaining an EPL or emit waste to the environment without conforming to stipulated standards, legal proceedings are adopted under the provisions of the NEA. (Refer to the link www.cea.lk for details.)

Thus, all procedures relating to issuing and renewal of an EPL affect almost all EM initiatives made by industrialists, from the beginning and throughout the business process. The entire responsibility in the affairs of the CEA falls to the MoE, aiming at integrating environment considerations into the development process (NEA, 1980).

Other institutions such as the Sri Lanka Standards Institution (SLSI) (www.slsi.lk), the Sri Lanka Accreditation Board (SLAB) (www.slab.lk), the Board of Investment (BOI) and the Labour Department play significant roles by promoting standardization, accreditation and quality control.

Zubair (2001) argues that, through a review of over 500 EIA and IEE reports in Sri Lanka, the introduction of EIA to Sri Lanka has been successful and robust and the EIA process is well understood throughout the government and by the public. Also, the EIA process has succeeded in introducing a mechanism for transparency and public review of projects. The drives behind this achievement are the initiatives taken to ensure success of the EIA process, such as training programs by the MoE, the CEA and the University of Peradeniya (which has produced over 200 trained personnel in the government, private sector, NGOs and academia), in addition to including it in planned courses at postgraduate level in several universities. He concludes that in Sri Lanka, the EIA process has succeeded in integrating environmental and other public concerns into the project planning process while recommending legal, policy, administrative and technological measures for the process to avoid any identified shortcomings.

Sigita (2016) shows that in Lithuania, current EIA practices assess manufacturing industry's negative impact relating to air emissions and direct consumption of natural resources and energy. The author further indicates that usually current EIA practice is focused on local and direct environmental impact assessment, and thus it has a shortcoming in assessing indirect and global impact. It also has a limitation in the evaluation of climate change issues and total cumulative effects of manufacturing industry on the environment.

Accordingly, in view of the gap in the literature, this study explores motivations for Sri Lankan listed companies operating within the regulatory framework and other factors to take measures towards ensuring environment protection while minimizing pollution. It largely concentrates on the types and extent of EM measures taken by listed companies in four industry sectors.

10.3   Research Question, Objective and Methodology

10.3.1 Research Question and Objective

Research question: What kind of environmental management (EM) measures have listed companies taken towards protecting the environment and why?

   Research objective: The main objective of this research is to explore motivation for listed companies engaging in businesses with varying potential for environmental sensitivity in different industry sectors and types of measures taken towards managing environmental concerns in the Sri Lankan context.

10.3.2 Methodology

10.3.2.1   Theoretical Drive, Core Component
and Supplemental Component

This study applies a mixed method research (MMR) approach, focusing on one of its eight paradigms in respect of methods and strategies applied simultaneously indicated as 'QUAL + *quan*'. Here, the theoretical drive is indicated with 'uppercase' and the supplemental strategy (component) with 'lowercase'. Relating to this study, the theoretical drive is qualitative (indicated as QUAL), that is, the complete method (identified as the core component) is a qualitative method that best answers most of the research question. Then the part of the question that cannot be answered by the selected qualitative method is addressed by either a qualitative or quantitative strategy, conducted at the same time (called simultaneous, shown with a + sign) or else immediately following the core component (called sequential, indicated with an arrow →) (Morse 2010). Accordingly, this study identifies 'QUAL' as core component, *'quan'* as supplemental strategy and thus the research approach as 'QUAL + *quan*'. Onwuegbuzie and Collins (2007) also present a similar interpretation on this time orientation of conducting MMR, stressing that most MMR designs utilize a time orientation dimension as their base.

10.3.2.2 Population and Sample

A sample of 34 companies was selected, using multi-stage purposeful sampling, representing 4 industry sectors out of 20 listed on the Colombo Stock Exchange: food beverage and tobacco (F&B, 08/22), chemicals and pharmaceuticals (CHEM, 03/12), diversified holdings (DVS, 05/16) and manufacturing (MNF, 18/39), aggregating to a population of 89 companies. Individual companies were selected using snowball, convenience and purposeful sampling, considering factors such as accessibility, relevance of businesses and nature of data and information required, so that the sample was the most suitable accessible one for the extents of investigation.

10.3.2.3 Data Collection and Analysis

Data were collected mainly through in-depth interviews and discussion with environmental officers and personnel involved in environment-related activities of the selected companies and with government authorities, mainly the CEA and SLSI. A questionnaire survey was conducted with the same officials of all companies parallel with interviews and discussions. The researchers accessed company policy documents; annual reports and sources, mainly environmental legislation, i.e. the NEA of 1980; and environment-related standards, i.e. the SLS ISO 14001: 2004 environmental management system (EMS) certification, pertinent to the Sri Lankan context. The study applied a 'personal visit approach' to each company to collect data, securing a 100% response rate and quality data. The main tools of analysis were thematic analysis and content analysis for qualitative data and frequency tables for quantitative data.

To ensure a meaningful complete analysis and interpretations, MMR design provides two *points of interface* for integrating core and supplemental components: *analytical point of interface* that transforms *qual* data into numerical form and *results point of interface* that adds *qual* data to QUAN results (Morse, 2010). In view of that, the researcher identified *results point of interface* as the suitable position for integrating the core component 'QUAL' and supplemental component *'quan'*. Although the qualitative data and information could not be transformed into numerical form, they are appropriate for adding to QUAN results to obtain meaningful complete analysis and interpretations for the study.

10.4   Findings and Discussions

The findings show that environment-related laws, regulatory measures and SLS ISO EMS standards are in effect in Sri Lanka for environmental protection. Of these, the NEA 1980 is the most important umbrella law, and the CEA is the key central government body empowered by the NEA to regulate the preservation of the environment. All responding companies typically take EM measures through their EMS in complying with environmental legislation and standards. Major findings are illustrated under four main categories as follows.

10.4.1 Influences for Companies/Sectors to Take Measures Towards Protecting the Environment

Findings are summarized in Table 10.1.

The results indicate that the most influencing factor for all companies (100%) is environmental legislation. This includes all provisions of the NEA and labour laws, particularly relating to safety, health and welfare of employees (under the Factories Ordinance), and other laws associated with specific aspects of the environment relevant for specific industry sectors/companies. All these are enacted in relation to industrial activities in Sri Lanka by way of strategies and actions for prevention and control of environmental pollution. The findings reveal that legislation relevant for all companies encompasses the NEA and labour laws: all in the sample have obtained and continued any EPL required for their businesses according to pollution control measures and criteria, all of which are mandatory under provisions of the NEA.

The second highest motivating factor is 'create a good image for the company', followed closely by 'sustainability of the business', rated as high by 88.2% and 85.3% of respondents, respectively. Company policies and mission and objectives are at a moderate level (fourth and fifth in the rank), with 55.9% and 47.1% of respondents, indicating these as 'high'. Competitors' actions seem to be least important, with only 29.4% as high and 23.5% as low.

Table 10.1 Influences for company management to take EM measures in their business processes

| Factors | Number of companies | | | | | | |
	High	%	Moderate	%	Low	%	Rank
Environmental legislation	34	100.0	–	–	–	–	1
Competitors' actions	10	29.4	16	47.1	08	23.5	8
Sustainability of the business	29	85.3	05	14.7	–	–	3
Create good image for the company	30	88.2	04	11.8	–	–	2
Company mission and objectives	16	47.1	18	52.9	–	–	5
Company policies	19	55.9	15	44.1	–	–	4
Influences from society	14	41.2	17	50.0	03	8.8	6
Stakeholders' interest	11	32.4	20	58.8	03	8.8	7

Notes: The ranking was based on values obtained by (high*3) + (moderate*2) + (low*1)

These further show that companies may not pay much attention to 'stakeholders' interest' or 'influence from society', so that these factors are less in evidence. It suggests that competitors' actions are not a causal factor in this regard. However, one company dealing with durable products stated that it strongly considers competitors' actions in EM issues because it has to compete with imported products.

10.4.2 Environmental Measures Taken at Different Stages of the Businesses

The results reveal that all responding companies typically pay attention to EM measures at each stage of the process and take actions required in complying with environmental legislation (NEA, labour laws, BOI laws) and standards (SLS ISO 14001: 2004 EMS certification and accreditation). Those companies apply novel EM strategies and initiatives by incorporating policies and strategies developed by the public sector through the National Environmental Action Plan (NEAP). All these EM initiatives are considered in the following sections in three principal stages: planning, pre-implementation and implementation.

(i) *Planning Stage: Capital Investment Project Appraisal and Product Design Stages*

Planning is the most influential and critical, because the decisions and actions taken involve adverse lifetime environmental impacts, if they arise from unsound decisions. Findings show that the NEA encourages companies through its EIA/IEE procedures to select and design business projects in an environmentally friendly manner. It can provide a greater contribution to environment protection. These findings agree with Zubair (2001). Such greater importance and attention by companies in their business planning stage may be attributed to the provisions of NEA that make it mandatory for all industrialists to obtain environmental approval for their projects, following EIA/IEE procedures from the conception phrase, and to follow EPL procedures from the commencement of operations throughout the business process.

Thus EIA/IEE assessments can be considered as the starting point of environmental concerns and actions relating to proposed industrial activities. EIA helps ascertain the possible effects of a particular project on the environment at an initial stage and empowers officials to incorporate mitigating measures identified in this assessment into the planning process before commencing the project, thereby reducing damage caused to the environment. It thus helps the industries implement their businesses more successfully in an environmentally friendly manner. Accordingly, the EIA is regarded as a major planning tool and one of the key techniques to achieve SD.

(ii) *The Pre-implementation Stage: Setting Up Machines and Surroundings*

In this stage, all companies essentially follow procedures and control measures prescribed under the Noise Control Regulations of the NEA in setting up machines to control noise emissions. All companies have obtained a Scheduled Waste Management Licence (SWML) by applying prescribed measures to manage under the NEA. Thus, the findings show that, following the EPL, IEE/EIA procedures and applicable NEA provisions, labour laws and other relevant laws (BOI regulations), all companies have taken initiatives to set up machines and surroundings so as to protect the environment from noise emissions, ensuring safety and health of workers. For example, most companies have specific equipment to alleviate noise, particularly inside the operations area, so as to provide a healthy working environment. Some who particularly deal with highly environmentally sensitive processes and/or operate machines with excessive noise emissions state that they have decided not to operate such machines after 10:00pm and instead they typically operate with less noise emission at night to avoid difficulties encountered by neighbours.

Where possible every company takes actions to replace old with new machines in order to avoid excessive noise and high energy consumption associated with older machinery. Finance managers of two companies in the DVS sector reveal that they have taken initiatives in securing machines to ensure maximum utilization of energy and other resources and avoiding or minimizing waste: the finance manager of one company explains their strategies thus:

> We apply certain strategies in setting up machines and surroundings to save energy consumption of machines. A sustainable energy manager has been allocated to each company in the group appointed under the Sri Lankan Sustainability Energy Authority. Each manager has formed an energy management team which works to reduce energy wastage through awareness programs, by applying activity-based costing (ABC), we divide spaces into cost centres based on machines, so that costs arising from that area goes to those particular machines, considering an individual machine as a separate activity, and allocating machine-related costs such as electricity, furnace oil, to that particular machine. Some machines produce more than one product with different volumes and thus those costs are allocated to different products based on volumes of each product items.
>
> Further, we have fixed up separate electricity meters for each machine in order to save energy: at month's end, it automatically counts energy consumption. Thus, we can just read meters and identify usage. We identify product items and related volumes processed on each machine and allocate energy costs accordingly to those products. Further, we have fixed plant-wise electricity meters in the factories, e.g. the soap section has a separate plant and a meter, and we calculate energy usage separately in each plant, and prepare plant-wise bills too.

The company's finance manager further stated that, through such strategies, it could accurately measure energy consumption and easily assign responsibility for operations to employees, so that all from labour and supervisory levels to managerial level are self-motivated to regulate their processes in the most effective way, contributing to saving energy consumption and minimizing associated costs and ultimately protecting the environment.

Thus, this stage involves taking measures to control noise effects inside and outside the manufacturing plants and justifies effective utilization of resources, assuring safety and health in complying with regulations. However, the mainstream EM measures relate to the implementation stage.

(iii) *Implementation Stage*

The results indicate that, compared to the previous two stages, most EM actions relate to implementation. All companies have obtained an EPL and maintain it throughout the operation, requiring it to operate in accordance with NEA provisions. All apply EM measures to prevent and control pollution in every aspect under the legislation. In the renewal of the EPL, the CEA or local authorities (LA) investigate whether the companies have violated conditions of a previous EPL, and, if any violation is observed, the CEA or LA requests the company to take relevant pollution control measures. After ensuring conformity of all aspects recommended, the renewal of EPL is granted. For this purpose, a team of CEA/LA carries out monitoring at regular intervals, inspecting industries and reviewing reports on wastewater analysis, noise/vibration measurements and efficiency/evaluation of pollution control systems adopted.

Accordingly, through this EPL process, companies are conscious that, if they continue to violate EPL conditions, legal action will be initiated in terms of cancellation or suspension of the EPL, rejection of an application for renewal of the EPL, sending legal notices and filing a case, all of which lead to termination of the business. Findings show that all companies have obtained SWML and manage their scheduled waste in accordance with the NEA and CEA. Thus, all companies generate, collect, transport, store, recover, recycle or dispose of waste properly, protecting air, water, soil, ground water and noise levels from pollution. Most procedures and criteria of SWML also cover the EPL.

10.4.3 Types and Extent of EM Measures Taken by Companies/ Industry Sectors

The study identifies the following as key EM activities taken and strategies applied typically in the implementation stage by most responding companies, motivated by and complying with licensing strategies, other provisions of legislation and standards. All these measures taken in this stage are analysed under four main categories identified based on the nature of those measures.

(i) *EM measures for efficient use of resources towards minimizing waste and pollution*

Energy Energy conservation initiatives at business unit level include monitoring energy, use of energy-efficient lighting and equipment and utilization of renewable energy sources, e.g. installing separate electricity meters for each machine and plant based on production section (lines) and by business unit, so as to monitor energy consumption. The most commonly used primary energy source by those sectors is the national grid. They switch off air conditioning prior to a specified time, e.g. 15 min before leaving the office; they use energy-efficient CFL bulbs throughout the premises. They produce by-products through power generation (e.g. burned ash from power generation used to manufacture cement, rather than channel to sea). They supply their own power with generation plants (e.g. the finance manager of a cement manufacturing company stated that they generate power for their operations and sell excess to national bidders). They use more furnace oil than electricity to generate steam for use in converting materials into liquid, as the electricity rate is higher than that of furnace oil. They replace old machines with high electricity consumption with energy-efficient machines (probably also reducing noise). They operate machines with high electricity consumption in off-peak hours and operate noisy machines by day and close them at night. They use solar power/red light to reduce energy costs. They reduce electricity consumption by opening windows and using glass to reduce darkness inside office areas. They use biomass instead of gas. They use hydropower instead of diesel (the finance manager of a food processing company stated that they are in the process of completing conversion of diesel power generator into hydropower and they are installing upgraded technology in the plant that contributes towards enhanced efficiency and increased utilization of by-products). They use electricity and furnace oil in the production process.

Water Companies take action to optimize usage of water in production processes – wherever possible, they seek to reuse water after treatment (e.g. the finance manager of a F&B company stated: 'We have adopted stringent water conservation measures for "dairy product" using water from effluent treatment plants for its entire production and operational needs'. Another finance manager of a company in the same sector stated: 'We use previously used water for washing salt to wash later stock that gains two advantages: saving water and adding salterns to salt, as it uses saltern water to wash salt'). They operate water treatment plants, recycling water and minimizing waste. They purify used water through water treatment plants and reuse it for gardening and cleaning machines in factories. They implement used water recycling system to use it for cleaning components (e.g. finance manager of a cable manufacturing company stated that they, with such a system, used recycled water to cool hot cables in the process).

Raw Materials Companies eliminate environmentally unfriendly raw materials from the manufacturing process. They purchase and store raw materials, ensuring maximum use and minimizing wastage. They employ recycling for used cane/bottles by collecting them from consumers and recycling to produce the same or any other products. They launch firm-wide initiatives to reduce use of paper materials (e.g. encourage use of double-sided printing; move from printed to electronic materials for training events and conferences). They sell waste plastics only for recyclers who use them for their own manufacturing purposes. They minimize waste of materials by recycling them. They use as input waste of one product line for another product line.

For example, the finance manager of a cable manufacturing company in the MNF sector stated:

> We use waste from the product line of 5000m cables for product lines producing 1000m and 100m, getting advantages of product lines with different sizes.

A finance manager of an F&B company operating with renewable resource use stated:

> With the assistance of training, practical knowledge and experience obtained, now we are changing traditional practices of extracting natural resources (saltern) in order to get maximum outcome in an environmentally friendly manner. Thus, instead of 'shallow based systems' now we practise 'deep tank systems' that provide high volume with high quality and high yield, but the time taken for the process is longer so that have to wait longer time to get yield.

(ii) *Pollution control measures and preventive EM activities*

For pollution control and preventive actions, there are commonly used measures: implementing effluent treatment plants; fixing up noise control equipment; establishing the best available odour (smell) control systems in factories; providing workers with masks to minimize risk and ensure safety; measuring and controlling lighting and noise levels; in processing, measuring emissions from boilers (CO_2); taking action to mitigate dust impacts and measuring them; creating sound barriers in the factory to alleviate pollution; and taking measures for dust control and effluent control.

In addition, there are the following initiatives and strategies applied for pollution control and prevention of environment harm.

Implementing cleaner production concepts and creating cleaner production team:

Most companies follow cleaner production concepts, and in some instances they have created a team to implement and monitor them. The finance manager of an F&B company explained:

> We implemented cleaner production concepts in collaboration with 'European Switch Asia' funded by European Union – we give targets for water, electricity, furnace oil, and implement options and monitor them, giving suggestions to minimise wastage. Also, these initiatives are audited in order to minimise consumption. For this purpose, the company has created a cleaner production team, representing all levels of employees, and they should implement those projects and reduce wastage. Moreover, our CEO has a particular interest in implementing those cleaner production projects, and, as a result, we received 'National Green Awards' from the CEA and a 'European Switch Asia Sustainability Award' for these activities. Moreover, we are working towards obtaining ISO 14001EMS certification.

However, according to the nature of the products, there is no large wastage, so that there is no need to proceed with bio gas.

Implementing power generation systems, manufacturing power houses and biomass projects:

Biomass is agricultural waste products used as a source of fuel. Two companies in the MNF sector use their own biomass power generation instead of hydropower. The finance manager of a cement manufacturing company in the MNF sector said that 'Our general manager and finance manager evaluate carbon projects and we have a technical training centre to train construction workers and other technical staff too'.

Taking actions on ozone depletion and global warming:

The finance manager of a MNF company dealing with durable products stated in the annual report:

We have two main concerns globally: ozone depletion and global warming. In 2012, we introduced new refrigerators under the GEO series and this uses the R600A gas (... as the refrigerant in the new product line), which does not result in global warming and has no impact on ozone depletion. It also has enormous electricity savings, like 20% energy savings from a refrigerator. This is the gas used in developed nations and recommended for use in the future. We are proud; we are the first manufacturer in South Asia to adopt R600A gas in its products. Our engineers and industry experts work tirelessly to achieve ever-greater efficiencies in energy consumption of our refrigerators and continue to make energy savings every year. We are looking to extend the use of this refrigerant across our entire range of refrigerators.

Appointing a cross-functional team and form energy management team:

Finance managers of five companies representing DVS and MNF sectors indicated that they have developed cross-functional teams, a combination of different personnel with different expertise (e.g. finance, production, sales, brand, quality, environment), so that they can easily develop sound decisions in every element, including EM measures. Also, eight companies in the DVS, MNF and F&B sectors have formed an 'energy management team' to work with reducing energy wastage through awareness programs. All such teams are centred on production and maintenance departments for decisions and follow-up actions. A company spreads duties across various teams, along with training and educating the workforce regarding the new EM concepts and their importance.

The finance manager of a MNF company stated:

Challenges of energy (as demand increases globally) encouraged us to strengthen our 'sustainable energy policy' through a well-established energy management system. We need to turn towards renewable energy to sustain our production. Thus, we already installed a renewable gas unit in the factory premises, reducing LPG consumption by 50% cylinders per year. This is a win-win situation, as input to the gas unit is food refused at the canteen. This unit also generates liquid fertiliser as a by-product.

Consultation with reputable specialists in the field and have them visit factories regularly and develop environmental policies and action plans for the company:

Finance managers of most companies in all sectors stated that they consult reputable specialists in the field, and thus regular visits to the factory have given management the proper guidance required. With this effort and commitment, they can develop environmental policies and action plans for the company.

Examples of such environmental policies of companies are:

X is committed to continually improve its EMS by reducing the generation of waste, optimising usage of resources and disposing waste effectively.

The company shall continually improve its EMS by establishing environmental objectives and targets and reviewing them periodically.

X is committed to comply with applicable legal requirements and other requirements related to environmental aspects.

X shall document the policy and communicate it to all employees and make it available to the public on request.

Obtaining SLS ISO 14001-EMS certification and accreditation

Almost all companies are working with this certification by adopting its guidelines and standards in their business processes. This is an independent acknowledgement of a company's sustainable business operations. Table 10.2 shows the progress of companies in this respect.

The findings show that 50% of companies considered (except CHEM) have already obtained EMS certification and accreditation, showing superior progress in DVS sector, while all others are working towards this. One MNF company with this certification was awarded a 'Merit Certificate' in the large-scale manufacturing category in 2012, at the 'National Cleaner Production Competition', in recognition of its sound, environmentally friendly manufacturing practices. Complying with EMS certification and accreditation means that those companies are essentially taking all

Table 10.2 Progress of companies in SLS ISO 14001-EMS certification and accreditation

Industry sector	Obtained SLS EMS certification	Working towards SLS EMS certification	Total no. of companies
F&B	4	4	8
CHEM	–	3	3
DVS	4	1	5
MNF	9	9	18
Total	**17**	**17**	**34**

kinds of possible EM measures and are innovative in their business processes to ensure green businesses while creating a green environment.

For example, the finance manager of the MNF company explained:

> Since we have obtained ISO 14001 EMS certification in late 2011, we have embarked on a new journey towards being a revolutionary business in a green economy. Based on ISO 14001: 2004 EMS, and supported by numerous resource efficient and cleaner production techniques, we have improved company processes to minimise environmental impacts from the point of raw material transportation to final product distribution. We will optimise use of raw materials, water and energy and minimise and control all waste. We believe that environmentally friendly energy sources, such as solar energy, have great future potential and we will consider extending our support for such projects. Working closely with the 'National Cleaner Production Competition' we could implement many cleaner production practices, including: process modification; waste elimination; energy savings; waste reuse potential and even achieved raw materials savings. We continuously improve its environmental performance by reducing the impact on the environment and by preventing pollution through economically feasible and technologically practical processes.

Create awareness among all employees regarding company responsibilities towards a green environment and communicate environmental policy stakeholders and the community:

All companies have taken initiatives regarding awareness of environmental policies and have recognized their responsibilities by conducting awareness programs, training programs and frequent discussion at team, department/division and board levels. All companies publish their EM measures, strategies applied for pollution control and protecting the environment, EM-related achievements, awards, certifications, accreditations, appreciation and future endeavours in their annual reports, reserving a separate section called 'corporate social responsibility (CSR) activities' or 'sustainability report'. Through such communication processes, the company management and all employees are motivated to continue and improve such EM strategies and measures while securing company reputation from an environmental perspective.

(iii) *Research and development (R&D) activities relating to environmental issues*

The findings show rather less attention to R&D activities by companies, mostly due to their belief that it is more feasible and cost-effective to implement EM strategies and measures recommended by authorized bodies, such as the CEA, rather than doing research on that by themselves. However, some major R&D activities by companies with specific businesses are as follows:

R&D with renewable resources

Companies involved in utilizing renewable resources undertake R&D projects to identify new technologies and systems to ensure the sustainability of the business while protecting the environment. The finance manager of a salt manufacturing company stated its experience:

> We usually undertake research, and so we could initiate construction of deep tanks in a newly acquired land area by developing new techniques to protect salt in rainy season and also to enhance the production capacities. Another significant benefit is these tanks provide 'brines' (salt water) for shallow crystal harvest operation, where necessary. We have determined saltern development activities, many of them involving construction of newly acquired land areas, adjoining the developed saltern, so that we can maximise yield, brine usage, and synergy in operations.

R&D with agro-inputs:

The finance manager of a company in the CHEM sector stated:

> We have a separate R&D Company in the group who engages in research fulltime to identify new products and product improvements that can be initiated in a healthy manner. That research is on 'how to bring new products to farmers'. For this purpose, they go to paddy fields and select a sample to cultivate and use chemicals. Then, the research team test the success and environment impacts, and other impacts. Based on outcomes of such experiments, new agro-inputs go to the market. Also, the R&D division has ties with multinational research-based companies from the world to introduce innovative crop protection solutions to [Sri Lankan] farmers. Their main focus is to promote target-specific, low-toxic, low-persistent, safe products to [Sri Lankan] agriculture.

(iv) *Initiatives made towards achieving CSR*

The findings indicate that all respondents typically recognize this aspect as an important activity they should attend to while business processes are going on.

Most companies undertake CSR activities by means of community development projects to assist schools, hospitals, temples and village communities; they take initiatives to create a protective healthy working environment and conduct awareness programs for employee safety and health and for raising their socio-economic condition. In addition, the following CRS activities have been undertaken by responding companies with particular attention to protecting the environment and minimize pollution. All companies publish their CSR activities in annual reports under a separate section 'sustainability report'.

Activities for protecting natural resources: The finance manager of a salt manufacturing company stated that it implemented a 'mangrove' strategy (using the tropical evergreen tree of the tidal coast) in coastal areas, such as Puttalam (removing mangroves is prohibited under the NEA). They further conduct workshops to support and educate small-scale salt suppliers about environmentally friendly practices. Another finance manager of a DVS company stated that it had implemented projects to grow plants in rural areas and help people there by providing water and other necessities. The finance manager of a company dealing with durable products in the

MNF sector that introduced new refrigerators with no impact on global warming and ozone depletion commented:

> Most people today are concerned about high electricity tariffs, so if we can produce some products with low power consumption, we can create competitive advantage by creating a good image. By introducing such environmentally friendly durable products, we have already achieved social responsibility for the society. Moreover, we provide training opportunities for students of technical colleges and the National Apprentice Board as a career development measure.

Activities towards pollution control in society: The finance manager of an agro-input company revealed that it is involved in activities such as conducting workshops to educate youngsters on 'prevention against the deadly mosquito', emphasizing the importance of a clean environment; conducting workshops in collaboration with the Department of Agriculture to educate farmers on weed ecology and integrated weed management practices; initiating a 'Pesticide Container Recycling Program', in collaboration with the Department of Agriculture, MoE & Crop Life of Sri Lanka, taking into account the increased number of accidents, due to empty glass containers lying around, and reduction of pollution; and initiating a waste management program with an aim of implementing proper waste management systems in a number of public organizations (the Sri Lanka Army, schools, municipal councils, the Sri Lanka Coconut Research Institute and cricket stadiums). This program helped in reducing the spread of dengue fever and in educating people in manufacture and use of 'compost' fertilizer.

A company in the DVS sector also introduced collection of e-waste, which is highly toxic to the environment, and the collection of paper for recycling. The finance manager of a MNF company stated that they have initiated an e-waste disposal system, in which they inform people about handing over their used electrical items (computers, plastics) to the nearest showroom or branch for recycling.

Celebrating world environment day (5 June): Together with this celebration, most companies initiate tree-planting campaigns on company premises with the participation of all employees, which will contribute towards offsetting their carbon footprint.

Conduct professional training programs in collaboration with universities: A cable manufacturing company with a memorandum of understanding (MOU) with the engineering faculty of a university has a program for increasing the skills and knowledge of electricians. This suggests that such professional training and educational qualification help increase the skills and earning capacity of these electricians in an environmentally friendly manner. Under the MOU, the university has provided a research desk at the faculty to contribute to the R&D requirements of the company, and, in turn, the company is providing in-plant training for final-year students of the faculty to enhance their academic knowledge with practical, hands-on work experience.

Maintaining biodiversity: A few companies are involved in such projects. For example, the finance manager of one F&B company stated:

> The group is committed to conserving biodiversity, wherever possible enhancing it through adherence to governmental laws and to best practices relating to conservation and protection of environment. For this purpose, the group has identified, through research, one location as an area of high biodiversity, where large-scale development has not been planned for the site in view of its environmental sensitivity.

The finance manager of an agro-input company in the CHEM sector stated that it mainly focused on maintaining biodiversity with its R&D.

These findings suggest that CSR activities undertaken by the companies greatly affect their good image and hence sustainability of their business; additionally, some CSR initiatives help them protect the environment. It is further clear from annual reports that some companies present their CSR activities together with EM initiatives and related achievements under the same heading in a sustainability report.

10.5   Interpretation of Findings

Agreeing with Zubair (2001), the CEA takes all required measures empowered under the NEA to protect the environment and minimize pollution. All responding companies typically pay attention to take EM measures at each stage of the process, typically at implementation stage, in complying with environmental legislation (NEA, labour laws, BOI laws) and standards (SLS ISO 14001: 2004 EMS certification and accreditation).

The NEA encourages companies (by granting approval for industrial proposals) to select and design business projects in an environmentally friendly manner. As the business planning stage is the most influential and critical, through this practice companies tend to select and implement businesses with minimum adverse lifetime environmental impacts. This can provide a greater contribution towards protecting the environment. Such greater importance and attention by companies in their business planning stage may be attributed to the provisions of the NEA that make it mandatory for all industrialists to obtain environmental approval for their projects, following EIA/IEE procedures from the conception phrase, and to follow EPL procedures from the commencement of operations throughout the business process.

Also, findings demonstrate that in the pre-implementation stage, following the EPL, IEE/EIA procedures and applicable NEA provisions, labour laws and other relevant laws (BOI regulations), all companies have taken initiatives to set up machines and surroundings so as to protect the environment from noise emissions, ensuring safety and health of workers. The findings indicate that, compared to the previous two stages, most EM actions relate to the implementation stage. Such greater attention to take EM measures by all companies is probably due to legislation enacted by the CEA through EPL procedures.

All companies have obtained an EPL and maintain it throughout their operations by applying EM measures to prevent and control pollution in every aspect under legislation. According to industry classification on their pollution potential, List 'A' projects (80% highly polluting industrial activities) require renewal of EPL annually while List 'B' and List 'C' projects (signifying 33% medium-level and 25% low-level polluting industrial activities, respectively) once in 3 years. The procedure for obtaining EPLs is somewhat different for industrial activities in List 'C' from those of Lists 'A' and 'B'. Renewal of the EPL is possible only after ensuring conformity with all aspects recommended.

These practices confirm with the findings that indicate environmental legislation as the most influencing factor for all companies (100%) for EM measures. These findings support the literature, for example, Tilt (1997), but are somewhat different from Schaltegger and Burritt's (2010) findings.

With regard to types of EM measures, as detailed in Sect. 4.3, findings show that by being motivated by environmental legislation and related standards institutionalized in Sri Lanka, listed companies tend to give priority to measures for efficient use of resources (energy, water and raw materials) that aim to minimize waste and pollution. Also, companies concentrate on pollution control measures and preventive EM activities, all of which lead to obtaining SLS ISO 14001-EMS certification and accreditation. Of the sample, 50% obtained and all others are working towards this certification. This trend is probably due to their trust that such EM measures together with EMS certification and accreditation influence a positive company image, hence ensuring survival of the business.

Relating to R&D activities, a few companies are involved in environment-related R&D projects, probably due to necessity and courage: for example, companies involved in utilizing renewable resources and companies with agro-inputs have shown greater interest in R&D than others. However, such a lesser attention to R&D by individual companies is mainly due to their perception that it is more feasible and cost-effective to implement EM strategies and measures recommended by authorized bodies, such as the CEA, rather than doing their own research on this. Companies have greater confidence in CEA's recommendations, as they are derived from large-scale research projects undertaken by its R&D divisions and most include EPL procedures for implementation as a requirement. Most respondents are of the view that they normally make developments or improvements for their business processes but rarely undertake research on EM issues because they have no proper infrastructure and qualified staff in the relevant fields. Most companies undertake CSR activities by means of community development projects, apart from some projects initiated towards protecting the environment while mitigating pollution. Companies trust that all of these attempts contribute to company image and business survival.

The findings showed certain differences between individual companies/sectors in potential and extent of measures taken. CHEM sector and some of individual companies in other sectors that are involved in environmentally highly sensitive businesses like poultry demonstrate higher impacts and greater potential for measures than others. Factors included nature of the business (varying potential: high, moderate or low), management and staff commitment, available expertise, costing systems, resources, infrastructure and international collaborations and agreements. Yet deficits also exist in implementation.

10.6 Conclusions and Recommendations

This study confirms that environment-related laws, regulatory measures and SLS ISO EMS standards are in effect in Sri Lanka for protecting the environment. In this endeavour, the NEA of 1980 is the most important, with extensive provisions on pollution control, regulation of development and preparation of management plans. The CEA is the key central government body empowered by the NEA to regulate the preservation of the environment. All responding companies typically take EM measures through their EMS in complying with environmental legislation and standards.

The NEA encourages companies intervening from business planning stage to select, design and implement business projects in an environmentally friendly manner, thereby ensuring sustainable businesses with minimum adverse lifetime environmental impacts. The pre-implementation stage involves taking measures to control noise effects inside and outside the manufacturing plants and justify effective utilization of resources assuring safety and health in complying with regulations. However, the mainstream EM measures relate more to the implementation stage than to the previous two, mainly due to its high impacts associated with industrial operations and legislation enacted by CEA through EPL procedures with tight control measures.

As far as concern with types of EM activities goes, companies tend to give greater attention to measures for efficient use of resources, to pollution control measures and to preventive EM activities. Companies normally pay less attention to R&D activities as the CEA undertakes the same research on their behalf with good quality and gives recommendations for companies through EPL procedures. Also, companies tend to show higher concern for CSR activities, most of which involve environmental protection, and they publish in annual report with a 'sustainability report'.

Differences are identified between individual companies/sectors, showing a greater extent and potential for EM measures in environmentally highly sensitive businesses than in other companies/sectors investigated. Some companies are concerned more with EM measures with their greater awareness and interest in such practices, regardless of the extent of environmental sensitivity of businesses.

Through such EM measures, strategies, SLS ISO EMS certification and accreditation and reporting to the public on proactive stances and achievements towards sustainability, listed companies strongly believe that, in addition to legal compliance, these efforts also influence a positive company image, hence ensuring survival of the business.

Businesses must improve awareness among all personnel on legal compliance and standards observance. All employees should be assigned EM responsibility through a sound monitoring system, which is more realistic and effective than assigning responsibility to individuals or a group, since environmental impacts may derive from actions of anyone in a company and are unbounded. The findings form the foundation for future directions and propose further research on the phenomena under consideration.

Five Takeaways

1. The importance of enacting legislation and environment-related standards for a country or organizational context towards protecting the environment.
2. Motivation for companies operating diverse businesses under different industry sectors to take measures in order to protect the environment and minimize pollution.
3. The implications of taking measures for managing environmental impacts in relation to company objectives, predominantly creating a good image for the company and ensuring sustainable business, apart from compliance to legislation.
4. Potential of environmental concerns under three main stages of a business process (planning, pre-implementation and implementation) and nature and extent of measures taken or to be taken at each stage of the process in complying with environmental legislation (NEA, labour laws, BOI laws) and standards (SLS ISO 14001: 2004 EMS certification and accreditation).
5. Apart from compliance with legislation and other motives (company image and survival), possible measures are to be taken by individual companies/sectors stipulating their greater awareness and interest to manage environmental concerns mostly with SLS ISO EMS certification and accreditation. These may include measures for efficient use of resources and pollution control measures and preventive EM activities, environment-related R&D activities and CSR activities to improve the businesses and processes while protecting the environment.

Reflection Questions

1. What are some of the impact of business activities on the environment?
2. Environmental pressures are different for companies according to their industry, region or country. Compare and contrast these differences.
3. How can sustainability provide a company with a competitive advantage?
4. Discuss the motives behind recording and reporting EM measures.
5. One of the key motivating factors for EM measures is to satisfy regulatory requirements. Do you agree? Discuss.

References

Albelda, E. (2011). The role of management accounting practices as facilitators of the environmental management: Evidence from EMAS organisations. *Sustainability Accounting, Management and Policy Journal, 2*(1), 76–100.

Babiak, K., & Trendafilova, S. (2011). CSR and environmental responsibility: Motives and pressures to adopt green management practices. *Journal of Corporate Social Responsibility and Environmental Management, 18*, 11–24.

Bennett, M., Schaltegger, S., & Zvezdov, D. (2011). Environmental management accounting. In M. Abdel Kader (Ed.), *Review of management accounting research* (pp. 53–84). Basingstoke: Palgrave Macmillan.

Bracke, R., Verbeke, T., & Dejonckheere, V. (2008). What determines the decision to implement EMAS? A European firm level study. *Environmental Resource Economics, 41*, 499–518.

Central Environmental Authority. (2009). *Guidelines for the Management of Scheduled Waste in Sri Lanka: In accordance to the National Environmental (Protection & Quality) Regulation No. 01 of 2008*. Battaramulla: Central Environmental Authority. www.cea.lk

Environmental Foundation Limited. (2006). *Your environmental rights and responsibilities: A handbook of Sri Lanka*. Colombo: Environmental Foundation Limited.

Hart, S. L., & Milstein, M. B. (2003). Creating sustainable value. *Academy of Management Executive, 17*(2), 56–69.

Indrani, M. W., Wickremasinghe, G., & Naidoo, M. (2019). Exploring environmental consideration of Sri Lankan context. In *Proceedings of 5th International Conference on Contemporary Management (ICCM) 2019* (pp. 16–45). Colombo: Faculty of Management Studies and Commerce, University of Jaffna.

International Federation of Accountants–IFAC. (2005). *Environmental management accounting: International guidance document*. New York: International Federation of Accountants.

Kollman, K., & Prakash, A. (2002). EMS-based environmental regimes as club goods: Examining variations in firm-level adoption of ISO 14001 and EMAS in U.K., U.S. and Germany. *Policy Sciences, 35*, 43–67.

Kokubu, K., & Nishioka, E. (2005). Environmental management accounting practices in Japan. In *Implementing environmental management accounting: Status and Challenges* (pp. 321–342). Springer: Netherlands.

Koontz, T. M., Steelman, T. A., Carmin, J., Korfmacher, K. S., Moseley, C., & Thomas, C. W. (2010). *Collaborative environmental management: What roles for government, resources for the future*. Washington, DC: Academic.

Melnyk, S. A., Sroufe, R. P., & Calantone, R. (2003). Assessing the impact of environmental management systems on corporate and environmental performance. *Journal of Operations Management, 21*, 329–351.

Ministry of Environmental and Natural Nesources. (1980). *National Environmental Act No. 47 of 1980*. Colombo: NEA.

Ministry of Environment – MoE (2012). Sri Lanka's Middle Path to Sustainable Development through Mahinda Chinthana-Vision for the future. United Nations Conference on Sustainable Development, Brazil (2012 edition).

Morse, J. (2010). Procedures and practice of mixed method design: Maintaining control, rigor, and complexity. In *Sage handbook of mixed methods in social & behavioural research* (2nd ed., pp. 339–353). Thousand Oaks: Sage.

Nawrocka, D., & Parker, T. (2009). Finding the connection: Environmental management systems and environmental performance. *Journal of Cleaner Production, 17*, 601–607.

Onwuegbuzie, A. J., & Collins, K. M. (2007). A typology of mixed methods sampling designs in social science research. *The Qualitative Report, 12*(2), 281–316.

Pajula, T., & Vatanen, S. (2017). Managing the life cycle to reduce environmental impacts. In *Dynamics of long-life assets: From technology adaptation to upgrading the business model* (pp. 93–113). New York: Springer.

Porter, M., & Kramer, M. (2006). Strategy and society: The link between competitive advantage and corporate social responsibilities. *Harvard Business Review, 82*(12), 78–92.

Savage, D., & Jasch, C. (2005). *International guidance document on environmental management accounting*. New York: International Federation of Accountants.

Schaltegger, S., & Burritt, R. L. (2010). Sustainability accounting for companies: Catchphrase or decision support for business leaders? *Journal of World Business, 45*(4), 375–384.

Sigita, Z. (2016). Environmental impact assessment of manufacturing industry projects. *Environmental Research, Engineering and Management*. https://doi.org/10.5755/j01. erem.72.1.11484.

Sri Lanka Accreditation Board. (2015). *Accreditation scheme for certification bodies*. Colombo: Sri Lanka Accreditation Board. www.slab.lk

Sri Lanka Standards Institution. (2015). *Sri Lanka standards on environmental management: SLSl ISO 14000*. Colombo: Sri Lanka Standards Institution. www.slsi.lk

Staniskis, J. K., & Stasiskiene, Z. (2006). Environmental management accounting in Lithuania: Exploratory study of current practices, opportunities and strategic intents. *Journal of Cleaner Production, 14*, 1252–1261.

Tilt, C. A. (1997). Environmental policies of major companies: Australian evidence. *The British Accounting Review, 29*(4), 367–394.

Watson, M., & Emery, A. R. T. (2004). Environmental management and auditing systems: The reality of environmental self-regulation. *Managerial Auditing Journal, 19*(7), 916–928.

Watzold, F. (2009). Explaining differences in EMAS participation rates across Europe: The importance of institutions, incomplete information and path dependance. *European Journal of Law & Economics, 28*, 67–82.

Zubair, L. (2001). Challenges for environmental impact assessment in Sri Lanka. *Environmental Impact Assessment Review, 21*(5), 469–478.

Do Green HRM Practices Matter in Shaping Sustainable Performance Among ISO 14001-Certified Malaysian Manufacturing Firms? A Mixed-Method Approach

11

Noor Ullah Khan, Roselina Binti Ahmad Saufi, and Asfia Obaid

11.1 Introduction

Human well-being, economic growth, and sustainability depend on how well we manage the environment (Kahle and Gurel-Atay 2013). It is factual that sustainability is vital for the manufacturing industry to address major environmental issues. Carbon emission (CO_2) from manufacturing firms results in harmful outcomes such as global warming, climate change, water and air pollution, and degradation of environmental performance (IEA 2015). Recently, a good number of studies provide evidence that there is pressure on manufacturers to improve environmental, social, and economic performance due to environmental awareness, the commitment of the government to climate change, and the emphasis of stakeholders (Ghazilla et al. 2015). The increase in CO_2 emission from manufacturing firms results in major atmospheric pollution, solid wastes, and reduction in environmental performance (Statistics 2015). The degradation of the environment as an outcome of industrial production creates an imbalance between economic and environmental performance (Khan et al. 2017a, b) because manufacturing firms are more considerate towards economic and financial gains while they ignore environmental and social aspects.

Sustainable performance (SP) is vital for manufacturing firms in reducing the imbalance between economic, environmental, and social performance (Maletič

N. U. Khan (✉) · A. Obaid
NUST Business School National University of Sciences and Technology, Islamabad, Pakistan
e-mail: noorullah.khan@nbs.nust.edu.pk; asfia.obaid@nbs.nust.edu.pk

R. B. A. Saufi
Fakulti Keusahawanan & Perniagaan, Universiti Malaysia Kelantan (UMK),
Kota Bharu, Malaysia
e-mail: roselina@umk.edu.my

S. Dhiman, R. Samaratunge (eds.), *New Horizons in Management, Leadership and Sustainability*, Future of Business and Finance,
https://doi.org/10.1007/978-3-030-62171-1_11

219

et al. 2016). It is quite challenging for firms to implement environmental initiatives and green HRM practices. Similarly, Malaysian manufacturing firms are facing barriers in adopting green initiatives and need to implement sustainable practices as indicated by several studies (Nordin et al. 2014). Only 18% of companies have ISO 14001 certification according to FMM (2015), and environmental performance has reduced significantly in the past 10 years (EPI 2016). Therefore, ineffective environmental policies of the government and industrial wastes are primarily responsible for the degradation in the environmental performance of Malaysia (Khan et al. 2017a, b). Hence, manufacturing firms must adopt sustainable HRM practices to ensure environmental protection and performance to address environmental problems (IEA 2015). A further aspect of sustainable HRM is the concept of green human resource management (GHRM), which was initially introduced by Renwick and his collogues. GHRM is a relatively new area of research that integrates traditional HRM practices and environmental management (EM) making HRM practices sustainable (Jabbour 2015; Renwick et al. 2013). The Eleventh Malaysian Plan (EMP) focuses on the sustainability agenda to improve sustainable performance.

Green human resource management aims to ensure sustainable performance (SP) and long-term survival of corporate sustainability. Most of the previous studies evaluated green HRM based on qualitative approaches (e.g., Ahmad 2015; Jabbour and de Sousa Jabbour 2016), while only a few have employed quantitative and empirical approaches (O'Donohue and Torugsa 2016). Thus, future studies need to empirically address this gap. According to Renwick et al. (2013), there is a need to integrate the fields of HRM and environmental management that result in green HRM. Hence, future studies should examine the impact of GHRM practices (selection and recruitment, training, and rewards) on environmental and organizational performance. GHRM involves specific HR policies and practices that create a balance between sustainable performance dimensions (economic, social, and environment) and financial performance to enhance overall sustainable performance. Accordingly, this study investigates the relationship between GHRM practices and sustainable performance. Moreover, this study also investigates the relationship between GHRM sub-dimensions, e.g., green selection and recruitment, green training and development, and green assessment and rewards, and sustainable performance, among Malaysian manufacturing firms that are ISO 14001-certified.

11.2 Review of Literature on Green Human Resource Management (HRM) Practices

The topic of green HRM is a relatively new area of research, and the term (GHRM) itself originated from the seminal work of Renwick and his colleagues (Renwick et al. 2008, 2013). The GHRM literature is largely dominated by western studies, so it is quite significant for future research to investigate the concept of GHRM in the context of Asian countries (Renwick et al. 2013) to fill this gap. Various contemporary scholars have researched to enhance their understanding of green HRM (Khan et al. 2017b; Renwick et al. 2013). Some have defined it based on the basic aspects of sustainability and environment such as Renwick et al. (2013), who define GHRM as integration of HRM and environmental objectives, while most authors defined green HRM based on HR policies and practices to meet the environmental objectives of an organization. This study refers to green HRM as the integration of environmental aspects in HRM practices to achieve environmental objectives, which is quite similar to the definition provided by Jabbour (2013): "Green HRM is concerned with the systemic, planned alignment of typical human resource management practices with the organization's environmental goals."

There is a growing need for the integration of literature on HRM and environmental management (Renwick et al. 2013) as research in this field is interdisciplinary and originates from sustainable HRM themes linked to performance management (Jabbour 2015). Globally, researchers have investigated HRM on the managerial perspectives to achieve environmental agenda for organizations (Khan et al. 2017b), while green HRM practices are also important for employees to align their environmental goals with the organizations' environmental strategy (Renwick et al. 2008). Therefore, to expand such a framework, it is a prerequisite that HRM practices, e.g., recruitment, training, appraisal, and reward systems, should be aligned with environmental strategy and prudent objectives (Jabbour 2013). The integration of environmental management and HRM is yet to be explored comprehensively (Khan et al. 2017a, b) as there should be synergy among the HR system and its environmental strategy within an organization. Consequently, an organization needs to adopt green HRM practices (Opatha and Arulrajah 2014) to meet a long-term sustainability agenda. This research mainly studies three key practices, i.e.:

First, green recruitment and selection, which refers to an organized activity that includes the environmental dimension, aiming at hiring motivated applicants with environmental knowledge for current and future job opportunities.

Second, green training and development, which means educating employees about environmental objectives and training them on how to save energy and reduce waste output. Thus, green organizations should train employees with green practices and also educate them on green values to achieve sustainable performance (O'Donohue and Torugsa 2016).

Third, green assessment and rewards that are vital for providing useful feedback and fostering firm environmental outcomes. Manufacturing companies have established environmental objectives for evaluating employee's environmental performance.

11.2.1 Sustainable Performance (SP)

Manufacturing organizations are facing growing demands from stockholders, shareholders, and regulatory bodies to address environmental issues and improve their corporate sustainability performance (Ghazilla et al. 2015). Organizations need to overcome the sustainability challenges resulting from an imbalance between

Fig. 11.1 Sustainable performance dimensions

economic, environmental, and social perspectives (Maletic et al. 2015), to accomplish sustainable performance (Nicolăescu et al. 2015). The concept of the triple bottom line (TBL) was proposed by Elkington (1994), which integrates with the three viewpoints, i.e., social, environmental, and financial. Currently, organizations use the TBL framework for evaluating sustainable performance; thus, the TBL approach can be applied to integrate sustainable performance (SP).

While sustainable performance (SP) integrates performance based on social and environmental aspects with economic dimensions, a few studies point to the limitations of TBL's measurement, for non-systemic approaches and compliance mechanisms (Sridhar and Jones 2013). Based on the primary assumption of TBL, performance should not be evaluated based on the economic dimension only (Fauzi et al. 2010). SP should consist of three measurement elements, namely, (i) economic, (ii) social, and (iii) environmental as illustrated in Fig. 11.1, and to achieve greater SP, organizations need to reduce the imbalance between these three dimensions through synergetic integration; otherwise, the outcome of SP may be negatively affected.

11.2.2 Hypothesis Development – Green HRM Practices and Sustainable Performance

GHRM practices are vital for improving performance (Tang et al. 2017), and companies should align HRM practices with the objectives of environmental management to achieve sustainability performance. GHRM is vital for the well-being of employees and organizational performance (Renwick et al. 2013); while traditional HRM practices only focus on the economic performance of an organization, green HRM practices focus on environmental performance along with organizational performance (Tang et al. 2017). Developing literature on GHRM emphasizes that a set of integrated HRM practices including recruitment, performance appraisal, learning and development, rewards, and employment relations can build a more environmentally sustainable workplace culture (Renwick et al. 2013). Based on previous literature, this study proposes the following hypotheses:

H1: Green HRM practices are positively related to sustainable performance (SP).
H1a: Green recruitment and selection are positively related to SP.
H1b: Green training and development are positively related to SP.
H1c: Green assessment and rewards are positively related to SP

11.2.3 Research Model and Theoretical Foundation

The proposed model for the current study consists of GHRM practices (green selection and recruitment, green training and development, green assessment and rewards) as exogenous variables and SP as the endogenous variable as shown in Fig. 11.2.

This study uses ability, motivation, and opportunity (AMO) as the underpinning theory which was proposed by Appelbaum (2000) to examine the relationship between HRM practices and organizational performance. However, some studies also used other theoretical conceptualizations, i.e., resource-based view (RBV) and contingency theory (CT), to examine HRM and performance relationships as the AMO framework has established foundations in industrial/organizational psychology literature (Paauwe 2009). Similarly, as compared with the two other theories, i.e., RBV and CT, the AMO theory is applied predominantly considering the effects of GHRM practices on firm performance (Boselie et al. 2005). In support of this,

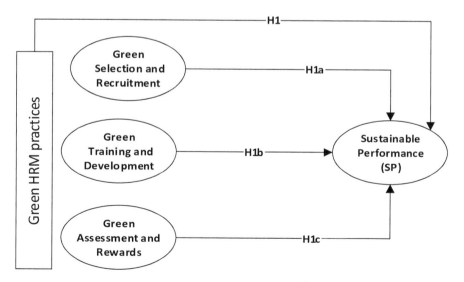

Fig. 11.2 Proposed research model

more than half of the articles published after the year 2000 have adopted the AMO framework (Paauwe 2009). According to the prime assumption of AMO theory, practices such as ability (selective hiring, training, education, and developing talented staff), motivation (incentive system, performance-based payments), and opportunity (involving employees in EM initiatives) positively affect discretionary behavior (Boxall and Purcell 2003), which ultimately leads to high performance (Renwick et al. 2013).

11.3   Mixed-Method: Explanatory Sequential Design

The purpose of this study is twofold. Firstly, this study investigates the direct relationship between green HRM practices (green selection and recruitment, green training and development, green assessment and rewards) and sustainable performance (SP). Secondly, this study bridges theoretical and empirical gaps based on the previous literature. The current study uses explanatory sequential design, which is composed of two phases, i.e., quantitative and qualitative proceeding sequentially. An explanatory sequential design based on sequential time orders more priority and value to quantitative data (Creswell et al. 2003). This design is more effective in the case of unexpected results from the quantitative part. One of the main strengths of this design is explaining quantitative results with qualitative findings. Conversely, this design needs sufficient time, financial resources, and researcher skills, which is considered as a major disadvantage (Wisdom and Creswell 2013). Figure 11.3 displays the application of explanatory sequential design which consists of quantitative and qualitative methods based on the complementarity approach for the current study. The quantitative method began with quantitative data collection and its analysis through the structural equation modelling (SEM) technique using AMOS 22. Subsequently, qualitative data was collected through semi-structured interviews and analyzed through thematic analysis using NVivo 11. Both the methods, i.e., quantitative and qualitative, used sequential order and were completed separately. However, during the final stage of the research, the quantitative results were explained and complemented with qualitative results using a complementarity approach (Creswell 2013) to better understand and address the research objectives. The next section discusses the quantitative phase in detail.

11.3.1 Quantitative Method Survey Instruments

This research employed probability sampling. Primary data was collected using standard questionnaires from a sample of 248 ISO 14001-certified manufacturing firms listed in standards achieved by the category of Federation of Malaysian Manufacturers (FMM) Directory 2015. The study used standard questionnaires as survey instruments composed of four latent variables, GHRM practices, and sustainable performance and measured and operationalized the GHRM practices using a 12-item survey instrument designed with a 5-point Likert scale adopted from

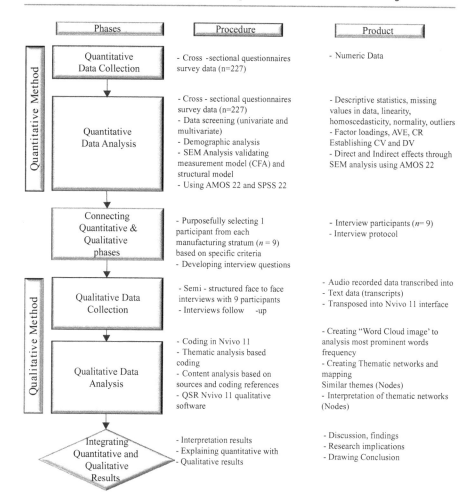

Fig. 11.3 Application of explanatory sequential mixed-method design

Jabbour (2011). The triple bottom line (TBL) approach was used to measure organizational performance beyond profit consideration including social and environmental aspects. This study used a 13-item measurement scale developed by Maletič et al. (2014) in measuring sustainable performance based on three dimensions, i.e., economic, social, and environment, with a 5-point Likert scale.

11.4 Quantitative Data Analysis and Results

Quantitative data was analyzed through structural equation modelling (SEM) technique using AMOS. SEM analysis assumptions were fulfilled such as univariate and multivariate normality, linearity and homoscedasticity, and multicollinearity.

Initially, a total of 350 self-administrated questionnaires (SAQs) were distributed among managers of ISO 14001-certified manufacturing firms in Malaysia. In response, 248 questionnaires were returned indicating a 71% response rate. Besides, normality tests confirmed that 21 cases had normality issues. Thus, 227 questionnaires were used for further SEM (Bryman and Bell 2015). Descriptive statistics analysis reported that a total of nine manufacturing groups participated in this study including (1) food, beverages, and tobacco, (2) chemical including petroleum, (3) electrical and electronics, (4) fabricated metals, (5) machinery, (6) plastic, (7) transport, (8) rubber, and (9) other industries as shown in Table 11.1.

To perform SEM analyses, the measurement model was initially analyzed by assessing standardized factor loadings, as well as the validity and reliability of each construct. Measurement of second-order constructs required error term on each dimension, as indicated in Fig. 11.4 (R1−R8). To achieve a good model fit, some adjustments were required, such as removing all items with a factor loading of less than 0.50 (Hair et al. 2010). After items such as ECOP02 and ECOP05 for which the standardized loadings were < 0.50 item loadings were removed, the model was

Table 11.1 Company background

Company background	N	%	Cum %
Industry			
Food, beverages, and tobacco	56	22.6	20.6
Chemical including petroleum	36	14.5	37.1
Electrical and electronics	45	18.2	55.3
Fabricated metal	25	10.0	65.3
Machinery	21	8.5	73.8
Plastic	16	6.5	80.3
Transport	20	8.0	88.3
Rubber	18	7.3	95.6
Others	11	4.4	100
Total	248	100	
Number of employees			
0–50	27	10.9	10.9
50–100	35	14.1	25.0
101–250	58	23.4	48.4
251–500	43	17.3	65.7
501–1000	67	27.0	92.7
1000+	18	7.3	100
Total	248	100	
Year of establishment			
Before 1970	09	3.6	3.6
1971–1980	23	9.3	12.9
1981–1990	30	12.0	24.9
1991–2000	78	31.5	56.4
2001–2009	62	25.0	81.4
2010–2016	46	18.6	100
Total	248	100	

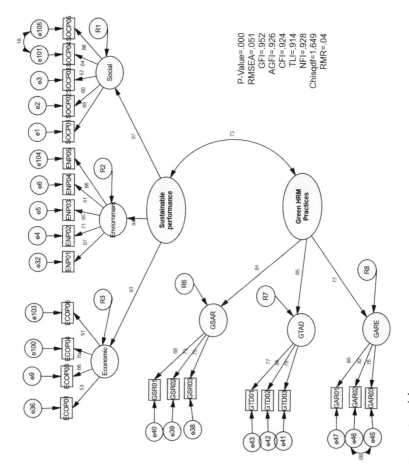

P-Value=.000
RMSEA=.051
GFI=.952
AGFI=.926
CFI=.924
TLI=.914
NFI=.928
Chisqdf=1.649
RMR=.04

Fig. 11.4 Second-order measurement model

revised. Besides, the error term e104 had to be correlated with e105 and e46 with e45. The goodness-of-fit values after making these adjustments were significantly improved, as shown in Fig. 11.4, i.e., CMIN/DF = 1.649, GFI = 0.952, AGFI = 0.926, CFI = 0.924, TLI = 0.914, NFI = 0.928, REMSA = 0.051, and RMR = 0.040, with the P-value of 0.000.

The proposed model was also evaluated in terms of convergent validity (CV), which was done by substantiating three basic criteria. First, all standardized loading estimates should be statistically significant with a value of 0.50 or higher, indicating that all items converge on their respective constructs. Second, the average variance extracted (AVE) must be at least 0.50, as this is indicative of adequate convergence. Third, construct reliability (CR) of 0.7 or higher is needed, as this indicates good reliability. All these criteria were met, thus confirming that the CV assumption was not violated in this study (Sekaran and Bougie 2016). All standardized factor loadings are reported in Table 11.2, where their respective values exceeded 0.50 (ranging from 0.674 to 0.959). Moreover, the AVE values ranged from 0.625 to 0.822, whereas the CR values ranged from 0.832 to 0.93, thus providing sufficient evidence of internal consistency and validity.

The extent to which a construct is truly distinct from other constructs was measured by discriminant validity. Discriminant validity assumption is violated if the value of correlation among exogenous variables exceeds the square root of the

Table 11.2 Convergent validity

Constructs	Dimensions	Items	Factor loading	Factor loading	CR	AVE
Sustainable performance (SP)	Economic	ECOP06	0.514	0.899	0.933	0.822
		ECOP04	0.694			
		ECOP03	0.663			
		ECOP01	0.535			
	Environmental	ENP05	0.655	0.859		
		ENP04	0.521			
		ENP03	0.651			
		ENP02	0.708			
		ENP01	0.658			
	Social	SOCP05	0.688	0.959		
		SOCP04	0.742			
		SOCP03	0.574			
		SOCP02	0.592			
		SOCP01	0.644			
Green human resource management practices (GHRMP)	Green selection & recruitment	GSR03	0.741	0.872	0.857	0.667
		GSR02	0.786			
		GSR01	0.697			
	Green training & development	GTD03	0.785	0.814		
		GTD2	0.862			
		GTD01	0.771			
	Green assessment & rewards	GAR03	0.775	0.760		
		GAR02	0.838			
		GAR01	0.798			

Table 11.3 Discriminant validity

	CR	AVE	SP	GHRMP
SP	0.933	0.822	**0.907**	
GHRMP	0.857	0.667	0.730	**0.817**

SP Sustainable performance, *GHRMP* green human resource management practices

Fig. 11.5 Collective green HRM practices and sustainable performance. *SP* Sustainable performance , *GHRMP* green human resource management practices

average variance extracted (AVE). As shown in Table 11.3, AMOS output confirmed that the square root of AVE value (shown in the diagonal and represented in bold) is greater than the inter-construct correlation value. Thus, the assumption of discriminant validity is not violated. As the measurement model has been confirmed, the structural model was assessed next, to test the proposed hypotheses.

This study used structural equation modelling (SEM) to evaluate the structural model performance after validating second-order measurement models. Although the aim was to test all research hypotheses, in the sections below, the focus is on the three sub-hypotheses related to the relationship between green HRM practices (GSR, GTD, and GAR) and SP, respectively. According to H1, green HRM practices relate positively to sustainable performance (SP). Structural model results confirmed a direct positive relationship between GHMRP and SP, with the path coefficient value $b = 0.440$, critical ratio $t = 12.698$, and $p = 0.000$, as shown in Fig. 11.5.

As evidenced by structural model results shown in Fig. 11.6 H1a: green selection and recruitment are related positively with sustainable performance with path coefficient value $b = 0.630$, critical ratio $t = 12.698$, and $p = 0.$ 000. Likewise, H1b: green training and development were also confirmed to have a positive relationship with sustainable performance path coefficient value $b = 0.201$, critical ratio $t = 2.983$, and $p = 0.000$. However, H1c: green assessment and rewards were not significantly related to sustainable performance with path coefficient value $b = 0.094$, critical ratio $t = 1.504$, and $p = 0.$ 133.

AMOS output as results indicate a good model fit such as Chisqdf = 30.054, GFI = 0.983, CFI = 0.978, TLI = 0.912, and NFI = 0.977, REMSA = 0.043, RMR = 0.036 with P value 0.000. In the next section, all three sub-hypotheses are discussed separately. Table 11.4 summarizes the structural model results and sub-hypotheses.

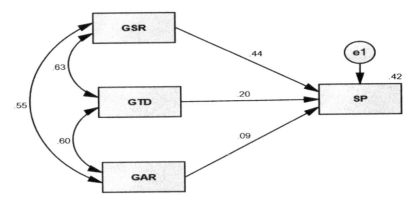

Fig. 11.6 Individual green HRM practices and sustainable performance

Table 11.4 Structural model hypotheses summary

S. No	Sub-hypothesis	S.E.	C.R.	P	Results
H1	GHRMP→SP	0.630	12.698	0.000	Accepted
H1a	GSR→SP	0.437	6.782	0.000	Accepted
H1b	GTD→SP	0.201	2.983	0.003	Accepted
H1c	GAR→SP	0.094	1.504	0.133	Rejected

SP Sustainable performance, *GSR* green selection and recruitment, *GTD* green training and development, *GAR* green assessment and rewards

11.4.1 Qualitative Data Analysis and Results

Semi-structured interviews were conducted with HR managers from ISO 14001-certified Malaysian manufacturing firms registered with FMM (2015). Purposive sampling was employed, and in total, nine participants were interviewed. Initially, interviews were recorded in the MP3 Audio gadget and later transcribed into Microsoft word document, which was uploaded as a file in NVivo 11. The main purpose of qualitative data analysis was to explore the basic and organizing themes within themes on green HRM practices and sustainable performance. First, word frequency analysis was performed to examine the most frequent words in the text. Next, data were coded in NVivo 11, and nodes were created. Finally, thematic network analysis was performed to explore basic, organizing, and global themes (Attride-Stirling 2001). NVivo 11 uses the terminology of nodes, where basic themes represent child nodes and, organizing, and global themes are represented by parent nodes. In total, nine (9) HRM managers from ISO 14001-certified manufacturing firms were interviewed. One manager was selected from each manufacturing firm stratum including (1) food, beverages, and tobacco, (2) chemical including petroleum, (3) electrical and electronics, (4) fabricated metals, (5) machinery, (6) plastic, (7) transport, (8) rubber, and (9) others. Manufacturing firms selected for interviews were mainly located in the central region (Kuala Lumpur, Selangor) and the southern region (Malacca, Johor Bahru) of peninsular Malaysia. This study employed a thematic network as a sophisticated qualitative technique step-by-step guide for thematic analysis (Attride-Stirling 2001). The thematic network is a tool for qualitative analysis to explore themes from the interview transcripts and organize them into a graphical representation. The thematic network consists of three stages: (a) reduction of the text, (b) exploration of the text, and (c) integration of exploration.

11.5 Mixed-Method Key Findings and Discussion

To achieve the targeted objective, this study proposed hypothesis H1: GHRM practices are positively related to sustainable performance. Besides, three sub-hypotheses such as H1a: Green selection and recruitment are positively related to sustainable performance, H1b: Green training and development are positively related to sustainable performance, and H1c: Green assessment and reward are positively related to sustainable performance were considered. The main hypothesis H1 was accepted. Similarly, two sub-hypotheses including H1a and H1b were also accepted. Results of H1, H1a, and H1b are consistent with the findings of Tang et al. (2017). However, only H1c sub-hypothesis was not supported as green assessment and rewards are not effective individually for explaining sustainable performance. Previous studies highlighted the reasons for making rewards more effective to improve environmental performance along with economic performance in achieving sustainable performance. Green compensation schemes should be associated with the performance of environmental objectives. Besides, poorly designed incentives may cause employees to avoid reporting environmental problems for the fear of being punished (del Brío et al. 2007). Companies should align HRM practices with the objectives of environmental management to enhance environmental sustainability (Jose Chiappetta Jabbour 2011).

11.5.1 Green HRM Practices and Sustainable Performance

The first probing interview question was, "In your opinion what are the important green HRM practices that explain the sustainable performance of the company?". Based on thematic analysis, three prominent green HRM practices include (1) green recruitment and selection, (2) green training and development, and (3) green assessment and rewards. Child nodes for green recruitment and selection were, e.g., selection criteria should be linked with environmental objectives, using green strategy to attract employees, and applicant knowledge about environmental aspects of the job. Similarly, child nodes for green training and development include environmental training as a priority, using environmental elements in training, and providing green programs. Finally, child nodes for green assessment and rewards are emerged as financial, non-financial, and rewards should be linked with environmental performance. All these sub-themes emerged to better understand and explain the concept of green HRM. Output generated through thematic analysis is shown in Fig. 11.7.

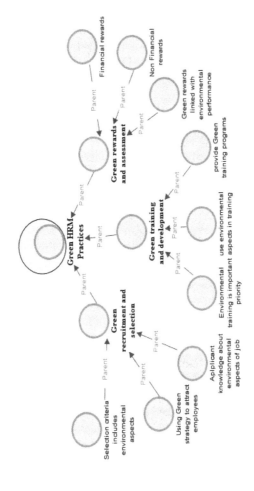

Fig. 11.7 Green HRM practices themes

Three sub-themes underpinned as a child node for each theme emerged (green recruitment and selection, training and development, assessment and rewards) that lead to the parent node, i.e., green HRM.

11.5.2 Assessment of Sustainable Performance Among Manufacturing Firms

The last part of thematic analysis explores sub-themes and their respective child nodes of sustainable performance as a central theme among ISO 14001-certified Malaysian manufacturing firms. Based on thematic analysis, three key themes including (1) economic performance, (2) environmental performance, and (3) social performance emerged. Child nodes for economic performance were return on investment (ROI), sales growth, and market share. Child nodes for environmental performance were efficiency and consumption of raw materials, the percentage of recycled materials, and resource consumption. Similarly, child nodes for social performance were employee satisfaction and motivation, employee training, education and safety, and turnover ratio. Figure 11.8 shows NVivo 11 output of the thematic analysis, explaining the sub-themes of sustainable performance and their child nodes.

11.5.3 Recommendations and Implications

This study brings several important implications for managers and manufacturing organizations. Manufacturing firms should implement GHRM practices to improve sustainable performance by reducing the imbalance between economic and

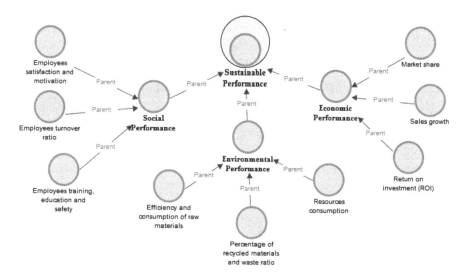

Fig. 11.8 Assessment of sustainable performance

environmental performance as suggested by Khan et al. (2017a). Green HRM practices (selection and recruitment) can also be used as an effective tool to build a green image and attract new talent for organizations. Manager's appraisal should be accountable for environmental performance outcomes as argued by Renwick et al. (2013). Currently, only 18% of manufacturing firms have EMS (ISO 14001) certification in Malaysia (FMM 2015) which is miserably low as compared to the most developed OECD countries. Thus, the findings of this study are quite relevant for Malaysia Environmental Performance Index (EPI), Global Environmental Performance Index (EPI), National Policy on the Environment (DASN), and Compendium of Environment Statistics Malaysia (CESM), to protect the environment from industrial waste and to strength environmental regulations.

11.6   Conclusion

This study makes a significant contribution in addressing important gaps identified in the literature on green HRM and provides a comprehensive insight into the sustainable performance of Malaysian manufacturing firms. By using the statistical techniques, this study established a direct positive relationship between green HRM practices and sustainable performance (SP) within ISO 14001-certified firms. To have a good outcome, one hypothesis and three sub-hypotheses are explored. Consequently, the major themes of green HRM practices emerged in explaining SP based on three dimensions, namely, economic, social, and environmental. This study makes a novel contribution to the field of green HRM and sustainable performance and recommends policy implications for Malaysian manufacturing firms that are the major engines for sustainable development and future growth of the economy.

Chapter Takeaways/Lessons

1. To highlight the importance of sustainability issues within manufacturing organizations in the Asian context.
2. To demonstrate the application of green HRM practices and how they can improve sustainable performance among Malaysian manufacturing firms.
3. To illustrate that by only employing green HRM practices, one cannot guarantee sustainability and organizational performance. Thus, the adoption of ISO 14001 certification is also one of the integral parts in addressing sustainability issues.
4. To highlight that the integration of both green HRM practices and ISO 14001certification helps manufacturing firms to minimize the imbalance between economic and environmental performance in improving overall sustainable performance.
5. To illustrate the application of mixed-method research design in green HRM practices and sustainable performance in manufacturing organizations.

Reflection Questions

1. Why is sustainability important for manufacturing organizations?
2. What are the key, green HRM practices that have been applied in Malaysian manufacturing firms?
3. How can manufacturing firms mitigate the imbalance between economic and environmental performance in achieving sustainable performance?
4. What are the major issues for manufacturing firms in adopting green HRM practices and ISO 14001 certification?
5. Why is mixed-method research design more effective as compared to mono-method research in the field of green HRM?

References

Ahmad, S. (2015). Green human resource management: Policies and practices. *Cogent Business & Management, 2*(1), 1030817.

Appelbaum, E. (2000). *Manufacturing advantage: Why high-performance work systems pay off.* Ithaca: Cornell University Press.

Attride-Stirling, J. (2001). Thematic networks: An analytic tool for qualitative research. *Qualitative Research, 1*(3), 385–405.

Boselie, P., Dietz, G., & Boon, C. (2005). Commonalities and contradictions in HRM and performance research. *Human Resource Management Journal, 15*(3), 67–94.

Boxall, P., & Purcell, J. (2003). *Strategy and HRM.* London: Palgrave.

Bryman, A., & Bell, E. (2015). *Business research methods.* New York: Oxford University Press.

Creswell, J. W. (2013). *Research design: Qualitative, quantitative, and mixed methods approaches.* Thousand Oaks: Sage.

Creswell, J. W., Plano Clark, V. L., Gutmann, M. L., & Hanson, W. E. (2003). Advanced mixed methods research designs. In A. Tashakkori & C. Teddlie (Eds.), *Handbook of mixed methods in social and behavioral research* (pp. 209–240). Thousand Oaks: Sage.

del Brío, J. Á., Fernandez, E., & Junquera, B. (2007). Management and employee involvement in achieving an environmental action-based competitive advantage: An empirical study. *The International Journal of Human Resource Management, 18*(4), 491–522.

Elkington, J. (1994). Towards the sustainable corporation: Win-win-win business strategies for sustainable development. *California Management Review, 36*(2), 90–100.

EPI. (2016). *Environmental Performance Index.* Retrieved from http://epi.yale.edu/reports/2016

Fauzi, H., Svensson, G., & Rahman, A. A. (2010). "Triple bottom line" as "sustainable corporate performance": A proposition for the future. *Sustainability, 2*(5), 1345–1360.

FMM. (2015). *Directory of Malaysian industries* (46th ed.). Kuala Lumpur: Federation of Malaysian Manufacturers.

Ghazilla, R. A. R., Sakundarini, N., Abdul-Rashid, S. H., Ayub, N. S., Olugu, E. U., & Musa, S. N. (2015). Drivers and barriers analysis for green manufacturing practices in Malaysian SMEs: A preliminary findings. *Procedia CIRP, 26*, 658–663.

Hair, J., Black, W., Babin, B., & Anderson, R. (2010). *Multivariate data analysis.* Upper Saddle River: Pearson Prentice Hall.

IEA. (2015). *World energy outlook special report: Energy and climate change.* Retrieved from https://www.iea.org/publications/freepublications/

Jabbour, C. J. C. (2013). Environmental training in organisations: From a literature review to a framework for future research. *Resources, Conservation and Recycling, 74*, 144–155.

Jabbour, C. J. C. (2015). Environmental training and environmental management maturity of Brazilian companies with ISO14001: Empirical evidence. *Journal of Cleaner Production, 96*, 331–338.

Jabbour, C. J. C., & de Sousa Jabbour, A. B. L. (2016). Green human resource management and green supply chain management: Linking two emerging agendas. *Journal of Cleaner Production, 112*, 1824–1833.

Jose Chiappetta Jabbour, C. (2011). How green are HRM practices, organizational culture, learning and teamwork? A Brazilian study. *Industrial and Commercial Training, 43*(2), 98–105.

Kahle, L. R., & Gurel-Atay, E. (2013). *Communicating sustainability for the green economy.* ME Sharpe.

Khan, N. U., Rasli, A. M., Hassan, M. A., Noordin, N. F. M., & Aamir, M. (2017a). Assessment of imbalance among environmental and economic performance within Malaysian manufacturing industry: A sustainable approach. *International Journal of Energy Economics and Policy, 7*(4), 149–155.

Khan, N. U., Rasli, A. M., & Qureshi, M. I. (2017b). Greening human resource management: A review policies and practices. *Advanced Science Letters, 23*(9), 8934–8938.

Maletič, M., Maletič, D., Dahlgaard, J. J., Dahlgaard-Park, S. M., & Gomišček, B. (2014). The relationship between sustainability–oriented innovation practices and organizational performance: Empirical evidence from slovenian organizations. *The Organ, 47*(1), 3–13.

Maletic, M., Maletic, D., Dahlgaard, J., Dahlgaard-Park, S. M., & Gomišcek, B. (2015). Do corporate sustainability practices enhance organizational economic performance? *International Journal of Quality and Service Sciences, 7*(2/3), 184–200.

Maletič, M., Maletič, D., & Gomišček, B. (2016). The impact of sustainability exploration and sustainability exploitation practices on the organisational performance: A cross-country comparison. *Journal of Cleaner Production, 138*, 158–169.

Nicolăescu, E., Alpopi, C., & Zaharia, C. (2015). Measuring corporate sustainability performance. *Sustainability, 7*(1), 851–865.

Nordin, N., Ashari, H., & Hassan, M. G. (2014). *Drivers and barriers in sustainable manufacturing implementation in Malaysian manufacturing firms.* Paper presented at the Industrial Engineering and Engineering Management (IEEM), 2014 IEEE International Conference on.

O'Donohue, W., & Torugsa, N. (2016). The moderating effect of 'Green'HRM on the association between proactive environmental management and financial performance in small firms. *The International Journal of Human Resource Management, 27*(2), 239–261.

Opatha, H., & Arulrajah, A. A. (2014). Green human resource management: Simplified general reflections. *International Business Research, 7*(8). Online, at http://www.ccsenet.org/journal/index.php/ibr/article/view/38976

Paauwe, J. (2009). HRM and performance: Achievements, methodological issues and prospects. *Journal of Management Studies, 46*(1), 129–142.

Renwick, D., Redman, T., & Maguire, S. (2008). Green HRM: A review, process model, and research agenda. *University of Sheffield Management School Discussion Paper, 2008*(1), 1–46.

Renwick, D. W., Redman, T., & Maguire, S. (2013). Green human resource management: A review and research agenda. *International Journal of Management Reviews, 15*(1), 1–14.

Sekaran, U., & Bougie, R. (2016). *Research methods for business: A skill building approach.* Hoboken: Wiley.

Sridhar, K., & Jones, G. (2013). The three fundamental criticisms of the triple bottom line approach: An empirical study to link sustainability reports in companies based in the Asia-Pacific region and TBL shortcomings. *Asian Journal of Business Ethics, 2*(1), 91–111.

Statistics, C. O. E. (2015). *Compendium of environment statistics.* Retrieved from https://www.statistics.gov.my/

Tang, G., Chen, Y., Jiang, Y., Paillé, P., & Jia, J. (2017). Green human resource management practices: Scale development and validity. *Asia Pacific Journal of Human Resources.*

Wisdom, J., & Creswell, J. (2013). *Mixed methods: Integrating quantitative and qualitative data collection and analysis while studying patient-centered medical home models.* Rockville: Agency for Healthcare Research and Quality.

An Analysis of Environmental Management in Developing Countries: Rubber Production in Sri Lanka

12

Lanumodara Fattrishiya Dedunu Zoysa Gunathilaka
and Kennedy D. Gunawardana

12.1 Introduction

The greatest environmental degradation of the planet started with the Industrial Revolution. At that point, environmental issues were not included in the global economic debate. Climate change is a universal challenge for the human race, requiring it to confront the significant challenges posed by reduction of carbon intensity from man-made activities in order to avoid irreversible catastrophic effects (Agan et al. 2013). In the broader perspective of sustainability, the natural environment is the pivot of the argument for organizations and their operations (Sarkis et al. 2010). Businesses need to consider the variety of events that may pose risks and take adequate steps to mitigate them. This will serve as an investment for the future of mankind, as well as a current need for organizations to contribute to environmental management (EM). EM is a management discipline and it should be protected by human beings by monitoring environmental hazards in order to minimize environmental degradation. It is highly politicized globally due to its value-laden nature, and it reflects the exercise of power by some groups over others. Barrow (2004, p. 8) posed a series of questions: "What exactly is environmental management? Is it a single field or discipline? Is it a process? Is it an agreed approach? Is it supposed to identify and pursue goals? Perhaps a philosophy? Or is it environment and development problem solving?" Sarkis et al. (2010) argued that environmental management has become a universal philosophy where individuals are involved in "greening"

L. F. D. Z. Gunathilaka (✉)
University of Sri Jayewardenepura, Nugegoda, Sri Lanka

K. D. Gunawardana
Department of Accounting, Faculty of Management Studies and Commerce, University of Sri Jayewardenepura, Nugegoda, Sri Lanka
e-mail: kennedy@sjp.ac.lk

S. Dhiman, R. Samaratunge (eds.), *New Horizons in Management, Leadership and Sustainability*, Future of Business and Finance, https://doi.org/10.1007/978-3-030-62171-1_12

237

their business organizations. There are many voices highlighting the importance of taking into consideration the restrictions imposed by environmentalists on the development of business activities (Salvadó et al. 2012).

Climatic changes produce major risk components that adversely affect businesses. Physical changes in the climate are anticipated risks in macro-circumstances which lead to extreme weather patterns and gradual transfiguration of the climate, which could affect the change in the equilibrium of businesses. It has already manifested itself in the sensitive rubber manufacturing process. Manufacturing has a role to play in both climate change mitigation and adaptation. Rubber is an essential agricultural commodity in the economy of Sri Lanka. The Central Bank report of Sri Lanka in 2014 highlighted that the foreign exchange earnings from rubber were 6 billion rupees in 2014. At present, the country ranks among the world's top ten largest producers and the seventh largest exporter in natural rubber. Unpredictable weather conditions and irregular seasonal changes created due to changes in the climate will adversely trigger irregular yields in raw rubber extraction. Organizations in the rubber sector are susceptible to weather sensitivity in the raw material stage.

12.1.1 History of the Rubber Industry

Though indigenous rainforest dwellers of South America have been using rubber for generations, it was not until 1839 that rubber had its first practical application in the industrial world. In the 1860s, Henry Wickham, a British citizen, smuggled some of the seeds from these rubber plants out of Brazil and sent 70,000 seeds to Sri Lanka for planting as commercial rubber in 1883. In 1998 the rubber industry was deemed to have produced equal amounts of raw rubber exports and quantity-wise the same for domestic consumption. It can be considered a remarkable year for the industry by being contingent or dependent on the use of latex for domestic purposes rather than for foreign trade. While domestic consumption has increased, the fluctuation of rubber prices may have caused a shift of the process to finished products and to get more value additions to 1 kg of processed rubber. The advancement of agro-based industries such as rubber is known to generate enormous quantities of solid and liquid waste. Environmental destruction is an inevitable consequence of human beings and has become more complex and multidimensional due to heavy utilization of resources and mounting up of by-products at a phenomenal rate, leading to high global pollution of air, land and water in the environment.

12.1.1.1 Climate Transition Risk in the Rubber Industry

The rubber manufacturing process is heavily dependent on heating which is the main cause of climate change due to emissions. Insufficient hydroelectric power and low rainfall in hydro catchment areas subject to weather changes have compelled industries to use furnace oil. Burning fossil fuel is a governing factor in increasing emissions (Gunathilaka and Gunawardana 2015). Environmental pollution, through the use of water in the industry, is yet another major concern. Environmental authorities have given organizations very strict norms to follow and are much more vigilant, as this issue has caused many problems in the recent past. Gunathilaka and Gunawardana (2015) found double the emission of conventional rubber compared to organic cultivation while operating other process parameters under the same conditions. The other danger associated with rubber cultivation highlighted by Houghton and Hackler (1999) is deforestation and burning of natural forest to convert land to rubber growth, which has reduced carbon stocks above- and below-ground, increasing the rate of carbon emissions (Table 12.1).

Rubber processing is categorized as one of the major polluting industries according to the published records by the CEA of Sri Lanka (Ranaweera 1991, as cited in Edirisinghe 2013). Edirisinghe (2013) stated that 40–50 l of effluents were discharged on average for 1 kg of rubber production. Further, due to total production of 114,700 metric tonnes in 2006, 4.5–5.7 billion litres of effluent have been produced and discharged to the environment (see Fig. 12.1). There are three main grades of natural rubber produced: ribbed smoked sheets (RSS), crepe rubber and centrifuge latex. Effluents generated by such production processes contain 30–40% rubber and 60–70% serum substances (Edirisinghe 2013). Rubber serum substances contain amino acids, carbohydrates and lactic acid. Substances required for plant growth and some chemicals such as sodium sulphite, ammonia or formalin, formic acid, acetic acid, oxalic acid, sodium bisulphite, metabisulphite and xylyl mercaptan are added in the processing of centrifuging. The most adverse effect that may be created due to influents is the pollution of groundwater. Effluents cannot be used for other purposes (Kudaligama et al. 2004, cited in Edirisinghe 2013). Heavy usage of energy is another factor in the industry contributing to more energy consumption. Another point of concern is solid and liquid waste generated from manufacturing operations. Thus, it is worthwhile investigating the real reasons for environmental transition from both environmental management and the environmental performance in the rubber industry.

Table 12.1 Central Environment Authority (CEA) standards for raw rubber processing effluent

Parameter	RSS	Crepe	TSR	Latex concentrate	Foam products	Dipped products	Regulatory standards
p^H	4.9	5.0	5.7	3.7	7.8	7.2	6.5–8.5
Settable solids	50	45	155	100	180	200	<250
Suspended solids	140	130	237	190	220	241	100
Total solids	3745	3500	1915	7576	2300	2457	1500[a]/1000
C.O.D	3300	3500	2740	6201	3500	2011	400
B.O.D	2630	2500	1747	3192	1700	1336	50/60[a]
Ammoniacal nitrogen	75	80	66	401	120	126	300[a]/40
Total nitrogen	500	550	147	616	156	180	300[a]/60
Sulphates	–	–	–	1610	69	72	1000

Source: Adapted from Seneviratne
[a]CEA standards centrifuged latex processing effluent (all values are in mg/l except for pH)

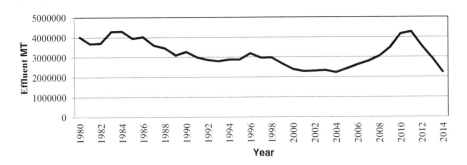

Fig. 12.1 Effluents discharged due to raw rubber processing. (Source: Author elaboration based on Rubber Development Department records)

One of the main targets of corrective action for climate change is to grow more rubber trees. The drive to grow more trees is now categorized under secondary "forest cover". This would certainly have better financial implications for the industry in general. Houghton and Hackler (1999) stress that burning of natural forest to convert land into rubber is feasible. Malhi et al. (2008) discuss the change in biomass carbon stocks. According to the Department of Census and Statistics, rubber cultivation has declined in recent years. In 2014, 134,000 hectares were cultivated, and in 2015 it was 135,000 hectares, showing a slight increase and a 0.7% growth compared to 2013/2014. The adverse weather conditions caused by climate change also resulted in calamitous landslides. Growing more rubber trees is considered a feasible solution that helps to reduce climate risks, while helping to reduce atmospheric carbon. This can be viewed as a good financial investment, as more rubber means better prices and also less interruption to manufacturing.

Montabon et al. (2007) emphasized that the contradiction between environmental management and solid performance has been of great interest in research literature. Whether or not EM improves on performance (Yang et al. 2011), knowledge of the topic is still limited and must grow to allow a unified theory to emerge. To some extent, results are isolated and conflicting. Some positive, others negative, some show mixed or no result, which is somewhat confusing. In recent literature there is a discrepancy in empirical findings within the framework to obtain the significant determinants of EM. Nevertheless, a few studies have investigated the role of environmental investment (EI) within the adoption of EM. The aim of this paper is to provide further insight into the role of EI in the adoption of EM to achieve business performance (BP) based on a four-concept balanced scorecard. We start with the relationship between BP and EM. We then present an integrated framework that includes EM, EI and BP. In the next section we provide a research model and a conceptual framework that presents key variables based on literature reviews. In the hypotheses development section, the inter-relationships between variables are defined and explained. We analyse whether the adoption of EM enhanced by BP is moderated by EI efforts within the organization. The results overwhelmingly show that, for the Sri Lankan rubber manufacturing industry, environmental investments negatively moderate the relationship between EM and BP. In subsequent sections we discuss the literature, research methodology and results, the theoretical and managerial implications, limitations and future research directions.

12.2 Theoretical Basis of the Study

12.2.1 Ostrom's View on the Collective Action Theory and Climate Change

In a study of the ecological system, Ostrom's theory is considered appropriate to address present-day ecological challenges. Ostrom (2008a) emphasizes that in the future, many of the pressing problems faced are more on a global scale, posing difficulty in establishing an effective governance arrangement on a global base rather than on a local scale and ignoring the protection of a common heritage. The challenge is to common-pool resources (CPRs) and the tragedy for human beings, the failure to halt massive overfishing of oceans, major deforestation and excessive emission of carbon dioxide to the atmosphere from works and much more. Protecting these resources without violating CPR through minimum impact on the environment will clearly improve environmental performance in the global context. Separateness of use is a characteristic derived from CPR, which means that used units of atmosphere, water and climate are a challenge for future generations to facilitate using units and/or joining use of nature due to rapid degradation. Failure to distinguish between the subtracting of used units and the joining of the natural resource system has contributed to confusion in the past about the attributing common-pool resources (Ostrom 1985). Water courses, air basins and global atmospheric sinks have a comparable capacity to absorb pollutants, but Ostrom (2010) argued atmospheric greenhouse gas (GHG) sinks fulfil the first priority more than water and air basins of CPR due to the use of units of sink services being different or deductible.

Thus the concept of maximum sustainable yield is important in the analysis of CPR management for environmental performances at the global level. Ostrom (2008a, b) defined CPRs as "the maximum numbers of use units that can be obtained from year to year while still maintaining the resource system's capability to continue to yield these units" (p. 5). Paavola argued that, with the distribution of sustainable capacity among the competing users to avoid deterioration of the atmosphere (damp yard) from global heat escalating, owing to the uncertainty of practice and the "crowding effect" or "over-use", the problem of air, the atmosphere and water problem, etc. do not occur in regard to the use of such collective goods (Ostrom 1985). The cost associated with exclusion of the tragedy of global climate change or environmental degradation depends on the type of resource system, technology associated with exclusion, entry and exit rules and resource boundaries (Ostrom 1985). Also, the condition of being a CPR is exclusion of unauthorized users and avoiding dumping (Paavola 2008b). The absence of clear borderlines and perfect mixing of emissions of GHGs in the atmosphere contribute to the difficulty of exclusion (Ostrom 2008a, b).

Ostrom suggested the requirement of analyses of macro-interface between humanity and the biosphere to get a better understanding of the social context of post-environmental change and the complexity of conceptualization of socially constructed and politicized biosphere in modern climate and environmental change. The atmosphere remains abstract in conceptualization. Social construction is difficult to communicate and is socially fragmented. Therefore it is very difficult to signify and is imbued with meaning (Rabinowitz 2010), but obstacles are associated with atmospheric conditions. Social science intervenes with the importance of implementing a better theoretical analysis to understand a coherent picture of climate change. The other aspect is that three decades of effort have been put into gaining theoretical insight into the abstract syndrome. Solving global climate change problems is not by acting alone. If one country solves that problem, there will be absence or dearth of wealthier countries participating to reduce risk in climate change (Ostrom 2010). Hence, it requires cooperation between countries through an internationally recognized framework and strong urgent collective action.

12.2.2 Ostrom's Institutional Behaviour and Environmental Change

Ostrom was preoccupied with paradoxes and contradictions surrounding human beings and their choices. She focused on communities' interface with their ecosystem and internal dynamics associated with securing long-term sustainable yields (Rabinowitz 2010). Empirical work on CPRs conducted by Ostrom provides a basic list of institutional characteristics that affect improvement of commonly held resources. Ostrom's list includes a clearly defined system of boundaries to the exclusion of non-members and rules governing resource usage which are suitable for local conditions and wide participation of local stakeholders in the design and implementation of rules and decisions governing the system. Ostrom generally was aware of social and cultural factors, "her work often seems to skim the surface of observable social and cultural data in linear, mono dimensional fashion" (Rabinowitz 2010, p. 106). Rabinowitz (2010) was disappointed in results when theorizing the global commons and the atmosphere through institutional analysis of CPR systems and defined the atmosphere and environment as an open access of universal commons. Paavola (2008a) explains atmospheric sinks for GHGs as a CPR. Her sinks are stock resources with the economics label "core variable" meaning "stock variable" of GHGs and the fringe variable which explains the flow variable as used units that mean GHGs embedded in the atmosphere.

A tertiary pressure is rooted in institutional sociology which proposes that firms respond to institutional pressure. Institutional theory places particular emphasis on the legitimation process and tendency for institutionalized organizational structures and procedures to be taken for granted, regardless of their efficiency implications (Hoffman and Ventresca 2002). Further emergence of global principles and standards is changing public expectations of companies, and triple-bottom-line reporting has increased demands for accountability, transparency and emphasis on financial, social and ecological performance. Jennings and Zandbergen (1995) were among the first to apply institutional theory to explain firms' adoption of EM practices. They argue that, because coercive forces, primarily in the form of regulations and regulatory enforcement, have been the main impetus for EM practices, firms in each industry have implemented similar practices.

Levy and Rothenberg (2002) describe several mechanisms by which institutionalism can encourage heterogeneity. First, they argue that institutional forces are transformed as they permeate organizational boundaries, because they are filtered and interpreted by managers according to firms' organizational unique history and culture. For example, "a firm's history with environmental technology influenced the degree to which future technological options were viewed as an opportunity or a threat". Second, they describe how an institutional field may contain conflicting institutional pressures that require prioritization by managers. Third, they describe how multinational and diversified organizations operate within several institutional fields both at social and organizational levels which expose them to different sets of institutionalized practices and norms. Hoffman (2001) cited nine institutional actors whom we believe most likely to directly influence environmental practices at the facility level, such as politicians, regulators, customers, competitors and local communities. Considering these points, institutional pressure is critical in converting a balanced scorecard into a green concept. This must be added into institutional theory because it shows the diversity of the institutions driving environmental pressures, including external and internal pressures to the organization and within each organization.

12.2.3 Ostrom's Conventional Collective Action Theory and Stakeholder Participation

Millions of actors favourably affect the global environment. All receive benefits from reduced greenhouse gas emissions, treated waste water, avoiding air pollution and protecting drinking water resources, but the problem is whether they benefit or not, do they pay any of the costs. In other words, the beneficiaries cannot be excluded from the benefit of cleaner air. Trying to solve the problem of providing good for the public is a classic collective action dilemma—and potentially the largest dilemma the world has ever knowingly faced (Ostrom 2009). Ostrom is asserting the fact of wide participation of local stakeholders, and Ostrom's social and cultural data combining with Paavola's (2011) collective ownership and management as well as the widely shared values associated with individual behaviour and voluntary engagement to mitigate atmospheric sinks for GHGs and degradation of CPRs encourage ascertaining who is having a stake in this issue and who are the interested parties that influence that matter in order to change to individual behaviours through wide participation of local stakeholders by combining social and cultural data in stakeholder network. The most interesting part highlighted by Rabinowitz (2010) is "like those of the other institutional analysts, it is admirably effective in shedding light on the dynamics governing the interface between the local groups and their immediate common" (p.108).

It further emphasizes the significance of social relationships among interested parties and individual social participation in network with better theoretical analysis to understand the coherent picture of environmental change. Social network analysis will give light to the theoretical analysis and empirical understanding to determine who the stakeholders are that have involved themselves in the present climate revolution issues and how the tie relationship is among each participant in the network. The constraint is the cultural and behavioural consideration among individual members who do not contribute any support to intensify the strength of the theoretical framework in the development of the debate on climate crisis. As the definition given by Freeman, public participation is increasingly embedded in national and international environmental policy, and it is necessary to identify who is affected by the action and decision-making that they take and which one has the power to influence their outcome (cited by Davis et al. 2009). Starik considered environment as a part of SH during the categorization among other SHs. Stakeholder theory also cannot satisfactorily treat enterprise in an environmentally ethical and responsible fashion considering the increasingly important problems of managing business enterprise in an environmentally ethical and responsible fashion, and Starik states most definitions of the concept of "stakeholder" include only human entities. This paper advances the argument that the non-human natural environment can be integrated into the stakeholder management concept. This argument includes the observations that the natural environment is finally becoming recognized as a vital component of the business environment, that the stakeholder concept is more than a human political/economic one and that non-human nature currently is not adequately represented by other stakeholder groups.

12.2.4 Natural Resource-Based View (NRBV) of the Firm and the Environment

The detailed analysis of firms' environmental management practices and their commitment towards the environmental achievement of the organization is needed to successfully tackle the socioeconomic challenges in society. Therefore, appropriately addressing environmental challenges imposed by a natural environment, researchers focus on two main theoretical streams:

1. The natural resource-based view (Hart 1995). This theoretical approach is the cornerstone of a researcher's argument; it attempts to answer to the challenge of sustainable development by taking a resource-based view as a reference.
2. Resource-based view of the firm (Peteraf 1993 as cited in Salvadó et al. 2012). The incorporation of environmental arguments to process, products and organizational modes to the firm require the development of a number of specific resources and capabilities.

Oliver (1991) discussed that organizations can have power over others by controlling scarce resources and argued that impacts of achieving institutional belief instead of scarce resources. Further, Oliver emphasized that organizational choice is controlled by a variety of external pressures as described in resource dependency and institutional perspectives. Using this theory in the fields of environmental performance started with Hart (1995), who presented the first theoretical paper that addressed the RBV (resource-based view) theory in the corporate environmental phenomenon. Hart is very concerned about the natural environment and thought that it has totally ignored the concept in the RBV. Hart believes that the NRBV approach is one of the major contributions to the field of environment/sustainability. NRBV emphasized that resource management and eco-development assumptions are combined in firms, in order to achieve competitive advantages through sustainable economic development. This theory attempts to combine the RBV with the constraints imposed by the natural environment. NRBV incorporates some of the important assumptions used by neoclassical logic when referring to competitive advantages through low-cost strategies. His argument was that cost reduction can be achieved by pollution prevention, waste management, recycling, emission control and other kinds of activities. Hart's theory is based on the condition that the three interrelated strategies, namely, pollution prevention, product stewardship and sustainability development, are used. Hart further mentioned that NRBV goes beyond pollution prevention and it incorporates eco-development. To fulfil the gap between resource management and eco-development, NRBV has proffered a better contribution. This theory delineated that proactive environmental management is a critical source for firm performance. Empirical research conducted by several researchers, namely, Russo and Fouts (1997), empirically found that higher levels of corporate environmental performance (CEP) relate positively to superior financial performances. This theory considers the natural environment as a source of new and imaging business opportunities and firms that are able to adapt their activity to those constraints will drive the economy of the future.

12.2.5 The Relationship Between Stakeholder Theory, BSC and BP

Orts and Strudler (2002) discussed that, however anyone redefines stakeholder's (SHs) and however one may balance SHs interest, the SH theory does not provide any detail for managers in the sense of how to do what is right. Based on this argument, we built up a rationale about "balancing stake holders" which is more vital than managing stakeholders.

Balance scorecard (BSC) is introduced by Norton and Kaplan in which a score system for managers is available to maximize stakeholder values. In particular, firms adapted it to the SH theory which politicized the firms. This will be a handicap for rivals due to the nature of empowerment of performance to exercise their own functions by spending resources of the firm. Jensen (2001) stated that at the same time, companies apply the so-called BSC approach as a managerial equivalent of stakeholder theory as a performance measurement system. Further, Jensen suggested that managers should be encouraged to use drivers of performance measures to comprehend how to improve their scores. With no way to keep scores, the stakeholder theory will lead to keeping managers unaccountable for their action or task to be performed. It is conscious that such a theory will encourage internal stake-holders to motivate self-interest in their firms. Cooperate purpose or vision and value maximization is not a technique to create energy and enthusiasm of employ-ees and managers. The assessment of the success and the failure of the firm depends on the long-term market value which becomes the scorecard of managers, directors and others who are used to assess success or failure of the organization. The value maximization is a complement from corporate vision, strategy and tactics as a coop-erate scorecard to withstand the rigours of present competitiveness. The abovemen-tioned previous knowledge of stakeholders encourage the BSC concept in applying measuring performance in the organization.

The sub-section below (discussion under the construct and core concepts) dis-cusses a comprehensive review of the BSC as a theory to measure firm's perfor-mance by incorporating environmental performance activities into cooperate scorecards. According to the researcher's discernment, the BSC has not discussed all aspects where the stakeholders are involved in the underlying issues, the internal performance perspectives it covered regarding internal stakeholders, learning and growth perspectives, the internally interested actors who involve themselves with the process, customer perspectives that go beyond the internal SHs and the more discussions on externally influencing parties, financial perspectives that cover the institutions' involvements with financing and other bodies who are engaged with profit maximization. But what is lacking here are the communities and other actors such as neighbour organizations who are interested with the issue to control envi-ronmental performances in organizations. There is a discrepancy in applying the SH theory into the BSC concept due to lack of participation of some interested actors in measuring performance through BSC. Further, it is critical to consider on how to incorporate environmental aspects to BSC as a separate perspective or include it into the current four perspectives. Based on the institutional aspects, the researcher aspires to investigate the theoretical aspects involved with institutionalism and their influence on organizations. Institutional theory has explained the theoretical basis.

12.3   Hypothesis Development

In this research, we have defined each construct in terms of essential characteristics with the support of the relevant literature base. Table 12.2 is a summary of each construct (definitions and supporting literature). Figure 12.2 is a research frame-work that represents how EM, environmental management practices (EMPs), envi-ronmental performance (EP) and business performance are related.

12.3.1 Environmental Management

According to Sharma and Vredenburg (1998), SMEs perform both proactively and reactively environmental practices towards elimination of environmental pollutants or waste. Further mentioned in some papers, such activities have ranged from waste

Table 12.2 Definitions and supporting literature

Variables	Definition	Supporting literature
Environmental management	The system that anticipates and avoids, or solves, environmental and resource conservation issues	
Environmental management practices	A set of programs to improve environmental performance of processes and products in the forms of environmental management system, life-cycle analysis, design for environment, environmental certification	Montabon et al. (2007)
Environmental performance	The degree to which an organization improves its performance in respect to its environmental responsibilities	Montabon et al. (2007)
Waste treatment	Stabilization, preferably by accelerated degradation, so that the final residues produced are either non-toxic and incapable of further change, that is, they are completely mineralized, or able to find ready entry into the various natural bio-geochemical (elemental) cycles that govern materials cycling in the environment, without causing distortion in any cycle relative to another	Hamer (2003 as cited in Agan et al. 2013)
Reduction	Focusing on preventing pollution at the source (in products as well as manufacturing process) rather than managing it	Srivastava (2007 as cited in Agan et al. 2013)
Internal recycling	The reuse of materials from returned products without conserving the product identity	Kapetanopoulou and Tagaras (2011, as cited in Agan et al. 2013)
Remanufacturing	The degree to which the firm rebuilds a product where some of the parts or components are recovered or replaced	Montabon, Sroufe and Narasimhan (2007)
Environmental design	Using environmentally sensitive design process does in fact result in greater product innovation and thus higher firm performance	Montabon et al. (2007)
Environmental management system	Supplier environmental relations, knowledge base of team members, environmental cost systems, environmental impact assessment, impact reduction and environmental training	
Environmental investment	Realized decisions to deploy resources and commitment to environmental management	
ROA	Profit before interest and tax (PBIT)/total assets (total equity + total debt)	
ROS	Profit before tax (operating profit)/total sales	
ROI/ROE	Profit after tax (PAT − profit for the year)/total equity	

Source: Author's own elaboration

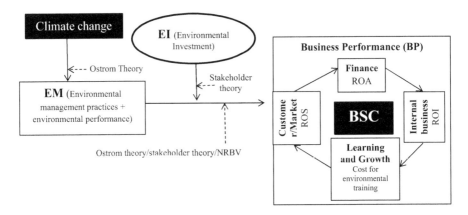

Fig. 12.2 Theoretical framework: climate change, EM, EI and BP. (Source: Authors' own elaboration)

treatment to developing sophisticated environmental management practices. Argan cleared that in the past literature, these activities were labelled as actions, performance, behaviours, applications, practices or systems. In the same paper, the researcher has discussed it as "process" because it fits their process framework. In this study the researcher categorized and labelled the term as "practices". The practices discussed in this paper are waste treatment, emission reductions, recycling, environmental innovations and environmental management system. Environmental management system (EMS) is a systematic approach to managing the environment which is reflected in the company's vision, mission, policy, strategies and actions. In addition to that, companies take it as top priority activity in environmental process to establish a standard EMS within boundaries. White et al. (1995) considered recycling, alternative energy and waste reduction in their research. Cohen et al. (1995) yet again highlighted that toxic emissions as Hart with different other variables such as superfund sites, environmental litigation, accident frequency and regulatory compliance record. Most researchers selected emission as an environmental performance variable in their research. Nonetheless some of them mixed it with other parameters as well. According to their selected variables, it is clear that there are different choices in selection of environmental variables.

12.3.2 Business Performance

Santos and Brito (2012) found six dimensions in connection with measuring firm performance and invited researchers to use subjective indicators to measure firm performance across industry. They stressed that "the dimensional structure" could also help scholars select performance indicators – for specific research problems that comprehensively cover the relevant dimensions of performance related to their investigation. Operating performance is the performance of a company based on the profit recorded in their financial statements. It is measured by return on equity

(ROE) and return on assets (ROA). ROE and ROA indicate how efficiently the company generates profits or earnings based on shareholders' equity and company's total assets, respectively. These ratios are the most basic and fundamental in analysing the profitability and performance of the company not only in empirical research but also by practitioners such as auditors, financial analysts and bankers. Moreover, many researchers also use these measurements as proxies for business performance.

Throughout the analysis, two different types of firm performance measures were used such as return on assets (ROA), return on sales (ROS) and return on equity (ROE). Market analysts widely used return on assets as a measurement tool for the firms' performance. Return on equity (ROE) is a measure of the performance of the firm relative to shareholder investment. Since the measure of shareholder returns is important, rather than overall firm profitability, interest expenses are subtracted out of income for this measure. As a test of robustness, an alternative formula was also used, where ROA is defined as income before extraordinary items, divided by average total assets plus accumulated depreciation. The researcher believes that if a company can implement good environmental practices, the company will indeed achieve benefits in operations. However, some may build an argument to say that to operate in an environmentally friendly manner, it has to incur additional expense in certification, annual audits, inspections, etc. that brings nothing in return. The author believes that the return on such investments cannot be measured by the profit which is only a tangible indication of the organization. Good will, reputation, market demand, competitiveness and the value passed on to the society are intangibles that will register the organization in the hearts of its customers, employees, the community and society and also as a global leader (Fig. 12.3).

12.3.3 Environmental Management and Business Performance

Material consumption, waste and emissions are problems associated with industrialization, and companies should have to represent an opportunity for companies to improve their capabilities in the field of pollution prevention and ecological efficiency (Hart and Milstein 2003). "Companies that carry out pollution prevention strategies focusing on environmental innovation have a resource base that enhances their ability to generate profits and also makes them able to protect themselves against future risk" (Shrivastava 1995, cited in Salvadó et al. 2012, p. 80). Environmental concern in strategic decision-making is relevant in incorporating with the natural environment. Reduction of waste emissions will enable to reduce cost and increase profits (Sharma and Vredenburg 1998) (Fig. 12.4).

Sharma et al. (1999) encouraged environmental features of a product and how that could add value to business (environmental design: environmental performance of products, packaging and sustainable business management). Small medium enterprises (SMEs) perform both proactively as well as reactively, and Environmental management practices towards elimination of environmental pollutants or waste (Sharma and Vredenburg 1998); Correa et al. 2008 as cited Agan 2013). Further

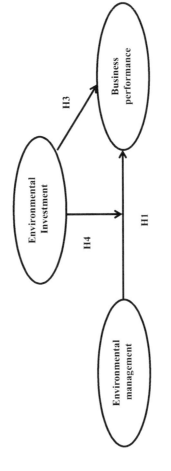

Fig. 12.3 Research model

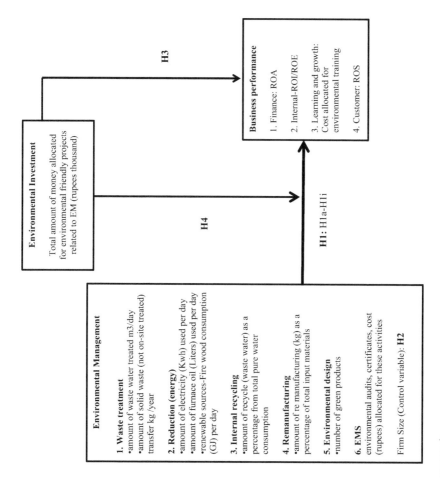

Fig. 12.4 Measurement framework

mentioned in some papers, such activities have ranged from waste treatment to developing sophisticated environmental management practices.

The determinants used to measure EM in this paper are waste treatment, energy reductions, recycling, environmental design and environmental management system (environmental training, certificates and audits). Environmental management system (EMS) is a systematic approach to manage the environment which is reflected in the company's vision, mission, policy, strategies and actions; in addition to that, companies take it as a top priority activity in environmental process to establish a standard EMS within boundaries. In 1992, the first EMS standard was applied in the UK. In 1996, the first EMS standard on the international scale, known as the ISO 14001, was introduced and further reviewed in 2004.

Therefore, the hypotheses are:

- *H1a: There is a significant relationship between amount of waste water treated m3/day and business performance.*
- *H1b: There is a significant relationship between solid waste (not on-site treated) transfer/kg/year and business performance.*
- *H1c: There is a significant relationship between amount of electricity (Kwh) used per day and business performance.*
- *H1d: There is a significant relationship between amount of furnace oil (litres) used per day and business performance.*
- *H1e: There is a significant relationship between renewable sources-firewood consumption (GJ) per day and business performance.*
- *H1f: There is a significant relationship between amount of recycled (waste water) as a percentage of total pure water consumption and business performance.*
- *H1g: There is a significant relationship between amounts of remanufacturing (kg) as a percentage of total input materials and business performance.*
- *H1h: There is a significant relationship between environmental design (number of green products) and business performance.*
- *H1i: There is a significant relationship between EMS (environmental training and audits, certificate, cost (rupees) allocated for these activities) and business performance.*

12.3.4 Environmental Management, Environmental Investment and Business Performance

Murovec et al. (2012) suggest that investments associated with environmental aspects have become very essential in today's context. Delmas and Pekovic (2015) stress that firms must reduce their natural resource consumption by investments in reusing and recycling of raw materials and waste management, due to the current environmental degradation. Financial viability of climate change mitigation and the associated financial risk in the performance of capital stock and business model portfolios need attention for long-term feasibility in business ventures. Testa et al. (2014) stress that requirements of best environmental management practices to mitigate negative environmental externalities are not yet settled. Figge and Hahn (2013) stress that environmental investment associates with company environmental growth, promotion of innovation, increasing productivity and resource efficiency. Lefebvre et al. (2003) emphasize that a higher amount of investments on environmental aspects and proactive environmental management issues may affect to create a positive association between the environmental performance in business and managerial actions. Heidrich and Tiwary (2013) emphasize the requirement of introducing environmental investment for achieving environmental performance by addressing small and micro firms. Ateş et al. (2012) tested the relationship between proactive environmental strategy and the large amount of environmental investment. The researcher found that environmental investments mediate the relationship between proactive environmental strategy and environmental performance. Cheng and Liao (2012) stress that financial allocation for environmental problems mitigation and adoption has often been contradicted in small companies; therefore, promoting environmental awareness and efficient environmental operation is necessary.

- *H2a: There is a significant relationship between environmental investment and firm performance.*
- *H2b: There is a significant relationship between environmental management practices and firm performance that grows stronger as environmental investment increases.*

12.4 Research Methodology

12.4.1 Research Database

In order to test the proposed hypotheses, we use the six determinants of EM. Secondary data was taken from 30 rubber manufacturing organizations from the time period 2012–2016, in Sri Lanka.

12.4.2 Research Design

We selected to conduct panel data to examine the driving effect of EM on BP. Prior studies are employed with event study, structural equation techniques and other statistical techniques based on perception measures of respondents, and only few studies had been carried out based on panel data techniques. Environmental measures should be better considered in long perspectives through different cross-sections (time series cross-sectional data). Therefore, we adopted the panel regression method to evaluate the impact of EM on BP from 30 rubber manufacturing companies from 2012 to 2016. The researcher decided to employ two different panel estimation methods: fixed effect (FE) and the random effect (RE) models to evaluate the relationships among variables.

12.4.2.1 Econometric Specifications

The analysis of the empirical relationship of environmental and business performance of organizations involves an estimation procedure based on panel data evaluation. Given the nature of the research work and the quantum of data, research studies data properties from econometric perspectives with the help of descriptive statistics and unit root test. This will help us by applying a random effect panel data model and a fixed effect panel data model. The model is derived in the traditional manner from the production function; the performance of a business is expressed as a function of environmental management such as furnace oil consumption, waste water treatment, waste water recycling, etc. Consequently the random effect model for specifying business performance is expressed as follows:

$$y_{it} = \beta_0 + \beta x_{it} + \mu_j + \varepsilon_{it} \tag{12.1}$$

$$
\begin{aligned}
y_{it} = {} & \beta_0 + \beta_1 \text{Size}_{it} + \beta_2 \text{ waste water treated} \\
& + \beta_3 \text{ solid waste transfer} + \beta_4 \text{ electricity use} \\
& + \beta_5 \text{ furnace oil use} + \beta_6 \text{ fire} - \text{woodconsumption} \\
& + \beta_7 \text{ recycling} + \beta_8 \text{ remanufacturing} \\
& + \beta_9 \text{ environmental design} + \beta_{10} EMS + \mu_j + \varepsilon_{it}
\end{aligned}
\tag{12.2}
$$

The equations of the model are grouped into two, Eqs. 12.2 and 12.3; Eq. 12.1 of the models signifies that the data are non-stationary meaning it cannot be co-integrated to convert the data to stationary; Eq. 12.3 was formed with first difference (Δ) on each variable which shows that the model is converted to first difference and the data has now become stationary.

$$
\begin{aligned}
\Delta y_{it} = {} & \beta_0 + \beta_1 \Delta (\text{Size})_{it} + \beta_2 \Delta (\text{waste water treated}) \\
& + \beta_3 \Delta (\text{solid waste transfer}) \\
& + \beta_4 \Delta (\text{electricity use}) + \beta_5 \Delta (\text{furnace oil use}) \\
& + \beta_6 \Delta (\text{fire} - \text{wood consumption}) + \beta_7 \Delta (\text{recycling}) \\
& + \beta_8 \Delta (\text{remanufacturing}) + \beta_9 \Delta (\text{environmental design}) \\
& + \beta_{10} \Delta (\text{training and audits}) EMS + \mu_j + \varepsilon_{it}
\end{aligned}
\tag{12.3}
$$

where i denotes the firm ($i = 1\ldots n$, $n = 30$ units under observation); j shows the industry = rubber industry and t ($t = 1\ldots t = 5$) years/time period of data collected. In this equation μ is the industry-related fixed effects; ε is the standard error term, where y_{it} denotes the observation of the dependent variable (business performance) of a firm I in a period of t. X_{it}, represents the set of time-variant independent variables (regresses), and μj is the time-invariant explanatory variables. Then the explanatory variables, size represents the firm size, and as the proxies for environmental management, the researcher takes furnace oil consumption, waste treatment, recycling, electricity use, furnace oil use, firewood consumption, remanufacturing, environmental design and environmental training and audits (EMS), respectively. Δ y_{it} is the first difference of firm performance; Δ (furnace oil) is the first difference of furnace oil consumption; Δ (waste treatment) is the Δ of waste water treatment; and Δ recycle is Δ of recycle of material. The same principle applies for the four aspects of BSC (finance, ROA; internal, ROI/ROE; sales, ROS; and cost allocated for environmental training and audit, T&D). In this analysis, two models of random and fixed effects were used, where the fixed effect model has the same issue of correlated time-invariant effects in repressors, but it does not appear in the random effect model. For the specification of fixed effects, panel data model is as follows,

$$\varepsilon_{it} = \xi i + \acute{\eta}_{it} \qquad (12.4)$$

where $\acute{\eta}_{it}$ is composed of the disturbance ξ_i reflecting left-out variables that are remaining broadly over each firm over the time period and idiosyncratic error (considered as time-persistent). The main assumption in fixed effect model is that individual effect ξ_i is correlated with time-variant independent variables X_{it}. In here ξ_i is a constant or dummy variable for each unit in analysis. In this model ξ_i is assumed to be time-variant independent variables.

12.5   Data Analysis and Results

12.5.1 Descriptive Statistics

This study mainly employed a quantitative approach; unit of analysis is rubber manufacturing firms. Figure 12.5 depicted that 90% of companies registered under BOI, and out of 90% of the companies, 70% were located inside the BOI promisors.

Figure 12.5 depicted that 90% of companies registered under BOI, and out of 90% of the companies, 70% were located inside the BOI promisors.

Figure 12.6 shows that of 30 companies, 14 produce gloves, 5 produce tyres, 3 produce natural foam, 7 produce centrifuge latex, etc. Seventeen percent of the companies manufactured dry rubber, and the other companies were manufacturing latex-based products.

12.5.2 The Summary of Statistics

In the econometric analysis, the researcher built up a panel data based on 30 rubber manufacturing companies in Sri Lanka from 2012 to 2016. Table 12.3 depicts the mean, the standard deviation, the maximum, the minimum and the number of observations for each of the variables and elaborates the correlation coefficients between the dependent, independent and control variables along with correlation matrix. Table 12.3 depicts the positive correlation between IV-D2-M2 and ROA, providing evidence to justify H1d. The correlation between IV-D1-M2 and ROA is negative, and the correlation between IV-D3 and ROA is positive, providing evidence to support Hb and Hf, respectively.

The mean and median in Table 12.4 were computed to find the central tendency of each variable for the 30 firms in the sample. The standard deviation indicates the

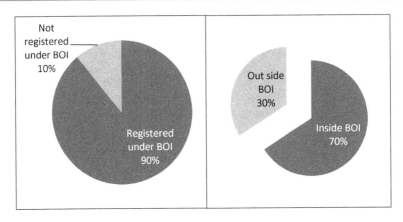

Fig. 12.5 Company (%) registered under Board of Investment and location (internal/out) BOI

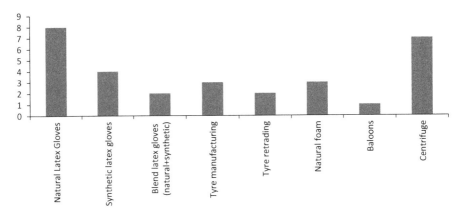

Fig. 12.6 Company (%) categorization – goods of manufacturing

sample's dispersion level of the variables. According to the above table, the average return on assets (ROA) is 31.2% which means about 31% of the return on assets of private sector rubber companies during 2012–2016. Further the average return on sales is almost 10.59% (median 2.6%) in private sector rubber companies in Sri Lanka over 2012–2016. When considering average waste generated -m³ per day of the companies (IV-D1-M1), the average cubic meters of waste generated per day is 274.96 cubic meters which means that 275 m³ of waste water was discharged from private sector rubber companies in Sri Lanka during the period 2012–2016 (Table 12.5).

Table 12.3 The correlation between dependent and independent variables (first-difference variables)

	DV-D1	DV-D2	DV-D3	DV-D4	IV-D1-M1	IV-D1-M2	IV-D2-M1	IV-D2-M2	IV-D2-M3	IV-D3	IV-D4	IV-D5	IV-D6	CONV	MV
DV-D1	1.000000														
DV-D2	0.015561	1.000000													
DV-D3	0.02456	0.04780	1.00000												
DV-D4	-0.135372	0.120145	-0.242120	1.00000											
IV-D1-M1	0.043434	-0.062226	0.105678	-0.111911	1.000000										
IV-D1-M2	-0.090707	-0.008892	0.098726	0.346445	0.080969	1.000000									
IV-D2-M1	0.221537	0.228304	-0.261320	0.070618	-0.114696	0.219260	1.000000								
IV-D2-M2	0.006853	0.011842	0.006853	0.155025	-0.089261	0.076453	-0.111911	1.000000							
IV-D2-M3	0.046548	-0.085295	0.052367	0.146686	0.016811	-0.006513	0.146686	-0.466247	1.000000						
IV-D3	0.070618	0.001071	0.150624	-0.139060	0.004525	0.261055	0.024412	0.018896	0.012535	1.000000					
IV-D4	0.308826	0.098726	0.033412	0.152614	0.012602	-0.116083	0.193792	-0.261320	0.070675	-0.115211	1.000000				
IV-D5	0.101525	0.209533	0.007834	0.124412	0.066989	0.050385	0.248280	-0.049943	0.086124	-0.073708	0.284199	1.000000			
IV-D6	-0.089261	0.076453	-0.031372	0.361145	0.070618	0.001071	0.004525	0.261055	-0.114696	0.219260	-0.109060	0.346445	1.000000		
CONV	0.143693	0.062241	0.146686	0.014366	0.069773	0.099080	0.177025	0.114366	-0.087584	-0.031372	0.150624	0.150784	-0.087584	1.000000	
MV	0.007478	0.060362	0.123781	-0.009060	-0.005956	-0.027799	-0.092442	-0.109060	0.346445	0.001368	0.012326	0.023667	0.346445	-0.038427	1.000000
	DV-D1	DV-D2	DV-D3	DV-D4	IV-D1-M1	IV-D1-M2	IV-D2-M1	IV-D2-M2	IV-D2-M3	IV-D3	IV-D4	IV-D5	IV-D6	CONV	MV

Table 12.4 Descriptive statistics of variables

	DV-D1 ROA	DV-D2 ROI/ROE	DV-D3 ROS	DV-D4 Cost-environmental training	IV-D1-M1 Waste water treated	IV-D1-M2 Solid waste transfer	IV-D2-M1 Electricity use	IV-D2-M2 Furnace oil use	IV-D2-M3 Firewood consumption	IV-D3 Internal recycling raw material	IV-D4 Remanufacturing	IV-D5 Environmental design	IV-D6 Environmental audits-ISO	CONV Firm size	MV Environmental investment projects
Mean	31.212	12.679	10.59	1.86	274.96	2636.65	2404	366.5	197	8.74	6.145	10.59	1.66	9705	10.587
Median	31.5	9.0	2.6	1.4	120	2800	355	0	0	4.5	5	2.6	1.3	7500	2.6
Standard deviation	9.116	14.84	19.9	2.13	391.6	1211.5	2997.6	792.3	293.1	10.68	4.87	19.9	1.54	10,874	19.91
Minimum	11	−26	0	0	17	100	0	0	0	0	0	0	0	440	0
Maximum	49.57	91	120	11	1480	5800	8247	4500	1300	37	27	120	15	55,000	120
Observations	150	150	150	150	150	150	150	150	150	150	150	150	150	150	150

Table 12.5 Clarification of descriptive statistics for dependent and independent variables

Dependent and independent variables	Statistical classification of descriptive statistics
Dependent variable measurement 1: return on assets (ROA)	The standard deviation indicates the sample's dispersion level of the variables. According to the above table, the average return on assets (ROA) is 31.2% which means that about 31% of the ROA of private sector rubber companies in Sri Lanka was achieved return due to assets during 2012–2016
Dependent variable measurement 2: return on investment (ROI)	The average return on investment (ROI) is 12.679% which means about 12.7% of the return due to investments over 2012–2016 in private sector rubber companies in Sri Lanka
Dependent variable measurement 3: return on sales (ROS)	The average return on sales (ROS) is 10.6% which means about 10.6% of the return due to sales was achieved by private sector rubber companies in Sri Lanka over 2012–2016
Dependent variable measurement 4: environmental training and development (T&D)	The average cost for training and development (T&D) is 1.86% which means about 1.86% of the cost invested for T&D over 2012–2016 in private sector rubber companies in Sri Lanka
Independent variable 1 measurement 1: amount of waste water generated m³ (cubic meters) per day (IV11)	Further, the amount of waste water generated m³ (cubic meters) per day is almost 274.96 cubic meters (median 120 m³) in private sector rubber companies in Sri Lanka over 2012–2016
Independent variable 1, measurement 2: amount of solid waste (not on-site treated) transfer kg per month (IV12)	The average 2636.65 kg of solid waste transfer per month in private sector rubber companies in Sri Lanka over 2012–2016
Independent variable 2, measurement 1: electricity (kwh) used per day (IV21)	The average electricity consumption per day is 2404 kwh per day in private sector rubber companies in Sri Lanka over 2012–2016
Independent variable 2, measurement 2: amount of furnace oil (litres) used per day (IV22)	Further the average furnace oil consumption is almost 366.5 l (median 0) in private sector rubber companies in Sri Lanka over 2012–2016
Independent variable 2, measurement 3: renewable sources-firewood consumption (GJ) per day (IV23)	Renewable sources-firewood consumption (GJ) per day is 197 GJ per day, and maximum and minimum consumption in a rubber company is 1300 and 0 GJ
Independent variable 3, dimension 1: amount of recycle (waste water) as a percentage from total pure water consumption (IV3)	The average of waste water recycle as a percentage from pure water per day in private sector rubber companies in Sri Lanka over 2012–2016
Independent variable 4: amount of remanufacture (kg) as a % from total input materials (IV4)	The average amount of remanufacturing as a percentage from total input is 6.145% in private sector rubber companies in Sri Lanka over 2012–2016
Independent variable 5: environmental designing (IV5)	The total average cost allocated for green environmental design is 10.59 million rupees in private sector rubber companies in Sri Lanka over 2012–2016

(continued)

Table 12.5 (continued)

Dependent and independent variables	Statistical classification of descriptive statistics
Independent variable 6: environmental training and audits (IV6), cost in rupees million	The total average cost allocate for environmental related training and development is 1.7 million rupees in private sector rubber companies in Sri Lanka over 2012–2016
Mediator variable (MV): amount of money (rupees in million) allocated for environmental friendly projects	The total average cost allocated for environmental friendly projects is 10.6 million rupees in private sector rubber companies in Sri Lanka over 2012–2016
Control variable (CONV): total sales (rupees in thousand)	The total average cost allocated for environmental friendly projects is 9705 rupees thousand in private sector rubber companies in Sri Lanka over 2012–2016

Source: Author's own elaboration

12.5.3 Empirical Results and Model Specification

12.5.3.1 Stationery Test (Unit Root Analysis)

In order to avoid spurious regressions, the researcher conducted the unit root test for panel data to assess stability before estimating panel regression. There are different estimation methods for unit root test in panel data. In this study two types were performed, that is, unit root test for the same root and different roots. Levin et al. (2002) explained that the Levin-Lin-Chu test (LLC test) can be applied for measuring the same root and a further Im-Pesaran-Shin test (IPS test) when different roots are considered. By performing unit root, taking all the data into a common platform is necessary to precede the analysis. Here the researcher intended to check whether all the variables are in the same order of interpretation. As per literature, Levin et al. (2002) stressed that H0 panel data has unit root (assuming common unit root process), while Ha panel data has no unit root. Im et al. (2003) mentioned that H0 panel data has unit root (assuming individual unit root process) (non-stationary), while Ha panel data has no unit root (stationary). The LLC and IPS tests revealed that all of the variables were statistically significant (see Table 12.6) at the first difference (Lag 1). Data was not stationary at level, but when it was converted into the first difference, it became stationary, and it means that data have no unit root in the first difference.

12.5.3.2 Diagnostics Tests

Multicollinearity Among Variables

The next step of the data analysis involves the relevant diagnostic tests to check on the regression assumptions. If there are any violations, the researcher could proceed with corrective actions to produce a robust model. Table 12.3 presents the correlation summary: according to the results, there is no multicollinearity among the variables since the inter-correlations among the explanatory variables are low. An

Table 12.6 Unit root test summary of all variables

Variable	LLC test probability (level-lo)	LLC test probability (level-l₁)	IPS test probability (level-lo)	IPS test probability (level-l₁)	Hadri test probability (level-l₁)
DV-D1	0.0000***	0.0000***	0.7115	0.0000	0.0158**
DV-D2	0.0000***	0.0003***	0.0579*	0.0000***	0.0000***
DV-D3	0.0000***	0.0000***	0.1509	0.0000***	0.0000***
DV-D4	0.2341	0.0000***	0.0144	0.0000***	0.0000***
IV-D1-M1	0.0000***	0.0000***	0.0000***	0.0000***	0.0000***
IV-D1-M2	0.0000***	0.0007***	0.8369	0.0001***	0.0000***
IV-D2-M1	0.0000***	0.0000***	0.0783+	0.0000***	0.0000***
IV-D2-M2	0.0000***	0.0000***	0.0553+	0.0470*	0.0000***
IV-D2-M3	0.0000***	0.0000***	0.0000***	0.0000***	0.0000***
IV-D3	0.0000***	0.0000***	0.5110	0.0007***	0.0000***
IV-D4	0.0000***	0.0000***	0.3760	0.0000***	0.0000***
IV-D5	0.1211	0.0000***	0.3421	0.0000***	0.0000***
IV-D6	0.0000***	0.0000***	0.8891	0.0000***	0.0000***
ICON	0.9959	0.0000***	1.0000	0.0604	0.0000***
MV	0.0000***	0.0000***	0.0000***	0.0000***	0.0000***

***Indicates a significant level of 1%, **indicates a significant level of 5%, *indicates a significant level of 10%

examination of Pearson correlation showed that none of the independent variables in all models have a correlation of 0.9 or above, indicating that the multicollinearity problem occurred in this study. According to the results in Table 12.3, the highest correlation recorded was 0.466247 between firewood consumption and furnace oil consumption (considered independent variables only). To check further, another diagnostic test for multicollinearity is used, with the variance inflation factor (VIF) calculated for independent variables as follows: $VIF = 1/ (1-r^2)$, where r^2 is the squared multiple correlation coefficient between independent variables. When r^2 is equal to zero, then VIF has its minimum value. The closer the value of VIF to 1, the lower the degree of multicollinearity. Gujarati stressed that, if one of the VIFs is greater than 10, then the multicollinearity is a problem. Based on the results of VIF, values are much lower than 10. With an average value of 1.3, multicollinearity does not exist among the independent variables. This confirms the high discriminant validity of the current study.

Serial Autocorrelation Among Residuals

A Breusch-Godfrey serial correlation test was performed to test whether there is a serial autocorrelation. Since the p value (0.09477) is higher than the 0.05, the researcher could not reject the null hypothesis, and the results revealed that there is no serial autocorrelation among the residuals which is desirable. One of the major issues arising from panel data is the problem of heteroscedasticity; the Breusch-Pagan test revealed that the p value (0.07819) is greater than 0.05. Hence, the researcher could not reject the null hypothesis, implying that the residuals are homoscedastic (same scatter), which is desirable. The Ramsey RESET Test for

Model Specification revealed that the p value of F-statistics (0.065) is higher than 0.05, so the researcher could not reject the null hypothesis since the model has not omitted any variable. Hence, this result emphasizes that there is no significant evidence for model misspecification.

12.5.3.3 The Determinants of EMPs

With the purpose of having robust results, the researcher used the Hausman test (with ROA, ROI, ROS and cost for training and development) to check which model is suitable to interpret results. Thus, the Hausman test is selected as the appropriate model for the analysis. The Hausman test related to each determinant of dependent variable is respectively (ROA-P = 0.0068; ROI-P = 0.7939; ROS-P = 0.0468 and training and development-P = 0.00023) revealed that the p values are <0.005 for the three determinants of dependent variable and only one ROI indicate that $p > 0.005$, so the null hypothesis of the appropriateness of the cross-section random effect model could be rejected. Table 12.7 depicts the summary results of the fixed and random effect panel. Least squares test related to each determinant of the dependent variable.

Since the significant value of the F-statistic is less than 0.1 ($p < 0.1$) at the 10% level of significance, the regression model is significant in explaining the BP (ROA). The adjusted R-squared value implies that 11% of the ROA variation could be explained through the model. Since the DW value is much higher than 2 which reflects a negative serial autocorrelation, the researcher decided to check whether it is a time-dependent serial autocorrelation, and it depicts that the DW related to that (2.8794) value is higher than in the previous model. Hence the researcher inferred that a higher DW value does not implicate with the time-dependent serial autocorrelation. The fixed effect model summary depicted (see Table 12.7) implied that Δ electricity, Δ furnace oil, Δ firewood and Δ recycle (proxy for environmental management) are significant determinants of BP (ROA). According to Table 12.7, the coefficient value of the Δ recycle (162.3) shows the highest positive impact on ROA, while Δ furnace oil (0.052633) and Δ firewood (0.222892) also show positive relationships with the ROA. Furthermore, Δ electricity (−0.150528) indicated a negative impact on the ROA.

Since the significant value of the F-statistic is less than 0.1 ($p < 0.1$) at the 10% level of significance, the regression model is significant in explaining the FP (ROI). The adjusted R-squared value implies that 2.8% of the ROI variation could be explained through the model. The Durbin Watson (DW) statistic is not a suitable explanation for non-correlation of errors in panel data. Hence, it is recommended to proceed with the serial correlation LM test, since the DW value (3.3) is much higher than 2 which reflects a negative serial autocorrelation. The researcher administered the model again with the first difference dependent variable to check whether there is a time-dependent serial correlation, and the new model (see Table 12.7) depicted that it was due to the time relevance, because the DW value of the new model with the first difference dependent variable DW value is 2.070603 which is closer to 2. It implies that the present model DW value (3.303583) is much higher than 2 due to the time relevance correlation among independent variables. The random effect

Table 12.7 The impact of environmental management practices on firms' performance using static panel data analysis

Dependent (ROA),(ROI), (ROS), (T&D)	Fixed (ROA)	Random (ROI)	Fixed (ROS)	Fixed (T&D)
C	−13.55769 (48.04649)	−0.197776 (2.505363)	−9.647747 (48.72069)	0.922964 (2.903308)
D waste water	0.133418 (0.133418)	−0.012330 (0.027045)	0.137521 (0.483964)	−0.016497 (0.033680)
D solid waste	0.143460 (0.390353)	0.253240 (0.005925)+	0.027967 (0.440248)	0.001342 (0.008479)
D electricity	−0.150528 (−0.150528)*	−0.026874 (0.007591)	−0.156879 (0.146446)	0.006208 (0.004420)*
D furnace oil	0.102633 (0.108742)**	0.004433 (0.003831)*	0.110013 (0.109942)+	0.001009 (0.005156)
D firewood	0.222892 (0.084599)+	0.001894 (0.004403)	0.218065 (0.085361)	0.001320 (0.009262)
D remanufacturing	−8.146912 (18.37208)	0.033568 (0.989100)	−9.092518 (18.52115)	−1.039821 (1.200988)
D recycle	162.3000 (48.85762)***	0.889536 (2.084299)	19.48431 (77.15059)	0.889536 (2.219128)
D no of green products	15.80222 (76.56781)	6.120403 (3.167275)+	165.9749 (49.47313)**	0.001591 (0.008412)*
D environmental training and audits	−7.121712 (15.31001)	0.004534 (2.00976)	−0.000180 (0.007113)	−0.104114 (1.01775)
D firm size	7.46E-05 (0.007070)	−2.17E-05 (0.000369)	0.903879 (1.568667)	−2.17E-05 (0.000399)
R-squared	0.388178	0.397050	0.390707	−0.637973
Adjusted R-squared	0.112111	0.320727	0.193676	0.397050
Prob (F-statistic)	0.09198	0.000008	0.09108	0.320727
Durbin-Watson stat	2.345354	3.303426	2.147322	2.070603
Hausman test		0.7939		
F-statistic	1.088104	1.578703	1.315376	0.000008
Number of observation	150	150	150	150

Note: (1) Figures in parentheses are standard errors robust to heteroscedasticity. (ii) Hausman is the Hausman test for fixed effects over random effects. (iii) Serial correlation is the test for first-order serial correlation in fixed effect models presented by Baltagi. $^+p < 0.1$, $^*p < 0.05$, $^{**}p < 0.01$, $^{***}p < 0.001$. D/Δ denotes fist difference

model summary stated in Table 12.7 implied that Δ furnace oil, Δ solid waste and Δ number of green products (proxy for environmental management practices) are significant determinants of FP (ROI). Accordingly, a second model is performed only with the significant variables. According to Table 12.7, the coefficient value of the Δ furnace oil (0.006208) shows the highest positive impact on ROI, while Δ solid waste disposed (0.001320) and Δ number of green products (0.001591) also show positive relationships with the ROI.

Since the significant value of the F-statistic is less than 0.1 ($p < 0.1$) at the 10% level of significance, the regression model is significant in explaining the FP (ROS). The adjusted R-squared value implies that 19% of the ROS variation could be explained through the model. The fixed effect model summary stated in Table 12.7 implied that Δ *furnace oil and* Δ *number of green products* (proxy for environmental management) are significant determinants of FP (ROS). Further the fixed effect model test summary related to T&D revealed that Δ *number of green products and* Δ *electricity* are proxy for environmental management. The determinant of EM based on ROA, ROI, ROS and T&D are named as D (electricity), D (furnace oil), D (firewood), D (recycle), D (solid waste) and D (number of green products).

12.5.3.4 Hypothesis Testing

The Impact of EM on BP (H1)

Environmental management impact on business performance is the first hypothesis (H1). The proposed relationship (H1) between environmental management and environmental performance is supported with six sub-hypotheses (H1b, H1c, H1d, H1e, H1f and H1h). H1a and H1b related to the waste treatment (the amount of waste water generated m3/day and amount of solid waste not on-site treated transfer kg/year). Only the amount of solid waste (not on-site treated) transfer had a significant determinant of BP. According to regression test result, it reveals that both measures of waste treatment have no significant relationship with BP. Further, correlation test results revealed that waste treatment (both solid waste transfer and waste water treatment) had a weak correlation with BP. Moreover, analysis shows that this variable (waste treatment-solid waste) has a significant relationship with BP in the category of ROI, indicating negative relationship between the amount of solid waste transfer and FP (see Table 12.8, ROA: $\beta = -0.131482, p > 0.1$; ROI: $\beta = -0.001215$, $p < 0.1$ and ROS, $\beta = -0.111202, P > 0.1$; T&D: $\beta = -0.001215, p > 0.1$), but waste water has no significant determinant for EM. Based on those results, the researcher rejected alternative hypothesis and accepted the null hypothesis of H1b and H1a.

This hypothesis of reduction consists of three sub-hypotheses of the electricity used per day (Kwh), furnace oil used per day (litters) and renewable sources-firewood consumption (GJ) per day had a significant relationship with BP. This study predicted a significant relationship between amount of electricity (kWh) used per day with a BP category of ROI, indicating positive relationship between the amount of electricity used per day and ROI (ROA: $\beta = 0.129029, p > 0.1$, ROI: $\beta =0.009262, p < 0.05$; ROS: $\beta = -0.171028, p > 0.1$ and T&D: $\beta = 0.009262, p > 0.1$). Thus, the amounts of furnace oil (litres) used per day with BP had a significant relationship between. Analysis implies that variable has a significant relationship with BP categories of ROA/ROS and ROI, indicating positive relationship between the amount of furnace oil used per day and BP (ROA: $\beta = 0.189671\ p < 0.05$; ROI: $\beta = -0.191167, p < 0.1$; ROS: $\beta = 0.002051\ p < 0.05$ and T&D $\beta = 0.191167$ $p < 0.05$). However, renewable firewood consumption had a significant relationship with BP categories of ROI, indicating positive relationship between the amount of firewood used per day and BP (ROA: $\beta =0.170537, p > 0.01$; ROI: $\beta = -0.108055$,

Table 12.8 Summary table – multiple regression outcomes with ROI/ROA/ROS and T&D: model 1

Variable	Hypothesis	ROS Fixed effect			ROI Random effect			ROA Fixed effect			T&D Fixed effect		
		Coefficient	Std. error	Prob.	Coefficient	Std. error	Prob.	Coefficient	Std. error	Prob.	Coefficient	Std. error	Prob.
C		19.02995	47.12312	0.4010	2.150985	2.795498	0.4439	59.02995	46.61933	0.2090	2.150985	2.795498	0.4439
D (solid waste)	H1b	−0.111202	0.37686	0.8917	−0.001215	0.008185	0.8824	−0.131482	0.152686	0.3917	−0.001215	0.008185	0.8824
D (electricity)	H1c	−0.171028	0.120173	0.9538	0.009262	0.006269	0.1435	0.129029	0.112283	0.2538	0.009262	0.006269	0.1435
D (finance oil)	H1c	0.002051	0.015030	0.0370*	0.191167	0.107649	0.0796+	0.189671	0.089460	0.0370*	0.191167	0.107649	0.0496+
D (firewood)	H1d	0.211436	0.112242	0.7131	−0.108055	0.004876	0.04701*	0.170537	0.462242	0.7131	−0.108055	0.004876	0.04701*
D (recycle)	H1e	1.215943	1.215169	0.8219	−1.136351	1.172328	0.3353	−4.397913	19.47018	0.8219	−1.136351	1.172328	0.3353
D (no. of green products)	H1h	15.23241	41.05423	0.0938+	3.376838	0.013409	0.0368*	5.738755	81.14593	0.0938+	3.376838	0.013409	0.0368*
D (firm size)	H2	0.001214	0.014471	0.9771	−1.81E-05	0.003082	0.9623	0.000216	0.007492	0.9771	−1.81E-05	0.003082	0.9623
D (environmental investment)	H3	1.207326	2.54133	0.8926	−0.000435	0.004865	0.9290	0.222326	1.641223	0.8926	−0.000435	0.004865	0.9290
		R-squared- 0.424125		Prob. (F-statistic 0.08701	R-squared 0.423738		Prob. (F-statistic 0.0000	R-squared 0.304729		Prob. (F-statistic 0.052702	R-squared- 0.614125		Prob. (F-statistic 0.05701

Note: (1) Figures in parentheses are standard errors robust to heteroscedasticity. (ii) Hausman is the Hausman test for fixed effects over random effects. (iii) Serial correlation is the test for first-order serial correlation in fixed effect models presented by Baltagi. $^+p < 0.1$, $^*p < 0.05$, $^{**}p < 0.01$, $^{***}p < 0.001$. D/Δ denotes fist difference

$p > 0.01$; ROS: $\beta = 0.211436$, $p > 0.05$, T&D: $\beta = -0.108055$ $p > 0.01$); and despite this situation, there was only one sub-hypothesis (furnace oil) that has a significant relationship with BP, and two hypotheses related to reduction (electricity and fire-wood) do not have a significant relationship with BP.

The recycle of waste has no significant relationship with ROA, ROI, ROS and T&D (ROA: $\beta = -4.397913$, $p > 0.01$; ROS: ROI: $\beta = 1.215943$, $P > 0.05$; $\beta = 0.255183$, $p > 0.0.1$). Therefore, it can be said with regard to the hypothesis that recycling has no significant relationship with BP. Remanufacturing also does not have a significant relationship with BP. This study predicted that remanufacturing is not a determinant of EM. Based on that, both H1f and H1g alternate hypotheses were rejected. When considered into variables, environmental design shows a posi-tive significant relationship with ROA, ROI, ROS and T&D (ROA: $\beta = 5.738755$, $p < 0.1$; ROI: $\beta = -3.376838$, $p < 0.1$, ROS: $\beta = 15.23241$ $p < 0.1$ and T&D: $\beta = 3.376838$, $p < 0.1$). In addition to that, the number of green products has a posi-tive correlation with BP. Therefore, the researcher has rejected the null hypothesis. Further, EMS has not a significant relationship with BP, and also it is not a determi-nant of EM (Table 12.9).

The Impact of EI and Firm Size on BP (H3 and H2)

This study predicted a significant relationship between EI and BP. However, EI does not imply a significant relationship with BP categories of ROA, ROI, ROS and T&D (ROA, $\beta = 0.222326$, $p > 0.1$; ROI, $\beta = 0.000435$, $P > 0.1$, ROS, $\beta = 1.207326$, $p > 0.05$ and T&D, $\beta = -0.000435$, $P > 0.05$). There is one control variable in this study, namely, the size of the firm. This study found that company size has no sig-nificant impact on all the BP indicators. This is inconsistent with resource depen-dence theory which suggests that larger the firm it gives better resources advantage for the company to perform well. Possibly, with the explosion of technology, resources like assets and infrastructure may not give a significant advantage to make profit, but exploitation of the latest technology and information to create value on products and services contributed more to the company in winning business over competitors. Another reason for the result can be viewed from the perspective of earnings management. Empirical research shows that a small company has more opportunity to manage earnings and avoid showing a loss in the financial statement as compared to bigger-sized companies (Albrecht & Richardson, 1990). Hence, it may appear that small companies are better performers than the large companies. This study predicted a significant relationship between firm size and BP. However, findings suggested that this variable has no significant relationship with BP catego-ries of ROA, ROI, ROS and T&D (ROA, $\beta = 0.001214$, $p > 0.1$; ROI, $\beta = -1.81E-05$, $P > 0.1$, ROS, $\beta = 0.000216$, $p > 0.05$ and T&D, $\beta = --1.81E-05$, $P > 0.1$). Therefore we have to reject the alternate hypotheses on both EI and firm size towards business performance.

Table 12.9 Summary table – moderator effect with ROA/ROI/ROS and T&D: model 2

Variable	Hypothesis	ROI			ROS			ROA			T&D		
		Coefficient	Std. error	Prob.	Coefficient	Std. error	Prob.	Coefficient	Std. error	Prob.	Coefficient	Std. error	Prob.
C		60.01925	42.34094	0.1600	−12.29445	44.25283	0.78117	−0.787865	2.373709	0.7408	−4.884773	3.076365	0.1152
D (furnace oil consumption)		0.183400	0.080929	0.0260*	0.219076	0.102967	0.03506	0.008950	0.004536	0.0308*	−0.010132	0.033209	0.7609
D (no. of green products)		27.93689	87.02588	0.0790+	−0.167142	0.072398	0.03105	0.036463	0.067186	0.5887	0.000711	0.009321	0.9393
D (firm size)		4.43E-05	0.007327	0.9952	0.437550	0.471895	0.35509	6.54E-05	0.000411	0.8738	−0.011215	0.007161	0.1202
D (furnace oil × ΔEI)	H4	0.002735	0.002383	0.0243*	0.105931	0.026907	0.01712	0.000170	0.000128	0.0279*	0.002931	0.005407	0.5888
D (no. of green products × ΔEI)	H4	0.260318	2.549827	0.0989+	0.149723	0.091023	0.05519	0.027091	0.013133	0.0872+	0.090584	0.024466	0.0003***
R-squared		0.228059	Prob(F-statistic)	0.041548	0.159799	Prob(F-statistic)	0.032653	0.287634	Prob(F-statistic)	0.099841	0.146004	Prob(F-statistic)	0.036330
Adjusted R-squared		0.05584	Durbin-Watson stat	2.046810	0.082716	Durbin-Watson stat	2.003147	0.090687	Durbin-Watson stat	2.181497	0.076131	Durbin-Watson stat	2.117007

Note: (1) Figures in parentheses are standard errors robust to heteroscedasticity. (ii) Hausman is the Hausman test for fixed effects over random effects. (iii) Serial correlation is the test for first-order serial correlation in fixed effect models presented by Baltagi. $^+p < 0.1$, $^*p < 0.05$, $^{**}p < 0.01$, $^{***}p < 0.001$. D/Δ denotes fist difference

The Relationship Between EMPs and FP Grows Stronger as the EI Increases (H4)

Prior results of this study showed that the majority of the EMPs did not have a unique relationship with FP. Some have suggested positive relationships, but others have concluded with negative, no or mixed relationships. However, environmental investment documented a positive significant relationship with several of the environmental practice indicators. Based on this, it was expected that a positive environment was created by the environmental investment, and it will foster EMPs to enhance the performance of the financial situation of the company. Findings support the hypothesis in which the moderating effect of the environmental investment established a stronger relationship between EM and BP of the company. Thus, H4 was accepted. This relationship is significant for all the performance measures (ROA, ROI, ROS and T&D). For ROA, the beta value of EM beta values for (furnace oil reduced from 0.008950 to 0.000170, number of green products beta value decreased 0.036463 to 0.027091). The beta value of furnace oil ($p < 0.05$) and the number of green products ($p < 0.05$) was significant as well as the moderating effect of furnace oil (furnace oil × EI) ($P < 0.1$). Further moderating effect of the number of green products (no. of green products × EI) ($P < 0.1$) was significant. The same improvement was also documented by ROI: the beta value of furnace oil decreased from 0.183400 to 0.002735, and the number of green products reduced from 27.93689 to 0.260318. The beta value of furnace oil ($p < 0.1$) and the number of green products ($p < 0.01$) was significant. But the moderating effect (furnace oil × EI) ($P < 0.01$) and moderating effect of number of green products (no. of green products × EI) ($P < 0.01$). Further, the same improvement was also documented by ROS, the beta value of EMPs (furnace oil decreased from 0.219076 to 0.105931, the beta value of number of green products reduced from 0.167142 to 0.149723. The beta value of furnace oil ($p < 0.1$) and the number of green products ($p < 0.01$) was significant. But the moderating effect (furnace oil × EI) ($P < 0.01$) and moderating effect of number of green products (no. of green products × EI) ($P < 0.01$) and T&D was (furnace oil decreased −0.010132 0.002931). The beta value of furnace oil ($p > 0.05$) and the number of green products ($p > 0.05$) was not significant as well as the moderating effect of furnace oil (furnace oil × EI) ($P > 0.1$). Further moderating effect of the number of green products (no. of green products × EI) ($P < 0.1$) was significant. Therefore, we can conclude based on the three aspects of business performance indicators that environmental investment is a negative significant moderator between EM and business performance for the company. All the model specifications were significant at the 1% significant level (ROA: $R^2 = 0.287634$, adjusted $R^2 = 0.090687$, Prob F-statistic = 0.099841; ROI: $R^2 = 0.228059$, adjusted $R^2 = 0.05584$, Prob F-statistic =0.041548 and ROS: $R^2 = 0.159799$, adjusted $R^2 = 0.08271$, Prob F-statistic = 0.032653, T&D: $R^2 = 0.146004$, adjusted $R^2 = 0.076131$, Prob F-statistic = 0.036330). Based on test results, the researcher inferred that environmental investment is capable to lift weaker environmental management practices to a weak business performance for the company.

12.6   Concluding Remarks

There is growing literature that refers to environmental management becoming more important and paramount in the business environment at the present time. This study examined the relationship between environmental management and BP and the interaction between environmental investment and EM on BP for the Sri Lankan rubber manufacturing companies for the period of 2012–2016. It documented the evidence on the significant EM that contributes to BP and the influence of the EI to moderate this relationship. This study is intended firstly to determine significant determinants of environmental management and secondly to identify the impact of these significant environmental determinants on BP based on the four aspects of BSC. There were four measurements employed to determine and measure business performance, namely, ROA, ROI, ROS and T&D. With regard to EM, this study was carried out based on the six (6) principles, namely, (1) waste treatment, (2) energy reduction, (3) recycle, (4) remanufacturing, (5) environmental design and (6) EMS. These principles were further divided into some sub-principles: waste water treatment, solid waste transfer, electricity use, furnace oil use, firewood consumption, waste recycling, remanufacture of raw material, environmental design and EMS; altogether there were nine (9) environmental management determinants to examine whether these determinants contributed to the BP of the company. Out of these nine variables, only two variables were revealed to have a significant relationship with financial performance (furnace oil use and environmental design). The remaining six variables were found as not having any significant effect on BP. After conducting the statistical analysis and as per results, this study only accepted three sub-hypotheses and rejected nine sub-hypotheses. Out of the three sub-hypotheses accepted, two hypotheses are related to the relationship between independent variables and dependent variable, one hypothesis is associated with the moderator effect. The hypotheses accepted are related to energy reduction (H1d) and environmental design (H1h) and moderator effect of environmental investment between EMPs and FP (H4).

This becomes more critical when regulations and laws are unable to curb volatility in an uncertain business environment. The result of the study shows that only several principles contributed to the performance of the company. The secondary data analysis based on industry records (descriptive secondary data: Chapter 5.1) also shows that many companies do not take EMPs seriously. Many companies have yet to fully disclose the EMPs as required by regulations and local government authorities to comply with required compliance to protect the business in the long run. A majority of them failed to reach a minimum of 50% disclosure practices. Besides, certain principles were poorly explained by the companies.

Thus, the policy makers and regulatory authorities like the Sri Lanka Standards Institution, certification bodies, the Board of Investment (BOI), the Central Environment Authority (CEA), Sri Lankan shareholders and other relevant agencies need to enhance their efforts, both on promoting significant determinants of environmental management and at the same time providing stern reminders on the repercussion of non-compliance to the private and public listed companies. More explanations also need to be provided on the positive impact of EM like reputation, attractiveness to foreign investors and favourable image in the eyes of shareholders and public that help a company to survive in business. In contrast, lack of EM may lead to fraud, malpractices and risk of bankruptcy during a financial crisis due to mismanagement. For the practitioner and company itself, particularly the board of directors, improvement and effort need to be taken. The results show that not many companies are making an effort to establish their own version of environmental protection measures. The directors need to provide a good leadership example to the employees of the company including the top management team. This can be done via the establishment of environmental protection measures relevant for directors themselves and codes that bind not only the employee in the company but any entities that have business transactions with the company like suppliers, vendors, distributors and customers. Environmental protection measures also need to be strictly enforced with good promotion and explanation, easily accessible to everybody and supported with transparent mechanisms for disciplinary action for those who do not comply with environmental protection measures or those who violate the environmental management practices.

The ultimate objective of this study is to find out whereby EM has a positive statistically significant relationship with respect to BP. There are a number of limitations within which need to be overcome in the period of research, such as EM is a novel concept and lack of research in Sri Lanka. The fact that there is no constant, uniform relationship between EM and BP which could be waiting to be discovered between firms environmental and BP presents more implications for future studies. Variation in the relationship between cases and over time should have to be separated to find out consistency in relationship. Further to get more consistency in results, sample selection should be conducted at industry level. Based on the above findings, it is evident that determinants of EM are not independent issues among business problems, but they are tightly related to different areas in business strategies. This kind of research will be of immense value to society due to emerging environmental and climatic issues. Development of a precise model to find out relationships between environmental and business performance in organizations will be a valuable contribution in the field of research for further investigation by future researchers.

References

Agan, Y., Acar, M. F., & Borodin, A. (2013). Drivers of environmental processes and their impact on performance: A study of Turkish SMEs. *Journal of Cleaner Production, 51*, 23–33.

Ateş, M. A., Bloemhof, J., Van Raaij, E. M., & Wynstra, F. (2012). Proactive environmental strategy in a supply chain context: The mediating role of investments. *International Journal of Production Research, 50*(4), 1079–1095.

Barrow, C. (2004). *Environmental management and development* (Vol. 5). London: Routledge.

Cheng, H. C., & Liao, W. W. (2012, February). Establishing a lifelong learning environment using IOT and learning analytics. In 2012 14th international conference on advanced communication technology (ICACT) (pp. 1178–1183). IEEE.

Cohen, J. C., Silva Dias, M. A., & Nobre, C. A. (1995). Environmental conditions associated with Amazonian squall lines: A case study. *Monthly Weather Review, 123*(11), 3163–3174.

Davis, J. L., Green, J. D., & Reed, A. (2009). Interdependence with the environment: Commitment, interconnectedness, and environmental behavior. *Journal of Environmental Psychology, 29*(2), 173–180.

Delmas, M. A., & Pekovic, S. (2015). Resource efficiency strategies and market conditions. *Long Range Planning, 48*(2), 80–94.

Edirisinghe, J. C. (2013). Community pressure and environmental compliance: Case of rubber processing in Sri Lanka. *Journal of Environmental Professionals Sri Lanka, 1*(1), 14–23.

Figge, F., & Hahn, T. (2013). Value drivers of corporate eco-efficiency: Management accounting information for the efficient use of environmental resources. *Management Accounting Research, 24*(4), 387–400.

Gunathilaka, L. F. D. Z., & Gunawardana, K. D. (2015). Carbon footprint calculation from cradle to grave: A case study of rubber manufacturing process in Sri Lanka. *International Journal of Business and Social Science, 6*(10), 82–94.

Hart, S. L. (1995). A natural-resource-based view of the firm. *Academy of Management Review, 20*(4), 986–1014.

Hart, S. L., & Milstein, M. B. (2003). Creating sustainable value. *Academy of Management Perspectives, 17*(2), 56–67.

Heidrich, O., & Tiwary, A. (2013). Environmental appraisal of green production systems: Challenges faced by small companies using life cycle assessment. *International Journal of Production Research, 51*(19), 5884–5896.

Hoffman, A. J. (2001). *From heresy to dogma: An institutional history of corporate environmentalism.* Stanford: Stanford University Press.

Hoffman, A. J., & Ventresca, M. J. (2002). *Organizations, policy and the natural environment: Institutional and strategic perspectives.* Stanford: Stanford University Press.

Houghton, R. A., & Hackler, J. L. (1999). Emissions of carbon from forestry and land-use change in tropical Asia. *Global Change Biology, 5*(4), 481–492.

Im, K. S., Pesaran, M. H., & Shin, Y. (2003). Testing for unit roots in heterogeneous panels. *Journal of Econometrics, 115*(1), 53–74.

Jennings, P. D., & Zandbergen, P. A. (1995). Ecologically sustainable organizations: An institutional approach. *Academy of Management Review, 20*(4), 1015–1052.

Jensen, M. (2001). Value maximisation, stakeholder theory, and the corporate objective function. *European Financial Management, 7*(3), 297–317.

Lefebvre, É., Lefebvre, L. A., & Talbot, S. (2003). Determinants and impacts of environmental performance in SMEs. *R&D Management, 33*(3), 263–283.

Levin, A., Lin, C. F., & Chu, C. S. J. (2002). Unit root tests in panel data: Asymptotic and finite-sample properties. *Journal of Econometrics, 108*(1), 1–24.

Levy, D. L., & Rothenberg, S. (2002). Heterogeneity and change in environmental strategy: Technological and political responses to climate change in the global automobile industry. In *Organizations, policy and the natural environment: Institutional and strategic perspectives* (pp. 173–193). Stanford: Stanford University Press.

Malhi, Y., Roberts, J. T., Betts, R. A., Killeen, T. J., Li, W., & Nobre, C. A. (2008). Climate change, deforestation, and the fate of the Amazon. *Science, 319*(5860), 169–172.

Montabon, F., Sroufe, R., & Narasimhan, R. (2007). An examination of corporate reporting, environmental management practices and firm performance. *Journal of Operations Management, 25*(5), 998–1014.

Murovec, N., Erker, R. S., & Prodan, I. (2012). Determinants of environmental investments: Testing the structural model. *Journal of Cleaner Production, 37*, 265–277.

Oliver, C. (1991). Strategic responses to institutional processes. *Academy of Management Review, 16*(1), 145–179.

Orts, E. W., & Strudler, A. (2002). The ethical and environmental limits of stakeholder theory. *Business Ethics Quarterly, 12*, 215–233.

Ostrom, E. (1985). The rudiments of a revised theory of the origins, survival, and performance of institutions for collective action. In *Bloomington, Indiana: Workshop in political theory and policy analysis*. Bloomington: Indiana University.

Ostrom, E. (2008a). The challenge of common-pool resources. *Environment: Science and Policy for Sustainable Development, 50*(4), 8–21.

Ostrom, E. (2008b). Institutions and the environment. *Economic Affairs, 28*(3), 24–31.

Ostrom, E. (2009). A general framework for analyzing sustainability of social-ecological systems. *Science, 325*(5939), 419–422.

Ostrom, E. (2010). A multi-scale approach to coping with climate change and other collective action problems. *Solutions, 1*(2), 27–36.

Paavola, J. (2008a). Livelihoods, vulnerability and adaptation to climate change in Morogoro, Tanzania. *Environmental Science & Policy, 11*(7), 642–654.

Paavola, J. (2008b). Governing atmospheric sinks: The architecture of entitlements in the global commons. *International Journal of the Commons, 2*(2), 313–336.

Paavola, J. (2011). Climate change: The ultimate 'tragedy of the commons'. In *Property in land and other resources* (pp. 417–434). Cambridge: Lincoln Institute of Land Policy.

Rabinowitz, D. (2010). Ostrom, the commons, and the anthropology of "earthlings" and their atmosphere. *Focaal, 57*, 104–108.

Russo, M. V., & Fouts, P. A. (1997). A resource-based perspective on corporate environmental performance and profitability. *Academy of Management Journal, 40*(3), 534–559.

Salvadó, J. A., de Castro, G. M., Verde, M. D., & López, J. E. N. (2012). *Environmental innovation and firm performance: A natural resource-based view*. London: Palgrave Macmillan.

Santos, J. B., & Brito, L. A. L. (2012). Toward a subjective measurement model for firm performance. *BAR-Brazilian Administration Review, 9*(SPE), 95–117.

Sarkis, J., Gonzalez-Torre, P., & Adenso-Diaz, B. (2010). Stakeholder pressure and the adoption of environmental practices: The mediating effect of training. *Journal of Operations Management, 28*(2), 163–176.

Sharma, S., & Vredenburg, H. (1998). Proactive corporate environmental strategy and the development of competitively valuable organizational capabilities. *Strategic Management Journal, 19*(8), 729–753.

Sharma, S., Pablo, A. L., & Vredenburg, H. (1999). Corporate environmental responsiveness strategies: The importance of issue interpretation and organizational context. *The Journal of Applied Behavioral Science, 35*(1), 87–108.

Testa, F., Rizzi, F., Daddi, T., Gusmerotti, N. M., Frey, M., & Iraldo, F. (2014). EMAS and ISO 14001: The differences in effectively improving environmental performance. *Journal of Cleaner Production, 68*, 165–173.

White, P. R., De Smet, B., Owens, J. W., & Hindle, P. (1995). Environmental management in an international consumer goods company. *Resources, Conservation and Recycling, 14*(3–4), 171–184.

Yang, M. G. M., Hong, P., & Modi, S. B. (2011). Impact of lean manufacturing and environmental management on business performance: An empirical study of manufacturing firms. *International Journal of Production Economics, 129*(2), 251–261.

Anticipating a Disrupted World: Levers for Sustainable Economic Development

13

Lanumodara Fattrishiya Dedunu Zoysa Gunathilaka
and Kennedy D. Gunawardana

13.1 Framing the Issues: From Ignorance to Awareness

Manufacturing plays a role in disruptive changes in mitigation and adaptation. Mitigation focuses on limiting the speed and scale of disruptive changes. It has typically received great attention in policy circles, such as debates over business model innovations, technological shift, multi-stakeholder collaboration, macro circumstance pressure (related issues and legal matters), and micro circumstance pressure (task-oriented pressure, stakeholder pressure, institutional pressure). Adaptation involves adjusting to actual or expected disruptive change effects. The mitigation management of disruptive change risk is included as a part of the transition, making allowances for sustainable economic development and exploitation opportunities to alter the financial viability of capital stock and the business models. This discussion focuses on the inclusion of disruptive change risks in financial, social, and environmental viability in the rubber manufacturing process in Sri Lanka. The aim of this discussion is twofold. Firstly, it examines the questions of long-term financial feasibility risk in disruptive transition to a sustainable future. It discusses different anticipatory options that interface with resolving and/or managing this risk, as well as the implication for bankers. Secondly, this review is on the risk associated with mitigation, labelled as challenges of disruptive change, and the associated long-term impact on the performance of assets and business portfolios. Hence it is explored in the rubber manufacturing industry, which has to ascertain the significance of the

L. F. D. Z. Gunathilaka (✉)
University of Sri Jayewardenepura, Nugegoda, Sri Lanka

K. D. Gunawardana
Department of Accounting, Faculty of Management Studies and Commerce,
University of Sri Jayewardenepura, Nugegoda, Sri Lanka
e-mail: kennedy@sjp.ac.lk

© The Author(s), under exclusive license to Springer Nature
Switzerland AG 2021
S. Dhiman, R. Samaratunge (eds.), *New Horizons in Management, Leadership and Sustainability*, Future of Business and Finance,
https://doi.org/10.1007/978-3-030-62171-1_13

anticipatory approach towards a tomorrow that is so important indeed for the entire world.

Because the way a challenge is perceived influences a business model, framing the issues, dynamics, and dilemmas is a critical responsibility of business leaders. Let us look, first, at the issue that arises when the challenge of disruptive change is perceived as a threat. Since its inception, socioeconomic development was always about innovation and change management. However, the focus has been on disruptive change, and not on incremental or dramatic change. "What exactly is disruptive change? Is it a single field or discipline? Is it a process? Is it an agreed approach? Is it an effort to identify and pursue goals? Perhaps a philosophy? Or is it development phase or problem-solving?" (Fig. 13.1).

An example: The focus was on how to stabilize the bags on the truck in a better way, instead of thinking about an entirely alternative transportation method. Disruptive change is a universal challenge for the whole human race to face significant challenges to reduce the economic intensity of man-made activities to avoid irreversible catastrophic impacts in society. Therefore disruptive change is a field of risk management or a dynamic construct; it has no a priori measured indicators, and the purpose is to arrive at a more parsimonious conceptual understanding of disruptive change. Recently, organizations have not much addressed disruptive transition risk and mitigation activities under the organization risk framework. The focus of

Source: Photo by Sabine Loetscher.

Fig. 13.1 Incremental versus disruptive change. (Source: Photo by Sabine Loetscher)

this discussion has been on disruptive change, and not on a gradualist approach (incremental or dramatic change) or the great leap approach (drastic change).

Business needs to consider the kinds of events that could pose a risk to a business and take adequate steps to mitigate them. This is an investment for the future of mankind and humanity that organizations can make. What working methods and tools can support disruptive challenges? For disruptive change, we will need to explore and invent, which means that we operate with many unknowns and high risks, and neither the end goal nor the solution path is known in advance. Developing ideas is not the most challenging part of disruptive innovation; the real challenge is in implementation and action while putting ideas into practice and making them work. With the Industrial Revolution, this balance of business and environment started to crack (disrupt), showing disrespect to long-term damage caused by our man-made selfish acts. The industrial sector is facing extraordinary disruptions. But leading industries are not afraid; they perceive massive opportunities are emerging, and they are looking forward to turning disruptive change as a challenge from ignorance to awareness. Challenges for disruptive change are initially framed as an opportunity, because the organization does not feel the threat: as Mark Twain famously said, "Every once in a while one stumbles across a good idea, but with any luck, you'll right yourself and pass it by."

13.2   Beyond Framing – from Awareness to Conflicts

There are three broad channels (physical risks, liability risk, and transition risks) through which disruptive change can affect the economic, social, and environmental stability of a business. Physical risks associated with the macro-oriented circumstances arise from climate- and weather-related events, such as floods, tsunami, storms, etc., that cause loss of life and damage to property or disruption to trade. Liability risk is the second associated risk that may arise tomorrow, and the parties who suffered loss or damage from the effects of disruptive risk seek compensation from those whom they hold liable. The final risk is the risk that ensues from the transition due to disruptions. Coercing issues, due to the adjustments the manufacturing sector makes, spend more time at the periphery, change the way you approach problems, recognize the early warning signs of disruptive change, and stay grounded while avoiding stagnation to keep the business alive in the long run. The broad concept of cradle-to-grave disruptive change is logical. It breaks down into recognized phases: business model innovations through corporates and start-ups, technological shifts in markets and industries as an opportunity for sustainable economic development, and multi-stakeholder collaboration and pressure.

On account of the phase of disruptive change, the process often contains certain chronic problems (see Fig. 13.2) in businesses. These sporadic problems are solved through "firefighting." Eventually, it becomes evident that something has to be done to eliminate chronic problems. They will not disappear on their own – that is the nature of disruptive change in business. The transition to the sustainable economy may lead to investing in standard physical assets that will generally impact

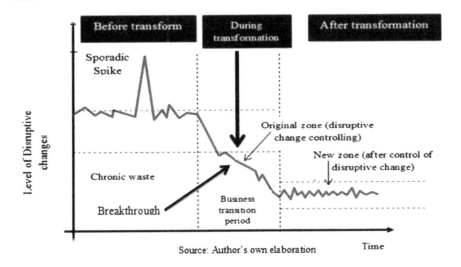

Fig. 13.2 Level of disruptive change and business risk transformation

investment decisions; therefore, the decision should be to prioritize for the most exposed assets' shadow pricing.

13.3   From Talk to Action

A comparison of traditional and modern products is not the way to face disruptive change. This step on the spiral of improvement activities concerns the process of translating the needs of the user, learned from field intelligence, innovation, research and development, new technologies, new product development, knowledge worker concept, learning organization, etc. So how can you develop a targeted approach to business performance during disruptive change? When we are setting objectives in the period of transformation, it is necessary to develop a breakthrough in attitudes, use the Pareto principle, organizing for a breakthrough in knowledge, creation of a steering arm, creation of a diagnostic arm, diagnosis itself, a breakthrough in cultural pattern action, and transition to a new level through an implicit approach than explicit orientation. In the phase of transformation (see Fig. 13.1 – breakthrough approach), the bank has a role to play both providing and expediting to guide the projects organized for diagnosis so as to find remedies: prove that the remedies are effective under operating conditions; provide for control to hold the gains. In 2017, KPMG International surveyed 120 bank CEOs to find out how they plan to grow, what opportunities they see in the market, and what steps they have taken to turn the current disruption into a competitive advantage.

As an example, emission control is directly related to the product carbon footprint in industries. Burning fossil fuel is a governing factor in increasing emissions in manufacturing processes. Currently, organizations are extremely conscious of reducing lifecycle emissions in the supply chain to enhance their organizational financial performance. Organizations now are very conscious of their carbon footprint and aggressively pursue action to re-engineer their process such as investing in biomass energy sources. Converting to biomass boilers requires *capital investments* that may delay implementation, depending on the financial position of the organization. Pending such investment, organizations do indeed have cut down on emissions by reducing consumption of furnace oil through rationalizing thermic boilers, optimizing burner efficiencies, power factor correction using new capacitor banks, and replacing high power-consuming motors with variable frequency drivers. Achievement of emission reductions directly leads to cash savings by reducing furnace oil consumption and electricity, resulting in profit growth, leading to the healthy financial performance of the organization. It is evident that converting to biomass boilers indeed gives significant savings with a quick return on investment.

This example further illustrates that banks will essentially need to improve their sensing capabilities and look around the corners to support green investment through steps beyond financing and crediting. Traditional banks can draw on deep experience in managing industries. *Are banks doing the right things to manage their money across their financial lifecycle in manufacturing sector organizations?* This key question is still open to debate. So what should banks be doing? "Outside-in sensing": banks need to understand how the manufacturing sectors around them are changing and how that will impact their services. Next, they will need to run "inside-out scenarios," taking all the information they gathered from their outside-in sensing (both on-line and off-line) and running scenarios to identify exactly how these trends apply to their service and operating models, what new opportunities they create, and what risks they need to avoid, such as enhancing green projects through hybrid loans and low interest rates for export industries to go for carbon-neutral products, enhancing new innovation by encouraging industries through ecological financing and strengthening credit facilities for carbon-free logistic activities, developing new facilities or fund-raising projects for water-saving projects, encouraging organic agro-management practices, new grant for eco-friendly projects, etc. Finally, they need to develop a simple yet translatable business strategy into operating model tactics: *ecologically sustainable business models.*

A good example is the introduction of "run-flat tires" in the automotive industry. This led to the elimination of the spare tire. If every vehicle sheds one tire, the saving in damage caused to the environment by way of input, and above all, no more dumping of old tires in our oceans, is unimaginable. For the car company, one tire less does not mean fewer profits but more profits indeed through the marketability of the technology to the consumer, incorporating the *concept of green into the brand.* Karl Marx was the first to elaborate the idea that changes in technology are significant, if not the primary, force acting on the shape and nature of society. The common view, that rapidly changing technologies are shaping our lives, stems from Marx's observation.

13.4   From Bark to the Root: Rubber Industry in Sri Lanka

In a disruptively changing business environment, financing vital industries such as the rubber industry is a challenge for leaders. However, in order to achieve sustainable economic development, it is important for industry leaders to understand the drastic change that had occurred in the industry over time. Hence, it is vital to briefly review the history of the rubber industry of Sri Lanka.

Though indigenous rainforest dwellers of South America have been using rubber for generations, it was not until 1839 that rubber had its first practical application in the industrial world. In the 1860s, Henry Wickham, a British citizen, smuggled some of the seeds from these rubber plants out of Brazil and sent 70,000 seeds to Sri Lanka for planting as commercial rubber in 1883. In 1998 the rubber industry was deemed to have produced equal amounts of raw rubber exports and in domestic consumption, and the year can be considered a remarkable year for the industry being contingent or dependent on using more latex for domestic purposes than for foreign trade. Domestic consumption increased, and fluctuation of rubber prices may have caused shifting the process to finished products to get more value additions to 1 kg of the processed rubber. The advancement of agro-based industries such as rubber generates enormous solid and liquid waste (roots of the disruptive change in manufacturing process). Environmental destruction is an inevitable consequence of human beings and has become more complex and multidimensional due to heavy utilization of resources and mounting by-products at a phenomenal rate, leading to high global pollution of air, land, and water in the environment. The Central Bank Report (2016) highlighted that foreign exchange earnings from rubber were more than 6 billion rupees in 2016 and recorded 7.83% of total exports in the first quarter of 2016 (see Table 13.1).

Table 13.1 Rubber and rubber-based product contribution to total merchandise exports 2006–2016 May

Year	Percentage share from total exports
2006	8.01
2007	7.74
2008	8.14
2009	6.78
2010	8.69
2011	10.89
2012	10.6
2013	9.6
2014	8.47
2015	7.7
2016 May	7.83

Source: Sri Lankan Export Development Board (http://www.srilankabusiness.com/blog/product/rubber.html – 29 April 2014)

At present, the country ranks among the world's top ten largest producers and the seventh largest exporter of natural rubber. The rubber industry consists of two closely related independent sectors: the rubber plantation industry, which produces raw rubber, and the high-value new product innovations in finished rubber goods. Starting from the stage of tapping latex to the manufacture of semi-finished or semi-processed rubber products, together with primary products, this sector is moving forward to the manufacturing of value-added products combined with those involved in trading in the rubber industry. The Sri Lanka Export Development Board (SLEDB) set out in 2016 the value addition of rubber and rubber-based products (Table 13.2). The Central Bank of Sri Lanka Report (2015) indicated that last year's total contribution to gross domestic product (GDP) was 3% and total production of rubber was 88.9 million Kg in 2015, which increased only to 98.6 million Kg in 2014, a 0.7% small increment. The noticeable drop in the growth rate of rubber and rubber products is mainly due to the global recession, which prevailed in 2009. SLEDB (2016) reports acknowledged that Sri Lanka can boast international acceptance in products such as Solideal branded industrial tires manufactured in-country by Loadstar Ltd.

There are other multinational companies that are engaged in the manufacture of this NR product while promoting more employment. For the population in the industry engaged in the production of rubber goods of the manufacturing sector, it comprises organizations categorized under small-, medium-, and large-scale manufacturers. These manufacturing organizations collectively have a large portfolio of different products that are manufactured either for local sale or predominantly for the lucrative export market. The wide range of products comprises such items as solid tyres, latex gloves, rubber bands, extrusions, beadings, mats, miscellaneous sports goods, mattress, pillows, etc. The versatility and experience of the technologists and designers ensure the manufacture of rubber products suits the stringent and

Table 13.2 Export performance of rubber products 2006–2016 May

Year	Value in USD million
2006	541.65
2007	592.24
2008	665.27
2009	483.18
2010	730.55
2011	1091.15
2012	981.77
2013	959.03
2014	935
2015	787.3
2016 May	323.84

Source: Sri Lankan Export Development Board (http://www.srilankabusiness.com/blog/product/rubber.html – 29 April 2014)

Fig. 13.3 Rubber
cultivation extent by other
countries. (Source:
Author's own elaboration)

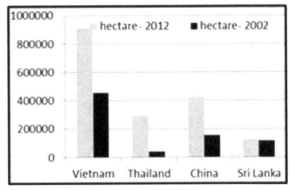

Source: Author's own elaboration

competitive requirements of the marketplace and these commodities are internationally acclaimed and accepted for their quality and durability. Sri Lanka produces rubber and rubber products for international brands such as Continental, Solideal, Wonder Grip, Mapa, Safety Work, etc. With the potential of its high value-adding capacity in the product manufacturing sector, the industry, together with relevant government institutions, has developed a long-term master plan for the development of the rubber industry (Fig. 13.3).

13.5   From Symptom to Cause – Developing Nations Darkened by Disruption?

The country today not boosts self-sufficiency in rice and even to have the capacity to imports. Organic cultivation has become a focal point within farming communities and needs the utmost attention to encourage organic farming and low-interest rates through ecologically benefited products for sustainable development. Figure 13.4 shows the growth rate of Sri Lankan rubber cultivation in comparison with countries involved in rubber cultivation. Sri Lanka remained in the lowest position of cultivation and remained the least developed in comparison with other rubber-producing countries. There was poor progress of cultivation and impact on futuristic demand for domestic consumption. Figure 13.3 shows the highest cultivation in 1982 and the lowest in 2002, with a slight improvement in 2010. The logical reason for this occurrence is due to the rubber price increase in the international market. In 1970 plantations recorded an extent of 224,000 hectares; in 1982 this declined to 171,726 hectares; in 2002 it was 114,681 hectares; and in 2010 it was 125,645 hectares. To date rubber cultivation has not attained the previous extent of rubber in 1970 and is far behind by 100,000 hectares in comparison with the rubber plantations of the same year. Increasing rubber cultivation in small farmer plots can result in significant increases in household income and in the eradication of poverty of communities. However, in the course of decision-making, this provides for growing rubber and will create a situation in the decades ahead for farmers to commit

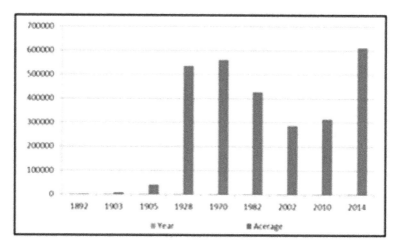

Source: Author's own elaboration

Fig. 13.4 Comparison of rubber extent from 1892 to 2014. (Source: Author's own elaboration)

themselves to earn money to get the return on their investments. Growing more rubber trees is considered a feasible solution for the neutralization of such adverse impact mitigation of climate risks while helping reduction of atmospheric carbon. This can be viewed as assigning a good financial implication because more rubber means better prices as well as less interruption to manufacturing moving towards a carbon-neutral economy (see the great leap approach in Thailand and Vietnam in Fig. 13.3).

Rubber can be categorized as an industrial cash crop, and it creates a demand that depends strongly on the dynamics of the world economy. The price of rubber depends on world demand, and it indicates the bust-and-boom cycle which will expose farmers to a risk situation due to unpredictable price fluctuations in the market (Fig. 13.5). Farmers regarding their yield are not able to build a short-term strategy to increase production in a dynamic market situation.

There are ecologically identified hazards due to crop diseases, pests, unfavorable weather conditions, or changes in climate. Previous research has emphasized the pollution of water resources, loss of natural vegetation and species, soil erosion, and climate change as consequences of rubber cultivation. More knowledge and understanding of economic risks associated with a monoculture crop and its ecological consequences for the environment and livelihoods is needed. A policy to keep growers attached to rubber is another area where government intervention is required. Minimum price levels, maintaining buffer stocks, and export grants for more rubber use in finished products are some steps that are needed urgently.

Growing more rubber trees is considered a feasible solution for the neutralization of such adverse impact mitigation of climate risks while helping reduction of atmospheric carbon. This can be viewed as assigning a good financial implication because more rubber means better prices, as well as less interruption to

Source: Singapore Commodity Exchange (SICOM)

Fig. 13.5 Rubber monthly price – US cents per pound. (Source: Singapore Commodity Exchange (SICOM))

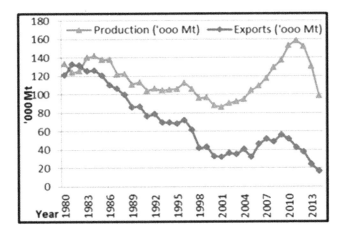

Fig. 13.6 Raw rubber production and exports. (Source: Author's own elaboration based on Rubber Development)

manufacturing. The Sri Lankan rubber industry has experienced a phenomenal growth in the late 1998s (Fig. 13.6), and it continues making headway as one of the stronger manufacturing sub-sectors in the country in terms of its contribution to GDP and value addition created in raw materials. If domestic consumption is increased at the current rate, the existing supply may not be enough to cater to that demand (Fig. 13.7). This will encourage importing raw rubber to cater to increasing demand for domestic consumption. We encourage replanting programs to increase rubber cultivation and support good ecosystem management for land utilization. A

Fig. 13.7 Raw rubber production and domestic consumption. (Source: Author's own elaboration based on Rubber Development)

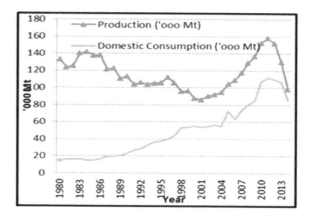

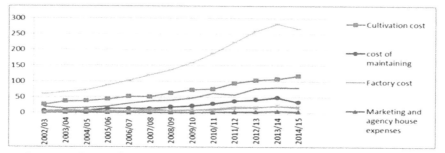

Source: Agriculture and Environment Statistics Division: Department of Census and Statistics, Sri Lanka.

Fig. 13.8 Relevant cost component associated with manufacturing of one kilogram of made. (Source: Agriculture and Environment Statistics Division: Department of Census and Statistic, Sri Lanka)

major reason for an increase in production is the failure to sustain a systematic and consistent long-term replanting program. This indicates a shift in processed raw rubber and export of standard end-products to higher value addition during an increase in the cost of production (Fig. 13.8). The significant growth of the cost of production and processing of raw rubber recorded with continuous effect over the past 12 years was supported by several factors, such as high labor cost, increase of cost of raw material, and tapping and collecting cost. These reforms also placed greater emphasis on export-driven industries due to unavoidable price increases associated with processing-related activities.

13.6   Harness the Power of Sustainability

Society modernization and population growth have forced adoption of fertilizers to obtain a higher yield of latex as harvest. Fertilizer application directly affects climate transition by changing organic land. Häuser (2015) argued that the application

Fig. 13.9 Fertilizer issue
in a rubber plantation in
0'MT and average yield.
(Author's elaboration
census of agriculture 2002;
estate sector – statistical
table)

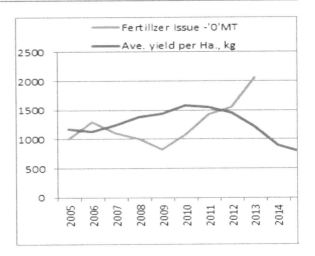

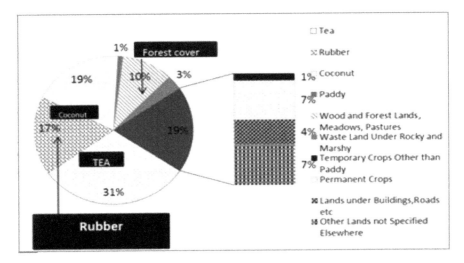

Fig. 13.10 Total extent under tea, rubber, coconut, and other cultivation in Sri Lanka. (Author's
elaboration Census of Agriculture 2002; Estate Sector – Statistical table)

of chemical or artificial manure (to increase fertility) has a negative correlation with
soil organic pools (Figs. 13.9 and 13.10).

Gunathilaka and Gunawardana (2015) found a double effect in the emission of
conventional rubber products compared to the organic product while operating
other process parameters in the same conditions. The other danger associated with
rubber cultivation highlighted by Houghton et al. (2000) was that, due to the effects
of deforestation and burning of natural forest to convert land to rubber, carbon
stocks are reduced above- and below-ground by increasing the rate of carbon emissions. Malhi et al. (2008) estimated the change in biomass carbon stocks due to
deforestation, and Ziegler et al. (2012) highlighted the risks to the ecosystem.

Changes in weather patterns interrupt tapping and cause bark disease and soil erosion, reducing the latex yield and output of rubber products. Hence, climate change has already conceived as the need for aggressive land conservation projects such as forest cover, and when transformed into rubber plantation, this may have mitigating effects on climate change as well as on water availability during the life cycle. There is good evidence to show the average temperature of rubber-producing areas and a reduced stream of flow and drying up of wells were to the adverse effect of regional water balance through rubber cultivation. The rapid loss of forest cover has been a major cause of concern in terms of climate transition. In the early season of natural rubber, fertilizer input or application is very low, and the surrounding soil appears to be enriched by abundant leaf fall and biodiversity, due to monoculture, excellent agronomic technique, and growing a wide variety of crops during the immature period.

In present-day society, people are moving from rubber to different cash crops due to low prices, applying fertilizers and pesticides, due to the monoculture nature of rubber production, and there is danger in using agro-fertilizers in run-off which can enter the aquatic system and threaten the quality of water for human use. For climate protection, it is necessary to move rubber plantation to organic menus for global sustainability and environment resilience against the effects of both climate change and sociocultural issues, such as protection of water base from pollution. The threat, however, is low yield due to absence of fertilizer application, and high rubber prices will create instability in the market when there is no proper agro-management. Hence the manufacturer is impelled to use more furnace oil boilers for heat consumption; there are no controls in emissions, in operation, etc. Based on these conditions, for both manufacturer and growers there is a necessity to establish a proper policy to mitigate such actions in long-run operations.

Whenever the price is relatively low, people look to introduce different cash crops. When considering such crops, it is essential to bear in mind this aspect of financial internal rates of return (FIRR) for crops. Figure 13.11 describes FIRR in the three main cash crops. FIRR indicates the need for ascertaining a feasibility study. In planting activities, the weighted average cost of capital (WACC) and the net present value (NPV) of the project are very important. The WACC calculation is considered with funding from various sources and assumes that the annual average interest rate of 13% and the corporate tax rate of 28% are included. The WACC after-tax related to the three main crops is computed as 5.1–24%. Figure 13.11 summarizes the FIRR of rubber per hectare as 15.44%, and this is well above the WACC. It highlights that planting rubber is financially more feasible than planting other cash crops, such as tea; palms and palm oil are the best cash crops in comparison with the main three cash crops. The Volume Index of Agricultural Production measures the aggregate production of a given set of goods and services over time. Figure 13.12 shows the volume index of rubber production in comparison with the other three main crops and the measured agricultural output changes. Figure 13.12 shows that rubber has the highest volume index of agricultural production in Sri Lanka.

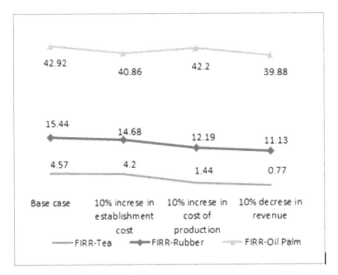

FIRR* = Financial Internal Rate of Return
Source: Asian Development Bank Independent Evaluation Department

Fig. 13.11 Financial internal rate of return for three cash crops. (*FIRR** financial internal rates of return. Source: Asian Development Bank Independent Evaluation Department)

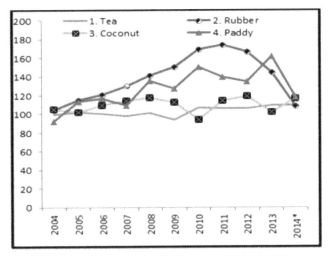

Source: Agriculture and Environment Statistics Division:
Department of Census and Statistics. Sri Lanka.

Fig. 13.12 Volume index of agriculture production 2004–2014. (Source: Agriculture and Environment Statistics Division: Department of Census and Statistics, Sri Lanka)

Table 13.3 Types of energy use in rubber product manufacturing

Industry division	Rubber products (more than 25 persons engaged factory)	Rubber & plastic (less than 25 persons engaged factory)
Fuel & electricity total (Rs.)	4,813,983,284	353,138,433
Electricity (Rs.)	2,614,359,207	260,424,778
Furnace (Rs.)	896,085,259	15,619,075
Diesel (Rs.)	314,977,700	24,944,532
Kerosene (Rs.)	52,972,080	737,867
Petrol (Rs.)	47,850,814	4,534,100
L.P.G. (Rs.)	20,530,227	37,888,271
Charcoal (Rs.)	208,096,259	14,600
Firewood (Rs.)	452,702,089	3,661,274
Water (Rs.)	190,168,153	3,536,752
Other fuel (Rs.)	16,241,497	1,777,183

Source: Annual industry survey (2011)

Heavy usage of energy has been addressed in previous sub-sections (Table 13.3) and is another contrasting factor in the industry in contributing more to energy consumption. Another concerning point is the solid and liquid waste generated from manufacturing operations. Thus, it is worthwhile investigating the real reasons for the environmental transition from both environmental management and environmental performance in the rubber industry. One of the main targets of corrective action for climate change is growing more rubber trees, and, in that context, the drive to grow more rubber trees, now categorized under secondary "forest cover," will certainly have better financial implications on balance for the industry.

Houghton and Hackler (1999) stress the burning of natural forest to convert land into rubber, and Malhi et al. (2008) discuss changes in biomass carbon stocks. According to the Central Bank (2014), growth of rubber cultivation in the last year periods declined, as recorded in total extent in 134,000 hectares in 2014; in 2015 it was 135,000 hectares, showing a slight rise in 2014–2015 or 0.7% growth. The adverse weather conditions caused by climate change also resulted in catastrophic landslides. Growing more rubber trees is considered a feasible solution that helps to reduce climate risks while helping to reduce atmospheric carbon. This has a good financial implication because more rubber means better prices and also less interruption to manufacturing. Effluent treatment is vital in operations in the management of used water, in modern treatment plants, that incurs high capital investment by organizations. Consequently, long-term feasibility in investment is raised for managers to find a realistic solution through water recycling or the use of treated water to avoid drinking water pollution. This has led to simultaneous benefits, such as cost reduction of water bills and mitigation of GHG emissions by way of effluent reduction. Edirisinghe (2013) stated that 40–50 liters of effluent are discharged on average for 1 kg of rubber production. For a total production of 114,700 metric tons in 2006, 4.5–5.7 billion liters of effluent were produced and discharged to the environment (Fig. 13.13).

There are three main grades of natural rubber produced: ribbed smoked sheets (RSS), crepe rubber, and centrifuged latex. Effluent generated by such production processes contains 30–40% rubber and 60–70% serum substances (Edirisinghe, 2013). Two hundred years after the Industrial Revolution, bad effects of climate change are already being experienced, and we do not have to wait for another 200 years for the revolution, as it is all happening so fast (Fig. 13.14). The world consists not only of humans; there are millions of living species. Our responsibility is to protect them all now and the future generations, without waiting for the global climate revolution to happen.

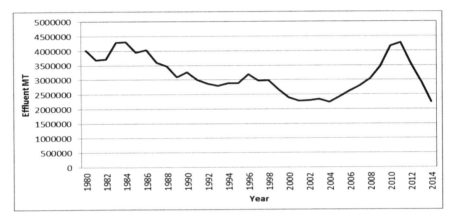

Fig. 13.13 Effluents discharged due to raw rubber processing. (Source: Authors)

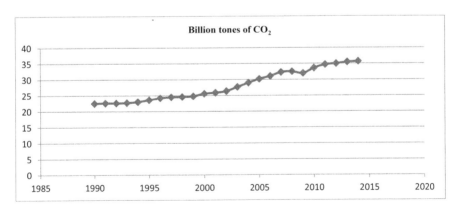

Fig. 13.14 Global trends in CO2 1990–2014 (unit: billion tons of CO2). (Source: 2015 Annual Publications by PBL Netherlands Environmental Assessment Agency and the European Commission's Joint Research Centre (JRC))

With ever-increasing populations, the quantities of their needs and requirements incrementally will be on the rise, and the rubber industry will play a big role in the future, not as a source of food, but as a facilitator for transport and supplier of health-related and household items. The whole world will depend on the speed of moving towards economic development. Understanding of global warming and corporate sector attitudes towards offsetting through sustainable economic development are essential for a business to predict the future of the firm. Today the pressure to reduce energy consumption will come from the twin drivers of reducing fossil fuel burn that helps to reduce carbon emission and also to be cost-competitive.

13.7 Conclusion

Kaplan and Norton have presented the balanced scorecard (BSC) concept in a series of articles in the *Harvard Business Review*. They have argued that traditional financial accounting measures like the ROI, ROE, ROA, payback period, etc. offer a narrow, incomplete picture of business performance and that reliance on such data hinders the creation of future business value. As a result, they suggest that financial measures be supplemented with additional ones that reflect customer satisfaction, internal business processes, and the ability to learn and grow. Their BSC is designed to complement "financial measures of past performance with measures of the drivers of future performance" (Kaplan and Norton 1996). The name of their concept reflects the intent to keep score of a set of items that maintain a balance "between short- and long-term objectives including opportunity loss due to disruptive change, between financial and non-financial measures, between lagging and leading indicators, and between internal and external performance perspectives." Bankers' attention to such a broad set of performance measures should not only help ensure good short-term financial results but also guide a business as it seeks to achieve its strategic goals in the face of challenges of disruptive change. By combining financial measures with non-financial measures in a single report (the $360°$ view), the BSC aims to provide managers with richer, more relevant information about activities they are managing than is provided by financial measures alone.

The findings of this study will redound to the benefit of society since challenges of disruptive change play an important role in rubber manufacturing technologies. The greater demand for companies with sustainable economic development justifies the need for more sustainable and green approaches to create a disruptive business model for a monetary reward. Thus banks that apply the recommended approach derived from the results of this discussion will be able to introduce manufacturing organizations to a better future. Challenges of disruptive change show bankers' commitments and substantive effort and action that will create a sustainable future. This may provide hope for the better, sustainable future.

References

Central Bank report, 2014. http://www.cbsl.gov.lk/pics_n_docs/10_pub/_docs/efr/annual_report/AR2014/English/content.htm.

Central Bank report, 2015. http://www.cbsl.gov.lk/pics_n_docs/10_pub/_docs/efr/annual_report/AR2015/English/content.htm.

Central Bank report, 2016. http://www.cbsl.gov.lk/pics_n_docs/10_pub/_docs/efr/annual_report/AR2016/English/content.htm.

Edirisinghe, J. C. (2013). Community pressure and environmental compliance: Case of rubber processing in Sri Lanka. *Journal of Environmental Professionals Sri Lanka, 1*(1).

Gunathilaka, L. F. D. Z., & Gunawardana, K. D. (2015). Carbon footprint calculation from cradle to grave: A case study of rubber manufacturing process in Sri Lanka. *International Journal of Business and Social Science, 6*(10), 82–94.

Houghton and Hackler (1999). Houghton, R.A. and Hackler, J.L., 1999. Emissions of carbon from forestry and land-use change in tropical Asia. *Global Change Biology, 5*(4), 481–492.

Houghton, R. A., Skole, D. L., Nobre, C. A., Hackler, J. L., Lawrence, K. T., & Chomentowski, W. H. (2000). Annual fluxes of carbon from deforestation and regrowth in the Brazilian Amazon. *Nature, 403*(6767), 301–304.

Häuser, I., Martin, K., Germer, J., He, P., Blagodatskiy, S., Liu, H., et al. (2015). Environmental and socio-economic impacts of rubber cultivation in the Mekong region: Challenges for sustainable land use. *CAB Reviews, 10*(27), 1–11.

Kaplan, R. S., & Norton, D. P. (1996). Linking the balanced scorecard to strategy. *California Management Review, 39*(1), 53–79.

Malhi, Y., Roberts, J. T., Betts, R. A., Killeen, T. J., Li, W., & Nobre, C. A. (2008). Climate change, deforestation, and the fate of the Amazon. *Science, 319*(5860), 169–172.

SLEDB (2016). Export Performance Report|Sri Lankan Exporters Performance | EDB (srilanka-business.com).

Ziegler, A. D., Phelps, J., Yuen, J. Q., Webb, E. L., Lawrence, D., Fox, J. M., et al. (2012). Carbon outcomes of major land-cover transitions in SE Asia: Great uncertainties and REDD+ policy implications. *Global Change Biology, 18*(10), 3087–3099.

Part IV

Macroeconomic Policy

An Empirical Study on the Impact of Political Shocks and Other Macroeconomic Variables on GDP of Sri Lanka

V. I. Amaratunge, A. R. Ajward, and R. M. A. K. Rathnayake

14.1 Introduction

Sri Lanka is a small island nation with limited economic resources. Despite this, Sri Lanka has often outperformed regional countries in terms of its economic development. In the 1940s Sri Lanka was on a par with Japan, and in the 1960s its economy was larger than that of newly industrialized countries (NICs). In 1956, on a diplomatic visit, Lee Kuan Yew declared that Sri Lanka was a country far richer in resources than Singapore (Jayaweera et al. 2003, cited in Ramanayake and Wijetunga 2017). However, the situation has now reversed for Sri Lanka, and today it has the lowest economic growth rate in comparison with its South Asian counterparts.

The country has faced much political turbulence, including the 30-year-long civil war and unrest in the 1970s and 1987/1989 periods, which has impacted economic growth (Easterly and Levine 1997). Ramanayeke and Wijetunge (2017, p. 13) observe: '[d]isagreements led to a civil war in the 1970s that lasted for three decades until the LTTE was destroyed by government forces in 2009. Sri Lanka's economic history can be divided into three major eras, namely, the colonial era (1505–1948), post-colonial era (1949–2013), and post-war era (after 2009)'. Despite having the

V. I. Amaratunge (✉)
Melbourne Business School, University of Melbourne, Melbourne, Australia
e-mail: vamaratunge@student.unimelb.edu.au

A. R. Ajward
Department of Accounting, Faculty of Management Studies and Commerce,
University of Sri Jayewardenepura, Nugegoda, Sri Lanka
e-mail: ajward@sjp.ac.lk

R. M. A. K. Rathnayake
Department of Business Economics, Faculty of Management Studies and Commerce,
University of Sri Jayewardenepura, Nugegoda, Sri Lanka
e-mail: rathnayake@sjp.ac.lk

© The Author(s), under exclusive license to Springer Nature
Switzerland AG 2021
S. Dhiman, R. Samaratunge (eds.), *New Horizons in Management, Leadership and Sustainability*, Future of Business and Finance,
https://doi.org/10.1007/978-3-030-62171-1_14

lowest growth rate in the region, Sri Lanka has maintained a more 'open economy' compared to any other economy. The late President, J.R. Jayawardena, was able to initiate open economic policies in Sri Lanka in 1978–1979 (Ramanayake and Wijetunga 2017).

Despite years of civil war, the country has been able to maintain around a 5% economic growth rate on average over the last three decades. Although the agricultural sector was the largest sector prior to 1956, now its contribution to GDP is only about 8%, and it is less than that of the industrial and services sectors. The economic growth of Sri Lanka today is thus basically determined by growth determinants (Kormendi and Meguire 1985) of industrial services sectors. At present, Sri Lanka is designated as a lower middle-income country with a GDP per capita of USD 4073 (Central Bank of Sri Lanka [CBSL] 2017). The main sectors of the Sri Lankan economy are tourism, tea exports, apparel, textiles and rice production. Remittances also constitute an important part of national revenue. Amidst these fluctuations in economic development, researchers also observe that Sri Lanka had undergone several political regime changes and other political shocks. However, despite these observations, researchers have found that there is a dearth of studies that examine how these political shocks, the open economy and other economic variables impact RGDP of Sri Lanka.

Accordingly, the main objective of this study is to examine the impact of political shocks and other macroeconomic variables on Sri Lanka's GDP. The impact of opening the economy in 1978 on economic growth will also be examined. The findings are expected to fill the observed empirical dearth in the local and empirical extant literature in the area. The findings are also expected to have significant policy implications for decision-makers and regulators of the economy.

The rest of the paper is structured as follows. The next section reviews local and international literature on the topic. Section three elaborates the methodology applied in achieving the objectives of this study. Section four details the main findings. The final section provides a discussion and concluding remarks and elaborates future research directions.

14.2 Literature Review

This section reviews the main theories that link RGDP with political instability and other macroeconomic variables. It includes a review on the relevant empirical literature on the impact of political instability on the RGDP. Based on the review of the literature, both the gap in the literature is identified and the basis of the conceptual framework that links political instability and other macroeconomic variables with RGDP established.

14.2.1   Theoretical Underpinnings in Trade Openness, FDI and Economic Growth

Although there are no specific theories on political shocks and economic growth, the discussion that follows establishes the link between trade openness (which was a politically motivated move in 1978), foreign direct investment and economic growth.

14.2.1.1   Endogenous Growth Model, Neoclassical Theories and Foreign Direct Investment (FDI)

Adhikary (2011) indicates that both endogenous growth and neoclassical models can be used as theoretical underpinning to explain the economic growth fuelled by FDI of a country. Under the endogenous growth model, Romer (1986) and Pugel (2007, as cited in Adhikary 2011) postulate that, through FDI, different types of skills (managerial, technical, human skills, etc.) as well as technological advancement, innovations and new knowledge are brought to a country. Pugel (2007, cited in Adhikary 2011) further elaborates that, in the expansion of international competition and strengthening the capacity of the production and sale of goods, 'technological spill over' via FDI plays a major role leading to higher economic growth. Discussing developing economies, Romer (1986) argues that increased efficiency due to FDI assists such economies to be on a par or converge with more economically advanced economies.

Adhikary (2011) explains that endogenous growth models explain that the growth of a nation in the long run does not only depend on physical investments, but in using such investments *efficiently*. Hence authors such as Nair-Reichert and Weinhold (2001) and Adhikary (2011) claim that, under the endogenous theoretical model, economic growth in the long run depends on progress in technology, which is based on knowledge and technology transfers. Neoclassical theories explain that FDI is a comparatively less volatile and more reliable means of capital infusion for the growth of developing countries (Moosa and Cardak 2006). Edwards (1992) also claims that, by absorbing modern innovative technologies, a country can grow faster than a country with lower openness.

Accordingly, in contrast to the endogenous model, neoclassical theories assume that the growth of a country in the long term depends on the FDI channelled to productive sectors of a country that is short of capital, rather than taking into account the technology and knowledge transferred via such investments. Thus neoclassical theories take a narrow view of FDI, limiting it only to the physical aspect of FDI.

In terms of the context of a developing country that has low levels of initial capital, neoclassical theories also suggest that, if additional capital is infused, higher marginal rates of returns can be achieved. This means that in economies short of capital stocks, the marginal productivity of new investment is higher (Adhikary 2011).

14.2.1.2   Transaction Cost Theory, Trade Openness and FDI

Transaction cost theory, propagated by scholars such as Coase (1937), can be used to as an argument that higher return on investment is provided for both local and foreign investors in a more open trade economic context. It is apparent that investors will not be motivated to invest in an economy where non-tariff and tariff barriers exist and where they will be unable to take back their capital and returns to their own countries. Adhikary (2011) argues that a country with trade openness has a competitive advantage over other countries, and investors will take that into account where it is advantageous for them to invest in such countries.

14.2.1.3   Classical Economists, Mercantilism, Heckscher-Ohlin Trade Theories and Trade Openness

Under classical economist theories, it is claimed that a country may not be able to continue to enjoy an indefinite positive trade balance; such countries should produce and export goods and services with a lower cost advantage and import only items with higher cost disadvantage (Khobai et al. 2018). Based on this argument, Keho (2017) and Nduka et al. (2013) also indicate that foreign trade, which is used as a proxy for trade openness, has a strong positive impact on the economic growth of a country. However, Khobai et al. (2018) argue that the economic benefit of one country is at the cost of another country and thus a zero-sum game. Based on this argument, Adedoyin and Ademola (2015, cited in Khobai et al. 2018) and Nduka et al. (2013) explain that exports should be greater than imports and the receiving country should take steps to protect its domestic industries from import competition. Contrary to these views, Heckscher and Ohlin (Heckscher 1919; Ohlin, 1933, cited in Khobai et al. 2018) claim that two countries should trade with each other if they have similar technology, returns of scale are constant and factor intensity of final products and services are similar. They further argue that the country with higher resources will manufacture at larger scale and enhance economic growth.

The next section reviews the extant literature on the impact of political instability and macroeconomic variables on economic growth.

14.2.2   Empirical Studies on Political Instability and Economic Growth

Chawdhury (2016) defines political instability as the 'propensity of a change in the executive, either by "constitutional" or "unconstitutional" means' (p. 4) and claims that political instability has become a major issue in both developing and developed nations. An analysis by Grossman (1991) of revolutions suggests an interesting argument on the negative association between political instability and economic growth: when the governors of a nation are comparatively weak, the incidence of occurrence of revolution is higher, and hence citizens of such a country will engage in revolutions rather than productive economic activity – and vice versa. This analysis is supported by Alesina and Perotti (1996), who claim that successful, as well as attempted, revolutions, coups and collective violence indicate anarchy and that they pose a threat to established property rights. Kuznets (1966, cited in Chawdhury 2016) argues that a basic level of political stability is required of a country so that citizens can plan for the future and ensure that they will get proper rewards for their extended contributions.

Shonchoy and Tsubota (2014) indicate that countries with conflicts and fragility are unable to develop proper governance functions or meaningful relationships within their communities. Roy and Borsha (2013) explain that political instability causes a plethora of negative impacts on a number of macroeconomic factors, such as growth in GDP, inflation and private investment. Memon et al. (2011, cited in Chawdhury 2016) argue that, when a country enjoys stability, individuals are empowered and can channel their energies to the development of their countries.

Chawdhury (2016) explains that there are at least two reasons why political instability has a negative effect on economic development. The first is that such instability disturbs market activities and relations with labour, impacting adversely on the productivity levels of a country. The second is that instability has a negative impact on the investment in a country, which negatively impacts the development.

In the Sri Lankan context, asserting the claims made by Chawdhury (2016), Herath and Amaratunge (2007) examined the association between the political changes (and other selected variables) in Sri Lanka and real effective interest rates and found that these changes had a significant impact on the interest rate during the period from January 1994 to December 2000. They had taken the Stock Market Index of the Colombo Stock Exchange to proxy the political changes and indicate that their selected period of study is a period where Sri Lanka had been seriously affected with civil war and other political instabilities. They further explain that, from the beginning of the 1994 period, Sri Lanka underwent a political change and the business community in Sri Lanka at that time believed that the government was not in favour of business.

However, MacCulloch (2005) concludes that empirical findings cited in a number of studies over two decades have produced divergent and sometimes contradictory findings on the association between conflict and inequality. Polachek and Sebastianova (2011) argue that conflicts negatively impact economic growth in the short run, but in the long run such economies recover from the negative effects between and among political parties.

The sections reviewed above identified several macroeconomic variables that could impact the economic growth of a country. They include political stability, FDI, population growth, inflation, trade openness and gross capital formation. Despite having found several local and foreign studies on the subject, the researchers did not come across recent Sri Lankan studies that had used all these variables, which indicates a gap for us to address. Another phenomenon observed was the mixed nature of evidence. The six variables cited here in some instances had a positive impact, while in others they had a negative impact on economic growth. This also warrants further investigation, particularly in light of the dearth identified in the Sri Lankan context.

14.3 Methods

This section discusses the methods deployed to examine the impact of political shocks and other macroeconomic variables on the GDP of Sri Lanka and to assess the impact of opening the economy in 1978. A quantitative approach in the positivistic research paradigm is used. Such an approach is deemed appropriate because the study examines the relationships between variables, and a similar approach is also observed in other studies.

Based on the endogenous growth model, the neoclassical theories and empirical studies discussed in the preceding section, the conceptual framework of the current study is present below (Fig. 14.1).

Based on this conceptual model, the following hypotheses are developed:

H1:   *Each production factor (i.e., gross fixed capital formation, population growth and FDI) has an association with real GDP.*

H2:   *Each technical factor (i.e., trade openness, political shocks and opening the economy) has an association with real GDP.*

In terms of data, secondary data from 1971 to 2016 are used to estimate the empirical model. RGDP, FDI, inflation, population growth and domestic capital data were obtained from World Bank databases; import and export data to calculate trade openness were collected from Central Bank reports in Sri Lanka.

Empirical Model

Since the original set of data was non-stationary, the first difference of each variable has been taken, and all variables were found to be stationary at the first difference. Accordingly, the following model has been estimated by the ordinary least squares (OLS) method.

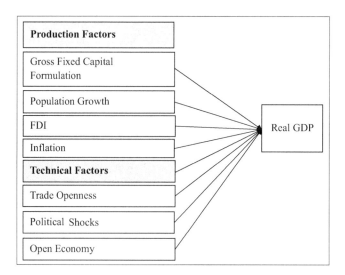

Fig. 14.1 Conceptual diagram. (Source: Authors, using the literature)

$$Y = f\left(X_1, X_2, X_3, X_4, X_5, X_6, X_7\right) \tag{14.1}$$

Y = GDP at constant prices (constant 2010 US$)
X_1 = Gross fixed capital formation (constant 2010 US$)
X_2 = Population growth rate (annual %)
X_3 = Foreign direct investment net inflows (constant 2010 US$)
X_4 = Inflation, GDP deflator (annual %)
X_5 = Trade openness
X_6 = Dummy variable which indicates whether the economy is an open economy or a closed economy (if X_6 = 0, Sri Lanka is a closed economy; if X_6 = 1 Sri Lanka is an open economy)
X_7 = Dummy variable which indicates whether Sri Lankan economy is in political instability or not (if X_7 = 0, Sri Lanka is in political instability; if X_7 = 1, Sri Lanka is in political stability)

GDP is the value of all goods and services which have been produced within the economy during a year, computed at market prices including inflationary effects. Therefore the study employed GDP at constant prices (constant 2010 US$). Capital is a crucial production factor which determines total output. Gross capital formation was employed as a proxy for capital. According to national accounting standards, gross domestic capital formation consists of three main components: gross fixed capital formation, changes in inventories and change in valuables. Since gross fixed capital formation has a direct effect on production capacity of the three components, gross fixed capital formation was employed for the model. Labour is another important production factor in any economy that determines the level of output. In many empirical studies, population growth rate has been used as a proxy for labour. Therefore the population growth rate has been employed for the model. FDI is a very important determinant of economic growth, especially in developing countries. According to data available, FDI net inflow has been employed in the model. FDI net inflow was computed by subtracting FDI outflow from FDI inflow. The relationship between inflation and economic growth/RGDP is still debated in the literature. There are a number of studies that argue that inflation has positive impact on economic growth in the short run and a negative impact in the long run. With this background, the GDP deflator (implicit price index) was employed in the model.

Trade openness is considered a crucial determinant of economic growth/RGDP in current open economies. Trade openness employed in the model is computed by the following formula.

$$TradeOpenness = \frac{Export + Import}{Gross\ Domestic\ Product}$$

X_6 is a dummy variable employed in the model to check whether an open economy has a significant impact on RGDP. Sri Lanka is a closed economy if $X_6 = 0$ and an open economy if $X_6 = 1$. X_7 is a dummy variable employed to check whether political shocks have significant impact on RGDP. Sri Lanka is in political shock/instability if $X_6 = 0$ and in political stability (free from political shocks) if $X_6 = 1$. Determination of the status of political stability or instability in each year of the sample has been based on a comprehensive analysis by an expert in political science.

Analytical Strategies

The empirical model of the study is estimated by employing time-series data. Since a non-stationary or unit root problem is an inherent problem associated with time-series data, all variables of the model must be stationary in order to derive reliable estimates. Thus the unit root problem of set of data has been tested by the Augmented Dickey-Fuller Test. Goodness of fit of the model or overall suitability of the model for a set of data is evaluated by the adjusted coefficient of determination. Overall significance of the model is tested by the 'F' test, and individual significance of each parameter estimated is tested by a 't' test.

14.4   Analysis and Findings

This section elaborates the analysis and the ensuing findings obtained via the application of the methodology elaborated in the preceding section. Accordingly, first the results of the diagnostic tests are elaborated and thereafter the results of the hypotheses testing presented.

Diagnostic Tests

The results of the outlier tests, unit-root tests and multicollinearity tests are discussed below.

Outlier Test Outliers of the set of data have been examined by utilizing Grubb's test. Outliers of the sample can reduce the accuracy of estimated parameters of the model. Therefore this test is important for identifying and removing unusual observations of the set of data.

According to Grubb's test, the 45th observation of net FDI inflows is found to be an outlier ($p < 0.05$) (Table 14.1). Therefore, the 45th observation (i.e. year 2015) of all variables has been removed from the sample in estimating the model.

Table 14.1 Outlier test

Variable	N	Mean	StDev	Min	Max	G	P
Y	46	30997085821	20176548587	8967036827	79706946035	2.41	0.595
X1	46	6975407408	5695566749	803142104	21361541421	2.53	0.416
X2	46	1.1463	0.4255	0.5551	1.9678	1.93	1.000
X3	46	3791005722	7338227795	-7765985	37313404649	4.57	0.000
X4	46	10.5890	5.7100	0.5840	24.3790	2.42	0.593
X5	46	0.5431	0.1445	0.2657	0.7741	1.92	1.000
X6	46	0.8478	0.3632	0.0000	1.0000	2.33	0.758
X7	46	0.5435	0.5036	0.0000	1.0000	1.08	1.000

Source: Data analysis by the authors

Variable	Row	Outlier
X3	45	3.73134E+10

Table 14.2 Unit root test

		t-statistics	Prob.
Augmented Dickey-Fuller test statistic		−2.319051	0.0451
Test critical values	1% level	−3.588509	
	5% level	−2.929734	
	10% level	−2.603064	

Source: Data Analysis by the authors

Table 14.3 Correlation metrics

	Y	X1	X2	X3	X4
X1	0.817				
	0.000				
X2	0.079	0.108			
	0.612	0.485			
X3	0.033	−0.046	0.012		
	0.833	0.765	0.936		
X4	−0.027	−0.049	−0.172	−0.517	
	0.860	0.752	0.265	0.0900	
X5	−0.083	0.140	0.141	0.168	−0.062
	0.592	0.364	0.362	0.274	0.688

Cell contents
Pearson correlation coefficient
p-value
Source: Data analysis by the authors

Unit Root Test Stationarity has been tested by the Augmented Dickey-Fuller test. Accordingly, all variables are found to be stationary at the first difference ($p < 0.05$) (Table 14.2).

Multicollinearity The multicollinearity problem is examined by correlation metrics of all predictor variables except dummy variables.

The model is free from multicollinearity, since almost all partial correlation coefficients are statistically insignificant at a 5% significance level (Table 14.3). This is further confirmed by the following matrix plot (Fig. 14.2).

Estimates of the Model

Having explored the results of the diagnostic tests in the preceding section, this subsection presents the results of the regression analysis involving the main model.

The F-test is used to check the overall significance of the model. The F-statistic is 14.89, and the p-value is closer to zero (Table 14.4). Therefore, it is concluded that the model is significant as a whole (Table 14.5).

Matrix Plot of Dy, DX1, DX2, DX3, DX4, DX5

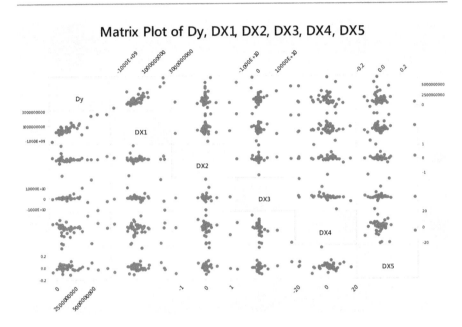

Fig. 14.2 Matrix plot of variables. (Source: Authors)

Table 14.4 Analysis of variance

Source	DF	Adj SS	Adj MS	F-value	p-value
Regression	7	7.28646E+19	1.04092E+19	14.89	0.000
X1	1	6.10497E+19	6.10497E+19	87.33	0.000
X2	1	2.41817E+17	2.41817E+17	0.35	0.560
X3	1	1.74097E+18	1.74097E+18	2.49	0.123
X4	1	8.28244E+17	8.28244E+17	1.18	0.284
X5	1	4.33320E+18	4.33320E+18	6.20	0.018
X6	1	1.67025E+18	1.67025E+18	2.39	0.131
X7	1	1.29932E+17	1.29932E+17	0.19	0.669
Error	36	2.51675E+19	6.99096E+17		
Total	43	9.80321E+19			

Source: Data analysis by the authors

Table 14.5 Model summary

S	R-sq	R-sq(adj)	R-sq(pred)
836,119,639	74.33%	69.34%	57.59%

Source: Data analysis by the authors

Table 14.6 Estimated parameters

Variable	Coefficient	Std. error	t-statistics	Prob.
Constant	2.9500	3.5400	0.8333	0.4100
X_1	1.5975	0.1863	0.5754	0.0000
X_2	1.9900	4.7400	0.4202	0.6768
X_3	0.0709	0.0267	2.6526	0.0117
X_4	23,114,664	18,686,006	1.2370	0.2239
X_5	−4.4400	1.8100	−2.4539	0.0190
X_6	6.3800	3.5500	1.7996	0.0801
X_7	−53,126,814	2.4400	−0.2181	0.8285

Source: Data Analysis by the authors

The adjusted R^2 value of the model is 69.34%, and this indicates that this percentage of GDP is explained by selected independent variables. Accordingly, it is observed that there is satisfactory goodness of fitness of the model with the data.

The individual significance of each variable in the model is presented in Table 14.6. It is observed that the variables population growth rate ($X2$), inflation ($X4$) and political stability ($X7$) are not statistically significant ($p > 0.10$), which means that there is no statistical evidences to confirm that these variables have significant impact on RGDP of Sri Lanka. Gross fixed capital formation ($X1$) is statistically significant at the 1% level ($p < 0.01$), and it has strong positive impact on RGDP. FDI ($X3$) is statistically significant at the 5% (p < 0.05), and it also has a strong positive impact on RGDP. However, trade openness ($X5$) is statistically significant at a 5% level ($p < 0.05$), but has negative impact on RGDP. The dummy variable, which indicates whether an economy is open or closed ($X6$), is found to be statistically significant at the 10% level ($p < 0.10$) and indicates that the open economy concept that was introduced after 1977 has a positive impact on RGDP.

14.5 Discussion and Conclusions

This section presents the discussion and conclusions. The first objective of this study was to examine the impact of macroeconomic variables on RGDP of Sri Lanka, and accordingly, FDI, domestic fixed capital formation, inflation, population growth rate and trade openness were taken into account. The second objective was to examine the impact of political shocks on RGDP. The third was to test whether RGDP was significantly affected by the open economy introduced in 1977. The study used secondary data from 1971 to 2016 to estimate the empirical model.

The regression results indicated that the population growth rate, inflation and political stability are not statistically significant, indicating that there is no statistical evidence to establish that these variables have significant impact on RGDP of Sri Lanka. The finding that political instability does not have a significant impact on

RGDP is consistent with the conclusions of MacCulloch (2005), who asserts that empirical findings elaborated in a number of studies over two decades have produced divergent, sometimes contradicting, findings on the association between conflict and inequality. Further, as indicated by Polachek and Sevastianova (2011), conflicts negatively impact economic growth in a short run, but in the long run such economies recover from the negative effects between and within political parties. Thus, after 30 years of war—which could be considered long-run—and political turbulence, Sri Lanka seems to be sensitized and normalized, so that such turbulence would not have any significant impact. It also could be claimed that the RGDP is quite low in the Sri Lankan context (especially compared to its Asian counterparts), and thus political instability in the long run would not have had an impact in any case. The insignificant impact of population growth rate on RGDP is also interesting to note, and this finding is consistent with researchers such as Landreth and David (2002, cited in Uddin 2016) and Feyrery (2002, cited in Uddin 2016), who claim that changes in population may not have an economic impact. Unless the *working* population grows significantly or their productivity grows significantly, it cannot be expected to have a significant impact on the economic growth (Kelley and Schmidt 2005). Therefore, mere increase of *total* population cannot be expected to have a significant impact. The findings indicate that these *internal*-oriented macroeconomic fundamentals do not have a significant impact on RGDP.

However, the findings indicate that gross fixed capital formation is statistically significant at a 1% level and it has strong positive impact on RGDP. It was also noted that FDI is statistically significant at a 5% level and has strong positive impact on RGDP. The dummy variable on the open economy is statistically significant at the 10% level. The open economy introduced after 1977 has thus positively affected RGDP and the closed economy prior to 1977 negatively affected GDP at that time. All these variables are *external*-oriented and assert that the Sri Lankan economy greatly depends on such *external* assistance. Similar to these findings, in the Indonesian context, Khaliq and Noy (2007) found that FDI had positively impacted the country's economic growth during the period from 1997 to 2006. In terms of gross capital formation, De Long and Summers (1991) indicate that there is a positive relationship between these two constructs. This positive relationship was also confirmed by Levine and Renelt (1992), Islam (1996) and Lauthier and Moreaub (2012).

Trade openness is statistically significant at the 5% level, and it has a negative impact on RGDP. Kwame (2013) found that liberalization of trade led to GDP growth in the long run, but it impacted negatively in the short run in Ghana. The period considered under this study is long run, and thus it is apparent that too many imports are detrimental to RGDP.

These findings have significant economic policy implications. Policymakers should promote FDI, open economic policies and thereby gross capital formation within Sri Lanka. Sri Lanka should promote exports over imports. In particular, through FDI, different types of skills (managerial, technical, human skills, etc.), as well as technological advancement, innovations and new knowledge, should be brought to Sri Lanka. Sri Lanka also needs to continue open economic policies and especially promote exports.

In terms of future research directions, it is proposed to examine the reasons behind some of the main findings of this study, as well as to consider additional macroeconomic variables. A comparative study with other developing nations is recommended.

Chapter Takeaways/Lessons

1. In terms of a country's economic growth, there may be various macroeconomic determinants such as foreign direct investment, inflation, population growth, fixed domestic capital formation and trade openness of a country, and 'political shocks' as a determinant has gained prominence particularly in the developing country context.
2. The endogenous growth and neoclassical models could be used as theoretical underpinning to explain the economic growth fuelled by FDI of a country.
3. The empirical evidence is mixed regarding the impact of political instability on economic development.
4. In a developing country context, the findings of this study suggest that population growth rate, inflation and political stability are not having a statistically significant impact on RGDP of Sri Lanka. But gross fixed capital formation and FDI were found to have a significant positive impact on RGDP.
5. As one of the first South Asian countries to adopt a full open economic model, the open economy concept introduced after 1977 has positively affected RGDP in Sri Lanka.
6. In an emerging country context, policymakers should promote FDI, open economic policies and thereby gross capital formation within Sri Lanka. Importantly, through FDI, different types of skills (managerial, technical, human skills, etc.), as well as technological advancement, innovations and new knowledge, should be brought to Sri Lanka.

Reflective Questions

1. Explain various macroeconomic determinants that could impact the RGDP of a country.
2. Compare and contrast the endogenous growth model and neoclassical theories on FDI and economic development.
3. 'Political instabilities will always have a negative impact on the economic growth of a country'. Critically evaluate this statement by using the findings of empirical studies.
4. What is an 'open economic system'? Discuss the benefits of such a system.
5. Evaluate why Sri Lanka as a developing country was not significantly impacted by political instability and shocks.

References

Adhikary, B. K. (2011). FDI, trade openness, capital formation, and economic growth in Bangladesh: A linkage analysis. *International Journal of Business and Management, 6*(1), 16–28.

Alesina, A., & Perotti, R. (1996). Income distribution, political instability and investment. *European Economic Review, 40*(6), 1203–1228.

Central Bank of Sri Lanka (CBSL). (2017). *Annual report of the central bank of Sri Lanka.* Colombo.

Chawdhury, J. (2016). *Political instability a major obstacle to economic growth in Bangladesh* (unpublished thesis). Centria University of Applied Sciences, Finland.

Coase, R. II. (1937). The nature of the firm. *Econometrica, 4,* 386–405.

De Long, J., & Summers, L. (1991). Equipment investment and economic growth. *Quarterly Journal of Economics, 106,* 445–502.

Edwards, S. (1992). Trade orientation, distortions and growth in developing countries. *Journal of Development Economies, 39,* 31–57.

Easterly, W., & Levine, R. (1997). Africa's growth tragedy: Policies and ethnic divisions. *Quarterly Journal of Economics, 112,* 1203–1250.

Grossman, H. (1991). A general equilibrium theory of insurrections. *American Economic Review, 81*(4), 912–921.

Herath, H. M. U. K., & Amaratunga, S. (2007). *The relationship between real effective exchange rate, inflation rate, interest rate and political change in Sri Lanka: an empirical test.* Proceedings of the Conference, Sabaragamuwa University.

Islam, N. (1996). Growth empirics: A panel data approach. *Quarterly Journal of Economics, 110,* 1127–1170.

Khaliq, A. & Noy, I. (2007). *Foreign direct investment and economic growth: Empirical evidence from sectoral data in Indonesia.* Working Papers from University of Hawaii at Manoa, Department of Economics – 200726, University of Hawaii at Manoa, Department of Economics.

Keho, Y. (2017). The impact of trade openness on economic growth: The case of cote d'Ivoire. *Cogent Economics & Finance, 5*(1), 1–14.

Kelley, A. C., & Schmidt, R. M. (2005). Evolution of recent economic-demographic modelling: A synthesis. *Population Economics, 18*(2), 275–300.

Khobai, H., Kolisi, N., & Moyo, C. (2018). The relationship between trade openness and economic growth: The case of Ghana and Nigeria. *International Journal of Economics and Financial Issues, 8*(1), 77–82.

Kormendi, R. C., & Meguire, P. G. (1985). Macroeconomic determinants of growth: Cross-country evidence. *Journal of Monetary Economics, 16,* 141–163.

Lauthier, M., & Moreaub, F. (2012). Domestic investment and FDI in developing countries: The missing link. *Journal of Economic Development, 37,* 1–22.

Levine, R., & Renelt, D. (1992). A sensitivity analysis of cross-country growth regressions. *American Economic Review, 82,* 942–963.

MacCulloch, R. (2005). Income inequality and the taste for revolution. *Journal of Law & Economics, 48*(1), 93–123.

Moosa, I. A., & Cardak, B. A. (2006). The determinants of foreign direct investment: An extreme bound analysis. *Journal of Multinational Financial Management, 16,* 199–211.

Nair-Reichert, U., & Weinhold, D. (2001). Causality test for cross country panels: A new look at FDI and economic growth in developing countries. *Oxford Bulletin of Economics and Statistics, 63*(2), 153–171.

Nduka, E. K., Chukwu, J. O., Kalu, I. K., & Nwakaire, O. N. (2013). Trade openness and economic growth: A comparative analysis of the pre and post structural adjustment programme (SAP) periods in Nigeria. *Asian Journal of Business and Economics, 3*(3), 1–12.

Polachek, S. W., & Sevastianova, D. (2011). Does conflict disrupt growth? Evidence of the relationship between political instability and national economic performance. *Journal of International Trade and Economic Development, 21*(3), 361–388.

Ramanayake, S. S., & Wijetunga, C. S. (2017). *Rethinking the development of post-war Sri Lanka based on the Singapore model.* Working Paper – WP-2017-009, Indira Gandhi Institute of Development Research, Mumbai, India.

Romer, P. M. (1986). Increasing returns and long-run growth. *Journal of Political Economy, 95*(5), 1002–1037.

Roy, M., & Borsha, F. H. (2013). Hartal: A violent challenge to the socio-economic development of Bangladesh. *International Journal of Scientific & Technology Research, 2*(8), 86–97.

Shonchoy, A., & Tsubota, K. (2014). *Economic impact of political protests (strikes) on manufacturing firms: Evidence from Bangladesh.* IDE Discussion Paper No. 523.

Uddin, G. A. (2016). *Population changes and implications for economic growth and the environment in Australia* (unpublished PhD dissertation). University of Southern Queensland, Australia.

The Relationship Between Macroeconomic Variables and Budget Deficit: A Comparative Study of Sri Lanka with Malaysia and South Korea

15

D. M. S. B. Dissanayake

15.1 Introduction

Year on year, striving for a balanced budget is a thorny question everywhere. For economic stability, countries need to reduce longstanding, sizable budget deficits and strive to maintain this as a trend. A country's unfavourable welfare trends are generally associated with balancing the budget and politically popular decisions. In general, the government budget is used to assess the fiscal health of a country. It is further differentiated by closely related terms of the primary balance and structural balance (also known as cyclically adjusted balance) of the government. The primary budget balance is the government budget balance before interest payments. The structural budget balance attempts to adjust the impacts of real GDP changes in the national economy (Dissanayake 2016).

Macroeconomic stability is a crucial component in meeting sustained growth and, along with reducing the size of the budget deficit, is a major determinant of economic stability. To maintain macroeconomic stability, economic policymakers need to consider current economic issues, historical trends and potential threats and future benefits. The budgetary process is multi-dimensional processes with many economic variables that affect the outcome and also depend on the country's economic behaviour.

Empirically, however, budget deficits are more common than a balanced budget internationally and locally for various economic reasons. This makes it important to study the impact of macroeconomic instability on an unmanageable, sizable, sustained budget deficit, identifying the selected macroeconomic variables (inflation, interest rates, exchange rates, real GDP growth rate and debts) and their relationship

D. M. S. B. Dissanayake (✉)
Aquinas College of Higher Studies, Colombo, Sri Lanka

309

to the budget deficit, and determine the potential of countries to achieve macroeconomic stability in the long term.

15.1.1 Budget Deficit Records

15.1.1.1 Sri Lankan Government
From 1980 to 2016, the Sri Lankan government budget deficit averaged 8.65% of GDP, with a record high of 19.20% in 1980. In 2017, the deficit increased to 5.5% from 5.4%, which was recorded in 2016 as a result of worsened government revenue collection. But in 2017 it represented a reduction in total government expenditure to 19.4% (% of GDP; see Fig. 15.1).

In 2017, the overall budget deficit of Rs.733.49 billion was financed largely through foreign sources (mainly international sovereign bonds (ISBs), foreign currency term financing facility (FTFF), T-bonds and T-bills). This foreign financing stood at Rs. 439,243 million (3.3% of GDP), and net domestic financing (2.2% of GDP) amounted to Rs. 294,251 million (CBSL annual report 2017).

15.1.1.2 International Trend
Malaysia recorded a government budget deficit equal to 3.20% of GDP in 2015. The budget averaged −3.0% of GDP from 2000 to 2015. South Korea recorded a deficit equal to 3% of GDP in 2015; the budget averaged −0.30% of GDP from 2000 to 2015 (IMF Factbook 2014).

In the 2000–2015 period, the global financial crisis of 2007–2008 is considered by many economists as the most terrible financial crisis after the Great Depression of the 1930s: many countries experienced their highest budget deficits in 2009 and 2010. In 2009 budget deficits (% of GDP) were the USA 13.3%, Ireland 7.3%, Greece 15.6%, Portugal 10.2%, Spain 11.2%, Japan 10.4%, and India 10%, and in 2010 the USA 11.2%, Ireland 30.9%, Portugal 9.8%, Spain 9.4%, Japan 9.4%, the UK 9.9%, and India 10% (IMF Factbook 2014).

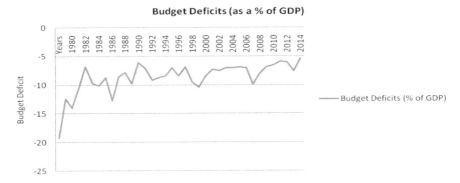

Fig. 15.1 Budget deficit record in Sri Lanka, 1980–2016. (Source: Author's analysis)

15.1.2 Impact of Budget Deficits on Economic Stability

A country with a larger budget deficit may struggle to attract sufficient foreign investors to buy government bonds. If this occurs, the Central Bank needs to print money to buy bonds, but, unless the economy is in a liquidity trap, printing money will cause inflation and reduce the value of savings. When a government tries to finance its large deficit domestically, the remaining reduced funds for private investment will lead to 'crowding out' in the private sector. Attraction of new investors to buy government bonds is required to increase the bond yield rate. This may lead to spending a higher amount of national income on debt interest repayment and will result in a larger deficit. When the budget deficit is above a certain level, national debt tends to increase on for deficit financing.

A sizable, sustained budget deficit may cause macroeconomic instability. According to Keynesian analysis, maintaining a sizable budget deficit during a recession will lead to increased aggregate demand, because, in a recession, private consumption and investment fall and increasing government expenditure are the only way to 'kick start' the economy. Hence government spending can help promote economic growth, which will enable collection of tax revenue from households and firms such that the deficit will fall over time. If a country tries to maintain a balanced budget during a recession, this can make the recession deeper. During such times there can be good reasons to run a deficit budget – at least for the short term (Keynes 2007).

15.1.3 Rationale

Macroeconomic stability can be measured by the volatility of key indicators: inflation, real GDP growth rate, changes in unemployment, fluctuations in the current account of the BOP (balance of payments), the size of the deficit, volatility of short-term policy interest rates and long-term interest rates such as the yield on government bonds and stability of the exchange rate in the currency market (Adam and Bevan 2005).

Macroeconomic stability provides a framework for improved supply-side performance and maintains that this is essential for healthy economic growth. Stable low inflation encourages higher investment, which is a determinant of improved productivity and non-price competitiveness. Controlling inflation also helps maintain price competitiveness for exporters and domestic businesses facing competition on imported goods. Maintaining the exchange rate helps international business confidence and also government debt servicing. The maintenance of short- and long-term low interest rates is important for private investment and will reduce the interest costs of those with mortgages and businesses with loans to repay. A stable real economy helps anchor a country's stability expectations, which can act as an incentive to attract inflows of foreign direct investment (Dornbush and Fisher 1994).

Impact of causes of and factors in macroeconomic instability have always been of great interest for researchers. Keynes's (2007) concept is based on the principle that the market economy is unstable and incapable of self-regulation. It requires external influences and regulation by the government, especially when the economy is in a recession or depression. It is the government's role to ensure macroeconomic stability by controlling aggregate demand and decide the amount of government spending, tax rates, and amount of money supply in the economy.

Macroeconomic instability may distort sustained growth: high or unstable inflation threatens economic growth, and high inflation alters the value of long-term contracts; volatile inflation creates uncertainty in the market and increases risk premiums, and, since many tax rates are adjusted by average inflation, volatile inflation can severely impact government revenue and individual liabilities. Higher national debt also points to government inflexibility in using tax revenue to address domestic needs instead of paying foreign creditors, whereas a low national debt permits lenient fiscal policy in a time of crisis. The Maastricht criteria cap that debt level at 60% of GDP. When the budget deficit is high, growth of national debt accelerates. The Maastricht criteria also cap the deficit needed at 3% of GDP. Real exchange rate stability allows importers and exporters to develop long-term growth strategies and reduces exchange rate risk for investors. In national accounting, a stable currency reduces the threat (currency depreciation) posed by the debt issue in terms of foreign currency. The Maastricht criteria permit exchange rate fluctuations of at most 2.5%. Increase of the exchange rate gap and increase of foreign exchange fluctuation cause increased risk and uncertainty in market decision-making. All these factors decrease the real growth of an economy in the short run (EMI Annual Report 1994). Put simply, the variables of budget deficit, inflation, interest rates, exchange rates, real GDP growth rate, current account deficit, debt and unemployment in an unmanageable situation represent macroeconomic instability.

Although numerous factors contribute to macroeconomic stability, policymakers can influence some of them in the short run. Proposing structural changes to deal with long-run stability may be of importance. The major issues for policymakers, in the context of a potential link between reducing the budget deficit and macroeconomic stability, are as follows: How to stimulate investment? How to increase the level of savings to lend funds for investment needs? How to attract foreign flows and maintain bilateral investment? How to manage international trade and the issues related to international trade? How to maintain an optimal level of interest rates? How to maintain an optimal level of exchange rates? How to control inflation to maintain price stability? How to maintain optimal debt levels? How to achieve sustained high economic growth? And how to raise the public's quality of life?

15.1.4 Research Questions

How do the selected macroeconomic variables influence the budget deficit in Sri Lanka? How do they influence the budget deficit in Malaysia? How do they influence it in South Korea? How do the variables negatively impact macroeconomic instability? And how do these circumstances affect achievement of high economic growth?

15.1.5 Problem Statement

Widening budget deficits have become a major concern, because of adverse impacts on macroeconomic instability. There are no guidelines for policymakers about the level of budget deficit that must be maintained. Therefore, there is a possibility of increasing budget deficit size to a level detrimental to macroeconomic stability, which might pose a greater risk of insolvency or, even worse, bankruptcy in the future. A country's lack of threshold levels to serve as guidelines in maintaining and reducing a budget deficit may lead to loss of control of the fiscal position.

15.1.6 Objective

The main objective of this study is to investigate selected macroeconomic variables' relationship to the budget deficits in Sri Lanka, South Korea and Malaysia from 2000 to 2016.

15.1.6.1 Specific Objectives

- To study the effect of budget deficit on selected macroeconomic variables in Sri Lanka, South Korea and Malaysia from 2000 to 2016;
- To undertake a comparative study; to identify the selected macroeconomics variable's relationship to the budget deficit during the post-liberalization era (2000–2016).

15.1.7 Hypotheses

The following null hypotheses are tested in the study of the Granger Causality test:
- H1: Inflation does not have any significant relationship to budget deficit.
- H2: Interest rate does not have any significant relationship to budget deficit.
- H3: Exchange rate does not have any significant relationship to budget deficit.
- H4: Real GDP growth rate does not have any significant relationship to budget deficit.
- H5: Debt does not have any significant relationship to budget deficit.
  The following hypotheses are tested in the study of the Hausman test;
- H6: The random-effect model is appropriate.
- H7: The fixed-effect model is appropriate.

15.1.8 Importance of the Study

In open economies, significant macroeconomic problems are liable to cause an unmanageable, sizable budget deficit, and ultimately this will lead to an economic crisis. The importance of the study is for making decisions on the level of future spending, national debt-level reduction and the opportunity cost of debt interest repayments, and for identifying possible pressures on inflation. The potential economic costs of budget deficits depend on economic climate, the exchange rate system, domestic interest rates and government borrowings, and finding solutions for these issues and maintaining a stable growth rate, which are even more important. Two Asian countries, South Korea and Malaysia, were selected as maintaining a lower budget deficit level in order to identify how to implement these two country's macroeconomic variables might positively impact on Sri Lanka's economic growth.

15.1.9 Limitations

The study involves a very complex array of relationships, and for study purposes it will be necessary to narrow the focus to a limited number of macroeconomic determinants of the budget deficit: inflation, interest rates, exchange rates, real GDP growth rate and debt. The main study also selected only 16 years (2000–2016) to minimize the macroeconomic variables' cyclical effect (if any). Further, it assumes error terms are uncorrelated when considering time series data.

15.2   Literature Review

A deficit budget is when government expenditure outweighs revenue. Fiscal policy is concerned with raising revenue through taxation and deciding the level of expenditure for economic activity. Fiscal policy decisions will affect achievement of certain desirable macroeconomic goals (Anyanwu 1993). Most studies suggest that inflation, interest rates, exchange rates, real GDP growth rate and debt cause budget deficits (and vice versa for reducing deficits).

The relationship between budget deficit and macroeconomic variables is one of the most widely debated topics among economists and policymakers in developed and developing economies. Budget deficit and these macroeconomic variable relationships can either be negative or positive (Saleh 2003).

In each period, the government must finance its planned expenditure and also pay any debt interest. For financing its expenditure, the government can use taxation or deplete fixed assets, sell new bonds or print money; one of these (and others) may be considered. In nominal terms, the government budget identity in each period can be written as Eq. 15.1:

$$G + iB \equiv T + \Delta B \qquad (15.1)$$

where G is government expenditure on goods and services in nominal terms; i, nominal interest rate; B, outstanding stock of bonds; T, tax revenue; and ΔB, value of new bonds issued in the current period (Carlin and Soskice 2013). Equation 2.1.1 is constructed considering the government budget of the expected revenue and level of expenditure.

Equation 15.2 is defined to identify the government debt level, relative to national income. We, therefore, write the equation:

$$\text{Gove}^n \text{debt to GDP ratio} \equiv b = \frac{B}{Py} \qquad (15.2)$$

where b is government debt-to-GDP ratio; B, government debt; P, price level; y, real national income; and Py, nominal national income (nominal GDP).

If the government decided to increase the money supply when the budget is not in equilibrium by selling government bonds or manipulating interest rates or printing money, this can be changed or increased via high-powered money (ΔH); by adding high-powered money to the right-hand side of Eq. 15.1, we can construct Eq. 15.3 as:

$$G + iB \equiv T + \Delta B + \Delta H \qquad (15.3)$$

$$\Delta B \equiv (G - T) + iB - \Delta H$$

$$\frac{\Delta B}{Py} = \frac{(G - T)}{Py} + \frac{iB}{Py} - \frac{\Delta H}{Py} \qquad \text{dividing by nominal GDP}$$

$$\frac{\Delta B}{Py} = d + ib - \frac{\Delta H}{Py} \qquad (A)$$

Where $\dfrac{B}{Py} = b =$ Gov^n debt to GDP ratio, $\dfrac{(G - T)}{Py} = d =$ Primary budget deficit to GDP ratio $B = b . Py$ from Eq. (15.2)

$$\Delta B \approx \Delta bPy + b\Delta Py + bP\Delta y$$

$$\frac{\Delta B}{Py} = \frac{\Delta bPy}{Py} + \frac{b\Delta Py}{Py} + \frac{bP\Delta y}{Py}$$

$$\frac{\Delta B}{Py} = \Delta b + b\pi + b\gamma_y \qquad (B)$$

where $\Delta P/P = \pi =$ rate of inflation, $\dfrac{\Delta y}{y} = \gamma_y =$ growth of real output

When (A) = (B)

$$d + ib - \frac{\Delta H}{Py} = \Delta b + b\pi + b\gamma_y$$

$$\Delta b = d + (i - \pi)b - b\gamma_y - \frac{\Delta H}{Py}$$

$$\Delta b = d + (r - \gamma_y)b - \frac{\Delta H}{H} \cdot \frac{H}{Py}$$

where $(i - \pi) = r =$ real interest rate, $M = kH$, $M =$ broad money, $H =$ High powered money, k(kappa) = banking multiplier

$$\Delta b = d + \left(r - \gamma_y\right)b - \gamma_H h \tag{15.4}$$

When $\dfrac{\Delta H}{H} = \gamma_H =$ growth rate of high powered money

$\dfrac{H}{Py} = h =$ ratio of high powered money to nominal GDPWhere $\Delta b=$ growth of the debt to GDP ratio, $b=$ ratio of government debt to GDP

Equation 15.4 provides a powerful way of understanding the relationship of the five key determinants of growth of debt-to-GDP ratio (Δb): (1) primary budget deficit ratio (d); (2) real interest rate (r); (3) growth of real GDP (γ_y); (4) ratio of government debt to GDP (b); and (5) growth of high-powered money (γ_H) (Carlin and Soskice 2013).

15.2.1 Budget Deficit and Selected Macroeconomic Variables

15.2.1.1 Budget Deficit and Inflation

The relationship between budget deficit, money supply and inflation is analysed as follows. Increase in monetary base balance, leading to increase in money supply, will result in more general inflation. Price growth tends to decrease the real value of money and forces the government to increase subsidies, which leads to an increase in the size of the budget deficit (Chimobi and Igwe 2010).

Devapriya and Masaru (2012) in a Sri Lankan study identified that budget deficit and inflation have a positive relationship, and there is a bi-directional causality between budget deficit and inflation. Their study suggests the main determinants of inflation rate are budget deficit, growth of money supply, interest rates and real exchange rates.

15.2.1.2 Budget Deficit and Interest Rate

Al-Khedir (1996) studied the relationship between budget deficit and macroeconomic performance of G7 countries for the period 1964–1993 using vector autoregression. He found a deficit budget that led to higher short-term interest rates. However, deficits did not manifest any impact on long-term interest rates. Knoester and Mak (1994) showed that only in Germany (of eight OECD economies) did government budget deficit contribute significantly to explanation of higher interest rates.

15.2.1.3 Budget Deficit and Exchange Rate

Krugman and Venables (1995) and Sachs (1985) argued that lower budget deficits lower the value of the dollar. Feldstein (1986) points out that appreciation of the dollar in the 1980s coincided with a high budget deficit; this study started a debate on the efficacy of cutting the budget deficit in the USA to strengthen the dollar. A similar phenomenon has been found in Canada by Wijnbergen (1989) where 'budget deficit contributed to an appreciation of the Canadian dollar'.

15.2.1.4   Budget Deficit and Real GDP Growth Rate

Ezeabasili et al. (2012) examined the relationship between economic growth and fiscal deficit in Nigeria. They utilized co-integration and structural method for 36 years (1970–2006) and revealed a negative effect of budget deficit on economic growth. Similarly, Fatima et al. (2012) investigated the consequential effect of budget deficit on the economic growth of Pakistan, using time series data for 31 years (1978–2009), also showing a negative impact of budget deficit on economic growth and suggesting that government should avoid a certain level of deficit to achieve a desired level of growth.

15.2.1.5   Budget Deficit and Debt

The national debt is the total amount of money payable by the government for goods and services bought but not paid for. As with the budget deficit, there are a number of views in regard to the national debt. When a government runs a budget deficit, meaning it spends more than it receives, in order to fund for this spending, the government needs loans. Mostly government finances its deficit by selling bonds. To sell bonds, the government must offer an interest rate which is attractive to investors. When the government increases the interest rate to finance the budget deficit, the debt-service level tends to increase. Financing the deficit in this manner may end with a debt trap (Michael 2011).

The government budget identity Eq. 15.1 shows the sources of the funds in any period to pay for the government's expenditure on consumption, transfers and investments and paying on debt servings (Carlin and Soskice 2013):

$$G + iB \equiv T + \Delta B$$
$$\Delta B = (G - T) + iB$$

Change in debt = primary deficit + interest on outstanding debt
Change in debt = actual deficit

$$\Delta b = d + (r - \gamma_y)b \tag{15.5}$$

Δb = change in debt to GDP ratio, d = primary deficit ratio, r = real interest rate, γ_y = grouth of real GDP, b = ratio of government debt to GDP.

The government's intertemporal budget identity can also be interpreted as to its solvency constraint and as a requirement for the absence of default risk on its debt. Also, there is a focus on the conditions necessary for the debt ratio not to increase zero $\Delta b \leq 0$:

$$\Delta b = d + (r - \gamma_y)b \tag{15.6}$$

$$\Delta b \leq 0$$

$$b \leq \frac{-d}{r - \gamma_y}$$

$$\frac{\text{Gov}^n \text{ Debt}}{\text{GDP}} = \frac{\text{primary budget surplus ratio}}{\left(r - \gamma_y\right)}$$

In order to interpret the budget constraint, we need to consider each variable's long-run value. For long-run sustainability, with an excess of expected long-run growth rate to give long-run real interest rates, there must be a long-run primary surplus if the debt-to-GDP ratio is constant (Carlin and Soskice 2013).

Dayarathna-Banda and Priyadrasanee (2014) have said Sri Lanka's public debt is not sustainable, so a change is required from foreign debt to other sources of financing for deficit reduction. In Sri Lanka, GDP growth rate, budget deficit, political instability and time trend positively affect increase of debt (Deyshappriya 2012). Financing the budget deficit by reducing the debt ratio and increasing the tax ratio is going to be a formidable challenge in the future development of Sri Lanka (Amirthalingam 2011/2012).

15.3   Methodology

This paper examined two different aspects to identify the nexus between selected macroeconomic variables and the budget deficit. Initially, the Granger Causality test was carried out to determine whether the selected variables' impact on budget deficit was uni- or bi-directional for Sri Lanka, Malaysia and South Korea, using annual time series data (2000–2016). Secondly, a comparative study used panel analysis for Sri Lanka, Malaysia and South Korea from 2000 to 2016. This utilized the Hausman test to identify the most suitable model between of the fixed-effect or random-effect models. The random effect's assumption is that the individual-specific effects are uncorrelated with the independent variables. The fixed effect's assumption is that the individual-specific effects correlate with the independent variables. The Durbin-Wu-Hausman test is often used to discriminate between the fixed and the random-effects models. All the non-stationary data were converted to a stationary level and employed EViews 9.5 econometric software for the data analysis.

Malaysia and South Korea were the two countries selected for the comparative analysis with Sri Lanka. The reason was that South Korea had the fourth-largest and Malaysia the third-largest economies in the Asian and Southeast Asian regions (respectively). They also maintained a lower budget deficit level and served to identify macroeconomic variables' positive impact applicable to Sri Lankan growth.

15.3.1 Data Collection

The secondary data collected for time series and panel data were obtained from the IMF international financial statistics database, World Bank data and a series of Central Bank of Sri Lanka annual reports. The economic interrelationships were grounded in theories extracted from relevant journals and textbooks. The study focused especially on macroeconomic variables during the post-liberalization period.

15.3.2 Model Specification

The proposed multiple regression model is to learn more about the relationship between selected independent variables – inflation (Inf), interest rate (r), exchange rate (ER), real GDP growth rate (y^g) and debts (debt) – and the budget deficit (Bd) as a dependent variable. Incorporating these explanatory variables, the budget deficit model specified in a linear form becomes:

$$Bd_{it} = \chi_0 + \chi_1 \inf_{it} + \chi_2 r_{it} + \chi_3 ER_{it} + \chi_4 y_{it}^g + \chi_5 debt_{it} + \phi_{it} \qquad (15.7)$$

where Bd = budget deficit as a % of GDP
Inf = rate of inflation; point to point price change %
r = 91 days T' bill rate, %
ER = US dollar exchange rate index
y^g = real GDP growth rate
debt = sum of cumulative domestic and foreign debts as a % of GDP
t = time (starting; 1980–2016 and 2000–2016)
i = indices for individuals
x_0 = intercept term (assume error terms are uncorrelated)
ϕ_{5t} = error term
$\sum_{a=1} x_a$ = coefficients

15.3.3 Granger Causality Testing

The Granger Causality test was carried out to determine whether the variable impacts were uni- or bi-directional. In fact, bi-directional causality may be valid for both series (see Abrego and Ross 2001; Sinha et al. 2011).

Simply put, the Granger Causality test is to represent six time series variables (budget deficit (Bd), debt (debt), exchange rate (ER), inflation (inf), interest rate (r) and real GDP growth rate (y^g)). The initial study concentrated on only two variables: budget deficit and inflation. Inf is said to cause Bd, if Bd can be better predicted using the histories of both inf and Bd than it can by using the history of Bd alone. Consequently, to determine the direction of causation between both series, the paper specifies regression models for the data series, which may be written more compactly as follows:

$$Bd_t = \alpha_1 + \sum_{i=1}^{k}\beta_{1i}Bd_{t-i} + \sum_{i=1}^{k}\lambda_{1i}\inf_{t-i} + \sum_{i=1}^{k}\mu_{1i}r_{t-i} + \sum_{i=1}^{k}\delta_{1i}ER_{t-i} + \sum_{i=1}^{k}\rho_{1i}y^g_{t-i} + \sum_{i=1}^{k}\sigma_{1i}\text{debt}_{t-i} + \varepsilon_{1i}$$
$$(15.8)$$

$$\inf_t = \alpha_2 + \sum_{i=1}^{k}\beta_{2i}Bd_{t-i} + \sum_{i=1}^{k}\lambda_{2i}\inf_{t-i} + \sum_{i=1}^{k}\mu_{2i}r_{t-i} + \sum_{i=1}^{k}\delta_{2i}ER_{t-i} + \sum_{i=1}^{k}\rho_{2i}y^g_{t-i} + \sum_{i=1}^{k}\sigma_{2i}\text{debt}_{t-i} + \varepsilon_{2i}$$
$$(15.9)$$

If $\sum_{i=1}^{k}\lambda_{1i} = 0$ then inflation does not Granger-cause budget deficit as in Eq. 15.7, and when $\sum_{i=1}^{k}\beta_{2i} = 0$ budget deficit does not Granger-cause inflation as in Eq. 15.8.

Causality was then examined between budget deficit and the component of inflation using Eqs. 15.7 and 15.8. If the budget deficit Granger-causes inflation, then inflation becomes a dependent variable, following Bandiere (2008) and Sinha et al. (2011). In each case, when probability value is less than 5%, a rejection of the null hypothesis implies there is a uni-directional causality from independent to dependent variable.

15.4 Data Analysis

15.4.1 Empirical Analysis for Sri Lanka, 2000–2016

This section discusses the empirical analysis for selected variables for Sri Lanka from 2000 to 2016. Figure 15.2 presents all selected variable behaviour at the stationary level.

15.4.2 Lag Selection Criterion for Sri Lanka, 2000–2016

According to the lag selection criterion, the lowest AIC (Akaike info criterion) and SC (Schwarz criterion) values mean a model is the best, and we utilize that lag model for the data analysis. According to Table 15.1, the lowest AIC and SC values belong to the Lag (2) model; we therefore applied the Lag (2) model for data analysis.

The probability values in Table 15.2 help identify the relationship between debt and the budget deficit. In this table, the probability value of 0.0216 is less than 0.05; hence we conclude that budget deficit Granger-causes debt (after rejecting the null hypothesis). Likewise, the rest of the findings suggested that there were uni-directional relationships between budget deficit and other selected variables: interest rate Granger-causes budget deficit, and inflation Granger-causes budget deficit. The study also identified a relationship between independent variables: debt Granger-causes real GDP growth rate, and interest rates Granger-cause inflation in Sri Lanka (see Table 15.10, Appendix 3).

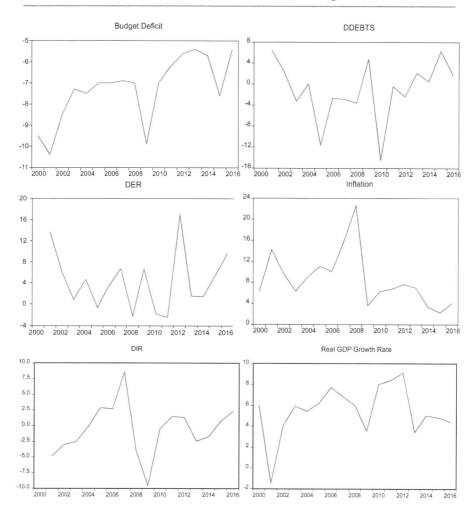

Fig. 15.2 Variables behaviour for Sri Lanka: 2000–2016. (Source: Estimates from E-Views Econometric package)

Null hypothesis (Ho) = Budget deficit does not Granger-cause debt
Alternative hypothesis (H1) = Budget deficit does Granger-cause debt

15.4.3   Debt Obligation Analysis for Sri Lanka, 2000–2016

Over recent decades, Sri Lankan government debt-to-GDP ratio remains high: during the 1988–1989 and 2001–2004 periods, it increased by 100%. The government debt-to-GDP ratio increased to 78.8% in 2016, amounting to Rs. 9387 Bn. The government debt-to-GDP ratio increased to 77.6% in 2017, amounting to Rs.10,313 Bn. Concessional loans declined to 49.6% in 2016, from over 90% before 2007, and this led to an increase in debt accumulation (CBSL annual report 2017).

Table 15.1 Comparison of Lag (1) and Lag (2) models

	Lag (1)	Lag (2)
AIC	30.12	0.31
SIC	32.13	0.91

Source: Author's analysis

Table 15.2 Pairwise Granger Causality test – Sri Lanka, 2000–2016

Null hypothesis:	Obs	F-statistic	Prob.
DDEBTS does not Granger-cause BUDGET_DEFICIT	14	0.24862	0.7851
BUDGET_DEFICIT does not Granger-cause DDEBTS		6.05289	0.0216

Source: Estimates from E-Views Econometric package

According to Fig. 15.3, domestic debt, the payment obligation will be at a high level from 2017 to 2020. Also, the foreign debt payment obligation will be at a higher level from 2017 to 2027 (see Fig. 15.4). When we consider the national debt payment obligation, the highest amount of service will be from 2107 to 2025. Because of these higher debt service obligations, Sri Lankan government policy-makers need to be more concerned when they take future policy decisions, especially on borrowing.

Because of higher debt, the ratio of debt service repayments to government revenue increased to 87.5% in 2017 from 80.2% in 2016 (CBSL Annual Report 2017) (see Table 15.3 for debt service payment comparative analysis).

15.4.4 Empirical Analysis for Malaysia, 2000–2016

In this section, the paper evaluates empirical analysis for the selected macroeconomic variables and the budget deficit for Malaysia from 2000 to 2016. Figure 15.5 presents all selected variables' behaviour at the stationary level.

15.4.5 Lag Selection Criterion

According to Table 15.4, the lowest AIC (Akaike info criterion) and SC (Schwarz criterion) values belong to the Lag (2) model, and we therefore selected the Lag (2) model for data analysis in the study.

There were no relationships revealed between budget deficit and the selected macroeconomic variables. Nevertheless, the findings confirmed the relationship between the independent variables. In Table 15.5, the given probability values are 0.0161 and 0.0424, and both values are less than 0.05 (5%), and thus we reject the null hypothesis and conclude that inflation Granger-causes debt and debt Granger-causes inflation. This represents a bi-directional Granger-cause situation. Likewise, the other findings suggest that there was a uni-directional causality between inflation and interest rates: inflation Granger-causes interest rates (see Table 15.11, Appendix 3).

DOMESTIC CURRENCY DEBT SERVICE OBLIGATIONS

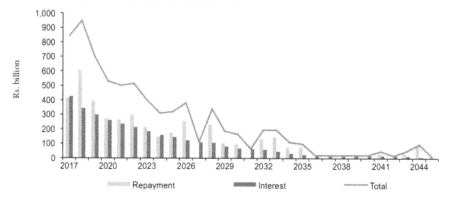

Fig. 15.3 Domestic currency debt service obligations. (Source: Public Debt Department, CBSL- 2017)

FOREIGN CURRENCY DEBT SERVICE OBLIGATIONS

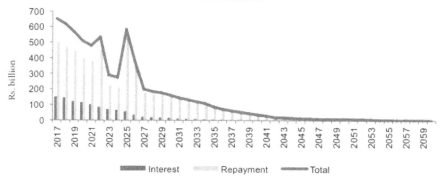

Fig. 15.4 Foreign currency debt service obligations. (Source: Public Debt Department, CBSL- 2017)

Table 15.3 Debt service payment comparison

Year	Government revenue (Rs.Bn)	Debt service payment (Rs.Bn)	Ratio
2014	1205	1076	89.34%
2015	1461	1318	90.60%
2016	1694	1352	80.20%
2017	1832	1603	87.5%

Source: Author's analysis

Null hypothesis (Ho) = Inflation does not Granger-cause debt
Alternative hypothesis (H1) = Inflation does Granger-cause debt

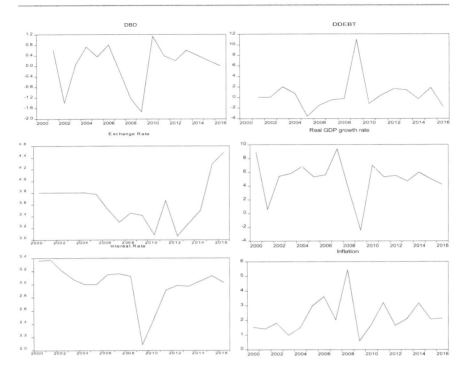

Fig. 15.5 Variables' behaviour for Malaysia, 2000–2016. (Source: Estimates from E-Views Econometric package)

Table 15.4 Comparison of Lag (1) and Lag (2) models

	Lag (1)	Lag (2)
AIC	13.11	1.53
SC	15.09	2.12

Source: Author's analysis

Table 15.5 Pairwise Granger Causality test

Null hypothesis:	Obs	F-statistic	Prob.
INFLATION does not Granger-cause DDEBT	14	6.75697	0.0161
DDEBT does not Granger-cause INFLATION		4.58514	0.0424

Source: Estimates from E-Views Econometric package

15.4.6 Empirical Analysis for South Korea, 2000–2016

In this section, the paper considers the empirical analysis of the selected variables for South Korea from 2000 to 2016. Figure 15.6 presents all selected variables' behaviour at the stationary level.

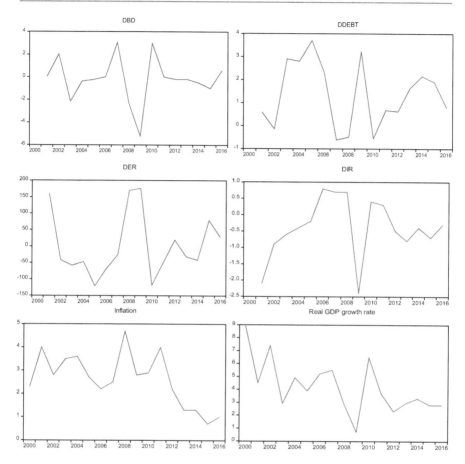

Fig. 15.6 Variables' behaviour in South Korea, 2000–2016. (Source: Estimates from E-Views Econometric package)

15.4.7 Lag Selection Criterion

According to Table 15.6, the lowest AIC (Akaike info criterion) and SC (Schwarz criterion) values belong to the Lag (2) model. Therefore we applied the Lag (2) model for the data analysis in the study.

In Table 15.7, the probability value 0.0231 is less than 0.05 (5%); hence we reject the null hypothesis and conclude that budget deficit Granger-causes exchange rates. Similarly, this study identified a relationship between budget deficit and real GDP growth rate: budget deficit Granger-causes real GDP growth rate. There were five uni-directional causalities between independent variables: debt Granger-causes exchange rate, debt Granger-causes interest rates, debt Granger-causes real GDP growth rate, exchange rate Granger-causes interest rate and inflation Granger-causes exchange rate (see Table 15.12, Appendix 15.3).

Table 15.6 Comparison of Lag (1) and Lag (2) models

	Lag (1)	Lag (2)
AIC	19.32	1.79
SC	21.30	2.38

Source: Author's analysis

Table 15.7 Pairwise Granger Causality test

Null hypothesis:	Obs	F-statistic	Prob.
DER does not Granger-cause DBD	14	2.25976	0.1602
DBD does not Granger-cause DER		5.89216	0.0231

Source: Estimates from E-Views Econometric package

Null hypothesis (Ho) = Budget deficit does not Granger-cause exchange rate
Alternative hypothesis (H1) = Budget deficit does Granger-cause exchange rate

15.4.8 Hausman Test

In the panel data series, the Hausman test evaluates the most suitable model to proceed from the fixed-effect and random-effect models. In Table 15.8, the probability value of the Hausman test is 0.0263, and this value is less than 0.05 (5%). Therefore we reject the null hypothesis and accept the alternative hypothesis. We conclude that the fixed-effect model is appropriate for the data analysis.
Null hypothesis (H0) = Random-effect model is appropriate
Alternative hypothesis (H1) = Fixed-effect model is appropriate
We utilized the fixed-effect model for data analysis. Table 15.9 shows that debts and real GDP growth rate probability values are, respectively, 0.001 and 0.0234. These selected values are less than 0.05. Therefore, we can conclude that debt and real GDP growth rate are significant variables in explaining the budget deficit.
The outcomes in Table 15.9: when identifying the link to prominent economic theories with debt, real GDP growth rate and budget deficit, the coefficient value of debt is −0.0946, and this minus sign represents the inverse relationship between budget deficit and debt. When a government decides to reduce its deficit while issuing debt securities, this may lead to accumulating debt stock level. In Keynesian theory, this circumstance is clearly emphasized. After considering the debt variable coefficient value (0.0946), the ratio between budget deficit and debt is 1:9 (*Bd*: debts = 1:9); this shows that, when the government decides to reduce its debt level by 9%, the deficit will increase by only 1%. A coefficient value of the real GDP growth rate is 0.185183, and this positive sign addresses Keynesian demand management theory: when government tends to increase expenditure while reducing taxes, with an objective of increasing GDP, this will lead to increase in the size of the budget deficit. According to Table 15.9, the ratio between budget deficit and real GDP growth rate is 1:18; this will appear when the government decides to increase GDP growth rate by 18%, so that the deficit will increase only by 1%.

Table 15.8 Hausman Test

Correlated random effect – Hausman test			
Test summary	Chi-Sq. statistic	Chi-Sq. d.f.	Prob.
Period random	12.704746	5	0.0263

Source: Estimates from E-Views Econometric package

Table 15.9 Fixed-effect model of Hausman test

Dependent variable: BUDGET_DEFICIT				
Variable	Coefficient	Std. error	t-statistic	Prob.
C	2.686242	2.149230	1.249862	0.2181
DEBTS	−0.094644	0.021956	−4.310709	0.0001
EXCHANGE_RATE	−0.005951	0.003090	−1.926280	0.0607
INFLATION	0.080128	0.077342	1.036019	0.3060
INTEREST_RATE	−0.051042	0.089169	−0.572416	0.5700
REAL_GDP_GROWTH_RATE	0.185183	0.078783	2.350553	0.0234

Source: Estimates from E-Views Econometric package

15.5 Conclusion and Recommendation

This paper examined the nexus between selected macroeconomic variables (inflation, interest rates, exchange rates, debt and real GDP growth rate) and the budget deficit from 2000 to 2016 and considered Sri Lanka, Malaysia and South Korea for comparative study.

The Sri Lankan finding suggested there were uni-directional causalities between budget deficit and debt, interest rates and budget deficit and inflation and budget deficit. Moreover, budget deficit Granger-causes debt, interest rates Granger-cause budget deficit and inflation Granger-causes budget deficit. In the Malaysian study, there were no relationships between the selected macroeconomic variables and budget deficit. The South Korean study found uni-directional causality between budget deficit and exchange rate and budget deficit and real GDP growth rate: budget deficit Granger-causes exchange rates, and budget deficit Granger-causes real GDP growth rate.

When implementing panel analysis for the comparative study, the test results revealed debt and real GDP growth rate were the two significant variables for explaining budget deficit. This observation suggested that debt and real GDP growth rate were the two significant variables in controlling the budget deficit. According to the statistical record, Malaysia and South Korea maintained a lower debt ratio level; consequently these two countries' budget deficits were also at a low level. Sri Lanka recorded a higher debt ratio level, and the country's budget deficit was also at a high level. Statistical data also show that a country's debt is a significant variable in managing the size of its budget deficit.

For a country like Sri Lanka, it is important to consider debt level in reducing the budget deficit and economic policy strategies adopted and how these were implemented by Malaysia and South Korea, in order to mitigate prevailing economic issues: sustained sizable budget deficits, significant debt maturities, weaker public finances and higher domestic and foreign currency debt portion. These are the main issues faced currently in achieving sustained economic growth.

Appendices

Appendix 15.1: Statistical Data for Sri Lanka, 1980–2016

Years	Budget deficits (% of GDP)	Inflation (CCPI %)	Interest rate (91 days T-bill rate)	Exchange rate (USD)	Real GDP growth rate (% of GDP)	Debt (% of GDP)
1980	−19.2	26.1	13	16.53	5.8	77.2
1981	−12.4	18	13	19.25	5.8	76.1
1982	−14	10.8	13	20.81	5.1	81.2
1983	−10.6	14	12	23.53	5	81
1984	−6.8	16.6	14	25.44	5.1	68.5
1985	−9.7	1.5	11.5	27.16	5	80.2
1986	−10.1	8	11.31	28.02	4.3	86.8
1987	−8.7	7.7	10.77	29.45	1.5	97
1988	−12.7	14	18.86	31.81	2.7	101
1989	−8.6	11.6	18.1	36.05	2.3	108.7
1990	−7.8	21.5	17.41	40.06	6.2	96.6
1991	−9.8	12.2	16.33	41.37	4.6	98.5
1992	−6.1	11.4	17.67	43.83	4.3	95.4
1993	−7.1	11.7	18.09	48.25	6.9	96.9
1994	−9.1	8.4	18.73	49.42	5.6	95.1
1995	−8.7	7.7	19.26	51.25	5.5	95.2
1996	−8.4	15.9	17.45	55.27	3.8	93.3
1997	−7	9.6	9.97	58.99	6.3	85.8
1998	−8.4	9.4	12.01	64.59	4.7	90.8
1999	−6.9	4.7	11.79	70.39	4.3	95.1
2000	−9.5	6.2	17.77	75.78	6	96.9
2001	−10.4	14.2	12.92	89.36	−1.5	103.3
2002	−8.5	9.6	9.92	95.66	4	105.6
2003	−7.3	6.3	7.35	96.52	5.9	102.3
2004	−7.5	9	7.25	101.19	5.4	102.3
2005	−7	11	10.1	100.5	6.2	90.6
2006	−7	10	12.76	103.96	7.7	87.9
2007	−6.9	15.8	21.3	110.62	6.8	85
2008	−7	22.6	17.33	108.33	6	81.4
2009	−9.9	3.5	7.73	114.94	3.5	86.2
2010	−8	6.2	7.24	113.06	8	81.9
2011	−6.9	6.7	8.68	110.57	8.2	78.5

(continued)

Years	Budget deficits (% of GDP)	Inflation (CCPI %)	Interest rate (91 days T-bill rate)	Exchange rate (USD)	Real GDP growth rate (% of GDP)	Debt (% of GDP)
2012	−6.5	7.6	10	127.6	6.3	79.2
2013	−5.9	6.9	7.54	129.11	7.2	78.3
2014	−6	3.3	5.74	130.56	7.4	75.5
2015	−7.6	2.2	6.45	135.94	4.8	77.6
2016	−5.4	4	8.72	145.6	4.4	79.3

Source: CBSL, Annual Reports

Appendix 15.2: Statistical Data for Sri Lanka, Malaysia and South Korea, 2000–2016

Country	Year	Budget deficit	Inflation	Interest rate	Exchange rate	Real GDP	Debts
Sri Lanka	2000	−9.5	6.2	17.77	75.78	6	96.9
Sri Lanka	2001	−10.4	14.2	12.92	89.36	−1.5	103.3
Sri Lanka	2002	−8.5	9.6	9.92	95.66	4	105.6
Sri Lanka	2003	−7.3	6.3	7.35	96.52	5.9	102.3
Sri Lanka	2004	−7.5	9	7.25	101.19	5.4	102.3
Sri Lanka	2005	−7	11	10.1	100.5	6.2	90.6
Sri Lanka	2006	−7	10	12.76	103.96	7.7	87.9
Sri Lanka	2007	−6.9	15.8	21.3	110.62	6.8	85
Sri Lanka	2008	−7	22.6	17.33	108.33	6	81.4
Sri Lanka	2009	−9.9	3.5	7.73	114.94	3.5	86.2
Sri Lanka	2010	−7	6.2	7.24	113.06	8	71.6
Sri Lanka	2011	−6.2	6.7	8.68	110.57	8.4	71.1
Sri Lanka	2012	−5.6	7.6	10	127.6	9.1	68.7
Sri Lanka	2013	−5.4	6.9	7.54	129.11	3.4	70.8
Sri Lanka	2014	−5.7	3.3	5.74	130.56	5	71.3
Sri Lanka	2015	−7.6	2.2	6.45	135.94	4.8	77.6
Sri Lanka	2016	−5.4	4	8.72	145.6	4.4	79.3
Malaysia	2000	−4.12	1.53	3.36	3.8	8.9	43
Malaysia	2001	−3.5	1.41	3.37	3.8	0.52	43
Malaysia	2002	−4.9	1.8	3.2	3.8	5.4	43
Malaysia	2003	−4.85	0.99	3.07	3.8	5.8	45
Malaysia	2004	−4.12	1.51	3	3.8	6.8	45.7
Malaysia	2005	−3.76	2.96	3	3.78	5.3	42.1
Malaysia	2006	−2.95	3.6	3.15	3.52	5.6	40.6
Malaysia	2007	−3.17	2.02	3.16	3.3	9.4	40.1
Malaysia	2008	−4.4	5.44	3.12	3.45	3.3	39.8

(continued)

Country	Year	Budget deficit	Inflation	Interest rate	Exchange rate	Real GDP	Debts
Malaysia	2009	−6.13	0.58	2.08	3.42	−2.5	50.8
Malaysia	2010	−5	1.71	2.5	3.08	7	49.6
Malaysia	2011	−4.61	3.2	2.91	3.67	5.3	50
Malaysia	2012	−4.4	1.64	2.98	3.06	5.5	51.6
Malaysia	2013	−3.8	2.09	2.97	3.28	4.7	53
Malaysia	2014	−3.4	3.17	3.05	3.5	6	52.7
Malaysia	2015	−3.2	2.08	3.13	4.29	5	54.5
Malaysia	2016	−3.2	2.12	3.03	4.49	4.2	52.7
South Korea	2000	1.08	2.3	7.9	1130.90	8.9	17.11
South Korea	2001	1.12	4	5.8	1292.01	4.5	17.7
South Korea	2002	3.15	2.8	4.9	1250.31	7.4	17.55
South Korea	2003	1	3.5	4.3	1192.08	2.9	20.45
South Korea	2004	0.63	3.6	3.9	1145.24	4.9	23.25
South Korea	2005	0.4	2.7	3.7	1023.75	3.9	26.96
South Korea	2006	0.4	2.2	4.5	954.32	5.2	29.27
South Korea	2007	3.47	2.5	5.2	928.97	5.5	28.65
South Korea	2008	1.16	4.7	5.9	1098.71	2.8	28.16
South Korea	2009	−4.1	2.8	3.5	1274.63	0.7	31.38
South Korea	2010	−1.1	2.9	3.9	1155.74	6.5	30.82
South Korea	2011	−1.1	4	4.2	1106.94	3.7	31.5
South Korea	2012	−1.3	2.2	3.7	1126.16	2.3	32.12
South Korea	2013	−1.5	1.3	2.9	1094.67	2.9	33.75
South Korea	2014	−2	1.3	2.5	1052.29	3.3	35.9
South Korea	2015	−3	0.7	1.8	1130.96	2.8	37.8
South Korea	2016	−2.4	1	1.5	1159.34	2.8	38.6

Source: The World Factbook

Appendix 15. 3: EViews Statistical Output

Table 15.10 Pairwise Granger Causality tests for all variables – Sri Lanka, 2000–2016

Pairwise Granger Causality tests			
Date: 09/05/18 Time: 12:58			
Sample: 2000 2016			
Lags: 2			
Null hypothesis:	Obs	F-statistic	Prob.
DDEBTS does not Granger-Cause BUDGET_DEFICIT	14	0.24862	0.7851
BUDGET_DEFICIT does not Granger-Cause DDEBTS		6.05289	0.0216
DER does not Granger-Cause BUDGET_DEFICIT	14	0.82632	0.4683
BUDGET_DEFICIT does not Granger-Cause DER		0.87243	0.4505
DIR does not Granger-Cause BUDGET_DEFICIT	14	4.33379	0.0481
BUDGET_DEFICIT does not Granger-Cause DIR		0.69782	0.5227
INFLATION does not Granger-Cause BUDGET_DEFICIT	15	6.22820	0.0175
BUDGET_DEFICIT does not Granger-Cause INFLATION		0.07295	0.9301
REAL_GDP_GROWTH_RATE does not Granger-Cause BUDGET_DEFICIT	15	0.27676	0.7639
BUDGET_DEFICIT does not Granger-Cause REAL_GDP_GROWTH_RATE		1.07370	0.3781
DER does not Granger-Cause DDEBTS	14	0.18234	0.8363
DDEBTS does not Granger-Cause DER		1.88703	0.2068
DIR does not Granger-Cause DDEBTS	14	1.61932	0.2508
DDEBTS does not Granger-Cause DIR		2.51331	0.1358
INFLATION does not Granger-Cause DDEBTS	14	1.87513	0.2086
DDEBTS does not Granger-Cause INFLATION		0.61945	0.5597
REAL_GDP_GROWTH_RATE does not Granger-Cause DDEBTS	14	0.75709	0.4967
DDEBTS does not Granger-Cause REAL_GDP_GROWTH_RATE		4.53868	0.0433
DIR does not Granger-Cause DER	14	0.66011	0.5401
DER does not Granger-Cause DIR		1.06879	0.3833
INFLATION does not Granger-Cause DER	14	0.29129	0.7541
DER does not Granger-Cause INFLATION		0.80341	0.4775
REAL_GDP_GROWTH_RATE does not Granger-Cause DER	14	0.11055	0.8965
DER does not Granger-Cause REAL_GDP_GROWTH_RATE		1.70248	0.2360
INFLATION does not Granger-Cause DIR	14	1.94935	0.1980
DIR does not Granger-Cause INFLATION		18.7791	0.0006
REAL_GDP_GROWTH_RATE does not Granger-Cause DIR	14	0.09866	0.9070
DIR does not Granger-Cause REAL_GDP_GROWTH_RATE		1.95374	0.1974
REAL_GDP_GROWTH_RATE does not Granger-Cause INFLATION	15	0.32722	0.7284
INFLATION does not Granger-Cause REAL_GDP_GROWTH_RATE		0.70733	0.5160

Table 15.11 Pairwise Granger Causality tests for all variables – Malaysia, 2000–2016

Pairwise Granger Causality tests			
Date: 09/07/18 Time: 12:47			
Sample: 2000 2016			
Lags: 2			
Null hypothesis:	Obs	F-statistic	Prob.
DDEBT does not Granger-Cause DBD	14	2.00415	0.1906
DBD does not Granger-Cause DDEBT		3.36743	0.0809
EXCHANGE_RATE does not Granger-Cause DBD	14	0.24323	0.7891
DBD does not Granger-Cause EXCHANGE_RATE		0.59025	0.5743
INFLATION does not Granger-Cause DBD	14	3.46719	0.0765
DBD does not Granger-Cause INFLATION		1.94765	0.1982
INTEREST_RATE does not Granger-Cause DBD	14	3.41098	0.0790
DBD does not Granger-Cause INTEREST_RATE		4.04870	0.0557
REAL_GDP_GROWTH_RATE does not Granger-Cause DBD	14	3.58834	0.0715
DBD does not Granger-Cause REAL_GDP_GROWTH_RATE		2.15980	0.1713
EXCHANGE_RATE does not Granger-Cause DDEBT	14	1.12881	0.3652
DDEBT does not Granger-Cause EXCHANGE_RATE		1.82346	0.2164
INFLATION does not Granger-Cause DDEBT	14	6.75697	0.0161
DDEBT does not Granger-Cause INFLATION		4.58514	0.0424
INTEREST_RATE does not Granger-Cause DDEBT	14	0.04439	0.9568
DDEBT does not Granger-Cause INTEREST_RATE		0.02577	0.9746
REAL_GDP_GROWTH_RATE does not Granger-Cause DDEBT	14	1.11594	0.3690
DDEBT does not Granger-Cause REAL_GDP_GROWTH_RATE		1.33015	0.3118
INFLATION does not Granger-Cause EXCHANGE_RATE	15	0.55177	0.5925
EXCHANGE_RATE does not Granger-Cause INFLATION		0.45948	0.6443
INTEREST_RATE does not Granger-Cause EXCHANGE_RATE	15	0.42780	0.6633
EXCHANGE_RATE does not Granger-Cause INTEREST_RATE		0.85120	0.4556
REAL_GDP_GROWTH_RATE does not Granger-Cause EXCHANGE_RATE	15	1.25942	0.3252
EXCHANGE_RATE does not Granger-Cause REAL_GDP_GROWTH_RATE		0.69463	0.5218
INTEREST_RATE does not Granger-Cause INFLATION	15	0.88380	0.4432
INFLATION does not Granger-Cause INTEREST_RATE		5.40783	0.0256
REAL_GDP_GROWTH_RATE does not Granger-Cause INFLATION	15	3.72079	0.0620
INFLATION does not Granger-Cause REAL_GDP_GROWTH_RATE		1.21012	0.3383
REAL_GDP_GROWTH_RATE does not Granger-Cause INTEREST_RATE	15	0.88830	0.4415
INTEREST_RATE does not Granger-Cause REAL_GDP_GROWTH_RATE		0.04134	0.9597

Table 15.12 Pairwise Granger Causality tests for all variables – South Korea, 2000–2016

Pairwise Granger Causality tests			
Date: 04/30/18 Time: 14:16			
Sample: 2000 2016			
Lags: 2			
Null hypothesis:	Obs	F-statistic	Prob.
DDEBT does not Granger-Cause DBD	14	1.94567	0.1985
DBD does not Granger-Cause DDEBT		0.34266	0.7187
DER does not Granger-Cause DBD	14	2.25976	0.1602
DBD does not Granger-Cause DER		5.89216	0.0231
DIR does not Granger-Cause DBD	14	0.05770	0.9443
DBD does not Granger-Cause DIR		2.73019	0.1184
INFLATION does not Granger-Cause DBD	14	1.24016	0.3344
DBD does not Granger-Cause INFLATION		2.38699	0.1473
REAL_GDP_GROWTH_RATE does not Granger-Cause DBD	14	0.22601	0.8021
DBD does not Granger-Cause REAL_GDP_GROWTH_RATE		7.06087	0.0143
DER does not Granger-Cause DDEBT	14	0.32254	0.7323
DDEBT does not Granger-Cause DER		5.76029	0.0245
DIR does not Granger-Cause DDEBT	14	1.77165	0.2245
DDEBT does not Granger-Cause DIR		5.05693	0.0337
INFLATION does not Granger-Cause DDEBT	14	0.51306	0.6152
DDEBT does not Granger-Cause INFLATION		1.76757	0.2252
REAL_GDP_GROWTH_RATE does not Granger-Cause DDEBT	14	0.67803	0.5318
DDEBT does not Granger-Cause REAL_GDP_GROWTH_RATE		6.17592	0.0205
DIR does not Granger-Cause DER	14	4.85440	0.0371
DER does not Granger-Cause DIR		4.99128	0.0348
INFLATION does not Granger-Cause DER	14	4.62704	0.0415
DER does not Granger-Cause INFLATION		1.44651	0.2853
REAL_GDP_GROWTH_RATE does not Granger-Cause DER	14	1.29382	0.3207
DER does not Granger-Cause REAL_GDP_GROWTH_RATE		1.49074	0.2759
INFLATION does not Granger-Cause DIR	14	2.14341	0.1733
DIR does not Granger-Cause INFLATION		0.63482	0.5522
REAL_GDP_GROWTH_RATE does not Granger-Cause DIR	14	1.01523	0.4003
DIR does not Granger-Cause REAL_GDP_GROWTH_RATE		0.96214	0.4181
REAL_GDP_GROWTH_RATE does not Granger-Cause INFLATION	15	2.34294	0.1464
INFLATION does not Granger-Cause REAL_GDP_GROWTH_RATE		1.02800	0.3926

Table 15.13 Hausman test (detailed)

Correlated random effects – Hausman test				
Equation: untitled				
Test period random effects				
Test summary		Chi-Sq. statistic	Chi-Sq. d.f.	Prob.
Period random		12.704746	5	0.0263
** WARNING: estimated period random effects variance is zero.				
Period random effects test comparisons:				
Variable	Fixed	Random	Var(Diff.)	Prob.
DEBTS	−0.079940	−0.105152	0.000004	0.0001
REAL_GDP_GROWTH_RATE	−0.066206	0.059786	0.000174	0.0234
EXCHANGE_RATE	0.002018	0.001464	0.000473	0.0607
INFLATION	−0.103599	−0.016585	0.009158	0.3632
INTEREST_RATE	0.052142	0.110778	0.007330	0.4934

Table 15.14 Fixed effect model (detailed)

Dependent variable: BUDGET_DEFICIT				
Method: panel least squares				
Date: 09/26/18 Time: 08:04				
Sample: 2000 2016				
Periods included: 17				
Cross-sections included: 3				
Total panel (balanced) observations: 51				
Variable	Coefficient	Std. error	t-statistic	Prob.
C	2.686242	2.149230	1.249862	0.2181
DEBTS	−0.094644	0.021956	−4.310709	0.0001
EXCHANGE_RATE	−0.005951	0.003090	−1.926280	0.0607
INFLATION	0.080128	0.077342	1.036019	0.3060
INTEREST_RATE	−0.051042	0.089169	−0.572416	0.5700
REAL_GDP_GROWTH_RATE	0.185183	0.078783	2.350553	0.0234
Effects specification				
Cross-section fixed (dummy variables)				
R-squared	0.887707	Mean dependent var		−3.872549
Adjusted R-squared	0.869427	S.D. dependent var		3.287514
S.E. of regression	1.187939	Akaike info criterion		3.325417
Sum squared resid	60.68154	Schwarz criterion		3.628448
Log likelihood	−76.79812	Hannan-Quinn criter.		3.441214
F-statistic	48.56115	Durbin-Watson stat		1.049976
Prob (F-statistic)	0.000000			

References

Abrego, L., & Ross, D. C. (2001). *Debt relief under HIPC initiative: Context and outlook for debt sustainability* (IMF working paper 01/144). Retrieved from https://www.imf.org/external/pubs/ft/wp/2001/wp01144.pdf

Adam, C. S., & Bevan, D. L. (2005). Fiscal deficits and growth in developing countries. *Journal of Public Economics, 89*(4), 571–597.

Al-Khedair, S. I. (1996). *The impact of the budget deficit on key macroeconomic variables in the major industrial countries.* PhD dissertation, Florida Atlantic University, United States. Retrieved from https://fau.digital.flvc.org/islandora/object/fau%3A9360

Amirthalingam, K. (2011/2012). Importance and issues of taxation in Sri Lanka. *Colombo Business Journal, 4*(1). Retrieved from http://docplayer.net/42852631-Colombo-business-journal-importance-and-issues-of-taxation-in-sri-lanka-abstract-1-introduction-k-amirthalingam-a.html

Anyanwu, J. C. (1993). *Monetary economics theory, policy and institutions.* Onitsha: Hybrid Publishers.

Bandiere, L. (2008). Public debt and its determinants in low income countries: Results from 7 country case studies. *Social Science Research Network.* Retrieved from https://papers.ssrn.com/sol3/papers.cfm?abstract_id=1143511

Carlin, W., & Soskice, D. (2013). *Macroeconomics: Imperfections, institutions and policies.* Oxford/London: Oxford University Press.

Central Bank of Sri Lanka. (2000–2017). *Annual reports.* Colombo. Retrieved from https://www.cbsl.gov.lk/en/publications/economic-and-financial-reports/annual-reports

Chimobi, O. P., & Igwe, O. L. (2010). Budget deficit, money supply, and inflation in Nigeria. *European Journal of Economics, Finance and Administration Sciences, 19*, 52–60.

Dayarathna Banda, O. G., & Priyadarshanee, A. A. S. (2014). Budget deficit and financial crowding-out: Evidence from Sri Lanka. *Sri Lanka Journal of Economic Research, 1*(1), 3–28.

Devapriya, T. N., & Masaru, I. (2012). *How does the budget deficit affect inflation in Sri Lanka?* Higashihiroshima: Graduate School for International Development and Cooperation, Hiroshima University.

Deyshappriya, N. P. R. (2012). Debt and fiscal sustainability in Sri Lanka. *International Journal Scientific and Research Publications, 2*(3). ISSN 2250-3153.

Dissanayake, D. M. S. B. (2016). Identifying the Relationships between Budget Deficit and Selected Macroeconomic Variables: A Study of Sri Lanka during the Post liberalization Era. *Social Science Research Network,* 13th International Conference on Business Management. Retrieved from https://ssrn.com/abstract=2910354

Dornbush, R., & Fisher, S. (1994). *Macroeconomics.* New York: McGraw Hill Book Company.

European Monetary Institute. (1994). *European Central Bank, European Union.* Retrieved from https://www.ecb.europa.eu/pub/pdf/annrep/ar1994en.pdf

Ezeabasili, V. N., Mojekwu, J. N., & Herbert, W. E. (2012). An empirical analysis of fiscal deficits and Inflation in Nigeria. *International Business Management, 4*(1), 105–120.

Fatima, G., Ahmed, M., & Rehman, W. (2012). Consequential effects of budget deficit on economic growth of Pakistan. *International Journal of Business, 3*(7), 203–208. Retrieved from http://ijbssnet.com/journals/Vol_3_No_7_April_2012/23.pdf.

Feldstein, M. S. (1986). *Budget deficits, tax rules, and real interest rates* (Working paper series, No. 1970). National Bureau of Economic Research. Retrieved from http://www.nber.org/papers/w1970.pdf

Keynes, J. M. (2007). *The general theory of employment, interest and money* (Collected works of Keynes) (P. Krugman, Ed.). London/New York: Harcourt Brace Jovanovich/Macmillan.

Knoester, A., & Mak, W. (1994). Real interest rates in eight OECD countries. *Rivista Internazionale, 41*(4), 325–344.

Krugman, P., & Venables, A. J. (1995). *Globalization and the inequality of nations.* Oxford/London: Oxford University Press.

Michael, S. O. (2011). Does fiscal deficit determine the size of external debt in Nigeria? *Journal of Economics and International Finance, 3*(10), 580–585.

Sachs, J. D. (1985). *Economic reform and the process of global integration*. London: Harvard University.

Saleh, A. S. (2003). *The budget deficit and economic performance: A survey* (Working Paper 03–12). Wollongong: Department of Economics, University of Wollongong. Retrieved from https://ro.uow.edu.au/commwkpapers/78/

Sinha, P., Arora, V., & Bansal, V. (2011). *Determinants of public debt for middle income and high income group Countries using panel data regression* (MPRA (Munich Personal RePEc Archive) Paper No. 32079). Retrieved from https://mpra.ub.uni-uenchen.de/32079/

Wijnbergen, S. (1989). External debt, inflation, and the public sector: Toward fiscal policy for sustainable growth. *The World Bank Economic Review, 3*(3), 297–320.

The Impact of Economic Variables, War, and Elections on the Behavior of All Share Price Index in the Colombo Stock Exchange

16

D. P. P. N. Peiris

16.1 Introduction

This paper mainly concentrates on the behavior of the Colombo Stock Exchange based on the All Share Price Index (ASPI). As an emerging stock market, CSE was the best performing stock exchange in the world in 2009 as ASPI jumped 125.2% during that year. Hence, the stock market has become a major method of investment among investors. Investors have a keen interest in the behavior of stock prices. Identifying the behavior of the ASPI on the variables considered in the study is important when it comes to the strategic decision-making state in investing. Identifying the variables that associate mostly with ASPI is important when it is needed to uplift the performance of the CSE, so that the identified variables can be taken into account with greater interest when developing the strategies. Even though studies have considered macroeconomic variables and exogenous factors separately, this study considers a combination of the variables.

16.2 Literature Review

The relationship between the performance of stock markets and macroeconomic variables has been discussed in many published researches. As cited in Yusof and Majid (2007), Fama (1981) has documented a significant relationship between stock returns and seven other macroeconomic variables, including inflation, national output, and industrial production. Nasseh and Straus (2000) conducted a Johansen Cointegration Test to investigate the long-run relationship between stock prices and both domestic and international economic activities in six European economies;

D. P. P. N. Peiris (✉)
Department of Statistics, Faculty of Science, University of Colombo, Colombo, Sri Lanka

© The Author(s), under exclusive license to Springer Nature
Switzerland AG 2021
S. Dhiman, R. Samaratunge (eds.), *New Horizons in Management, Leadership and Sustainability*, Future of Business and Finance,
https://doi.org/10.1007/978-3-030-62171-1_16

their findings had concluded that stock price levels are significantly related to industrial production, short- and long-term interest rates as well as foreign stock prices. Variance decomposition methods support the strong explanatory power of macroeconomic variables in contributing to the forecast variance of stock prices.

Being inspired by the literature, Yusof and Majid (2007) conducted a study on stock returns of the Malaysian stock market and macroeconomic variables. Their study investigated the extent to which the macroeconomic variables affect the stock market behavior in the emerging market of Malaysia, in the post-1997 financial crisis period. They suggest that the real effective exchange rate, money supply, industrial product index, and federal funds rate seem to be suitable variables for the government to focus on, to stabilize the stock market. It is stated in their study that any changes in US monetary policy affect the Malaysian stock market.

Rashid (2008) has investigated the dynamic interactions between four macroeconomic variables and stock prices in Pakistan. He used cointegration and Granger causality. The macroeconomic variables that have been used are consumer price, industrial production, exchange rates, and market rates of interests. Rashid concludes that estimates of bivariate error-correction models reveal that there is long-run bidirectional causation between the stock prices and all the said macroeconomic variables, except for consumer prices, which only lead to stock prices. The results have also provided some evidence that the stock prices are Granger-caused by changes in interest rates in the short run. However, his analysis was unable to explore any short-run causation between the stock prices and the remaining three macroeconomic variables. Thus, he concludes that the association between the health of the stock market in the sense of rising share prices and the health of the economy is only a long-run phenomenon.

Financial economists agree in general that the oil price has significant associations with economic activities. Hamilton (1983) has shown that a significant increase in oil price preceded every post-World War II recession in the USA.

Kling (1985) has investigated the relationship between the crude oil price changes and stock market activities between 1973 and 1982 in the USA with a method of illustration. He concludes that crude oil price changes affect the future stock prices in the industries which use oil as input factors.

Sadorsky (1999) has investigated the dynamic interaction between the oil price and other economic variables which also included the stock returns. The study was conducted using an unrestricted vector auto-regression (VAR) with US data. The study has identified that the oil price changes and oil price volatility have a significantly negative impact on the real stock returns. It also showed that oil price movements explain a larger portion of the forecast error variance in real stock returns than interest rates.

Similarly, Papapetrou (2001) has also studied the dynamic relationship among the oil price, real stock prices, interest rates, real economic activity, and employment with data from Greece. The study concluded that an oil price shock has an immediate negative impact on the stock market as well as industrial production and employment. This implies that a positive oil price shock depresses real stock returns. However contrary to the literature, Papapetrou showed that stock returns do not rationally signal (or lead) to changes in real activity and employment, since growth in industrial production and employment respond negatively to real stock returns.

In general, the political situation in a country directly influences the economy. Since the country is governed by the politicians who are selected by the public, their principles and policies towards the economy directly influence the behavior of the economy. Keeping that in mind, it is important to investigate the behavior of the stock market around the elections.

Karachi Stock Exchange returns were analyzed on the effect of multiple political events covering up to the year 2006 by Masood and Sergi (2008). They focused on measuring the political risk in the Pakistan stock market and the probability of events that took place in the following year as compared to previous years. Bayesian modeling and Markov Chain Monte Carlo techniques were used for the analysis and forecasting. The results indicated that the probability of an event in any year is higher than the previous year with an average arrival rate of 1.5 events per year with no time trend. The forecast suggested that the level of political risk would remain unchanged in the future. In the end, they found that Pakistan's political uncertainty has a risk premium of 7.5–12%.

Following the literature based on GARCH models, Wang and Lin (2008) examine the relationship between political activities and the TAIEX stock market by asymmetric GARCH. They find that the congressional effect is negative on stock returns, but volatility is not significant. The congressional effect on stock market returns, which was followed by financial reform, significantly dropped before financial reform and significantly exceeded the volatility in the same circumstances. These results provide some evidence that investors would hold a conservative position during the congressional sessions.

Moving from international literature to the literature based on local stock market data, an interesting study can be found. Jayasinghe (2014) examines the behavior of stock returns and the volatility of the returns around both parliament and general elections in Sri Lanka. The study is based on daily data from January 1985 to September 2009. In this study, he concludes that there exists strong evidence that the movement of the volatility of the returns is upward around both presidential and general elections. Furthermore, he documents that when it gets close to the election date, the degree of volatility hike is observed to be stronger. In addition to that, he suggests that negligence of conditional heteroscedasticity in estimation may result in failures in capturing the impact of elections on stock returns. Moreover, he emphasizes the fact that most of the developed countries hold their elections at regular intervals. But in certain emerging countries like Sri Lanka, elections are not held at regular intervals. And as a result, the decision to hold an election on a certain date itself is news that may influence the performance of the stock market.

Yatiwell and Silva (2011) have investigated the calendar anomalies on the evidence from CSE over a period from 1985 to 2005. The regression results suggest that stock returns in the CSE to a certain extent are not consistent with the random walk hypothesis during the period 1995–2005. Moreover, the paper declares largely negative and significant regression coefficients relating to international crises suggesting that such events have triggered an adverse impact on the stock market performance over the period under study. In addition to that, they claim particular combinations of trading days concerning both general and presidential elections appear to be significant with varying effects. Furthermore, they conclude that the extended study by Elyasiani et al. in 1996 had decisively proven the presence of the turn-of-the-year. Additionally, they state that the study strengthens the findings by Abeysekara (2001), which asserts that substantial autocorrelation is present on the CSE.

Chesney et al. (2011) have studied the impact of several significant terror attacks on international stock markets, bond markets, and commodity markets. They have used an event study approach, a non-parametric approach, and a GARCH-based approach. They also study the impact of the inclusion of the effects of natural disasters and financial crashes. They report that terror attacks often have a significant negative effect on stock markets, where terror attacks also affect stock markets at the industry level.

Most recently, Balcilar et al. (2018) have used a novel nonparametric causality-in-quantiles test to study the effects of terror attacks on stock market returns and volatility in G7 countries. They also use the novel test to study the international repercussions of terror attacks. Test results show that terror attacks often have significant effects on returns, whereas the effect on volatility is significant only for Japan and the UK for several quantiles above the median.

Even though some literature has considered all the variables that were considered in this study, this review on the previous work clearly shows the lack of studies that have considered the influence of macroeconomic variables, terrorism, and the elections together.

16.3   Research Question

"How does the All Share Price Index behave under the variations of imports, exports, exchange rates, and crude oil price with elections and terrorism?"

Along with the above research question, this study has fulfilled the following objectives.

I. Identifying the interactional relationships among the macroeconomic variables.
II. Identifying the behavior of the ASPI on the period that the war was present and in the post-war period.

16.4   Methodology

16.4.1 Dependent Variable

ASPI is the broad market price index of the Colombo Stock Exchange. It is designed to measure the movements of the overall market. The index is calculated in real-time as a market capitalization weight index, which constitutes all voting and non-voting ordinary shares listed on the CSE (Colombo-Stock-Exchange 2018).

$$ASPI = \frac{\text{Market capitalization of all listed companies}}{\text{Base market capitalization}} \times 100 \qquad (16.1)$$

16.4.2 Independent Variables

Imports, exports, and the exchange rates were incorporated into this study as the macroeconomic variables. In addition to the aforesaid macroeconomic variables, the crude oil price has been included in the research. The crude oil price has been used in this research as a proxy for international economic variation. Another suitable candidate for this purpose is the gold price. Since the Sri Lankan economy is more sensitive to the crude oil price, it was chosen as the proxy. Apart from the macroeconomic perspective, another two perspectives were considered in this study. One perspective was the influence of the elections towards the ASPI, while the other perspective is the influence of the 30-year civil war with the L.T.T.E.

16.4.3 ARCH and GARCH Models

Since the dependent variable of this analysis was possessed with conditional heteroscedasticity (time varied volatility), a model that could address this scenario was needed. The ARCH model of Engle (1986) is a systematic framework for volatility modeling. Even though the ARCH model is simple, it has a trade-off between the number of parameters, which are needed to adequately describe the volatility process. Taking that into concern, Bollerslev (1986) proposed an extension for the ARCH model which is known as the generalized ARCH model (GARCH model). As a result of the aforesaid necessity and trade-offs, the generalized autoregressive conditional heteroscedasticity (GARCH) model was used along with time series regression techniques.

16.4.4 Data Preparation

All Share Price Index series was directly purchased from the Colombo Stock Exchange data library. They provide all the series that are interested in researchers in a single disk. From that disk monthly series of ASPI was extracted as the response variable. There were no missing values in the series.

The series of the three macroeconomic variables, namely, imports, exports, and foreign exchanges were collected from the e-research center, an online data library maintained by the Central Bank of Sri Lanka. The database allows the user to query data using the selections they have provided. Unfortunately, some of the series had missing data points. So they were filled up by referring to the Central Bank Report of the respective years. Originally the imports and exports were produced in US dollars. In favor of changing the units of the variables that are measured in currency into a single unit, all the variables were converted into Sri Lankan rupees. The conversion process was done using the exchange rates of the respective months.

The list of elections with their respective dates was also collected from the official website for the Sri Lankan elections which is maintained by the Election Commission of Sri Lanka. All the dates of the elections are extracted from the dates of the official results that have been attached to the website. Apart from that, the official site of the Parliament of Sri Lanka was also referred to extract election dates (Parliament of Sri Lanka 2019).

As declared by the former president Mahinda Rajapaksa at the Parliament on 19 May 2009, Sri Lanka was liberated from the civil war which was engaged with the Liberation Tigers of Tamil Eelam. The time window before that date was taken as the war period, and the time window after that date was taken as the post-war period.

In this study, apart from the presence and the absence of the war, bomb attacks that happened in the district of Colombo are considered a special case. Since the Colombo District is considered the heart of the Sri Lankan economy, there are suggestions that if something happens in Colombo, it will influence the Sri Lankan economy. That issue is the motivation to select the bomb blasts that happened in the Colombo District. As the limits of the selections were too broad when selecting the bomb attacks, the following criteria were used as a selection frame:

1. The bomb blast should be within the Colombo District.
2. It should be an attack that affected the general public, not a specific person. Even though the attack is for an individual and if the public had been affected, then the blast is taken into consideration.
3. It should be within the time frame from January 1994 to December 2017.

Eleven bomb blasts that took place in Colombo District were selected according to the above criteria. Even though Katunayaka International Airport bomb blast took place in the Gampaha District, it was considered as it was the only international airport at that time (Table 16.1).

16.4.5 Variable Selection

Even though the available literature supports the claim that the variables influence the stock market, proper statistical evidence was needed within the context of this study. To do that the best subset selection algorithm was used. The algorithm is as follows:

1. Let M0 denote the null model with no variables.
2. For k = 1,2,...,p
   (a) Fit all (p_k) models that contain exactly k predictors.
   (b) Pick the best among these models, and call it Mk. Here the best is defined as having the smallest RSS or equivalently the highest R squared values.
3. The best model is selected from M0, ..., Mk using the cross-validated prediction error, BIC, AIC, or adjusted R squared values (James et al. n.d.).

In this study "Leaps" R package (Lumley and Miller 2017) was used to run the best subset selection algorithm. Moreover, the adjusted R squared values were used to select the model.

Table 16.1 List of bomb blasts that happened in Colombo District

Attack	Date	Location
1. Thotalanga bombing (assassination of Gamini Dissanayake)	1994-10-24	Thotalanga, Colombo
2. Attack to the oil storage complexes at Kolonnawa and Orugodawatta	1995-10-20	Kolonnawa, Colombo
3. Colombo Central Bank bombing	1996-01-31	Central Bank of Sri Lanka, Colombo
4. 1996 Dehiwala train bombing	1996-07-24	Dehiwala, Colombo
5. 1997 Colombo World Trade Centre bombing	1997-10-15	Colombo World Trade Centre
6. Colombo Town Hall bombing (assassination attempt on Chandrika Bandaranaike Kumaratunga)	1999-12-18	Colombo Town Hall
7. Bandaranaike Airport attack	2001-07-24	Katunayake, Western Province
8. Nugegoda shopping mall bombing	2007-11-28	Nugegoda
9. 2008 Fort Railway Station bombing	2008-02-03	Fort Railway Station, Colombo
10. Piliyandala bus bombing	2008-04-26	Piliyandala, Colombo
11. 2008 Dehiwala train bombing	2008-05-26	Dehiwala, Colombo

16.4.6 Model Selection

According to the results of the variable selection process, only a subset of the variables were selected to be included in the model:

1. ElectionsProv – Dummy variable for the provincial elections
2. TerrNo_Terr – Dummy variable for the absence of terrorism
3. CrudeOil_LKR – Crude oil price in Sri Lankan rupees
4. ExchRate – Exchange rate of US dollar
5. Imports_LKR_mill – Imports in Sri Lankan rupees millions
6. Exports_LKR_mill - Exports in Sri Lankan rupees millions

Surprisingly the dummy variables for general and presidential elections as well as the dummy variables for the presence of war and bomb blasts in Colombo were excluded in the optimum model. This result is contrary to the results of the study carried out by Jayasinghe (2014). In his study, it is concluded that there are abnormal returns and changes in returns relative to the previous day's returns during election periods, which indirectly implies the influence of the elections towards the performance of the stock market.

This result splits the analysis into two paths. One considered the subset of the variables, while the other path considered the full set of variables.

In both procedures, initially, an ARIMA model was fitted with the exogenous variables. The process was done using the *auto.arima* function with *stepwise* and *approximation* parameters disabled as well as the conventional method of observing the ACF and PACF plots. The two results were overlapped in both procedures. Then that selected

ARIMA model was used in the "rugarch" R package (Ghalanos 2018). Using the aforesaid package, a GARCH model is fixed with the ARMA model as well as the exogenous variables. In each procedure GARCH models with orders (0,0), (0,1), (0,2), (0,3), (1,0), (1,1), (1,2), (1,3), (2,0), (2,1), (2,2), (2,3), (3,0), (3,1), (3,2), and (3,3) were fitted. From the 16 models that had been fitted, the models which still had the ARCH effect were removed. Then the models that did not have stationary residuals were removed. And finally, from the remaining models, one model from each of the two procedures was selected using the mean absolute percentage error on the test set.

16.5   Key Findings

16.5.1 Descriptive Analysis

Before the advanced analysis, a thorough univariate descriptive analysis was carried out. The following findings were obtained from the descriptive analysis.
1. All Share Price Index
   (a) ASPI has a non-linear increasing trend. It shows a noticeable increase from January 2009 (1821.24) to January 2011 (7174.90) which is the post-war-time period.
   (b) ASPI has a slight seasonal variation. In addition to that January, February, November, and December months also show a relative decrement of ASPI.
2. Crude oil price
   (a) Crude oil price also shows an increasing trend. It also possesses two notice-able drops. One is from Rs.7782.05 to Rs.5102.52 in January 2009. The other drop is from Rs.11397.42 to Rs.6323.64 in January 2015 which is almost a 50% decrement. The aforesaid decrements were the results of the financial crisis of the respective years as well as the significant oil produc-tion in the USA in the middle of 2014.
   (b) Crude oil price has got a quite noticeable variation. But until 2005 the sea-sonal fluctuation is very low. Furthermore, crude oil price shows a slight increment over the months up to June and then shows a decrement towards the latter part of the year.
3. Exchange rate
   (a) The exchange rate also shows an increasing trend which is very close to a linear trend.
   (b) The exchange rate is the only variable that lacks seasonal variation. Even though it lacks seasonal variation, it possesses a relatively high increasing trend.
4. Imports
   (a) Imports show an increasing trend with a very strong seasonal variation.
   (b) March, August, and October show relatively high values, whereas April July, and November show relatively low values.
5. Exports
   (a) Exports also have an increasing trend which is very close to a linear trend.

(b) Exports showed relatively higher fluctuations after the year 2015. The reason behind this unusual increment of the magnitude of the fluctuations might be the political change that took place in the year 2015. As the two political parties possess two different economic strategies, this unusual pattern might be present.

(c) Relatively exports show higher values in March, July, and August, while relatively lower values are shown in April and November.

6. If the results were observed clearly, it can be seen that both imports and exports have relatively high values in March and August every year. Furthermore, both imports and exports have relatively low values in April or November in every year.

16.5.2 Advanced Analysis

For both models, the model with all variables and the model with the selected variables, the following model selection method was applied. When fitting a GARCH model using the "rugarch" R package, it allows the user to parse the specifications of the interested model. "sGARCH," the standard GARCH model, was used in this study. An ARMA model should be parsed into the specification as the mean model. To find the suitable ARMA model, two methods were used. One is the conventional method of observing the PACF and ACF. The other method was using the "auto.arima" function in "forecast" R package with "stepwise" and "approximation" parameters set to FALSE. The two methods converged to the same results. The selected ARIMA model was ARIMA (2,0,1).

With that ARIMA model being the mean model, 12 models were fitted to the series by changing the GARCH order. The used GARCH orders are (0,0), (0,1), (0,2), (0,3), (1,0), (1,1), (1,2), (1,3), (2,0), (2,1), (2,2), (2,3), (3,0), (3,1), (3,2), and (3,3). For all these models, the last six observations were left out as the test set to measure the performance. The measurement of the performance used in this study is the RMSE (root mean squared error). Only the models which had stationary residuals and absence of ARCH effect were selected to measure the performance.

16.5.3 The Model with All Variables (Table 16.2)

According to the performance measures, the model with the smallest MAPE was selected. Table 16.3 represents the coefficients of the selected model.

16.5.4 The Model with the Selected Variables

Table 16.4 represents the performance measures of the model with the selected variables.

Table 16.5 represents the coefficients of the selected model with selected variables.

Table 16.2 Performance measures of the fitted models with all variables

Performance measure	(1,1)	(1,2)	(1,3)	(2,1)	(2,2)	(2,3)	(3,1)	(3,2)	(3,3)
RMSE	299.65	299.63	364.12	392.42	392.42	384.36	404.73	407.06	410.78
MAPE	4.38	4.38	5.30	5.73	5.73	5.61	5.91	5.94	5.99

Table 16.3 Coefficients of the selected model with all variables

Parameter	Estimate	Standard error
Mu	1425.2652	259.0400
Ar1	0.7886	0.0244
Ar2	0.2134	0.0256
Ma1	0.2822	0.0809
TerrTerr_North	10.4761	14.7039
TerrNo_Terr	100.00	142.6266
Eelction_Presi	26.4535	21.5743
Election_Gen	18.2216	15.8806
Election_Prov	−11.308	13.3437
CrudeOil	0.028	0.0186
Exports	−0.0004	0.006
Imports	−0.0016	0.007
Exch	−2.1181	4.7821
Omega	113.433	100.1956
Alpha1	0.2209	0.1435
Beta1	0.8109	0.8625
Beta2	0.0000	0.7470

16.5.5   Influence of the War Towards ASPI

To analyze the behavior of the ASPI with the presence and the absence of war, the ASPI series was first divided into two sets. The series is divided using the date May 2009. The period before the date was considered as the period in which the war is present. And the period after the time is considered as the period in which the war is not present.

Then two models were fitted separately for the two time periods to analyze the behavior of the ASPI on the presence and absence of war. Initially, the best ARIMA model was fitted to the series with other variables as the exogenous regressors. Both the conventional method and "auto.arima" function was used to fit the ARIMA model. Then the model which had the lowest AIC value was considered as the optimum model. Then the model was checked for the presence of the ARCH effect using both the Ljung-Box test for the squared residuals and ARCH-LM test. Ljung-Box test supported the claim that the model when the war is present possesses an ARCH effect with a confidence level of 99%. The results of the test are mentioned in Table 16.6.

The Ljung-Box test supported the claim that the model when the war is not present does not possess an ARCH effect with a confidence level of 99%. The results of the test are mentioned in Table 16.7.

Table 16.4 Performance measures of the model with selected variables

Performance measure	(1,1)	(1,2)	(1,3)	(2,1)	(2,2)	(2,3)	(3,1)	(3,2)	(3,3)
RMSE	307.77	277.46	277.47	379.42	379.42	334.74	354.97	354.40	354.55
MAPE	4.49	4.05	4.05	5.54	5.54	4.86	5.15	5.14	5.14

Table 16.5 Coefficients of the selected model with selected variables

Parameter	Estimation	Standard error
Mu	1425.2653	280.4193
Ar1	0.6972	0.0321
Ar2	0.3043	0.0429
Ma1	0.3918	0.1919
Ma2	0.0691	0.0653
Ma3	0.0096	0.1748
TerrNo_Terr	100.00	262.0947
Elections_Prov	−9.5712	10.6067
CrudeOil	0.0238	0.0335
Exports	−0.0005	0.0009
Imports	−0.0017	0.0010
Exch	−2.4891	5.0961
Omega	123.3450	266.8363
Alpha1	0.2188	0.5473
Beta1	0.8112	3.1762
Beta2	0.0000	2.7255

Table 16.6 Results of the Ljung-Box test for the squared residuals when the war is present

Order	P-value
4	7.87e-13
8	2.40e-11
12	1.60e-11
16	8.13e-14
20	1.11e16
24	0.00e+0

Table 16.7 Results of the Ljung-Box test for the squared residuals when the war is not present

Order	P-value
4	0.597
8	0.891
12	0.740
16	0.792
20	0.927
24	0.839

16.6   Conclusions

In the procedure of variable selection, surprisingly dummy variables for the presidential and general elections were left out. However, Jayasinghe (2014) concludes that there are abnormal returns and changes in returns relative to the previous day's returns during election periods. If this fact is discussed more deeply, it can be found that there are some major differences between this study and the study carried out by him.

The first and most important difference is the frequency of the data. This study considers the monthly data, while the aforesaid literature considers daily data. When this fact is considered deeply, it can be argued that the influence that can be felt upon the ASPI for several days might be significant, but when the gap between two data points is a month, which is a relatively higher gap considered to daily data points, it might miss the significant movements that take place between several days.

When a country is freed from a long-term civil war or any rebellion equivalent, it becomes a fountain of novel opportunities. Thus, investors pay considerable attention to such countries. This position would be in favor of the companies, where the revenues will increase and their dividends will rise, which makes the stock market perform well.

It is a known fact that since the provincial councils were invented by the thirteenth amendment to the constitution of Sri Lanka (13A), the country had never held a provincial election on the same date for all the provinces, since the influence of the elections of different provinces towards the stock market might be different. Moreover, the power that had been granted to the provincial councils towards the economy of the whole country is relatively low. Also, when the influence of the presidential and general election is discussed, both had a positive influence on the ASPI. When such an election comes, the governing party will provide concessionaries towards the public as well as the business community most of the time which will result in a good performance in the market.

Surprisingly the oil price has a positive effect on the ASPI. It is a quite interesting result when it is compared to Billmeier and Massa (2009), since in their study they indicated that the increase in the oil prices had a positive impact on the stock yields of the oil exporter countries but a negative impact on the stocks of the oil importer countries. Contrary to the results of them, Sri Lanka is an oil importer country but ended up with a positive influence upon the increase of the crude oil price. The top ten companies which hold more than 40% of the market capitalization are indirectly related to the crude oil price. However, almost all of these companies have the capability of surviving a sudden increment of crude oil prices by changing the prices of their goods and services.

The exchange rate also has a negative influence on the ASPI. It is a known fact that for a long time Sri Lanka has been importing goods and services more than exporting which will result in higher demand in the foreign currency. Moreover, when the currency rate increases, the expenditures of companies are increased and will reduce the cash flow of the companies which will eventually decrease the dividends and the performance of the stock market.

During the period of civil war, foreign interventions in the political perspective and economical perspective were present. Moreover, investments were relatively low in the country due to the instability, the lack of peace, and the high risk of terrorist attacks on the island. Due to these facts, the performance of the stock market was also subjected to sudden changes which were the main reasons behind the conditional heteroscedasticity.

In addition to the facts that have been mentioned so far, another noticeable drop in the ASPI can be observed around the years 2011 and 2012. It was the time that the country was accused of war crimes which led to losing investor confidence towards the market.

However, considering the whole post-war period as a single period, the stock market has attracted more foreign investors and had taken the full out of the benefits of the post-war period.

16.7   Limitations of the Study and Recommendations

This study can be extended with the daily data with proper access to the other macroeconomic variables. The influence of the war, as well as the elections, can be analyzed through a functional time series approach. The functional time series approach is separating the original series into natural time intervals and analyzing the behavior of the series. Considering the sudden peak after the war in 2009 and the sudden drop around 2011 and 2012, an approach which addresses the phenomenon of structural breaks can be used in a future study. The macroeconomic variables that are available in quarterly values can be used with the spline smoothing.

Chapter Takeaways/Lessons
1. Presidential elections as well as the general elections in Sri Lanka have a positive influence on the behavior of the ASPI compared to the absence of the elections. Moreover, presidential elections have a slightly higher magnitude on the influence compared to the influence of the general elections.
2. Provincial elections have a negative influence but with a slightly lower magnitude than presidential and general elections towards the ASPI when compared to the absence of elections.
3. The absence of the war has a higher influence on ASPI when compared to the presence of the war and the presence of severe bomb attacks in Colombo District.
4. The crude oil price has a positive influence on the ASPI, whereas the export, imports, and exchange rates have a negative influence upon the ASPI.
5. The absence of war has stabilized the performance of the stock market by removing the conditional heteroscedasticity which was present when the war is present.

Reflection Questions

1. Will these results remain the same if the same study is done using the daily data? What will be the performance of the statistical models if more macroeconomic variables like GDP, gold prices, interest rates, etc. of Sri Lanka were included?
2. Since more than a decade has passed after the civil war, under the assumption that the economy of Sri Lanka has now adjusted to the war-free environment, how do these findings respond to the aforesaid changes?
3. As the whole world has faced a pandemic situation at the moment this chapter is being written, what adjustments do we need to make to this study to identify the behavioral pattern of ASPI?
4. If a sudden civil war arises in Sri Lanka again due to any possible reason, can ASPI be expected to behave the same as it behaved at the 30-year Eelam Civil War?
5. Is there a possibility of applying the same findings with extremely minor adjustments to a similar economy like the Sri Lankan economy?

References

Abeysekera, S. (2001). Efficient markets hypothesis and the emerging capital market in Sri Lanka: Evidence from the Colombo stock exchange – a note. *Journal of Business Finance & Accounting, 28*, 249–261. https://doi.org/10.1111/1468-5957.00373.

Balcilar, M., Gupta, R., Pierdzioch, C., & Wohar, M. E. (2018). Terror attacks and stock-market fluctuations: Evidence based on a nonparametric causality-in-quantiles test for the G7 countries. *The Europian Journal of Finance, 24*(4), 333–346.

Billmeier, A., & Massa, I. (2009). What drives stock market development in emerging markets-institutions, remittances or natural resources? *Emerging Markets Review, 10*(1), 23–35.

Bollerslev, T. (1986). Generalized autoregressive conditional heteroskedasticity. *Journal of Econometrics, Elsevier, 31*(3), 307–327. April.

Chesney, M., Reshetar, G., & Karaman, M. (2011). The impact of terrorism on financial markets: An empirical study. *Journal of Banking and Finance, 35*, 253–267.

Colombo-Stock-Exchange. (2018). *Colombo Stock Exchange*. Retrieved 2018, from Colombo Stock Exchange: https://www.cse.lk/home/market

Fama, E. F. (1981). "Stock returns, real activity, inflation, and money," American economic review. *American Economic Association, 71*(4), 545–565. September.

Ghalanos, A. (2018). *rugarch: Univariate GARCH models*. R package version 1.4–0. Retrieved from https://CRAN.R-project.org/package=rugarch

Hamilton, J. (1983). Oil and the macroeconomy since World War II. *The Journal of Political Economy, 91*, 829–853.

James, G., Witten, D., Hastie, T., & Tibshirani, R. (n.d.). *An introduction to statistical learning with applications in R*. New York: Springer.

Jayasinghe, P. (2014). The behavior of stock returns and volatility around elections: Evidence from Colombo stock exchange. *Journal of Multidisciplinary Research, 1*(1), 187–210.

Kling, J. (1985). Oil price shocks and stock market behavior. *Journal of Portfolio Management, 12*, 34–39.

Lumley, T., & Miller, A. (2017). *Leaps: Regression subset selection*. Retrieved from https://CRAN.R-project.org/package=leaps

Masood, O., & Sergi, B. (2008). How political risks and events have influenced Pakistan's stock markets from 1947 to present. *Economic Policy in Emerging Economies, 1*, 427–444.

Nasseh, A., & Strauss, J. (2000). Stock prices and domestic and international macroeconomic activity: A cointegration approach. *The Quarterly Review of Economics and Finance, Elsevier, 40*(2), 229–245.

Papapetrou, E. (2001). Oil price shocks, stock market, economic activity and employment in Greece. *Energy Economics*, (23), 511–532.

Parliament of Sri Lanka. (2019, 11 18). Retrieved from Parliament of Sri Lanka: https://www.parliament.lk/dates-of-elections

Rashid, A. (2008). Macroeconomic variables and stock market performance: Testing for dynamic linkages with a known Structiral break. *Savings and Development, 32*, 77–102.

Sadorsky, P. (1999). Oil price shocks and stock market activity. *Energy Economics, 21*, 449–469.

Wang, Y.-H., & Lin, C.-T. (2008). Empirical analysis of political uncertainty on TAIEX stock market. *Applied Economics Letters, 15*, 545–550.

Yatiwella, W. B., & Silva, J. D. (2011). Calendar anomalies: Evidence from the Colombo stock exchange. *Economics, Management and Financial Markets, 6*(2), 84–105.

Yusof, R. M., & Majid, S. A. (2007). Macroeconomic variables and stock returns in Malaysia: An application of the ARDL bound testing approach. *Savings and Development, 31*, 449–469.

Part V

Higher Education Management

Use of Social Media in Student Learning and Its Effect on Academic Performance

G. D. T. D. Chandrasiri and S. M. Samarasinghe

17.1 Introduction

The widespread use of social media sites has become a global phenomenon in recent years (Acheaw and Larson 2015). It facilitates communication between people, shares information, sends messages, creates blogs and conducts real-time conversations (Al-rahmi et al. 2015). The term "social media" has been defined as electronically mediated technologies to facilitate sharing and creation of information, ideas and interests (Bajpai 2018). According to El-Badawy and Hashem (2015), social media provide a platform that uses two-way communication to facilitate interaction between people who have online accounts. Due to speed, reach and ease of use, social media are changing the public discourse in the society and making new trends (Asur and Huberman 2014). Such media have a variety of applications and tools, including social networks, blogs, online videos and other online and electronic tools (Tenopir et al. 2013). Growing attention to social media can be seen in disciplines as different as economics, marketing, health, education and other industries (Phillips and Shipps 2012).

Social media have changed not only communication between people but also the way students learn (Mingle and Adams 2015). According to Al-rahmi et al. (2015), a considerable number of social media users are young people engaged in higher education. Higher education institutes use social media to connect with students and alumni and to deliver instructional content (Al-rahmi et al. 2016). The incorporation of social media within the educational context is easy, because most students tend to create accounts on many social media sites such as Facebook, Twitter, Instagram,

G. D. T. D. Chandrasiri (✉) · S. M. Samarasinghe
Department of Information Technology, Faculty of Management Studies and Commerce, University of Sri Jayewardenepura, Nugegoda, Sri Lanka
e-mail: thamali.chandrasiri@sjp.ac.lk; malkanthi@sjp.ac.lk

YouTube, Google, etc. (Tess 2013). Collaborative learning, information distribution and communication between peers have been the common benefits of using social media in higher education (Collins and Hide 2010; Nicholas et al. 2014; Al-rahmi et al. 2016). Further, social media facilitate investigation-based and collaborative learning among students in higher education and make them active learners (Al-rahmi and Othram 2013).

However, other studies identify an adverse effect of social media on academic performance. Many students are unfocused on their lessons and highly distracted because of using social media during lectures (Bajpai 2018). A significant negative relationship between social media usage and academic performance has been cited (Acheaw and Larson 2015; Kirschner and Karpinski 2010; Brooks 2015). According to Mingle and Adams (2015), undergraduates have had negative experiences such as lack of time to study, late assignment submissions and poor spelling and grammar due to heavy use of social media. El- Badawy and Hashem (2015) have argued that there is no relationship between social media use and academic performance – positive or negative.

Although a considerable number of studies have explored the impact of social media in higher education, the findings have been inconclusive. Thus, further research is important to identify the effect of social media use on students' academic performance (Melani and Andrew 2018; Thuseethan and Vasanthapriyan 2015). Little attention has been given to studying the impact of social media on students' academic performance, specifically in the Sri Lankan higher education context. The purpose of this study was, therefore, to develop an integrated multi-dimensional model to provide a more comprehensive view of the impact of social media usage on performance.

The rest of the paper is organized as follows. The review of literature is presented in section two. Section three presents the conceptual model developed based on the literature, followed by formulation of hypotheses in section four. The methodology used is presented in section five. Section six provides the results and section seven discussion of findings. Section eight reports the conclusion, and in section nine practical implications are provided.

17.2 Literature Review

Due to the invention of social media, the online world has changed drastically. Billions of people exchange their opinions, personal information, pictures and videos at an amazing rate (Acheaw and Larson 2015). This has transformed communication and all areas reliant upon it. Social media comprise electronic tools such as blogs, collaborative projects, social networking sites, virtual social worlds, virtual games, virtual second world and content communities (Kaplan and Haenlein 2010). Examples include Facebook, Twitter, Myspace (Asur and Huberman 2014) and YouTube (Al-rahmi and Zeki 2016). Al-rahmi and Othman (2013) and Nicholas et al. (2014) have identified Wikipedia also as part of social media. In this study, "social media" refers to the applications, services and systems that allow users to create, remix and share content (Junco 2012).

Khurana (2015) emphasizes that most social media users are in the 15–25 age range, representing the youth generation. The majority of users are college students or undergraduates (Al-rahmi et al. 2016). Hence a number of researchers have examined the impact of social media in education (Al-rahmi and Othram 2013; González et al. 2016; Lau 2017). Wheeler et al. (2008) found four major advantages of using social media: improved motivation for learning, enhanced relationships, personalized course materials and enhanced collaborative learning. With the popularity of social media, universities use them as a marketing tool and as a tool to communicate with students and alumni (Al-rahmi et al. 2014).

Studies report positive effects (Al-rahmi and Othram 2013; Bajpai 2018; Michikyan et al. 2015) and negative effects (Acheaw and Larson 2015; Mingle 2015) on students' academic performance. Phillips and Shipps (2012) indicate that use of social media increases collaborative information sharing without considering time and geographical barriers and it is helpful for educational purposes. College students can have opportunities to enhance creative work, get support from peers and alumni and have mutual contacts with their institution by associating with social media (Al-rahmi and Zeki 2016). As positive outcomes, social media usage improves writing skills and vocabulary and reduces spelling mistakes (Yunus and Salehi 2012). Social media also help students become active learners (Rutherford 2010). Al-rahmi and Othman (2013) highlight that social media enhance academic performance through collaborative learning along with the interactivity with teachers, peers and engagement. Said, Alshuaibi et al. (2018) argue that people can learn from other's multiple intelligences, by creating and sharing information via social media, which means they can analyse the way others think. Moghavvemi et al. (2018) have identified YouTube as an effective medium for students in a learning process if the videos are relevant to their courses.

Using social media for non-academic purposes and multitasking in social media have negatively affected academic performance (Lau 2017). To examine multitasking performance, Sweller (1994) used cognitive load theory, which explains the role of working memory in educational aspects. Despite the advantages of social media, misuse leads to negative impacts on learning such as less study time, late submissions and spelling and grammar mistakes (Mingle and Adams 2015). According to Bandura's (1998) social learning theory, individuals, peers and situations may affect individuals' learning outcomes. Higher usage levels of social media lead to lower performance of tasks as well as increased technostress and lower happiness (Brooks 2015). Kolan (2018) argues that, although students gain many advantages by using social media, such as information sharing, discussions with others and building relationships, usage may lead to addictions to an extent, resulting in reduced concentration that seriously affects academic lives. Considering these aspects, Kolan called social media a "useful servant but a dangerous master" that can be further described as a "two-edged sword". Bajpai (2018) argue that there should be a balance between social media usage for academic and non-academic purposes. They stress that restrictions on social media are undesirable in this globalized era; students should be encouraged to use social media more and more for academic purposes (see also Mingle and Admas 2015).

A review of literature highlights that prior studies have used the technology acceptance model (TAM) (Davis 1989), the theory of reasoned action (TRA) (Fishbein and Ajzen 1975), the theory of planned behaviour (TPB) (Ellen and Ajzen 1992) and the unified theory of acceptance and use of technology (UTAUT) model (Venkatesh 2000) to predict the acceptance and adoption of information technology, and these are also commonly applied in social media research (Lu et al. 2009; Phillips and Shipps 2012; Fan et al. 2013). TAM and TPB have been commonly used in predicting IT acceptance and adoption (Fan et al. 2013; Choi and Chung 2013; Lu et al. 2009; Pavlou and Fygenson 2006; Liao et al. 2007). Much research on social media usage in higher education has emphasized TAM and TPB as prominent models in explaining user behaviour. However, to better understand the role played by social media in higher education, apart from usage, how social media impact students' academic performance is equally important. Thus, the literature lacks models providing an integrated view of the impact of social media on students' intention to use such tools in their learning and the impact on academic performance.

TAM (Davis 1989) and TPB (Ajzen 1991) are models used to explain and predict beliefs and behaviour of individuals. TAM predicts that perceived usefulness (PU) and perceived ease of use (PEOU) determine attitudes towards using and intention to use a specific technology; TPB states that attitude toward behaviour, subjective norms and perceived behavioural control (PBC) shape an individual's behavioural intentions and behaviour. Delone and McLean (1992) proposed the IS success model and updated it (Delone and McLean 2003) to predict the net benefits in the updated version. The IS success model provides the theoretical foundation to predict the system's success through the outcomes (net benefits) determined by the intention to use or indeed use a system and user satisfaction (Isaac et al. 2019). Hence the current study hypothesized a comprehensive model synthesizing the concepts of TAM, TPB and IS success model in a complementary manner to predict students' academic performance (outcome) based on user beliefs and user behaviour.

17.3 Research Model

A comprehensive review of the literature revealed the importance of identifying the impact of students' intention to use social media in their learning, as well as identifying the effect of social media on their academic performance. Although the TAM and TPB alone properly reflect behavioural intention, there was no prior research to demonstrate the impact of students' beliefs on intention to use social media in their learning and how it affects their academic performance. This study therefore seeks to synthesize the important aspects from the TAM, TPB and IS success models to predict students' intention to use social media and its academic performance impact. The conceptual model in Fig. 17.1 reflects the relationships between all the theoretical constructs used in the model. Perceived usefulness (PU) and perceived ease of

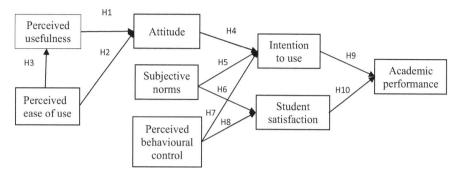

Fig. 17.1 Research model

use (PEOU) were taken from TAM to reflect students' perception about system features. Attitude, subjective norm and perceived behavioural control (PBC) were taken from TPB to reflect the effect of individuals' control beliefs and normative beliefs on their behaviour. Intention to use, student satisfaction and academic performance (net benefit) were three success dimensions from the IS success model to reflect how control beliefs and normative beliefs impact user satisfaction and intention to use, which in turn affect individuals' perception of the impact of social media on their academic performance. Academic performance is "The apparent demonstration of understanding, concepts, skills, ideas and knowledge of a person and proposed that grades clearly depict the performance of a student" (Tuckman 1975, p. 15).

17.4   Hypotheses of the Study

17.4.1 Perceived Usefulness

PU refers to "The degree to which individuals believe that their performance will enhance by using the technology" (Davis 1989, p. 320). Fan et al. (2013) have identified PU as a key motivator of consumers' intention and attitudes towards using blog services. Lu et al. (2009) show that there is a significant positive relationship between PU and attitude towards using instant messaging. Dumpit and Fernandez (2017), in their study on use of social media in higher educational institutes, emphasize that PU influences attitudes and this in turn leads to intention to use social media. Phillips and Shipps (2012) adopted TAM in their study and found a positive relationship between PU and attitude towards use of social media. Based on the justification above, the following hypothesis was formulated:

H1: Perceived usefulness has a positive effect on attitude towards using social media in student learning.

17.4.2 Perceived Ease of Use

Davis (1989, p. 320) defined PEOU as "The degree to which an individual feels that using a particular technology will be free of effort". PEOU has a positive effect on intention to use systems as well as PU. The less the effort in using a system, the better the performance (Venkatesh and Davis 2000). In the social media context, PEOU can be described as the degree to which a student believes that social media e-learning systems (ELS) will be easy to use and free of effort in that use. Lee (2006) emphasizes that PEOU positively affects attitudes towards using ELS. Gu et al. (2009) have identified PEOU as the main determinant of PU and that it has a direct and indirect effect on intention to use in mobile banking. Hence, the following hypotheses were formulated:

H2: Perceived ease of use has a positive effect on attitude towards using social media in student learning.
H3: Perceived ease of use has a positive effect on perceived usefulness of social media in student learning.

17.4.3 Attitude

In both TAM and TPB, attitude is the antecedent of intention to use (Davis 1989; Ajzen 1991). It can be defined as "An individual's positive or negative feelings about performing the target behavior" (Ajzen 1991, p. 188). Pavlou and Fygenson (2006) found that attitude has a positive effect on intention to purchase products online. Park (2009) showed a significant positive effect of attitude on intention to use e-learning systems. According to Alqasa et al. (2014), there is a positive relationship between students' attitude and behavioural intention to use banking systems. Hussain (2016) emphasizes that attitude towards e-learning positively impacts on students' intention to use it. Irianto (2015) shows that consumers' attitudes positively affect their intentions when they are purchasing organic foods in the market. Alharbi and Drew (2014) have found a positive relationship between attitude towards the usage of learning management systems (LMS) and the behavioural intention to use LMS among academics. Another study has found that attitude positively influences the intention to use bike-sharing systems in today's sharing economy (Yu et al. 2018). Based on this discussion, the following hypothesis was formulated:

H4: Attitude has a positive effect on intention to use social media in student learning.

17.4.4 Subjective Norms

Subjective norms refer to "The degree to which a person perceives that others believe he/she should use the technology" (Taylor and Todd 1995, p. 150). In the TRA model, Fishbein and Ajzen (1975) tested social influence on behavioural intention and reported that a person thinks that he should or should not perform a behaviour according to a social referent. These referents may be parents, teachers, friends, classmates, etc. (Taylor and Todd 1995). For example, if a teacher believes students should use ELS, students may be strongly motivated to comply with the teacher's expectations, and they tend to use ELS more and more (Lee 2006). Alnaser et al. (2017) show a significant relationship between subjective norm and satisfaction. Hence the following hypotheses were formulated:

H5: Subjective norms have a positive effect on intention to use social media in student learning.
H6: Subjective norms have a positive effect on student satisfaction of social media use in their learning.

17.4.5 Perceived Behavioural Control

Ajzen (1991, p. 183) defined behavioural control as "People's perception of ease or difficulty in performing the behavior of interest", which simply means the degree to which an individual believes that there is a control factor which supports or hinders the performance of his/her behaviour. According to TPB (Ajzen 1991), perceived behavioural control (PBC) affects intention, which ultimately determines the behaviour. Chen (2013) emphasizes that PBC directly influences intention to use Web 2.0. Guo et al. (2009) have reported a significant effect of PBC on user satisfaction. In this study PBC is referred to as students' belief that using social media is under their control. Accordingly, the following hypotheses were formulated:

H7: Perceived behavioural control has a positive effect on intention to use social media in student learning.
H8: Perceived behavioural control has a positive effect on student satisfaction of social media in their learning.

17.4.6 Intention to Use

Intention is defined as the "Individual's intention to perform or not to perform a behavior" (Fishbein and Ajzen 1975). According to both TAM and TPB, intention to use systems leads to performing a behaviour or actual use. Some studies demonstrate the relationship between intention to use social media and actual usage (Salloum et al. 2018; Dumpit and Fernandez 2017). Intention to use also predicts the net benefits of using information systems, as included in the IS success model (Delone and McLean 2003). In this study, intention to use refers to students' intention to use social media in their learning. Hence the following hypothesis was formulated:

H9: Intention to use social media has a positive effect on students' academic performance.

17.4.7 Student Satisfaction

User satisfaction is a key indicator of deciding continued use (Eom 2014; Pereira et al. 2015). User satisfaction is defined as "whether the user feels the system is useful and plans to be a repeat visitor" (Xinli 2013, p. 59). Eom (2012) also finds that there is a positive relationship between user satisfaction and system use. Satisfaction is a predecessor of net benefits of a behaviour, found in the IS success model (Delone and McLean 2003). Al-Rahmi and Zeki (2016) report a positive relationship between satisfaction and learner performance in social media. Hence the following hypothesis was formulated:

H10: Student satisfaction has a positive effect on students' academic performance.

17.5   Methodology

The current study addressed the question "What is the impact of social media on students' academic performance?" To answer it, a quantitative research design was used. Data were gathered from undergraduate students of a leading university in Sri Lanka to obtain information about their experience of the impact of social media on their academic performance. A convenient but reasonably representative sample was used for data collection through an online questionnaire survey. The questionnaire was developed with already validated items from prior research. A seven-point Likert scale, anchored from "Strongly agree" to "Strongly disagree", was used to measure all the constructs in the research model. The questionnaire consisted of 34 questions in relation to model constructs and informants' demographic information; 312 usable responses were taken for the analysis after removing incomplete responses. SPSS (Version 23) and SmartPLS (Version 3.0) were used to analyse the data.

17.6   Results

SmartPLS (Version 3.0) was used to test the research model. Partial least squares (PLS) is a second-generation multivariate statistical technique that can evaluate both the measurement model and the structural model at the same time, in a single operation. PLS is a more appropriate technique to use with predictive-oriented and exploratory type of models (Hair et al. 2011; Richter et al. 2016). Thus PLS was chosen as the primary data analysis technique. Using the two-step analysis procedure (Hair et al. 2011), the measurement model was first evaluated, followed by the structural model analysis.

17.6.1 Measurement Model Analysis

In the measurement model analysis, indicator reliability, internal consistency reliability and construct validity were tested. According to Chin (1998), to establish indicator reliability, factor loadings should be greater than 0.7. In this study, all factor loadings were greater than 0.7 except for two items (see Table 17.1): PU4 and

Table 17.1   Factor loadings

Measures	AP	Att	BI	PBC	PEOU	PU	Sat	SN
AP1	0.872							
AP2	0.880							
AP3	0.891							
AP4	0.873							
AP5	0.875							
ATT1		0.891						
ATT2		0.929						
ATT3		0.906						
ATT4		0.849						
IU1			0.919					
IU2			0.909					
IU3			0.883					
IU4			0.910					
IU5			0.896					
PBC1				0.743				
PBC2				0.763				
PBC3				0.870				
PBC4				0.857				
PEOU1					0.815			
PEOU2					0.802			
PEOU3					0.798			
PEOU4					0.770			
PU1						0.784		
PU2						0.847		
PU3						0.819		
PU4						0.650		
PU5						0.674		
SAT1							0.856	
SAT2							0.903	
SAT3							0.863	
SN1								0.828
SN2								0.885
SN3								0.910
SN4								0.906

Note: *AP* academic performance, *ATT* attitude, *IU* intention to use, *PBC* perceived behavioural control, *PU* perceived usefulness, *PEOU* perceived ease of use, *SAT* student satisfaction, *SN* subjective norm

PU5 had factor loadings below the threshold value. However, as the factor loadings were very close to 0.7, (PU4 = 0.650; PU5 = 0.674), the two items were retained.

Internal consistency reliability refers to "The degree to which the items on a test jointly measure the same construct" (Henson 2001, p. 177). To assess the internal consistency reliability, Cronbach's alpha and composite reliability were used (Hair et al. 2009). The threshold value considered for Cronbach's alpha was 0.7 (Hair et al. 2009). As shown in Table 17.2, all the Cronbach's alpha values and composite reliability values fulfilled the requirements for establishing internal consistency reliability. Construct validity is defined as the extent to which a set of measures precisely represent the concept of interest (Hair et al. 2009). Construct validity was established using convergent validity and discriminant validity. Hair et al. (2017, p. 137) defined convergent validity as "The extent to which a measure correlates positively with alternative measures of the same construct" and discriminant validity as "The extent to which a construct is truly distinct from other constructs by empirical standards". This implies that a construct is unique, and it describes the phenomenon which is not represented by other constructs (Hair et al. 2017). To measure convergent validity, factor loadings and the AVE values of the constructs were used (Bagozzi et al. 1991; Hair et al. 2011). As Table 17.2 shows, AVE values of all constructs of the model were above the threshold value, 0.5 (Hair et al. 2011). Thus convergent validity was established.

Following Hair et al. (2017, p. 138), discriminant validity was established using the square root of AVE values of each construct (Fornell and Larcker 1981). Accordingly, AVE should be greater than the construct's highest squared correlation with any other latent construct. As the square root of AVE values given in the diagonal (see Table 17.3) is greater than the correlation values, discriminant validity was established.

17.6.2 Structural Model Analysis

Structural model testing verifies the model's prediction of the variance towards dependent variables (Hair et al. 2017). The most commonly used measure to evaluate the model fit is the coefficient of determination (R^2 value). This measures the predictive power of the model, and it is calculated as the squared correlation between

Table 17.2 Internal consistency reliability and convergent validity of measures

Constructs	Cronbach's alpha	Composite reliability	AVE
Academic performance	0.926	0.944	0.771
Attitude	0.916	0.941	0.800
Intention to use	0.944	0.957	0.816
Perceived behavioural control	0.825	0.884	0.657
Perceived ease of use	0.809	0.874	0.635
Perceived usefulness	0.812	0.870	0.576
Student satisfaction	0.846	0.907	0.764
Subjective norm	0.905	0.934	0.779

Table 17.3 Discriminant validity

Constructs	AP	Att	IU	PBC	PEOU	PU	Sat	SN
AP	**0.878**							
ATT	0.708	**0.895**						
IU	0.795	0.708	**0.904**					
PBC	0.636	0.562	0.682	**0.81**				
PEOU	0.586	0.581	0.554	0.650	**0.797**			
PU	0.675	0.733	0.657	0.600	0.653	**0.759**		
SAT	0.725	0.622	0.732	0.746	0.597	0.636	**0.874**	
SN	0.652	0.699	0.630	0.537	0.386	0.620	0.662	**0.883**

Note: *AP* academic performance, *ATT* attitude, *IU* intention to use, *PBC* perceived behavioural control, *PU* perceived usefulness, *PEOU* perceived ease of use, *SAT* student satisfaction, *SN* subjective norm

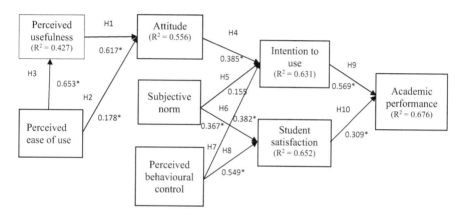

Fig. 17.2 Structural model results. (Note: "*" denotes the significant paths (p < 0.05))

a specific endogenous construct's actual and predicted values (Henseler et al. 2014). After testing reliability and validity, SEM focuses on coefficients of determination (R^2 values) and significance of path coefficients (Hair et al. 2017). As a rule of thumb, R^2 values of 0.75, 0.50 or 0.25 could be described as substantial, moderate or weak, respectively, for endogenous latent variables (Hair et al. 2011). Based on the structural model analysis, the model explained 67.6% of variance in students' academic performance, 55.6% of variance in attitudes, 63.1% of variance in intention to use, 42.7% of variance in perceived usefulness and 65.2% variance in student satisfaction (Fig. 17.2).

The bootstrapping process in SmartPLS 3.0 was used to test the hypotheses. Hair et al. (2017) have emphasized that 5% of significance level is more favourable, which indicates that the p value must be smaller than 0.05 (95% level of confidence). Accordingly, of the ten hypotheses, nine were supported (Table 17.4).

Table 17.4 Hypothesis testing results

Hypotheses	Path coefficients	p values	Supported/not supported
Attitude – intention to use	0.385	0.001	Supported
Intention to use – academic performance	0.569	0.000	Supported
Perceived behavioural control – intention to use	0.382	0.000	Supported
Perceived behavioural control – student satisfaction	0.549	0.000	Supported
Perceived ease of use – attitude	0.178	0.003	Supported
Perceived ease of use – perceived usefulness	0.653	0.000	Supported
Perceived usefulness – attitude	0.617	0.000	Supported
Student satisfaction – academic performance	0.309	0.001	Supported
Subjective norm – intention to use	0.155	0.109	Not supported
Subjective norm – student satisfaction	0.367	0.000	Supported

17.7 Discussion

The purpose of this study was to identify the impact of social media on students' academic performance. The results reveal that there is a significant positive effect of perceived usefulness on perceived ease of use ($\beta = 0.653$, $p = 0.000$). The finding was consistent with prior research. In TAM, Davis (1989) proposed that, if an individual feels that using a technology is free of effort, he or she will understand the usefulness of that particular technology. Lee (2006) found that, when students perceive ELS as easy to use, they consider ELS useful for their learning. Gu et al. (2009) found that perceived ease of using mobile banking applications was a key determinant of predicting the usefulness of them. It therefore implied that, if students believe that using social media in their e-learning is easy, they will consider it useful for better performing in academic activities. According to the findings, perceived usefulness had a significant positive effect on attitude ($\beta = 0.617$, $p = 0.000$), and perceived ease of use also had a significant positive effect on attitude ($\beta = 0.178$, $p = 0.003$). These findings were consistent with previous study findings.

Phillips and Shipps (2012) found that perceptions of ease of use and usefulness led to positive attitudes in using social networking websites. Lu et al. (2008) showed this in a study examining user acceptance of instant messaging. Attitude also had a significant positive effect on intention to use ($\beta = 0.385$, $p = 0.001$). This finding is consistent with the findings of other studies (Ajzen 1991; Pavlou and Fygenson 2006). In TPB, Ajzen (1991) proposed that the individual's positive or negative feelings about performing the target behaviour positively affected their intention towards the behaviour. Pavlou and Fygenson (2006) found that, when customers are buying products online, their attitudes towards the website had a positive effect on intention to purchase products.

According to the study findings, subjective norm did not have a significant effect on intention to use ($\beta = 0.155$, $p = 0.109$). However, Lee (2006) found that there was a significant positive effect of subjective norm on intention to use ELS. The insignificance of this hypothesis may be because this study used a sample of undergraduates who were using social media voluntarily. If it was mandatory, this could have provided a supportive outcome for the hypothesized relationship. However, the finding was consistent with some prior studies. Venkatesh et al. (2003) suggested that subjective norm only mattered in a case where use of technology was compulsory. Here, perceived behavioural control had a significant positive effect on intention to use ($\beta = 0.382$, $p = 0.000$), as suggested in TPB. Ajzen (1991) emphasized that, if individuals believed that there was a control factor which supported or hindered their performance of behaviour, this would determine their intention to perform the behaviour. This indicates that, if students believe social media use is under their control, they will tend to use social media more.

Student satisfaction had a significant positive effect on intention to use ($\beta = 0.549$, $p = 0.000$). Guo et al. (2009) also found that customer's perceived behavioural control had a positive impact on customer satisfaction about the organization. According to the findings of the study here, subjective norm had a significant positive effect on student satisfaction ($\beta = 0.367$, $p = 0.000$), showing that, if a social referent believed that students should use social media, students were highly satisfied with using social media in their learning. This was consistent with findings of Lee (2006) and Alnaser et al. (2017). Alnaser et al. (2017) emphasize that subjective norm positively affects satisfaction of customers in banks.

Intention to use had a significant positive effect on students' academic performance ($\beta = 0.569$, $p = 0.000$). As suggested by DeLone and McLean (2003) in the IS success theory, intention towards a behaviour has a significant positive relationship with net benefits which can be gained by performing the behaviour. Student satisfaction also had a significant positive effect on students' academic performance ($\beta = 0.309$, $p = 0.001$). This finding was supported by Eom (2012), who found a positive relationship between user satisfaction and use of systems. Al-Rahmi and Zeki (2016) also found an effect of student satisfaction of using social media on their academic performance.

17.8 Conclusion

Social media is becoming the most important tool for communication among students, especially in higher educational institutes. The current study focused on formulating an integrated model to investigate the effect of social media on students' academic performance, based on the concepts of the technology acceptance model, the theory of planned behaviour and the IS success model. Model fitness was empirically tested using survey data. The measurement model analysis showed that the model constructs have adequate reliability and validity; structural model analysis verified the model as having a good model fit with empirical data. The integrated model combining TAM, TPB and the IS success model provided better explanatory power. According to the study findings, the model predicted a substantial variance in students' academic performance ($R^2 = 0.676$, or 67.6%). Thus, practitioners should concentrate on incorporating social media effectively in their courses to enhance student learning.

Although this study provided many meaningful findings, it does have some limitations. The sample was from a single university with a comparatively small sample size. Therefore future research is recommended to use a more comprehensive student sample from different higher education contexts. To generalize this model, further studies are needed to examine its appropriateness. Future studies could include additional constructs that would be meaningful for examining the impact of social media on students' academic performance in higher education. However, since social media are widely used by students, the findings of this study will be very useful for administrators, content developers/lecturers and students in higher education institutes.

17.9   Practical Implications

The findings of this study provide useful implications for stakeholders in higher education. This study filled the theoretical gap in the literature to an extent by developing a comprehensive model in assessing the impact of social media on students' academic performance. Students are using social media for academic and non-academic purposes. However, in this millennial era restricting the use of social media is not advisable. Students should be educated on how to use social media productively for academic purposes rather than just persuaded towards mere socializing. The findings here revealed that integrating social media in teaching and learning can assist in enhancing students' academic performance.

Chapter Takeaways

1. Social media is an electronically mediated platform, which facilitates sharing and creation of information, ideas and interests.
2. Students in higher educational institutes are widely using social media for academic and non-academic purposes.
3. A model integrating TAM, TPB and IS success established a strong reliability and validity of model constructs.
4. The integrated model had high predictive power in students' intention to use social media and the impact on academic performance.
5. Incorporating social media in teaching and learning can assist in enhancing academic performance.

Reflection Questions

1. What are the positive and negative impacts of using social media in student learning?
2. Suggest ways that social media can be used to enhance academic performance of students in higher educational institutes.
3. Identify other theoretical models used to examine the impact of social media on students' academic performance.
4. Explain how social media could be used effectively in teaching and learning.
5. Investigate other technology-mediated factors that could affect students' academic performance.

References

Acheaw, M. O., & Larson, A. G. (2015). Use of social media and its impact on academic performance of tertiary institution students: A study of students of Koforidua Polytechnic, Ghana. *Journal of Education and Practice, 6*, 94–101.

Ajzen, I. (1991). The theory of planned behavior. Organizational behavior and human decision processes, *50*(2), 179–211.

Alharbi, S., & Drew, S. (2014). Using the technology acceptance model in understanding academics' behavioural intention to use learning management system. *International Journal of Advanced Computer Science and Application, 5*(1), 143–155.

Alnaser, F. M., Ghani, M., Rahi, S., & Abed, H. (2017). The impact of SERVQUAL model and subjective norms on Customer's satisfaction and customer loyalty in Islamic banks: A cultural context. *International Journal of Economics & Management Sciences, 6*(5), 455. https://doi.org/10.4172/2162-6359.1000455.

Alqasa, K. M., Isa, F. M., Othman, N. S., & Zolait, A. H. S. (2014). The impact of students' attitude and subjective norm on intention to use of banking systems. *International Journal of Business Information Systems, 15*(1), 105–122.

Al-rahmi, W. M., & Othram, M. S. (2013). The Impact of Social Media use on Academic Performance among university students: A Pilot Study. *Journal of Information Systems Research and Innovation*, 1–10. At https://www.academia.edu/27575207/The_Impact_of_Social_Media_use_on_Academic_Performance_among_university_students_A_Pilot_Study

Al-rahmi, W. M., & Zeki, A. M. (2016). A model of using social media for collaborative learning to enhance learners' performance on learning. *Journal of King Saud University - Computer and Information Sciences, 29*(4), 526–535. https://doi.org/10.1016/j.jksuci.2016.09.002.

Al-rahmi, W. M., Othman, M. S., & Yusuf, L. M. (2015). The role of social Media for Collaborative Learning to improve academic performance of students and researchers in Malaysian higher education. *The International Review of Research in Open and Distributed Learning, 16*(4), 177–204.

Al-rahmi, W. M., Othman, M. S., & Musa, M. A. (2014). The improvement of students' academic performance by using social media through collaborative learning in Malaysian higher education. *Asian Social Science*, 10(8), 210.

Alshuaibi, M. S. I., Alshuaibi, A. S. I., Shamsudin, F. M., & Arshad, D. A. (2018). Use of social media, student engagement, and academic performance of business students in Malaysia. *International Journal of Educational Management*.

Asur, S., & Huberman, B. A. (2014). Predicting the Future with Social Media, (May). In *2010 IEEE/WIC/ACM international conference on web intelligence and intelligent agent technology* (Vol. 1, pp. 492–499). IEEE. https://doi.org/10.1109/WI-IAT.2010.63.

Bagozzi, R. P., Yi, Y., & Phillips, L. W. (1991). Assessing construct validity in organizational research. *Administrative science quarterly*, 421–458.

Bajpai, P. (2018). Analyzing effect of social media on academic performance of university graduates, (June). https://doi.org/10.1145/3234825.3234830.

Bandura, A. (1998). Self-efficacy (reprint). In V. S. Ramachaudran (Ed.), *Encyclopedia of human behaviour* (Vol. 4, 1994) (pp. 71–81). New York: Academic.

Brooks, S. (2015). Computers in human behavior does personal social media usage affect efficiency and Well-being? *Computers in Human Behavior, 46*, 26–37. https://doi.org/10.1016/j.chb.2014.12.053.

Chen, C. (2013). The exploration on network behaviors by using the models of theory of planned behaviors (TPB), technology acceptance model (TAM) and C-TAM-TPB. *African Journal of Business Management, 7*(30), 2976–2984. https://doi.org/10.5897/AJBM11.1966.

Chin, W. W. (1998). The partial least squares approach to structural equation modeling. *Modern methods for business research, 295*(2), 295–336.

Choi, G., & Chung, H. (2013). Applying the technology acceptance model to social networking sites (SNS): Impact of subjective norm and social capital on the acceptance of SNS. *International Journal of Human-Computer Interaction, 29*, 619–628. https://doi.org/10.1080/1044731 8.2012.756333.

Collins, E., & Hide, B. (2010). *Use and relevance of Web 2.0 resources for researchers* (pp. 271–289). At https://elpub.architexturez.net/system/files/pdf/119_elpub2010.content.pdf

Davis, F. D. (1989). Perceived usefulness, perceived ease of use, and user acceptance of information technology. *MIS Quarterly, 13*(3), 319. https://doi.org/10.2307/249008.

DeLone, W.H., & McLean, E.R. (1992). Information systems success: The quest for the dependent variable. *Information Systems Research, 3*(1), 60–95.

Delone, W., & McLean, E. (2003). The Delone and McLean model of information systems success : A ten-year update. *Journal of Management Information Systems, 19*(4), 9–30. https://doi.org/10.1080/07421222.2003.11045748.

Dumpit, D. Z., & Fernandez, C. J. (2017). Analysis of the use of social media in higher education institutions (HEIs) using the technology acceptance model. *International Journal of Educational Technology in Higher Education, 14*(1), 5. https://doi.org/10.1186/s41239-017-0045-2.

El-Badawy, T. A., & Hashem, Y. (2015). The impact of social media on the academic development of school students. *International Journal of Business Administration, 6*(1), 46–52. https://doi.org/10.5430/ijba.v6n1p46.

Ellen, P. S., & Ajzen, I. (1992). A comparison of the theory of planned behavior and the theory of reasoned action. *Personality and Social Psychology Bulletin, 18*(1), 3–9. https://doi.org/10.1177/0146167292181001.

Eom, S. B. (2012). Effects of LMS, self-efficacy, and self-regulated learning on LMS effectiveness in business education. *Journal of International Education in Business, 5*(2), 129–144. https://doi.org/10.1108/18363261211281744.

Eom, S. B. (2014). Understanding eLearners' satisfaction with learning management systems. *Bulletin of the IEEE Technical Committee on Learning Technology, 16*(2), 10–13.

Fan, W. S., Haung, Y. K., Hsu, H. C., & Chen, C. C. (2013). An analysis of the Blog-User' attitude employing structural equation modeling combine TAM and TPB model, 414, 90–93. https://doi.org/10.4028/www.scientific.net/AMM.411-414.90.

Fishbein, M., & Ajzen, I. (1975). Belief, attitude, intention and behavior: An introduction to theory and research.

Fornell, C., & Larcker, D. F. (1981). Structural equation models with unobservable variables and measurement error: Algebra and statistics.

González, M. R., Gasco, J., & Llopis, J. (2016). Facebook and academic performance : A positive outcome. *The Anthroplogist, 23*(1-2), 59–67. https://doi.org/10.1080/09720073.201 6.11891924.

Gu, J., Lee, S., & Suh, Y. (2009). Determinants of behavioral intention to mobile banking. *Expert Systems with Applications, 36*, 11605–11616. https://doi.org/10.1016/j.eswa.2009.03.024.

Guo, L., Jian, J., & Tang, C. (2009). Understanding the psychological process underlying customer satisfaction and retention in a relational service. *Journal of Business Research, 62*(11), 1152–1159. https://doi.org/10.1016/j.jbusres.2008.10.020.

Hair, J. F. et al. (2009). *Multivariate data analysis.* New Delhi: Pearson Education.

Hair, J. F., Ringle, C. M., & Sarstedt, M. (2011). PLS-SEM: Indeed a silver bullet. *Journal of Marketing Theory and Practice, 19*(2), 139–151. https://doi.org/10.2753/MTP1069-6679190202.

Hair, J. F., Hult, T. M., Ringle, C. M., & Sarstedt, M. (2017). *A Primer on Partial Squares Structural Equation Modeling (PLS-SEM)* (2nd ed.). SAGE Publications.

Henson, R. K. (2001). Understanding internal consistency reliability estimates: A conceptual primer on coefficient alpha. *Measurement and evaluation in counseling and development, 34*(3), 177–189.

Henseler, J., Dijkstra, T. K., Sarstedt, M., Ringle, C. M., Diamantopoulos, A., Straub, D. W., ... & Calantone, R. J. (2014). Common beliefs and reality about PLS: Comments on Rönkkö and Evermann (2013). *Organizational research methods, 17*(2), 182–209.

Hussain, Z. (2016). Leading to intention: The role of attitude in relation to technology acceptance model. *Procedia Computer Science*, 159–164.

Irianto, H. (2015). Consumers' attitude and intention towards organic food purchase: An extension of theory of planned behavior in gender perspective. *International Journal of Management, Economics and Social Sciences, 4*(1), 17–31.

Isaac, O., Aldholay, A., Abdullah, Z., & Ramayah, T. (2019). Online learning usage within Yemeni higher education: The role of compatibility and task-technology fit as mediating variables in the IS success model. *Computers & Education, 58*(1), 113–129. https://doi.org/10.1016/j.compedu.2019.02.012.

Junco, R. (2012). The relationship between frequency of Facebook use, participation in Facebook activities, and student engagemnet. *Computers and Education, 58*(1), 162–171.

Kaplan, A. M., & Haenlein, M. (2010). Users of the world, unite! The challenges and opportunities of social media. *Business Horizons, 53*(1), 59–68. https://doi.org/10.1016/j.bushor.2009.09.003

Khurana, N. (2015). The impact of social networking sites on the youth. *Journal of Mass Communication Journalism, 5*(12), 10–13. https://doi.org/10.4172/2165-7912.1000285.

Kirschner, P. A., & Karpinski, A. C. (2010). *Facebook® and academic performance.* Centre for Learning Sciences and Technologies.

Kolan, B. J. (2018). *Effect of social media on academic performance of students in Ghanaian universities: A case study of University of Ghana, Legon* (February).

Lau, W. W. F. (2017). Computers in human behavior effects of social media usage and social media multitasking on the academic performance of university students. *Computers in Human Behavior, 68*, 286–291. https://doi.org/10.1016/j.chb.2016.11.043.

Lee, Y. C. (2006). An empirical investigation into factors influencing the adoption of an e-learning system. *Online Information Review, 30*. https://doi.org/10.1108/14684520610706406.

Liao, C., Chen, J., & Yen, D. C. (2007). Theory of planning behavior (TPB) and customer satisfaction in the continued use of e-service: An integrated model. Computers in Human Behavior, 23(6), 2804-2822https://doi.org/10.1016/j.chb.2006.05.006

Lu, Y., Zhou, T., & Wang, B. (2009). Computers in human behavior exploring Chinese users' acceptance of instant messaging using the theory of planned behavior, the technology acceptance model, and the flow theory. *Computers in Human Behavior, 25*(1), 29–39. https://doi.org/10.1016/j.chb.2008.06.002.

Melani, A., & Andrew, A. (2018). *Social media and academic performance of undergraduate students* (November 2017).

Michikyan, M., Subrahmanyam, K., & Dennis, J. (2015). Computers in human behavior Facebook use and academic performance among college students: A mixed-methods study with a multi-ethnic sample. *Computers in Human Behavior, 45*, 265–272. https://doi.org/10.1016/j.chb.2014.12.033.

Mingle, J., & Adams, M. (2015). Social media network participation and academic performance in senior high schools in Ghana. *Library Philosophy and Practice*, 1.

Moghavvemi, S., Sulaiman, A., & Jaafar, N. I. (2018). The international journal of social media as a complementary learning tool for teaching and learning: The case of youtube. *The International Journal of Management Education, 16*(August 2017), 37–42. https://doi.org/10.1016/j.ijme.2017.12.001.

Nicholas, D., Farm, W., & Rowlands, I. (2014). *Social media use in the research workflow* (May). https://doi.org/10.3233/ISU-2011-0623.

Park, S. Y. (2009). An analysis of the technology acceptance model in understanding university student's behavioral intention to use e-learning. *Journal of Educational Technology & Society, 12*(3), 150–162. https://doi.org/10.1007/s00340-009-3513-0.

Pavlou, P. A., & Fygenson, M. (2006). Understanding and predicting electronic commerce adoption: An extension of the theory of planned Behavio. *MIS Quarterly, 30*(1), 115–143.

Pereira, F. A. D. M., Ramos, A. S. M., Gouvêa, M. A., & Da Costa, M. F. (2015). Satisfaction and continuous use intention of e-learning service in Brazilian public organizations. *Computers in Human Behavior, 46*, 139–148. https://doi.org/10.1016/j.chb.2015.01.016.

Phillips, B., & Shipps, B. (2012). Frequency of usage: the impact of technology acceptance factors versus social factors. *International Journal of Virtual Communities and Social Networking* (IJVCSN), 4(2), 30-45.

Richter, N. F., Rudolf, S. R., Ringle, C. M., & Schlagel, C. (2016). A critical look at the use of SEM in international business research. *International Marketing Review, 33*(3), 376–404. https://doi.org/10.1108/IMR-04-2014-0148.

Rutherford, C. (2010). Using online social media to support preservice student engagement. *MERLOT Journal of Online Learning and Teaching, 6*(4), 703–711.

Salloum, S. A., Maqableh, W., Mhamdi, C., & Kurdi, B. Al. (2018). *Studying the Social Media Adoption by university students in the United Arab* (December).

Sweller, J. (1994). Cognitive load theory, learning difficulty, and instructional design. *Learning and Instruction*, 4(4), 295–312, 4, 295–312.

Taylor, S., & Todd, P. A. (1995). Understanding information technology usage: A test of competing models. *Information Systems Research, 6*(2), 144–176.

Tenopir, C., Volentine, R., & King, D. W. (2013). Social media and scholarly reading. *Information Review, online*. https://doi.org/10.1108/OIR-04-2012-0062.

Tess, P. A. (2013). The role of social media in higher education classes (real and virtual)–A literature review. *Computers in human behavior, 29*(5), A60–A68.

Thuseethan, S., & Vasanthapriyan, S. (2015). Social media as a new trend in Sri Lankan digital journalism : A surveillance. *Asian Social Science, 11*(10), 86. https://doi.org/10.5539/ass.v11n10p86.

Venkatesh, V. (2000). Determinants of perceived ease of use: Integrating control, intrinsic motivation, and emotion into the technology acceptance model. *Information Systems Research, 11*(4), 342–365.

Venkatesh, V., & Davis, F. D. (2000). Studies linked references are available on JSTOR for this article : A theoretical extension of the technology acceptance model : Four longitudinal field studies. *Management Science, 46*(2), 186–204.

Venkatesh, V., Morris, M. G., Davis, G. B., & Davis, F. D. (2003). User acceptance of information technology: Toward a unified view. *MIS quarterly*, 425–478.

Wheeler, S., Yeomans, P., & Wheeler, D. (2008). The good, the bad and the wiki: Evaluating student-generated content for collaborative learning. *British Journal of Educational Technology, 39*(6), 987–995. https://doi.org/10.1111/j.1467-8535.2007.00799.x.

Xinli, H. (2013). Effectiveness of information technology in reducing corruption in China. *The Electronic Library, 33*(1), 52–64. https://doi.org/10.1108/EL-11-2012-0148.

Yu, Y., Yi, W., Feng, Y., & Liu, J. (2018). *Understanding the intention to use commercial bike-sharing systems: An integration of TAM and TPB*. Hawaii International Conference on System Sciences.

Yunus, M. M., & Salehi, H. (2012). The effectiveness of Facebook groups on teaching and improving writing: Students' perceptions. *International journal of education and information Technologies, 1*(6), 87–96.

The Role of an Entrepreneurial Leader in Developing an Entrepreneurial University: A Case Study of a State University in Sri Lanka

18

R. Senathiraja, K. K. Kapiyangoda, and S. Buvanendra

18.1 Introduction

18.1.1 Background of the Study and the Research Issue

The materialization of entrepreneurial activities has become popular worldwide in the recent decades, and promoting entrepreneurial spirit has become a social phenomenon which is considered as a solution for unemployment and poverty alleviation through stimulating economic growth and innovation (Porter 2003; Andersson et al. 2010; Errasti et al. 2018). In such a context, universities have become pioneers in developing skills of the young, creating and disseminating knowledge (Gibb and Haskins 2014) and building national and international linkages in order to develop as an entrepreneurial university (EU). This concept is further explored by the Sustainable Development Goals (SDGs) under Goal 4 (education) by UNESCO (Sustainable Development Goals 2019), and it is expected that universities would facilitate in producing a number of young adults who possess skills suitable for decent jobs, while creating entrepreneurs through providing equal quality education, and promoting lifelong learning opportunities for all, which ultimately leads to sustainable development.

The concept of EU has emerged, giving a new definition to traditional universities. An EU is broadly defined as a university that has the ability to innovate,

R. Senathiraja (✉) · K. K. Kapiyangoda
Department of Management and Organization Studies, Faculty of Management and Finance, University of Colombo, Colombo, Sri Lanka
e-mail: laxumy@mos.cmb.ac.lk; kumudukapiyangoda@mos.cmb.ac.lk

S. Buvanendra
Department of Finance, Faculty of Management and Finance, University of Colombo, Colombo, Sri Lanka
e-mail: bkshanthy@dfn.cmb.ac.lk

© The Author(s), under exclusive license to Springer Nature
Switzerland AG 2021
S. Dhiman, R. Samaratunge (eds.), *New Horizons in Management, Leadership and Sustainability*, Future of Business and Finance,
https://doi.org/10.1007/978-3-030-62171-1_18

recognize, and create opportunities, take risks, respond to challenges (Etzkowitz 2003a, b, 2004), and engage with industry (Charles 2006; Owen-Smith et al. 2002) as to arrive at a more promising posture for the future (Clark 1998). Sound leadership practices of the institutional leader play a vital role in directing a university to develop as an EU. Accordingly, entrepreneurial leaders direct a group of people to achieve a common goal, using proactive entrepreneurial behavior by optimizing risk, taking personal responsibility, and managing change to create sustainable value through innovation and technology transfer (Surie and Ashley 2008).

Under this background few studies have explored how institutional leaders, who take the form of entrepreneurial leaders, build EUs (Gibb 2012). Our study, therefore, aims to fill this lacuna in research in the areas of EUs and entrepreneurial leadership through investigating how entrepreneurial leaders (previous and current Vice Chancellors) build an EU through incorporating the Triple Helix Model in a case of a Sri Lankan leading state university (Etzkowitz et al. 2008; Thorn and Soo 2006; Zhou 2008).

18.2   Theoretical Background and Review of Literature

18.2.1 Theoretical Background

18.2.1.1   Triple Helix and EU

The Triple Helix Model was invented at Stanford University (Triple Helix Association, under the leadership of Professor Henry Etzkowitz), which elaborated that universities and governments act as entrepreneurs, demonstrating that innovation and entrepreneurship are not limited to business. EUs play a key role in the triple helix through facilitating technology transfer, incubating new firms, and taking the lead in regional renewal efforts and development. Universities are widening their teaching and research activities to reshape the firms through entrepreneurial education and incubation programs (Broström 2011), while universities, firms, and governments each take the role of the other in triple helix interactions, even though they maintain their primary roles and distinct identities. Accordingly, the universities initiate the development of new organizations, start-ups, and spinoffs through research and innovation; business entities conduct training programs and support sharing knowledge; and governments play the role of a regulator (Etzkowitz 2013a, b; Etzkowitz and Zhou 2017).

An EU is a source which facilitates interactions among the actors of tripe helix of university-industry-government. According to Clark (1998), the ability to act as an independent entity is necessary but an insufficient condition. The main characteristics of an EU are research output with potential for commercialization, patenting, creating start-ups, inculcating an entrepreneurial culture, obtaining intellectual property rights, generating revenues, and ultimately influencing regional development. When compared with the traditional universities, EUs adopt a holistic approach rather than an individualistic stand. Over the period, universities have expanded the scope of their duties while contributing to regional development together with the industry and government. Supporting this fact, Link and Siegel (2003) and Shane (2004) mentioned that universities receive enhanced public attention as a generator of jobs and regional innovation. However, the Triple Helix Model is emerging globally, despite uneven development, with academic culture changing at different rates in different societies. According to Gibb (2012), universities are becoming entrepreneurial in order to address the needs of its own environment and to contribute to regional and national economic development. This explains that triggered by diversity and complexity of the environment the universities are naturally becoming entrepreneurial in order to survive and thrive within their ecosystem.

18.2.2 Entrepreneurial Leadership

Leadership is the process of influencing people and creating the environment to achieve goals. Studies have highlighted that as new organizational designs, new thinking patterns and new information systems emerge, new leadership styles should also emerge, in order to sustain and lead such institutions efficiently and effectively (Tarabishy et al. 2005). The concept of entrepreneurial leadership has emerged in order to provide leadership to such entrepreneurial institutions (Tarabishy et al. 2005) while providing an opportunity to shape thinking in both entrepreneurship and leadership (Leitch and Volery 2016). Moreover, entrepreneurial leaders are expected to create and lead an entrepreneurial culture (Harper-Anderson 2018), inculcating ethics (Surie and Ashley 2008) and strengthening institutional norms (Harper-Anderson 2018) while building business linkages (Coyle 2014). Roomi and Harrison (2011) have recently defined entrepreneurial leadership as communicating the vision to engage teams to identify, develop, and take advantage of opportunity in order to gain competitive advantage. This indicates that application of entrepreneurial competencies together with personal and functional competencies of a leader could lead towards achieving common goals (Cogliser and Brigham 2004; Vecchio 2003). Therefore, entrepreneurial leaders are viewed as creators or innovators of an economy (Surie and Ashley 2008) who can ensure continuous innovation while sustaining trust and confidence to develop their organizations beyond the horizon.

18.2.3 Entrepreneurial Leadership and EUs

As discussed earlier under the Triple Helix Model, universities are no longer isolated, but are increasingly involved with external partners such as industry and government. Under such a context, the importance of entrepreneurship education has been popularized as a field of study in many different fields (Zhang et al. 2013; Honig 2004; Neck and Greene 2011). The study of EC (European Commission) and OECD (Organisation for Economic Co-operation and Development) has developed a guiding framework for EUs which measures the level of entrepreneurial bent of universities through seven criteria, which includes leadership and governance as a criterion. Furthermore, Clark (1998) also identified five key elements that explain the EU paradigm which included "strengthened core of leadership" as one of the elements which defines EUs. Therefore it could be concluded that leadership plays a vital role in directing the organization towards developing into an entrepreneurial institution through inculcating an entrepreneurial culture (Coyle 2014).

There are some principal definitions elaborating the concept of EUs. Among them, Clark (1998) defined EU as "a university which actively seeks to innovate in how it goes about its business, seeks to work out a substantial shift in organizational character so as to arrive at a more promising posture for the future while becoming a 'stand-up' university that are significant actors on their own terms" (p. 4). In addition, Etzkowitz (2003a) described EU as a natural incubator, providing support structures for teachers and students to initiate new ventures. These definitions clearly explain that universities become entrepreneurial by engaging in innovative research; commercializing research outcomes through licensing and patenting; and facilitating creation of new ventures, spinoffs, start-ups, and new industries for social development.

In organizations, the leader plays a vital role in the process of establishing vision and mission and channeling the organizational resources towards achieving the established goals. Similar to the other organizations, in the universities the head of the institution (Vice Chancellor) plays a vital role in molding the institutional practices. The leader is involved directly in influencing and motivating the institutional members towards achieving the organizational goals, which involves recognizing and exploiting entrepreneurial opportunities with a particular emphasis on shaping the university into an EU. As explained above, along with the concept of EUs, entrepreneurial leaders play a vital role in shaping and developing an EU. Under such a context, only few studies have explored how institutional leaders build EUs. Therefore, the aim of this study is to examine how entrepreneurial leader(s) built an EU through identifying their role in developing such a university by illustrating a case of a leading Sri Lankan state university.

18.3 Methodology

18.3.1 Qualitative Methodology

The socially constructed nature of reality and the intimate relationship between the researcher and what is studied, as well as the situational constraints that shape inquiry, are acknowledged in qualitative researches. The way the social experience is created and the meaning given are investigated through these researches (Vaivio 2008) while capturing actors' perspective by detailed interviewing and observations (Qu and Dumay 2011). Therefore, it was decided to incorporate qualitative methodology in order to explore deeply how leaders of a state university contribute in building an EU.

According to Lillis (2008), qualitative researches focus on "how" and "why" research questions in a real organizational setting. Accordingly, our study aims to understand how entrepreneurial leader(s) build an EU (University of Delta). Consequently, the qualitative approach was considered as the most suitable research methodology in order to investigate the role of entrepreneurial leaders in building an EU.

18.3.2 Case Study Approach

Case study is an empirical inquiry that investigates a contemporary phenomenon in depth and within its real-life context, when the boundaries between the phenomenon and context are not clearly evident (Yin 2009). Thus, in order to analyze and understand how the institutional leaders build an EU, it was decided that case study method is the most suitable for this research. Accordingly, University of Delta which is one of the leading and earliest established state universities in Sri Lanka was selected as the case to be explored.

18.3.3 Data Collection Methods

In-depth interviews were the mode of primary data collection. Through this method, views of the current Vice Chancellor and the former Vice Chancellor were captured. Probing questions were raised in order to facilitate gathering rich data (Qu and Dumay 2011). A documentary analysis was also conducted through observing the university strategic plan, university website, and university newsletters (university magazine) in order to obtain an understanding of the institutional leaders' role in building an EU. Moreover, documentary evidence was utilized as a part of evidence which facilitated data triangulation to ensure validity and reliability.

18.3.4 Data Collection

Data was collected initially from the former Vice Chancellor of the university through an interview guide prepared in accordance with the OECD Framework (2012) and the Triple Helix Model. During this initial interview, an overview of the university, history of the university, and the initiatives taken to develop University of Delta into an EU during his term of 3 years were elaborated along with examples drawn from the context of University of Delta. The other interview was held with the current Vice Chancellor of University of Delta which provided ideas on developments yet to be undertaken as well as initiatives taken to keep up with the momentum towards developing into an EU. This interview was also based on an interview guide which contained not only open-ended questions but also probing questions to gather rich in-depth data. These interviewees were selected based on purposive sampling technique, which facilitated the selection of the most appropriate people who would provide the most relevant rich data related to the research question.

18.3.5 Data Analysis

Special focus was given to the thematic analysis of Braun and Clarke (2013) which was followed in the analysis of data. As the initial step, the data collected through interviews were transcribed. Then all the collected and transcribed data were read and familiarized, while taking note of items of potential interest. Next the data set was coded giving relevant words or phrases for group of ideas expressed by the two interviewees (Miles et al. 2014), while identifying and categorizing the similar ideas expressed by the interviewees under themes. Subsequently the themes were reviewed to identify and understand similar themes, while analyzing relationships among different themes. After reviewing these themes, they were related to the Triple Helix Model (Etzkowitz 2013a, b). Finally, the discovered themes were elaborated and the analysis was finalized.

18.4   Findings

18.4.1 University of Delta

University of Delta (the name "University of Delta" was incorporated because the authors did not want to divulge the actual name of the university which was incorporated in this study) is a state-owned university which was established in the early twentieth century and currently operates as the pioneer in facilitating higher education in Sri Lanka. This consists of a campus, a school, seven institutes, and nine faculties with fifty-six academic departments and is one of the oldest and most reputed universities in Sri Lanka. At present, it provides education for more than 27,000 students including more than 10,000 undergraduates and nearly 17,000 post-graduate and certificate level students (information obtained from University of Delta Strategic Plan, 2018–2022).

18.4.2 Role of an Entrepreneurial Leader in Developing an EU

As the head of the institution, the Vice Chancellor has the main responsibility of making the key decisions and leading the university towards success. As the institution's leader, his/her perception on entrepreneurship and emphasis given to become an EU has a major influence in building an EU. As the interviewees revealed, the institutional leader needs to be creative and innovative in utilizing current trends emerging from the education industry and implement new projects in order to sustain the quality of higher education, while ensuring that the staff possess the required competencies to become an EU.

Being Creative and Innovative: Utilizing the Current Trends Emerging from the Education Industry

When focusing on the role of a leader in building an EU, he/she should come up with innovative ideas in order to improve the services rendered through identifying the current trends of the education industry. Our study revealed that the former institutional leader took a prime initiative in identifying the upcoming trends of the industry and reacting accordingly. As he suggests, the way in which universities were perceived in the past is different from that at present:

> The universities in the past were seen as **undergraduate universities** and we did not focus on the role of the students after their graduation. We do our maximum to teach the students well and after graduation we didn't even have a mechanism to trace and see what they were doing. Furthermore, the state was also having the vision of improving the economy and generating employment opportunities for the youth, thereby facilitated universities in achieving this vision of producing competent and knowledgeable graduates.

> There was a move all over the world two or three decades ago to emphasize the importance of developing universities to become EUs because there was this debate on meeting the demand generated from the job market. Therefore, it was our role to supply competent graduates who possessed required skills in order to fulfil this demand. So, market forces came into operation. Thus, there was a need to place everything within that context. Current generation of students demand their needs and want to be innovative and creative. This gave rise to the concept of universities becoming a **knowledge hub**. Since the students themselves want to be entrepreneurs, why not the universities?

The former institutional leader has captured the current trends of the industry and market forces in the process of leading the institution to become an EU. He identified that even though in the past, education was provided as a means of generating knowledge, at present the academics have a responsibility of creating employable graduates in addition to their duty of inculcating knowledge. Under the above circumstances, the university has placed a higher importance on promoting entrepreneurship (through collaboration with the industry) and innovation through inclusion of these aspects into the university mission statement as below:

> To discover and disseminate knowledge; *enhance innovation*; ...and beyond the university through *engagement and collaboration with industry* and community. (Information obtained from University of Delta Strategic Plan, 2018-2022)

In the above context, creativity was perceived as the key to grow into an EU. Instances which the former Vice Chancellor embraced creativity on behalf of the institution is illustrated below.

The former head of the institution has introduced new programs such as human resource development, manpower planning, and business demography into the Faculty of Arts which were very popular among the students. These programs were created through analyzing the current trends in the education sector and the demands of the industry with the aim of increasing the employability of the students and developing links with the industry. Adding to the above points, the current Vice

Chancellor has also illustrated how the leaders' creativity plays a crucial role as she explained importance of opening up new faculties and introducing new degree programs as means of acknowledging current trends of the industry. Furthermore, the traditional teaching and learning methods have been replaced by outcome-based learning and student-centered learning through the intervention of the head of the institution. Initiatives have also been taken in order to build interactive classrooms through embedding a computer-based learning environment including learning management systems (LMS), video conferencing, virtual campus, and M-learning facilities, which further illustrates how innovations on teaching and learning have been embedded within the university environment with the intervention of the head of the institution.

Developing Staff in Order to Enhance Their Competencies
Staff attached to the university plays a major role in developing it into an EU. The former institutional leader perceives that the staff needs to become entrepreneurial in order to make the university entrepreneurial. As he explained, more attention was directed on recruitment of competent, dynamic, and enthusiastic staff with the intention of inculcating an entrepreneurial culture within the university. As the former Vice Chancellor explains:

> During the last four years I was very much interested in recruitment, I have chaired all the selection panels and if you look at the people we have recruited they are dynamic and full of enthusiasm to facilitate the process of building an entrepreneurial culture within the university. We need to understand how the new generation thinks and what attracts them. In the Sri Lankan context, unless people receive benefits or incentives from the process they hardly move towards achieving these goals. Thus, the institution needs to develop an incentive scheme which triggers entrepreneurship through inclusion of these practical aspects in to the proposals we make in future.

A center for staff development has been established by the University of Delta with the intention of providing systematic training and development workshops for academic staff attached to universities in Sri Lanka. This center has received international accreditation for its academic staff training and development programs as well (information obtained from University of Delta Strategic Plan, 2018–2022).

Engaging in Projects to Uplift Quality of Education in the University of Delta
The institutional leaders have taken up a number of initiatives in order to uplift the quality of education through providing leadership to university-wide projects. Accordingly, blended learning program has been initiated in order to upgrade the traditional education system with the incorporation of technology and reforming delivery of selected courses of the University of Delta with the intention of taking the university education into the next level. Furthermore, projects such as "Higher Education for the 21st Century" (World Bank-funded project in collaboration with the Ministry of Higher Education); HETC project; AHEAD project; "Improving Relevance and Quality of Undergraduate Education" (IRQUE) – World Bank-funded project; self-assessment for ICT-driven innovation project; and capacity

development programs have been taken up with the intervention of the leadership of the institution, in order to uplift the quality of the higher education institution.

18.4.3 Moving Towards an EU in Light of the Triple Helix Model

As the above data suggests, the current and former heads of the institution have been directly involved in the process of developing the University of Delta into an EU. Accordingly, the Triple Helix Model is utilized as a theoretical lens to illuminate how the head of the university has developed linkages with the industry and the government. This section highlights how the head of the university acts as a key agent who links the university, government, and industry in light of the Triple Helix Model.

18.4.3.1   Initiatives Taken to Link with the Industry

Following the vision of making the university entrepreneurial, the former institutional leader has strengthened Career Guidance Units (CGUs), established UBL (University Business Linkage) Cell, strengthened UDSTEC (University of Delta Science and Technology Cell), upgraded international unit, and encouraged research and development activities in order to link the university with the industry as explained below.

Strengthening CGUs

As the former Vice Chancellor suggests:

> If you need to make the students more employable, we need to strengthen our CGUs and bring experts who have competency in that area. I have invested a lot of money in these areas and I have linked the university with reputed companies such as MAS and JKH to bring up that initiative through holding career fairs. Accordingly, we have developed a university wide network through the CGUs. Also, I made it compulsory for the final year students to undergo an internship period of six months, which was another good initiative. We can't give jobs for everybody but it's a good start.

Establishing CGUs was perceived by the Vice Chancellors as a worthy initiative to link with the industry while creating job opportunities for the passing out graduates.

Establishing UBL Cell

The former Vice Chancellor of the University of Delta took the initiative to appoint a director for the UBL Cell, in order to set up business linkages with the industry, while facilitating transfer of technology:

> Through UBL Cell we adopted IP (Intellectual Property) policy and we worked with World Intellectual Property Organization (WIPO) and the National Intellectual Property Organization. Now we have a technology transfer officer at University of Delta. So, all these were done during my time in order to make the university an EU.

The UBL Cell functions as the main technology transfer entity of the university, which would aid in fulfilling the University of Delta's mission of linking with the industry. Accordingly, the UBL Cell has initiated actions to strengthen the relationships with the industry through a variety of strategies: closely working with CGU; supporting invention, research, and start-ups of undergraduate students; engaging with local business community; and organizing networking events at the university.

Strengthening UDSTEC

UDSTEC was established in 2009 with the vision of collaborating with the private sector to develop industry-linked research (information obtained from the University of Delta Strategic Plan, 2018–2022). UDSTEC is engaged in facilitating transfer of knowledge and technology to the benefit of society; creating an awareness in the public/private sector about the advisory and consultancy capabilities in teaching, research, and professional services that can be provided by the university; and undertaking consultancy projects with private/public sector organizations.

UDSTEC has been involved in initiating a number of research projects through playing a major role in connecting the industry and the University of Delta. Some of these researches include Bio-Ethanol Feasibility Assessment (in partnership with B.C.R. Trading Company (Pvt) Ltd.), development of a toilet bowl cleaner (in partnership with Darley Butler), analysis of total available phosphorus content in bio-fertilizers (in partnership with Bio Power Lanka (Pvt) Ltd), testing of contaminated air (in partnership with UNFPA office), and the project of adding value to graphite (in partnership with Kahatagaha Graphite Lanka Ltd). Both the former Vice Chancellor and the current Vice Chancellor confirmed the above findings while highlighting the importance of the UDSTEC.

Upgrading the International Unit

In order to strengthen the international collaborations, the International Unit has been upgraded in order to work with many international universities and local institutions. In this relation, the University of Delta has entered into more than 75 MOUs so far, and collaborations have been made with more than 15 countries including European and Asian countries. These collaborations with foreign universities are aimed at developing research collaborations and academic exchange programs which are meant to be mutually beneficial for the local and global academic partners while facilitating national and international knowledge dissemination.

Encouraging Research and Development Activities

The University of Delta has taken a number of steps in developing research and inculcating a research-oriented culture within the institution. The annual research symposium was initiated as a regular event in 2008 with the objective of disseminating new knowledge acquired by the academic community of the University while promoting interaction between the faculties and institutes of the University. Furthermore, the University of Delta Review (the Journal of the University) is published annually by the University of Delta which covers multidisciplinary researches.

In addition to the university journal, faculty-based journals are also being published annually and biannually. Furthermore, university research symposium and faculty-wide international research conferences are being held annually to inculcate a research-oriented culture.

The research and development committees, which operate both faculty-wide and university-wide, engage in evaluation of research projects submitted by the university academics, with the aim of providing financial support. Research grants such as university research grant, university travel grant, and foreign PhD grant are being provided upon the recommendation of the above committees, in order to encourage the academics to engage in research while inculcating a research-oriented culture within the university.

18.4.3.2 Linking with the Government

The Sri Lankan government considers development of education as a method of achieving economic development. The concept of providing free education has been promoted from primary education in which the government provides free text books and free school uniforms in order to encourage children to attend schools. When it comes to university education, it is also provided free of charge for the students who get the highest scores in General Certificate of Education Advanced Level (G.C.E A/L) subject to district-wise merit. Furthermore, benefits such as *mahapola* and *bursary* are provided as financial assistance for the less privileged students who achieve requisite academic excellence. Accordingly, government policies have been implemented favorably in promoting higher education throughout the past decades.

As a fully state-owned institution, the University of Delta operates with the treasury funds, which is utilized to develop infrastructure facilities and provide other services with the prime intention of securing free education for the future generation of the country. However, Sri Lankan state universities at present do not totally depend on funds provided by the state and try their maximum to generate funds internally. With the intervention of the institutional leaders, the University of Delta is conducting extension courses such as PhD programs, masters programs, diploma programs, higher diploma programs, etc. which assist in generating funds internally without depending solely on the government treasury. The former leader strongly believed in his ability and the potential of the university, when developing the University of Delta into an EU. He believed that the university has the ability to build up as an independent EU, without depending on the funds of the state. Therefore, it could be concluded that the leader played an important role in securing the autonomy of the university while developing it to become an EU.

However, the government provides grants, research allowances, and project-focused funds which are being distributed among various parts of the university. As the authoritative institutional leader appointed from the government, the Vice Chancellor plays the role of a collaborating and coordinating agent that links the government and the university and takes the initiatives in distributing the grants and funds among the respective faculties and institutes connected to the university.

18.4.4 Role of a Leader in Developing an EU: In Light of the Triple Helix Model

Figure 18.1 encapsulates above data and illustrates the role of a leader in developing an EU through incorporating the Triple Helix Model as a theoretical lens. As above data suggests, the leaders of the University of Delta (previous and current Vice Chancellors) play a vital role in acting as the key collaborating agents that link the university, industry, and government into a single platform. The government facilitates free education and provides grants, research allowances, and funds in order to strengthen the infrastructure facilities and promote research activities of the university. As the intermediary between the government and the university, the Vice Chancellor plays the role of disseminating the funds among the relevant parties and different sectors attached to the university. In addition, as the key intermediary that links the university and the industry, the Vice Chancellor takes steps to strengthen the CGUs, establish UBL Cell, strengthen UDSTEC, upgrade the international unit, and encourage industry-collaborated research.

Furthermore, the Vice Chancellors of the University of Delta take the leadership in strengthening the staff, being creative and innovative through utilizing the current trends emerging from the education industry and initiating projects to uplift quality of education while acting as the key collaborating agent in combining the university, industry, and government into a single platform. Finally, all these collaborations among the university, industry, and the government led through the Vice Chancellor would contribute in producing knowledgeable graduates possessing entrepreneurial behavior while ensuring convergence of academic entrepreneurship and securing quality of the higher education institution.

18.5 Discussion and Conclusion

18.5.1 Discussion

18.5.1.1 Entrepreneurial Leadership and EUs

The study on the University of Delta reveals that the entrepreneurial leader (Vice Chancellor) plays a major role in the process of inculcating an entrepreneurial culture within the university (Harper-Anderson 2018; OECD Framework 2012; Clark 1998; Coyle 2014). Accordingly, the head of the institution plays a prominent role in recruiting competent, enthusiastic staff and developing their skills through training while promoting innovation and value creation within the institution (Hisrich 1986). As the study of Roomi and Harrison (2011) reveals, the entrepreneurial leader has to embrace the concept of entrepreneurship and communicate institution's entrepreneurial orientation via its vision. The University of Delta has taken significant steps to incorporate the concept of entrepreneurship into its mission (i.e., enhance innovation, engagement, and collaboration with industry) and embed it in

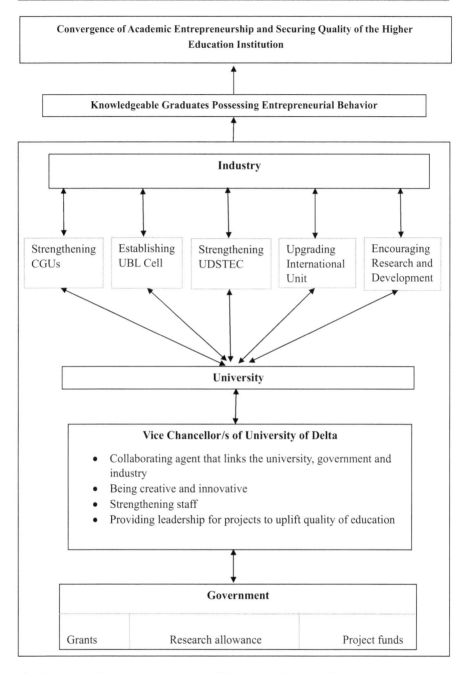

Fig. 18.1 Role of a leader in developing an EU: in light of the Triple Helix Model

the culture of the university. However, our study does not specifically reveal how the intervention of an entrepreneurial leader contributes to inculcate ethics (Surie and Ashley 2008) and strengthen institutional norms (Harper-Anderson 2018). Our study highlights the key role institutional leader plays in building and strengthening commercial linkages with the industry (Coyle 2014) through strengthening the support structure (Etzkowitz 2003a). Accordingly, it was revealed that the head of the institution has taken necessary steps in strengthening CGUs, establishing UBL Cell, strengthening UDSTEC, upgrading international division, and encouraging industry-collaborated research in order to link the university with the industry.

Our study also identified the unique competencies of an entrepreneurial leader. The proactive nature (Chen 2007; Kuratko 2007; Gupta et al. 2004) of the entrepreneurial leader could be identified through the actions of the previous Vice Chancellor as he identified the current trends of the education industry and embedded those into the curriculum to make the potential graduates competent for the job market. Furthermore, the heads of institution have been creative and innovative (Chen 2007; Kuratko 2007; Gupta et al. 2004) in designing new courses and introducing new programs such as Master of Business Studies (MBS) to open up avenues for the graduates to enter new job markets (Morris and Schindehutte 2004). Furthermore, as proposed by Swiercz and Lydon (2002), our study also identified initiatives such as developing the human resource through training and focusing on internally generated funds as prominent functional competencies of the former Vice Chancellor. Accordingly, it could be concluded that the above characteristics and competencies of an entrepreneurial leader aided in the process of developing the university into an EU.

18.5.1.2 The Triple Helix Model in Illuminating the Role of an Entrepreneurial Leader

As suggested by Etzkowitz and Leydesdorff (2000), the Triple Helix Model illuminates the university-industry-government network and how the university can play a superior role in disseminating innovation in knowledge-based societies through transforming its functions (Gibb 2012) from "undergraduate universities" into "knowledge creating hubs." In relation to our study based on the University of Delta, we attempt to uncover how the entrepreneurial leader influences development of an EU through acting as a collaborator who strengthens the linkages among the university, industry, and government.

As suggested by Zhou (2008), the University of Delta falls into the category which combines university pushed model and government pulled model in which the university initiates generation of knowledge-based innovation and facilitates technology transfer through UBL Cell and UDSTEC Cell, while government plays an important role in promoting knowledge creation through providing grants, allowances, and funds for research activities in order to sustain knowledge generation and dissemination through universities. However, the corporate-led model is still emerging in the context of Sri Lanka, and therefore, currently the industry joins hands with the universities to continue their research activities rather than engaging in research independently.

As revealed in our case study, the University of Delta acts as a knowledge producer which facilitates mobility and exchange of knowledge while creating a platform for social interaction (Romano et al. 2014). The university links with the industry and government through the intervention of the head of the institution. Accordingly, the head of institution links the university with the industry through strengthening CGUs, establishing UBL Cell, strengthening UDSTEC, upgrading international division, and encouraging industry-collaborated research. Furthermore, the government provides grants, research allowances, and funds which are distributed through the intervention of the head of the institution. Therefore, the Vice Chancellor of the university acts as the main coordinating agent who links the university, government, and industry while bringing these three helices into one platform, enabling exchange of knowledge and facilitation of social interaction.

18.6   Conclusion

The research objective of our study is to explore how the entrepreneurial leaders build an EU. The Vice Chancellors (both previous and current) as the leaders of the institution contribute in building an EU in several ways: acting as the key agent that links the university, government, and industry into a single platform; being creative and innovative; strengthening staff; providing leadership for projects to uplift quality of higher education institution. As the chief coordinator who links the industry and the university, the Vice Chancellor takes the leading role in strengthening CGUs, establishing UBL Cell, strengthening UDSTEC, upgrading international division, and encouraging industry-collaborated research. Furthermore, the Vice Chancellor, as the key authoritative agent, also plays the role of connecting the university with the government. Finally, all these activities link together in building an EU which ensures producing knowledgeable graduates who possess entrepreneurial behavior, bringing out convergence of academic entrepreneurship and securing quality of the higher education institution.

Chapter Takeaways

1. The Triple Helix Model can be incorporated as a theoretical lens to illuminate the role of a leader in developing an EU.
2. The Vice Chancellor of a university contributes in building an EU through acting as the key agent that links the university, government, and industry into a single platform; being creative and innovative; strengthening staff; and providing leadership for projects to uplift quality of the higher education institution.
3. The government supports free education and provides grants, research allowances, and funds in order to strengthen the infrastructure facilities and to promote research projects as means of leading the university to become an EU.
4. The institutional leader takes steps to strengthen the CGUs, establish UBL Cell, strengthen UDSTEC, upgrade the international unit, and encourage

industry-collaborated research in the process of strengthening linkages between the university and the industry.

5. The Vice Chancellor of a university should act as a change agent to accommodate the demands of the dynamic environment and make sure that the graduates possess the required entrepreneurial competencies and entrepreneurial behavior while ensuring convergence of academic entrepreneurship which ultimately leads to secure quality of the higher education institution.

Reflection Questions

1. Explain the role of an institutional leader in the process of building an EU incorporating the Triple Helix model.
2. How do the leaders of a state university develop the ecosystem in the process of building an EU?
3. Explain how the government facilitates the state universities in the process of developing them as EUs.
4. Explain how the state universities link with the industry in the process of developing as EUs.
5. How could a country at large benefit from emerging as an entrepreneurial nation through the contribution of entrepreneurial leaders of the state EUs?

References

Andersson, T., Formica, P., & Curley, M. G. (2010). *Knowledge-driven entrepreneurship: The key to social and economic transformation*. New York: Springer New York.

Braun, V., & Clarke, V. (2013). Teaching thematic analysis: Overcoming challenges and developing strategies for effective learning. *The Psychologist, 26*(2), 120–123.

Broström, A. (2011). Book review of Henry Etzkowitz, "The triple helix: University–industry–government innovation in action". *Papers in Regional Science, 90*(2), 441–442.

Charles, D. (2006). Universities as key knowledge infrastructures in regional innovation systems. *Innovation: The European Journal of Social Science Research, 19*(1), 117–130.

Chen, M. H. (2007). Entrepreneurial leadership and new ventures: Creativity in entrepreneurial teams. *Creativity and Innovation Management, 16*(3), 239–249.

Clark, B. R. (1998). *Creating entrepreneurial universities: Organizational pathways of transformation*. Paris: IAU Press.

Cogliser, C. C., & Brigham, K. H. (2004). The intersection of leadership and entrepreneurship: Mutual lessons to be learned. *The Leadership Quarterly, 15*(6), 771–799.

Coyle, P. (2014). How entrepreneurial leadership can engage university staff in the development of an entrepreneurial culture. *Industry & Higher Education, 28*(4), 263–269.

Errasti, N., Bezanilla, M. J., García-Olalla, A., Auzmendi, E., & Paños, J. (2018). Factors and maturity level of entrepreneurial universities in Spain. *International Journal of Innovation Science, 10*(1), 71–91.

Etzkowitz, H. (2003a). Innovation in innovation: The triple helix of university-industry-government relations. *Social Science Information, 42*(3), 293–337.

Etzkowitz, H. (2003b). Research groups as 'quasi firms': The invention of the entrepreneurial university. *Research Policy, 32*, 109–121.

Etzkowitz, H. (2004). The evolution of the entrepreneurial university. *International Journal of Technology and Globalization, 1*(1), 64–77.

Etzkowitz, H. (2013a). *Can a teaching university be an entrepreneurial university?: Civic entrepreneurship and the formation of a cultural cluster in Ashland Oregon* (Center for Innovation Management Working Paper Series). London: University of London. Retrieved from http://www.bbk.ac.uk/innovation/publications/docs/WP11.pdf.

Etzkowitz, H. (2013b). Anatomy of the entrepreneurial university. *Social Science Information, 52*(3), 486–511.

Etzkowitz, H., & Leydesdorff, L. (2000). The dynamics of innovation: From national systems and "mode 2" to a triple Helix of university–industry–government relations. *Research Policy, 29*(2), 109–123.

Etzkowitz, H., & Zhou, C. (2017). *The triple helix: University–industry–government innovation and entrepreneurship.* London: Routledge.

Etzkowitz, H., Ranga, M., Benner, M., Guaranys, L., Maculan, A. M., & Kneller, R. (2008). Pathways to the entrepreneurial university: Towards a global convergence. *Science and Public Policy, 35*(9), 681–695.

Gibb, A. (2012). Exploring the synergistic potential in entrepreneurial university development: Towards the building of a strategic framework. *Annals of Innovation & Entrepreneurship, 3*(1), 1–24.

Gibb, A. A., & Haskins, G. (2014). The university of the future: An entrepreneurial stakeholder learning organisation? In A. Fayolle & D. T. Redford (Eds.), *Handbook on the entrepreneurial university* (pp. 25–63). Cheltenham: Edward Elgar Publishing Limited.

Gupta, V., MacMillan, I. C., & Surie, G. (2004). Entrepreneurial leadership: Developing and measuring a cross-cultural construct. *Journal of Business Venturing, 19*(2), 241–260.

Harper-Anderson, E. (2018). Intersections of partnership and leadership in entrepreneurial ecosystems: Comparing three U.S. regions. *Economic Development Quarterly, 32*(2), 119–134.

Hisrich, R. D. (1986). Entrepreneurship and intrapreneurship: Methods for creating new companies that have an impact on the economic renaissance of an area. In R. D. Hisrich (Ed.), *Entrepreneurship, intrapreneurship, and venture capital* (pp. 71–104). Toronto: Lexington Books.

Honig, B. (2004). Entrepreneurship education: Toward a model of contingency-based business planning. *Academy of Management Learning & Education, 3*(3), 258–273.

Kuratko, D. F. (2007). Entrepreneurial leadership in the 21st century: Guest editor's perspective. *Journal of Leadership & Organizational Studies, 13*(4), 1–11.

Leitch, C. M., & Volery, T. (2016). Entrepreneurial leadership: Insights and directions. *International Small Business Journal, 35*(2), 147–156.

Lillis, A. (2008). Qualitative management accounting research: Rationale, pitfalls and potential – A comment on Vaivio. *Qualitative Research in Accounting & Management, 5*(3), 239–246.

Link, A. N., & Siegel, D. (2003). *Technological change and economic performance.* London: Routledge.

Miles, M. B., Huberman, A. M., & Saldana, J. (2014). *Qualitative data analysis: A methods sourcebook.* California: Sage Publications. Retrieved from https://issuu.com/annisa.fikriyah_tasya/docs/_matthew_b._miles__a._michael_huber.

Morris, M. H., & Schindehutte, M. (2004). Entrepreneurial values and the ethnic enterprise: An examination of six subcultures. *Journal of Small Business Management, 43*(4), 53–97.

Neck, H. M., & Greene, P. G. (2011). Entrepreneurship education: Known worlds and new frontiers. *Journal of Small Business Management, 49*(1), 55–70.

OECD Framework. (2012). *A guiding framework for Entrepreneurial Universities.* European Commission and OECD joint publication. Retrieved on June 6, 2019, from https://www.oecd.org/site/cfecpr/EC-OECD%20Entrepreneurial%20Universities%20Framework.pdf

Owen-Smith, J., Riccaboni, M., Pammolli, F., & Powell, W. W. (2002). A comparison of US and European university-industry relations in the life sciences. *Management Science, 48*(1), 24–43.

Porter, M. (2003). The economic performance of regions. *Regional Studies, 37*(6–7), 549–578.

Qu, S. Q., & Dumay, J. (2011). The qualitative research interview. *Qualitative Research in Accounting & Management, 8*(3), 238–264.

Romano, A., Passiante, G., Del Vecchio, P., & Secundo, G. (2014). The innovation ecosystem as booster for the innovative entrepreneurship in the smart specialisation strategy. *International Journal of Knowledge-Based Development, 5*(3), 271–288.

Roomi, M. A., & Harrison, P. (2011). Entrepreneurial leadership: What is it and how should it be taught? *International Review of Entrepreneurship, 9*(3), 1–44.

Shane, S. A. (2004). *Academic entrepreneurship: University spinoffs and wealth creation.* Cheltenham: Edward Elgar Publishing Limited.

Surie, G., & Ashley, A. (2008). Integrating pragmatism and ethics in entrepreneurial leadership for sustainable value creation. *Journal of Business Ethics, 81*(1), 235–246.

Sustainable Development Goals. (2019). Website of United Nations, Department of Economics and Social Affairs – Statistics Division. Retrieved on June 6, 2019, from https://unstats.un.org/sdgs/report/2019/goal-04/

Swiercz, P. M., & Lydon, S. R. (2002). Entrepreneurial leadership in high-tech firms: A field study. *Leadership & Organization Development Journal, 23*(7), 380–389.

Tarabishy, A., Solomon, G., Fernald, L. W., & Sashkin, M. (2005). The entrepreneurial leader's impact on the organization's performance in dynamic markets. *The Journal of Private Equity, 8*(4), 20–29.

Thorn, K., & Soo, M. (2006). *Latin American universities and the third mission: Trends, challenges, and policy options.* Policy Research Working Paper no. WPS 4002, Washington, DC: World Bank. Retrieved from http://documents.worldbank.org/curated/en/305971468266684626/Latin-American-universities-and-the-third-mission-trends-challenges-and-policy-options

Vaivio, J. (2008). Qualitative management accounting research: Rationale, pitfalls and potential. *Qualitative Research in Accounting & Management, 5*(1), 64–86.

Vecchio, R. P. (2003). Entrepreneurship and leadership: Common trends and common threads. *Human Resource Management Review, 13*(2), 303–327.

Yin, R. K. (2009). *Case study research: Design and methods.* Thousand Oaks: SAGE Publications.

Zhang, Y., Duysters, G., & Cloodt, M. (2013). The role of entrepreneurship education as a predictor of university students' entrepreneurial intention. *International Entrepreneurship and Management Journal, 10*(3), 623–641.

Zhou, C. (2008). Emergence of the entrepreneurial university in evolution of the triple helix: The case of Northeastern University in China. *Journal of Technology Management in China, 3*(1), 109–126.

Linkages with Micro Small Medium Enterprises (MSMEs) for Sustainable Higher Education in Management

19

19.1 Introduction: The Role of Universities as Knowledge Producers

Universities are progressively predictable in developing links with the business community. At the same time, micro small medium enterprises (MSMEs) need to improve their skills and knowledge via collaborative work with the knowledge community. Improving competitiveness of innovative ideas for the business community is determined through a healthy relationship with the knowledge community and leaders. Collaboration between the university and the business community provides a win-win situation for both parties. Many researchers suggest that the development of that relationship and linking agendas lead universities to have a greater number of job opportunities. In the contemporary higher education sector, the greatest challenge faced by a higher education institution is to create job opportunities. Graduates seek jobs from the government. Many graduates have a negative attitude toward private employment, and most are job seekers rather than job creators.

One of the problems behind this issue is that universities do not seriously concern themselves with the relationship between the knowledge community and practical workers. But just producing management graduates will not lead to creating jobs in the market. During their studies, it is essential to motivate students to create and collaborate in job opportunities. The university is a social institution with a long history. It has gone through many stages in growth. Uniersity is considered an institution with the mission of teaching, learning, and researching, it has developed collaborative work with the business community to enhance knowledge through research and innovations. In recent years, universities have been expected to have

S. Shivany (✉)
Faculty of Management Studies and Commerce, University of Jaffna, Jaffna, Sri Lanka
e-mail: shanshivany@univ.jfn.ac.lk

© The Author(s), under exclusive license to Springer Nature
Switzerland AG 2021
S. Dhiman, R. Samaratunge (eds.), *New Horizons in Management, Leadership
and Sustainability*, Future of Business and Finance,
https://doi.org/10.1007/978-3-030-62171-1_19

another role that contributes to the social and economic sector. The faculties in universities have responsibilities in their output of human capital that services society. To achieve the sustainable development goals in the twenty-first century, human capital should also have the ability to contribute to the economy for sustainable development.

MSMEs would like to hire graduates who have an impact of innovativeness on the firms and hire those with management training backgrounds and who have significant positive impact on the frequent organizational changes. The low demand for graduates in the private sector reflects the barriers that restrict the hiring of graduates, but more important is stagnation in terms of technical and organizational change. The flow of graduates into industry is the most powerful mechanisms through which knowledge creation at universities can contribute to innovation in business (Brundenius et al. 2009). The University, facing global challenges that extend well beyond the economy, innovation, and entrepreneurship provides a way forward by building sustainable development, creating self-employment, reducing unemployment, generating renewed economic growth, and advancing human welfare. The triple helix model states that a knowledge-based organization can play an enhanced role in innovation in increasingly knowledge-based activities (Etzkowitz and Leydesdorff 2000).

19.2   Education for Sustainability

Sustainability can be deconstructed into three pillars: environmental (the planet), social, and economic. These need to be considered in a balanced way in order to achieve a sustainable outcome. Environmental sustainability includes issues surrounding transport, energy, water, biodiversity, resources such as computer paper and ink, and other resources and packaging. Environmental sustainability addresses issues that environmental education covers. Yet, increasingly, social sustainability plays a significant role in the sustainability agenda (Hammond and Churchman 2008). Social responsibility includes issues surrounding the well-being of staff and students, such as workplace health and safety, ethics, inclusive community, interconnectedness, quality of life, Democratic integrity, respect, partnerships, and the ability to work in teams as an opportunity to listen to and understand others' viewpoints. A national sustainable development strategy can be defined as a coordinated participatory and iterative process of thoughts and actions to achieve economic environmental and social objectives in a balanced and integrative manner.

The principle of sustainability is the foundation. The three pillars are also informally used to describe profit, people, and the planet. Social sustainability includes cultural and corporate sustainability and sometimes economic sustainability. Cultural sustainability includes issues surrounding the diversity of staff and students, equity in recruitment to the workplace, and promotion acceptance for all staff and students. Inclusive communication provides a cross-cultural and international outlook. Economic sustainability includes consideration of the short- and long-run costs that are not only financial. For any faculty, economic sustainability specifically means having a viable number of students in each unit or course so that the university will be sustainable in the long run. However, like any corporation, the cost for a university in maintaining any number of students depends on how assets and services are managed and ensuring that all staff and students are able to do their job and study well, with access to training needs and support.

Education for sustainability is to equip all people with the awareness, knowledge, skills, values, and motivation to live sustainably in order that future generations can meet their own needs. Education is fundamental to enabling people to achieve this goal. Many universities are starting to address these ideas. With the many definitions of sustainability education, grown from environmental education, it is important to offer explanations for environmental, social, economic, cultural, and corporate social responsibility.

Sustainable education is often referred to as education for sustainable development (ESD), which allows every human being to acquire the knowledge, skills, attitudes, and values necessary to shape a sustainable future (UNESCO 2014): sustainable development that meets the needs of the present without compromising the ability of future generations to meet their own needs. Given its primary role as a knowledge producer, higher education can serve as a powerful means to help create a more sustainable future. A university has the responsibility to teach in such ways that graduates have knowledge and skills necessary to live reasonability and also to help transform their workplaces toward sustainable practices (DEWHA 2009a; Ferrer-Balas et al. 2008). Ferrer-Balas et al. (2008) have suggested that the key characteristics of a sustainable university are transformative education, conducting inter- and transdisciplinary research, a societal problem-solving orientation, and networks, as well as university leadership and vision that promote proactive responses to society's changing needs. Transformative education is interactive and learner-centric with a strong emphasis on developing critical thinking skills; this prepares students to become capable of addressing complex sustainability challenges, whereas transmission education is often a one-way process of learning and may not develop, assess, or reward these attitudes in students.

The degree to which sustainability is duplicitous in actions that are the results of giving advantage to groups in society, often dishonestly, in order to give an appearance of fairness (Sherren 2006) is easily checked by answering these questions: are the students learning and being assessed on knowledge about the topic, and are they becoming equipped with the knowledge, skills, and understanding necessary to make decisions based on their full environmental and social implications? Sustainable higher education will be transformative, as its goal is to equip all people with the knowledge, skills, and understanding necessary to make decisions based on their full environmental, social, cultural, and economic implications (DEWHA 2009b), rather than transmissive, with a goal to provide students with knowledge alone. It will not be specialized in content-driven units of study on sustainability but will be integrated across courses and units. Education for sustainability and education for sustainable development have gained international usage (Shrivastava 2010). It is in this context that new educational programs, research institutions, and scientific publications with an emphasis on sustainability in higher education have emerged (Wang et al. 2013; Scott 2012; Sterling and Scott 2008). A sustainable curriculum is based on seven principles: education for all and lifelong learning, system thinking, problem-solving, critical thinking and reflection, participation, and partnership for change (DEWHA 2009b).

Sustainability is a paradigm that requires educators and learners to examine their own values, hidden assumptions and motivations, beliefs, and actions (Holdsworth et al. 2008). How eductators and learners live and work impact on environment , economy and people in the society at local, regional, national as well as global levels. We build respect for the planet and what it provides for us; conserve and manage resources for present and future generations; build respect for life in all its diversity; use active, reflective, transformative, and participative learning strategies; use correct case studies of local, national, and global examples; allow and instigate discussions that expose students to diverse viewpoints; devise viable solutions to complex problems rather than one single way of doing things; consider the consequences of possible actions; and accept responsibility for creating a sustainable future. Lang (2007) suggests that the ideal approach to designing and providing a curriculum related to sustainability is to embed the values and principles of sustainability through a whole-school approach that reorients the existing curriculum rather than through an add-on approach, a theme, or a special event. This style of curriculum design is holistic and integrated.

There are many practical ways that a curriculum can be designed to enhance student participation in thinking about these issues, solve problems, reflect on their own practices, and more. Pedagogies for sustainability include any strategies that equip students with such decision-making skills and enhance their understanding from environmental, social, cultural, economic, and political viewpoints. They include cooperative, problem-based, and experience learning.

Sustainability is an ongoing learning process that actively involves stakeholders in understanding (DEH 2005). Desha et al. (2009) list three core phases for curriculum renewal: an ad hoc exploration initiated and driven by staff, a flagship approach that is market driven, and an integrated approach that is institution driven. Several universities are grappling with ways to teach social responsibility to students because decision-making is complex with its number of technical, economic, environmental, social, and ethical constraints (El-Zein et al. 2008). Recognition of the integrated nature of indigenous cultural values and understanding of the environment (DEH 2005) would be an important addition to some units and courses.

The Global Seminar (GS) model provides a broader notion of teaching and learning for sustainability that incorporates greening and education for sustainability into the curriculum. This participatory model shows the emerging shift toward a new paradigm for teaching and learning for sustainability in academia (Savelyeva and McKenna 2011). It is recognized that there are many drivers of curriculum development—most importantly the needs and desires of employers for educated people who have the skills and competencies that can help their organizations survive and succeed. Employers constitute the ultimate marketplace for the output of educational institutions (Dubicki 2010). Good practice identified in the incorporation of sustainability within the curriculum is to use a problem-based approach supported by real-life projects to enhance the students' authentic leaning experience. Good practice for successfully incorporating sustainability into the property is to have a clear vision of what it has planned to achieve and to ensure that there is a balance between sustainability and value for money (Poon 2017). Integrating a framework for addressing sustainable development in the university curriculum, research engagement activities, and operations consistently and comprehensively through a whole institutional approach identifies the challenges and lessons on effective change management and leadership for sustainability transformation initiatives in universities and colleges (Mader et al. 2013).

The execution of university sustainable programs enables national and global level sustainable achievements (Su and Chang 2010). There is a widely held belief that sustainable development policies are essential for universities to successfully engage in matters related to sustainability and are an indicator of the extent to which they are active in this field. Good sustainable practices in universities contribute to models of economic growth consistent with sustainable development (Leal Filho et al. 2018). The level of incorporation depends on the nature of the course or unit, largely driven by the initiation of individual academics.

Quality higher education has spilled over at the macro-economic level. The role of universities in social and economic development cannot be refuted. Tertiary education equips individuals with skills to fit the job market. It is now recognized that improving university education has a positive impact on gross domestic product.

Numerous policy announcements have been produced over the past 20 years calling for higher education institutions to give greater focus on social, cultural, economic, and environmental sustainability in their curriculum, research engagement activities, and operations. However, there has been much less attention paid to establishing how to ensure these desired developments are successfully initiated, implemented, and sustained.

19.3   Sustainable Higher Education

Acceptable education is an alteration of informative thinking, which develops and demonstrates the theory and practice of sustainability in a way that is aware. It is a transformative paradigm that values, sustains, and realizes human potential in relation to the need to attain and sustain social, economic, and ecological well-being, recognizing that they must be part of the same dynamic (Sterling 2001).

The higher education system is designed to redesign the value system, families, and study system in terms of maintaining quality of life (Bateson 1997). Sustainable education is often referred to as education for sustainability development that allows human beings to obtain new knowledge, skills, attitudes, and values necessary to shape sustainable future (UNESCO 2014). Education for sustainable development means including key sustainable development issues into teaching and learning. It also requires participatory teaching and learning methods that motivate and empower learners to change their behavior and take actions for sustainable development. Education for sustainable development therefore promotes competencies like critical thinking, imagining future scenarios, and making decisions in a collaborative way. Education for sustainable development requires far-reaching changes in the way education is often practiced today. There is need for new pedagogy for the sustainability education, owing to that fact there is broad consensus that it requires a shift toward active participative , and experience based learning, methods that engage the learner and make the real difference in their understanding and thinking ability to act.

Researchers have identified five pedagogic elements that cover a host of pedagogical approaches or methods that can be used in higher education in management for achieving suitability:

1. *Critical reflection*, including old-style lecture methods, thoughtful accounts, learning journals, education journals, and deliberations groups
2. *Systematic thinking and analysis*: the use of MSME case studies and critical incidence, project-based learning, stimulus activities, and the use of field visits as a source of learning about current industrial trends
3. *Participatory learning* with a group or peer learning, developing dialogs, experiential, and developing case studies with local community groups and businesses
4. *Thinking creatively for future scenarios* by using role play, real-world inquiry, future visioning, problem-based learning, and providing space for emergence
5. *Collaborative learning*, including collaborative guest speakers, work-based learning, interdisciplinary and multidisciplinary working, and collaborative learning and coinquiry.

The knowledge economy needs institutions with the ability to discover new knowledge, develop innovative applications of these discoveries, and transfer them into the marketplace through entrepreneurial activities. Knowledge accumulation is increasingly at the core of a country's competitive advantage. During the last two decades, an increasing concern has been expressed about the quality of university education. The World Bank (2009) reiterated that the establishment of a quality assurance system for the higher education sector was of great importance. The value added to the curriculum with management decisions is embraced by management students. They also begin to comprehend how environmental literacy, as well as outdoor educational experiences, can be integrated into higher education efficiency (Lo Mun Ling 2013). In this ever-fluctuating world, handling our natural systems and making a maintainable future seem to be one of the main tests facing humanity.

This challenge is further enhanced by the ignorance or apathy of people toward the concept of sustainability. In most cases, students, who are our future cohort, are left without any insights, promise, or even understanding of their part and accountability toward creating any meaningful beliefs and actions related to sustainability. Sustainability teaching is becoming significant mainly for the young so that they have a comprehension of concepts such as economic affluence, resource equity, energy use, and environmental health and concern (Sengupta et al. 2020).

Sustainability is about lowering our ecological footprint while concurrently refining the quality of life that we value as livability in society (Newman and

Kenworthy 1999). Education for sustainability is both present and future oriented. It is learning; it is designing and implementing actions for the present, in the knowledge that the impact of these actions will be experienced in the future. In this way it leads to students developing an overall capacity to contribute to a more sustainable future in terms of environmental integrity, economic viability, and a just society for present and future generations (UNESCO 2009). In an era marked by concern about the future of the planet, education for sustainability can be empowering. It equips students to act individually and collectively in ways that can contribute to sustainability. It provides the opportunity for students to explore and evaluate contested and emerging issues, gather evidence, and create solutions for a sustainable future. Education for sustainability can enable students to become effective citizens and active change agents by helping them to deal with complexity and uncertainty. It can also help them understand that there is rarely a single solution, because new knowledge is continuously generated, and diverse viewpoints exist in society. Embedded in this curriculum framework is the principle that education for sustainability is not simply the acquisition of knowledge or skills but the total approach that generates motivation and commitment to take sustainability actions for improved outcomes for a sustainable world.

19.4 Sustainable Higher Education in Management

Over the last decade, educators in postsecondary institutions have launched numerous courses, programs, and initiatives in sustainability in management (Caeiro et al. 2013; Rands and Starik 2009). Thus, an increasing number of management educators have contributed to transforming the method of training of future business leaders and managers based on the assumption that companies need to recognize their pivotal roles and responsibilities in achieving sustainable societies. Waddock (2007) points out that this shift toward sustainability challenges educators in existing firm- or organization-centered management programs to take both the environment and society into account in their teaching. Erskine and Johnson (2012) summarize that the business is embracing a triple bottom line (TBL), and higher education institutions need to prepare students for triple bottom-line thinking.

Higher education is expected to play a pivotal role in sustainable development, economic growth, recent work, gender equality, and responsible global citizenship in all regions. Higher education and its role are considered as a debate agenda (Adomßent et al. 2014). The promotion of education on sustainability in higher education is key to building a sustainable future while also bringing youth to the center of sustainability concerns (Wals 2014; Leal Filho et al. 2015; Guerra et al. 2016). Thus, education for sustainability as a matter of environmental education shares knowledge and experience and stimulates environmental awareness and ethical behaviors (Teixeira 2013; Leal Filho et al. 2016; Guerra et al. 2016). There has been a growing demand from societies on higher education institutions regarding actions of sustainability, therefore turning these institutions into agents of change (Stephens and Graham 2010; Lozano et al. 2013a, b; Ramos et al. 2015; Leal Filho et al. 2015). Consequently, having upheld this status, an increasing number of HEIs are becoming aware of their roles in building a sustainability paradigm (Hancock and Nuttman 2014; Lozano et al. 2015a, b; Ramos et al. 2015; Verhulst and Lambrechts 2015). It has been recognized by many scholars that higher education with sustainable education is essential for building sustainable societies by adopting and institutionalizing sustainability in their systems (Lozano et al. 2013a, b, 2015a, b; Foo 2013; Romas et al. 2015; Verhulst and Lambrechts 2015).

Education in environmental matters for the young generation as well as adults, giving due consideration to the underprivileged, is essential in order to broaden the basis for an informed opinion and responsible conduct by individuals. Universities have a moral obligation to act and behave according to socio-environmental concerns (De Vega et al. 2008; Zhang et al. 2011). Several authors have highlighted the importance of developing and implementing an internal agenda of sustainability in these institutions by adopting administrative processes and campuses to effectively establish sustainability-based strategic planning that seeks to identify the economic environmental and social viability of institutions (Lozano et al. 2013b; Waheed et al. 2011; Zhang et al. 2011; Kościelniak 2014; Gómez et al. 2015; Ramos et al. 2015; Mintz and Tal 2014; Coral et al. 2003). Sustainable management of internal factors in higher education institutions (HEIs) can enhance productivity and efficiency by utilizing resources such as energy, water, etc.; stimulating sustainable waste management and recycling practices; reducing the institutional ecological footprint; and enhancing market visibility (Rauen et al. 2015; Adomßent et al. 2014).

Through the involvement of the people in the sustainable environment, higher education institutions can make a positive impact on students, professors, and other staff members, making them mindful about the importance of reducing water and energy consumption, teaching them to diminish waste production and to recycle, and changing their habits into more sustainable ones (Katiliūtė et al. 2014). These changes in institutional routine require planning and strategies to be implemented, leading it to be a process of societal transformation (Waheed et al. 2011; Ferrer-Balas et al. 2010; Velazquez et al. 2006). According to the literature, the implementation of sustainability in HEIs goes beyond the need to educate its members. It focuses on internal processes, establishing and following an institutional agenda of sustainability.

Sustainability is a relatively new area in management education. However, studies have shown, for example, that there is evidence of a positive correlation between stock price and sustainable business practices (Holliday 2010; Seidman 2008; Waddock and Graves 1997). Sustainable practices may even offer a new proxy for management performance (Bradbury 2003; Nicholson and DeMoss 2009). In addition, as regulatory compliance becomes more complex and costly, sustainable practices may enable organizations to comply more readily with these more comprehensive regulations (Rands 2009). By broadening their vision to sustainable development, business leaders are recognizing the impact of the organization on the social and natural environment.

The process of change in labor market and shifts in the world economy demand a radical reshaping of HEI provision if universities are to be the vehicle for meeting this need. The consequence of this is a reassessment of the relationship between higher education and small firms and the entrepreneurial sector. In order to meet the emerging needs of society, HEIs have had to change, for example, by expanding student numbers, introducing new learning styles and processes, altering and adding to the curricula to meet the needs of businesses and industry, improving accessibility and openness, and introducing a more diverse academic program. This process of transition is underway but not complete, and it is clearly the case that different HEIs are responding individually to these forces of change. Over the past 20 years, the knowledge base in the field of university-SME linkage has grown immensely. There are many examples of initiatives that seem to work, and these have been captured in a variety of manuals and publications with a view to disseminating best practices to other potential providers. However, it is fair to say that these descriptions of best practice have had a reduced impact because the developers of specific initiatives are often closely involved in the review process. The number of publications with titles, such as lessons from experiences, is exhaustive and does little to raise academic debate.

19.5   Linkage with MSMEs

For boosting multidimensional productivity, a holistic national process ensures that management graduates are linked with the MSMEs to learn and live with the business society and take a role as a manager for sustainable business outcomes in future.

Universities and MSMEs both recognize the mutual benefits and potential spillovers to the economy. Universities know that, if they are to remain relevant, they need to train graduates to fit the job market and concretize and test the concepts created in the real world. Many industries now acknowledge that, to successfully innovate, they cannot exclusively rely on internal research and development. They know that universities could open up great opportunities to an enormous global pool of talent and skills. The challenges are how to close the gap between the two. The barriers include the fact the match-making process can be problematic.

Universities and industries have different expectations. Universities are interested in chasing linkages and technology transfer but do not know where to look for companies that need certain technologies. For their part, industries may find it difficult to get expertise from universities. This makes engagement ad hoc, fragmentary, and short term. MSMEs can get up-to-date expertise and networks of contact in academia. The university obtains reality-based knowledge and connections to the business sector. Students can complete a degree and gain research-related work experience at the same time. Universities should have a framework for tracking alumni who have joined the world of business. While higher education institutions require practical attachments for their students, there is little follow-up after attachments.

It is now widely accepted that, in a knowledge and global economy, graduate education is the primary driver of social and political progress (Mundy 2000). Education has been presented as a means of increasing the productivity of individuals, communities, and nations (Collins and Rhoads 2008). The ability of the graduate education system to strengthen its leadership linkages with local communities is important for any university and society. The graduate education system produces individuals who possess the necessary context-specific and university-relevant capabilities to continue to develop in an interlinked global context (Lynn and Kantini 2015).

Universities, being seats of higher learning, not only produce highly qualified and skilled human resources; they also help in fostering new ideas and businesses. According to Tipple et al. (2012), higher education institutions should be contributing to students to place connection events for SMEs. These events could be linked with the student society to maintain continuity. University graduates and researchers are the key resources when it comes to the commercialization of new ideas based on technical and economic skills; cooperation with universities is of immense value to sustainable development (Tijana et al. 2013). The significance of this to the economy is obvious enough. In addition, the process of commercializing original ideas is a major issue in MSME development. Entrepreneurial universities have attracted the attention of policy makers and researchers of developing countries to discover human resource production of universities in order to acquire more important roles (Farsi et al. 2012).

MSMEs have been identified as an important strategic sector for promoting growth and social development. Over time, MSMEs have gained wide recognition as a major source of employment, income generation, poverty alleviation, and regional development. SMEs are the backbone of the economy: according to recent research, 45% percent of employment and 75% of total enterprises. The policy framework toward MSME development focuses on six key policy intervention strategies for creating a more conducive environment for the MSMEs, as well as the creation of regional balance and resource efficiency in doing business for entrepreneurial culture, skill development, and market facilitation. There is therefore a need for a specific study on MSMEs for graduates who seek employment opportunities. Studying entrepreneurship benefits students and learners from different social and economic backgrounds because it teaches students to cultivate unique skills and think outside the box. It creates opportunities, instills confidence, ensures social justice, and stimulates the sustainable economy. Linking with MSMEs also provides budding entrepreneurs with the skills and knowledge to develop business ideas and their own ventures. This will increase the intake of graduates into private sector employment.

Innovation is considered to be the most important driving factor for sustainable economic development. Knowledge transfer is widely recognized as a key element in the innovation process in knowledge-driven economies. The creation and transfer of knowledge are the basis for competitive advantage in organizations (Argote and Ingram 2000). For knowledge transfer, institutes of higher education are considered to be essential, and most enterprises cannot operate without external knowledge (Muizer 2003). A smooth transfer of knowledge is therefore crucial to ensure that the available knowledge reaches small organizations. Universities as sources of knowledge are important as well, though in a different way, because we expect them to play an important role in addressing the needs of micro and small businesses. SME-size enterprises are not assumed to have the same absorption capabilities as have large organizations in order for them to be able to interact with universities in the same manner (Freel 2006). If universities have a more practical education approach with, for instance, compulsory internships for their students, closer relations with the industry should enhance their accessibility and approachability for small firms. Therefore, it is expected that colleges will have a higher collaboration level with SMEs than universities—large firms tend to be more often engaged in knowledge transfer with higher education institutions than are small-sized enterprises (Malecki 2008).

SMEs play an important role in any economy and are increasingly being encouraged to engage with higher education institutions (Lockett et al. 2008). SMEs are highly heterogeneous; they are a source of innovation and entrepreneurship, by which means they create healthy competition (Risseeuw and Thurik 2003). Given their significance, there is a vast and growing literature stressing the importance of university linkages, including with small firms (De Jong and Hulsink 2010; Lockett et al. 2008; Niosi 2006; Wright et al. 2004). However, these studies tend to focus on technological transfer and technology-based SMEs.

Argote and Ingram (2000) describe knowledge transfer as the process through which one unit is affected by the experience of another. Colleges translate knowledge into applications for companies that affect such organizations. Simultaneously, these organizations create new knowledge and new contexts that can be used in HEIs, with each innovation that occurs. Small organizations expect new knowledge from students. This new knowledge can be shared as forms of joint supervision, guest lectures, joint research, and collaborative work (Bekker and Bodas Freitas 2008; Schartinger et al. 2002). Many SMEs expect informal contacts with the students during their studies; they believe that these contacts may bring sustainable development to their enterprises (Cohen and Levinthal 1990; De Jong and Hulsink 2010). University research centers also want to collaborate with industry because they increasingly need to find new ways of generating income since government intends to reduce research and development (R&D) funding. The universities that maintain industry-business linkages gain access to students as potential future employees and for aid on product development.

Universities provide major inputs for industrial innovation processes in terms of human capital, either through the education of graduates who become industry researchers or through personal mobility from universities to firms (Schartinger et al. 2002). The triple helix involves the state, academics, and industry and charts the relationships between them. University-industry interactions cover a wide range of relationships that include seminars, workshops, training contract research, consultancy, spin-offs, etc. Traditionally, universities have been reckoned as places of invention, education, and research (Wallmark 1997), while industry is the home of innovation. But with present trends, this is no longer the case as it has become clear that academics and industry must necessarily cooperate to bring about development. The new university functions have been described as the translation of knowledge into economic activity alongside research and teaching. A contract is drawn up between the university research center and the contractor in which costs associated with the work are shared. The two parties can work together from the stage of R&D through to commercialization. There must be mutual benefits to industry and research centers, and commercially valuable data may be protected for a limited period. This provides some assurance that the best brains in the business will be brought together to focus on the problem and that there will be a balance between long-term, high-risk research and short-term work that can be promptly commercialized (Moses 1985).

Universities and SMEs are two players in a broad range of stakeholders, with stakeholder theory (see Freeman and Medoff 1984; Freeman et al. 1987; Donaldson and Preston 1995; Johnson 1998) as a potentially viable organizing model, and it allow us to move beyond a dual partner relationship to a multistakeholder relationship, including other potential stakeholders, such as governments, large firms, and banks (Wheeler and Sillanpaa 1997). Future development on loyal inclusive stakeholder relationship will become one of the most important determinants of commercial viability and business success.

Recent research has empirically found constraints on the linkage between a management faculty and MSMEs, using an institutional case study method (Shivany 2020, forthcoming). These constraints are reluctant participation in social contribution, lack of motivation on social participation, a curriculum not encouraging field visits, lack of infrastructure facilities, work overload with academic activities, instruction methods that do not facilitate voluntary social work, lack of awareness among staff and students about community-related work, lack of support from the administration, an immense gap that exists between the academic community and the business sector, and a negative attitude toward community participation. From the stakeholders' point of view, this study recommended eight approaches to linking MSMEs:

1. Altering pedagogical methods for students to center on learning with an industry-based curriculum
2. Incorporating field visits for the cocreation of knowledge
3. Motivating faculty-level centers for linking with MSMEs
4. Attitude-change programs inducing self-start-up businesses
5. Inviting stakeholder partners for networking and student leadership
6. Outcome-based measures for academic performance
7. Introducing an award for best solution-oriented thesis
8. Quality led approach for student involvement

These eight approaches are suggested to improve linkages with the MSMEs from the stakeholder perspective of a management faculty that produces management graduates to the society.

19.6   Conclusion

The old concept that management degree holders only work at large multinational companies is dead and gone. These days, many management graduates are opting for opportunities with micro and small business organizations. These enterprises are actively recruiting management and administrative graduates for prominent positions in their businesses so they can take advantage of the skills these professionals possess. Twenty-first-century enterprises look very different from their precursors—nimbler, more transient, less graded, less steady. Yet management education has insulated change in organizations. To keep pace, management education needs new guidance to accomplish its aims. Sustainable development goals for educating future managers provide a solid framework for higher education in management. This framework develops sustainability via educating future managers who will manage enterprises which have more influence on sustainable developments.

Business and management are a means not an end. The purpose of management is to serve human needs; meeting those needs effectively is the ultimate measure of business success. We do not need to fetishize the tools of human collaboration; we should train our students in rigorous doubt about determining the best vehicle for accomplishing the ends of management. The skills needed to manage small businesses on a world platform are rather different from those of the traditional large corporation.

The world of organizations is changing radically, the world of management education, much less so. There is no better time to reconsider the 'what' and 'how' of management education for the twenty-first century. Training managers to use new tools of collaboration in the service of sustainable development goals, while energetically questioning the methods, will help create the world we want to live in.

Education for sustainable development (ESD) promotes the development of knowledge and skills and understands the values and actions required to create a sustainable world that ensures environmental protection and conservation, promotes social equity, and encourages economic sustainability. Educational institutions must consider this as their responsibility to deal intensively with sustainable development competencies and to develop the specific learning outcomes related to all sustainable development goals (SDGs). There is no one right way for a university to engage with SDGs. ESD aims to empower and equip current and future generations to meet their needs using a balanced and integrated approach to the economic, social, and environmental dimensions of sustainable development.

When MSMEs invest in management graduates, they know that they are getting an individual who brings a unique mix of classroom education and real work experience to their company. Many management graduates possess professional experience and a specialized degree in order to advance their career. The benefit that the MSMEs enjoy when hiring management graduates is immediate because these professionals can hit the ground running and be instant contributors to their workplace without a lengthy onboarding process. Therefore, to satisfy that expectation, business sector graduates should have prior knowledge and engagement with MSMEs during their studies.

MSMEs crave real-world experiences, and the knowledge these graduates possess is just as important. The knowledge that management graduates gain in universities provides them with an understanding of the essential roots of businesses and how businesses work. When hired, management graduates are then able to translate that knowledge into real-work applications for their small businesses. This knowledge can be used to create a company budgets, business plans, cost-benefit analyses, or marketing campaigns.

One of the greatest strengths unique to MSMEs is their ability to solve problems quickly and efficiently when compared to their larger corporate competitors. The education obtained at the universities empowers graduates with a skill set of best practices in problem-solving. In addition, their experience allows them to look at existing problems with a fresh eye, offering suggestions and instituting improvements for the betterment of the MSME. MSMEs know better than most that their successful operations require all staff members to wear several hats. Management graduates have been trained to recognize tasks that can be appropriately partnered, and they are able to work efficiently at accomplishing tasks successfully as soon as possible. While larger companies may worry that a given role does not provide enough challenges for a management graduate, MSMEs will benefit from the expediency that graduates possess.

Experts of the professional world know that earning a management degree is hard work and that only the most dedicated individuals accomplish this feat. While a management graduate is learning the skills they will take into the world of businesses, they are also learning the self-discipline necessary to accomplish the task of getting their degree. Discipline and dedication are traits that management graduates carry with them into their professional life, and both traits make them a perfect fit for the growing demands of MSMEs. Management graduates land in leadership positions in MSMEs because they have learned leadership skills as part of their curriculum in universities. These graduates should have such skills as part of their curriculum in universities. They should have the skills necessary to influence teams and have a lasting positive impact on MSMEs which hire them.

Universities are social institutions that have responsibilities in the sustainable development of their countries. They are knowledge producers and have an impact on the three pillars of sustainability. An education system that considers sustainable development can influence the sustainable future of a country. For these reasons, many universities are concerned about sustainability in their curriculums. Higher education in management faces challenges in employing people after graduation. Reducing unemployment and innovation for job opportunities come under sustainable goals for the twenty-first century. Management faculties of universities can enhance the employability rate of their graduates through linkages with MSMEs that have the power to create jobs—which leads to sustainability in society, economy, as well as environment.

Reflection Questions

1. What are the three core phases for curriculum renewal to link higher education in management with the current market needs?
2. How can environmental literacy, as well as outdoor educational experiences, be integrated into higher education efficiency in management teaching?
3. Why does higher education in management need problem-based approach supported by real-life projects to enhance the students' authentic learning experience?
4. What are the constraints and approaches for linkages with MSMEs?
5. Do graduates have engagement and collaborative experience with MSMEs during their studies with relevant knowledge to sustain their future?

References

Adomßent, M., Fischer, D., Godemann, J., Herzig, C., Otte, I., Rieckmann, M., & Timm, J. (2014). Emerging areas in research on higher education for sustainable development in management education, sustainable consumption and perspectives from Central and Eastern Europe. *Journal of Cleaner Production, 62*, 1–7. https://doi.org/10.1016/j.jclepro.2013.09.045.

Argote, L., & Ingram, P. (2000). Knowledge transfer: A basis for competitive advantage in firms. *Organizational Behavior and Human Decision Processes, 82*(1), 150–169.

Bateson, M. C. (1997). Understanding natural systems. In C. Zelov & P. Cousineau (Eds.), *Design outlaws on the ecological frontier*. Philadelphia: Knossus Publishing.

Bekker, R., & Bodas Freitas, I. M. (2008). Analysing knowledge transfer channels between universities and industry: To what degree do sectors also matter? *Research Policy, 37*, 1837–1853.

Bradbury, H. (2003). Sustaining inner and outer worlds: A whole-systems approach to developing sustainable business practices in management. *Journal of Management Education, 27*, 172–187.

Brundenius, C., Nuñez, J., & Pérez Ones, I. (2009). *Capacity building for the knowledge economy: The Cuban experience (1959–2009)*. Georgia Institute of Technology.

Caeiro, S., Leal Filho, W., Jabbour, C., & Azeiteiro, U. M. (Eds.). (2013). *Sustainability assessment tools in higher education institutions: Mapping trends and good practices around the world*. Cham: Springer International Publishing.

Cohen, W. M., & Levinthal, D. A. (1990). Absorptive capacity: A new perspective on learning and innovation. *Administrative Science Quarterly, 35*(1, special issue: Technology, organizations, and innovation), 128–152.

Collins, C. S., & Rhoads, R. A. (2008). The World Bank and higher education in the developing world: The cases of Uganda and Thailand. The Worldwide Transformation of Higher Education. *International Perspectives on Education and Society, 9*, 177–221.

Coral, E., Rossetto, C.R., & Selig, P.M. (2003). Planejamento Estratégico para a Sustentabilidade Empresarial: uma proposta para convergência das estratégias econômicas, ambientais e sociais. Available at: http://www.anpad.org.br/diversos/trabalhos/EnANPAD/enanpad_2003/ESO/2003_ESO1303.pdf. Accessed on 26 Mar 2016.

De Jong, P.J., & Hulsink, W. (2010). Patterns of innovation networking in Dutch small firms. EIM research reports, January 2010, Zoetermeer.

De Vega, A. C., Ojeda Benítez, S., & Ramírez Barreto, M. E. (2008). Solid waste characterization and recycling potential for a university campus. *Waste Management, 28*, S21–S26. https://doi.org/10.1016/j.wasman.2008.03.022.

DEH. (2005). *Educating for a sustainable future: A national environmental education statement for Australian schools*. Canberra: Australian Government, Department of the Environment and Heritage.

Desha, C. J., Hargroves, K., & Smith, M. H. (2009). Addressing the time lag dilemma in curriculum renewal towards engineering education for sustainable development. *International Journal of Sustainability in Higher Education, 10*(2), 184–199.

DEWHA. (2009a). *Living sustainably: The Australian Government's National Action Plan for education for sustainability*. Canberra: Australian Government, Department of the Environment, Water, Heritage and the Arts.

DEWHA. (2009b). *Education for sustainability: The role of education in engaging and equipping people for change*. Canberra: Australian Government, Department of the Environment, Water, Heritage and the Arts.

Donaldson, T., & Preston, L. E. (1995). The stakeholder theory of the corporation: Concepts, evidence, and implications. *Academy of Management Review, 20*(1), 65–91.

Dubicki, E. (2010). Research behavior patterns of business students. *Reference Services Review, 38*(3), 360–384.

El-Zein, A., Airey, D., Bowden, P., & Clarkeburn, H. (2008). Sustainability and ethics as decision-making paradigms in engineering curricula. *International Journal of Sustainability in Higher Education, 9*(2), 170–182.

Erskine, L., & Johnson, S. D. (2012). Effective learning approaches for sustainability: A student perspective. *Journal of Education for Business, 87*(4), 198–205.

Etzkowitz, H., & Leydesdorff, L. (2000). The dynamics of innovation: From National Systems and "mode 2" to a triple Helix of university–industry–government relations. *Research Policy, 29*(2), 109–123.

Farsi, J. Y., Imanipour, N., & Salamzadeh, A. (2012). Entrepreneurial university conceptualization: Case of developing countries. *Global Business and Management Research: An International Journal, 4*(2), 193–204.

Ferrer-Balas, D., Adachi, J., Banas, S., Davidson, C. I., Hoshikoshi, A., Mishra, A., Motodoa, Y., Onga, M., & Ostwald, M. (2008). An international comparative analysis of sustainability transformation across seven universities. *International Journal of Sustainability in Higher Education, 9*(3), 295–316.

Ferrer-Balas, D., Lozano, R., Huisingh, D., Buckland, H., Ysern, P., & Zilahy, G. (2010). Going beyond the rhetoric: System-wide changes in universities for sustainable societies. *Journal of Cleaner Production, 18*, 607–610. https://doi.org/10.1016/j.jclepro.2009.12.009.

Foo, K. Y. (2013). A vision on the role of environmental higher education contributing to the sustainable development in Malaysia. *Journal of Cleaner Production, 61*, 6–12. https://doi.org/10.1016/j.jclepro.2013.05.014.

Freel, M. (2006). Innovation and the characteristics of cooperating and non-cooperating small firm. In *Managing complexity and change in SMEs: Frontiers in European research* (pp. 103–135). Cheltenham/Northampton: Edward Elgar.

Freeman, R. B., & Medoff, J. L. (1984). What do unions do? *Industrial & Labour Relations Review, 38*, 244.

Freeman, R. E., Gilbert, D. R., & Jacobson, C. (1987). The ethics of greenmail. *Journal of Business Ethics, 6*(3), 165–178.

Gómez, F. U., Sáez-Navarrete, C., Lioi, S. R., & Marzuca, V. I. (2015). Adaptable model for assessing sustainability in higher education. *Journal of Cleaner Production, 107*, 475–485. https://doi.org/10.1016/j.jclepro.2014.07.047.

Guerra, J. B. S. O. A., Garcia, J., Lima, M. A., Barbosa, S. B., Heerdt, M. L., & Berchin, I. I. (2016). A proposal of a balanced scorecard for an environmental education program at universities. *Journal of Cleaner Production (In Press)*. https://doi.org/10.1016/j.jclepro.2016.11.179.

Hammond, C., & Churchman, D. (2008). Sustaining academic life: A case for applying principles of social sustainability to the academic profession. *International Journal of Sustainability in Higher Education, 9*(3), 235–245.

Hancock, L., & Nuttman, S. (2014). Engaging higher education institutions in the challenge of sustainability: Sustainable transport as a catalyst for action. *Journal of Cleaner Production, 62*, 62–71. https://doi.org/10.1016/j.jclepro.2013.07.062.

Holdsworth, S., Wyborn, C., Bekessy, S., & Thomas, I. (2008). Professional development for education for sustainability: How advanced are Australian universities? *International Journal of Sustainability in Higher Education, 9*(2), 131–146.

Holliday, S. (2010). The relationship between sustainability education and business: An interview with Chad Holliday. *Academy of Management Learning & Education, 9*, 532–541.

Johnson, D. (1998). *A stakeholder mode of university links with the entrepreneurial society, research into entrepreneurship conference, Lyon E.M.*, Lyon, France, November.

Katiliūtė, E., Daunorienė, A., & Katkutė, J. (2014). Communicating the sustainability issues in higher education institutions World Wide Webs. *Procedia – Social and Behavioral Sciences, 156*, 106–110. https://doi.org/10.1016/j.sbspro.2014.11.129.

Kościelniak, C. (2014). A consideration of the changing focus on the sustainable development in higher education in Poland. *Journal of Cleaner Production, 62*, 114–119. https://doi.org/10.1016/j.jclepro.2013.06.006.

Lang, J. (2007). *How to succeed with education for sustainability.* Carlton: Curriculum Corporation.

Leal Filho, W., Shiel, C., & Paço, A. (2015). Integrative approaches to environmental sustainability at universities: An overview of challenges and priorities. *Journal of Integrative Environmental Sciences, 12*, 1–14. https://doi.org/10.1080/1943815X.2014.988273.

Leal Filho, W., Shiel, C., & Paço, A. (2016). Implementing and operationalising integrative approaches to sustainability in higher education: The role of project-oriented learning. *Journal of Cleaner Production, 133*, 126–135. https://doi.org/10.1016/j.jclepro.2016.05.079.

Leal Filho, W., Brandli, L. L., Becker, D., Skanavis, C., Kounani, A., Sardi, C., Papaioannidou, D., Paço, A., Azeiteiro, U., de Sousa, L. O., Raath, S., Pretorius, R. W., Shiel, C., Vargas, V., Trencher, G., & Marans, R. W. (2018). Sustainable development policies as indicators and pre-conditions for sustainability efforts at universities: Fact or fiction? *International Journal of Sustainability in Higher Education, 19*(1), 85–113. https://doi.org/10.1108/IJSHE-01-2017-0002.

Ling, L. M. (2013). Curriculum, pedagogy and educational research. The work of Lawrence Stenhouse. *International Journal for Lesson and Learning Studies, 23*, 300–304. https://doi.org/10.1108/IJLLS-05-2013-0031.

Lockett, N., Cave, F., Kerr, R., & Robinson, S. (2008). Multiple perspectives on the challenges for knowledge transfer between higher education institutions and industry. *International Small Business Journal, 26*(6), 661–681.

Lozano, R., Lozano, F. J., Mulder, K., Huisingh, D., & Waas, T. (2013a). Advancing higher education for sustainable development: International insights and critical reflections. *Journal of Cleaner Production, 48*, 3–9. https://doi.org/10.1016/j.jclepro.2013.03.034.

Lozano, R., Lukman, R., Lozano, F. J., Huisingh, D., & Lambrechts, W. (2013b). Declarations for sustainability in higher education: Becoming better leaders, through addressing the university system. *Journal of Cleaner Production, 48*, 10–19. https://doi.org/10.1016/j.jclepro.2011.10.006.

Lozano, R., Ceulemans, K., & Seatter, C. S. (2015a). Teaching organisational change management for sustainability: Designing and delivering a course at the University of Leeds. *Journal of Cleaner Production, 106*, 205–215.

Lozano, R., Ceulemans, K., Alonso-Almeida, M., Huisingh, D., Lozano, F. J., Waas, T., Lambrechts, W., Lukman, R., & Hugé, J. (2015b). A review of commitment and implementation of sustainable development in higher education: Results from a worldwide survey. *Journal of Cleaner Production, 108*, 1–18. https://doi.org/10.1016/j.jclepro.2014.09.048.

Lynn, I., & Kantini, M. S. (2015). Universities as leaders in community development: The case of the University of Zambia. In *Collective Efficacy: Interdisciplinary Perspectives on International Leadership* (pp. 137–162). Published online: 8 Mar 2015.

Mader, C., Scott, G., & Abdul Razak, D. (2013). Effective change management, governance and policy for sustainability transformation in higher education. *Sustainability Accounting, Management and Policy Journal, 4*(3), 264–284. https://doi.org/10.1108/SAMPJ-09-2013-0037.

Malecki, E. J. (2008). *Higher education, knowledge transfer mechanisms and the promotion of SME innovation. Entrepreneurship and higher education*. Paris: OECD.

Mintz, K., & Tal, T. (2014). Sustainability in higher education courses: Multiple learning outcomes. *Studies in Educational Evaluation, 41*, 113–123.

Moses, M. D. (1985). *Research and Development linkages to production in developing countries*. Boulder: Westview Press.

Muizer A. (2003). Knowledge transfer. In *Entrepreneurship in the Netherlands. Knowledge transfer: developing high-tech ventures*, Ministerie van Economische Zaken.

Mundy, K. (2000). Retrospect and prospect: Education in a reforming World Bank. *International Journal of Education Development, 22*, 48350.

Newman, P., & Kenworthy, J. (1999). *Sustainability and Cities*, Island Press, and adopted by the WA State Sustainability Strategy in 2003, by the House of Representatives Environment Committee Sustainable Cities Sustainability Strategy in 2003, the House of Representatives Environment Committee Sustainable Cities report in 2005 and by the Australian State of the Environment Reports in 2001 and 2006, etc.

Nicholson, C. Y., & DeMoss, M. (2009). Teaching ethics and social responsibility: An evaluation of undergraduate business education at the discipline level. *Journal of Education for Business, 84*, 213–218.

Niosi, J. (2006). Introduction to the symposium: Universities as a source of commercial technology. *Journal of Technology Transfer, 31*, 399–402.

Poon, J. (2017). Engaging sustainability good practice within the curriculum design and property portfolio in the Australian higher education sector. *International Journal of Sustainability in Higher Education, 18*(1), 146–162. https://doi.org/10.1108/IJSHE-09-2015-0149.

Ramos, T. B., Caeiro, S., Hoof, B., Lozano, R., Huisingh, D., & Ceulemans, K. (2015). Experiences from the implementation of sustainable development in higher education institutions: Environmental Management for Sustainable Universities. *Journal of Cleaner Production, 106*, 3–10. https://doi.org/10.1016/j.jclepro.2015.05.110.

Rands, G. P. (2009). A principle-attribute matrix for environmentally sustainable management education and its application. *Journal of Management Education, 33*, 296–322.

Rands, G., & Starik, M. (2009). The short and glorious history of sustainability in north American management education. In C. Wankel & J. A. Stoner (Eds.), *Management education for global sustainability* (pp. 19–49). Charlotte: Information Age Publishing.

Rauen, T. R. S., Lezana, A. G. R., & da Silva, V. (2015). Environmental management: An overview in higher education institutions. *Procedia Manufacturing, 3*, 3682–3688. https://doi.org/10.1016/j.promfg.2015.07.785.

Risseeuw, P., & Thurik, R. (2003). *Handboek Ondernemers & Adviseurs: Management en Economie van het Midden- en Kleinbedrijf*. Deventer: Kluwer.

Savelyeva, T., & McKenna, J. R. (2011). Campus sustainability: Emerging curricula models in higher education. *International Journal of Sustainability in Higher Education, 12*(1), 55–66. https://doi.org/10.1108/14676371111098302.

Schartinger, D., Rammer, C., Fischer, M. M., & Fröhlich, J. (2002). Knowledge interactions between universities and industry in Austria: Sectoral patterns and determinants. *Research Policy, 31*, 303–328.

Scott, W. (2012). Sustainability education perspectives and practice across higher education. *Environmental Education Research, 18*(5), 722–726.

Seidman, D. (2008, December 5). Outgreening delivers sustainable competitive advantage. *Business Week*. Retrieved from http://www.businessweek.com/managing/content/dec2008/ca2008125029230.htm

Sengupta, E., Blessinger, P., & Yamin, T. S. (2020). Introduction to integrating sustainability into curriculum. In Sengupta, E., Blessinger, P. & Yamin, T.S. (Eds.), *Integrating Sustainable Development into the Curriculum* (*Innovations in Higher Education Teaching and Learning, Vol. 18*), emerald publishing limited, pp. 3-14. https://doi.org/10.1108/S2055-364120200000018018.

Sherren, K. (2006). Core issues: Reflections on sustainability in Australian university coursework programs. *International Journal of Sustainability in Higher Education, 7*(4), 400–413.

Shrivastava, P. (2010). Pedagogy of passion for sustainability. *The Academy of Management Learning and Education, 9*(3), 443–455.

Shivany, S. (2020). Impediments and approaches for faculty and SME linkage: Institutional case study, *American International Journal of Business Management (AIJBM), 3*(3), 08–18. ISSN- 2379-106X.

Stephens, J. C., & Graham, A. C. (2010). Toward an empirical research agenda for sustainability in higher education: Exploring the transition management framework. *Journal of Cleaner Production, 18*, 611–618. https://doi.org/10.1016/j.jclepro.2009.07.009.

Sterling, S. (2001). *Sustainable education – Re-visioning learning and change* (Schumacher Society Briefing no. 6). Dartington: Green Books.

Sterling, S., & Scott, W. (2008). Special issue: Education for sustainable development in higher education. *Environmental Education Research, 14*(4), 383–504.

Su, J. H., & Chang, T. (2010). Sustainability of higher education institutions in Taiwan. *International Journal of Sustainability in Higher Education, 11*(2), 163–172. https://doi.org/10.1108/14676371011031883.

Teixeira, S. R. (2013). The environmental education as a path for a global sustainability. *Procedia - Social and Behavioral Science, 106*, 2769–2774. https://doi.org/10.1016/j.sbspro.2013.12.318.

Tijana, et al. (2013). Developing SME's through university support centers: A comparative analysis. *Management Journal for Theory & Practice Management, 67*, 15–27.

Tipple, N., Cumming, M., Taylor, P., & Tan, S.-Y. (2012). *Interaction between HEIs and SMEs the student perspective*. Proceedings of the HEA STEM learning and teaching conference. https://doi.org/10.11120/stem.hea.2012.052.

UNESCO Education Sector, United Nations Decade on Education for Sustainable Development (2005–2014): International Implementation Scheme, 2009., at http://unesdoc.unesco.org/images/0014/001486/148654E.pdf, p. 5.

United Nations Educational, Scientific and Cultural Organization (UNESCO). (2014). UNESCO roadmap for implementing the global action programme on education for sustainable development.

Velazquez, L., Munguia, N., Platt, A., & Taddei, J. (2006). Sustainable university: What can be the matter? *Journal of Cleaner Production, 14*(9–11), 810–819. https://doi.org/10.1016/j.jclepro.2005.12.008.

Verhulst, E., & Lambrechts, W. (2015). Fostering the incorporation of sustainable development in higher education. Lessons learned from a change management perspective. *Journal of Cleaner Production, 106*, 189–204. https://doi.org/10.1016/j.jclepro.2014.09.049.

Waddock, S. (2007). Leadership integrity in a fractured knowledge world. *Academy of Management Learning & Education, 6*(4), 543e557.

Waddock, S. A., & Graves, S. B. (1997). The corporate social performance–financial performance link. *Strategic Management Journal, 18*, 303–319.

Waheed, B., Khan, F., Veitch, B., & Hawboldt, K. (2011). Uncertainty-based quantitative assessment of sustainability for higher education institutions. *Journal of Cleaner Production, 19*, 720–732. https://doi.org/10.1016/j.jclepro.2010.12.013.

Wallmark, J. (1997). Inventions and patents at universities: The case of Chalmers Institute of Technology. *Technovation, 17*(3), 127–139.

Wals, A. E. J. (2014). Sustainability in higher education in the context of the UN DESD: A review of learning and institutionalization processes. *Journal of Cleaner Production, 62*, 8–15. https://doi.org/10.1016/j.jclepro.2013.06.007.

Wang, Y., Wang, R., Shi, H., Huisingh, D., Hansson, L., & Hong, J. (2013). Special issue: Green universities and environmental higher education for sustainable development in China and other emerging countries. *Journal of Cleaner Production, 61*, 1e138.

Wheeler, D., & Sillanpaa, M. (1997). *The stakeholder corporation*. London: Pitman Publishing.

World Bank. (2009). World Development Report 2009: Reshaping Economic Geography. World Bank. © World Bank. https://openknowledge.worldbank.org/handle/10986/5991 License: CC BY 3.0 IGO.

Wright, M., Birley, S., & Mosel, S. (2004). Entrepreneurship and university technology transfer. *Journal of Technology Transfer, 29*, 235–246.

Zhang, N., Williams, I. D., Kemp, S., & Smith, N. F. (2011). Greening academia: Developing sustainable waste management at Higher Education Institutions. *Waste Management, 31*, 1606–1616. https://doi.org/10.1016/j.wasman.2011.03.006.

Part VI

Human Resource Management

Impact of Envy on Job Engagement: A Study of Academic Staff Members in the Private Higher Education Sector in Sri Lanka

20

W. A. Menaka Imashi Abeyratna
and Bhadra J. H. Arachchige

20.1 Introduction

Robbins et al. (2009, p. 275) define an emotion as 'an intense feeling that is directed at someone or something'. People experience many emotions, such as anger, contempt, enthusiasm, envy, fear, frustration, disgust, happiness, hate, surprise, sadness etc. Emotions have a profound effect on almost everything we do in the workplace. Hochschild (1983/2003), as cited in Truta, claims that slightly above 66% of jobs inevitably involve emotions in work.

Smith and Kim (2007, p. 49) define envy as 'an unpleasant and often painful blend of feelings characterized by inferiority, hostility, and resentment caused by a comparison with a person or group of persons who possess something we desire'. Tai et al. (2012, p. 107) state that envy is 'rampant' in the workplace.

In general, envy is a frustrating emotion (Ven et al. 2009, p. 426) that produces feelings of inferiority (Smith et al. 1988, p. 407) and dissatisfaction with one's current state, which can have both negative and positive implications for individuals and their environment. Despite the size of the organisation, envy works in varying degrees as we experience it on a day-to-day basis. Experts' attention on the subject of envy has not been as great as it should be. The reason for this is that the subject of envy is subtle, and as a result, scholars may not discuss this in an open forum. Even though the subject is subtle, the quality of being envious is observed in any human being.

W. A. M. I. Abeyratna (✉)
Faculty of Graduate Studies, University of Sri Jayewardenepura, Nugegoda, Sri Lanka

B. J. H. Arachchige
Faculty of Management Studies and Commerce, University of Sri Jayewardenepura, Nugegoda, Sri Lanka
e-mail: bhadra@sjp.ac.lk

© The Author(s), under exclusive license to Springer Nature Switzerland AG 2021
S. Dhiman, R. Samaratunge (eds.), *New Horizons in Management, Leadership and Sustainability*, Future of Business and Finance,
https://doi.org/10.1007/978-3-030-62171-1_20

In the literature, engagement has been defined and measured in different ways, such as employee engagement, work engagement, job engagement. Kahn (1990, p. 694) defined 'engagement as the harnessing of organization members' selves to their work roles; in engagement, people employ and express themselves physically, cognitively, and emotionally during role performances'. However, engagement reflects the simultaneous investment in cognitive, affective and physical energies wholly involved in the full performance of a role, which means a holistic investment of self to one's role (Rich et al. 2010). To make employees more engaged through their body, mind and soul, it is needed to manage employee emotions. In fact, research on emotions and well-being highlights a connection between positive feelings at work and levels of engagement. Saks (2006, cited in Erdil and Muceldili 2014, p. 449), states that 'job engagement is characterized by the active use of emotions'. Therefore, managing employees' emotions is seen as one of the main ways to be successful in the global environment.

Even though there are various factors that directly influence job engagement, this research focuses only on the emotion envy and its impact on job engagement as envy is a factor that has received less scholarly attention. Following the background of the study and evidence from the literature, this study seeks to answer the research question 'Is there an impact of envy on job engagement?' Also, an attempt is made to provide extensive empirical evidence of envy on job engagement in the context of private-sector higher educational institutions in Sri Lanka.

This paper is organised as follows. The literature review is followed by the conceptual model, which discloses the hypotheses development. The methodology section describes the sample and instruments of the current study, followed by the findings of the research and discussion.

20.2   Literature Review

20.2.1 Employee Emotions

Writers and readers in the emotion literature are usually challenged by the varying definitions of the term 'emotion', as well as terms that overlap with the term. Authors use terms such as emotion, mood, affect and feelings almost synonymously (Ashkanasy 2003). This results in a vague definition of the term 'emotions'.

According to McShane and Young (2010, p. 98), 'emotions are physiological, behavioral, and psychological episodes experienced toward an object, person, or event that create a state of readiness'. These 'episodes' are very brief events that diminish or last for milliseconds to a few minutes. However, Barclay et al. (2005) have said that emotions are fundamentally a social phenomenon, and they define emotions as an individual's dynamic reactions to an object or event. Robbins et al. (2009, p. 275) define emotions as 'intense feelings that are directed at someone or something'. According to these definitions, it is clear that emotions are a psychological state, and it can be simply defined as a person's response towards someone or something.

Emotions are temporary and peculiar in nature (Ashkanasy 2003). Employees in an organisation have to face several issues and unexpected situations. To these situations and events, people often react emotionally. These affective experiences have direct influences on behaviours and attitudes (Weiss and Cropanzano 1996, cited in Basch and Fisher 1998). Envy is categorised under emotions. Social sciences consider envy as a key aspect of human experience (Patient et al. 2003) that takes place in the minds of individuals even without them knowing that it is happening. Envy, therefore, is an involuntary and uncontrollable reaction to external stimuli (Stein 2000).

20.2.2 Envy

Smith and Kim (2007, p.49) define envy as 'an unpleasant and often painful blend of feelings characterized by inferiority, hostility, and resentment caused by a comparison with a person or group of persons who possess something we desire'. Webster's online dictionary, cited in Tai et al. (2012), explains that 'envy' is derived from the Latin term 'invidere', which means to 'look at another with malice'.

Robbins et al. (2009, p. 296) define envy as 'an emotion that occurs when a person feels worried about someone's possession of something that you don't have but that you strongly desire-such as a better work assignment, larger office or higher salary'. Parrott and Smith (1993, cited in Cohen-Charash and Mueller 2007) describe envy as a negative emotion felt when a person lacks another's superior quality, achievement, or possession and either desires it or wishes that the other lacked it.

Protasi (2016, p. 536) has stated: 'Envy is a negative reaction to a perceived inferiority to a similar other with regard to a good that is relevant to the sense of identity of the envier.' Explaining this definition, Protasi stated that the aversive character of envy emphasises that it is unpleasant and painful. This aversive nature leads to the perception of inferiority within a person. Furthermore, he stated that this definition is connected to the phenomenon of social comparison, which discusses people comparing themselves with people who are like them in capabilities, endowments, values and aspirations. Therefore, according to Protasi, people envy only those who are similar to them. According to these definitions, envy could be defined as an emotion that arises in you towards someone who possesses something that you really desire but unfortunately you do not have.

Explaining the features of envy, Tai et al. (2012) emphasise envy as having two aspects: the object of desire (what we covet) and the object of envy (the person who has what we covet). The object of desire creates a relational bond or tie between the envious person and the envied person, while the object of envy is often the target of negative appraisals and feelings. Tai et al. (2012) state that 'Envy is a painful emotion, much like jealousy, guilt, and shame'. The feeling of envy is inseparably connected with the notion of *Schadenfreude*, which means malicious joy (Piskorz and Piskorz 2009).

Envy is different from jealousy. Klein (1975, cited in Tai et al. 2012) stated that envy directly focuses on the object of love itself and wants to obtain its good properties, while jealousy aims to get the object of love and eliminate the competitor. Anderson (2002) states that in envy, the other has the advantage you do not. It is that difference that evokes envy. In jealousy, you have the advantage and you want to keep a rival from taking the advantage from you. Envy involves two people – the envier and the envied – whereas jealousy involves three elements: 'oneself, a person with whom one has a valued relationship, and a third party who one fears will disrupt the relationship' (Bedeian 1995, cited in Cleary et al. 2016, p. 15).

According to these explanations, it is clear that envy and jealousy are two different emotions: envy focuses on getting the benefits of something that you do not have but someone else has, while jealousy focuses on eliminating the competitor to keep the advantages of something that one already has.

20.2.3 Types of Envy

Various scholars have identified different types of envy. Tai et al. (2012) have identified two types. The traditional view talks about malicious envy with negativity and hostility towards others and negative outcomes for the self. The alternative view talks about benign envy, which leads to positive outcomes. Cohen-Charash and Larson (2017) also explain the same two types of envy. Differentiating benign and malicious envy, they also stated that 'benign' envy involves the motivation to improve self, leading to socially desirable reactions; 'malicious' envy involves the motivation to harm the envied other, leading to socially undesirable reactions.

Lelord and Andre (2003, cited in Andries 2011) also describe three types of envy: envy depressed, hostile envy and jealousy admiration. In English, the default form of envy seems to be malicious envy, though people often use it in a more positive way as well. People sometimes say 'I envy you' to express that they are impressed and would like to also have what the other has (Ven et al. 2009). However, Vecchio (2005) identified two aspects of envy at work: feeling envied by others and feeling envy towards others.

People with high self-esteem usually tend to be envied by others rather than those with low self-esteem. The people who are being envied by others or the people who are targets of envy may feel achievement or satisfaction, or they might regard it as a source of tension. Despite this, the envied are likely to experience higher levels of job satisfaction than enviers. Being envied is more positive than envying someone. To feel envied, one must perceive antagonism and resentment from others, but to feel envious, one must believe others enjoy better standing and status (Vecchio 2005).

Foster (1972, cited in Greshman 2014, p. 410), states that 'a man fears being envied for what he has, and wishes to protect himself from the consequences of the envy of others'. This is further emphasised by Ven et al. (2009): Schoeck (1969, cited in Ven et al. 2009) claims that feeling afraid of being envied by someone has some negative consequences as the envied person stops working for excellence, which ultimately obstructs the success of the organisation.

Explaining the ways in which envy can be seen, Joseph (1986) postulates that if someone has something better than him or her, it will lead that person to get what the other person has. Until he or she gets the same thing or a better one, he/she will be envious of the person who possesses that object. A person who envies others may act aggressively and initiate professionally damaging behaviour in the workplace. They may demean others' work and misrepresent their own accomplishments. Further, they may provide incorrect misleading communication and information to others while withholding information and delaying correspondence (Cleary et al. 2016).

Perceived injustice or unfairness may lead to both feeling envious of others and being envied by others. However, comparing one's own outcomes relative to the other's outcomes according to the inputs of both persons is not an essential requirement for experiencing envy (Kim et al. 2010). Envy is not essentially accompanied with feelings of unfairness or vice versa. Therefore, even if there is no social support for the perceived unfairness, people still could feel envy, especially under competitive circumstances (Kim et al. 2010). Therefore, it is unclear to state which situation or event causes the occurrence of being envied by others and feeling envious of others.

20.2.4 Job Engagement

Kahn (1990, p. 694) originally described engagement as a unique and important motivational concept: 'the harnessing of an employee's full self in terms of physical, cognitive, and emotional energies to work role performances'. Leiter and Bakker (2010, cited in Inceoglu and Warr 2011, p. 177) defined job engagement as 'a positive, fulfilling, affective-motivational state of work-related well-being'. Roberts and Davenport (2002, p. 21) defined job engagement as 'a person's enthusiasm and involvement in his or her job'. He further states that people who are highly engaged in their jobs identify personally with the job and are motivated by the work itself.

In the literature, engagement has been defined and measured in different ways, such as employee engagement, work engagement and job engagement. Schaufeli and Bakker (2004 cited in Bakker 2011, p. 265) defined work engagement as an active, positive, and work-related state that is characterised by vigor, dedication, and absorption. Robinson et al. (2004, p. ix) defined employee engagement as 'a positive attitude held by the employee towards the organization and its values'.

However, work engagement and employee engagement are interchangeably used terms. 'Work engagement refers to the relationship of the employee to his or her work, while employee engagement refers to the relationship of the employee to his or her work and also with the organization' (Schaufeli 2013, p. 1).

There are several definitions of engagement. Of all these definitions, Kahn's definition for engagement has been accepted and discussed in most of the scholarly articles.

20.2.5 Aspects or Dimensions of Engagement

Kahn (1990, cited in Rich et al. 2010) states that engagement is a motivational concept and is unique from one employee to another. It develops an employee's full potential physically, cognitively and emotionally according to the work role performance. Alvi et al. (2014) also explain the process of employee engagement as people employing and expressing themselves psychically, cognitively and emotionally during role performances.

Kahn's work has given rise to three kinds of engagement, and employee engagement is visualised as a desire for work. According to Rich (2006, as cited in Alvi et al. 2014), physical engagement means extending physical energies towards a particular task while being actively involved with the task physically. This ranges from laziness to vigorous involvement or lethargy to active participation. If a person is physically involved with an assistant's work who is physically away from his or her work, it is as an example of physical engagement. According to Rothbard (2001, as cited in Alvi et al. 2014), cognitive engagement is being involved with a certain task highly attentively, which will lead to thorough absorption and unwillingness to face disturbances. Cognitively engaged employees can focus on their duties, ignoring the competitors who distract them. The opposite of cognitive engagement is cognitive detachment, which means little attention is given to job duties (Kahn 1990, as cited in Alvi et al. 2014). Emotional engagement focuses on the employees' feelings, ideas and views about the job and enthusiasm and the pride in the job. The opposite of emotional engagement is emotional absence or detachment from the job. From this statement, it is clear that emotional engagement is different from the term 'cynicism', which is part of burnout.

Schaufeli and Bakker (2004) identified three aspects of work engagement: vigor, dedication and absorption. Vigor is described as extending high levels of energy and being rigid mentally when working and, despite the difficulties that come along the way, investing effort willingly and diligently. Dedication refers to being strongly involved in one's work and experiencing a sense of significance, enthusiasm, inspiration, pride and challenge. The third dimension, absorption, is characterised by being fully concentrated and happily occupied in work, whereby time passes quickly and the person has difficulty detaching himself or herself from work (Csikszentmihalyi 1990, as cited in Schaufeli et al. 2002).

The idea of employee engagement has many dimensions. There are three such dimensions presented by Kahn: meaningfulness, safety and availability. Explaining these three dimensions, May et al. (2004) have stated that the degree to which one engages in his/her role at work is influenced by these three psychological conditions. Meaningfulness has to do with how valuable a work goal is in relation to an individual's own ideals or standards. Psychological safety should lead to engagement at work because it reflects one's belief that he/she can employ himself/herself without fear of negative consequences. Finally, availability refers to an individual's belief that he/she has the necessary physical, emotional and cognitive resources in order to immerse himself/herself in their roles.

According to the Insync Surveys' model of employee engagement, there are three components: heart, head and hand (White paper: Employee Engagement Survey n.d.). Also, it states that these three components are positively correlated. This means that an engaged employee should possess an emotional commitment to the organisation (the heart) and enthusiasm for work (the head) and should engage in positive discretionary behaviour (the hand) for the benefit of the organisation.

20.2.6 Employee Envy and Job Engagement

Corporate Leadership Council (2004, as cited in Kumar and Sia 2012, p. 33), engaged employees perform 20% better; organisations with disengaged employees underperform compared to organisations with engaged employees (Meere 2005, cited in Kumar and Sia 2012, p. 33). Therefore, paying attention to the reasons behind employees being disengaged from work is essential.

Working today: understanding what drives employee engagement (n.d.) has identified emotions and rationality as the core components of job engagement. Emotional factors relate to employee's individual satisfaction towards their job and the feeling of being part of their job. Rational factors generally relate to the relationship between the individual and the broader corporation, for instance the extent to which employees understand their role and their unit's role relative to company objectives.

Emphasising the relevance of emotions on job engagement, Saks (2006, as cited in Erdil and Muceldili 2014, p. 449) stated that job engagement is characterised by the active use of emotions. Wilson (2004, p. 99) argues that 'feelings connect us with our realities of lives however, when we are in organizations we experience worry, envy, hurt, sadness, boredom, excitement and other emotions'. Thus, employees experience various emotions at their workplaces.

Being a behavioural response of envy, job engagement is affected by reward and recognition as well (Maslach et al. 2001). One cause for employees to be disengaged from work roles is their understanding that there is high injustice among coworkers. Saks (2006, cited in Erdil and Muceldili 2014) highlights that a lack of fairness could be the reason for disengagement. It has been found that competition among coworkers for rewards generates feelings of envy that lead to burnout, the opposite concept of engagement (Maslach et al. 2001). Tai et al. (2012) also state that 'envy can function as a signal that someone or something is obstructing one's course of action'. It is observed that in workplaces, the envied person may go to the extent of quitting the job due to the negative impact that the envious party may have on them. This is caused by the lack of support from peers, being neglected by them, and organisations not treating them fairly.

However, Ven et al. (2009, p.784) state that envy is a more productive emotion than admiration as 'admiring someone feels positive but may not lead to a motivation to improve oneself (happy self-surrender), whereas being (benignly) envious of someone feels frustrating and as such may promote a motivation to improve oneself (unhappy self-assertion)'.

The competition for scarce resources, for time and for promotions generates and triggers envy in most organisations. Employees compare their benefits, advantages and salaries with colleagues through formal and informal mechanisms, resulting in competition among co-workers. Thus, differentiation promotes competition among employees in an organisation and may foster levels of hostility and distrust, especially in the members of staff who think that their work is assessed in terms of winning or losing (Vecchio 2005; Tai et al. 2012). However, this envy can motivate people to excel, thus reducing the gap that exists between them and the envied targets by raising themselves rather than bringing them down. This may promote an employee to be more engaged or disengaged with their job.

20.3   Conceptual Model

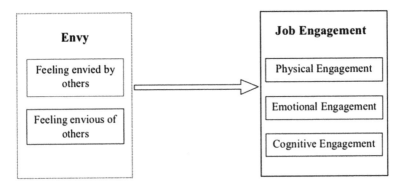

20.4   Development of Hypotheses

The conceptual framework shown above depicts six hypotheses of two phenomena: feeling envied by others and feeling envious of others. For this study, Kahn's definition has been used as the operational definition, and his work was used to explain relationships between employee envy and job engagement using three dimensions: physical, emotional and cognitive engagement.

According to Kahn (1990, 1992, as cited in Rich et al. 2010), extending physical energy throughout would contribute to the achievement of organisational goals as it increases the level of individual effort over an extended period of time, whereas investing in emotional energy to work roles meets individual demands of work roles resulting in complete and authentic performance. Moreover, investing in cognitive energy in work roles also aids in the achievement of organisational goals as it helps individuals to be more vigilant, attentive and focused.

As job engagement is characterised by the active use of emotions (Saks 2006, as cited in Erdil and Muceldili 2014, p. 449), for this study the two aspects of envy that are explained in Vecchio (2005), namely feeling envied by others and feeling envious of others, have been used. Smith and Kim (2007, p. 49) define 'envy [as] an unpleasant and often painful blend of feelings characterized by inferiority, hostility, and resentment caused by a comparison with a person or group of persons who possess something we desire'.

Schoeck (1969, cited in Ven et al. 2009) stated that being afraid of being envied by someone has some negative consequences as the envied person stops working for excellence, which ultimately obstructs the success of the organisation.

When considering the two aspects of envy at work, some people act socially, building valuable interactions among members of the groups due to the fear of being envied by others. This will make members understand inequalities in each other. This inequality may lead to envy and hinders the survival of the organisation (Ven et al. 2010). Some people tend to work below their capacities because their outstanding performance may make others envious (Vidaillet 2007). This may lead to job disengagement. Based on the above evidence, the following three hypotheses have been developed to test how feeling envied by others affect three dimensions of job engagement separately:

H1: There is an impact of feeling envied by others on physical engagement.
H2: There is an impact of feeling envied by others on emotional engagement.
H3: There is an impact of feeling envied by others on cognitive engagement.

As stated in Tai et al. (2012), using equity theory, it can be argued that employees who compare themselves with others on what they gain as opposed to their peers lead to feeling envious. Employees physically, emotionally and cognitively disengage themselves from their work roles due to lack of fairness (Saks 2006, cited in Erdil and Muceldili 2014).

Masclach et al. (2001, cited in Erdil and Muceldili 2014) state that in workplaces, the existence of competitive reward systems engenders feelings of envy and reward and recognition is associated with job engagement. Therefore, competition among coworkers for rewards generates feelings of envy that lead to burnout, the opposite concept of engagement.

The following three hypotheses have been developed to test the impact of feeling envious of others on three dimensions of job engagement:

H4: There is an impact of feeling envious of others on physical engagement.
H5: There is an impact of feeling envious of others on emotional engagement.
H6: There is an impact of feeling envious of others on cognitive engagement.

20.5   Method

20.5.1 Sample

Full-time academic staff members in private higher educational institutes in the Colombo District were selected as the sample for this study. This sample is considered as ideal for the investigation of the research question. Hudak (2000), reflecting his views as a professor, stated that, while experiencing job satisfaction as an academic, 'all too often I have experienced the debilitating pain of alienation and marginalization because others envy either my work or my enthusiasm, or both'. He further stated that every academic suffers from the pain of 'ruthless envy' and especially this is evident within institutions that have 'loose-yet binding structure'. Hudak (2000) emphasised the fact that envy operates as an unmitigated factor within rankings and departments, and forms of elitism, racism, sexism, and homophobia, which link with addictions to careerism are foundations of envy. As such, the particular empirical context has been utilised to study the emotion of envy and its impact on job engagement.

One hundred and sixty-two full-time academic staff members in the private higher educational institutes in the Colombo District were selected as a sample size using a convenience sampling technique to obtain a large number of responses quickly and economically when other means of sampling were impractical (Zikmund et al. 2009). Therefore, respondents were selected from the sample frame, allowing academics to voluntarily respond to the questionnaires, which were distributed through the Internet.

This study was based on primary data. A questionnaire was utilised as the data collection method and was self-administered.

20.5.2 Measures

The questionnaire consists of eight indicators to measure envy and eighteen items for measuring job engagement. The indicators of two dimensions of envy, namely feeling envied by others and feeling envious of others, were solely based on the literature of Vecchio (2005). Feeling envied by others was measured using a 7-point Likert scale ranging from 1 = Very inaccurate to 7 = Very accurate (Vecchio 2005). Five questions were developed to measure feeling envious of others using a 5-point Likert scale ranging from 1 = Never to 5 = Often (Vecchio 2005). The indicators of three dimensions of job engagement, namely physical engagement, emotional engagement and cognitive engagement, were based on the past literature of Rich et al. (2010) and Schaufeli and Bakker (2004). It was measured using a 5-point Likert scale ranging from 1 = Strongly disagree to 5 = Strongly agree. In addition, three questions were formed categorically to collect the data on the gender, age and work experience of the sample respondents.

20.6   Data Analysis

Collected data were analysed using Statistical Packages Social Sciences (SPSS) version 20. Firstly, data were screened using missing value analysis and by identifying outliers. The Little's MCAR test was performed to check whether the missing cases were randomly distributed, and it was found that the Little's MCAR test is insignificant ($p > 0.05$) at the 0.088 level. The boxplots were used to identify outliers, and in this analysis, there are only suspected outliers that are slightly more 'central' versions of outliers.

20.6.1   Sample Distribution

Table 20.1 shows that the sample includes 45.7% males and 54.3% females. The majority of respondents belong to the age group of 30 years or younger and are more than 50% of the sample. The majority of respondents belong to the experience category of 1 to 5 years, with a percentage of 55.6.

20.6.2   The Validity of the Measures

Content validity was ensured with a careful assessment of the scale items as the items were adopted from previous studies. However, as stated in Malhotra and Birks (2007, p. 358), relying only on content validity is not sufficient as it is 'common sense of interpretation of scores of scale'; thus, construct validity was assessed using the Kaiser-Meyer-Olkin (KMO) test and Bartlett's test. According to Yusoff (2011), the sample is considered adequate if the KMO value is more than 0.5 and Bartlett's test is significant ($p < 0.05$). According to the obtained results, KMO values and Bartlett's test for all the variables fulfil the requirement, confirming the construct validity of the questionnaire.

Table 20.1   The sample distribution

	Variable	Frequency	Percentage (%)
Gender	Male	74	45.7
	Female	88	54.3
Age	30 or younger	86	53.1
	31–40	54	33.3
	41–50	12	7.4
	51 or older	10	6.2
Work experience	Less than 1 year	14	8.6
	1–5 years	90	55.6
	6–10 years	34	21.0
	11–15 years	12	7.4
	16–20 years	6	3.7
	21 years or over	6	3.7

Note: $N = 162$
Source: Survey data (2017)

Principal Component Analysis was used to check *discriminant validity*. According to the analysis, the percentage of average variance explained by the third factor (physical engagement (PE)) is less than 50%, while all the other factors were above 50%. Furthermore, PE factors were loaded to two, resulting in no factor loading. Therefore, PE1 was removed to take everything to one factor loading and to fulfil the standards of validity.

20.6.3 Reliability of the Measures

Prior to the data analysis, reliability of the measurement was analysed using the Cronbach's alpha reliability test. Kline (1999) noted that, although the generally accepted Cronbach's alpha value of 0.8 is appropriate for cognitive tests such as intelligence tests, for ability tests a cut-off point of 0.7 is more suitable. The results of Cronbach's alpha for each construct were above the threshold value of 0.7 and therefore acceptable.

20.6.4 Descriptive Statistics

Based on the mean values derived from the analysis, it can be identified that the existing level of feeling envied by others (mean value of 4.218) and feeling envious of others (mean value of 2.716) are of a moderate level, whereas physical engagement, emotional engagement and cognitive engagement are high (4.442, 4.296 and 3.998) (Table 20.2).

20.6.5 Assumptions in Regression

Several assumptions must be true to conclude a population based on a regression analysis done on a sample. According to the analysis, residuals have shown no autocorrelation and homoscedasticity and the error terms were normally distributed.

Table 20.2 Means and standard deviations of the variables

	Minimum	Maximum	Mean	Std. deviation
	statistic	statistic	statistic	statistic
Feeling envied by others	1.00	7.00	4.2181	1.54809
Feeling envious of others	1.20	4.60	2.7160	0.87866
Physical engagement	2.60	5.00	4.4420	0.47362
Emotional engagement	2.00	5.00	4.2963	0.57013
Cognitive engagement	2.33	5.00	3.9983	0.58478

Source: Survey data (2017)

Table 20.3 Hypotheses testing

Hypothesis	β	P***	Result
H1: there is an impact of feeling envied by others on physical engagement	0.036	0.137	Rejected
H2: there is an impact of feeling envied by others on emotional engagement	−0.089	0.002	Accepted
H3: there is an impact of feeling envied by others on cognitive engagement	0.093	0.002	Accepted
H4: there is an impact of feeling envious of others on physical engagement	0.059	0.163	Rejected
H5: there is an impact of feeling envious of others on emotional engagement	−0.116	0.023	Accepted
H6: there is an impact of feeling envious of others on cognitive engagement	0.121	0.021	Accepted

Note: *** $P < 0.05$

20.6.6 Hypotheses Testing (Table 20.3)

20.7   Discussion

20.7.1 Findings and Discussion

The regression analysis reveals that there is no impact of feeling envied by others and feeling envious of others on physical engagement. This result is consistent with the study of Erdil and Muceldili (2014) as it did not find any correlation between feelings of envy and physical engagement.

However, the regression analysis results of the hypotheses of 'there is an impact of feeling envied by others on cognitive engagement' and 'there is an impact of feeling envious of others on cognitive engagement' were accepted as the P values were significant at 95% level of significance ($P < 0.05$). Therefore, there was enough evidence to say that there is an impact of feeling envied by others and feeling envious of others on cognitive engagement. Moreover, there is a positive impact of feeling envied by others and feeling envious of others on cognitive engagement, which means that when feeling envied by others and feeling envious of others increases cognitive engagement also increases. This result is contrary to the study of Erdil and Muceldili (2014), which did not find any correlation between feelings of envy and cognitive engagement.

The developed hypothesis to test the impact of feeling envied by others on emotional engagement and the hypothesis that was developed to find out the impact of feeling envious of others on emotional engagement were accepted as the P values were significant at 95% level of significance ($P < 0.05$). Also, the impact of feeling envied by others and feeling envious of others on emotional engagement is negative, which means that when feeling envied by others and feeling envious of others increases emotional engagement decreases. This result is consistent with the study of Erdil and Muceldili (2014) as the study illustrated that feelings of envy are negatively associated with emotional engagement.

The current study findings could be contradictory for various reasons, such as industrial, organisational, and individual factors. However, as some of the findings are contradictory to previous research findings, further research will need to be carried out with respect to this area so as to provide a vivid conclusion that can be applicable to all types of organisational settings.

20.7.2 Theoretical and Managerial Implications

Being a negative emotion, the envy literature reveals that envy in the workplace can have many consequences, and it is typically dysfunctional in nature. As stated in Duffy and Shaw (2000), envy can also significantly undermine individual and group performance, potentially leading to job dissatisfaction, supervisor dissatisfaction, and a tendency to quit. It is claimed that envy can have a negative impact on the productivity and efficiency of a workplace. It also has a direct impact on a worker's dedication and attitudes and behavior as well. This may weaken the competitive position of an organisation in its industry.

Conversely, the literature states that there are positive consequences associated with envy. For example, unfavourable social comparison, which is one of the major reasons highlighted by many scholars, may promote feelings of envy among employees. However, this may motivate goal achievement in order to equalise outcomes with a strong referent other. As a result, it will provide an intrinsic motive, leveraging extrinsic motives such as earning more money. Therefore, a person who envies others may be intrinsically motivated and show high engagement towards the job (Beach and Tesser 2000, as cited in Duffy et al. 2008). Thus, the literature has emphasised that there is an impact of envy on job engagement, regardless of whether the impact is positive or negative.

This research has suggested several possible managerial implications. The findings of the study indicate that there is a significant impact of feeling envied by others and feeling envious of others on cognitive and emotional engagement. The cause may be that envious employees remove themselves from particular task behaviors and that it is the root of employee disengagement, which means employees having aggressive feelings might become less engaged with their job (Erdil and Muceldili 2014). Envious employees sweat to put their physical, cognitive and emotional energies into role performance contexts and tend to lower engagement in their job (Erdil and Muceldili 2014) due to exhaustion ultimately.

In general, envy can have unpleasant implications for individuals' interactions with others and for their own general happiness. Because they persist in comparing their own situations with those of others, enviers seem to experience unflattering comparisons with greater frequency than do their less envious counterparts (Bedeian 1995). Therefore, when rewarding employees, management should establish a fair benefit system and encourage managers to create supportive and fairness conditions as employees frequently experience envy as a result of comparison benefits and advantages at work with their colleagues.

Envy is an inherent emotion of today's competitive workplace. Therefore, management should attempt to establish an organisational culture to include negative emotions and their positive consequences. Specifically, human resource managers have to deal with employees' emotions (Muchinsky 2000). Therefore, organisations can implement good human resource management (HRM) practices like equitable compensation systems and effective training and career development programs to enhance job engagement of employees. This may help employees to understand their performance deficiencies in comparison to employees who are envied and improve their performances while being more engaged in their current jobs.

20.8   Conclusion

This study is about the impact of envy on job engagement. Envy is an invisible issue in today's business context due to competitiveness. For the developed objectives, a model was constructed and tested to explain job engagement and feelings of envy. The regression analysis has found that there is a significant impact of feeling envied by others and feeling envious of others on emotional and cognitive engagement. Notably, no impact has been found on physical engagement through feeling envied by others and feeling envious of others. Moreover, the study illustrated that feeling envied by others and feeling envious of others are negatively associated with emotional engagement, whereas feeling envied by others and feeling envious of others are positively associated with cognitive engagement.

20.8.1 Limitations and Future Research

The present study has some limitations. Most significantly, the data for the study were collected from 162 full-time academic staff members of private higher educational institutes in Sri Lanka. The generalizability of the findings for other higher educational institutes such as state universities, therefore, may not be appropriate. Moreover, the generalizability of the results to non-academic staff may be an issue. Finally, the generalizability of research findings to other industries may not be suitable due to the diversity of job roles, work practices, appraisal patterns and cultures etc. Therefore, a future study could replicate this study by comparing data across all types of universities, including government universities. As the experience of envy will differ from context to context, it could be beneficial if a future study is carried out by replicating the same study in different industries and at different managerial levels. Consequences of envy could also be investigated in terms of both benign and malicious envy. Even the same research could also be extended by examining factors that moderate the impact of envy on job engagement.

Chapter Takeaways

1. Envy could be defined as an unpleasant and frustrating emotion, which is rampant in the workplace.
2. Envy and jealousy are two different emotions experienced by human beings.
3. Job engagement is a motivational concept where employees are considered to be involved in the job physically, emotionally and cognitively.
4. Employees' feeling of envy in the workplace has not received enough attention in research, and it often plays an underestimated role in relation to job engagement.
5. Organisations need to constantly manage envy as an underlying, powerful and impactful emotion, which might need to be converted from a negative emotion to a positive emotion within organisations themselves to enhance job engagement.

Reflection Questions

1. What is envy, and how is it linked to job engagement of employees?
2. Describe, in your own words, the difference between envy and jealousy.
3. What are the common dimensions/aspects that you can identify in job engagement literature?
4. Consider the literature on types of envy in this chapter and describe in your own words how you consider the emotion envy to be viewed as a positive emotion.
5. How could organisations manage the employees' feelings of envy to enhance job engagement?

Appendices

Appendix 20.1: Operationalisation of Variables

Construct	Dimension	Indicator	Source	Measure	Scale	Question no
Envy	Feeling envied by others	Success causing resentment	Vecchio (2005)	7-scale Likert	Interval	4
		Closeness of the working relationship with supervisor causing resentment	Vecchio (2005)	7-scale Likert	Interval	5
		Envied on accomplishments	Vecchio (2005)	7-scale Likert	Interval	6

Construct	Dimension	Indicator	Source	Measure	Scale	Question no
	Feeling envious of others	Co-workers having something better	Vecchio (2005)	5-scale Likert	Interval	7
		Supervisor valuing the efforts of others	Vecchio (2005)	5-scale Likert	Interval	8
		Never having a job as good as someone is having	Vecchio (2005)	5-scale Likert	Interval	9
		Seems to be the underdog at work	Vecchio (2005)	5-scale Likert	Interval	10
		Others having luck in getting the best assignments	Vecchio (2005)	5-scale Likert	Interval	11
Job engagement	Physical engagement	Intensity on job	Rich et al. (2010)	5-scale Likert	Interval	12
		Working for very long periods at a time	Schaufeli and Bakker (2004)	5-scale Likert	Interval	13
		Giving all energy to job	Rich et al. (2010)	5-scale Likert	Interval	14
		Trying hardest to perform well on job	Rich et al. (2010)	5-scale Likert	Interval	15
		Trying hard to fully complete all given tasks	Rich et al. (2010)	5-scale Likert	Interval	16
		Working at full capacity in all job duties	Rich et al. (2010)	5-scale Likert	Interval	17
	Emotional engagement	Enthusiasm in job	Rich et al. (2010)	5-scale Likert	Interval	18
		Feeling energetic at job	Rich et al. (2010)	5-scale Likert	Interval	19
		Interest in job	Rich et al. (2010)	5-scale Likert	Interval	20
		Being proud of job	Rich et al. (2010)	5-scale Likert	Interval	21
		Positivity about job	Rich et al. (2010)	5-scale Likert	Interval	22

Construct	Dimension	Indicator	Source	Measure	Scale	Question no
		Excitement about job	Rich et al. (2010)	5-scale Likert	Interval	23
	Cognitive engagement	Focus on job	Rich et al. (2010)	5-scale Likert	Interval	24
		Forgetting everything else around naturally	Schaufeli and Bakker (2004)	5-scale Likert	Interval	25
		Focusing a great deal of attention on job	Rich et al. (2010)	5-scale Likert	Interval	26
		Time passing quickly when performing job	Schaufeli and Bakker (2004)	5-scale Likert	Interval	27
		Getting carried away when working	Schaufeli and Bakker (2004)	5-scale Likert	Interval	28
		Difficulty to detach from job	Schaufeli and Bakker (2004)	5-scale Likert	Interval	29
	Gender				Nominal	1
	Age				Ordinal	2
	Work experience				Ordinal	3

Appendix 20.2: Validity and Reliability of the Measures

Variable	No of items	Cronbach's alpha reliability	KMO Kaiser-Meyer-Olkin Measure	Bartlett's test Chi-Square	Sig.	Average variance explained	Factor loading
Feeling envied by others (FEBO)	3	0.889	0.739	275.895	0.000	81.781%	✓
Feeling envious of others (FEOO)	5	0.729	0.744	183.386	0.000	49.216%	✓
Physical engagement (PE) – before	6	0.730	0.689	317.934	0.000	–	x

Variable	No of items	Cronbach's alpha reliability	KMO Kaiser-Meyer-Olkin Measure	Bartlett's test		Average variance explained	Factor loading
				Chi-Square	Sig.		
Physical engagement (PE) – after (removed PE1)	5	0.744	0.694	289.312	0.000	52.045%	✓
Emotional engagement (EE)	6	0.874	0.848	504.259	0.000	62.836%	✓
Cognitive engagement (CE)	6	0.793	0.734	313.486	0.000	50.618%	✓

Source: Survey data (2017)

References

Alvi, A. K., Haider, R., Haneef, M., & Ahmed, A. A. (2014). A critical review of model and theory of employee engagement. *Science International (Lahore), 26*(2), 821–824.

Anderson, R. E. (2002). Envy and jealousy. *American Journal of Psychotherapy, 56*(4), 455–479. https://doi.org/10.4337/9781843767008.00013.

Andries, A. M. (2011). Positive and negative emotions within the organisational context. *Global Journal of Human Social Science, 11*(9), 26–40. https://doi.org/10.4324/9781315163475-3.

Ashkanasy, N. M. (2003). Emotions in organisations: A multi-level perspective. *Research in Multi-Level Issues Multi-Level Issues in Organisational Behavior and Strategy, 2*, 9–54. https://doi.org/10.1016/s1475-9144(03)02002-2.

Bakker, A. B. (2011). An evidence-based model of work engagement. *Current Directions in Psychological Science, 20*(4), 265–269. https://doi.org/10.1177/0963721411414534.

Barclay, L. J., Skarlicki, D. P., & Pugh, S. D. (2005). Exploring the role of emotions in injustice perceptions and retaliation. *Journal of Applied Psychology, 90*(4), 629–643. https://doi.org/10.1037/0021-9010.90.4.629.

Basch, J., & Fisher, C. D. (1998). Affective events-emotions matrix: A classification of work events and associated emotions. In *Affective events-emotions matrix: A classification of work events and associated emotions*. Gold Coast: Bond University.

Bedeian, A. G. (1995). Workplace envy. *Organizational Dynamics, 23*(4), 49–56. https://doi.org/10.1016/0090-2616(95)90016-0.

Cleary, M., Walter, G., Halcomb, E., & Lopez, V. (2016). An examination of envy and jealousy in nursing academia. *Nurse Researcher, 23*(6), 14–19. https://doi.org/10.7748/nr.2016.e1405.

Cohen-Charash, Y., & Larson, E. C. (2017). An emotion divided. *Current Directions in Psychological Science, 26*(2), 174–183. https://doi.org/10.1177/0963721416683667.

Cohen-Charash, Y., & Mueller, J. S. (2007). Does perceived unfairness exacerbate or mitigate interpersonal counterproductive work behaviors related to envy? *Journal of Applied Psychology, 92*(3), 666–680. https://doi.org/10.1037/0021-9010.92.3.666.

Duffy, M. K., & Shaw, J. D. (2000). The salieri syndrome. *Small Group Research, 31*(1), 3–23. https://doi.org/10.1177/104649640003100101.

Duffy, M. K., Shaw, J. D., & Schaubroeck, J. M. (2008). Envy in organisational life. *Envy*, 167–189. https://doi.org/10.1093/acprof:oso/9780195327953.003.0010.

Erdil, O., & Müceldili, B. (2014). The effects of envy on job engagement and turnover intention. *Procedia – Social and Behavioral Sciences, 150,* 447–454. https://doi.org/10.1016/j.sbspro.2014.09.050.

Gershman, B. (2014). The two sides of envy. *Journal of Economic Growth, 19*(4), 407–438. https://doi.org/10.1007/s10887-014-9106-8.

Hudak, G. M. (2000). Envy and goodness in academia. *Peace Review, 12*(4), 607–612. https://doi.org/10.1080/10402650020014717.

Inceoglu, I., & Warr, P. (2011). Personality and job engagement. *Journal of Personnel Psychology, 10*(4), 177–181. https://doi.org/10.1027/1866-5888/a000045.

Joseph, B. (1986). Envy in everyday life. *Psychoanalytic Psychotherapy, 2*(1), 13–22. https://doi.org/10.1080/02668738600700021.

Kahn, W. A. (1990). Psychological conditions of personal engagement and disengagement at work. *Academy of Management Journal, 33*(4), 692–724. https://doi.org/10.5465/256287.

Kim, S., O'Neill, J. W., & Cho, H.-M. (2010). When does an employee not help coworkers? The effect of leader–member exchange on employee envy and organisational citizenship behavior. *International Journal of Hospitality Management, 29*(3), 530–537. https://doi.org/10.1016/j.ijhm.2009.08.003.

Kline, P. (1999). *Handbook of psychological testing* (2nd ed.). London: Routledge.

Kumar, R., & Sia, S. K. (2012). Employee engagement. *Management and Labour Studies, 37*(1), 31–43. https://doi.org/10.1177/0258042x1103700104.

Malhotra, N. K., & Birks, D. F. (2007). *Marketing research: An applied approach* (3rd ed.). Harlow: Prentice Hall.

Maslach, C., Schaufeli, W. B., & Leiter, M. P. (2001). Job burnout. *Annual Review of Psychology, 52*(1), 397–422. https://doi.org/10.1146/annurev.psych.52.1.397.

May, D. R., Gilson, R. L., & Harter, L. M. (2004). The psychological conditions of meaningfulness, safety and availability and the engagement of the human spirit at work. *Journal of Occupational and Organizational Psychology, 77*(1), 11–37. https://doi.org/10.1348/096317904322915892.

McShane, S. L., & Young, V. G. M. A. (2010). *Organisational behavior: Emerging knowledge and practice for the real world* (5th ed.). Boston: McGraw-Hill/Irwin.

Muchinsky, P. M. (2000). Emotions in the workplace: The neglect of organisational behavior. *Journal of Organizational Behavior, 21*(7), 801–805. https://doi.org/10.1002/1099-1379(200011)21:7<801:aid-job999>3.3.co;2-1.

Patient, D., Lawrence, T. B., & Maitlis, S. (2003). Understanding workplace envy through narrative fiction. *Organisation Studies, 24*(7), 1015–1044. https://doi.org/10.1177/01708406030247002.

Piskorz, J., & Piskorz, Z. (2009). Situational determinants of envy and schadenfreude. *Polish Psychological Bulletin, 40*(3), 137–144. https://doi.org/10.2478/s10059-009-0030-2.

Protasi, S. (2016). Varieties of envy. *Philosophical Psychology, 29*(4), 535–549. https://doi.org/10.1080/09515089.2015.1115475.

Rich, B. L., Lepine, J. A., & Crawford, E. R. (2010). Job engagement: Antecedents and effects on job performance. *Academy of Management Journal, 53*(3), 617–635. https://doi.org/10.5465/amj.2010.51468988.

Robbins, S. P., Judge, T. A., & Sanghi, S. (2009). *Organisational behavior* (13th ed.). New Delhi: Dorling Kindersley (India) Pvt. Ltd.

Roberts, D. R., & Davenport, T. O. (2002). Job engagement: Why it's important and how to improve it. *Employment Relations Today, 29*(3), 21–29. https://doi.org/10.1002/ert.10048.

Robinson, D., Perryman, S., & Hayday, S. (2004). *The drivers of employee engagement.* Brighton: Institute for employment studies.

Schaufeli, W. B. (2013). What is engagement? In C. Truss, K. Alfes, R. Delbridge, A. Shantz, & E. Soane (Eds.), *Employee engagement in theory and practice.* London: Routledge.

Schaufeli, W., & Bakker, A. (2004). *Utrecht work engagement scale.* Occupational Health Psychology Unit: Utrecht University.

Schaufeli, W. B., Martínez, I. M., Pinto, A. M., Salanova, M., & Bakker, A. B. (2002). Burnout and engagement in university students. *Journal of Cross-Cultural Psychology, 33*(5), 464–481. https://doi.org/10.1177/0022022102033005003.

Smith, R. H., & Kim, S. H. (2007). Comprehending envy. *Psychological Bulletin, 133*(1), 46–64. https://doi.org/10.1037/0033-2909.133.1.46.

Smith, R. H., Kim, S. H., & Parrott, W. G. (1988). Envy and jealousy. *Personality and Social Psychology Bulletin, 14*(2), 401–409. https://doi.org/10.1177/0146167288142017.

Stein, M. (2000). After eden: Envy and the defences against anxiety paradigm. *Human Relations, 53*(2), 193–211. https://doi.org/10.1177/a010558.

Tai, K., Narayanan, J., & McAllister, D. J. (2012). Envy as pain: Rethinking the nature of envy and its implications for employees and organisations. *Academy of Management Review, 37*(1), 107–129. https://doi.org/10.5465/armr.2009.0484.

Truță, C. (n.d.). Organisational management of emotions at work: motives and forms. *Management and Socio-Humanities*, 39–42.

Vecchio, R. (2005). Explorations in employee envy: Feeling envious and feeling envied. *Cognition & Emotion, 19*(1), 69–81. https://doi.org/10.1080/02699930441000148.

Ven, N. V. D., Zeelenberg, M., & Pieters, R. (2009). Leveling up and down: The experiences of benign and malicious envy. *Emotion, 9*(3), 419–429. https://doi.org/10.1037/a0015669.

Ven, N. V. D., Zeelenberg, M., & Pieters, R. (2010). Warding off the evil eye. *Psychological Science, 21*(11), 1671–1677. https://doi.org/10.1177/0956797610385352.

Vidaillet, B. (2007). Lacanian theory's contribution to the study of workplace envy. *Human Relations, 60*(11), 1669–1700. https://doi.org/10.1177/0018726707084304.

White paper: Employee engagement survey. (n.d.). Retrieved from https://insyncsurveys.com.au/media/65492/employee_engagement_survey_white_paper.pdf/

Wilson, F. M. (2004). *Organisational behaviour and work: A critical introduction* (2nd ed.). Oxford: Oxford University Press.

Working today: Understanding what drives employee engagement. (n.d.). Retrieved from http://www.keepem.com/doc_files/Towers_Perrin_Talent_2003(TheFinal).pdf.

Yusoff, M. S. B. (2011). *The reliability and validity of the postgraduate stressor questionnaire (psq) among postgraduate medical trainees.* Retrieved November 18, 2017, from http://www.webmedcentral.com/article_view/558

Zikmund, W. G., Babin, B. J., Carr, J. C., & Griffin, M. (2009). *Business research methods* (8th ed.). Mason: South-Western College Publications.

Towards Organisational Sustainability: A Model for a Successful Implementation of HR Analytics

21

R. Navodya Gurusinghe, Bhadra J. H. Arachchige, and N. W. K. D. K. Dayarathna

21.1 Introduction

At present, data analytics is a growing trend that plays a critical role in business to achieve efficiency and effectiveness and thereby gain a competitive advantage. The application of data analytics makes an impact on functional areas such as finance, accounting, marketing, supply chain and even human resource management (HRM). HRM is a latecomer to the data analytics bandwagon (Strategic Human Resource Management (SHRM) Foundation 2016).

According to Research and Markets (2019), North America is projected to hold the largest market size (35%) in HR analytics by 2024. The second largest will be Europe (27%). The Asian region will hold 23% of the market size in HR analytics by 2024. Further, Asia is expected to grow fastest in HR analytics due to rapid digital transformation in the region, which has increased the requirement of HR analytics solutions and services. HR analytics enables organisations to make strategic business decisions. Even though Asia is expected to grow fastest in HR analytics, it is still questionable as to what extent executives in the region are ready to implement HR analytics in the HR function.

The use of data analytics in HR is referred to as HR analytics. This term is also called "people analytics" (Charted Institute of Personnel and Development (CIPD) 2018; Fecheyr-Lippens et al. 2015; Waber 2013; Walford-Wright and Scott-Jackson 2018), "workforce analytics" (Durai et al. 2019; Simón and Ferreiro 2017), "talent analytics" (CIPD 2013; Harris et al. 2011; Lawler III 2015) and "human capital analytics" (Boudreau and Cascio 2017; Minbaeva 2017). Even though there are

R. N. Gurusinghe (✉) · B. J. H. Arachchige · N. W. K. D. K. Dayarathna
Faculty of Management Studies and Commerce, University of Sri Jayewardenepura, Nugegoda, Sri Lanka
e-mail: bhadra@sjp.ac.lk; dushar@sjp.ac.lk

S. Dhiman, R. Samaratunge (eds.), *New Horizons in Management, Leadership and Sustainability*, Future of Business and Finance, https://doi.org/10.1007/978-3-030-62171-1_21

437

different names, all these terms have several things in common (Marler and Boudreau 2017): they cover analysing people-related data using information technology to collect, manipulate and report diverse types of structured and unstructured data that are internal and external to the organisation. These analytics support people-related decision-making and link HR decisions to business outcomes and thereby organisational performance (Davenport et al. 2010; Falletta 2014; Lawler III et al. 2004; McIver et al. 2018; Minbaeva 2017; van den Heuvel and Bondarouk 2017).

According to Lawler III (2015), in the 1940s, some large organisations (LOs) used analytics to improve talent selection and management. However, today with advanced technology, it is possible to collect new sources of data using wearable technology, emails, calendars, short message service (SMS) and social media (Angrave et al. 2016; McIver et al. 2018; van der Laken et al. 2017). Further, these data sources can be analysed to assist in the understanding of the behaviour of employees and enable the deployment of strategies to improve employee performance. Previously, these techniques were not thought to be possible.

This evolution of analytics and evidence-based decision-making is the key today to achieving organisational efficiency and effectiveness and thereby gaining competitive advantage (Falletta 2014; Minbaeva 2017; SHRM Foundation 2016). However, there is still a significant gap in understanding how organisations can successfully use HR analytics to influence strategic organisational outcomes. Even though many large organisations have built HR analytics teams to gain vital insights from data, the output of these teams is still lagging. For example, according to the Deloitte University Press (2017) survey, 71% of companies believe in HR analytics as a high priority in their organisations. However, only very few companies are said to have usable data (8%), and not many believe that they have a sound understanding of which talent dimension drives performance in their organisations (9%). Further, only 15% of companies have broadly deployed HR and talent scorecards for line managers (Deloitte University Press 2017). This survey shows that organisations are struggling with moving from interesting statistics to strategic outcomes. The necessity to explore the challenges and barriers to implementing HR analytics is, therefore, significant. The objectives of this chapter are to (1) understand the current status of HR analytics, (2) explore the challenges and barriers to implementing HR analytics and (3) build a theoretical framework to understand the relationship between the contextual factors and HR analytics implementation.

21.2 Literature Review

21.2.1 Evolution of HR Analytics

HR analytics is new to some extent in human resource literature. According to Marler and Boudreau (2017), the term HR analytics initially appeared in Lawler III et al. (2004), published by the Centre for Effective Organisations. In their study, they conducted 37 surveys using several Fortune 500 corporations and assessed whether and how HR metrics and analytics were used in these corporations. Results indicated that HR departments often collect data on their efficiency but not on the business impact of their programmes and practices. Their findings suggested that if HR needs to perform a strategic role in the organisations, it is essential to develop its ability to measure how decisions of human capital affect the business and how business decisions affect human capital. Organisations that are capable in strategic analysis could be positioned as strategic partners. Hence, it is crucial to develop better HR metrics and analytics concerning organisational effectiveness and strategy. Consequently, these measures should be able to indicate whether HR programmes and practices make a difference in organisational effectiveness. Further, it is crucial to measure whether and how improving talents would affect business processes and business outcomes, especially towards strategic success. Lawler III et al. (2004) concluded that many organisations are required to develop better metrics in terms of talent, organisational capabilities and core competencies. Furthermore, they need to build better analytical skills to assess which HR practices would impact organisational performance and to what extent organisational capabilities would impact organisational performance. In summary, they have distinguished the difference between HR metrics and HR analytics.

21.2.2 Importance of HR Analytics

According to Lawler III et al. (2004), there is a burning requirement for HR managers to address critical business decisions and solve strategic business issues with the use of better metrics and analytical capabilities. At the same time, they need to be aware of their capacity for employing metrics and analytics. Nonetheless, with the growth of information technology, they have the opportunity to develop the required skills and data needed to effectively evaluate the link between HR policies, practices and organisational performance. Further, analytical skills can be considered as an essential HR competency, and the capability of HR metrics and analytics will be increasingly developed over time.

Davenport (2006) has discussed how leading companies build their strategies around data-driven insights, providing different examples from different business sectors, and how the extensive use of data, statistical and quantitative analysis, explanatory and predictive models and evidence-based management help to make strategic business decisions. He concluded that HR analytics could be used for better decision-making and thereby to provide a competitive advantage.

Fitz-enz (2009, p. 1) defined human capital analytics as "a method of logical analysis that uses objective business data as a basis for reasoning, discussion or calculation". His study indicates five steps of analytics to identify what matters, at what time and the purpose of the organisation. The first step is recording work (e.g. hiring, training, supporting, retaining etc.), the second step is relating to one's organisational work (e.g. quality, innovation, productivity, service), the third step is comparing results with others' (e.g. benchmarking) and the fourth step is understanding past behaviours and outcomes (e.g. descriptive analytics). The final step is predicting future possibilities (e.g. prescriptive analytics). To improve the return on investment (ROI) in HR services, the workforce can be segmented into four groups (mission critical, differentiations, important and moveable) in capability planning. From this segmentation, an organisation can optimise its resource commitments to the workforce, and thereby HR would be able to become a strategic partner. Predictive analytics provides meaning or insight from the patterns revealed by descriptive analytics and thus predicts the future. Data should be carefully selected, suiting the right context before performing predictive analytics.

According to Levenson (2011), HR analytics and metrics improve the quality of decision-making on people-related issues of the organisations. The higher are the impediments in applying HR analytics, the more are the required time, resources and understanding of what type of analytics, when to use it and how to apply it. In this respect, the application of the capability-opportunity-motivation (COM) model, the labour market model and the organisation design model is proposed.

Bassi (2011) describes HR analytics as answering what, why, who, when and where. She defined HR analytics as "an evidence-based approach for making better decisions on the people side of the business; it consists of an array of tools and technologies, ranging from simple reporting of HR metrics all the way up to predictive modelling" (Bassi 2011, p. 16). In her study, she emphasised the need for HR analytics to improve organisational and individual performance. HR must take the lead in developing HR analytics by extending their capacities and capabilities. Principles and regulations need to be created to decide when to use or when not to use HR analytics as ethical issues could be raised.

Concurrently, Mondore, Douthitt and Carson (2011, p. 21) defined HR analytics as "demonstrating the direct impact of people data on important business outcomes". They argued that efficiency metrics, scorecards, alignment to the business, gap analysis (which does not show a business impact), correlation analysis and benchmarking could not be considered as HR analytics as they do not analyse data. Instead, these are ways of looking at data. They have also provided a comprehensive practical road map on how to conduct HR analytics, highlighting that proper implementation of HR analytics will lead HR to becoming a strategic partner in the organisation.

According to Worth (2011), HR analytics is an offshoot of HR metrics that leads to business predictability and thereby business intelligence. He defined analytics as "the process of obtaining an optimal or realistic decision based on existing data" (Worth 2011, p. 59). The importance of analytics is that it uncovers and understands patterns of historical data that make it capable to predict the future and thereby improve business performance. Further, he emphasised that the reason organisations should use HR analytics is that they help organisations to be more competitive and profitable. Moreover, managers can identify high performers and create strategies to retain them by using HR analytics.

Falletta (2014) also indicated that leading organisations are building strategic capabilities and competitive advantage using advanced HR analytics that is beyond simple metrics and scorecards. Further, he stressed that the HR profession itself has a lot more to do to become a more influential strategic business partner. However,

Kapoor and Kabra (2014) revealed that even though functional business areas such as finance, marketing, supply chain and accounting use advanced analytics for business advantage, HR's usage of analytics is still at a dashboard level. Using data from leading job search engines (SimplyHired.com and Indeed.com), authors have modelled trends in hiring analytics professionals in different functional areas in business, such as supply chain, finance, accounting and marketing.

Nevertheless, Rasmussen and Ulrich (2015) argued that HR analytics is a fad, adding controversy to the existing literature. Fads are "largely insignificant, nonrational swings that come and go, with little or no lasting impact on the language of management techniques and on organisations themselves" (Abrahamson and Eisenman 2008, p. 720). Rasmussen and Ulrich (2015) suggested several recommendations to transform HR analytics from being a fad to being a part of management decision-making. If the HR profession does not take the necessary measures to make HR analytics realistic, it will end up being a fad. Angrave et al. (2016) also suggested that HR analytics is a fad to some extent at present as it is highly unlikely that existing HR analytics practices will deliver a transformational change in business. They argued that HR practitioners should be thoroughly aware of the ups and downs of this emerging field and should actively engage operationally and strategically to develop better methods and systems.

21.2.3 HR Analytics – Definition

In reviewing existing literature, Marler and Boudreau (2017, p. 15) defined HR analytics as "A HR practice enabled by information technology that uses descriptive, visual, and statistical analyses of data related to HR processes, human capital, organisational performance, and external economic benchmarks to establish business impact and enable data-driven decision-making".

According to Tursunbayeva et al. (2018), HR analytics is

An area of HRM practice, research and innovation concerned with the use of information technologies, descriptive and predictive data analytics and visualization tools for generating actionable insights about workforce dynamics, human capital, and individual and team performance that can be used strategically to optimize organisational effectiveness, efficiency and outcomes, and improve employee experience. (p. 231)

21.2.4 The Current State of HR Analytics

21.2.4.1   Global Context

According to Deloitte University Press (2017), Nordic countries, Western Europe and Asia have rated HR analytics as "very important" (above 83%), while Latin America-South America, North America, Africa, Middle East and Central and Eastern Europe rated HR analytics as "important" (over 75%). These figures indicate that analytics plays a vital role in the global HR context.

21.2.4.2   Asian Context

It is observed that interest in HR analytics is high in the Asian region. India and China are among the top three countries rating HR analytics as "very important". According to Research and Markets (2019), the Asian region will hold 23% of the market size in HR analytics by 2024. Moreover, Asia is expected to grow fastest in HR analytics due to rapid digital transformation in the region. However, HR implementation is still lagging in Asia despite its significance (Ahmed 2019).

21.2.4.3   Sri Lankan Context

While it is noted that there is some discussion on HR analytics among Sri Lankan HR professionals at a primary level, we could not find any research on HR analytics in Sri Lanka. We, therefore, decided to choose Sri Lanka as the empirical point of study to examine why HR analytics adoption is at a lower level in the Asian region.

21.2.5 Theoretical Underpinnings of HR Analytics

21.2.5.1   Diffusion of Innovation Theory

Even though HR analytics has been discussed for many years, HR analytics still can be identified as an innovation (Marler and Boudreau 2017). Hence, we base our study on diffusion of innovation theory (Rogers 1983) as the basis for understanding HR analytics adoption and diffusion (Marler and Boudreau 2017). Rogers (1983, p. 11) defined diffusion of innovation theory as "the process by which (1) an innovation (2) is communicated through certain channels (3) over time (4) among the members of a social system". Here, innovation is an "idea, practice, or object that is perceived as new by an individual or other unit of adoption" (Rogers 1983, p. 11). Rogers' (1983) model of the innovation-decision process consists of five stages: (1) knowledge, (2) persuasion, (3) decision, (4) implementation and (5) confirmation.

It has been noted that organisations are sceptical about adopting HR analytics, or they are slow at the rate of taking HR analytics irrespective of the competitive business outcomes it gains for the organisations (Ahmed 2019). Hence, it is crucial to investigate this matter from an organisational point of view to uncover the exact picture or the reasons why organisations are sceptical about adopting HR analytics. This study examines why organisations are slow to adopt HR analytics from the lens of Rogers' (1983) model of the innovation process in organisations. The innovation process in organisations also consists of similar sequences as those of the five stages involved in the innovation-decision process by individuals. However, the innovation process in organisations is much more complicated compared to the innovation-decision process by individuals since organisations entail a number of individuals who will play different roles in the process. Rogers (1983) formed a model for the innovation process in organisations, which consists of five stages: (1) agenda setting, (2) matching, (3) redefining/restructuring, (4) clarifying and (5) routinising. This study will investigate what factors should be considered when adopting HR analytics in organisations based on Rogers' model for the innovation process.

21.2.5.2   LAMP Model

Accordingly, a credible measurement system will be able to gain the senior management's interest and investment to address the above challenge (Cascio and Boudreau 2011). Boudreau and Ramstad (2007) introduced the LAMP model as an HR measurement system, arguing that there are four critical elements that are necessary to uncover evidence-based relationships and to encourage informed decisions based on the analyses. They are (a) logic, ensuring a clear causal logic connecting measures and relevant business outcomes; (b) analytics, engaging in analysis that tests relationships between measures and outcomes; (c) measures, identifying the right data and ensuring high-quality data; and (d) processes, ensuring a process for incorporating insights from rigorous analytics into business decision-making (Kryscynski et al. 2017). They further suggested that these elements may be the key to understanding the cause and effect relationship between HR processes and strategic HRM and business outcomes. Hence, the LAMP model can be applied to measure the effectiveness of HR analytics strategy.

21.3   Methodology

An exploratory qualitative study has been adopted to ascertain new insights and to dig deep into uncovering what is happening when reviewing a phenomenon in a new light (Robson 2002). In-depth interviews were used as a primary data source. Twenty-two interviews were conducted. A senior HR manager (1), HR managers (13), HR analysts (4), a talent analyst (1), HR executives (2) and a data evangelist (1) were interviewed to understand the current status of HR analytics and to identify the challenges and barriers in implementing HR analytics in Sri Lanka. The sample of managers was chosen from five Sri Lankan large-scale firms, and the seventeen organisations were multinational corporations (MNCs). Interviews lasted for 30–60 min. Data were analysed by using the constant comparison method (Glaser and Strauss 1967).

21.4   Results and Discussion

21.4.1 Interview Results Summary

An interview result summary is provided in Table 21.1. Results of the interviews will be discussed based on the Rogers model, in detail in the following sections.

Overall, it was observed that only MNCs in Sri Lanka are currently using HR analytics to some extent. Out of those MNCs, very few practice HR analytics to a moderate level, while the majority practice HR analytics at a primary level. The study was unable to identify at least one large organisation that practices HR analytics in Sri Lanka. The interviews with the HR practitioners revealed that implementing HR analytics is vital to make strategic business decisions, and it is possible in Sri Lanka. However, it was revealed that there are some contextual factors that may

Table 21.1 Classifying the implementation of HR analytics in the innovation process of organisations

Organisation	Industry	Whether MNC or LO	Designation of the interviewee	Initiation		Implementation		
				1 Agenda setting	2 Matching	3 Refining/restructuring	4 Clarifying	5 Routinising
ORG 01	FMCG	MNC	HR manager	Yes	Yes, to moderate extent	Yes, to little extent	No	No
ORG 02	FMCG	MNC	HR manager	Yes	Yes, to moderate extent	Yes, to moderate extent	No	No
ORG 03	Beverages	MNC	HR executive	Yes	Yes, to moderate extent	Yes, to moderate extent	No	No
ORG 04	Apparel	MNC	Senior HR manager	Yes	Yes, to moderate extent	Yes, to moderate extent	No	No
ORG 05	Telecommunication	MNC	HR manager	Yes, but to very little	Yes, but to very little	No	No	No
ORG 06	Apparel	MNC	Data evangelist	Yes	Yes	Yes, to moderate extent	Yes, to little extent	No
ORG 07	Information technology	MNC	HR manager	Yes	Yes, to moderate extent	Yes, to moderate extent	No	No
ORG 08	Tobacco	MNC	HR manager	Yes	Yes, to moderate extent	Yes, to moderate extent	No	No
ORG 09	Software	MNC	Talent analyst	Yes	Yes	Yes, to moderate extent	Yes, to moderate extent	Yes, to moderate extent

Organisation	Industry	Whether MNC or LO	Designation of the interviewee	Initiation		Implementation		
				1 Agenda setting	2 Matching	3 Refining/restructuring	4 Clarifying	5 Routinising
ORG 10	Stock market	MNC	HR analyst	Yes	Yes, to moderate extent	Yes, to moderate extent	No	No
ORG 11	Information technology	MNC	HR analyst	Yes	Yes, to moderate extent	Yes, to moderate extent	No	No
ORG 12	FMCG	LO	HR manager	No	No	No	No	No
ORG 13	FMCG	MNC	HR manager	Yes	Yes, to moderate extent	Yes, to little extent	No	No
ORG 14	FMCG	LO	HR manager	No	No	No	No	No
ORG 15	Banking	LO	HR manager	No	No	No	No	No
ORG 16	Banking	LO	HR manager	No	No	No	No	No
ORG 17	Banking	LO	HR manager	No	No	No	No	No
ORG 18	Banking	LO	HR manager	No	No	No	No	No
ORG 19	Rubber	MNC	HR executive	Yes	Yes, to moderate extent	Yes, to moderate extent	No	No
ORG 20	BPO	MNC	HR analyst	Yes	Yes, to moderate extent	Yes, to moderate extent	No	No
ORG 21	Accounting	MNC	HR analyst	Yes	Yes, to moderate extent	Yes, to moderate extent	No	No
ORG 22	Banking	LO	HR manager	No	No	No	No	No

present as challenges and barriers to implementing HR analytics. They are lack of leadership support, lack of analytical skills of employees, organisational culture, lack of advanced technology, legal and ethical issues, traditional HR practices, data quality, lack of awareness and lack of proper business plan and HR strategy. Further discussion of results based on Rogers' (1983) model for the innovation process in organisations is presented below.

21.4.2 Initiation Stage

In Rogers' (1983) model, the initiation stage refers to seeking all the relevant information relating to the adoption of an innovation and planning for the adoption of the innovation. The initiation stage consists of agenda setting and matching.

21.4.2.1   Agenda Setting

According to Rogers (1983), agenda setting could be either problem initiated or innovation initiated. Problem initiation is when one or more individuals in the organisation identify a significant problem and search for innovation as one way of solving that problem. On the other hand, most organisations are in search of new ideas that are beneficial for them by scanning the environment. In this study, we could identify HR analytics as an innovation that will be used as a solution to solve the problem of how to increase organisational effectiveness by deploying HR analytics as a competitive advantage. As one of the managers said:

> Of course, HR analytics is the latest innovative solution not only for HR related concerns but also it helps to make better business decisions so that we can improve our ways of doing things. Actually, if we can do right, HR analytics is the new way to gain the competitive advantage. (ORG 06, Data Evangelist)

It is vital to have a proper corporate plan for organisations to focus on what business goals they need to achieve to gain sustainable competitive advantage. Accordingly, an organisation can decide on its business priorities. Based on this prioritisation, the HR department can align its HR strategy to the organisation's business goals. Here, HR analytics plays a critical role in making strategic business decisions based on evidence-based information and thereby increasing organisational effectiveness and gaining competitive advantage.

21.4.2.2   Business Strategy

According to Huselid (2015), HR analytics matters in that it focuses on executing the organisation's business strategy through its workforce. Levenson (2017) recommended starting HR analytics implementation with the business strategy and the primary business objectives that the top management of an organisation aims to achieve in the marketplace. He further argued that it is very vital to identify and address critical business issues first and take necessary measures to solve them. The presence of business strategies and measures was evident in the MNCs interviewed.

For instance, one MNC reported that with its business plan, it would identify the areas of changes in future for respective designations and work accordingly. As one MNC HR manager said:

> We are in touch with the changes of technologies happening around us and we always keep our eye on new technologies coming in, especially the technologies that matter to us and then we train our people to apply such tech. At times we have sent our guys for foreign training where such technologies were available. (ORG 08, HR manager)

This is more productive for them, even in cost, instead of recruiting new people. If they hire new people, once such technology has emerged in their industry, of course, they have to spend a lot of money recruiting such professionals who will be in high demand.

Accordingly, HR departments must have an in-depth understanding of the business beyond the HR's function (Minbaeva 2017) and identify what business goals an organisation is trying to achieve from medium to long term in order that the HR department can understand what workforce size and what skills it would likely require to achieve those goals. By doing this, the HR department can quantify and qualify the gap between its current and idyllic workforce profile.

Two MNCs revealed that it is imperative to first have a proper business plan and strategy and to align the HR analytics strategy to achieve crucial organisational objectives to gain a competitive advantage. However, according to them, in the context of Sri Lanka, it is observed that some organisations at least do not have a proper business plan. Hence, the significant value we could obtain from HR analytics is when such analytics projects have a strategic impact on the organisation's business (Minbaeva 2017).

21.4.3 Matching

According to Rogers (1983, p. 363), under this stage, "A problem from the organisation's agenda is considered together with innovation, and the fit between them is planned and designed". In other words, an organisation must test the feasibility of its chosen innovation, whether it could be practically implemented to solve the organisation's problems before implementing it. The problem that we are trying to fix in this study is to increase organisational effectiveness through strategic business decision-making using HR analytics as evidenced-based information. Hence, now it is essential to explore how we could match the fit between organisational effectiveness and HR analytics. We consider HR analytics as a strategy answering our research questions.

21.4.3.1   HR Analytics Strategy

HR analytics strategies depend on the organisational context and accessibility to macro and micro factors. Not all organisations have full accessibility to all macro and micro factors, which is required for them to fully implement HR analytics strategies. Such strategies need to be flexible and adaptable with the resources available. Hence, they will be different from organisation to organisation (CIPD 2018). However, organisations should have accessibility to the core factors to implement HR analytics strategies. For instance, one MNC reported that the minimum requirement for organisations to implement an HR analytics strategy is to digitise its organisational data and have a mechanism to analyse these data. The level of digitising data and analysing data can be varied from organisation to organisation. Some organisations are financially capable of investing in costly and more sophisticated analytical software, while some organisations are not. Yet the organisations that are not that financially strong can also implement HR analytics strategies using Excel Advanced Analytics. In fact, this MNC still uses only Excel Advanced Analytics manually in its organisation.

21.4.3.2 Assessing Organisational Readiness

The first step that the HR department should do is to assess their organisational readiness to adopt HR analytics. It is essential to identify both the macro and micro factors when assessing organisational readiness (Marler and Boudreau 2017). These factors may act as challenges or barriers when trying to adopt HR analytics.

Macro Factors

Technology
With regard to technology, different countries and organisations are at different levels in their technology. Based on the interview data, it was revealed that while some organisations have accessibility to and affordability for advanced technology, some organisations do not. For instance, they might have affordability only for advanced Excel. However, one MNC revealed that it performs HR analytics manually using advanced Excel.

Legal Practices
HR analytics mostly use data related to people. Today, organisations can monitor the contents of people's e-mails, SMS, social media and mobile phone records using advanced technology. Thus, most of these personal data can be highly sensitive, causing a severe concern for organisations to use these data responsibly.

Legal practices and standards vary from country to country. For instance, in the United States, it is legitimate to collect data from their employees, and they consider these data as the company's property (Levenson and Pillans 2017). Conversely, organisations of the European Union are responsible for justifying why they need to collect the personal data of their employees. At the same time, it is illegitimate to monitor employees' private emails in Canada (SHRM Foundation 2016). According to Levenson and Pillans (2017), in some countries, organisations are required to inform employees, employee representatives or work councils about the purpose of collecting data and what potential benefits employees can gain by doing so and are required to obtain their consent to gather data. However, getting permission over some critical matters could be challenging. Issues related to the legality of how organisations can collect, analyse and act upon people-related data are yet to be addressed in most countries (Bassi 2011; International Business Machines (IBM) Corporation 2014; Levenson and Pillans 2017; McAbee et al. 2017; SHRM Foundation 2016). Therefore, it is required to define and address the legal and ethical boundaries of HR analytics before implementing them.

Micro Factors

Awareness of HR Analytics

According to Rogers (1983), the adoption of innovation primarily depends on the awareness, knowledge and level of interest in such innovation. Organisations must be aware of innovative HR analytics practices. Out of twenty-two organisations, seven do not implement HR analytics. Out of those seven organisations, two were aware of HR analytics, even though they have not taken any measures to implement it. All of the remaining five organisations indicated that they were unaware of HR analytics. In fact, all responded with a question, "HR analytics? What is HR analytics?"

Analytical Competencies

Analytical competencies are the ability to measure variables, build casual models, test them using rigorous statistical methods and tell a compelling story (Minbaeva 2017; Minbaeva and Vardi 2019; Simón and Ferreiro 2017). While all these steps are equally important, telling a compelling story is the most challenging (Minbaeva and Vardi 2019). The team must be able to present its findings in a much simpler and understandable way and must link the results to the organisation's business strategy (Minbaeva and Vardi 2019). Here, what the senior management is interested in is whether the relationships between variables are equally strong in all situations or finding any conditions that make them stronger or weaker (Minbaeva 2017). These conditions could have been linked to organisational culture, managers' or line managers' characteristics or team compositions, which are governance mechanisms manipulated by the organisation (Minbaeva 2017). As a result, HR analysts must have an in-depth understanding of the business beyond HR's function to build the right casual model, to operationalise and to test it using rigorous statistical methods.

Many of the MNCs reported that the most challenging barrier they currently experience is that the majority of people in the management do not have a strong analytical background. They therefore often lack analytical motivation and refrain from engaging in related discussions due to their lack of statistical and econometric skills. According to Minbaeva (2017), to build analytical competencies, analytics projects must be linked with HR processes justifying the value added to business outcomes, in terms of not only activities but also deliverables. For instance, there is no value in the training and development programmes offered to employees unless they genuinely aim at achieving the business objectives of a unit or organisation.

Further, Kryscynski et al. (2017, p. 3) defined analytical ability as an individual's ability to "(a) develop causal 'logic' connecting critical components of the organisational system, (b) leverage appropriate 'analytics' to test causal relationships in the data, (c) ensure appropriate 'measures' for the components of the system, and (d) ensure a 'process' for incorporating insights into organisational decision making".

Accordingly, HR analysts who have strong analytical competencies must have the ability to access and obtain accurate quality data (Dulebohn and Johnson 2013) and also to analyse and interpret such data generating valuable insights (Levenson 2011). The reason it is important for HR professionals to have analytical capability is that it enables them (a) to make better decisions using their analytical skills, (b) to influence decisions taken at the board by leveraging insights from data, (c) to discover new insights that other HR professionals may not see by using and interpreting data and (d) to better communicate and coordinate with other data-driven functions such as sales, finance and research and development (Kryscynski et al. 2017).

However, it is not sufficient for HR professionals to have only analytical capabilities. They also need to be able to generate rich insights from their analysis. What truly matters are the insights. Analytical insights enable an organisation to achieve a competitive advantage by (a) identifying where talent has the highest potential for strategic impact, (b) connecting HR practices to organisational performance, (c) assessing and improving the HR strategy of the organisation and (d) assessing the feasibility of new business strategies (Levenson 2011). However, in a practical context, it was reported by the MNCs that generating valuable insights is lacking and is the real challenge. They further informed that performing advanced statistical analytics can be managed either internally or externally. Still, the real challenge is to identify what data should be collected and analysed, turning those analytical results to meaningful information in an understandable manner for decision-makers.

Data Quality

Data quality is the most basic and crucial resource to build a credible HR analytics strategy in organisations. According to Minbaeva (2017), data quality could be measured in terms of their completeness, accuracy, structure, timeliness, reliability and perceived value. Further, she informed that most organisations do not know what type of data they require, what type of data is already available to them, how they collect data and how they store and structure such data. She further emphasised the importance of proper organisation of data to reduce costs.

Information obtained from our survey of MNCs revealed that it is a real challenge to collect data in the structure they need from respective departments and units. Some claimed that it was truly difficult for them to train other departments to collect data as the departments have to do it from scratch since they have not practised collecting and digitising their data in a proper system. Also, almost all MNCs indicated that they have to deal with missing data, wrong entries and data duplication, which causes them difficulty in combining such data sets.

MNCs that manually analyse data said that, even though the analysis can be done manually, it is more efficient and faster if this could be done using advanced software, which is very expensive. However, they still analyse their data manually and make an effort to add value to their business outcomes, believing that it would persuade the management to invest in such software.

Leadership Support

MNCs reported that leadership support matters for the success of HR analytics projects. The right leadership will lead the projects towards success in conjunction with the ability to manage the changes in organisational culture, process, behaviour and capabilities caused by the analytics projects (Harris et al. 2011). It is most suitable if senior executives who are interested in HR analytics and evidence-based decision-making could lead these HR analytics projects. If an organisation can implement the above factors, we believe that it is in a position to implement HR analytics.

21.4.4 Implementation

Rogers (1983) defined the implementation stage as including all the events, actions, and decisions involved in putting innovation into use. The implementation consists of three stages: redefining/restructuring, clarifying and routinising.

21.4.4.1 Redefining/Restructuring

Rogers (1983) stated that innovation needs to be modified and reinvented to fit the situation of a particular organisation and its perceived problem. Organisational structures directly relevant to innovation have to be altered to accommodate innovation.

This was supported by data from our interview. For example, some MNCs reported that they use Oracle software to analyse data, while some MNCs use Excel Advanced Analytics. MNCs that use Oracle are the firms that have the ability and willingness to invest in advanced software to implement HR analytics compared to the MNCs that use Excel Advanced Analytics. MNCs using Excel Advanced Analytics can gain the support of their senior leaders if they could prove the value of HR analytics towards achieving a sustained competitive advantage. Once senior leaders are convinced, then they will invest in sophisticated analytics software. On the other hand, organisations that do not have the financial capacity to invest money on HR analytics also can gain the advantage of HR analytics using Excel Advanced Analytics.

Another example is that organisations can decide whether a centralised or decentralised organisation structure is the most suitable for implementing an analytics regime and whether it is better to incorporate the analytics team into the same HR department or whether having a separate HR analytics team is better for effective HR analytics implementation. These are few restructures that HR departments and organisations can consider for an effective implementation of HR analytics strategies in their organisations. This will depend on available resources, facilities and the level of impact HR analytics projects make.

Further, organisations can use the HR measurement system to monitor the effectiveness of their HR analytics projects and thereby decide what type of redefining and restructuring need to be made. Based on the LAMP (logic, analytics, measures, process) model, there must be a clear, logical link between what is being measured and the expected outcome. This means that there should be a business case to clarify the logical depth of the relationships that will identify the important connections between numbers and effects, which will lead to attracting the interest of senior leaders' decision-making. Here, it is important to ask strategically relevant questions and present them in a logical framework, showing the intervening linkages between HR investment and critical organisational business outcomes to act on such crucial findings (Boudreau and Cascio 2017).

Analytics must be able to draw the right conclusion from quality data. Once the organisation is in a position to implement an HR analytics strategy aligning the organisational business strategy along with the key elements, it is important to draw the practical analytical insights from the analytics projects. In order to make necessary changes in the process and perform the function of maximising business outcomes, these analytical insights must be communicated to the stakeholders to make the right strategic decisions. It is crucial that insights from HR analytics projects be effectively communicated in simpler, sensible ways using visualisation and storytelling (Boudreau and Cascio 2017; Green 2017; Minbaeva and Vardi 2019). Green (2017, p. 174) emphasised this fact: "You can create the best insights in the world, but if you don't tell the story in a compelling way that resonates with your audience then it is highly likely that no action will be taken."

The Sri Lankan MNCs that have implemented HR analytics to a certain extent reported that it is very crucial to present analytical insights to the senior management of an organisation in a simplified way as much as possible since most of them do not have an analytical background. Further, they informed that analytics projects that address the key strategic issues of the organisations and presenting analytical insights from these projects using storytelling and visualisation have the ability to draw the attention of the senior leaders as such effective insights will assist them in achieving their business objectives. These organisations further informed that this is a major challenge acting as a barrier to the implementation of HR analytics in their organisations.

With regard to measures, large organisations have invested millions of dollars to collect, organise and integrate people-related data (Boudreau and Cascio 2017). Effective data management is very significant for the more widespread adoption of HR analytics. Organisations should take necessary actions for proper data integration and acquire error-free quality data. Having more quality data is the key to a more effective analytics (Boudreau and Cascio 2017).

Finally, the process involves using discovered data to influence decision-making. It is important to show the clear rational connections between HR processes and organisational effectiveness. For instance, simple measures on how employee turnover affects organisational effectiveness will persuade and encourage senior members of management to pay their attention more to the value of HR analytics strategies and their future commitment.

21.4.4.2   Clarifying

Rogers (1983) argued that when innovation is gradually put into wider use in the organisation, the significance of the new idea becomes clearer to the members of the organisation. He further stressed that if an organisation tries to implement the innovation fast at the clarifying stage, it may result in failure to accept the innovation. There is a high possibility of having misunderstandings and undesirable side effects occurring during the early stage of innovation. However, if these could be identified at the right time, corrective actions can be taken. Once the innovation is established in the organisation, it may become embedded in the organisational structure.

As a result, it is recommended not to rush when implementing HR analytics in the organisation. Some MNCs reported that there are instances when the outcome of the analytics does not provide clear insights into the specific problem. When they investigated the reason, they found out that some required data have not been included in the data set or sometimes required data have not been entered into the analytic model.

21.4.4.3 Routinising

According to Rogers (1983), in this stage, innovation loses its separate identity and becomes incorporated into the regular system of the organisation. If HR analytics could be implemented successfully, HR analytics projects will be a normal activity in the organisation. The time taken to implement HR analytics in an organisation can be considerable. One MNC, which is from the apparel industry, reported that it had to spend 3 years just to make a data collection system and to report the data in real time. Another apparel manufacturer, which is also an MNC, informed that it is now in its fifth year of implementing HR analytics, yet it still could not reach the predictive analytics stage. This appears to be a somewhat unavoidable situation when implementing HR analytics. But this does not mean that they could not achieve any business outcomes. A respondent from one garment manufacturer reported that, for the first time, they were able to refuse the factory location that was suggested by the senior management. Instead, they were able to inform the senior management why they refuse that location and suggested an ideal location for their next new factory with supporting facts and evidence gained from HR analytics. The management has accepted and approved that location. It may be possible to draw two assumptions from this example. Firstly, HR analytics has become a normal activity in their organisation and, secondly, that even though HR analytics take years to implement, once it is implemented correctly it provides immense results for the business' success.

21.5 Strategic Decision-Making

Strategic business decisions focus on long-term goals and the longer term vision of the organisation. In this study, what we argue is that HR analytics can be used to make strategic business decisions, and thereby organisational effectiveness can be improved. As already explained previously, the most effective approach is, firstly, to start with the business plan of the organisation, identifying the most critical organisational objectives to be achieved, and then execute HR analytics projects focusing upon them. These HR analytics projects should then determine which metrics are relevant and which data elements are required to be incorporated into the analysis. The analytical insights from these HR analytics projects, in turn, assist senior leaders to make strategic business decisions, thereby improving organisational effectiveness (Carlson and Kavanagh 2012).

21.6   Organisational Effectiveness

HR analytics must be considered both inside and outside the HR department, but primarily outside the HR department, to improve the organisational process as a whole (Carlson and Kavanagh 2012). Here, the objective is to use the HR professionals' technical competence with regard to their understanding of how best to recruit, select, board, job design, train, motivate, develop, evaluate and retain employees in order to support all organisational units in accomplishing their objectives effectively. For instance, the desired business outcomes of a manufacturing department can be measured through operational metrics such as operational downtime, cost per unit, units sold, lost time accidents and percentage of on-time deliveries. Analytical insights can identify what sort of changes in HRM practices contribute to improving their operational effectiveness. Carlson and Kavanagh (2012) argued that HR managers are required to first identify what processes can most effectively accomplish organisational objectives at multiple unit levels and then discover ways to maximise the efficiency and effectiveness of the implementation of such processes in the organisation. This requires the close coordination of line managers, unit managers and departmental managers. In conclusion, insights from HR analytics assist senior leaders in making strategic business decisions that enable them to improve organisational effectiveness and thereby to gain a competitive advantage (Durai et al. 2019). Based on the above argument, we suggest the following theoretical framework for a successful implementation of HR analytics strategies (Fig. 21.1).

21.7   Conclusion

Although results cannot be generalised in relation to other countries, this study is the first to have examined the adoption of HR analytics in a Sri Lankan context. Based on the study, it can be concluded that the practice of HR analytics is at primary level in Sri Lanka compared to Western countries, as well as some countries in the Asian region, including India, China and Singapore. Results suggested that there are a small number of MNCs using HR analytics to a moderate level. According to HR practitioners, HR analytics is an emerging trend in Sri Lanka. Further, contextual factors such as lack of leadership support, lack of analytical skills of employees, organisational culture, lack of advanced technology, legal and ethical issues, data quality, lack of awareness and lack of proper business plan and HR strategy should be addressed for its successful adoption and implementation.

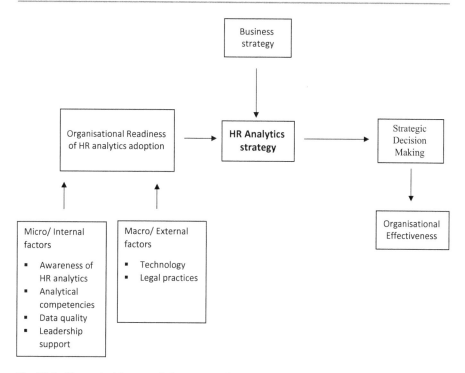

Fig. 21.1 Theoretical framework for a successful implementation of HR analytics strategies

Limitations

There are some inherent methodological limitations to an exploratory study of this nature. All data were obtained from a carefully chosen sample of organisations that are operating in Sri Lanka. Hence, it is important to investigate other countries in Asia to discover whether the same factors have a significant impact on the adoption and implementation of HR analytics. Further research examining organisational culture and the adaptation of innovative practices like HR analytics is recommended in order to broaden the scope of HR analytics research.

Chapter Takeaways/Lessons

1. Today, new technologies, digitisation and artificial intelligence create a demand for organisations to adopt new and different skill sets, as well as new ways of working.
2. HR analytics empowers organisations to make evidence-based strategic business decisions to understand what new skill sets and what new ways of working would benefit a sustained competitive advantage.
3. There is a lag in the adoption and diffusion of HR analytics in emerging markets.
4. The factors that mainly affect the adoption of HR analytics are lack of leadership support, lack of analytical skills of employees, organisational culture, lack of

advanced technology, legal and ethical issues, traditional HR practices, data quality, lack of awareness and lack of a proper business plan.

5. The challenges in applying HR analytics are understanding what type of data and analytics to be used, when to use and how to apply them, generating meaningful insights from analytics and how to present these insights to the management in a manner they understand.

Reflection Questions

1. Why is HR analytics important for organisations?
2. How does HR analytics improve the capability of organisations to gain sustained competitive advantage?
3. Why are organisations in the emerging markets slow in adopting HR analytics?
4. Why are effective data visualisation and storytelling vital in presenting the outcomes of HR analytics?
5. What are the challenges and barriers to the adoption and implementation of HR analytics?

References

Abrahamson, E., & Eisenman, M. (2008). Employee-management techniques: Transient fads or trending fashions? *Administrative Science Quarterly, 53*(4), 719–744. https://doi.org/10.2189/asqu.53.4.719.

Ahmed, M. (2019, January 16). *HR analytics is a high priority in APAC, but the adoption is sluggish.* Retrieved January 25, 2019, from https://www.peoplemattersglobal.com/article/talent-analytics/hr-analytics-is-a-high-priority-in-apac-but-the-adoption-is-sluggish-20532

Angrave, D., Charlwood, A., Kirkpatrick, I., Lawrence, M., & Stuart, M. (2016). HR and analytics: Why HR is set to fail the big data challenge. *Human Resource Management Journal, 26*(1), 1–11. https://doi.org/10.1111/1748-8583.12090.

Bassi, L. (2011). Raging debates in HR analytics. *People & Strategy, 34*(2), 14–18.

Boudreau, J., & Cascio, W. (2017). Human capital analytics: Why are we not there? *Journal of Organizational Effectiveness: People and Performance, 4*(2), 119–126. https://doi.org/10.1108/joepp-03-2017-0021.

Boudreau, J., & Ramstad, P. (2007). *Beyond HR: The new science of human capital.* Boston: Harvard Business School Press.

Carlson, K., & Kavanagh, M. (2012). Human resources metrics and workforce analytics. In M. Kavanagh, M. Thite, & R. Johnson (Eds.), *Human resource information systems: Basics, applications, and future directions* (2nd ed., pp. 150–174). Thousand Oaks: Sage. Retrieved from https://pdfs.semanticscholar.org/3a48/1e185d6489c9e6f43e727d677dff261c1e56.pdf.

Cascio, W., & Boudreau, J. (2011). *Investing in people: Financial impact of human resource initiatives* (2nd ed.). Upper Saddle River: FT Press.

Chartered Institute of Personnel and Development. (2013, November 7). *Talent analytics and big data: The challenge for HR.* Retrieved July 29, 2019, from http://www.cipd.co.uk/knowledge/strategy/analytics/hr-challenge-report

Chartered Institute of Personnel and Development. (2018, November 27). *Getting started with people analytics: A practitioner's guide.* Retrieved May 13, 2019, from https://www.cipd.co.uk/knowledge/strategy/analytics/practitioner-guide

Davenport, T. (2006, January). *Competing on analytics.* Retrieved April 9, 2019, from https://hbr.org/2006/01/competing-on-analytics

Davenport, T., Harris, J., & Shapiro, J. (2010, October). *Competing on talent analytics.* Retrieved May 12, 2019, from https://hbr.org/2010/10/competing-on-talent-analytics

Deloitte University Press. (2017). *Rewriting the rules for the digital age: 2017 Deloitte global human capital trends.* Retrieved July 30, 2019, from https://www2.deloitte.com/content/dam/Deloitte/us/Documents/human-capital/hc-2017-global-human-capital-trends-us.pdf

Dulebohn, J., & Johnson, R. (2013). Human resource metrics and decision support: A classification framework. *Human Resource Management Review, 23*(1), 71–83. https://doi.org/10.1016/j.hrmr.2012.06.005.

Durai, D. S., Rudhramoorthy, K., & Sarkar, S. (2019). HR metrics and workforce analytics: It is a journey, not a destination. *Human Resource Management International Digest, 27*(1), 4–6. https://doi.org/10.1108/hrmid-08-2018-0167.

Falletta, S. (2014). In search of HR intelligence: Evidence-based HR analytics practices in high performing companies. *People & Strategy, 36*(4), 28–37.

Fecheyr-Lippens, B., Schaninger, B., & Tanner, K. (2015, March 1). *Power to the new people analytics.* Retrieved April 9, 2019, from https://www.mckinsey.com/business-functions/organization/our-insights/power-to-the-new-people-analytics

Fitz-enz, J. (2009). Predicting people: From metrics to analytics. *Employment Relations Today, 36*(3), 1–11. https://doi.org/10.1002/ert.20255.

Glaser, B., & Strauss, A. (1967). *The discovery of grounded theory: Strategies for qualitative research.* Chicago: Aldine.

Green, D. (2017). The best practices to excel at people analytics. *Journal of Organizational Effectiveness: People and Performance, 4*(2), 137–144. https://doi.org/10.1108/joepp-03-2017-0027.

Harris, J., Craig, E., & Light, D. (2011). Talent and analytics: New approaches, higher ROI. *Journal of Business Strategy, 32*(6), 4–13. https://doi.org/10.1108/02756661111180087.

Huselid, M. (2015). Workforce analytics for strategy execution. In D. Ulrich, W. Schiemann, & L. Sartain (Eds.), *The rise of HR, wisdom from 73 thought leaders* (pp. 309–316). Alexandria: HR Certification Institute.

International Business Machines Corporation. (2014). *Unlock the people equation: Using workforce analytics to drive business results.* Retrieved April 9, 2019, from https://www.ibm.com/downloads/cas/7JEENPAQ

Kapoor, B., & Kabra, Y. (2014). Current and future trends in human resources analytics adoption. *Journal of Cases on Information Technology, 16*(1), 50–59. https://doi.org/10.4018/jcit.2014010105.

Kryscynski, D., Reeves, C., Stice-Lusvardi, R., Ulrich, M., & Russell, G. (2017). Analytical abilities and the performance of HR professionals. *Human Resource Management, 57*(3), 715–738. https://doi.org/10.1002/hrm.21854.

Lawler III, E. (2015, May 20). *Talent analytics: Old wine in new bottles?* Retrieved May 10, 2019, from https://www.forbes.com/sites/edwardlawler/2015/05/20/talent-analytics-old-wine-in-new-bottles/#3524118b1c90

Lawler, E., III, Levenson, A., & Boudreau, J. (2004). HR metrics and analytics: Use and impact. *Human Resource Planning, 27,* 27–35.

Levenson, A. (2011). Using targeted analytics to improve talent decisions. *People & Strategy, 34,* 34–43.

Levenson, A. (2017). Using workforce analytics to improve strategy execution. *Human Resource Management, 57*(3), 685–700. https://doi.org/10.1002/hrm.21850.

Levenson, A., & Pillans, G. (2017, November). *Strategic workforce analytics.* Retrieved July 3, 2019, from https://www.concentra.co.uk/uploads/sites/2/2020/05/strategic-workforce-analytics-report.pdf?__hstc=4447468.a04055ced70067d4b0303258273cd03e.1594789053647.1594789053647.15947890 53647.1&__hssc=4447468.2.1594789053648&__hsfp=898855238

Marler, J., & Boudreau, J. (2017). An evidence-based review of HR analytics. *The International Journal of Human Resource Management, 28*(1), 3–26. https://doi.org/10.1080/09585192.201 6.1244699.

McAbee, S., Landis, R., & Burke, M. (2017). Inductive reasoning: The promise of big data. *Human Resource Management Review, 27*(2), 277–290. https://doi.org/10.1016/j.hrmr.2016.08.005.

McIver, D., Lengnick-Hall, M., & Lengnick-Hall, C. (2018). A strategic approach to workforce analytics: Integrating science and agility. *Business Horizons, 61*(3), 397–407. https://doi.org/10.1016/j.bushor.2018.01.005.

Minbaeva, D. (2017). Building credible human capital analytics for organizational competitive advantage. *Human Resource Management, 57*(3), 701–713. https://doi.org/10.1002/hrm.21848.

Minbaeva, D., & Vardi, S. (2019). Global talent analytics. In D. Collings, H. Scullion, & P. Caligiuri (Eds.), *Global talent management* (2nd ed., pp. 197–217). New York: Routledge.

Mondore, S., Douthitt, S., & Carson, M. (2011). Maximizing the impact and effectiveness of HR analytics to drive business outcomes. *People & Strategy, 34*(2), 20–27.

Rasmussen, T., & Ulrich, D. (2015). Learning from practice: How HR analytics avoids being a management fad. *Organizational Dynamics, 44*(3), 236–242. https://doi.org/10.1016/j.orgdyn.2015.05.008.

Research and Markets. (2019, June). *HR analytics market by component, application area (workforce management, recruitment, and employee development), organization size, deployment type, vertical (BFSI, manufacturing, and IT and telecom), and region global forecast to 2024.* Retrieved July 23, 2019, from https://www.researchandmarkets.com/reports/4778261/hr-analytics-market-by-component-application?utm_source=CI&utm_medium=PressRelease&utm_code=vsswsc&utm_campaign=1267374+-+Global+HR+Analytics+Market+Size+is+Expected+to+Grow+from+USD+1.9+Billion+in+2019+t

Robson, C. (2002). *Real world research: A resource for social scientists and practitioner-researchers* (2nd ed.). Malden: Blackwell.

Rogers, E. M. (1983). *Diffusion of innovations* (3rd ed.). New York: Macmillan.

Simón, C., & Ferreiro, E. (2017). Workforce analytics: A case study of scholar-practitioner collaboration. *Human Resource Management, 57*(3), 781–793. https://doi.org/10.1002/hrm.21853.

Strategic Human Resource Management Foundation. (2016, May). *Use of workforce analytics for competitive advantage.* Retrieved April 9, 2019, from https://www.shrm.org/foundation/ourwork/initiatives/preparing-for-future-hr-trends/Documents/Workforce%20Analytics%20Report.pdf

Tursunbayeva, A., Di Lauro, S., & Pagliari, C. (2018). People analytics – A scoping review of conceptual boundaries and value propositions. *International Journal of Information Management, 43*(1), 224–247. https://doi.org/10.1016/j.ijinfomgt.2018.08.002.

van den Heuvel, S., & Bondarouk, T. (2017). The rise (and fall?) of HR analytics: A study into the future application, value, structure, and system support. *Journal of Organizational Effectiveness: People and Performance, 4*(2), 157–178. https://doi.org/10.1108/JOEPP-03-2017-0022.

van der Laken, P., Bakk, Z., Giagkoulas, V., van Leeuwen, L., & Bongenaar, E. (2017). Expanding the methodological toolbox of HRM researchers: The added value of latent bathtub models and optimal matching analysis. *Human Resource Management, 57*(3), 751–760. https://doi.org/10.1002/hrm.21847.

Waber, B. (2013). *People analytics: How social sensing technology will transform business and what it tells us about the future of work* (1st ed.). Upper Saddle River: Pearson Education.

Walford-Wright, G., & Scott-Jackson, W. (2018). Talent rising: People analytics and technology driving talent acquisition strategy. *Strategic HR Review, 17*(5), 226–233. https://doi.org/10.1108/shr-08-2018-0071.

Worth, C. (2011). The future talent shortage will force global companies to use HR analytics to help manage and predict future human capital needs. *International Journal of Business Intelligence Research, 2*(4), 55–65. https://doi.org/10.4018/jbir.2011100105.

Part VII

Corporate Governance

CSR Reporting Practices of Chinese MNCs

22

Chao Ren and Heng Hee Ting

22.1 Introduction

Multinational corporations (MNCs), which are defined as companies that '(…) engage in foreign direct investment (FDI) and own or control value-adding activities in more than one country' (Dunning 1992), have become economically and socially significant players in the global economy. How MNCs manage sustainability practices has attracted considerable attention (Momin and Parker 2013; Sotorrío and Sánchez 2010; Tewari and Dave 2012). Sustainability reporting is playing a critical role in MNCs' successful international business operations as there has seen a rapid increase in accountability pressure for MNCs to report more information on social and environmental impacts. A variety of agreements, treaties and initiatives has been launched that aims to promote more sustainable development and transparency by MNCs. Despite the widespread adoption of global sustainability reporting frameworks, research has raised concerns that corporate sustainability reporting may be failing to meet the information requirements of stakeholder constituents. The same holds for MNCs (Kolk 2008; Kolk and Lenfant 2010).

It has been pointed out that developed market MNCs (DMNCs), many of which are prestigious ones, departing from their home country, fall short of maintaining adequate minimum corporate social responsibility (CSR) policies or adopt strategies to the loose CSR restrictions (see, for example, Beddewela and Herzig 2013; Kapelus 2002; Narwal and Singh 2013; Tewari and Dave 2012). Although CSR literature into the DMNCs is well established, research on the emerging market MNCS (EMNCs) has been largely unexplored (Park 2018), albeit there is a rapid

C. Ren (✉)
Department of Management, Monash University, Melbourne, Australia

H. H. Ting
College of Business and Law, RMIT University, Melbourne, Australia

© The Author(s), under exclusive license to Springer Nature
Switzerland AG 2021
S. Dhiman, R. Samaratunge (eds.), *New Horizons in Management, Leadership and Sustainability*, Future of Business and Finance,
https://doi.org/10.1007/978-3-030-62171-1_22

increase in emerging markets' outward foreign direct investment (OFDI). Compared with those traditional MNCs, which have typically better management practices, MNCS from non-Western and emerging economies generally have a much shorter history of internationalisation and may not accumulate rich experience in addressing sustainability at the corporate level. Furthermore, due to different institutional profiles and features, developing countries sometimes favour economic interests over social and environmental concerns, leading to less stringent CSR regulations and lower labour costs (Apostol 2015; Belal et al. 2013; De Villiers and Van Staden 2006; Lauwo et al. 2016). This, in turn, raises issues on the impact of the EMNCs' business activities on their country of origin and their host country. In this article, we contend that fruitful insights could be gained from drawing on the theoretical and applied insights afforded by the broader CSR literature rather than the international business outlets only.

The discussions are forged with the case of China for several reasons. Foremost, as a leading emerging economy, China has the most promising foreign investments among all the non-developed nations (Unctad 2017). Moreover, China has a long history from a feudal to an industrialised society and has a rich experience in closing and opening its doors to stop or speed up interactions between the East and the West over the last hundred years. The unprecedented transition towards a market-driven economy shows evidence of distinctly different institutional contexts and various stages of economic and CSR development and internationalisation. Also, as organisations worldwide are increasingly seeking to enhance legitimacy through developing sustainability reporting practices, it is in part under this pressure that sustainability reporting has gained popularity in China, and a growing number of articles has focused on this phenomenon (He and Loftus 2014; Marquis and Qian 2014). Nevertheless, Chinese MNCs' CSR reporting practices and the quality of disclosure in foreign countries are missing from the literature. Given the increasing call for considering context in CSR reporting practices (Tilt 2016, 2018; Yang et al. 2014) and that CSR research in China has developed rapidly in recent years, it will be beneficial to take stock of what we know in this field to facilitate future research.

Our intention is twofold: to provide a relatively comprehensive appraisal of the CSR field and to offer research directions to researchers. Since the extant literature pays little attention to the cross-border situations of MNCs, we provide a concrete example by reinterpreting the similarities and differences between the Western and Chinese practices in the Australian mining industry. The contextual differences indicate that Chinese MNCs with their institutional logics find it challenging to incorporate the emerging institutional logic of the host country. These challenges are likely to resonate broadly in the hybrid organisational setting since they similarly confront a multitude of competing logics (Pache and Santos 2013). This may even be compounded by the high visibility, operations and impacts of MNCs. Our study endeavours to make two key contributions. First, our study draws attention to the development of CSR research as it is vital to assess how the CSR scholarship has matured. Second, we shed light on how the field can be further developed by adopting a broader research agenda, and theoretical underpins, which we believe would be helpful for future research on Chinese MNCs.

The review starts with the development of CSR research in general. The paper next reviews the literature on CSR reporting in the context of China. Then we situate the focus on the Australian mining industry and map out the implications of future research on CSR reporting and management in the context of Chinese MNCs. The paper concludes with a research agenda and explores how the literature may be extended to other EMNCs.

22.2 Corporate Social Responsibility (CSR)

The notion of CSR has appeared on the radar for many companies. This section provides a comprehensive overview of CSR and sustainability reporting, along with the analysis of disclosures in multiple contexts. The studies of the critical determinants, the uses, the content, theoretical underpinnings and the rhetoric of sustainability reporting are also presented.

CSR is often related to corporate community engagement as organisations have a long history of donating their resources to communities and societies at large (Muthuri et al. 2012). Whilst Friedman (2007) proposes that the only social responsibility for business is to maximise profits for its shareholders within legally acceptable margins, debates are stating that business plays a significant role in giving back to the communities and noting the political role companies take on (Carroll 1991; Scherer et al. 2014). Scholars have supported the idea that engaging CSR can create long-term value by adopting a business approach that is equally mindful of economic, social and environmental implications (Caprar and Neville 2012; Dhanda 2013).

An important driver contributing to the growing perfernce for CSR reporting is the increase in moral requirements imposed on enterprises as a result of a growth of the social impact of companies' activities (Donaldson and Preston 1995). Organisational engagement in CSR activities creates shared values to allow organisations to gain benefits and competitiveness from addressing societal concerns while simultaneously advancing the economic and social conditions in the communities in which they operate (Porter and Kramer 2006). Organisations committing to CSR practices not only bring internal benefits, such as improved employee commitment and reduced employee turnover (Dawkins and Lewis 2003; Maio 2003), but also enhance corporate image (Choi and Ng 2011; Miles and Covin 2000; Nybakk and Panwar 2015), attract new and quality employees (Greening and Turban 2000; Kim and Park 2011), improve customer loyalty (Marin et al. 2009), increase sales revenue and sustain financial performance (Cheung 2011; Robinson et al. 2011; Wagner 2010; Weber 2008). However, research points to the difficulties in translating corporate CSR commitment into competitive advantages. For example, the relationship between corporate sustainability performance and financial performance is found to be positive but weakly associated (Becchetti et al. 2012; Gao and Bansal 2013; Garcia-Castro et al. 2010; Schreck 2011; Surroca et al. 2010). Gao and Bansal (2013) state that stakeholders are unaware of relatively small improvements in the organisation's social and environmental management because operations are not entirely transparent. As such, small improvements are difficult to measure. In addition to instrumental motivations in driving CSR implementation in business, organisations, such as MNCs, face increasing pressures from their stakeholders to implement and report CSR practices (Adams 2002; Kolk 2008; Richter 2011). With rising expectations, CSR communications play a vital part in minimising stakeholder conflicts and ensuring continued corporate sustainability (Madsen and Ulhøi 2001).

22.2.1 CSR Communications

The CSR communications literature is mainly based on a transmission model wherein social and environmental communications are labelled as a corporate function to perform the transfer of information for the benefits of organisations and stakeholders (Amaladoss and Manohar 2013; Arvidsson 2010; Du et al. 2010; Goodman et al. 2011; Schoeneborn and Trittin 2013; Spence 2009). Terms like 'tools', 'means' or 'messages' or attributes like 'strategic' or 'effective' suggest an instrumental notion of CSR communications (Schoeneborn and Trittin 2013).

However, CSR communications are not merely a mechanism through which organisations convey their CSR objectives, intentions and progress to stakeholders but also a continuous process through which stakeholders explore, construct, negotiate and modify what could be considered as legitimated organisations (Schultz et al. 2013). CSR communications assume the involvement of stakeholders in corporate CSR decision-making process (Morsing and Schultz 2006). Research has focused on corporate CSR communications with stakeholders, such as employees (Morsing et al. 2008), shareholders (Hockerts and Moir 2004; Rehbein et al. 2013), non-governmental organisations (NGOs) (Van Huijstee and Glasbergen 2008) and customers. Ongoing dialogues with stakeholders throughout the implementation of CSR policy arguably help fix weaknesses and correct deficiencies, which then promotes the institutionalisation of the CSR vision and processes and increases the credibility of published sustainability information. In doing so, it enables organisations to respond to stakeholder concerns (Maon et al. 2009). In this line of reasoning, CSR communications take accounts of organisations' and stakeholders' concerns and materialise CSR ideas, which is different from the transmission model.

22.2.2 Sustainability Reporting

Sustainability reporting is one form of CSR communications and is referred to as CSR reporting in some organisations. Scholars agree that CSR and sustainability terms can be used interchangeably (Lodhia 2018; Metcalf and Benn 2013; Perez-Batres et al. 2010). Although sustainability reporting remains a voluntary activity in most jurisdictions (Lackmann et al. 2012; Searcy and Buslovich 2014), it has become a global trend (Mori et al. 2014). Organisations seem to have put an end to the debate of whether they should or should not engage in sustainability reporting and are focusing on the quality of sustainability reporting and the best means to reach relevant audiences.

There has been a large and growing body of literature on key determinants in sustainability reporting. Some reasons that influence companies to engage in social and environmental reporting include to conform with legal or industry regulations, to consider CSR information within economic rationality, the belief in accountability, to consider the organisation's reputation or legitimacy treats and to manage diverse stakeholder group (Bebbington et al. 2008; Deegan et al. 2002; Unerman 2008). Empirical studies were conducted in developed countries, such as the study undertaken by Ho and Taylor (2007) in the US and Japan, Moore (2001) in the United Kingdom, Adams et al. (1998) and Reverte (2009) in European countries and Hackston and Milne (1996) in New Zealand. Others have explored the drivers in emerging countries, such as Liu and Anbumozhi (2009) in China and Islam and Deegan (2008) in Bangladesh.

These drivers can be explained by the institutional theory, the stakeholder theory and the legitimacy theory. Powell and DiMaggio (2012) describe the way in which isomorphic pressures (mimetic, coercive and normative) constrain organisations, attitudes and behaviours. With the upward trend in sustainability reporting, mimetic pressure is formed when organisations feel obligated to imitate the same practices as other peers have done (Escobar and Vredenburg 2011). Coercive pressure refers to the legal standards that require organisations to be socially and environmentally responsible. In Sweden, for example, the government makes it mandatory for state-owned enterprises (SOEs) to report sustainability performance according to the Global Reporting Initiatives (GRI) guidelines. Also, organisations face normative pressure in creating a positive corporate citizen image, adopting CSR practices or engaging in sustainability reporting. De Villiers et al. (2014) find that normative isomorphism is characterised by professionalisation, shaping individual beliefs towards shared norms. Especially in industries that have significant CSR risks, organisations face normative pressure to ensure the safety and health of their employees, as well as to adopt ecological practices to minimise environmental harms.

Prior research on CSR disclosures has adopted the stakeholder theory in explaining many factors on sustainability reporting, as well as stakeholder engagement and management, that might influence the companies' legitimacy strategies (Deegan and Islam 2014; Morsing and Schultz 2006; O'Dwyer 2005; O'Dwyer et al. 2005). This body of literature argues that organisations need to consider the expectations of all stakeholders, which form part of social contract expectations. In this regard, sustainability reporting is an indicator of stakeholder accountability, which facilitates the pursuit of social acknowledgement.

A rich and extensive literature has also shown that organisations strive for legitimacy by reporting on their corporate values and their economic, social and environmental impacts (Du and Vieira 2012; Pellegrino and Lodhia 2012). Suchman (1995) defines legitimacy as a generalised perception or assumption that the actions of an entity are desirable, proper or appropriate in society and identifies three dimensions of personal evaluative assessments to examine stakeholder attitudes towards organisations: pragmatic, moral and cognitive. By demonstrating the congruence of corporate values with societal values, CSR reporting provides a social licence to operate and a tool for managing risks. However, in garnering successful legitimisation from sustainability reporting, many organisations have been accused of building up an appearance of hypocrisy (or greenwashing) in terms of avoiding public accusations or gaining external verification. Newson and Deegan (2002) found the large MNCs used CSR disclosures to respond to national expectations but not to meet global expectations. Slack (2012) suggests that organisations should proactively communicate with potentially affected communities about the social benefits that its operations can and cannot deliver, keep the promises they make to communities and regularly report publicly on the progress made on these commitments.

22.2.3 The Content of Sustainability Reporting

Organisations that voluntarily engage in sustainability reporting often use guidelines to specify the published content. The Global Reporting Initiative (GRI), which covers more than 100 CSR indicators, as well as a wide range of sustainability issues, principles and processes, is now the globally accepted standard. Most organisations' reports include the three 'triple bottom line' dimensions of economic, social and environmental. More specially, economic indicators focus on sales and benefits, environmental indicators focus on energy and water and social indicators focus on donations, labour practices and the breakdown of the workforce (by employment type and region). Perez and Sanchez (2009) evaluated the evolution of sustainability reporting in the mining industry, arguing that the highest reporting focus has been put on social performance and the lowest on economic performance.

The literature suggests that the content and quality of sustainability reporting are inconsistent across different industries and different countries (Cho and Patten 2007; Farooq et al. 2018; Perez and Sanchez 2009). Cho and Patten (2007) tested the use of monetary and non-monetary environmental disclosures between environmentally sensitive and non-sensitive companies. They found that high-profile companies had more CSR disclosures, along with more quantitative information, whereas low-profile companies had more non-monetary disclosures regarding negative social and environmental performance. Alazzani and Wan-Hussin (2013) discover that oil and gas companies in countries where stakeholder engagement and involvement are more pronounced, such as Canada, show more commitment to environmental issues. Jose and Lee (2007) find that environmental sustainability is not a top corporate priority, especially for MNCs. Although environmental policies and corporate ecological principles are in place, the MNCs do not use predetermined targets and objectives to guide their environmental management efforts. Rather, they tend to highlight their achievement of environmental goals and are less likely to reveal the variances between their actual performance and goals. Sections like CEO statements, corporate governance and the structure of board committees are included by MNCs in their sustainability reporting, in their hope to increase transparency and accountability (Kolk 2008). As alluded to above, there is a bourgeoning of research demonstrating that corporations tend to camouflage negative corporate performance and potential risks (Adams 2004; Quaak et al. 2007; Ruffing 2007). Searcy and Buslovich (2014) note that organisations have not done enough in conveying accountability and transparency. Cheng et al. (2014, p. 91) find that 'the extent of CSR-related information in such reports is often overwhelming in quantity' for reasons including the absence of regulation. This has led to problems in relation to the quality of the report, including issues of objectivity and materiality (Beck et al. 2014).

Further, the definition of sustainability is found to be inconsistent across different countries and industries (Chen and Bouvain 2009; Freeman and Hasnaoui 2011). For example, English-speaking countries such as the United Kingdom and the United States look to the individual taking responsibility for their actions. Maintaining sustainability has become a responsibility for each individual. In France and Germany, high involvement of their government in societies relieves individuals from social actions and highlights the role of the government in promoting sustainability. While detailed disclosures are not yet standard, some common patterns and practices can be found, such as low levels of CSR disclosures and the use of sustainability reporting as public activities in developing countries (De Villiers and Van Staden 2006; Liu and Anbumozhi 2009).

22.2.4 The Rhetoric of Sustainability Reporting

In a prior research on sustainability reporting, rhetorical strategies (logos, ethos and pathos) are studied to understand how reporting relates to Suchman's (1995) legitimacy perspective (Brennan and Merkl-Davies 2014; Castelló and Lozano 2011; Marais 2012). Suddaby and Greenwood (2005) describe rhetorical strategies as shifts in logic and shaping perceptions through language selection and the use of metaphors and common referents. Some scholars describe them as discursive moves that enable organisations to gain control over meaning made in a context (Lucas and Fyke 2014). Brennan and Merkl-Davies (2014) state that organisations use rhetoric techniques to reframe situations in ways hoped to be understood.

Aristotle (2010) states that rhetoric is the art of persuasion and introduces three modes of persuasion: *logos*, *ethos* and *pathos*. Firstly, *logos* is about facts and logic and is used to achieve pragmatic legitimacy. Information, such as improved reputation, increased new investments, attraction of skilled employees and other positive impact of corporate CSR practices, is included in sustainability reporting in order to convince stakeholders that their best interests are in good hands. Secondly, *ethos* concentrates on communicating ethics or character to persuade and is used to show that organisations comply with regulations and support normative principles in society. *Ethos* improves the organisations' worthiness and social acceptance and hence promotes cognitive legitimacy (Castelló and Lozano 2011). *Ethos* also includes expertise and knowledge and can be used to show practical skills and the wisdom of an organisation in making important decisions. Thirdly, *pathos* is concerned with persuading based on emotions and promotes moral legitimacy. In the context of sustainability reports, pathos creates an engaged dialogue with stakeholders to make sure that they feel included and valued and promotes common good and mutual respect (Castelló and Lozano 2011). For examples, the use of images evokes emotions and makes them feel attached to the issues raised (Rämö 2011), while the development of code of conducts makes stakeholders feel confident and assured towards an organisation's operations and future direction.

In the business world, the use of euphemisms is related to the rhetoric *pathos* in sustainability reporting to convince stakeholders of the obligation that an organisation has towards its society. McGlone et al. (2006) define euphemism as a word or phrase considered as a polite manner of referring to a topic than its literal designation. For example, the term 'neighbour' is chosen to replace 'corporation' to present stakeholders the philanthropic duty a company has other than being profitable (La Cour and Kromann 2011). According to Lucas and Fyke (2014), euphemism can reduce ethics awareness and encourage unethical decision-making as it alters meanings to reframe a critical situation. This says that too much use of euphemism in sustainability reports hides corporate crises and allows the stakeholders to focus only on positive corporate issues.

22.3   China and CSR Research

China is the second-largest economy in the world and, as a result, is a significant contributor to and employer in the global manufacturing sector. As part of China's economic reform process, environmental pollution, workers' health, increasing safety problems, social injustice and inequality have primarily been tolerated by the CPC to help boost growth in gross domestic product (GDP). Nevertheless, the Chinese government began to exhibit more interest in CSR. In 2005, the government proposed the idea of 'Building a Harmonized Socialist Society', aiming to 'harness the Scientific Outlook on Development harmonious human-to-human and human-to-nature relationships through democracy, the rule of law, fairness, justice, integrity and fraternity' (Ji and Parker 2016, p. 7). Promoting public awareness of Chinese companies' environmental stewardship and transparency has been the propaganda used by the government to develop overall societal balance and harmony. China has enforced a broad array of laws, regulations and reporting guides in order to address increasing environmental challenges, and many international policies and guidelines are also being applied. Sustainability reporting is an activity that the Chinese government believes signals the organisation as legitimate (Marquis and Qian 2014). This trend is mirrored by an increasing level of Global Reporting Initiative (GRI) participation, as well as the development of domestic CSR reporting guidebooks—the Chinese CSR Report Preparation Guide (CASS-CSR 3.0) and ISO26000 in China. Another notable feature of Chinese CSR development is the country's growing number of industry CSR initiatives. In line with the increase of stand-alone CSR reporting practices, initiatives to form voluntary reporting standards to guide company reporting practices have been developed and promulgated by industry associations in China. While there are significant overlaps between these guidelines and GRI reporting guidelines, some disclosure items and associated metrics emerged that are unique to the Chinese context.

With a different political system from other countries—particularly the Western system—the Chinese capital market is in the process of transitioning from a centrally planned economy to a market economy. Many public-listed Chinese companies remain controlled by the Chinese government and are referred to as state-owned enterprises (SOEs) (Lin 2001; Tan and Tan 2003). Contrary to the rule-based system in Western capitalist countries, a distinctive feature of the Chinese capital market is that China has progressed from relation-based governance to rule-based governance (Li 2012). This changing situation can affect the form of CSR activities. For instance, market-based models that prioritise shareholders' interests means that human capital in terms of employee well-being is, to some extent, ignored in managerial decisions (Gospel and Pendleton 2005). China is also experiencing an institutional transition from bureaucratic secrecy to an open information disclosure environment (Yang et al. 2014). This is remarkable given the Chinese government's release of Open Government Informaton (OGI 2007) and Open Environment Information (OEI 2007) regulations, and its encouragement of environmental reporting in China. These have propelled Chinese firms to institute CSR reporting and management practices.

Chinese enterprises' CSR reporting and management practices had received considerable attention in recent years. A dominant theme is that social and environmental accountability research in China is heavily clustered around environmental reporting performance of high-polluting industries (Du et al. 2014; Wang et al. 2014), which may be subject to government intervention and orientations, and public interest. It is noted that the CSR disclosures of Chinese companies seem to be oriented towards 'window dressing' rather than stimulated CSR awareness (Hung et al. 2013). Another emerging research focus is the relationship between corporate characteristics and CSR actions, with authors empirically testing governance controls and ownership structures to see how reporting practice could be affected (Chu et al. 2012; He and Loftus 2014; Marquis and Qian 2014; Situ and Tilt 2012; Xiao and Yuan 2007). He and Loftus (2014), for example, find that environmental sensitivity of corporations and size have significant relationships with sustainability reporting, and the government pressure proxy is the dominant factor. Overal, there is a gap between CSR reporting in China and that in developed countries, and the inadequate disclosures may be a result of less pressure from stakeholders (Li 2014).

Chinese outward foreign direct investment (OFDI) increased rapidly when the 'Go-Out' policy was initiated. Taking economic, legal, ethical and philanthropic responsibilities is regarded as a must for MNCs to stay in host countries (Du and Vieira 2012). However, Chinese OFDI has not always been well perceived by host communities, and many countries doubt the ability of Chinese firms to fulfil social responsibilities (Burgoon and Raess 2014; Hilson et al. 2014). When going abroad, changes in political influence and stakeholders' make it challenging for Chinese MNCs to operate, particularly in socially and environmentally sensitive areas. While scholars have made efforts toward studying and provided insightful evaluations of Chinese CSR practices, empirical contributions for evaluating CSR disclosures of Chinese MNCs operating in foreign countries are rare, as are studies on the implementation and outcomes of CSR disclosures (Tan 2009). Thus, CSR research focusing on Chinese MNCs is worthy of critical examination.

22.4   An Example: The Australian Mining Industry

The section sets a scene for Chinese MNCs operating in Australia's mining industry by reviewing the difference in CSR policies, measures and legitimising the strategies used. The extractive industry is significant economically from an international and national context. Over the last two decades, the dramatic increase in Chinese OFDI into Australia has made Australia one of the key destinations for Chinese OFDI. China is interested in securing natural resources and technology, leading to significant investment in Australian mining companies. Chinese investments in Australia's mining industry provide increased capital to the Australian economy.

The Australian mining industry has a high profile. It is often seen as performing relatively well in aspects of CSR reporting. Given the dirty and dangerous nature of its business, Chinese invested companies are generally perceived by sectors of the community and media as having little regard for the environment and communities in which they operate. The negative sentiment imposed by the media and restrictive foreign investment policies reflects material differences in the business practices of China and Australia, particularly in the areas of sustainable governance, disclosures and transparency. Although a set of policies has been initiated in order to balance national extensive economic growth with the social and environmental effects of industrial growth, CSR norms and regulations in China are still in their primary stage of development. Uncertainties exist in the institutional environment, leading to mimicking of global CSR trends. CSR disclosures in Chinese companies are seemingly oriented towards 'window dressing' rather than stimulated CSR awareness (Hung et al. 2013). This has been reflected in Chinese mining companies' silence on several significant issues, including human rights and biodiversity loss, indicating that Chinese companies need fewer legitimising strategies in their local sustainability reporting because of a lack of institutional pressures (Guan and Noronha 2013).

In contrast, CSR is often touted as the solution to social and environmental ills associated with the Australian mining boom, albeit with some legitimising strategies adopted to gain, maintain or repair legitimacy from organisations' relevant publics (Bice 2013). In Australia, the early adopters of sustainability reporting are mining, utility and energy companies (Higgins et al. 2015). They take up sustainability reporting guidelines because the government seems to loom large in reporting companies. Companies that are government suppliers receive supply-chain pressure to report, suggesting that legitimacy plays a significant part in the uptake of sustainability reporting in Australia. Moreover, continued criticism, particularly by NGOs, and increased attack by the media have highlighted the increasing scrutiny that stakeholders are prepared to subject this industry to. In these situations,

Australian mining companies have been aware that the increasing scrutiny may lead to increasing levels of regulation that may potentially threaten their viability. Thus, they prefer to disclose their social and environmental impact. Taken together, a lack of acceptance of stakeholders and different institutional spheres underlie that Chinese MNCs may face substantial challenges and pressures when trying to apply their home country practices and models in Australia with different regulations, norms and business operations.

22.5   Future Research Directions

In this special issue on 'New Horizons in Management, Leadership and Sustainability', we consolidate our review and highlight several avenues in the existing knowledge base for further empirical research to advance the study of sustainability reporting of Chinese MNCs and subsidiaries in other regions. It is recognised that these gaps highlighted are illustrative, but not exhaustive, and have been studied to varying degrees in the existing research but are applicable to this specific context.

Over the last decades, CSR as a research field has emerged in China, and Chinese scholars have benefited enormously from learning from and interacting with Western counterparts. Many Western and local CSR concepts and practices have been advocated and undertaken in Chinese firms in multiple ways. This development has laid the foundations to link research dialogues between Chinese researchers and the research community in the world. Nonetheless, research on the evolution of CSR reporting in Chinese foreign companies is under-represented in the literature, which is a critical gap since learning the best CSR practices of host countries can be significant for overseas expansion. This is a question that requires serious consideration, which is associated with both the content of the CSR disclosures and the implementations and uses. For example, developing key performance indicators (KPIs) for measuring and reporting sustainability performance might be challenging for Chinese companies because they do not possess a rich experience. The literature could benefit significantly from identifying changes in sustainability reporting after Chinese acquisition, in comparison with disclosure changes in a similar group of Australian domestic acquisitions and other local Chinese enterprises.

Further research can address the gap in the literature as to how Chinese foreign-invested firms deal with the legitimacy threats that they face in other countries. For example, there is still a lack of research into how rhetorical techniques are employed in sustainability reporting to assist Chinese investors in securing a social licence to operate. Also, it is essential to consider both the quantity and quality of sustainability reporting by focusing on the broad aspects that have been less well explored but are deemed necessary, such as the area of labour issues. Moreover, research should extend the scale and scope of examining both high-profile and low-profile Chinese companies to investigate how the use of sustainability reporting differs by industry sectors.

Future studies should acknowledge the importance of economic, political and social contexts in which disclosures are made and the contextual effects, such as the role of local governments, civil society, NGOs and external stakeholders and their impact on the reporting and accountability practices. There is a need for much more work on the effects that the investor's country of origin (e.g. the socio-cultural and institutional background) would have on the development and use of CSR reporting practices. Doing this would deepen our understanding of the impact of the home country on firms' CSR practices, supplementing the traditional focus on the host country effects.

The possible broadening of what is being reported will potentially influence internal management practices and dynamics. There is an overarching need to address the gaps between the design, implementation and actual use of sustainability reporting in practice. The relative absence of attention to the relationship between corporate control and related firm-level practices represents a fascinating area of research on the extent to which and the ways sustainability practices are deployed in their governance, organisation-wide decision-making process, planning and performance measurements. Several issues associated with internal management practices require additional research. It includes investigating the factors affecting the success and failure in the implementation of sustainability reporting, identifying the perception of the preparers of the reports since CSR reporting represents not only the product of context but also of the choices of the senior management, revealing underlying dilemmas and complexities for managers in dealing with accountability to stakeholders and uncovering the internalisation of social and environmental values into managerial practices as well as assurance-related issues. Related to this topic would be the strong potential of examining the role of accounting and accountability in practically leveraging the implementation of sustainability reporting in various operating and functional units and subsidiaries and headquarters, as well as the capitals that MNCs use or affect.

In understanding the sustainability reporting of Chinese MNCs, critically, there is a need to better connect the research on sustainability reporting to theory. There remains a need for more holistic accounts on the application of micro-theories to understanding micro-level socio-institutions and those focusing on macro-level socio-traditions. Institutional logic theory is a popular theoretical paradigm that provides a conceptual basis for analysing how MNCs operate and respond to the multiple pressures they face from home country integration and host country orientation. The concept was first introduced by Friedland (1991), who argues that multiple rationalities that provide meaning to the social reality constitute society. Dunn and Jones (2010, p. 114) define institutional logics as '(. . .) cultural beliefs and rules that shape the cognitions and behaviours of actors (. . .)' and that provide those actors with means-ends designations and rationales for goals and actions (see also Thornton 2002; Thornton et al. 2012). Institutional logics further provide a collective understanding of how organisational decision-makings are framed and are a 'taken-for-granted social prescription' that legitimates actions (Battilana and Dorado 2010, p. 1420). The extent of dissimilarity between the different institutional environments in which MNCs confront with multiple and conflicting institutional demands and pressures (Kostova and Roth 2002; Kostova et al. 2008; Marano and

Kostova 2016) is known as 'institutional distance' (Kostova and Zaheer 1999). Indeed, how MNCs obtain legitimacy in the local host country and the wider social setting and environment are among the key challenges faced by MNCs (Kostova and Roth 2002; Kostova and Zaheer 1999; Xu and Shenkar 2002). Extending this line of enquiry, institutional logics could provide an opportunity to explore how Chinese MNCs cope with a plurality of institutional demands and request for stakeholder accountability as a form of transparency, disclosure and responsibility. As MNCs are simultaneously embedded in their country of origin and their host country (Ferner et al. 2001), institutional logics offer a useful toolkit with which to investigate issues regarding what extent Chinese MNCs apply their home standards when going abroad or rely on the standards and logic of their host country and how their responses shift over time.

More broadly abd fundamentally, it is necessary to collect data from different sources to address the 'what', 'how' and 'why' questions on Chinese MNCs' sustainability reporting practices. To fully understand this topic, qualitative studies such as case studies and interviews should also be used to ascertain inside and in-depth insights. There is a need for longitudinal case studies that document and reflect on the entire process and intra-organisational ties through uncovering the dissemination and imposition of sustainability strategies from outside the firm.

22.6   Conclusion

Developments in global politics and nation policy have brought about many changes in the way Chinese MNCs (re)configure their business models. Chinese MNCs face growing challenges in managing the complexity of logics of accountability and pressures in their host locations. Hence, developing sustainability initiatives is critical for the success of Chinese outward FDI. While existing studies often focus on CSR reporting practices in MNCs, the literature accords significant attention to traditional and large MNCs from developed economics. Given that the CSR reporting practices of non-Western and emerging MNCs appear to be less researched, our understanding of the state of affairs in this field remains partial. As one of the largest OFCI investors among developing countries, few have looked at how Chinese MNCs manage their CSR disclosures in the host countries. Based on this extensive literature review, we take stock of relevant research themes from academic articles in the field. Using the Australian mining industry as an example, we illustrate differences in contexts and challenges that Chinese MNCs may encounter when dealing with sustainability issues. We highlight several avenues, including theoretical and empirical guidelines, for future research in this less-studied area. We argued that a stronger momentum in researching Chinese MNCs and their CSR reporting practices might be developed to shed light on their business activities, especially the way they manage and adjust CSR strategies to survive or succeed in the host country. This paper has implications for Chinese FDI literature, foreign investment policies and legislations and has relevance to MNCs from other emerging economies in developing international footprints.

Takeaway Messages

- This study reviews the state of knowledge on CSR, together with specific literature on China.
- There is a need for more holistic accounts on the role of sustainability reporting in emerging MNCs, drawing on insights from cognate fields.
- Most research attention may be given to how sustainability is practised in Chinese foreign-invested firms, given their significance to FDI and unique macro-level socio-traditions and meso- and micro-level socio-institutions.
- It identifies key themes at the intersection of CSR-MNC-China.
- It points out several research opportunities as a guide for future empirical studies.

Reflection Questions

- How far has CSR reporting travelled in Chinese foreign-invested companies?
- How do Chinese MNCs respond to the plurality of institutional logics and pressures over time?
- What type of legal enforcement can be implemented to address shadowing the environmental disclosures or absence of some sensitive disclosures?
- How are the number of disclosures (environmental, economic and social) measured?
- Can a small number of disclosures be more impactful in value?

References

Adams, C. A. (2002). Internal organisational factors influencing corporate social and ethical reporting. *Accounting, Auditing & Accountability Journal, 15*(2), 223–250.

Adams, C. A. (2004). The ethical, social and environmental reporting-performance portrayal gap. *Accounting, Auditing & Accountability Journal, 17*(5), 731–757.

Adams, C. A., Hill, W. Y., & Roberts, C. B. (1998). Corporate social reporting practices in Western Europe: Legitimating corporate behaviour? *British Accounting Review, 30*(1), 1–21.

Alazzani, A., & Wan-Hussin, W. N. (2013). Global reporting Initiative's environmental reporting: A study of oil and gas companies. *Ecological Indicators, 32*, 19–24.

Amaladoss, M. X., & Manohar, H. L. (2013). Communicating corporate social responsibility–a case of CSR communication in emerging economies. *Corporate Social Responsibility and Environmental Management, 20*(2), 65–80.

Apostol, O. M. (2015). A project for Romania? The role of the civil society's counter-accounts in facilitating democratic change in society. *Accounting, Auditing & Accountability Journal, 28*(2), 210–241.

Aristotle. (2010). *Rhetoric*. New York: Cosimo.

Arvidsson, S. (2010). Communication of corporate social responsibility: A study of the views of management teams in large companies. *Journal of Business Ethics, 96*(3), 339–354.

Battilana, J., & Dorado, S. (2010). Building sustainable hybrid organizations: The case of commercial microfinance organizations. *Academy of Management Journal, 53*(6), 1419–1440.

Bebbington, J., Larrinaga, C., & Moneva, J. M. (2008). Corporate social reporting and reputation risk management. *Accounting, Auditing & Accountability Journal, 21*(3), 337–361.

Becchetti, L., Ciciretti, R., Hasan, I., & Kobeissi, N. (2012). Corporate social responsibility and shareholder's value. *Journal of Business Research, 65*(11), 1628–1635.

Beck, J., Clowes, C., Deegan, C., Gallagher, P., Martin, A., & Tunny, J. (2014). *Corporate social responsibility* (4th ed.). Geelong: CPA Australia Ltd.

Beddewela, E., & Herzig, C. (2013). Corporate social reporting by MNCs' subsidiaries in Sri Lanka. *Accounting Forum, 37*(2), 135–149.

Belal, A. R., Cooper, S. M., & Roberts, R. W. (2013). Vulnerable and exploitable: The need for organisational accountability and transparency in emerging and less developed economies. *Accounting Forum, 37*(2), 81–91.

Bice, S. (2013). No more sun shades, please: Experiences of corporate social responsibility in remote Australian mining communities. *Rural Society, 22*(2), 138–152.

Brennan, N. M., & Merkl-Davies, D. M. (2014). Rhetoric and argument in social and environmental reporting: The dirty laundry case. *Accounting, Auditing & Accountability Journal, 27*(4), 602–633.

Burgoon, B., & Raess, D. (2014). Chinese investment and European labor: Should and do workers fear Chinese FDI? *Asia Europe Journal, 12*(1–2), 179–197.

Caprar, D. V., & Neville, B. A. (2012). "Norming" and "conforming": Integrating cultural and institutional explanations for sustainability adoption in business. *Journal of Business Ethics, 110*(2), 231–245.

Carroll, A. B. (1991). The pyramid of corporate social responsibility: Toward the moral management of organizational stakeholders. *Business Horizons, 34*(4), 39–48.

Castelló, I., & Lozano, J. M. (2011). Searching for new forms of legitimacy through corporate responsibility rhetoric. *Journal of Business Ethics, 100*(1), 11–29.

Chen, S., & Bouvain, P. (2009). Is corporate responsibility converging? A comparison of corporate responsibility reporting in the USA, UK, Australia, and Germany. *Journal of Business Ethics, 87*(1), 299–317.

Cheng, M., Green, W., Conradie, P., Konishi, N., & Romi, A. (2014). The international integrated reporting framework: Key issues and future research opportunities. *Journal of International Financial Management & Accounting, 25*(1), 90–119.

Cheung, A. W. K. (2011). Do stock investors value corporate sustainability? Evidence from an event study. *Journal of Business Ethics, 99*(2), 145–165.

Cho, C. H., & Patten, D. M. (2007). The role of environmental disclosures as tools of legitimacy: A research note. *Accounting, Organizations and Society, 32*(7–8), 639–647.

Choi, S., & Ng, A. (2011). Environmental and economic dimensions of sustainability and price effects on consumer responses. *Journal of Business Ethics, 104*(2), 269–282.

Chu, C. I., Chatterjee, B., & Brown, A. (2012). The current status of greenhouse gas reporting by Chinese companies: A test of legitimacy theory. *Managerial Auditing Journal, 28*(2), 114–139.

Dawkins, J., & Lewis, S. (2003). CSR in stakeholder expectations: And their implication for company strategy. *Journal of Business Ethics, 44*(2–3), 185–193.

De Villiers, C., & Van Staden, C. J. (2006). Can less environmental disclosure have a legitimising effect? Evidence from Africa. *Accounting, Organizations and Society, 31*(8), 763–781.

De Villiers, C., Low, M., & Samkin, G. (2014). The institutionalisation of mining company sustainability disclosures. *Journal of Cleaner Production, 84*, 51–58.

Deegan, C., & Islam, M. A. (2014). An exploration of NGO and media efforts to influence workplace practices and associated accountability within global supply chains. *The British Accounting Review, 46*(4), 397–415.

Deegan, C., Rankin, M., & Tobin, J. (2002). An examination of the corporate social and environmental disclosures of BHP from 1983–1997: A test of legitimacy theory. *Accounting, Auditing and Accountability Journal, 15*(3), 312–343.

Dhanda, K. K. (2013). Case study in the evolution of sustainability: Baxter international inc. *Journal of Business Ethics, 112*(4), 667–684.

Donaldson, T., & Preston, L. E. (1995). The stakeholder theory of the corporation: Concepts, evidence, and implications. *Academy of Management Review, 20*(1), 65–91.

Du, S., & Vieira, E., Jr. (2012). Striving for legitimacy through corporate social responsibility: Insights from oil companies. *Journal of Business Ethics, 110*(4), 413–427.

Du, S., Bhattacharya, C. B., & Sen, S. (2010). Maximizing business returns to corporate social responsibility (CSR): The role of CSR communication. *International Journal of Management Reviews, 12*(1), 8–19.

Du, X., Jian, W., Zeng, Q., & Du, Y. (2014). Corporate environmental responsibility in polluting industries: Does religion matter? *Journal of Business Ethics, 124*, 485–507.

Dunn, M. B., & Jones, C. (2010). Institutional logics and institutional pluralism: The contestation of care and science logics in medical education, 1967–2005. *Administrative Science Quarterly, 55*(1), 114–149.

Dunning, J. H. (1992). *Multinational enterprises and the global economy* (International business series). Wokingham/Reading/Menlo Park: Addison-Wesley.

Escobar, L. F., & Vredenburg, H. (2011). Multinational oil companies and the adoption of sustainable development: A resource-based and institutional theory interpretation of adoption heterogeneity. *Journal of Business Ethics, 98*(1), 39–65.

Farooq, M. B., Ahmed, A., & Nadeem, M. (2018). Sustainability reporter classification matrix: Explaining variations in disclosure quality. *Meditari Accountancy Research, 26*(2), 334–352.

Ferner, A., Quintanilla, J., & Varul, M. Z. (2001). Country-of-origin effects, host-country effects, and the management of HR in multinationals: German companies in Britain and Spain. *Journal of World Business, 36*(2), 107–127.

Freeman, I., & Hasnaoui, A. (2011). The meaning of corporate social responsibility: The vision of four nations. *Journal of Business Ethics, 100*(3), 419–443.

Friedland, R. (1991). Bringing society back in: Symbols, practices, and institutional contradictions. The new institutionalism in organizational analysis, (pp. 232–263).

Friedman, M. (2007). The social responsibility of business is to increase its profits. In W. C. Zimmerli, K. Richter, & M. Holzinger (Eds.), *Corporate ethics and corporate governance* (pp. 173–178). Berlin/Heidelberg: Springer.

Gao, J., & Bansal, P. (2013). Instrumental and integrative logics in business sustainability. *Journal of Business Ethics, 112*(2), 241–255.

Garcia-Castro, R., Arino, M. A., & Canela, M. A. (2010). Does social performance really lead to financial performance? Accounting for endogeneity. *Journal of Business Ethics, 92*(1), 107–126.

Goodman, M. B., Johansen, T. S., & Nielsen, A. E. (2011). Strategic stakeholder dialogues: A discursive perspective on relationship building. *Corporate Communications: An International Journal, 16*(3), 204–217.

Gospel, H. F., & Pendleton, A. (2005). *Corporate governance and labour management: An international comparison.* Oxford: Oxford University Press.

Greening, D. W., & Turban, D. B. (2000). Corporate social performance as a competitive advantage in attracting a quality workforce. *Business & Society, 39*(3), 254–280.

Guan, J., & Noronha, C. (2013). Corporate social responsibility reporting research in the Chinese academia: A critical review. *Social Responsibility Journal, 9*(1), 33–55.

Hackston, D., & Milne, M. J. (1996). Some determinants of social and environmental disclosures in New Zealand companies. *Accounting, Auditing & Accountability Journal, 9*(1), 77–108.

He, C., & Loftus, J. (2014). Does environmental reporting reflect environmental performance?: Evidence from China. *Pacific Accounting Review, 26*(1–2), 134–154.

Higgins, C., Milne, M. J., & Van Gramberg, B. (2015). The uptake of sustainability reporting in Australia. *Journal of Business Ethics, 129*(2), 445–468.

Hilson, G., Hilson, A., & Adu-Darko, E. (2014). Chinese participation in Ghana's informal gold mining economy: Drivers, implications and clarifications. *Journal of Rural Studies, 34*(0), 292–303.

Ho, L. C. J., & Taylor, M. E. (2007). An empirical analysis of triple bottom-line reporting and its determinants: Evidence from the United States and Japan. *Journal of International Financial Management and Accounting, 18*(2), 123–150.

Hockerts, K., & Moir, L. (2004). Communicating corporate responsibility to investors: The changing role of the investor relations function. *Journal of Business Ethics, 52*(1), 85–98.

Hung, M., Shi, J., & Wang, Y. (2013). *The effect of mandatory CSR disclosure on information asymmetry: Evidence from a quasi-natural experiment in China.* Paper presented at the Asian Finance Association (AsFA) 2013 Conference, Jiangxi.

Islam, M., & Deegan, C. (2008). Motivations for an organisation within a developing country to report social responsibility information: Evidence from Bangladesh. *Accounting, Auditing and Accountability Journal, 21*(6), 850–874.

Ji, S., & Parker, L. (2016). *A decade of CSR, reporting and research in the People's Republic of China: Towards a harmonious social society?* Paper presented at the 8th Asia-Pacific Interdisciplinary Research in Accounting Conference, Melbourne.

Jose, A., & Lee, S.-M. (2007). Environmental reporting of global corporations: A content analysis based on website disclosures. *Journal of Business Ethics, 72*(4), 307–321.

Kapelus, P. (2002). Mining, corporate social responsibility and the" community": The case of Rio Tinto, Richards Bay minerals and the Mbonambi. *Journal of Business Ethics, 39*(3), 275–296.

Kim, S.-Y., & Park, H. (2011). Corporate social responsibility as an organizational attractiveness for prospective public relations practitioners. *Journal of Business Ethics, 103*(4), 639–653.

Kolk, A. (2008). Sustainability, accountability and corporate governance: Exploring multinationals' reporting practices. *Business Strategy and the Environment, 17*(1), 1–15.

Kolk, A., & Lenfant, F. (2010). MNC reporting on CSR and conflict in Central Africa. *Journal of Business Ethics, 93*(2), 241–255.

Kostova, T., & Roth, K. (2002). Adoption of an organizational practice by subsidiaries of multinational corporations: Institutional and relational effects. *Academy of Management Journal, 45*(1), 215–233.

Kostova, T., & Zaheer, S. (1999). Organizational legitimacy under conditions of complexity: The case of the multinational enterprise. *Academy of Management Review, 24*(1), 64–81.

Kostova, T., Roth, K., & Dacin, M. T. (2008). Institutional theory in the study of multinational corporations: A critique and new directions. *Academy of Management Review, 33*(4), 994–1006.

La Cour, A., & Kromann, J. (2011). Euphemisms and hypocrisy in corporate philanthropy. *Business Ethics: A European Review, 20*(3), 267–279.

Lackmann, J., Ernstberger, J., & Stich, M. (2012). Market reactions to increased reliability of sustainability information. *Journal of Business Ethics, 107*(2), 111–128.

Lauwo, S. G., Otusanya, O. J., & Bakre, O. (2016). Corporate social responsibility reporting in the mining sector of Tanzania. *Accounting, Auditing & Accountability Journal, 29*(6), 1038–1074.

Li, S. (2012). The inevitable and difficult transition from relation-based to rule-based governance in China. *Modern China Studies, 21*(1), 145–171.

Li, Y. (2014). A study of the new trend in the development of corporate social responsibility in China. *International Journal of Innovation and Sustainable Development, 8*(2), 112–124.

Lin, Y.-m. (2001). *Between politics and markets : Firms, competition, and institutional change in post-Mao China.* Cambridge: Cambridge University Press.

Liu, X., & Anbumozhi, V. (2009). Determinant factors of corporate environmental information disclosure: An empirical study of Chinese listed companies. *Journal of Cleaner Production, 17*(6), 593–600.

Lodhia, S. (2018). Is the medium the message? *Meditari Accountancy Research, 26*(1), 2–12.

Lucas, K., & Fyke, J. P. (2014). Euphemisms and ethics: A language-centered analysis of Penn State's sexual abuse scandal. *Journal of Business Ethics, 122*(4), 551–569.

Madsen, H., & Ulhøi, J. P. (2001). Integrating environmental and stakeholder management. *Business Strategy and the Environment, 10*(2), 77–88.

Maio, E. (2003). Managing brand in the new stakeholder environment. *Journal of Business Ethics, 44*(2–3), 235–246.

Maon, F., Lindgreen, A., & Swaen, V. (2009). Designing and implementing corporate social responsibility: An integrative framework grounded in theory and practice. *Journal of Business Ethics, 87*(1), 71–89.

Marais, M. (2012). CEO rhetorical strategies for corporate social responsibility (CSR). *Society and Business Review, 7*(3), 223–243.

Marano, V., & Kostova, T. (2016). Unpacking the institutional complexity in adoption of CSR practices in multinational enterprises. *Journal of Management Studies, 53*(1), 28–54.

Marin, L., Ruiz, S., & Rubio, A. (2009). The role of identity salience in the effects of corporate social responsibility on consumer behavior. *Journal of Business Ethics, 84*(1), 65–78.

Marquis, C., & Qian, C. (2014). Corporate social responsibility reporting in China: Symbol or substance? *Organization Science, 25*(1), 127–148.

McGlone, M. S., Beck, G., & Pfiester, A. (2006). Contamination and camouflage in euphemisms. *Communication Monographs, 73*(3), 261–282.

Measures on Open Environmental Information (for Trial Implementation), State Environmental Protection Administration, February 8, 2007, effective May 1, 2008 (Chinese I English).

Metcalf, L., & Benn, S. (2013). Leadership for sustainability: An evolution of leadership ability. *Journal of Business Ethics, 112*(3), 369–384.

Miles, M. P., & Covin, J. G. (2000). Environmental marketing: A source of reputational, competitive, and financial advantage. *Journal of Business Ethics, 23*(3), 299–311.

Momin, M. A., & Parker, L. D. (2013). Motivations for corporate social responsibility reporting by MNC subsidiaries in an emerging country: The case of Bangladesh. *The British Accounting Review, 45*(3), 215–228.

Moore, G. (2001). Corporate social and financial performance: An investigation in the U.K. supermarket industry. *Journal of Business Ethics, 34*(3), 299–315.

Mori, R., Best, P. J., & Cotter, J. (2014). Sustainability reporting and assurance: A historical analysis on a world-wide phenomenon. *Journal of Business Ethics, 120*(1), 1–11.

Morsing, M., & Schultz, M. (2006). Corporate social responsibility communication: Stakeholder information, response and involvement strategies. *Business Ethics: A European Review, 15*(4), 323–338.

Morsing, M., Schultz, M., & Nielsen, K. U. (2008). The 'Catch 22' of communicating CSR: Findings from a Danish study. *Journal of Marketing Communications, 14*(2), 97–111.

Muthuri, J. N., Moon, J., & Idemudia, U. (2012). Corporate innovation and sustainable community development in developing countries. *Business & Society, 51*(3), 355–381.

Narwal, M., & Singh, R. (2013). Corporate social responsibility practices in India: A comparative study of MNCs and Indian companies. *Social Responsibility Journal, 9*(3), 465–478.

Newson, M., & Deegan, C. (2002). Global expectations and their association with corporate social disclosure practices in Australia, Singapore, and South Korea. *The International Journal of Accounting, 37*(2), 183–213.

Nybakk, E., & Panwar, R. (2015). Understanding instrumental motivations for social responsibility engagement in a micro-firm context. *Business Ethics: A European Review, 24*(1), 18–33.

O'Dwyer, B. (2005). Stakeholder democracy: Challenges and contributions from social accounting. *Business Ethics: A European Review, 14*(1), 28–41.

O'Dwyer, B., Unerman, J., & Bradley, J. (2005). Perceptions on the emergence and future development of corporate social disclosure in Ireland. *Accounting, Auditing & Accountability Journal, 18*(1), 14–43.

Pache, A.-C., & Santos, F. (2013). Inside the hybrid organization: Selective coupling as a response to competing institutional logics. *Academy of Management Journal, 56*(4), 972–1001.

Park, S. B. (2018). Multinationals and sustainable development: Does internationalization develop corporate sustainability of emerging market multinationals? *Business Strategy and the Environment, 27*(8), 1514–1524.

Pellegrino, C., & Lodhia, S. (2012). Climate change accounting and the Australian mining industry: Exploring the links between corporate disclosure and the generation of legitimacy. *Journal of Cleaner Production, 36*, 68–82.

Perez, F., & Sanchez, L. E. (2009). Assessing the evolution of sustainability reporting in the mining sector. *Environmental Management, 43*(6), 949–961.

Perez-Batres, L., Miller, V., & Pisani, M. (2010). CSR, sustainability and the meaning of global reporting for Latin American Corporations. *Journal of Business Ethics, 91*(Supplement 2), 193–209.

Porter, M. E., & Kramer, M. R. (2006). The link between competitive advantage and corporate social responsibility. *Harvard Business Review, 84*(12), 78–92.

Powell, W. W., & DiMaggio, P. J. (2012). *The new institutionalism in organizational analysis.* Chicago: University of Chicago Press.

Quaak, L., Aalbers, T., & Goedee, J. (2007). Transparency of corporate social responsibility in Dutch breweries. *Journal of Business Ethics, 76*(3), 293–308.

Rämö, H. (2011). Visualizing the phronetic organization: The case of photographs in CSR reports. *Journal of Business Ethics, 104*(3), 371–387.

Rehbein, K., Logsdon, J., & Buren, H. (2013). Corporate responses to shareholder activists: Considering the dialogue alternative. *Journal of Business Ethics, 112*(1), 137–154.

Regulations of the People's Republic of China on Open Government Information, April 5, 2007, effective May 1, 2008 (Chinese I English).

Reverte, C. (2009). Determinants of corporate social responsibility disclosure ratings by Spanish listed firms. *Journal of Business Ethics, 88*(2), 351–366.

Richter, U. H. (2011). Drivers of change: A multiple-case study on the process of institutionalization of corporate responsibility among three multinational companies. *Journal of Business Ethics, 102*(2), 261–279.

Robinson, M., Kleffner, A., & Bertels, S. (2011). Signaling sustainability leadership: Empirical evidence of the value of DJSI membership. *Journal of Business Ethics, 101*(3), 493–505.

Ruffing, L. (2007). Silent vs. shadow reports: What can we learn from BP's sustainability report versus the financial times? *Social and Environmental Accountability Journal, 27*(1), 9–16.

Scherer, A. G., Palazzo, G., & Matten, D. (2014). The business firm as a political actor: A new theory of the firm for a globalized world. *Business & Society, 53*(2), 143–156.

Schoeneborn, D., & Trittin, H. (2013). Transcending transmission: Towards a constitutive perspective on CSR communication. *Corporate Communications: An International Journal, 18*(2), 193–211.

Schreck, P. (2011). Reviewing the business case for corporate social responsibility: New evidence and analysis. *Journal of Business Ethics, 103*(2), 167–188.

Schultz, F., Castelló, I., & Morsing, M. (2013). The construction of corporate social responsibility in network societies: A communication view. *Journal of Business Ethics, 115*(4), 681–692.

Searcy, C., & Buslovich, R. (2014). Corporate perspectives on the development and use of sustainability reports. *Journal of Business Ethics, 121*(2), 149–169.

Situ, H., & Tilt, C. (2012). Chinese government as a determinant of corporate environmental reporting: A study of large Chinese listed companies. *Journal of the Asia Pacific Centre for Environmental Accountability, 18*(4), 251–286.

Slack, K. (2012). Mission impossible?: Adopting a CSR-based business model for extractive industries in developing countries. *Resources Policy, 37*(2), 179–184.

Sotorrío, L. L., & Sánchez, J. L. F. (2010). Corporate social reporting for different audiences: The case of multinational corporations in Spain. *Corporate Social Responsibility and Environmental Management, 17*(5), 272–283.

Spence, C. (2009). Social and environmental reporting and the corporate ego. *Business Strategy and the Environment, 18*(4), 254–265.

Suchman, M. C. (1995). Managing legitimacy: Strategic and institutional approaches. *Academy of Management Review, 20*(3), 571–610.

Suddaby, R., & Greenwood, R. (2005). Rhetorical strategies of legitimacy. *Administrative Science Quarterly, 50*(1), 35–67.

Surroca, J., Tribó, J. A., & Waddock, S. (2010). Corporate responsibility and financial performance: The role of intangible resources. *Strategic Management Journal, 31*(5), 463–490.

Tan, J. (2009). Institutional structure and firm social performance in transitional economies: Evidence of multinational corporations in China. *Journal of Business Ethics, 86*(2), 171–189.

Tan, J., & Tan, D. (2003). A dynamic view of organizational transformation: The changing face of Chinese SOEs under transition. *Journal of Leadership & Organizational Studies, 10*(2), 98–112.

Tewari, R., & Dave, D. (2012). Corporate social responsibility: Communication through sustainability reports by Indian and multinational companies. *Global Business Review, 13*(3), 393–405.

Thornton, P. H. (2002). The rise of the corporation in a craft industry: Conflict and conformity in institutional logics. *Academy of Management Journal, 45*(1), 81–101.

Thornton, P. H., Ocasio, W., & Lounsbury, M. (2012). *The institutional logics perspective: Foundations, research, and theoretical elaboration.* Oxford: Oxford University Press.

Tilt, C. A. (2016). Corporate social responsibility research: The importance of context. *International Journal of Corporate Social Responsibility, 1*(1), 1–9.

Tilt, C. A. (2018). Making social and environmental accounting research relevant in developing countries: A matter of context? *Social and Environmental Accountability Journal, 38*(2), 145–150.

Unctad, U. (2017). *World Investment Report 2017: investment and the digital economy.* Paper presented at the United Nations Conference on Trade and Development, United Nations, Geneva.

Unerman, J. (2008). Strategic reputation risk management and corporate social responsibility reporting. *Accounting, Auditing & Accountability Journal, 21*(3), 362–364.

Van Huijstee, M., & Glasbergen, P. (2008). The practice of stakeholder dialogue between multinationals and NGOs. *Corporate Social Responsibility and Environmental Management, 15*(5), 298–310.

Wagner, M. (2010). The role of corporate sustainability performance for economic performance: A firm-level analysis of moderation effects. *Ecological Economics, 69*(7), 1553–1560.

Wang, F., Cheng, Z., Keung, C., & Reisner, A. (2014). Impact of manager characteristics on corporate environmental behavior at heavy-polluting firms in Shaanxi, China. *Journal of Cleaner Production, 108*, 707–715.

Weber, M. (2008). The business case for corporate social responsibility: A company-level measurement approach for CSR. *European Management Journal, 26*(4), 247–261.

Xiao, H., & Yuan, J. (2007). Ownership structure, board composition and corporate voluntary disclosure: Evidence from listed companies in China. *Managerial Auditing Journal, 22*(6), 604–619.

Xu, D., & Shenkar, O. (2002). Note: Institutional distance and the multinational enterprise. *Academy of Management Review, 27*(4), 608–618.

Yang, H., Craig, R., & Farley, A. (2014). A review of Chinese and English language studies on corporate environmental reporting in China. *Critical Perspectives on Accounting, 28*, 30–48.

Compliance of Listed Companies with Codes of Corporate Governance and Impact on Corporate Performance: Evidence from Sri Lanka

D. H. S. W. Dissanayake, D. B. P. H. Dissabandara, and A. R. Ajward

23.1 Introduction

At the beginning of the twenty-first century, fraud cases involving Enron (USA), One.Tel (Australia), WorldCom (USA), Tyco (USA), Adelphia (USA), Parmalat (Italy), Ahold (Netherlands), Notel (Canada), Satyam Computer Services (India), Golden Key (Sri Lanka), and Pramuka Bank (Sri Lanka) were corporate scandals experienced in the world. These reiterated the need for better corporate governance in the economies, and new corporate governance codes have been adopted and various researches conducted to implement this system (Tricker 2015). The corporate governance concept of the twenty-first century indicated a culture and climate of consistency, responsibility, accountability, fairness, transparency, and effectiveness deployed throughout the organization, thereby increasing organizational performance. On the other hand, various scholars have measured the impact of the concept of corporate governance on corporate performance on the basis of the agency theory and the stakeholder theory and examined it on the basis of the equilibrium variable analysis and the corporate governance index (CGI) model (Ntim 2009). Under the

D. H. S. W. Dissanayake (✉)
Department of Accountancy, Faculty of Business Studies and Finance,
Wayamba University of Sri Lanka, Kuliyapitiya, Sri Lanka
e-mail: hiranya@wyb.ac.lk

D. B. P. H. Dissabandara
Department of Finance, Faculty of Management Studies and Commerce,
University of Sri Jayewardenepura, Nugegoda, Sri Lanka
e-mail: dissa@sjp.ac.lk

A. R. Ajward
Department of Accounting, Faculty of Management Studies and Commerce,
University of Sri Jayewardenepura, Nugegoda, Sri Lanka
e-mail: ajward@sjp.ac.lk

© The Author(s), under exclusive license to Springer Nature
Switzerland AG 2021
S. Dhiman, R. Samaratunge (eds.), *New Horizons in Management, Leadership and Sustainability*, Future of Business and Finance,
https://doi.org/10.1007/978-3-030-62171-1_23

CGI model, some researchers have used already established indices, while other researchers have constructed an index of their own, which renders the results of these research studies inconclusive.

The academic research in corporate governance was initiated in the early 1980s, and up to today a continuous research process is taking place (Tricker 2015). The main objective of the research in this field is to solve the problems that arose in the world based on the corporate scandals. These scandals occurred mainly due to non-compliance with corporate governance. The main inconclusive area of corporate governance research, however, is the relationship between corporate governance and corporate performance, which according to some researchers is a positive relationship between corporate governance and corporate performance (Gompers et al. 2003; Drobetz et al. 2004; Beiner et al. 2006). Corporate governance mechanisms result in improving shareholder perceptions and solving agency problems and, thus, improving corporate performance. On the other hand, some researchers (Bebchuk et al. 2009; Chhaochharia and Grinstein 2007) have shown a negative relationship between corporate governance and corporate performance. They have shown that restrictive corporate governance provisions may restrict the management as to its performance, which may lead to a reduction of corporate performance. The validity of this research is limited to small and medium firms, and its findings may vary with the size of the firm.

Sri Lankan researchers have also studied the level of corporate governance and the impact on corporate governance based on the agency theory. Heenetigala and Armstrong (2011) focused on the 2003–2007 period, when the country faced political and financial instability, using 37 companies for their research, which was conducted in economic settings different from today and using only secondary data from annual reports. Manawaduge (2012) used 60 companies and covered the 2001–2009 period and applied the CGI model to analyze the impact of corporate governance on corporate performance on an overall basis, and he conducted an in-depth investigation of the relationship of ownership concentration and corporate performance. He constructed the CGI model for his study, which was based on the Corporate Governance Code of Sri Lanka (2008), Listing Rules of the Colombo Stock Exchange (CSE) (2009), and the Organisation for Economic Co-operation and Development (OECD) Code (2004).

Sri Lanka was embroiled in an internal armed conflict from about 1980 to 2009, and the postwar economic situation (i.e., after 2009) in the country is different from that of the prewar period. In 2018, per capita gross domestic product was USD 4102, which in 2005 was only USD 1241 (Central Bank of Sri Lanka 2018). This reveals the growth of the economy and positioning of the country in the upper middle-income category in 2019 (World Bank 2019). The economic background to the corporate governance issues of the time is different from that of studies conducted in the prewar period in Sri Lanka. Furthermore, in 2017, an updated corporate governance code was introduced by the Chartered Accountants of Sri Lanka (CASL) to meet the current ongoing requirements arising from the changes taking place in the country (CASL 2017). Research conducted in other countries reveals that the impact on corporate performance has changed with time and changes in governance.

In accordance with the information discussed above, the main objective of this study is to construct a comprehensive CGI to measure corporate governance based on the overall level of compliance of listed companies in Sri Lanka with the Chartered Institute of Sri Lanka Code (2017), OECD Code (2015), and the United Kingdom (UK) Code (2016) and to examine the relationship between compliance with these corporate governance principles and the corporate performance of Sri Lankan listed companies.

The remainder of this study is organized as follows: the subsequent section discusses the theoretical perspectives of corporate governance and performance, followed by a discussion of the existing empirical literature. The next section addresses the methodology, and section 4 discusses the key findings of the study. The final section presents the conclusions and also notes the limitations of the study and future research directions.

23.2 Review of Current Literature

23.2.1 Theoretical Perspective of Corporate Governance and Firm Performance

Corporate governance is vital to the management and operation of modern companies, and there is an ongoing debate about which theoretical models are appropriate (Letza et al. 2004). Furthermore, a lack of consensus on the definition of corporate governance has resulted in researchers from different backgrounds (finance, economics, sociology, and psychology) proposing different theoretical views that are all aimed at understanding the complex nature of the concept (Lawal 2012).

A number of diverse fundamental theories underlie corporate governance, including the original agency theory, stewardship theory, stakeholder theory, resource dependency theory, transaction cost theory, and political theory (Abdullah and Valentine 2009). Nevertheless, most discussions on corporate governance theories have focused on the shareholders and the stakeholders' perspectives (Letza et al. 2004; Vinten 2001). The purpose of the corporation and its associated structure of governance and arrangements are determined by two paradigms, each suggesting a different way of understanding governance (Ayuso and Argandona 2009). Consequently, this research used two theories, namely the agency theory and the stakeholder theory, to establish the relationship between corporate governance and performance in listed companies based in Sri Lanka, which are discussed next.

23.2.1.1 Agency Theory

The separation of ownership and control is one of the key features of modern corporations, and corporate governance mechanisms have become necessary to mitigate the principal-agent problem (Berle and Means 1932). The agency problem was first highlighted by Smith (1776) in the eighteenth century and explored by Ross (1973), with the first detailed description of the theory presented by Jensen and Meckling in 1976. The agency relationship is described by Jensen and Meckling (1976) as a contract under which one or more persons (the principals) engage another person (the agent) to perform some service on their behalf, which involves delegating some decision-making authority to the agent.

Fama and Jensen (1983a, b), Williamson (1987), and Aghion and Bolton (1992) further explicated this problem over the next two decades. The agency theory evolved from the economic literature and developed along two separate streams: the positivist agency theory and the principal agent theory. The positivist agency theory describes the conflicting relationship in terms of the goals between principals and agents and explains that governance mechanisms are established to resolve these conflicts. On the other hand, the principal-agent theory discusses this relationship as a general relationship between principals and agents (Eisenhardt 1989). Both streams concern the contracting problem of self-interest as a motivator for both the principal and the agent, and they share common assumptions regarding people, organizations, and information. However, they differ in mathematical orientation, modeling effects, and constraints used (Jensen 1983). The objectives of corporate governance mechanisms are to "protect shareholder interests, minimize agency cost and ensure agent–principal interest alignment" (Davis et al. 1997, p. 23). According to Shleifer and Vishny (1997) and Kiel and Nicholson (2003), the agency theory suggests that the separation of the positions of chairman and CEO leads to higher performance. Fama (1980) contends that the appointment of nonexecutive directors to a board is designed to control management issues and is intended to have a positive effect on the firm's performance (Fama and Jensen 1983b; Jensen and Meckling 1976). Barnhart and Rosenstein (1998) emphasized that larger boards seem to be less helpful and more difficult to coordinate, resulting in a negative effect on performance.

23.2.1.2   Stakeholder Theory

The stakeholder theory has been developing continuously over the past three decades. Freeman (1984) was one of the first theorists to present the stakeholder theory as inherent in management discipline. Freeman also proposed a general theory applicable to firms based on the premise that firms should be accountable to a broad range of stakeholders (Solomon and Solomon 2004). Freeman (1984, p. VI) defines stakeholders as "any group or individual who can effect or is effected by the achievement of a corporation's purpose." Thus, the term stakeholder may cover a large group of participants; in fact, it applies to anyone who has a direct or indirect stake in the business (Carroll and Buchholtz 2007). Stakeholders include shareholders, employees, suppliers, customers, creditors, and communities within the vicinity of the company's operations, in addition to the public (Solomon and Solomon 2004).

According to Clarke (2004), if corporate managers are there to maximize the total wealth of the organization, they must take into account the effects of their decisions on all stakeholders. Pesqueux and Damak-Ayadi (2005) show that the practice of stakeholder management will result in higher profitability, stability, and growth and will thus affect the firm's performance. Consequently, good corporate governance must focus on creating a feeling of security that a company will consider the interests of stakeholders, as the board of directors is responsible for the company as well as its stakeholders (Ljubojevic and Ljubojevic 2011). According to Jensen (2001), the stakeholder theory solves the problems caused by multiple objectives as it seeks to maximize value in the long term. Moreover, if the management of a firm does not take into account the interests of all of its stakeholders, the firm cannot be maximizing its value.

The integration of the agency and stakeholder theories stresses the special role of the company towards the shareholders and all other stakeholders. Hill and Jones (1992) proposed that the stakeholder-agency paradigm explicitly focused on the causes of conflict between managers and stakeholders. In addition, the stakeholder-agency theory highlights the concepts underlying the alignment of management and stakeholder interests in the conflict of such interests. The agency theory calls for governance mechanisms to provide sufficient monitoring or control methods to protect shareholders from conflicts of interests with agents. The stakeholder theory, however, enables fostering good relationships with a range of stakeholders and emphasizes corporate efficiency in a social context; it also underpins the corporation's purpose of maximizing shareholders' wealth. Hence, using both theories is the most effective approach, as compared to other governance theories, because it involves combining all the elements of corporate governance to improve the firm's performance. This study relies on the agency theory-stakeholder theory, which suit the nature and scope of the empirical work. Hence, the stakeholder-agency theories could provide some useful insights in the current research.

23.2.2 Compliance Index Model and Firm Financial Performance: Developed Countries

The study of Gompers et al. (2003) is considered to be a pioneering study investigating the relationship between a composite corporate governance index and the firm's performance (Bauer et al. 2010). They constructed the Gompers, Ishii, and Metrick (GIM) index, consisting of 24 governance provisions extracted from the Investor Responsibility Research Centre (IRRC). Using a sample of 1500 large US firms from 1990 to 1999, Gompers et al. (2003) found that good corporate governance practices improved the firm's value, profitability, and sales growth. Subsequently, in a number of studies, the GIM index was adopted to further investigate the governance-performance relationship among US listed firms (e.g., Cremers and Nair 2005; Bhagat and Bolton 2008; Bebchuk et al. 2009). For example, Brown and Caylor (2006) found a significant and positive link between the constructed governance index and Tobin's Q among 1868 US firms.

Similarly, Bauer et al. (2010) adopted a corporate governance quotient (CGQ) index consisting of 61 provisions to examine its relationship with financial performance, using a sample of about 210 US firms from 2003 to 2005. They found a significant and positive relationship between the CGQ index and financial performance. Giroud and Mueller (2011) used the governance ratings of GIM to examine the relationship in US firms. They found out that weak corporate governance practices lead to lower equity returns, poor operating performance, lower firm value, and lower propensity to pay dividends. Recently, Gordon et al. (2012) revealed that financial performance measured by the Q-ratio is positively related to a constructed corporate governance index in a small sample of Canadian firms. Similarly, Drobetz et al. (2004) constructed a broad corporate governance rating index (CGR) consisting of 30 governance provisions. Using a sample of 91 publicly traded German firms in 2002, they found that firms with better corporate governance showed good financial performance. In the UK, Clacher et al. (2008) found a positive relationship between the level of compliance with corporate governance and Tobin's Q/ROA in a sample of 63 firms from 2003 to 2005. To investigate this relationship, they developed a corporate governance index using the UK Combined Code (2003), which was derived from the main recommendations of the London Stock Exchange. These findings are consistent with the theoretical expectation that a high level of compliance with corporate governance standards can help reduce agency costs and increase shareholders' returns (e.g., Jensen and Meckling 1976; Shleifer and Vishny 1997).

In contrast to the findings of previous US studies reviewed above, Chhaochharia and Grinstein (2007) revealed a negative relationship between corporate governance and the firm's performance. They constructed a governance index of five main provisions to examine a sample of 312 US firms in 2001 and 2002. Similarly, Bebchuk et al. (2009) revealed a negative relationship between a composite corporate governance index (entrenchment index, hereinafter "E-index") and a firm's value. This negative relationship may imply that the costs of implementing good corporate governance practices possibly outweigh the associated benefits (see Ammann et al. 2013).

However, other studies conducted in the US and Canada suggest that there is no significant relationship between corporate governance indices and a firm's performance (e.g., Klein et al. 2005; Koehn and Ueng 2005; Epps and Cereola 2008; Daines et al. 2010). Lehn et al. (2007) used both GIM and Bebchuk, Cohen, and Ferrell's (BCF) 29 indices to examine 1500 firms in a six-year window from 1990 to 2002. They reported that there is no significant relationship between corporate governance practices and firm performance, as measured by the market-to-book ratio. Similarly, Epps and Cereola (2008) revealed no statistically significant evidence to support the correlation between the CGQ index and firms' operating performance, as measured by ROA and ROE among 230 US listed firms from 2002 to 2004. In Canada, Klein et al. (2005) and Gupta et al. (2009) used the report on business (ROB) index, and both found no evidence of overall governance mechanisms helping to improve the firm's performance. Interestingly, Daines et al. (2010) used four corporate governance indices, CGQ, Governance Metrics International (GMI), AGR, and TCL (The Corporate Library), to study a large sample of 6827 US listed firms. They revealed no significant relationship between compliance with good corporate governance practices and the firm's value.

The summary of literature related to CGI and corporate performance in developed countries is depicted in Appendix 23.1.

23.2.3 Compliance Index Model and Firm Financial Performance: Emerging Countries

A number of studies examined the link between governance compliance indices and financial performance in emerging economies (Cheung et al. 2011; Garay and Gonzalez 2008; Price et al. 2011; Black et al. 2012; Munisi and Randøy 2013; Tariq and Abbas 2013). Appendix 23.2 gives a summary of the findings of previous studies conducted in emerging countries on the relationship between composite corporate governance indices and the firm's financial performance.

Bai et al. (2004) reported a positive effect of corporate governance on the firm's value, as measured by Tobin's Q, among 1051 Chinese listed firms from 1999 to 2001. In the same context, Cheung et al. (2011) analyzed 168 large Hong Kong firms and constructed a corporate governance index based on the OECD standards and the Hong Kong Code. They found a positive governance-performance relationship using the market-to-book ratio. Similarly, Varshney et al. (2012) constructed a corporate governance index of 11 provisions using 105 Indian listed firms in 2012 and reported a positive effect of governance on performance. Haldar and Nageswara Rao (2013) also revealed that the firm's performance is positively affected by good corporate governance practices among a sample of Indian listed firms. Specifically, they studied 500 Indian firms from 2008 to 2011 using firm and market performance measures. Furthermore, Garay and Gonzalez (2008) constructed a corporate governance index of 17 provisions using 46 Venezuelan listed firms in 2004 and reported a positive effect of governance on performance.

In contrast to the evidence of a positive effect of good corporate governance on the firm's performance reported in studies elaborated above in the context of developing countries, Price et al. (2011) revealed that the firm's performance is not affected by good corporate governance practices among a sample of Mexican listed firms. Specifically, they studied 107 Mexican firms from 2000 to 2004 using firm and market performance measures.

Generally, the evidence in Appendix 23.2 suggests that the findings of the majority of previous studies conducted in emerging economies show a positive association with the firm's financial performance.

23.3 Development of Research Hypotheses

In the Sri Lankan context, corporate governance principles are considered a vibrant element in improving a firm's performance, and the conceptual framework (see Fig. 23.1) of this study based on the extant literature establishes the link between the corporate governance elements and the firm's performance. Accordingly, the independent variable used in this study is the corporate governance index constructed with 200 elements of different corporate governance dimensions and its main sub-indexes, including elements based on the main governance principles: board of directors, transparency and disclosure, shareholders, stakeholders, and CEO and management. The dependent variables were identified as the firm's performance

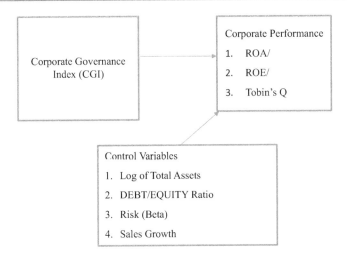

Fig. 23.1 Conceptual framework. (Source: Constructed by the authors)

proxied by Tobin's Q, return on assets (ROA), and return on equity (ROE), whereas the control variables used in this study are firm growth, leverage, firm size, and firm risk. The extant literature has established a positive relationship between superior corporate governance and financial performance (Gompers et al. 2003; Black et al. 2006), and thus the following hypothesis is established in this study:

H_1: The degree of compliance with good corporate governance principles is positively associated with corporate financial performance.

Empirical evidence suggests a positive relationship between corporate governance and market performance proposed by various scholars (Brown and Caylor 2006; Garay and Gonzalez 2008). Therefore, the second hypothesis of this study is as follows:

H_2: The degree of compliance with good corporate governance principles is positively associated with corporate market performance.

23.4   Methodology

This study is based on a positivist paradigm and therefore uses deductive reasoning and quantitative techniques, which are deemed appropriate for examining the relationship between the level of compliance and the degree of corporate financial performance. The data for the study were collected from secondary data sources, and the population consisted of public companies incorporated under the Companies Act No. 7 of 2007 (Sri Lanka) and listed in the Colombo Stock Exchange. The time period of 2009–2016 was selected because Sri Lanka has reached an upper middle-income status in 2017 (CBSL, 2019) and several corporate governance codes were introduced to meet global governance requirements during 1997 to 2017.

Table 23.1 Sample selection

Sector	No. of companies in CSE	First sample selected	Exclusion of firms listed after 2009	Final sample	Representation from the total population
Bank finance and assurance	60	38	16	22	36.67
Beverage food and tobacco	21	14		14	66.67
Chemicals and pharmaceuticals	10	5		5	50
Construction and engineering	4	3	1	2	50
Diversified holdings	19	17	6	11	57.89
Footwear and textiles	3	0	0	0	0
Closed end	0	0	0	0	0
Health care	6	6	1	5	83.33
Hotels and travels	37	15		15	40.54
Information and technology	2	0		0	0
Investments	9	5		5	55.56
Land and property	19	7		7	36.84
Manufacturing	37	18	2	16	43.24
Motors	6	3		3	50
Oil palm	5	5	·	5	100
Plantations	19	5		5	26.32
Power and energy	8	5	1	4	50
Services	8	5	2	3	37.5
Store supplies	4	4		4	100
Telecommunication	2	2		2	100
Trading	8	5		5	62.5
	287	150		133	46.34

Source: Constructed by the authors

The data used cover the 2009 to 2016 period, and the stratified sampling method was applied to select firms with the sector-wise highest market capitalization as at December 31, 2016. Table 23.1 shows the sample for this study. The conceptual framework (Fig. 23.1) illustrates the link between the theoretical framework and the operationalization of the corporate governance variables and performance of the firms investigated in this study.

Operationalization of the Variables

Table 23.2 elaborates the operationalization of the variables in this study.

Table 23.2 Operationalization of variables

Variable and denotation	Measurement	Related studies
Corporate governance (CGI)	See *Note 01* below	
Return on equity (*ROE*)	Net profit after tax/book value of equity	Mapitiya (2015)
Return on assets (*ROA*)	Earnings before interest and tax/book value of assets	Price et al. (2011)
Tobin's Q	Market capitalization/assets' replacement cost	Black et al. (2006)
Leverage (*DE*)	Total liabilities/total equity	Cheung et al. (2011)
Firm size (*lnTA*)	Natural logarithm of total assets	Cheung et al. (2011)
Firm risk (*Risk*)	Beta (covariance/variance of the stock market)	
Firm growth (*Growth*)	Sales growth	Cheung et al. (2011)

Source: Constructed by the authors

Table 23.3 Weights of CGI

Area	BO	SH	CEO	DI	ST	CGI
Assessor 1	45	10	20	15	10	100
Assessor 2	45	20	10	15	10	100
Assessor 3	60	10	10	10	10	100
Assessor 4	35	20	20	15	10	100
Assessor 5	90	10	0	0	0	100
Final weight assigned	275	70	60	55	40	500
CGI	55	14	12	11	8	100

Source: Constructed by the authors

Note 1: CGI is calculated from the information gathered from the selected sample of Sri Lankan listed companies by means of performing a structured content analysis and measures corporate governance practices in the listed companies, which consist of 200 diverse evaluation measures set as per the OECD Principles of Corporate Governance (OECD 2015), CA Sri Lanka Code (2017), and UK Code (2016). These measures are then classified into five categories, namely, responsibilities of the board of directors (*BO*), the role of stakeholders (*ST*), the role of shareholders (*SH*), disclosure and transparency (*DI*), and chief executive officer and management (*CEO*). The five main criteria were weighted according to five experts. The weights assigned by the five expert assessors are given in Table 23.3.

The weighting of marks is determined in order to allocate each of the abovementioned governance criteria according to the importance of such areas on corporate governance based on a survey conducted by research involving five professionals and academics, as detailed below, who, at the time of the survey, held the following positions:

Assessor 1 – the Chairman of Securities and Exchange Commission (SEC) Sri Lanka
Assessor 2 – a director of SEC

Assessor 3 – a senior academic specialized in corporate governance and finance
Assessor 4 – a director from CSE
Assessor 5 – a director from CASL

The checklist used under the structured content analysis was prepared according to the weights. Likert scale questions were prepared, and the checklist was completed based on the contents of the annual reports of the respective companies. The construction of the index was straightforward. Each attribute of the 200 items within a specified governance mechanism was scored on a scale of 0 to 5 for each checklist component, which was based on the response to the satisfactory implementation of corporate governance practice within the firm. Next, the score across all the attributes within the specific subindex were divided by the maximum possible score and multiplied by the weight. For each of the five corporate governance components (which were elaborated above), i.e., *SH*, *ST*, *DI*, *BO*, and *CEO*, subindexes were developed. The next step was calculating the mean of the scores calculated separately for each company. The scores of the index included the responses mentioned in the content analysis of annual reports regarding corporate governance. The formula below was used to calculate the CGI:

$$\text{CGI}(100) = \text{SH}(14) + \text{ST}(8) + \text{DI}(11) + \text{BO}(5) + \text{CEO}(12)$$

It was used to determine the ranking of each company, which varied according to the corporate governance score (out of 100) the company gained. These scores form the basis of the subsequent analyses.

23.5   Analytical Strategies

The first objective of this study was achieved by computing descriptive statistics of the governance index to measure the level of corporate governance in Sri Lanka. As explained in the preceding section, a measure of corporate governance was created by awarding weighted points for each of the principles that a company was compliant with, giving each company its own corporate governance score. This corporate governance measure was used to determine the ranking of each company as high, medium, or low based on the corporate governance score (out of 100) that the company gained. In compliance with CGI, the researchers classified the companies into four main groups, namely, low CGI (with a CGI score of 0–40), low medium CGI (with a CGI score of 40–60), upper medium CGI (60–80), and higher CGI (with a CGI score of 80–100).

Second, the impact of compliance with corporate governance practices on the firm's performance was examined using the CGI and financial and market performance. The impact was statistically verified using correlation analysis and panel regression analysis after conducting diagnosis tests and the Hausman test. The general regression equations are as follows:

$$\text{ROA} = \beta_0 + \beta_1 \text{CGI} + \beta_2 \ln\text{TA} + \beta_3 \text{DE} + \beta_4 \text{Growth} + \beta_5 \text{Risk} + \varepsilon \qquad \text{Model 01}$$

$$\text{ROE} = \beta_0 + \beta_1 \text{CGI} + \beta_2 \ln\text{TA} + \beta_3 \text{DE} + \beta_4 \text{Growth} + \beta_5 \text{Risk} + \varepsilon \qquad \text{Model 02}$$

$$\text{Tobin's Q} = \beta_0 + \beta_1 \text{CGI} + \beta_2 \ln\text{TA} + \beta_3 \text{DE} + \beta_4 \text{Growth} + \beta_5 \text{Risk} + \varepsilon \qquad \text{Model 03}$$

23.6   Key Findings

According to the descriptive analysis (Table 23.4), the mean compliance level with corporate governance principles (as measured via the corporate governance index (CGI)) during the 2009 to 2016 period was 54.27%. Manawaduge (2012), in his study, found that the mean compliance level was 61.17%, and Dissabandara (2010) found that the mean compliance level of the board index was 56%. Accordingly, it is observed that the overall level of compliance is quite low and consistent with extant studies. Table 23.4 also depicts the descriptive statistics of CGI and performance variables.

According to the CGI, as reported in Table 23.5, in 2016 companies had been classified as firms with high compliance, moderate compliance, and low compliance. The main groups fall in the 20–40 range, 40–60 range, 60–80 range, and 80–100 range. In the sample, in 2016, 14 companies scored CGI values below 40 and 11 companies above 80, while most of the companies (62) scored a CGI value between 40 and 60, as shown in Table 23.5.

According to the findings of Dissabandara (2010), in the year 2008, the number of companies with low CGS scores was 10 out of 59 and corresponded to a percentage of 17%. However, based on our findings presented in Table 23.5 above, the number of low-compliance companies are 14 in the year 2016, which is 10% of the total sample. This indicates an improvement of corporate governance over time in terms of compliance.

Results of the sectoral comparison of CGI for the year 2016 are shown in Table 23.6. The highest mean of compliance level (79.845) is in the telecommunication sector. According to the empirical findings of Dissabandara (2010), the banking sector's CGI score (with board components) is highest in 2009 but is the third highest in 2016, according to this study (Table 23.6). Furthermore, the second highest CGI (68.973) is in the diversified sector, which is consistent with the findings of Dissabandara (2010). Moreover, the lowest score is observed in the service sector (27.091).

Table 23.7 indicates the extent of correlation between the overall index score and performance variables used in this study. It shows a positive relationship between

Table 23.4 Descriptive statistics of CGI and performance variables

Variable	Mean	Skewness	Kurtosis	Minimum value	Maximum value
CGI	54.273	0.343	−0.554	32.543	78.800
CGI-SH	49.910	2.020	2.760	42.860	84.760
CGI-ST	50.570	0.060	−1.430	0.000	100.000
CGI-DI	76.520	−1.130	0.380	43.750	93.750
CGI-BO	52.960	0.700	−0.400	32.730	84.940
CGI-CEO	47.160	−0.380	−1.630	12.500	75.000
ROA	0.060	1.330	4.590	−0.030	0.230
ROE	0.130	1.320	4.630	−0.060	0.492
Tobin's Q	0.760	2.290	8.720	0.590	4.220

Source: Constructed by the authors

Table 23.5 Classification of firms according to CGI levels in 2016

Category	CGI 2016 Levels	Mean	Obs.
Low	[20, 40]	34.396	14
Low medium	[40, 60]	53.069	62
Upper medium	[60, 80]	67.023	46
High	[80, 100]	83.401	11
	All	58.438	133

Source: Constructed by the authors

Table 23.6 CGI comparison of sectors in the year 2016

Sector	Mean (2016)
Telecommunication	79.845
Diversified	68.973
Banking	65.252
Hotels	64.549
Manufacturing	62.785
Energy	61.782
Chemicals	58.93
Beverage	57.151
Investments	56.935
Motors	55.755
Plantations	54.011
Construction	53.431
Trading	47.243
Land	47.23
Health care	46.882
Oil palms	45.533
Stores	37.411
Services	27.091

Source: Constructed by the authors

CGI and the financial performance measure. The overall sample showed a statistically significant positive relationship between the CGI and ROE at the 1-percent level ($p < 0.01$), indicating increased financial performance with increased compliance with corporate governance.

However, in the overall sample, Tobin's Q is negatively related to CGI, suggesting that high compliance with corporate governance causes an unexpected negative impact on market performance. Thus, it is difficult to establish a clear relationship between corporate governance and performance of Sri Lankan firms. The relationship between corporate and *financial* performance is positive, whereas it is negative for *market* performance measures.

The panel data regression analysis (Table 23.8) shows a positive relationship between the degree of compliance with corporate governance practices and company financial performance in terms of ROA and ROE, as proposed by the

Table 23.7 Results of Pearson correlation

Variables	CGI	ROA	ROE
CGI	1		
ROA	0.020	1	
ROE	0.111**	0.710**	1
Tobin's Q	−0.130**	0.389**	0.297**

The definitions of these variables are indicated in Table 23.4

For the sample of 133 firms

$*p < 0.05; **p < 0.01$

Table 23.8 Results of panel regression

Models	Model 01-ROA		Model 02-ROE		Model 03-*Tobin's Q*	
	Coefficient	Standard error	Coefficient	Standard error	Coefficient	Standard error
CGI	0.0012**	0.0004	0.0011**	0.0007	−0.0078**	0.003
Risk	0.0034	0.0026	0.0046	0.0052	0.0848**	0.0217
DE	−0.0070**	0.0015	−0.0016	0.0030	0.0136	0.0126
Growth	0.0005**	0.0001	0.0011**	0.0002	0.0025**	0.0006
lnTA	−0.0110**	0.0028	−0.0055	0.0056	−0.2584**	0.0234

The definitions of these variables are given in Table 23.4

For the sample of 133 firms

$*p < 0.05; **p < 0.01$

conceptual framework of the study. According to Table 23.8, the regressions are significant at the 95% confidence level. Since the results show a significant positive relationship between corporate governance and financial performance, hypothesis H_1 is supported. These results are supported by prior research on the relationship between corporate governance practices and financial performance. One of the earliest studies of the relationship of governance and performance was by Gompers et al. (2003), who found a strong positive correlation between the firms' performance and the quality of their corporate governance. Furthermore, studies such as by Okike and Turton (2009), Bauer et al. (2010), and Chang et al. (2014) found a positive relationship between corporate governance and financial performance. Also, a positive relationship between corporate governance and firm financial performance was found for emerging market studies (Bai et al. 2002; Campbell II and Keys 2002; Klapper and Love 2004; Black et al. 2003; Durnev and Kim 2005, as cited by Klein et al. 2005). Mapitiya (2015) showed that governance practices have a significant positive relationship with corporate financial performance in terms of profitability in public listed companies in Sri Lanka.

Nevertheless, market performance (i.e., measured via Tobin's Q) showed a negative relationship with corporate governance compliance (Table 23.8), which is inferred as due to the market anomalies that prevailed in the Sri Lankan market at that time. The results of the market performance are consistent with the findings of previous researches carried out based on the quality of corporate governance and firms' performance in Sri Lanka. Manawaduge (2009) specifically found out that compliance with corporate governance principles caused a negative impact on market prices in Sri Lanka due to market anomalies. In addition to these findings, differences in compliance were noted in the industry sectors, where in certain sectors (telecommunication, diversified industry, and banking) high compliance was noted and in other sectors (service, store, and trading) a low level of compliance was observed.

23.7   Conclusions and Recommendations

This study helps to fill the wide gap in the literature on corporate governance practices in Sri Lanka. Its main contribution stems from the investigation of corporate governance in Sri Lanka from a broader and more comprehensive approach where a comprehensive corporate governance index was used in this study, which was based on the CA Sri Lanka, OECD, and UK codes of corporate governance. Furthermore, this is a pioneering study to use a weighted average corporate governance index to measure compliance with corporate governance principles. This study also used a sample of 133 firms out of the 297 listed companies, which is close to half the population. Thus, this study used a relatively higher sample than in other extant studies. This investigation is also expected to contribute to knowledge of corporate governance not only in Sri Lanka but also in other developing countries.

In terms of findings, the mean compliance level of corporate governance in Sri Lanka indicated a quite low level of compliance of 54.27 (out of 100). Furthermore, it was also noted that there are significant differences among different sectors considered in this study in terms of the level of compliance. In addition, this study indicates that companies that comply with good corporate governance practices can expect to achieve better *financial* performance. These findings have significant implications and can be recommended for using good corporate governance practices across developing countries in general and in emerging countries in particular. Further, the findings provide a clear understanding of quite lower compliance levels and sectoral differences in the compliance levels in Sri Lanka and points out that policy makers, regulators, academics, the community, CA Sri Lanka, and SEC should take active steps to improve the situation. The implications for a policy from this research are expected to help policy makers and regulators identify areas of development in corporate governance that are in need of immediate attention.

The findings of the study provide extensive evidence regarding corporate governance practices and their effect on firms' performance. However, certain limitations of the study should be taken into account when considering the conclusions that can be drawn. One of the limitations of this study is that the research is based on secondary data and only considers the annual reports owing to the difficulty of obtaining primary data from 133 companies. Another limitation is that it used only two financial performance indicators (ROA and ROE) and one measure of the market (Tobin's Q) to determine company performance. Furthermore, this research covers only a seven-year period due to the nonavailability of data. Future research could examine corporate governance best practices and firms' performance over a longer period as well as perform comparative studies among countries using a comprehensive compliance index as well as mixed methods of study.

Chapter Takeaways

1. The level of compliance with corporate governance principles by firms could be comprehensively measured by a corporate governance index (CGI), which provides a broader picture on corporate governance. This index could include five broad subindexes: board of directors subindex, shareholders subindex, chief executive officer (CEO) and management subindex, communication and disclosure subindex, and stakeholders subindex.
2. Corporate governance and performance relationship is formulated based on various theories, including mainly the agency theory and the stakeholder theory.
3. The findings on the relationship between corporate governance and performance vary with the time period, country, industry sector, the way the variables are measured, and the data analysis method used.
4. In the context of an emerging country, the level of compliance of corporate governance has increased over time. Furthermore, sectoral differences are noted in terms of compliance levels.
5. The main findings of this study indicate that the level of compliance with corporate governance principles in Sri Lanka is quite low with sectoral differences, and the relationship between corporate governance compliance and financial performance is positive. The firms have to improve their level of compliance of corporate governance to increase their financial performance.

Reflective Questions

1. In the measurement of compliance with corporate governance principles, explain how to use an index and the importance of using such.
2. Using the agency theory and the stakeholder theory, discuss how you could establish the relationship between higher compliance with corporate governance principles of firms and better corporate performance.
3. "Empirical evidence always indicates a positive relationship between compliance with corporate governance principles of firms and better corporate performance." Do you agree? Evaluate this statement.
4. Discuss and comment on the level of overall and sectoral compliance with corporate governance principles by firms in Sri Lanka as an emerging economy.
5. In this study, contrary to expectations, a negative relationship is observed between the firms' compliance with corporate governance principles and the "market" performance of such firms. Explain.
6. Emerging economies could improve their economic growth by improving their economic performance of corporate sector. This could be achieved by increasing the compliance level of corporate governance. Do you agree? Explain with reasons.

Appendices

Appendix 23.1: Summary of Literature on CGI and Performance in Developed Economies

Year	Author/s	Country	Sample	Independent variable	Dependent variable	Relation-ship
2003	Gompers et al.	USA	1500 firms	GIM index	Tobin's Q, net profit margin, ROE, sales growth	Positive
2004	Drobetz et al.	Germany	91 public firms	CG index constructed	Tobin's market to book value, historical returns, dividend yield, sales, and asset growth	Positive
2006	Beiner et al.	Switzerland	109 firms	CG index based on Swiss Code	Tobin's market to book value	Positive
2004	Fernandez-Rodriguez et al.	Spain	57 listed firms	CG index based on Spanish Code	Daily abnormal returns	Positive
2005	Cremers and Neir	USA	1500 firms	Adopting GIM index and constructing takeover protection index	Tobin's Q, stock returns	Positive
2008	Gruszczynski	Poland	37 firms	CGI	Operating profit margin	Positive
2007	Chhaochharia and Grinstein	USA	312 firms	Self-constructed CG index	Stock returns	Negative
2008	Clacher et al.	UK	63 firms	CGI based on Combined Code	Tobin's Q, IAROA	Positive
2008	Kowalewski	Poland	298 firms	Corporate governance index	ROA and Tobin's Q	Positive
2006	Brown and Caylor	USA	1868 firms	Gov. score	Tobin's Q	Positive
2009	Bebchuk et al.	USA	IRRC firms	Enrichment index (E-index)	Tobin's stock returns	Negative
2009	Okike and Turton	UK	18 banks	CGI	ROE	Positive
2010	Bauer et al.	USA	509 firm year observations	CGQ index	Tobin's Q, net profit margin, ROE, ROA, sales growth	Positive
2012	Gordon	Canada	Small listed firms	CG index based on Toronto SE	Tobin's Q	Positive

Year	Author/s	Country	Sample	Independent variable	Dependent variable	Relation-ship
2012	Hassan and Ahmed	United Arab Emirates	23 national banks	CGQ index	Performance	Positive
2012	Mariani and Panaro	Italy	12 firms	CGI	EBIT	Positive
2010	Daines	California	2106 firms	CGI	Book-to-market ratio, NP margin	Mixed
2013	Ntim and Soobaroyen	South Africa	169 firms	SA CG index	Tobin's Q	Positive
2014	C. Chang et al.	Taiwan	886 firms	CGI	ROA and Tobin's Q	Positive
2015	Shahwan	Egypt	86 nonfinancial firms	Corporate governance index	Tobin's Q	Positive
2015	Rossi et al.	Italy	215 firms	CGQI	ROE, ROA, and Tobin's Q	Positive and negative
2015	Orazalin	Kazakhstan	38 commercial banks	Corporate governance index	ROA and ROE	Positive
2016	Outa and Waweru	Canada	520 firms	CG guidelines issued in 2002 by Capital Markets Authority	ROA and Tobin's Q	Positive
2018	Liu et al.	Australia	20,706 firms	Corporate governance index	Tobin's Q	Moderate and negative
2018	Ajili and Bouri	Gulf Cooperation Council (GCC) countries	44 firms	CG index	ROA and Tobin's Q	No relationship
2018	Bernini et al.	Italy	98 firms	CGI	ROI and CAR	Positive
2019	Guney et al.	USA	1203 firms	CGI	ROA	Negative

Source: Constructed based on the literature

Appendix 23.2: Summary of Literature on CGI and Performance in Emerging Economies

Year	Author/s	Country	Sample	Independent variables	Firm performance	Relationship
2004	Bai et al.	China	1006 firms	CGI index	Market-to-book value (MTBV)	Positive
2006	Black et al.	Korea	515 firms	KCGI	Tobin's Q, market-to-book value, market-to-sales ratio, ordinary income, EBIT, EBITPA	Positive
2006	Javed and Iqbal	Pakistan	50 firms	CGI	Tobin's Q	Positive
2007	Wahab et al.	Auckland	440 firms	CGI	Stock performance	Positive
2007	Abdo and Fisher	South Africa	97 firms	Governance scorecard	MTBV and P/E ratios	Positive
2007	Nishat and Shaheen	Pakistan	226 firms	Gov. score	ROE, NP margin	Positive
2008	Garay and Gonzalez	Venezuela	46 firms	CG index	Tobin's Q	Positive
2011	Cheung et al.	Hong Kong	168 listed firms	CG index based on OECD and Hong Kong Code	MTBV	Positive
2011	Price et al.	Mexico	107 firms	CG index based on Mexico best practice	ROA, Tobin's Q, sales growth, stock market returns	No association
2011	Braga and Shastri	Brazil	15 firms	Composite index	Tobin's Q and EBIT to assets	Negative
2012	Varshney et al.	India	105 firms	CGI	EVA, ROCE, RONW, Tobin's Q	Positive
2013	Haldar and Nageswara Rao	India	50 firms	CGI	Tobin's Q	Positive
2013	Tariq and Abbas	Pakistan	119 firms	CG index based on Pakistani CG Code	ROA, ROE, ROCE	Positive

Year	Author/s	Country	Sample	Independent variables	Firm performance	Relationship
2014	Tu et al.	Vietnam	110 firms	CGI	ROA, ROE	Positive
2015	Love and Rachinsky	Russia and Ukraine	107 banks from Russia and 50 banks from Ukraine	CGI	ROA, ROE	Positive
2016	Haque and Arun	Bangladesh	140 firms	CGI	Tobin's Q	Positive
2016	Hwang and Jung	South Korea	278 firms	CGI	EBIT/sales, Tobin's Q, and market-to-book value	Positive
2017	Bhatt et al.	Malaysia	113 listed companies	CGI	ROE, ROA, and RIC	Positive
2018	Ramachandran et al.	Singapore, Malaysia	43 firms	R-index	ROE, ROA, and NP margin	Positive

Source: Constructed based on the Literature

References

Abdo, A., & Fisher, G. (2007). The impact of reported corporate governance disclosure on the financial performance of companies listed on the JSE. *Investment Analysts Journal, 36*(66), 43–56.

Abdullah, H., & Valentine, B. (2009). Fundamental and ethics theories of corporate governance. *Middle Eastern Finance and Economics, 4*(4), 88–96.

Aghion, P., & Bolton, P. (1992). An incomplete contracts approach to financial contracting. *The Review of Economic Studies, 59*(3), 473–494.

Ajili, H., & Bouri, A. (2018). Corporate governance quality of Islamic banks: Measurement and effect on financial performance. *International Journal of Islamic and Middle Eastern Finance and Management, 11*(3), 470–487.

Ammann, M., Oesch, D., & Schmid, M. M. (2013). Product market competition, corporate governance, and firm value: Evidence from the EU area. *European Financial Management, 19*(3), 452–469.

Ayuso, S., & Argandoña, A. (2009). Responsible corporate governance: Towards a stakeholder board of directors? *Corporate Ownership & Control, 6*(4), 9–19.

Bai, C. E., Liu, Q., Lu, J., Song, F. M., & Zhang, J. (2004). Corporate governance and market valuation in China. *Journal of Comparative Economics, 32*(4), 599–616.

Barnhart, S. W., & Rosenstein, S. (1998). Board composition, managerial ownership, and firm performance: An empirical analysis. *Financial Review, 33*(4), 1–16.

Bauer, R., Eichholtz, P., & Kok, N. (2010). Corporate governance and performance: The REIT effect. *Real Estate Economics, 38*(1), 1–29.

Bebchuk, L., Cohen, A., & Ferrell, F. (2009). The society for financial studies what matters in corporate governance? *The Review of Financial Studies, 22*(2), 783–827.

Beiner, S., Drobetz, W., Schmid, M. M., & Zimmermann, H. (2006). An integrated framework of corporate governance and firm valuation. *European Financial Management, 12*(2), 249–283.

Berle, A., & Means, G. (1932). *The modern corporation and private property*. New York: Macmillan.

Bhagat, S., & Bolton, B. (2008). Corporate governance and firm performance. *Journal of Corporate Finance, 14*(3), 257–273.

Bhatt, P. R., & Bhatt, R. R. (2017). Corporate governance and firm performance in Malaysia. *Corporate Governance, 17*(5), 896–912.

Black, B. S., Jang, H., & Kim, W. (2006). Does corporate governance predict firms' market values? Evidence from Korea. *Journal of Law, Economics, and Organization, 22*(2), 366–413.

Black, B. S., De Carvalho, A. G., & Gorga, É. (2012). What matters and for which firms for corporate governance in emerging markets? Evidence from Brazil (and other BRIK countries). *Journal of Corporate Finance, 18*(4), 934–952.

Braga-Alves, M. V., & Shastri, K. (2011). Corporate governance, valuation, and performance: Evidence from a voluntary market reform in Brazil. *Financial Management, 40*(1), 139–157.

Brown, L. D., & Caylor, M. L. (2006). Corporate governance and firm valuation. *Journal of Accounting and Public Policy, 25*(4), 409–434.

Carroll, A. B., & Buchholtz, A. K. (2007). *Business and society: Ethics and stakeholder management* (7th ed.). Mason: South-Western Cengage Learning.

CBSL, Sri Lanka. (2019). *Central Bank annual report (2018)*. Colombo.

Chang, Y. K., Chou, R. K., & Huang, T. H. (2014). Corporate governance and the dynamics of capital structure: New evidence. *Journal of Banking & Finance, 48*, 374–385.

Cheung, Y.-L., Connelly, J. T., Jiang, P., & Limpaphayom, P. (2011). Does corporate governance predict future performance? Evidence from Hong Kong. *Financial Management, 40*(1), 159–197.

Chhaochharia, V., & Grinstein, Y. (2007). Corporate governance and firm value: The impact of the 2002 governance rules. *The Journal of Finance, 62*(4), 1789–1825.

Clacher, I., Doriye, E., & Hillier, D. (2008). *Does corporate governance matter? New evidence from the United Kingdom*. https://doi.org/10.2139/ssrn.1293188.

Clarke, T. (2004). *Theories of corporate governance*. New York: Routledge.

Cremers, M., & Nair, V. (2005). Governance mechanisms and equity prices. *Journal of Finance, 60*, 2859–2894.

Daines, R. M., Gow, I. D., & Larcker, D. F. (2010). Rating the ratings: How good are commercial governance ratings? *Journal of Financial Economics, 98*(3), 439–461.

Davis, J. H., Schoorman, F. D., & Donaldson, L. (1997). Toward a stewardship theory of management. *Academy of Management Review, 22*, 20–47.

Dissabandara, H. (2010). *Corporate governance and best practices and current views based on evidence from Sri Lankan Corporate Boards*. Retrieved from http://www.cmetsec.gov.lk/wp-content/uploads/2012/05/Current-Views-on-Corporate-Governance-in-Sri-Lanka-Evidence-from-Srilankan-Corporate-Bonds.ppt

Drobetz, W., Schillhofer, A., & Zimmermann, H. (2004). Corporate governance and expected stock returns: Evidence from Germany. *European Financial Management, 10*(2), 267–293.

Eisenhardt, K. (1989). Agency theory: An assessment and review. *The Academy of Management Review, 14*(1), 57–74.

Epps, R. W., & Cereola, S. J. (2008). Do institutional shareholder services (ISS) corporate governance ratings reflect a company's operating performance? *Critical Perspectives on Accounting, 19*(8), 1135–1148.

Fama, E. F. (1980). Agency problems and the theory of the firm. *Journal of Political Economy, 88*, 288–307.

Fama, E. F., & Jensen, M. C. (1983a). Agency problems and residual claims. *Journal of Law and Economics, 26*(2), 327–349.

Fama, E. F., & Jensen, M. C. (1983b). Separation of ownership and control. *Journal of Law and Economics, 26*(2), 301–325.

Fernández-Rodríguez, E., Gómez-Ansón, S., & Cuervo-García, Á. (2004). The stock market reaction to the introduction of best practices codes by Spanish firms. *Corporate Governance: An International Review, 12*(1), 29–46.

Freeman, R. E. (1984). *Strategic management: A stakeholder approach*. London: Pitman.

Garay, U., & González, M. (2008). Corporate governance and firm value: The case of Venezuela. *Corporate Governance: An International Review, 16*(3), 194–209.

Giroud, X., & Mueller, H. M. (2011). Corporate governance, product market competition, and equity prices. *The Journal of Finance, 66*(2), 563–600.

Gompers, P., Ishii, J., & Metrick, A. (2003). Corporate governance and equity prices. *The Quarterly Journal of Economics, 118*(1), 107–156.

Gordon, I. M., Hrazdil, K., & Shapiro, D. (2012). Corporate governance in publicly traded small firms: A study of Canadian venture exchange companies. *Business Horizons, 55*(6), 583–591.

Gruszczynski, M. (2008). Corporate governance ratings and the performance of listed companies in Poland. *Przegląd Statystyczny, 1*(55), 113–129.

Guney, Y., Hernandez-Perdomo, E., & Rocco, C. M. (2019). Does relative strength in corporate governance improve corporate performance? Empirical evidence using MCDA approach. *Journal of the Operational Research Society, 1*(26). https://doi.org/10.1080/01605682.201 9.1621216.

Gupta, P., Kennedy, D., & Weaver, S. (2009). Corporate governance and firm value: Evidence from Canadian Capital Markets. *Corporate Ownership and Control Journal, 6*(3), 293–307.

Haldar, A., & Nageswara Rao, S. V. D. (2013). Governance practices of Indian firms: An empirical analysis. *The Empirical Economic Letters, 12*(9), 975–984.

Haque, F., & Arun, T. G. (2016). Corporate governance and financial performance: An emerging economy perspective. *Investment Management and Financial Innovations, 13*(3), 228–236.

Hassan, S. U., & Ahmed, A. (2012). Corporate governance, earnings management and financial performance: A case of Nigerian manufacturing firms. *American International Journal of Contemporary Research, 2*(7), 214–226.

Heenetigala, K., & Armstrong, A. F. (2011). The impact of corporate governance on firm performance in an unstable economic and political environment: Evidence from Sri Lanka. Paper presented at the *Financial Markets & Corporate Governance Conference*. https://doi.org/10.2139/ssrn.1971927

Hill, C. W. L., & Jones, T. M. (1992). Stakeholder – Agency theory. *Journal of Management Studies, 29*, 131–154.

Hwang, S. W., & Jung, Y. R. (2016). The relationship between corporate governance, foreign investors' shareholdings, and corporate performance: The case of South Korea. *Afro-Asian Journal of Finance and Accounting, 6*(4), 318–338.

Javed, A. Y., Iqbal, R., & Hasan, L. (2006). Corporate governance and firm performance: Evidence from Karachi Stock Exchange [with comments]. *The Pakistan Development Review, 45*(4), 947–964.

Jensen, M. C. (1983). Organization theory and methodology. *The Accounting Review, 58*(2), 319–339.

Jensen, M. (2001). Value maximisation, stakeholder theory, and the corporate objective function. *European Financial Management, 7*, 297–317.

Jensen, M. C., & Meckling, W. H. (1976). Theory of the firm: Managerial behavior, agency costs, and ownership structure. Journal of Financial Economics, *3*(4), 305–360. Reprinted in *The modern theory of corporate finance* (M. C. Jensen & C. W. Smith Jr., Eds.). New York: McGraw-Hill, 1984.

Kiel, G. C., & Nicholson, G. J. (2003). Board composition and corporate performance: How the Australian experience informs contrasting theories of corporate governance. *Corporate Governance: An International Review, 11*(3), 189–205.

Klein, P., Shapiro, D., & Young, J. (2005). Corporate governance, family ownership and firm value: The Canadian evidence. *Corporate Governance: An International Review, 13*(6), 769–784.

Koehn, D., & Ueng, J. (2005). Evaluating the evaluators: Should investors trust corporate governance metrics ratings? *Journal of Management & Governance, 9*(2), 111–128.

Kowalewski, O., Stetsyuk, I., & Talavera, O. (2008). Does corporate governance determine dividend payouts in Poland? *Post-Communist Economies, 20*(2), 203–218.

La Rosa, F., & Bernini, F. (2018). Corporate governance and performance of Italian gambling SMEs during recession. *International Journal of Contemporary Hospitality Management, 30*(3), 1939–1958.

Lawal, B. (2012). Board dynamics and corporate performance: Review of literature, and empirical challenges. *International Journal of Economics and Finance, 4*(1), 22–35.

Lehn, K., Patro, S., & Zhao, M. (2007). Governance indices and valuation: Which causes which? *Journal of Corporate Finance, 13*, 907–928.

Letza, S., Sun, X., & Kirkbride, J. (2004). Shareholding versus stake holding: A critical review of corporate governance. *Corporate Governance: An International Review, 12*(3), 242–262.

Liu, L., Qu, W., & Haman, J. (2018). Product market competition, state-ownership, corporate governance and firm performance. *Asian Review of Accounting, 26*(1), 62–83.

Ljubojević, Ĉ., & Ljubojević, G. (2011). Improving the stakeholder satisfaction by corporate governance quality. *Škola biznisa, 1*, 22–35.

Love, I., & Rachinsky, A. (2015). Corporate governance and bank performance in emerging markets: Evidence from Russia and Ukraine. *Emerging Markets Finance and Trade, 51*(sup2), S101–S121.

Manawaduge, A. (2012). *Corporate governance practices and their impact on corporate performance in an emerging market: The case of Sri Lanka.* PhD thesis, University of Wollongong, New Zealand. Retrieved from http://ro.uow.edu.au/theses/3676

Manawaduge, A., De Zoysa, A., & Rudkin, K. (2009). Performance implications of ownership structure and ownership concentration: Evidence from Sri Lankan firms. Presented at *Performance Management Association conference* (pp. 1–12). Dunedin: Performance Measurement Association. Retrieved from http://www.pma.otago.ac.nz/pma-cd/papers/1040.pdf

Mapitiya, G. S. (2015). *Degree of compliance with corporate governance best practices and corporate financial performance of public listed companies in Sri Lanka.* Presented at 12th international conference on Business Management (ICBM), University of Sri Jayewardenepura, Sri Lanka. https://doi.org/10.2139/ssrn.2699719

Mariani, G., & Panaro, D. (2012). Corporate governance and performance in turnaround: A synthetic index. *Corporate Ownership & Control, 10*(1), 62–74.

Munisi, G., & Randøy, T. (2013). Corporate governance and company performance across Sub-Saharan African countries. *Journal of Economics and Business, 70*, 92–110.

Nishat, M., & Shaheen, R. (2007). Corporate governance and firm performance in an emerging market – An exploratory analysis of Pakistan. *Corporate Ownership & Control, 4*(2–1), 216–225.

Ntim, C. G. (2009). *Internal corporate governance structures and firm financial performance: evidence from South African listed firms.* Doctoral dissertation, University of Glasgow, United Kingdom. Retrieved from http://theses.gla.ac.uk/1282/1/2009ntimphd.pdf

Ntim, C. G., & Soobaroyen, T. (2013). Corporate governance and performance in socially responsible corporations: New empirical insights from a neo-institutional framework. *Corporate Governance: An International Review, 21*(5), 468–494.

OECD. (2015). *G20/OECD principles of corporate governance.* https://doi.org/10.1787/9789264236882-en

Okike, E., & Turton, A. (2009). Corporate governance reform within the UK banking industry and its effect on firm performance. *Corporate Ownership and Control, 456.*

Orazalin, N., Makarov, R., & Ospanova, M. (2015). Corporate governance and firm performance in the oil and gas industry of Russia. *Journal of Business, Economics & Finance, 4*(4), 710–722.

Outa, E. R., & Waweru, N. M. (2016). Corporate governance guidelines compliance and firm financial performance. *Managerial Auditing Journal, 31*(8/9), 891–914.

Pesqueux, Y., & Damak-Ayadi, S. (2005). Stakeholder theory in perspective. *Corporate Governance: The International Journal of Business in Society, 5*(2), 5–21.

Price, R., Román, F. J., & Rountree, B. (2011). The impact of governance reform on performance and transparency. *Journal of Financial Economics, 99*(1), 76–96.

Ramachandran, J., Chen, K. K., Subramanian, R., Yeoh, K. K., & Khong, K. W. (2018). Corporate governance and performance of REITs. *Managerial Auditing Journal, 33*(6/7), 586–612.

Ross, S. A. (1973). The economic theory of agency: The principal's problems. *American Economic Review, 62*(2), 134–139.

Rossi, M., Nerino, M., & Capasso, A. (2015). Corporate governance and financial performance of Italian listed firms. The results of an empirical research. *Corporate Ownership & Control, 12*(2), 628–643.

Shahwan, T. M. (2015). The effects of corporate governance on financial performance and financial distress: Evidence from Egypt. *Corporate Governance, 15*(5), 641–662.

Shleifer, A., & Vishny, R. W. (1997). A survey of corporate governance. *Journal of Finance, 52*(2), 737–783.

Solomon, J., & Solomon, A. (2004). *Corporate governance and accountability* (3rd ed.). Chichester: Wiley.

Tariq, Y. B., & Abbas, Z. (2013). Compliance and multidimensional firm performance: Evaluating the efficacy of rule-based code of corporate governance. *Economic Modelling, 35*, 565–575.

The Institute of Chartered Accountants of Sri Lanka. (2008). *Code of best practice on corporate governance.* Colombo: ICASL. Retrieved from https://www.casrilanka.com/casl/images/stories/content/members/corporate_governance_code.pdf.

The Institute of Chartered Accountants of Sri Lanka. (2017). *Code of best practice on corporate governance.* Colombo: ICASL. Retrieved from https://www.casrilanka.com/casl/images/stories/2017/2017_pdfs/code_of_best_practice_on_corporate_governance_2017_final_for_web.pdf.

Tricker, B. (2015). *Corporate governance, principles, policies, and practices.* Oxford: Oxford University Press.

Tu, T. T. T., Son, N. H., & Khanh, P. B. (2014). Testing the relationship between corporate governance and bank performance – an empirical study on Vietnamese banks. *Asian Social Science, 10*(9), 213–226.

UK Listing Authority (UKLA). (2016). *The combined code, annex to UK listing rules.* Retrieved from http://www.fsa.gov.uk/ukla

Varshney, P., Kaul, V. K., & Vasal, V. K. (2012). *Corporate governance index and firm performance: Empirical evidence from India.* https://doi.org/10.2139/ssrn.2103462

Vinten, G. (2001). Shareholder versus stakeholder–is there a governance dilemma? *Corporate Governance: An International Review, 9*(1), 36–47.

Wahab, E. A. A., How, J. C., & Verhoeven, P. (2007). The impact of the Malaysian code on corporate governance: Compliance, institutional investors and stock performance. *Journal of Contemporary Accounting and Economics, 3*(2), 106–129.

Williamson, O. E. (1987). Transaction cost economics: The comparative contracting perspective. *Journal of Economic Behavior & Organization, 8*(4), 617–625.

World Bank. (2019). *New country classifications by income level: 2018–2019* Retrieved from blogs.worldbank.org/opendata/new-country-classifications-income-level-2018-2019

Part VIII

Health Policy and Healthcare Management

Behaviour Change to Improve Dietary Diversity of Pregnant Mothers Through Counselling: A Lesson from Sri Lanka

24

R. B. B. S. Ramachandra, L. D. J. U. Senarath,
N. Hemachandra, and S. H. P. de Silva

24.1 Introduction

Sri Lanka, while being a developing country in the South Asian region, shows improvement in health indicators such as life expectancy, death rates and fertility rates which are comparable with those of developed countries (World Health Organization 2018). Despite having a reasonably higher literacy rate, a well-established public health system and continuous public health interventions to uplift its nutritional status, the country is still struggling to reach the desired level of nutritional indicators (UNICEF & WHO 2004). Prevalence of anaemia, low body mass index (BMI) among pregnant mothers, incidence of low birth weight, and childhood nutritional indicators are still higher in Sri Lanka even though they show gradual improvement (Family Health Bureau Sri Lanka 2017). The health system of the country has taken many efforts in improving the situation. Mass-scale distribution to all pregnant mothers of food supplements called 'Triposha' (Ministry of Health and Nutrition 2016) and multivitamin supplements have been practised in the country for more than two decades continuously, investing large allocation from public funds. Each pregnant mother is registered with a public health midwife (PHM) from the day she is eligible for pregnancy, her nutritional status is assessed and she is

R. B. B. S. Ramachandra (✉)
District General Hospital, Embilipitiya, Sri Lanka

L. D. J. U. Senarath
University of Colombo, Colombo, Sri Lanka

N. Hemachandra
Family Health Bureau, Colombo, Sri Lanka

S. H. P. de Silva
Department of Research and Evaluation, National Institute of Health Sciences, Katukurunda, Sri Lanka

© The Author(s), under exclusive license to Springer Nature
Switzerland AG 2021
S. Dhiman, R. Samaratunge (eds.), *New Horizons in Management, Leadership and Sustainability*, Future of Business and Finance,
https://doi.org/10.1007/978-3-030-62171-1_24

507

given dietary advice to correct any malnutrition during the pre-pregnancy period and throughout the pregnancy. And national-level information revealed that 50% of pregnant mothers fall into the risk category at the beginning of pregnancy just due to inappropriate body mass index (BMI) (Family Health Bureau 2017).

Failing many blanket measures of correcting nutritional status itself describes the need for a tailed intervention addressing individuals according to their requirement. A review by Gernand et al. (2016) has focused on micronutrient deficiencies and consequences of longer-term outcomes of offspring. This review showed that the survival, cognition and cardio-metabolic risks in the offspring improve with the intake of micronutrients. Multiple micronutrient intake is an effective strategy during the critically vital biological period of pregnancy, according to their findings.

Utilization of evidence found in global literature addressing nutritional problems starting right from conception is a worthwhile exercise for a country like ours, with a target of better health indicators for the future generation. Furthermore, the public health system of the country provides a robust platform for experimenting such an intervention. Thus, the importance of dietary diversity and the possibility of increasing diversity through improved utilization of locally available food are the main emphasis of this study.

24.1.1 Objective

The study was conducted to improve the dietary diversity of pregnant mothers through nutritional counselling. The primary target group was pregnant mothers in the first trimester of their pregnancy, for testing hypothesis 1. The dietary counselling by PHM of pregnant mothers and their family is an effective method to improve the dietary diversity of pregnant mothers. The counselling was delivered through PHMM as they are the usual health caregivers to this category of the population. Identification of the feasibility of delivering the intervention through PHM is the secondary objective of the study as this facilitates the sustainability of the intervention when it is implemented into the health system of the country. Thus, hypothesis 2 was a short training incorporated with knowledge and skill updates as an in-service training can improve the dietary counselling skills of PHMM.

24.2   Literature Review

24.2.1 Dietary Diversity

Dietary diversity is defined as the number of different foods consumed over a given reference period (Ruel 2003), which is the main measure of a healthy diet. Dietary pattern is widely different among countries and, even within the country, shows cultural differences. The consumption of individuals will also depend on the age, sex, activity level, personal favouritism and other medical conditions. Dietary pattern may also show seasonal variation as some food types are available in one season of the year and eaten only in that period. Dietary diversity (DD) is an important finding in designing a nutritional intervention. It acts as an indirect measure of the micronutrient adequacy of an individual (Savy et al. 2018). There are many tools developed by researchers in measuring the DD with different objectives. While 'household DD questionnaires' are designed to measure food purchasing power, 'individual DD questionnaires' are designed to measure the adequacy of micronutrient intake (El Bilali et al. 2017). DD of pregnant mothers a crucial factor as survival, cognition, and cardio-metabolic risk in the offspring improve with adequate micronutrient in pregnancy (Gernand et al. 2016; Viteri and Gonzalez 2003). These reasons made women's nutritional status especially important as it compromises her quality of life as well as her children's lives due to its generation effect (Ransom and Elder 2003).

Though the DD is an important factor in nutritional outcomes, the consumption of varieties depends on many other factors (Savy et al. 2006), such as seasonal variation of staple, purchasing power, personal favour, knowledge on the nutritional value of food, age, gender and membership status within the family in some cultures. The nutritional status of the pregnant mother is considered important in many cultures and is given priority irrespective of scientific evidence. Thus, the pregnant mother receives the best diet possible within the family. As the DD varies in several factors other than individual selection, the World Health Organization (WHO) highlights the importance of addressing nutritional issues through integrated initiatives using health programmes for sustainable outcomes (WHO 2016). It is essential to identify measures for improving DD using locally available food items for a better acceptance of the intervention and sustainability in a setting with low food purchasing power (Demment et al. 2018).

24.2.2 Behavioural Change Towards Increase in DD

Availability of varieties of food, ability to buy (food purchasing power), access to available food and selecting preferences from available food (food purchasing behaviour) are the most important factors for individuals' DD. Individuals' awareness of the nutrient value of food, knowledge in selecting the correct combination of foods, knowledge of low-cost methods in improving the nutrition value of a particular food portion and influence of the immediate environment are well known to affect the consumption of nutrient supplements or nutritious food (Tinago et al. 2017). Knowledge and perception of food items can change the food purchasing behaviour of an individual (Rimal et al. 2001). Therefore, improving food purchasing behaviour can positively influence dietary diversity, especially in a country like Sri Lanka, which is a setting with large varieties of food items available locally.

24.2.3 Dietary Counselling

Unlike other health issues, most individuals do not have a self-understanding of what they face regarding nutritional issues. Usually, most prominent nutritional problems are extreme BMI values or iron, folate or vitamin deficiencies. Though these nutritional issues can be a sign of an underlying disease, usually these result in improper dietary habits, which eventually become a causative factor for many lifestyle diseases (Sanders 2004). Nutrition counselling by a health professional targets to assess the individual's dietary intake, habit and preferences and identifies areas where changes are needed (Sanders 2004). The nutrition counsellor provides information, educational materials, support and follow-up to help the individual to make and maintain the required dietary changes.

There are many pieces of evidence from the global literature stating that dietary counselling can work as an effective intervention for altering food habits. Forouhi et al. (2018) identified that dietary counselling is an effective method for changing diets, but changes made are hard to sustain without frequent counselling sessions as many other factors affect the food habit of an individual. Many studies around the developed world are targeting to reduce consumption and weight gain as most developed countries are facing problems of over-nutrition. A randomized control trial done in Finland has adopted dietary counselling as intervention to improve the quality of essential fatty acids in their offsprings and found a statistically significant higher 'essential fatty acids' levels in the intervention group's infants. They highlight the importance of maternal diet for child health, calling for dietary counselling for pregnant women in primary health care settings (Niinivirta et al. 2011). Ilmonen et al. (2011) have adopted dietary counselling as intervention to reduce waist circumference after 12 months of delivery, and 256 pregnant women were assigned to the intervention arm in the first trimester of their pregnancy. The intervention lasted until the end of exclusive breastfeeding, which is until 6 months post-delivery. The number needed to treat (NNT) was four to prevent females from developing 80-cm or more waist circumference, according to this study.

24.3 Method

The study was conducted as a community-based cluster-randomized trial in Kalutara district in Sri Lanka. The public health midwife (PHM) area, which is the functional unit of 'maternal and child health service delivery', was taken as the cluster in this study. Inclusion of clusters in all possible communities to improve the representation of the study was a special concern in selecting clusters. PHM areas of the district were divided into three sectors (urban, rural, estate) according to living areas, and the number of clusters was randomly selected from each sector proportionate to the population size.

Fifty-four selected clusters were randomly divided into the intervention and control arms. This allowed a random allocation of both pregnant mothers and midwives, who are the primary and secondary target groups of the study arms.

Counselling intervention was delivered through PHMM as they are the grassroots-level health care officers. This facilitated the studying feasibility of delivering the planned intervention utilizing the established system. The possibility of utilizing established system is an uttermost important in a public intervention as if the intervention is successful; where it can be easily incorporated into the system and deliver country-wise without major investment.

Ten mothers from each cluster with a pregnancy period of less than 12 weeks were recruited into the sample as they get registered with the midwife for antenatal care. The final sample size was 540, with 270 mothers per study arm.

24.3.1 Training of PHMM to Deliver the Intervention

24.3.1.1 Testing Hypothesis 2

Though basic counselling concepts and skills were incorporated into the PHM training curriculum, nutrition counselling training was given to 27 PHMM in the intervention arm. This requirement was identified with a qualitative study conducted by the same scholar before this study (unpublished data) with the following reasons. The selected PHMM were with different service period who had undergone their basic training at different years in the past. Their basic curriculum focuses on contraceptive usage and nutritional advice rather than counselling. As many mothers do not have an insight of their own nutritional status, PHMM need special efforts to make them aware of their nutrition and to highlight the need for corrective actions. Updating the knowledge of pregnant mothers on the nutritional requirement during pregnancy, monitoring their nutritional status regarding pregnancy weight gain (which is the universally accepted method in pregnancy nutritional status) and informing them about the nutritional values of locally available food items, food items with high nutritional value, the different methods of food preparation while preserving nutrition value, the influence of family and the environment, and the myths and beliefs influencing food habits were also made during the training.

Further, improving counselling skills was also incorporated into the training with practical sessions. This training was delivered as a 'three days in-service training' starting on a Saturday and ending on the Monday of the next week. The fifth week of the month was selected for this as in that week, PHMM were not conducting field clinics and the training had a minimum influence on their routing work. The counselling skills of PHMM were assessed using the same tools applied in the basic midwifery training in Sri Lanka. These were used prior to the training, immediately after the training and six months post training. A 20-item checklist similar to the tool used to measure the counselling skills in the basic PHM training was developed to also measure the counselling skills after this in-service training. A handbook on nutritional counselling, a quick reference material used at the field and a food menu book with preparation methods of local food were prepared as resource materials for the intervention. Further, the training highlighted the importance of counselling both the pregnant mother and her immediate family members as the family plays a major role in selecting the food items for a pregnant mother in the Sri Lankan context.

24.3.2 Measuring Dietary Diversity of Pregnant Mothers

24.3.2.1 Testing Hypothesis 1

Nutrition counselling was delivered to pregnant mothers and their families by the PHMM in the intervention arm during antenatal home visits. The intervention started before completing the 12 weeks of gestation and was repeated during pregnancy to conduct a minimum of three counselling sessions during the pregnancy. Those who were in the control arm was given the routine care, which may include counselling too, but those PHMM were without special training for nutrition counselling.

A positive change in dietary diversity was the primary outcome expected for the study. DD of all pregnant mothers in the study (both arms) was recorded using the women's dietary diversity questionnaire used in the FANTA II project in the year 2009 (FAO 2016) as the tool is recommended for international use and adaptation. The same tool was previously used in Sri Lanka for national-level research by the Medical Research Institute. Subsequently, DD was recorded at the end of 36 weeks of pregnancy in both groups.

DD was recorded by trained data collectors independent from PHMM. Data collectors were trained to question on each food group, probing on food items which were not mentioned during the data collection. The tool was designed to have two components: first, one with several food groups, including examples of food items belonging to each group, and, second, a checklist to identify consumption according to the portion size of the consumed food. For example, rice was considered as consumed if it was used as the staple food in a minimum of two meals out of three. A pictorial guide on portion size was developed for data collectors to be utilized during data collection as dietary diversity was based on the recall of food consumed during the last 24 hours. The collection of data during pre and post-intervention DD, in both arms of the study, has facilitated the demonstration of changes in DD before and after the intervention and the differences in intervention and control arms.

24.4 Results

The analysis targeted to identify both the effectiveness of the dietary counselling training to improve the counselling skills of PHMM and the ability of the counselling intervention to change the dietary diversity of pregnant mothers.

24.4.1 Effectiveness of Training in Improving Counselling Skills

Each study arm comprised 27 PHMM, and the training on dietary counselling was given only to the 27 PHMM who were in the intervention arm. Demographic characteristics and pieces of training received by PHMM in the two groups showed no statistically significant differences (Table 24.1). Table 24.1 describes that the two groups of PHMM showed no differences in basic characteristics. Each PHM in the

Table 24.1 Demographic characteristics and basic skills of PHMM in two groups

	Intervention arm		Control arm		
	No. of PHM	%	No. of PHM	%	Level of significance
Counseling trainings					
Received during the basic training	12	44.4	13	48.1	P = 0.69
Received as in-service training	11	40.8	12	44.5	
Received both trainings	4	14.8	2	7.4	
Service experience					
Less than 5-years experience	2	7.4	1	3.7	P = 0.74
5–10-years experience	3	11.1	5	18.5	
11–20-years experience	21	77.8	18	66.7	
More than 21-years experience	1	3.7	3	11.1.	
Counselling skill before the training					
Poor	25	92.6	24	88.9	
Moderate	1	3.7	2	7.4	P = 0.58
Excellent	1	3.7	01	3.7	
Total	**27**	**100**	**27**	**100**	

Table 24.2 Changes in counselling skills with training in intervention arm PHMM

	First assessment		Second assessment		Third assessment	
Skill category	No. of PHMM	%	No. of PHMM	%	No. of PHMM	%
Poor skill	25	92.6	3	11.1	0	0.0
Moderate skill	1	3.7	23	85.2	16	59.3
Excellent skill	1	3.7	1	3.7	11	40.7
	Paired t = 17.48					
	Df = 26					
	P = 0.000					
			Paired t = 4.481			
			Df = 26			
			P = 0.000			
Percentage of mean score	29.76		53.61		63.79	
Total	**27**	**100**	**27**	**100**	**27**	**100**

study has received counselling training somewhere during their career. The two groups have no differences in service experience.

Counselling skills of both groups were assessed at the beginning with a tool of 20 skill areas. The assessment shows no statistically significant different in two groups on counselling skills at the begining of the training (p = 0.58).

The counselling skills of the intervention arm PHMM were subsequently assessed with the same tool as that used after the counselling training and after six months of the training (Table 24.2).

The results showed a statistically significant improvement following the training (paired $t = 17.48$, $df = 26$, $p = 0.000$), and the skills further improved after practising counselling for a 6-month duration (paired $t = 4.481$, $df = 26$, $p = 0.000$).

24.4.2 Effectiveness of Dietary Counselling in Improving Dietary Diversity

Socio-demographic characteristics of pregnant mothers in the two arms showed no difference (Table 24.3).

As the counselling was targeted to family members too, the characteristics of the family were also compared in the two study arms. Marital status of pregnant mother, the family type of the pregnant mother and parity to show no difference in mothers in the study. Furthermore, the starting BMI and use of folic acid were similar in the two categories (Table 24.4).

There was no difference in the comparison of selected risk factors in the study arms (Table 24.5).

By the time that the pre-intervention data collection had taken place, the advice on expected weight gain according to the pre-pregnancy weight gain plan has been received by pregnant mothers during health education. Receiving of personal health education had shown a statistically significant difference in the two study arms (Table 24.6).

Dietary changes in the two study groups showed a remarkable difference in general, as described in the below table (Table 24.7).

DD was measured according to FAO recommendation. Though the questionnaire comprised 18 food groups altogether, nine main food groups were taken for calculating DD. The consumption of three or fewer food groups was taken as poor DD, the consumption of four to five food items was taken as moderate and the consumption of six or more food groups was taken as good DD. The consumption of different food items and the mean DD score showed statistically significant differences, with better DD observed in the intervention group (Table 24.8).

At the end of the intervention, the mean dietary diversity score showed a statistically significant difference with p value <0.000. The consumption of individual food groups except organ meat was higher in the intervention group, with a statistically significant difference. There were significantly a smaller number of mothers in the intervention arm who avoided food items linked with myths and beliefs ($p < 0.001$).

Intervention arm mothers showed better adherence to recommended weight gain according to the starting BMI (Table 24.9).

Out of all mothers who had inappropriate weight gain, intervention arm mothers mostly showed excessive weight gain, which is an alarming observation. Further analysis showed that family members of the intervention arm subjects had been counselled better for improving dietary diversity, and mothers in the intervention arm had received better family support ($p < 0.0001$ in both occasions).

Table 24.3 Distribution of socio-demographic characteristics among pregnant mothers in two study arms

	Intervention arm		Control arm		Significance (using chi-square test)
	No.	%	No.	%	
Age					
Teenage (<20 years)	13	4.8	10	3.7	P = 0.34
21–25 years	46	17.0	51	18.9	
26–30 years	95	35.2	76	28.1	
31–35 years	76	28.1	81	30.0	
Elderly mothers (>35 years)	40	14.8	52	19.3	
Ethnicity					
Sinhala	222	82.2	219	81.1	P = 0.52
Sri Lankan Tamil	5	1.9	9	3.3	
Indian Tamil	6	2.2	3	1.1	
Sri Lankan Moor	37	13.7	39	14.4	
Religion					
Buddhist	195	72.2	202	74.8	P = 0.77
Catholic	25	9.3	19	7.0	
Hindu	12	4.4	10	3.7	
Islam	38	14.1	39	14.4	
Educational level					
Less than grade 6	7	2.6	13	4.8	
Grades 6–10	73	27.0	68	25.2	
O/L passed	91	33.7	92	34.1	P = 0.72
A/L passed	81	30.0	81	30.0	
Higher education	18	6.7	16	5.8	
Occupation					
Related to professions (nursing, teaching etc.)	2	0.7	1	0.4	
Technical officers and other officers	7	2.6	6	2.2	
Clerical and related jobs	15	5.6	11	4.1	
Service and business related	7	2.6	1	0.4	
Agricultural work, carpenters, masons and other skilled jobs	4	1.5	4	1.5	P = 0.55
Hand crafting and related jobs	4	1.5	2	0.7	
Machine operators, fixers and factory workers	13	4.8	12	4.4	
Basic jobs (unskilled)	7	2.6	10	3.7	
Uncategorized like army soldiers	0	0	3	1.1	
Housewife	211	78.1	220	81.5	
Total	**270**	**100**	**270**	**100**	

Classification according to the SL labour department

Table 24.4 Distribution of some basic family characteristics and nutritional status related to pregnancy at the beginning of pregnancy

Description	Intervention arm		Control arm		Statistical significance
	No.	%	No.	%	
Marital status of pregnant Mother					
Married	267	98.8	267	98.9	
Living together	1	0.4	3	1.1	
Separated	1	0.4	0	0.0	
Widowed	1	0.4	0	0.0	$P = 0.41$
Family type of pregnant Mother					
Nuclear family	124	45.9	121	44.8	
Extended family	146	54.1	149	55.2	$P = 0.79$
Parity					
1st pregnancy	99	36.7	104	38.5	
2nd pregnancy	111	41.1	109	40.4	
3rd pregnancy	40	14.8	41	15.2	
4th pregnancy	16	5.9	13	4.8	
5th pregnancy or above	4	1.5	3	1.1	$P = 0.96$
BMI category					
Low BMI (<18.5 kg/m^2)	52	19.3	56	20.7	
Normal BMI (18.5–24.99 kg/m^2)	158	58.5	156	57.8	
Overweight (25–29.99 kg/m^2)	47	17.4	46	17.0	
Obese (>30 kg/m^2)	13	4.8	12	4.4	$P = 0.97$
Use of folic acid	255	94.4	249	92.2	$P = 0.82$
Total	**270**	**100.0**	**270**	**100.0**	

Table 24.5 Comparison of selected risk factor distribution between two study arms

Risk factor	Intervention arm		Control arm		Statistical significance
	No.	%	No.	%	
Risk factors related to a previous pregnancy					
H/O LBW	12	4.4	10	3.7	$P = 0.91$
H/O premature deliveries	2	0.7	1	0.4	
H/O abortions	19	7.0	14	5.2	
Total	**33**	**12.1**	**25**	**9.3**	

Table 24.6 Receiving personalized health messages from the PHMM between two study arms

Advice on expected weight gain	Intervention arm		Control arm		Statistical significance
	No.	%	No.	%	
Advised	184	68.2	134	49.6	
Not advised	86	31.8	136	50.4	
Total	**270**	**100**	**270**	**100**	**$P < 0.00$**

Chi square = 19.122

Table 24.7 Differences elicited in the main aspects of meal following intervention in two study groups

Description	Intervention arm		Control arm		Level of significance
	No.	%	No.	%	
Perceived differences					
The number of meals consumed in a day changed appropriately	208	78.7	105	39.7	$P < 0.001$
Portion size changed appropriately	215	81.4	87	32.9	$P < 0.001$
Dietary diversity increased	209	77.4	167	63.2	$P < 0.001$
Abstained from some food items	55	20.8	136	51.6	$P < 0.001$
$N =$	264		264		
Loss to follow-up	6		6		

Table 24.8 Consumption of selected food groups by pregnant mothers and dietary diversity

Food item consumed	Intervention arm		Control arm		P
	No. of mothers	%	No. of mothers	%	
Carbohydrate sources					
Rice	264	100	264	100	
Bread	40	15.2	62	23.5	$P < 0.000$
Roots	83	31.4	44	16.7	$P < 0.000$
Other starch/ cereals	64	24.2	14	5.3	$P < 0.000$
Micronutrient sources					
Green leaves	245	92.8	166	62.9	$P < 0.000$
Vitamin-A-rich fruit and vegetables	220	83.3	173	65.5	$P < 0.000$
Other vegetables	229	86.7	206	78.0	$P = 0.006$
Other fruits	258	97.7	158	59.8	$P < 0.000$
Protein sources					
Organ meat	80	30.3	117	44.3	$P = 0.001$
Flesh meat	129	48.9	91	34.5	$P = 0.001$
Eggs	206	78.0	91	34.5	$P < 0.000$
Fish and seafood	225	85.2	130	49.2	$P < 0.000$
Nuts and legumes	154	58.3	87	33.0	$P < 0.000$
Milk and dairy products	254	96.2	210	79.5	$P < 0.000$
Oil	260	98.5	247	93.6	$P = 0.003$
Mean dietary diversity	**7.2348**		**5.6274**		**$P < 0.000$**

Table 24.9 Adherence to weight gain recommendation among pregnant mothers in two arms

Percentage of weight gain in categories		Intervention arm	Control arm
Appropriate weight gain	No. of mothers	159	128
	%	60.2%	48.5%
Inappropriate weight gain	No. of mothers	105	136
	%	39.8%	41.5%
Total	**No. of mothers**	**264**	**264**
	%	**100.0%**	**100.0%**
$X^2 = 7.336, p < 0.007$			
Inappropriate weight gain		105	136
Poor weight gain	No. of mothers	33	105
	%	23.9%	39.8%
Excessive weight gain	No. of mothers	72	31
	%	27.3%	11.7%

24.5   Discussion

Though all PHMM have been trained on counselling both during basic training and in-service training, it was demonstrated that the nutrition counselling skills of Sri Lankan PHMM were not up to satisfactory level. But the skills can be improved with a well-planned, structured training programme. It was an exciting observation that the counselling skills were improving over time as they kept on practising the skills (Table 24.2). As counselling is a skill, it was expected to be improved with repeated practice, and this was facilitated during the training through reference materials discussing the further use of PHMM. At field-level intervention, it is proved that nutrition counselling is a successful method in modifying the DD of pregnant mothers positively. It further proved that utilizing PHMM is feasible for DD. This finding is very important for a country like Sri Lanka, which has a well-established public health care delivery system. This facilitates improving the nutritional status of pregnant mothers, which had been an unsolved problem of the system for decades because of lack of major structural changes and investment. But further care needs to be considered in the training of PHMM regarding expected weight gain for pregnant mothers according to the pre-pregnancy BMI, especially in counseling obese mothers to control gaining excessive weight.

24.6   Conclusion and Recommendation

Nutrition counselling was a successful tool in improving the DD of pregnant mothers in the Sri Lankan setting. Studies need to be continued in identifying needed changes for the already developed nutrition counselling training to streamline pregnancy weight gain. Further, a well-established antenatal care system in the country is a strength in delivering interventions targeted to pregnant mothers. Finally, it is recommended that nutrition counselling can be used as an effective mode of improving dietary diversity of pregnant mothers using the current health system of the country.

Reflection Questions

1. Why was a cluster-randomized trial selected as the study method?

   As the research was conducted in the community and the Sri Lankan health system finds geographical demarcation pertaining to preventive health care delivery, it was very convenient to conduct the study as a community trial. The areas of public health midwives (PHMM) in Sri Lanka include small clusters with almost homogenous communities living together in the same area. This demographic division is identified in the country, mainly targeting the easy delivery of maternal and child health. In the epidemiological research, cluster-randomized trials are identified as the best method of testing an intervention in the community.

2. What are the measures taken to minimize the contamination of the intervention?

   After studying basic characteristics in community clusters, pairs of clusters were made, putting almost equal population sizes and geographic variations together. A total of 380 PHM areas were paired into 190, and 27 cluster pairs (54 clusters) were randomly selected for the study. One cluster from each pair was randomized to the intervention arm, leaving the other cluster for the control. Measures were taken not to include adjoining PHM areas in a pair and to maintain adequate distance to minimize the contamination of the intervention. PHMM in the intervention arm were taken separately for the training and educated about the importance of uncontaminated results. Still, some level of contamination was expected as there were PHMM in both intervention arm and control arm belonging to the same administrative area.

3. Why was the intervention delivered through public health midwives rather than delivering it by the researcher?

   Though the research needs to identify the effectiveness of the intervention, it is equally important to identify the practical issues that can arise when we incorporate it into the existing health care delivery system of the country. As this research was planning an improvement to the existing health system of the country, it was especially important to check the feasibility of the intervention in the system. Therefore, it was very much justifiable to deliver the intervention by PHMM rather than by a group of researchers.

4. Was the intervention found to be effective?

   Yes. The intervention was effective in changing pregnant mothers' behaviour towards better dietary diversity, and the training on dietary counselling identifies as an effective method for improving the counselling skills of PHMM.

5. What are the possible modifications for applying this intervention in other settings?

Food items in dietary counselling can differ according to the locally available food items and their nutrition value. The number of family members addressed in the counselling can be changed according to the type of family. The frequency of counselling too can be changed according to the education level of the mother, husband or family members. With these modifications, this intervention can be applied to any type of community in any region across the globe.

References

Demment, M. W., Young, M. M., & Sensenig, R. L. (2018). Providing micronutrients through food-based solutions: A key to human and national development. *The Journal of Nutrition*. https://doi.org/10.1093/jn/133.11.3879s.

El Bilali, H., O'Kane, G., Capone, R., Berry, E. M., & Dernini, S. (2017). Exploring relationships between biodiversity and dietary diversity in the Mediterranean region: Preliminary insights from a literature review. *American Journal of Food and Nutrition*. https://doi.org/10.12691/ajfn-5-1-1.

Ransom, E. I., & Elder, L. K. (2003). *Nutrition of women and adolescent girls: Why it matters*. Population Reference Bureau.

Family Health Bureau. (2017). *Anual report*. Retrieved from https://drive.google.com/file/d/1sIAn kf1okrinQI3VDCtOokPtf9vvc94o/view

FAO. (2016). Minimum dietary diversity for women – A guide to measurement. *Minimum Dietary Diversity for Women: A Guide for Measurement*. https://doi.org/10.1016/S0167-6393(00)00055-8.

Forouhi, N. G., Misra, A., Mohan, V., Taylor, R., & Yancy, W. (2018). Dietary and nutritional approaches for prevention and management of type 2 diabetes. *BMJ, 361*. https://doi.org/10.1136/bmj.k2234.

Gernand, A. D., Schulze, K. J., Stewart, C. P., West, K. P., & Christian, P. (2016). Micronutrient deficiencies in pregnancy worldwide: Health effects and prevention. *Nature Reviews Endocrinology, 12*(5), 274–289. https://doi.org/10.1038/nrendo.2016.37.

Ilmonen, J., Isolauri, E., Poussa, T., & Laitinen, K. (2011). Impact of dietary counseling and probiotic intervention on maternal anthropometric measurements during and after pregnancy: A randomized placebo-controlled trial. *Clinical Nutrition, 30*(2), 156–164. https://doi.org/10.1016/j.clnu.2010.09.009.

Ministry of Health and Nutrition, S. L. (2016). *General circular N0: 01–04/2016: Selection of Thriposha beneficiaries and distribution of Thriposha*. Retrieved from http://www.health.gov.lk/CMS/cmsmoh1/upload/english/01-04-2016-eng.pdf

Niinivirta, K., Isolauri, E., Laakso, P., Linderborg, K., & Laitinen, K. (2011). Dietary counseling to improve fat quality during pregnancy alters maternal fat intake and infant essential fatty acid status. *The Journal of Nutrition, 141*(7), 1281–1285.

Rimal, A., Fletcher, S. M., McWatters, K. H., Misra, S. K., & Deodhar, S. (2001). Perception of food safety and changes in food consumption habits: A consumer analysis. *International Journal of Consumer Studies, 25*(1), 43–52. https://doi.org/10.1111/j.1470-6431.2001.00162.x.

Ruel, M. T. (2003). Operationalizing dietary diversity: A review of measurement issues and research priorities. *The Journal of Nutrition, 133*(11), 3911S–3926S. https://doi.org/10.1093/jn/133.11.3911S.

Sanders, T. A. B. (2004). Diet and general health: Dietary counselling. *Caries Research, 38*(Suppl 1), 3–8. https://doi.org/10.1159/000074356.

Savy, M., Martin-Prével, Y., Traissac, P., Eymard-Duvernay, S., & Delpeuch, F. (2006). Dietary diversity scores and nutritional status of women change during the seasonal food shortage in rural Burkina Faso. *The Journal of Nutrition*. https://doi.org/10.1093/jn/136.10.2625.

Savy, M., Delpeuch, F., Eymard-Duvernay, S., Traissac, P., & Martin-Prével, Y. (2018). Dietary diversity scores and nutritional status of women change during the seasonal food shortage in rural Burkina Faso. *The Journal of Nutrition*. https://doi.org/10.1093/jn/136.10.2625.

Tinago, C. B., Annang Ingram, L., Blake, C. E., & Frongillo, E. A. (2017). Individual and structural environmental influences on utilization of iron and folic acid supplementation among pregnant women in Harare, Zimbabwe. *Maternal and Child Nutrition*. https://doi.org/10.1111/mcn.12350.

UNICEF & WHO. (2004). *Low birthweight: Country, regional and global estimates* (E. Å. T. Wardlaw, A. Blanc, J. Zupan, Eds.). UNICEF, Editorial and Publications Section.

Retrieved from https://data.unicef.org/wp-content/uploads/2015/12/low_birthweight_from_EY_107.pdf

Viteri, F. E., & Gonzalez, H. (2003). Adverse outcomes of poor micronutrient status in childhood and adolescence. *Nutrition Reviews*. https://doi.org/10.1301/00296640260130795.

WHO. (2016). *Double-duty actions for nutrition: Policy brief*. WHO.

World Health Organization. (2018). *Disease burden by cause, age, sex, by country and by region. 2000–2016*. Geneva.

Part IX

Democratic Governance

Perplexing Coexistence of Democracy, Transparency and Development in the Contemporary Era

Miskat Jahan

25.1 Introduction

For the time being, 123 of 192 countries follow democracy as one of their state principles. Democracy is one of the most conventional state principles, and it has made the path of development easier through ensuring transparency, accountability and the overall rule of law in state operations. Similarly, transparency as a legal phenomenon is not altogether new. The importance of transparency as a policy principle has been growing as its various beneficial effects are being celebrated worldwide (Banisar 2006). The nexus and interdependence of democracy, transparency and development have become debatable issues in contemporary global politics. Many scholars have undertaken studies on this perspective.

But currently a different wind of democracy is blowing in countries that do not exactly define any specific nature of the relationship between democracy, development and transparency. Right-wing populists have risen to power, rejecting transparency requirements based on documents while claiming that they 'hide nothing' (Roelofs 2019). The correlation between economic development and democratization is probably one of the strongest we find in the social sciences; no matter what measure of democracy or of development is employed, a positive correlation between them is always present in data (Cheibub and Vreeland 2012). Recently different dimensions have been added to global politics. Populism has taken hold in many countries that may shrink the space of liberal democracy and the existence of transparency as the core element of good governance. Yet the process of development cannot be put off for want of a perfect democracy or transparency. Although the coexistence of democracy and transparency is considered inevitable for

M. Jahan (✉)
Department of Public Administration, Comilla University, Cumilla, Bangladesh

© The Author(s), under exclusive license to Springer Nature Switzerland AG 2021
S. Dhiman, R. Samaratunge (eds.), *New Horizons in Management, Leadership and Sustainability*, Future of Business and Finance, https://doi.org/10.1007/978-3-030-62171-1_25

development, many countries are developing without following statutory democracy or proper transparency.

This paper explores the deceptive coexistence of democracy, development and transparency in the contemporary world based on secondary data and empirical knowledge to gain a clear view of the current global issues related to the coexistence of democracy, development and transparency.

25.2 Objectives of the Study

This study explores the interrelation between democracy and development from a global perspective. Its specific objectives are as follows:

1. To point out the substantive definitions of democracy, transparency and development
2. To undertake a literature review on the interrelation of democracy, transparency and development
3. To compose a compact understanding about the recent vexatious contemporary affairs related to democracy, transparency and development
4. To analyze the current deceptive coexistence of democracy, transparency and development.

25.3 Methodology

Quantitative and qualitative data from secondary sources have been used in this study. Substantive definitions have been reviewed to provide the exact connotations of democracy, transparency and development. The literature has been reviewed to determine the interlinkage of democracy, transparency and development. The study has sought to depict the current perplexing state of democracy, transparency and development based on secondary source analysis and empirical knowledge. Secondary sources include journal articles, research reports, relevant websites, newspapers, books and the author's empirical knowledge. Secondary sources have been investigated in depth to make the study viable. The author's empirical knowledge has been used to analyze the current state of the democracy, development and transparency.

25.4 Substantive Definitions of Democracy, Development and Transparency

Though the work of defining democracy and development began a long time ago, different propagation of these propositions now demands more substantive definitions.

25.4.1 Defining Democracy

Prior definitions of democracy give more emphasis to electoral voting to define the nature of democracy. In 1942, political scientist Schumpeter remarked on the competitive struggle for the people's vote as a means of democracy (Schumpeter 1942). Another political scientist, Robert A. Dahl, defined a new terminology, 'polyarchy', identifying seven key criteria; among the relatively frequent criteria, fair and free elections was foremost.

For a long time, the international community only focused on the importance of elections as the determinant of democracy. But there was an implicit assumption that elections will not just be a foundation stone but over time will be a key generator of further democratic reforms (Carothers 2002). Yet it has become increasingly clear with the emergence of new democracies in many regions of the developing world since the 1980s that the process of democratization entails not only a transition to formal democracy but also the consolidation of such a democratic system (Menocal 2011).

The US Department of State's Bureau of International Information Programs has defined democracy as more than a set of constitutional rules and procedures that determine how a government functions. In a democracy, government is only one element coexisting in a social fabric of many and varied institutions, political parties, organizations and associations. This diversity is called pluralism, and it assumes that the many organized groups and institutions in a democratic society do not depend upon the government for their existence, legitimacy or authority.

According to American political scientist Larry Diamond, democracy consists of four key elements: a political system for choosing and replacing the government through free and fair election; the active participation of the people, as citizens, in politics and civic life; protection of the human rights of all citizens; and a rule of law, in which the laws and procedures apply equally to all citizens (Diamond 2004).

Changes in the definitions of democracy occurred in the twentieth century. In his *Theory of Justice*, Rawls puts this focus upfront: 'The definitive idea for deliberative democracy is the idea of deliberation itself. When citizens deliberate, they exchange views and debate their supporting reasons concerning public political questions' (Sen 2009).

However, Amartya Sen has said in *The Idea of Justice* that 'Ballots do, of course, have a very important role even for the expression and effectiveness of the process of public reasoning, but they are not the only thing that matters, and they can be seen just as one part – admittedly a very important part – of the way public reason operates in a democratic society'.

So it can be said that in contemporary political science literature, people's participation has been emphasized together with elections to define democracy.

25.4.2 Defining Transparency

Transparency, as one of the important indicators of good governance, became popular in the last decade of the twentieth century. Basically, transparency as an accounting principle was founded in the 1980s to discuss 'macro-economic transparency'. Transparency dispels opacity, the first refuge of corruption, inefficiency and incompetence, and it addresses asymmetries that prevent reliable information from serving as building blocks for resilient democracies and markets. It depends on two necessary and jointly sufficient conditions: the visibility of information and its inferential ability – the ability to draw accurate conclusions from it (Michener and Bersch 2013). Other studies investigate and assess transparency as the degree to which organizations convey information related to governance and financing to their stakeholders (Bushman and Smith 2003).

Various studies explain transparency as the timely disclosure of accurate information. In this case, both senders and receivers have an important role in ensuring accurate information dissemination and in ensuring transparency. Theorization of transparency as a matter of information disclosure assumes that successful transmission occurs when the cognitive abilities and information processing requirements of both the sender and receiver are taken into account (Rasmussen 1991). Vishwanath and Kaufmann (1999) define transparency as the 'increased flow of timely and reliable economic, social and political information, which is accessible to all relevant stakeholders'. In addition, stakeholders should identify relevant content that may meet their informational needs.

However, all approaches use indicators such as relevance, timeliness, understandability and reliability to explore the relationship between transparency, disclosure and observability (Rawlins 2009).

25.4.3 Defining Development

Basically, development began with the invention of fire and the growth of civilization. One of the simplest definitions of development can be considered the objective of moving towards a state relatively better than the one that previously existed (Chambers 1997). In this view, development could mean any positive change in life (Sikuka 2017).

Many early theorists defined development as only the economic progression of a state. But now it is considered that development is not purely an economic phenomenon but rather a multi-dimensional process involving reorganization and reorientation of the entire economic and social system. Recent debates on a rights-based approach to development also focus on participation, accountability and other elements that are very similar to those values underlying substantive forms of democracy (UNDP 2000).

Stiglitz (2003) also defined development as a 'transformation of society' that goes beyond economic growth to include social dimensions such as literacy, distribution of income, life expectancy etc.

Economist Amartya Sen (1999) has also focused on development as freedom – a suitably broad definition that incorporates not only economic indicators but also freedoms like human and political rights, social opportunities, transparency guarantees and protective security.

According to Ben Daley (2014), development can be defined as bringing about social change that allows people to achieve their human potential. An important point to emphasize is that development is a political term: it has a range of meanings that depend on the context in which the term is used, and it may also be used to reflect and to justify a variety of different agendas held by different people or organizations.

Definitions of development vary from institution to institution as well as context to context. Development is not only the rise of gross domestic product (GDP) or gross national product (GNP) but also the improved accumulation of socio-political synergies.

25.5 The Literature

Many intellectual and theoretical analyses of democracy, transparency and development interrelations by academicians and experts are available to study. To get an explicit overview of democracy, transparency and development interrelation, previous literature is noted here briefly.

Martin Lipset observed that democracy is related to economic development, a view first advanced in 1959, and has generated the largest body of research on any topic in comparative politics. It has been supported and contested, revised and extended, buried and resuscitated (Przeworski and Limongi 1997). However, Lipset, in his famous essay 'Some Social Requisites of Democracy', argued that there is one of the strongest and most enduring relationships of democracy and development in the social sciences. And generally transparency has become the absolute repercussion of democracy. As Shapiro (2003) suggests, 'democratic leaders can never be entirely free from a commitment to truth-telling'. Democracy and transparency have thus been conceived as having multiple dimensions, and some of these dimensions overlap explicitly (Hollyer et al. 2011). Both of these are practised to accelerate the way of development through ensuring good governance.

Today, even after the prolonged democratization wave that started in the 1970s and accelerated in the 1990s, the distribution of democracies remains highly skewed by level of per capita income (Boix 2011). One of the simplest explanations is that once people start to acquire higher levels of economic development and social maturity, they will begin to seek more transparency and accountability from their governments, thus achieving better democracy (Sikuka 2017). Hence, it seems that the practice of democracy and transparency is interlinked with development.

It is also significant that global historical events like world wars, the Cold War etc. introduced the practice of democracy in many countries as an effect of development on political institutions, and this development of political institutions later prompted the provision of transparency. Transparency pertains to questions of who rules, how governments might be replaced and, indeed, how elections are contested in countries that fill key offices through an electoral process. In other words, transparency may pertain to the very question of whether one can call a political regime 'democratic' (Hollyer et al. 2011).

If one follows Sen (1999) and adopts a definition of development as 'freedom', then by definition democracy as well as transparency must lead to development (Menocal 2011).

In the same vein, Stiglitz (2003) argues that transparency could set up a virtuous circle where increased legitimacy, democratic participation and trust would lead to a dynamic change in the government. However, it can be said that democracy also has some intrinsic values that lead to policy decisions in a way that is inclusive, participatory and transparent, which accelerates development.

In international business research, transparency is deemed an ideal condition for democratic societies since it means that citizens are able to observe and access all information about public affairs – a situation that Fung (2013) has called an 'infotopia'.

Trust is another consequence of transparency. A statesman may gain citizens' trust through practising democracy in a true sense and ensuring transparency of those important state affairs that make the state progress. Hence good governance, for example, is understood to coincide with transparency in many contemporary organizational and regulatory contexts (Braithwaite and Drahos 2000). Empirical research supports the claim that transparency has positive effects, suggesting a correlation between transparency and, for example, low inflation rates and a decreased occurrence of famine (Besley and Burgess 2002). There is a clear link between transparency and democracy, in the sense that more transparency is supposed to reinforce democratization (Héritier 2003).

From this discussion, it is clear that the coexistence of democracy and transparency plays an inevitable role in making the path of development smooth.

25.6 Understanding How Contemporary Affairs Lead to the Perplexing Coexistence of Democracy, Transparency and Development

The following figure depicts the relationship between the practice of democracy, transparency and development (Fig. 25.1).

In this section, contemporary affairs are reviewed that assert the perplexing coexistence of democracy, transparency and development across the globe. Through describing contemporary affairs, light will be shed on the current status of democracy, transparency and development in different countries.

Francis Fukuyama, an American political scientist, has noted in his renowned book *The End of History and the Last Man* that 'What we may be witnessing is not just the end of the Cold War, or the passing of a particular period of post-war history, but the end of history as such: that is, the end point of mankind's ideological evolution and the universalization of Western liberal democracy as the final form of

Fig. 25.1 Relationship between democracy, transparency and development

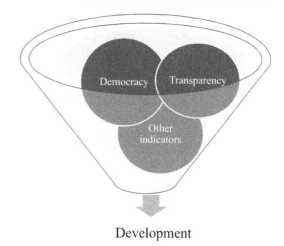

Development

human government' (Fukuyama 1992). Fukuyama declared the introduction of liberal democracy against the perspective of abolition of socialism (as communism) in the Soviet Union. But at present, grief about the state of liberal democracy is increasing day by day in different countries. Yet advocates of transparency also celebrate it for its role in realizing democracy, equality, economic development, improvement in education, poverty relief and a decline in corruption (Banisar 2006).

Roberts (2006) indicates that there has been a decline in transparency in the United States since the beginning of this century. The United States of America, known as the 'Lighthouse of Democracy', has chosen a leader who has no political background and does not practise the principles of the Republican Party at all. Moreover, he does not appear to care for democratic values or the institutionalization of democracy. The President continually argues against the freedom of the press as well as people's opinions, which results in a severe lack of transparency. *The Economist* in its Democracy Index (2017) has also described the American political system as a 'flawed democracy'. In the name of the 'America First' slogan, the USA has become isolated from the international community. The President's irrational speeches and controversial policies have made the people distrust him. He is accused of corrupt practices and sexual harassment. So the question is, how will democracy be sustained in the regime of such an ill-practised, opaque state leader? Although the condition of democracy is not so flourishing in the USA, and the transparency of various state affairs is questionable, the economic influence of the USA in the world economy remains a very important factor. Despite facing challenges at the domestic level, along with a rapidly transforming global landscape, the US economy is still the largest and the most important in the world. The US economy represents about 20% of total global output and is still larger than that of China. Moreover, according to the International Monetary Fund (IMF), the US has the sixth highest per capita GDP (PPP) (Focus Economics 2018) (Fig. 25.2).

Thus, it can be said that undemocratic and opaque practices of America are not influencing the progress of the economy. Although less than one third of the younger

	2013	2014	2015	2016	2017
Population (million)	317	319	321	324	326
GDP per capita (USD)	52,737	54,657	56,411	57,559	59,501
GDP (USD)	16,692	17,428	18,121	18,624	19,391
Economic Growth (GDP, annual variation in %)	1.7	2.6	2.9	1.5	2.3

Fig. 25.2 United States economy data. (Focus Economics 2018)

generation in America thinks that democracy is obvious for development, economic growth is taking place there at full speed.

India, the largest country practising democracy in the world, has developed its own incremental trends, primarily based on the influence of a pluralistic society with many minorities in terms of religion, caste and language (Kainikara 2017). Fair electoral practice is one important indicator of democracy, which was flawed in the elections in India in 2014 and 2019. According to the Association of Democratic Reform (ADR), the source of the funds spent on the election in India is turbid. Transparency about the background of the candidates in the election is absent. ADR identified the other more alarming characteristic of the Indian Lok Shova – that 30% of the candidates have criminal cases against them. The Bharatiya Janata Party (BJP)-led government has also given in to majoritarian assertiveness, disregarding the basic rights of minority communities. The corrosive influence of money plays a decisive role in the minds of a majority of voters (815,000,000, 2014), who are poor and illiterate (Hasan 2018). In spite of having political anomalies, India has the fastest growing economy in the region. GDP is on a recovery path after a slowdown in the first quarter of 2017–2018, and real GDP growth for the second quarter (fiscal year (FY) 2018) increased to 6.3% from 5.7% in the previous quarter. The second half of 2017–2018 witnessed a higher growth rate, and this is further expected to consolidate in the coming year as the benefits of other reforms gain traction (CII Economy Matters 2018) (Fig. 25.3).

The sectoral growth data of India are cited here from the report of the Confederation of Indian Industry, 'Indian Economy in 2018: Current Status, Prospects and Challenges'. The agricultural sector registered moderate growth as erratic monsoons in several areas and flooding in some states impacted performance. Industrial growth accelerated sharply during the second quarter of FY 2018 and jumped to 6.9% from 1.5% in the previous quarter, on account of a sharp increase in manufacturing and electricity, gas, water supply and utility services. Manufacturing registered an impressive growth of 7% in Q2 FY 2018 compared to 1.2% posted in the first quarter. The service sector grew only marginally at 6.6% in the second quarter compared to 7.8% in the previous quarter (Fig. 25.4).

Fig. 25.3 GDP of India in FY 2017 and FY 2018. (Confederation Indian Industry Economy Matters (November Issue) 2018)

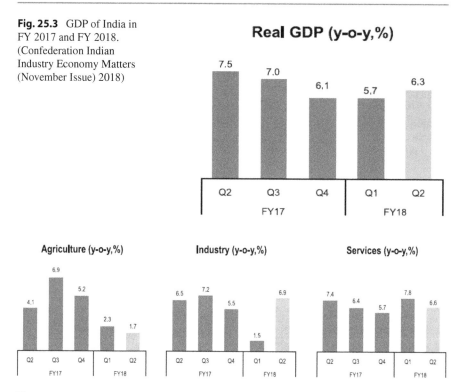

Fig. 25.4 Sectoral growth data of India. (Confederation Indian Industry Economy Matters (November Issue) 2018)

Thus, it is revealed that, in spite of undemocratic and opaque practices, the Indian economy is growing continuously. Pranab Bardhan (2010) has said that it is a paradox even for those who believe in a positive relationship between economic equality or social homogeneity and democracy. India's wealth inequality (say, in land distribution and even more in education or human capital) is one of the highest in the world. Indian society is also one of the most heterogeneous in the world (in terms of ethnicity, language, caste and religion), and social inequality, a legacy of the caste system, is considerable.

China is another rising member in the cohort of the next global superpower worldwide. According to Wikipedia, the socialist market economy of the People's Republic of China is the world's second largest economy by nominal GDP and the world's largest economy by purchasing power parity. Until 2015, China was the world's fastest-growing major economy, with growth rates averaging 10% over 30 years. Due to historical and political facts of China's developing economy, China's public sector accounts for a bigger share of the national economy than the burgeoning private sector (Democracy from Wikipedia 2018). China reached all the Millennium Development Goals (MDGs) by 2015 and made a major contribution to the achievement of the MDGs globally. Although China's GDP growth has gradually showed since 2012, it is still impressive by current global standards. Focus Economics has revealed the following economic data of China (Fig. 25.5).

However, the matter for analysis here is the political development in line with the economic development of China. The politics of the People's Republic of China takes place in a framework of a socialist republic run by a single party, the Communist Party of China, headed by General Secretary. State power within the People's Republic of China (PRC) is exercised through the Communist Party, the Central People's Government (State Council) and their provincial and local representation (Democracy from Wikipedia 2018). Liaberthal et al. (2014) opined that China's path to political reform over the last three decades has been slow, but discourse among Chinese political scientists continues to be vigorous and forward thinking. So it is noticeable that without following the practice of democracy and transparency, China has become the second largest economy of the world through its authoritarian regime.

The re-elected President of Turkey is also taking Turkey towards authoritarianism instead of democratization, which causes an absence of transparency in the state mechanism. In late June 2018, the presidential election in Turkey returned incumbent Recep Tayyip Erdogan. Turkey, which was seen as a Muslim democracy, has now converted into an authoritarian state, giving Erdogan massive presidential powers (Hasan 2018). Recently Turkey's economy has become hampered by the disagreeable relationship between America and Turkey. There are many complaints of irregularities against Turkey's President and the political leaders of his party (Goldstone 2018). So development under this authoritarian ruler may become questionable in Turkey.

Empirical evidence shows that authoritarianism is also especially rising in developing countries like Bangladesh. Bangladesh is a country where democracy has been stipulated as a state principle. But a recent huge 'partyarchy' of government and political turmoil have made the country undemocratic and turbid to date. General elections were held in Bangladesh on 5 January 2014 in accordance with

	2013	2014	2015	2016	2017
Population (million)	1,361	1,368	1,375	1,383	1,390
GDP per capita (USD)	7,124	7,662	7,948	8,103	8,806
GDP (USD bn)	9,694	10,480	10,925	11,204	12,241
	2013	2014	2015	2016	2017
Economic Growth (GDP, annual variation in %)	7.8	7.3	6.9	6.7	6.9

Fig. 25.5 Economy data of China. (Focus Economics 2018)

the constitutional requirement that the election must take place within the 90-day period before the expiration of the term of the *Jatiya Sangshad* on 24 January 2014. Since then, bitter politics have continued to dominate the political landscape, having wider ramifications on the country's democratic governance. The situation remains tense and volatile as major political parties are yet to come to any consensus as to the mechanism under which free, fair and credible elections could be arranged (Zakaria 2018). In spite of undemocratic practices and lack of adequate transparency of state affairs, Bangladesh is making faster socio-economic growth. It has already become one of the fastest developing countries in South Asia.

Gross domestic product (GDP) growth rate of the last 10 years in Bangladesh is set out below (Fig. 25.6).

Despite a poor governance record, the country demonstrated remarkable success in socio-economic development indicators, which is termed by many experts as a Bangladesh Paradox (World Bank Annual Report 2016). The life expectancy of people has also marked a sharp increase from about 58 in 1990 to 72 in 2015 (Zakaria 2017). So without following democracy properly and practising the provision of transparency adequately, Bangladesh is making astounding socio-economic development.

The Russian Federation is fundamentally structured as a multiparty representative democracy (Democracy from Wikipedia 2018). But through the last election, President Vladimir Putin has strengthened his authoritarian regime, which leads to the lack of transparency of the state. Misdeeds like controlling media and authoritarianism etc. were argued against Putin from long ago. But a firm labour market, higher commodity prices and rising oil production are expected to boost growth this year. However, high geopolitical uncertainty and the possibility of further economic sanctions remain key risks to the outlook (Focus Economics 2018). The Economist Intelligence Unit describes Russia as 'authoritarian'. Others have labelled it as a 'hybrid regime' and 'fake democracy' (Hasan 2018).

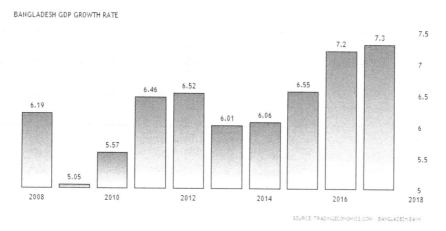

Fig. 25.6 Gross domestic product (GDP) growth rate of the last 10 years in Bangladesh. (www. tradingeconomics.com, Bangladesh Bank)

Amartya Sen has said that Middle Eastern history and the history of Muslim people also include a great many accounts of public discussion and political participation through dialogue. But now the illusion of an inescapably non-democratic destiny of the Middle East is both confused and very seriously misleading – perniciously so – as a way of thinking about either world politics or global justice today (Sen 2009).

In the case of Africa, for a long time authoritarianism has been rising. The presidential election in Zimbabwe in late July 2018 also came under international criticism for the violence that led to several deaths. The presidential election in Egypt in March 2018 was even heavier handed. Only one candidate was allowed to run for the presidency, along with incumbent General Abdel Fatah Al-Sisi, who overthrew the democratically elected government of Mohammed Morsi in July 2013 (Hasan 2018). In many African countries like the Congo, Sierra Leon and Libya, predators have ruled for many years. The economic development of these countries is also not good.

From this discussion, it is clear that, in spite of having a history of democratic practice, many countries are experiencing authoritarian regimes. It is noticeable that, after the economic recession of 2007–2008, decay of democracy has been occurring. According to the Economist Intelligence Unit, about 89 countries are backsliding in terms of democratic practice as well as in maintaining transparency. Development of democracy is taking place in only 27 countries. But populist leaders may not be sustained because of their corruption and misdeeds. Malaysia is a glaring example in this case.

25.7 Discussion and Conclusion

Discussion on the interrelationship between democracy, transparency and development is not a new thing. But the contemporary diversified nature of democracy and the lack of adequate transparency demand more discourse to demark the interrelation of democracy, transparency and development. From this study, it has been found that many countries are backsliding in the practice of liberal democracy in spite of their economic growth. In point of fact, it can be said that rulers are misusing democracy to hold their power for longer periods, and also they are not maintaining transparency in the state mechanism. Yet, in most cases, economic growth is not being affected by these authoritarian rulers. As they want to stay longer in power, they show economic growth as the most important indicator of the development of their regime. This is to deceive citizens. Selim Jahan, Director of the Human Development Report Office, has said that to understand how developed a country is, we must also grasp how people's lives are affected by progress. And to understand that, we must consider the 'quality' of the change that is being reported (Jahan 2017). So not only economic growth but also quality of people's living should be considered as development indicators. Economic growth may take place under authoritarian regimes, but people's lives are better in democratic regimes because transparency, rule of law, separation of powers and, overall, social justice may take place. Deterioration of liberal democracy and simultaneous lack of adequate transparency may not be a good sign for overall human development.

References

Bardhan, P. (2010). *Democracy and development in India: A comparative perspective*. Retrieved from https://eml.berkeley.edu/~webfac/bardhan/papers/DemDevIndia.pdf

Banisar, D. (2006). *Freedom of information around the world*. Retrieved from https://www.privacyinternational.org/article/freedominformation-around-world-2006-report

Besley, T., & Burgess, R. (2002). The political economy of government responsiveness. *The Quarterly Journal of Economics*.

Boix, C. (2011). Democracy, development and the international system. *American Political Science Review, 105*(4), 809–828.

Braithwaite, J., & Drahos, P. (2000). *Global business regulation*. Cambridge: Cambridge University Press.

Bushman, R., & Smith, A. J. (2003). Transparency, financial accounting information, and corporate governance. *Economic Policy Review, 9*(1), 65–87.

Carothers, T. (2002). The end of the transition paradigm. *Journal of Democracy, 13*, 1.

Chambers, R. (1997). Responsible well-being: A Personal agenda for development. *World Development, 25*(11), 1743–1754.

Cheibub, J. A. & Vreeland, J. R. (2012). *Economic development, democratization and democracy*. International Conference on Democracy as Idea and Practice, University of Oslo.

Democracy from Wikipedia. (2018). The free encyclopedia. Retrieved from https://en.wikipedia.org/wiki/Democracy

Diamond, L. (2004). *What is democracy*. Retrieved from https://en.wikipedia.org/wiki/Democracy

Daley, B. (2014). *Understanding sustainable development*. Retrieved from https://www.soas.ac.uk/cedep-demos/000_P501_USD_K3736-Demo/index.htm

Economic Forecasts from the World's Leading Economists. Retrieved from https://www.focus-economics.com/

Fukuyama, F. Y. (1992). *The end of history and the last man*. New York: Free Press.

Fung, A. (2013). Infotopia: Unleashing the democratic power of transparency. *Politics and Society, 41*, 183–212.

Goldstone, J. A. (2018). *Corruption will fracture in the popularity of populism*. Retrieved from https://www.prothomalo.com/opinion/article/1526896/

Hasan, M. (2018). Democracies in decline. *The Daily Star*, p. 6.

Héritier, A. (2003). Composite democracy in Europe: The role of transparency and access to information. *Journal of European Public Policy, 10*(5), 814–833.

Hollyer, J. R., Rosendorff, B. P., & Vreeland, J. R. (2011). Democracy and transparency. *The Journal of Politics, 73*(4), 1191–1205.

Indian Economy in 2018: Current Status, Prospects and Challenges. (2018). Retrieved from https://www.cii.in/

Jahan, S. (2017). Counting what counts in development. Retrieved from https://www.project-syndicate.org/commentary/human-development-quality-over-quantity-by-selim-jahan-2017-09?barrier=accesspaylog

Kainikara, S. (2017). *Changing face of democracy in India-analysis*. Retrieved from https://www.eurasiareview.com/30052017-changing-face-of-democracy-in-india-analysis/

Liaberthal, K. G., Li, C., & Keping, Y. (2014). *China's political development*. Washington, DC: Brookings Institution Press.

Menocal, A. R. (2011). Analysing the relationship between democracy and development: defining basic concepts and assessing key linkages. *Commonwealth Good Governance 2011/12*.

Michener, G., & Bersch, K. (2013). Identifying transparency. *Information Polity, 2013*, 233–242.

Przeworski, A., & Limongi, F. (1997). Modernization: Theories and facts. *World Politics, 49*(2), 155–183.

Rasmussen, R. V. (1991). A communication model based on the conduit metaphor. *Management Communication Quarterly, 4*, 363–374.

Rawlins, B. (2009). Give the emperor a mirror: Toward developing a stakeholder measurement of organizational transparency. *Journal of Public Relations Research, 21*(1), 71–99.

Roberts, A. (2006). *Blacked out: Government secrecy in the information age* (p. 2006). Cambridge: Cambridge University Press.

Roelofs, P. (2019). Transparency and mistrust: Who or what should be made transparent? *Governance,* published by Wiley Periodicals, Inc.

Schumpeter, J. (1942). *Capitalism, socialism and democracy*. London: Harper Perennial.

Sen, A. (1999). *Development as freedom*. Oxford: Oxford University Press.

Sen, A. (2009). *The idea of justice*. London: Penguin Group.

Shapiro, I. (2003). *The moral foundations of politics*. New Haven, CT: Yale University Press.

Sikuka, K. (2017). *Is there a link between Democracy and Development in Africa?* Retrieved from http://www.accord.org.za/conflict -trends/editorial-2017-3/

Stiglitz, J. (2003). Towards a new paradigm of development. In J. H. Dunning (Ed.), *Making globalization good*. Oxford: Oxford University Press.

UNDP. (2000). *Human rights and human development: Human development report.* New York: UNDP.

United States Economy Data. Retrieved from https://www.focus-economics.com/countries/united-states

Vishwanath, T. & Kaufmann, D. (1999). Towards transparency in finance and governance. Available at SSRN: https://ssrn.com/abstract=258978 or http://dx.doi.org/10.2139/ssrn.258978

World Bank Annual Report. (2016). Retrieved from https://openknowledge.worldbank.org/handle/10986/24985

Zakaria, S. M. (2017). *Relationship between Democracy and Development: Evidence from Bangladesh*. Retrieved from http://bigd.bracu.ac.bd/index.php/resources/sub-menu-item-4/working-paper/11.

Zakaria, S. M. (2018, August 10). Where do we stand in democratic governance? *The Daily Star*, p. 7.

Part X

Disaster Management

Evaluating Seismic Vulnerability of Residential Buildings by Rapid Evaluation Method (REM)

26

Md Faiz Shah, Orsolya K. Kegyes-Brassai, Anas Ahmed, and Parves Sultan

26.1 Introduction

Increased development and urbanization of a city may cause higher risk from seismic events, even in areas of moderate seismicity, such as the area of investigation of the present study. The city of Jeddah in Saudi Arabia is expanding rapidly in terms of building and population. The objective of the study is to specifically address the rapid evaluation of many buildings in Jeddah with steps to determine hazard, assess building stock, and compute vulnerability through a scoring method.

Earthquake hazard mitigation research focuses on evaluating potential building damage scenarios from different magnitude events. The methods facilitate prevention by gathering information about building condition and expected damage so that the most vulnerable buildings can be strengthened to mitigate risk (Shah et al. 2018). When many buildings are too irregular and have a wide variety of material properties, comprehensive structural analysis and evaluation are time-consuming. Alternative methods have been applied in many cases and provide a

M. F. Shah (✉) · P. Sultan
School of Business and Law, CQUniversity, Melbourne, Australia
e-mail: m.shah3@cqu.edu.au

O. K. Kegyes-Brassai
Faculty of Architecture, Civil Engineering & Transport Sciences, Szechenyi Istvan University, Győr, Hungary
e-mail: kegyesbo@sze.hu

A. Ahmed
Faculty of Engineering, University of Jeddah, Jeddah, Saudi Arabia
e-mail: anas@uj.edu.sa

© The Author(s), under exclusive license to Springer Nature Switzerland AG 2021
S. Dhiman, R. Samaratunge (eds.), *New Horizons in Management, Leadership and Sustainability*, Future of Business and Finance,
https://doi.org/10.1007/978-3-030-62171-1_26

541

reasonable compromise of time, cost and efficiency. The visual screening method, a low-cost or cost-effective method developed by researchers, is based on the inspection of structural systems, time and mode of construction, and materials used. Assessing buildings by means of the rapid evaluation method (REM) requires less expertise and time. As a preseismic assessment tool, score assignments from REM may be applied to evaluate the relative vulnerability of structures in a neighborhood. This study follows previous research methods and interprets score assignment values of FEMA (2002) to buildings in the case study area with a research question: to what extent can the rapid evaluation method (REM) assess the vulnerability of residential buildings in Jeddah?

26.2   Evaluating Vulnerability

The seismic vulnerability of building stock can be determined by expert opinions offering the possibility to estimate damage before an earthquake occurs. For the assessment, one of the main ingredients in a loss model is an accurate, transparent, and conceptually sound algorithm to assess the seismic vulnerability of the building stock, and in fact many tools and methodologies have been proposed over the past 30 years for this purpose (Calvi et al. 2006). In the case of analytical approaches, vulnerability is expressed as a critical acceleration causing a damage mechanism to occur based on the identification of collapse mechanisms, yielding the equivalent shear capacity (Benedetti and Pezzzoli 1996). Detailed analyses are time-consuming, and these evaluations correspond to the methods of structural analysis and design. The main disadvantage is that they should be performed for every investigated building individually; therefore, alternative methods have been developed to enable the rapid evaluation of large building stock.

Visual screening methods, based on systems calibrated by experts, allow for the quantification of structural vulnerabilities more easily than do analytical approaches. There is no need for detailed calculations and multiple scenarios. In the case of observed vulnerability (Haddar 1992; Castano and Zamarbide 1992), the damage is defined as a ratio of the replacement cost or the degree of loss of all affected buildings considering the number of casualties, too. The relationship between damage and earthquake intensity is valid only for the region where it was developed. Another method is to ask experts to estimate the expected percentage of damage caused by a given intensity, which is implied in macroseismic scales, e.g., the European macroseismic scale (EMS) (Grünthal 1998). These scales are used to evaluate the possible damages after an earthquake (Fäh et al. 2001).

Score assignment methods determine seismically hazardous structures by identifying structural deficiencies. Quantitative information is gathered to determine the level of damage according to the severity of a potential seismic event. Potential structural deficiencies are identified from observed correlations between damage and structural characteristics. The main aim is to determine if a building needs a more detailed investigation or not. Score assignment methods have been successfully applied recently to seven European cities in the RISK-UE European project

(Mouroux et al. 2004). In Japan, the JBDPA (Japanese Seismic Index Method) describes three seismic screening procedures to estimate the seismic performance of a building: a seismic performance index (strength, ductility etc.), time-dependent deterioration of the building, and a seismic judgment index for the safety of structure (Fukuyama et al. 2001).

26.3   The REM Procedure

The REM procedure can be used for ranking a neighborhood's seismic rehabilitation needs by designing seismic hazard mitigation programs, developing inventories of buildings with specific seismic vulnerability information, planning postearthquake building safety evaluation efforts, and determining insurance ratings. The REM approach relates common building structural, material and construction features to the seismic building capacity curves. The building capacity curve (also known as the push-over curve) is a plot of a building's lateral-load resistance as a function of some characteristic lateral displacement. This is derived usually from a static push-over analysis that defines the relationship between static equivalent base shear versus a building's roof displacement. Standard building capacity curves for different classes of buildings have been developed from many possible combinations of structural systems and materials. It is assumed that the final push-over state corresponds to building collapse or ultimate limit state. The capacity curve of the building is compared to the demand spectrum corresponding to a low-, moderate-, or high-demand seismic event. Depending on the relation between the capacity (resilience) of the building and the demand (intensity) of the seismic event, the building will have some probability of collapse. A low capacity with high demand will generate a high probability of collapse, while a high capacity with low demand will generate a low probability of collapse.

The REM procedure by commonly used methods (EMS, FEMA 155) does not require the performance of any structural analyses; rather, the evaluator must collect data to determine (i) the primary structural lateral-load-resisting system scoring with a basic structural score and (ii) building attributes that modify the seismic performance expected of this lateral-load-resisting system, such as applied code, height, irregularity of the building, and soil conditions. To complete the evaluation process, a wide variety of data is required. The collected data are classified (grouped) into one of many (perhaps as many as ten) categories. An essential step in a risk analysis is to ensure a uniform interpretation of data and results. When dealing with vulnerability models, the classification system should group together structures that would be expected to behave similarly during a seismic event. The need for a deeper diversification of building behaviors has led to more elaborate classification systems, where consideration is given to primary parameters affecting building damage and loss characteristics, such as the basic structural system, the seismic design criteria (code level), the building height (low-rise, midrise, high-rise), as well as nonstructural elements affecting nonstructural damage. For masonry buildings, the EMS (European Microseismic Scale) classification considers seven typologies, various materials, techniques of installation, and construction. FEMA 155 classifies masonry structures according to reinforcement only. The detailed EMS classification was not needed in the study because this type of building in Jeddah would fall into the category of "unreinforced masonry", regardless of its other features.

For reinforced concrete, the EMS differentiates the construction only about the seismic-resistant system (frame or shear wall); FEMA also determines one more category for RC: a concrete frame with unreinforced masonry infill, which is typical of this region as well. These differences favored the use of FEMA 155 for this research tailored to the most used building construction of the area and creating a checklist. According to FEMA 155, the probability of collapse is represented by a Basic Structural Hazard Score (BSH), which represents the average probability of surviving a seismic event, the maximum considered earthquake (MCE) (Eq. 26.1). The BSH scores are estimated from the building fragility and capacity curves of the HAZUS Technical Manual (NIBS 1999), representing an 'average' score for buildings in each class used for large-scale economic studies:

$$BSH = -\log 10 \left[P\left(collapse\, given\, MCE \right) \right] \tag{26.1}$$

Additional building features, so-called Score Modifiers (SMs) specific to that building, may increase or decrease the BSH score, resulting in the final Structural Score (S) (Eq. 26.2).

$$S = BSH \pm SMs \tag{26.2}$$

26.4 Data Collection

Conducting a cluster analysis with population and building data, two districts were selected for the investigation and to carry on a survey. The objective of the survey was to collect information on residential buildings in two districts. One of the districts represents a developing urbanized area, Al-Salamah, and the other a typical old area, Al-Balad. This selection offers the possibility to compare the vulnerability of buildings constructed according to different seismic codes and to make assumptions about the rest of the city based on typical structures of districts. In accordance with previous inventories for score assignment (Kegyes-Brassai 2014) and knowledge about the most used building construction of the area, a checklist was prepared to group the building points into three major areas:

- Identification of the buildings (district, street, number)
- General data (age and function of the buildings, regularity in plan and elevation, the position of the building, changes in function, previous damages etc.)
- Structural data (construction system, quality of materials, workmanship); and
- Other remarks

The visual inspection was conducted by trained staff during the field survey done through the period of June to August 2016. Data were uploaded onto an online

Table 26.1   Main features of examined buildings

Analyzed buildings	Al-Balad	Al-Salamah
Number of buildings	308	714
General building condition		
Good	54%	**81%**
Minor restoration needed	46%	17%
Construction period		
1965–1975	**32%**	–
1976–1982	**31%**	6%
1983–2007	13%	**64%**
After 2007	1%	30%
Structural system		
Column beam system with fitted walls (steel, RC, wood)	12.34%	2.94%
Column beam system with infill walls (steel, RC, wood)	**72.08%**	**95.66%**
Load-bearing walls (masonry, stone, mixed, clay)	12.34%	1.26%
Others	3.25%	0.14%

interface with a total number of 1192 filled questionnaires (Shah et al. 2016). After a validation procedure, the remaining 1022 buildings (11–15% of the buildings in a district) were evaluated and scores were assigned based on FEMA 155. The primary findings (Table 26.1) show that the typical structure of the buildings was a column beam system with infill walls. The proportion of this type of building was even higher in the recently built area of Al-Salamah District (Shah et al. 2016).

26.5   The Database

The survey data were entered into an Excel spreadsheet. For some complex decisions, a series of evaluation functions were programmed in Visual Basic for Applications (VBA), which resides within the Excel software. These functions could read a building record, decide the basic hazard score, then read additional information to determine score modifiers. The only general requirement was that the building records remained consistent in their description of the various features of the building. A similar set of VBA routines was developed for evaluating hazards in Gyor, Hungary (Kegyes-Brassai 2014), and more detailed information about the routines can be found there. Using the programmed functions also made it easier to detect data entry errors and to examine possible scenarios where soil types or building performance can be modified.

26.6   The Results

Classification of the buildings was the first step to perform in the analysis considering the vertical structure of the building and the material of this structure. Most structures were classified as concrete moment-resisting frames with infill walls (Table 26.2).

The basic structural score was determined for each building based on the visual inspection considering the structural system and the moderate seismicity of the region (Table 26.3).

Additional modifiers were applied to account for the proximity of neighboring buildings, construction practices, the building code used for the design, and plan/profile irregularities:

1. Vertical irregularity modifier was determined based on mass compactness or irregularity and the relation to adjacent buildings in the case of the older city part. There are strict rules according to new codes for the distance between the adjacent buildings from 1.8 to 2 m. However, in the Al-Balad area, the buildings are built closely having separate infill walls with a few centimeters of dilatation.
2. Construction code modifier was used in case of buildings built before 1983 with a pre-code modifier, and a post-code modifier was taken into account for buildings constructed after 2007 according to the new code. The Saudi Building Code was enacted in 2007.
3. Mid-rise modifier was determined for buildings having more than four stories.
4. Soil score modifier was evaluated based on interviews with a soil testing company (Al Jazar Consultant Office). According to their finding (Table 26.4), the typical soil is a mix of coral in the top level of the soil and *sabkhas* in most of the areas in Al-Salamah District. Mud soil is usually in Al-Balad District.

Soil type D was assumed for this analysis based on information from soil testing companies and publications concerning the soil analysis of the area.

Based on BSH scores and score modifiers, a final structural score can be obtained. A final score greater than or equal to 2.0 would indicate that no further seismic

Table 26.2 Number of examined buildings concerning structural class

Analyzed buildings	Al-Balad	Al-Salamah
W1 (wood frame)	1	–
S3 (light metal buildings)	1	2
S5 (steel frame with infill walls)	–	5
C1 (concrete moment-resistant frame)	37	19
C2 (concrete shear walls)	9	6
C3 (concrete frame with infill walls)	176	676
RM1 (reinforced masonry)	46	2
URM (unreinforced masonry)	38	4
Total	**308**	**714**

Table 26.3 Typical BSH scores and examined buildings

BSH of analyzed buildings	Al-Balad	Al-Salamah
3,00	37	19
3,20	176	676
3,40	38	4
3,60	55	13
3,80	1	2
5,20	1	0
Total	**308**	**714**

Table 26.4 Soil analysis in Al-Salamah

Depth [m]	Soil type
1	Sand silt with mud and brownstone – medium density
2	
3	Coral crumbly has been extracted gravel or sand graded light grey to white – very incoherent to medium density
4	
5	
6	
7	
8	
9	Soft sand to an average roughness with brown silt – medium density
10	

Al-Mhaidib (2002)

evaluation is needed. Scores lower than 2.0 indicate that additional evaluation is warranted.

A bar chart of scores for Al-Balad and Al-Salamah are shown in Figs. 26.1 and 26.2. In Al-Balad, most of the 300 structures evaluated fall well below the 2.0 level, with some reaching a negative score. The distribution shown in Fig. 26.1 is typical when there are only a few varieties of buildings examined. This means that there is a limited combination of features and scores to be counted, and so there are four clusters of scores: the lowest around -0.7, the next 0.4, a third around 1.1, and finally a few buildings at 2.3. Negative scores would indicate unreinforced masonry construction of multiple stories with a "soft" ground floor, irregular plan or profile, and perhaps neighboring buildings directly attached to it.

In the newer Al-Salamah District, the buildings are generally reinforced concrete with masonry infill, built according to more recent codes, with a higher quality of construction. Most of the buildings pass the 2.0 score threshold. Since more than 700 buildings were examined in this district, the bar chart is somewhat misleading; there are still a significant number of structures below the 2.0 threshold.

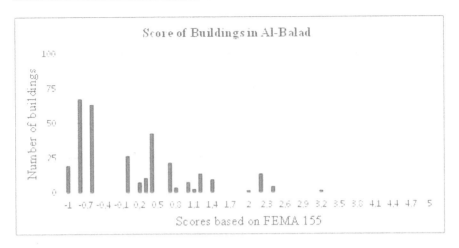

Fig. 26.1 Scores of buildings in Al-Balad District

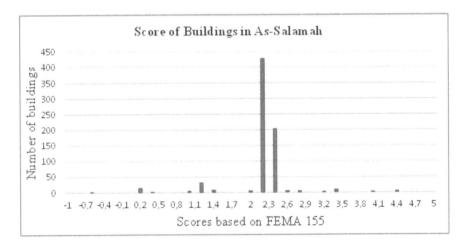

Fig. 26.2 Scores of buildings in Al-Salamah District

26.7   Comparison of Results

Figure 26.3 illustrates the influence of time of construction as well as the type of building. In Al-Balad District, most of the buildings are older, while in Al-Salamah District, a much higher percentage is newer construction. The impact is perhaps due to the changes to Saudi Arabian building codes in the 1980s and 1990s. The same trend can be found in many cities. Note that the tops of the two highest bars were shortened to fit the graph more easily. Thus, the applied REM could access the vulnerability of residential buildings in the study area and brought results for the relevant actors for further action.

Fig. 26.3 Final Structural Score distribution of evaluated buildings

26.8   Conclusions and Further Research

Seismic risk is a public safety issue that requires appropriate risk management measures and intends to protect citizens, properties, and infrastructure. A seismic risk analysis aims to estimate the consequences of seismic events in an investigated area on a regional or state level. The evaluation demonstrates the relative ease and low cost of the REM system. Districts, or even city blocks, can be delineated on the basis of how much seismic rehabilitation will be needed. However, since most of the scoring is based on experience in the US and other countries, a more rigorous evaluation of structural performance under seismic loads would be helpful. Calibrating the scoring system to a specific building stock will create more confidence in the evaluation system.

The results of the investigation so far show the influence of age on expected seismic performance, the different levels of vulnerability, and the areas where intervention is needed. This is due mainly to the evolution of building codes, building material quality, and construction methods. Modern designs tend to be more regular in form as well. The presented case study is offering the steps that should be performed to determine the seismic risk of a city rather than being a finalized risk assessment for the city of Jeddah. This study offers the method that can be applied for further analysis of the city but stressing the clear differences of vulnerabilities for residential buildings constructed based on different seismic codes. Further research will be directed toward other districts in the city, as well as performing more rigorous analyses (pushover, dynamic response) on selected typical building types. Additional work on determining the impact of soft, *sabkhas* soils on the response of short, medium, and tall buildings is also necessary.

Lessons Learned

1. Earthquake hazard mitigation research is focused on evaluating potential building damage scenarios from different magnitude events.
2. Mitigation methods facilitate prevention by gathering information about building condition and expected damages, and therefore the most vulnerable buildings can be strengthened to mitigate risk.
3. If many buildings are too irregular and have a wide variety of material properties, comprehensive structural analysis and evaluation would be time-consuming and expensive.
4. Alternative mitigation methods could be applied to provide a reasonable compromise of time, cost, and efficiency.
5. The visual screening method is a low-cost or cost-effective method, which is based on the inspection of structural systems, time and mode of construction, and materials used. As a preseismic assessment tool, score assignments from REM may be applied to evaluate the relative vulnerability of structures in a neighborhood.

Reflection Questions

1. What is the focus of earthquake mitigation research for potential residential buildings?
2. What are the alternative mitigation methods that could be applied for residential buildings to provide reasonable time, cost, and efficiency?
3. What methodology could be applied to assess the seismic vulnerability of residential buildings in an easy and low-cost way?
4. What could be done for seismic vulnerable residential buildings by applying REM?
5. What could be the easiest application of vulnerability assessment method for residential buildings?

References

Al-Mhaidib, A. I. (2002). Sabkha soil in the Kingdom of Saudi Arabia: Characteristics and treatment. *King Abdulaziz Journal: Engineering Science, 14*, 29–80.

Benedetti, D., & Pezzoli, P. (1996). *Shaking table tests on masonry buildings, results and comments: Experimental evaluation of technical interventions to reduce the seismic vulnerability of masonry buildings.* Bergamo: IMSES.

Calvi, G. M., Pinho, R., Magenes, G., Bommer, J. J., Restrepo-Vélez, L. F., & Crowley, H. (2006). Development of seismic vulnerability assessment methodologies over the past 30 years. *ISET Journal of Earthquake Technology, 43*, 75–104.

Castano, J. C., & Zamarbide, J. L. (1992). A seismic risk reduction program for Mendoza City, Argentina. In *Tenth world conference on earthquake engineering.* Madrid: International Association for Earthquake Engineering.

Fäh, D., Kind, F., Lang, K., & Giardini, D. (2001). Earthquake scenarios for the city of Basel. *Soil Dynamics and Earthquake Engineering, 21*, 405–413.

FEMA. (2002). *155 SECOND EDITION rapid visual screening of buildings for potential seismic hazards: Supporting documentation.* Washington, DC: Federal Emergency Management Agency.

Fukuyama, H., Tumialan, G., & Matsuzaki, Y. (2001). Outline of the Japanese guidelines for seismic retrofitting of RC buildings using FRP materials. In *Non-metallic reinforcement for Concrete Structures – FRPRCS-5.* Cambridge, UK.

Grünthal, G. (Ed.). (1998). *European Macroseismic Scale.* Luxembourg: European Seismological Commission.

Haddar, F. N. (1992). Urban seismic vulnerability analysis: The case of Algeria. In *Proceedings of the Tenth World Conference on Earthquake Engineering.* Madrid: IAEE.

Kegyes-Brassai, O. K. (2014). *Earthquake hazard analysis and building vulnerability assessment to determine the seismic risk of existing buildings in an urban area.* PhD dissertation, Szechenyi I. University, Gyor. http://mmtdi.sze.hu/kegyes-brassai-orsolya

Mouroux, P., Bertrand, E., Bour, M., Le Brun, B., Depinois, S., & Masure, P. (2004). The European RISK-UE project: An advanced approach to earthquakes risk scenarios. In *13th WCEE,* Vancouver.

NIBS. (1999). *Earthquake loss estimation methodology technical manual* (HAZUS99 Service Release 2 (SR2)). Washington, DC: National Institute of Building Sciences for the Federal Emergency Management Agency.

Shah, M. F., Ahmed, A., Al-Ghamadi, A., Kegyes-Brassai, O. K., & Ray, R. P. (2016). Rapid visual screening method to determine seismic vulnerability in Jeddah City, SA: 1 Methodology background. In *New technologies for urban safety of mega cities in Asia,* Tacloban, The Philippines.

Shah, M. F., Kegyes-Brassai, O. K., Ray, R. P., Ahmed, A., & Al-Ghamadi, A. (2018). Vulnerability assessment of residential buildings in Jeddah: A methodological proposal. *International Journal of GEOMATE, 14*(44), 134–141.

Part XI

Spirituality and Management

The Influence of Buddhist Philosophy on Sustainability Reporting in Sri Lanka

Prabanga Thoradeniya

27.1 Introduction

This study explores the influence of Buddhist philosophy on sustainability reporting[1] (SR) of Sri Lankan companies.

Sri Lanka is classified as a developing country in the South Asian region. It has also been known as the 'Pearl of the Indian Ocean' from ancient times. With the conclusion of a 30-year war in 2009, the country is now accelerating in rapid economic growth. It is a multi-religious country, but the majority are Buddhist (70.1% of its population of 21.67 million), following the Buddhist philosophy (CBSL 2019). Sri Lankan society has been shaped by the teachings of Buddhist philosophy (Ven. Sumangala 1952; Ven. Rahula 1959; Wijesekera 1990), which closely linked to the idea of sustainability practices leading to SR.

The concept of SR is evolving, and the literature shows an increasing trend of SR in Sri Lanka. However, the level and quality of SR in Sri Lanka is still in its infancy compared to developed countries (ACCA 2005; Abeydeera et al. 2016; Senaratne 2009; Senaratne and Liyanagedara 2009). There is only a nominal understanding as to whether the Buddhist philosophy that concerns itself with the society and the environment has an influence on companies' SR. Thoradeniya et al. (2015) argue that Sri Lankan non-listed company managers' Buddhist religious background influences their beliefs, shaping their intention to engage in SR, but this was not

---

[1] 'Sustainability report is a report published by a company or organization about the economic, environmental and social impacts caused by its everyday activities. Sustainability reporting can be considered as synonymous with other terms for non-financial reporting; triple bottom line reporting, corporate social responsibility reporting, and more' (GRI 2020, p. 1).

P. Thoradeniya (✉)
Department of Accounting, Monash Business School, Monash University, Clayton, Australia
e-mail: prabanga.thoradeniya@monash.edu

© The Author(s), under exclusive license to Springer Nature Switzerland AG 2021
S. Dhiman, R. Samaratunge (eds.), *New Horizons in Management, Leadership and Sustainability*, Future of Business and Finance,
https://doi.org/10.1007/978-3-030-62171-1_27

observed for the listed companies. Abeydeera et al. (2016) have found only minimal evidence of Buddhist values influencing SR. Given the mixed results of Thoradeniya et al.'s (2015) study, which used a quantitative research approach through a survey, and Abeydeera et al.'s (2016), who content analysed only 16 sustainability reports, the intention of this study is to further explore broader managerial views and insights on the influence of Buddhist philosophy on SR through semi-structured interviews to address the gap in literature. Hence, the following research question was formulated for this exploratory study: does Buddhist philosophy influence SR by Sri Lankan companies? Given that Sri Lanka's national and cultural orientation is heavily influenced by the effect of Buddhist philosophy, Sri Lanka provides a rich research context to explore the influence of Buddhist philosophy on SR.

The findings indicate that Sri Lankan society has been practising corporate social responsibility (CSR) and sustainability for centuries, long before the advent of the concepts of CSR and sustainability in the Western world. It was also found that listed and non-listed company managers' beliefs, thinking patterns and mindset are influenced by Buddhist philosophy from their childhood, and they translate these values into corporate values by undertaking sustainability activities and SR. In contrast, managers from a large conglomerate and a subsidiary of a multinational company (MNC) indicated that Buddhist philosophy had no influence on SR, showing that local values may not be appreciated by such companies.

This study contributes to the limited SR literature from a developing country perspective by studying an under-researched area of the influence of Buddhist philosophy on SR.

The remainder of this chapter is organised as follows. Section 27.2 provides a literature review. Section 27.3 outlines the research method. Section 27.4 presents findings, discussed in Sect. 27.5. The concluding remarks are presented in Sect. 27.6.

27.2 Literature Review

Literature on the role of Buddhism in environmental preservation, how Buddhism is linked to ancient literature and the cultural perspectives of Sri Lanka and the nature of SR practices in Sri Lanka are discussed and reviewed here.

27.2.1 The Role of Buddhism in Environmental Preservation

As a predominantly Buddhist country, Sri Lanka's appreciation of the environment and the inculcation of sound environmental values have been promoted from ancient times due to Buddhist teachings. Its culture is fashioned and influenced by Buddhist teachings of Lord Buddha from the time Buddhism was introduced to Sri Lanka, more than 2600 years ago. Teachings of Lord Buddha are 'the actual words used by the Buddha as they are to be found in the original Pali texts of the "Tripitaka", universally accepted by scholars as the earliest extant records of the teachings of the Buddha. It has come down to us through oral tradition' (Ven. Rahula 1959, p. 11).

Amongst the well-known essentials and fundamental teachings of Lord Buddha are doctrines of the Four Noble Truths and the Nobel Eightfold Path. Theravada and Mahayana are the two main forms of Buddhism practised globally. 'Theravada, which is regarded as the original orthodox Buddhism, is practiced in Sri Lanka' (Ven. Rahula 1959, p. 12). Hence Sri Lankan culture is imbued by Theravada Buddhism: Sri Lankan Buddhists have preserved Theravada Buddhism in its purest form (Wijesekera 1990).

'Among the world religions Buddhism has great promise as a basis for an environmental ethic, because it teaches a concern for the other animals and nature as well as our fellow humans' (Gunn 1998, p. 13). De Silva (1998) has attempted a Buddhist diagnosis of the human domination of nature, constructing a Buddhist orientation towards the non-human world. He explored an ethic of sustainability in green economics and Buddhist economics. He also pointed out that the self and the transformation of nature go together. 'Buddhism reiterates that other than homo sapiens our planet is inhabited by a countless number of living beings of different forms, shapes and sizes. It emphasises the intrinsic value and contribution of our planet and animal life in the preservation of ecological integrity and biodiversity. Further, it highlights the interrelationships and interdependencies between and among different ecosystems in maintaining the natural equilibrium so essential for environmentally sound and sustainable development' (Wijayadasa 2007, p. 4).

Mihintale, the place where Buddhism was officially introduced to Sri Lanka, is the world's first declared sanctuary, dating back to the third century BCE. The Mahameuna Uyana, Nandana Uyana and Ranmasu Uyana ('Uyana' means park or garden) at Anuradhapura (the first Kingdom of Sri Lanka) were declared as royal parks by King Devanampiya Tissa (247–207 BCE) (Ven. Sumangala 1952).

27.2.2 How Buddhism is Linked to the Ancient Literature and Cultural Perspectives of Sri Lanka

Sri Lanka has a written literature that dates back to several centuries. Writing was known to Sri Lanka from ancient days of her Aryan colonization, and it soon spread with the establishment of Buddhism in the country (Godakumbura 1996).

Sri Lanka's religious and literary mythology, legends and folklore provide a large number of examples of social and environmental concerns (Swan 1987). In ancient times, writers of both prose and verse included descriptions of nature and many elements of the environment in their literary works. Thus, forests, rivers, mountains, the dawn of the day, sunset and nightfall were treated artistically in describing the beauty of nature. The best example for such a work is 'Pansiya Panas Jataka Potha' or 'Jataka Tales' (stories of Lord Buddha's previous births) (Godakumbura 1996).

Sri Lanka boasts of an ancient literature eulogizing sacred trees. The sacred 'Jaya Siri Maha Bodhi' in Anuradhapura is accepted as the oldest surviving angiosperm and human-planted tree in the world. It was brought to Sri Lanka by Theri Sangamitta, daughter of Emperor Asoka of India, and was planted in the Mahameuna

Gardens in Anuradhapura in 249 BCE by King Devanampiya Tissa. It is said to be the southern branch of the 'Jaya Siri Maha Bodhi' at Buddha Gaya in India under which Lord Buddha attained enlightenment. Sri Lanka is the home of this sacred Bo Tree, revered by Buddhists the world over and admired by naturalists as the world's oldest tree with a recorded planting date. 'Mahavamsa', an ancient chronicle in Sri Lanka written in the fifth century CE, describes in two chapters how the Bo sapling was brought to Sri Lanka from India and planted in the Gardens (Ven. Sumangala 1952).

The following aspects may have been embedded in Sri Lankan culture due in part to Buddhist teachings: personal development; personal effort and intelligence; recognition of human endeavour and human intelligence; individual responsibility; avoidance of ignorance and false views; liberation from doubt and ways of resolving or dispelling doubt; tolerance and understanding; idea generation from seeing, knowing and understanding things; not becoming attached to one view; avoiding extremes; giving vision and knowledge; leading to calm; insight and enlightenment; collectivism; selflessness; development of the community; willingness to listen and right speech; universal love; compassion; rejoicing in others' success; equanimity; and recognition of the impermanence of things (Ven. Rahula 1959; Wijesekera 1990).

Buddhism is a philosophy reflecting all aspects of human behaviour. Sri Lankan society and culture are also influenced by the Buddhist teaching of 'kamma'. 'Kamma' means action (meritorious and demeritorious volition) that constitutes both good and evil. The law of 'kamma' denotes that 'good begets good. Evil begets evil. Like attracts like' (Ven. Naraka 2010, p. 43). 'Kamma' and rebirth are interrelated and fundamental doctrines in Buddhist philosophy (Ven. Narada 1988). According to Buddhist teachings, 'kamma' is not the only reason that influences life. Effort and courage should be given priority for a successful life.

Sri Lankan culture is designated as collectivist, oriented to high-power distance and security, and is deemed to be concerned with spiritual and family values (Weathersby 1993). Thus, when comparing similar traits with Western countries, Sri Lanka sits virtually at the opposite end of the work-related values that are hallmarks of developed Western cultures – individualism, moderate power distance and risk taking, achievement and materialism. Sri Lanka's national and work culture is therefore more attuned towards a concept of social empathy. The significance of this research is paramount in laying the foundation for the exploration of the influence of Buddhist philosophy on SR in a scenario where social responsibility is part and parcel of a nation's way of life.

27.2.3 SR in Sri Lanka

In Sri Lanka, as in many countries, separate sections on environment and sustainability are included in the annual reports of companies. Stand-alone corporate social disclosure reports, sustainability reports, corporate videos, newsletters, company brochures and other site reports reveal the embryonic stage of SR. However, there is no legal requirement for environmental, social and SR in annual reports or stand-alone reports in Sri Lanka. This kind of reporting is purely voluntary for Sri Lankan companies. The use of the Global Reporting Initiative's (GRI's) guidelines in SR is becoming popular in Sri Lanka (SheConsults and Emagewise 2015; Abeydeera et al. 2016). In November 2003, the Association of Chartered Certified Accountants (ACCA-Sri Lanka) launched the first environmental, social and SR awards in Sri Lanka, which provided an impetus to popularising the concept of SR in the country (ACCA 2005).

ACCA (2005) surveyed environmental and social disclosures in annual reports, targeted 100 Sri Lankan companies and found a very low level of environmental or social disclosure. Jariya (2015) found that companies disclose environmental information in their annual reports, and the level of disclosure varies across industries. However, Akram and Thilakarathne (2016) reported that society-related information is largely disclosed, noting that there is a lack of SR. Similarly, Dissanayake et al. (2016) reported that companies disclose more social indicators than environmental indicators.

Senaratne and Liyanagedara (2009) noted that companies do not consider GRI guidelines in SR: a few companies have included some form of disclosure related to environmental and social impact. It was argued that Sri Lankan companies are at a nascent stage in respect of SR. Possible attributable factors are lack of awareness of SR and awareness of the benefits of SR by key persons involved in the preparation of annual and sustainability reports. The accounting profession has a role to play in creating awareness in companies about the importance and benefits of SR. SheConsults and Emagewise (2015) noted that the chief executive officer and the board should lead the processes to encourage a change in the culture, creating greater awareness of SR. Reward and recognition programmes by way of award programmes provide an impetus for growth in SR. Beddewela and Herzig (2013) report that subsidiaries of MNCs are unable to publish a separate social report to achieve accountability to their local stakeholders.

Thoradeniya et al. (2015), in a study focussing on the behavioural perspective of Sri Lankan managers, found that managers' psychological factors influenced their intention to engage in SR. However, whilst managers exhibited the intention to engage in SR, their intentions by and large did not translate into actual SR. A more recent study by Thoradeniya, Lee, Tan and Ferreira (2019) found that organisational factors facilitate or inhibit SR in Sri Lankan companies more than individual and institutional factors do in both war and post-war periods in Sri Lanka.

Recent studies (SheConsults and Emagewise 2015; Abeydeera et al. 2016; Dissanayake et al. 2016, 2019) show that the use of GRI guidelines is becoming popular in SR of Sri Lankan companies. Dissanayake et al. (2019) argue that companies have paid greater attention to GRI guidelines and global practices after the war in the re-development stage in order to attract foreign investment, initiate new activities, enter new markets and negotiate contracts. SheConsults and Emagewise (2015), Abeydeera et al. (2016) and Dissanayake et al. (2016) also found that more companies are using GRI guidelines. In 2015, 59 public listed companies (30%) prepared their annual report using either the G3.1 or G4 guidelines. A few non-listed companies are also using GRI guidelines for SR (SheConsults and Emagewise 2015). Alawattage and Fernando (2017) argue that corporate philanthropy is used to satisfy the demands of global reporting protocols.

Thoradeniya et al. (2015) found that Sri Lankan non-listed company managers' Buddhist religious background influences their intention to engage in SR, but Abeydeera et al. (2016) found only a little evidence of Buddhist values influencing SR.

The current SR literature on Sri Lanka is mainly focused on disclosure types and motivational factors influencing SR, paying less attention to how Buddhist philosophy may influence such reporting practices, except for Thoradeniya et al. (2015) and Abeydeera et al. (2016), which exhibited mixed results, yet in a country that is heavily influenced by Buddhist philosophy. This study addresses this gap in the literature.

27.3   Research Method

Qualitative research approach was pursued to explore whether there is any influence of Buddhist philosophy on SR. Data collected through semi-structured interviews are useful to gain insights into managers' views (Kvale 1996). The qualitative nature of the research method allows for a broader discussion on motivations for SR in relation to personal value systems and beliefs.

Thirteen interviews were conducted with top- and middle-level managers of four listed and nine non-listed companies across different industry sectors in Sri Lanka. This included managers from a large conglomerate, one of the subsidiaries of this conglomerate and a subsidiary of an MNC. Managers from a cross-section of managerial roles were interviewed to obtain a representative view. As a first step, potential interviewees were contacted via telephone and email with a request to take part in the interviews. The interviews were conducted at company premises. The interview protocol guided the interviews. The recruitment of new interviewees was stopped when similar insights were expressed by a number of interviewees. Interviews lasted an average of 30 min. All interviews were transcribed and manually analysed by the researcher. Table 27.1 represents the interviewees' profile.

27.4   Findings

Interviewees from listed and non-listed companies explained how Buddhist philosophy is related to the concept of CSR and sustainability, elaborating how well Buddhist teachings and festivals of CSR nature were deep-rooted in Sri Lankan culture, society and companies well before the concept of CSR was introduced in the Western world. Manager E from a listed company said:

Table 27.1 Interviewee profile

Interviewee	Company type	Industry	Title/Position
A	Listed (Conglomerate)	Diversified Holding	Head, Sustainability, Enterprise Risk Management
B	Non-listed (Subsidiary of a MNC)	Fast Moving Consumer Goods	Manager, Sustainable Business & Communications
C	Listed (Subsidiary of a Conglomerate)	Insurance	General Manager, Finance & Planning
D	Listed	Bank	Chief Marketing Officer
E	Listed	Bank	Deputy General Manager, Marketing
F	Non-listed	Trading Company (Spice Exporter)	Export Director
G	Non-listed	Pharmaceutical Company	Managing Director
H	Non-listed	Authorised Tile and Bath Ware Distributor	Director
I	Non-listed	Nutraceutical Company	Chief Executive Officer & Managing Partner
J	Non-listed	Advertising	Managing Director (joint)
K	Non-listed	ICT Company	Managing Director/Chief Executive Officer
L	Non-listed	Trading Company (Pharmaceutical Products)	Chief Executive Officer
M	Non-listed	Knowledge Process Outsourcing (KPO)	Vice President

I think CSR has a very strong relationship with Buddhism and sustainability too, because Buddhism is a philosophy that talks about sustainability, social aspects, environmental aspects. That is very close to Buddhism. I think if you take Sri Lanka, CSR was practised even before the discipline of CSR came in. During our Buddhist festivals such as 'Vesak', people are given free food throughout the day. In such a context CSR has been in our DNA and systems way before the discipline of CSR evolved in the world. The charitable causes of Sri Lankan organizations may have existed for a long time. So, there is a direct influence of sustainability from Buddhism.

Managers from non-listed companies also held the same views regarding how CSR and sustainability were practised in Sri Lankan society and companies from ancient times. Interviewee G from a non-listed company said:

CSR is a western term. But in Sri Lanka we have been using this from ancient times. We have 'dansals', almsgiving and everything is in our culture. Mainly we are doing CSR because of our Buddhist teachings and Sri Lankan culture. Everybody thinks we have to do something to the society. We will continue to do this for our next generation.

Interviewee I from a non-listed company further elaborated on how CSR and sustainability were practised in Sri Lankan companies well before CSR became a corporate 'fad' globally and how CSR and sustainability activities were linked to businesses and SR:

> Religion and culture have a direct influence because it's pretty much who we are as opposed to something that we need to do. I think sustainability and CSR are probably something that we have been doing for many centuries before it became one of these corporate fads really. It's been something that we've being doing as a community. I mean as a whole our entire culture, Sri Lankans have practising over 2500 years of Buddhism in Sri Lanka, so it's nothing new to us. It's probably now that we label it sustainability and CSR that it has become fashionable the world over in a sense. Say it's something we have being doing and it's nothing new and the fact that now we are transposing what we do as individuals into our corporate life is probably again nothing new. As corporates in Sri Lanka have done it for many years, but we are just labelling it and bring it to business perspectives now in terms of probably reporting it.

Three of the interviewees representing two separate listed companies (a large conglomerate and its subsidiary and a non-listed company subsidiary of an MNC) explained that Buddhist philosophy has a direct influence on SR. Some observations were as follows:

> Definitely, there is a direct influence from Buddhist teachings on SR (Interviewee J).

> Buddhism and culture go together. The thought of giving is there. In Buddhism it says you get what you give. That affects the people a lot. Buddhism plays a big part. The Buddhist impact on SR is very direct (Interviewee K).

> Yes, definitely, a lot of empathy is there, employees have leant them from their Buddhist cultural background to help less fortunate. I think Buddhist culture influences on SR is more or less direct (Interviewee M).

The remaining managers from listed companies acknowledged how the influence of Buddhist teachings of social empathy influence managers' feelings and actions resulting in SR. Manager D reflected:

> Yes, Buddhist culture and teaching are hugely influencing. That is because they are getting that sensitivity from the cultural and religious background. They emotionally feel the obligation to help the less fortunate and improve certain things mostly because of the religious things and that background.

Manager D further elaborated how Buddhist values and teachings of good and bad 'kamma' (actions) influence the managers' and employees' beliefs, thinking pattern and mindset to undertake SR:

> It's not that people are deeply religious but that spirit and the value system has been instilled in them by that religious and cultural situations and backgrounds. Those values shape their thinking and mindset. They believe when you do something good, in addition to the immediate improvements in that particular area, there could be after effects in terms of 'kamma' or that sort of belief is there and have a direct influence from the religious background on SR.

Manager E from a listed company went further in reflecting on the influence of Buddhist teaching of 'kamma' and how it shaped managerial beliefs, thinking patterns and mindset towards undertaking sustainability activities leading to SR:

Being a Buddhist, I believe that, as Buddhism teaches, if I may sum it up, doing good work, good 'kamma', I think it has an influence. Buddhism is about doing good to the society, the individual must do good, and it also talks about certain qualities like giving and concern for the environment. Maybe an individual's religious beliefs and religious qualities of top management would have influenced their mindset. Buddhism being the biggest religion in the country, there is a positive influence on the people of the country. But mostly the individual managerial thinking and background may be influenced by Buddhism.

Managers from non-listed companies also further elaborated that top management's beliefs and mindset are influenced by Buddhist teachings. As Interviewee F said:

I think that our religion teaches us that to do whatever possible we should do to people in less advantaged positions and that would shape our mindsets. Religion has a direct influence. Top management will have a cultural and religious influence.

In Buddhist philosophy, rebirth is interrelated to 'kamma'. The belief of rebirth, too, influences the top management mindset to undertake sustainability activities and SR. Interviewee G, from a non-listed company, further explained how Buddhist teachings influence the mindset of managers from childhood and how top managers spread that message throughout the organization and also to the next generation:

According to our religion we believe that we have another life after. The Buddhist teaching has an impact. Stemming from Buddhist culture, from our childhood we were taught to do good things. This is a factor which brought us to this level, to do something from our organization. If top management is thinking that way, that message is going through the organization. We got the good habits through our religion. It is a direct influence for us to make our mindset. Our society believes that we have to do good things. From doing that we are teaching our children as well.

Interviewee H from a non-listed company confirmed this:

We are coming from Buddhist culture. Buddhist teaching has a direct impact on our mindsets.

Interviewee I, who is part of the top management team of a non-listed company, explained how top managers' beliefs and mindset influenced by Buddhist teachings translate into corporate values and beliefs to engage in SR:

My beliefs as a person are congruent or they get passed on to the corporate beliefs and corporate values. I do think so, because I am Buddhist, and I think as a culture in Sri Lanka, people are a lot more giving, and they have that openness to give and openness to help. So, Buddhism and our religious beliefs influence us very much in terms of undertaking CSR activities. Because, I think in Buddhism, there is this concern for the wellbeing of everyone else aside from yourself. Its representative in its own culture and our traditional way of living. So pretty much, I think in Sri Lanka when you look at CSR, how we go about doing CSR, I am not talking about only our organization but other organizations as well, is that when they see that there is a need, people always somehow come together and assist. I think it is part and partial to our way of life. So, I believe that would sort of transfer to CSR initiatives and SR in companies.

Interestingly, not only the top managers but also young employees were keen to practise Buddhist teachings in the organizational setting. The practice stems without conscious effort from perpetuating sustainability practices and SR within the organization. As verbalised by Interviewee L from a non-listed company:

> Buddhist culture has a very positive impact on sustainability. Simply speaking, Buddhism talks about impermanence, helping each other and respecting each other. There has been a very positive influence from the Buddhist culture. Even very young employees are very particular about this philosophy. When they start practising it without their knowledge certain critical aspects of sustainability have been met (Interviewee L).

In contrast, a manager from a listed company representing a large conglomerate of the country expressed his negative views about the influence of Buddhist teachings on SR:

> No. Not for a business. I don't think that. This is my personal opinion, I don't think that culture enables either (Interviewee A).

Interviewee C from a listed company that is one of the subsidiaries of the large conglomerate also did not see the connection, opting instead to stress the need to balance sustainability and financial interests:

> I don't see any direct link there. As a corporate there are so many stakeholders, the basic existence of the corporate is to provide returns to the shareholders. Sustainability has a long-term impact to the business to sustainably grow. Organizations are not charitable organizations. So, in that sense, I don't know whether it has a cultural influence.

A manager from a non-listed company that is a subsidiary of an MNC was unable to comment on it:

> I really don't know. I don't see that within this company (Interviewee B).

However, this manager expressed that Sri Lankan companies have a philanthropical and charitable culture that is influenced by Buddhist teachings.

The findings highlight that Buddhist teachings influence managerial beliefs and the mindset of listed and non-listed company managers in Sri Lanka. However, the value system in a large conglomerate, its subsidiary and a subsidiary of an MNC seemed unaffected by Buddhist philosophy. Managers in these organisations did not appreciate or correlate the sustainability practice or SR to Buddhist philosophy. This may be attributable to the fact that the managerial beliefs and values of these companies have been shaped by other factors outside of Buddhist teachings, which translate into corporate values to engage in SR.

27.5   Discussion

The prominent Buddhist philosophy in Sri Lanka (Swan 1987; Ven. Sumangala 1952) is related to CSR and sustainability practices. Sri Lankan society has been practising CSR and sustainability from ancient times. Buddhist teachings play a positive role in influencing managers' beliefs and mindset towards engagement in SR. Thoradeniya et al. (2015) indicate that Buddhist beliefs and values influence non-listed company managers to engage in SR. This present study finds that managers of listed and non-listed companies (except a large conglomerate and a subsidiary of an MNC) articulated the nexus between Buddhist teachings, managers' beliefs and mindset and how those ultimately guide sustainability practices and SR. According to the theory of planned behaviour (Ajzen 1991), behavioural beliefs influence attitudes towards behaviour. Managers' beliefs and positive attitude towards sustainability initiatives and SR seem to stem from a combination of personal and social value systems inspired by Buddhist philosophy. Managers' beliefs and mindset to engage in SR are shaped by Buddhist teachings of 'kamma', rebirth and concern for the environment and society, which promotes achieving balance. Other studies find that religious beliefs influence managers' values and morals (Cialdini and Goldstein 2004; Conroy and Emerson 2004; Quazi 2003). Managers also highlighted how the Buddhist teachings influenced their mindset from their childhood and how the top managers spread that message throughout the organization in order to translate their values influenced by Buddhist philosophy into corporate values.

For a large conglomerate, one of its subsidiaries and a subsidiary of an MNC, Buddhist philosophy is not a strong factor influencing managers' beliefs, individual thinking and thus their decision towards SR. These types of companies may have other dominant factors shaping their SR practices. They may have different corporate cultures more exposed to the global business environment. They may also be appreciative of global SR frameworks such as GRI guidelines in SR, which are lacking in the consideration of local prominent factors, such as how religious and cultural factors influence SR. Subsidiaries of MNCs in Sri Lanka are unable to publish a separate social report for accountability to their local stakeholders (Beddewela and Herzig 2013). This may be another reason why local beliefs and values such as Buddhist teachings are not appreciated and not relevant in the context of SR of a subsidiary of an MNC.

27.6   Conclusion

This study explored the possible influence of Buddhist philosophy on SR of Sri Lankan companies through semi-structured interviews with managers. It found that, due to Buddhist philosophy, Sri Lankan society has been practising CSR and sustainability for centuries. The culture and value systems that pervade Sri Lankan society, stemming primarily from the pervasive influence of Buddhism and inherent social ethic, shape managers' beliefs and mindset from their childhood. Managers translate their values and beliefs inspired by Buddhism into corporate values, leading them to appreciate sustainability and engage in SR. The study also finds that managers of a large conglomerate, one of its subsidiaries and a subsidiary of an MNC may not appreciate the influence of Buddhist teachings in SR due in large to broader corporate ethics stemming from global influence.

The study contributes to the limited research on SR from a developing-country perspective by exploring an under-researched area on the influence of Buddhist philosophy on SR. It also contributes to the literature by showing that long-rooted local Buddhist teachings are not appreciated by a large conglomerate, one of its subsidiaries and a subsidiary of an MNC.

The study limitation is that only three managers were interviewed to represent a large conglomerate, a subsidiary and a subsidiary of an MNC. Therefore, results should be interpreted in context. The study opens an area for future research in the form of exploration of factors that influence SR in large conglomerates and subsidiaries of MNCs operating in Sri Lanka.

Five Chapter Takeaways/Lessons
1. Buddhist philosophy is deep-rooted in Sri Lankan culture and society.
2. Buddhist teachings are related to the concept of CSR and sustainability practice, with Sri Lankan companies engaging in CSR and sustainability well before these concepts were articulated and formalised amongst companies in the Western world.
3. Buddhist values and teachings of 'kamma', rebirth, concern for the environment and society etc. influence managers' and employees' beliefs and thinking patterns from their childhood.
4. Both listed and non-listed company managers' and employees' beliefs, thinking patterns and mindset are shaped by Buddhist teachings, and their personal values are translated into corporate values to undertake sustainability activities and SR.
5. Managers' values and beliefs in the setting of a large conglomerate, one of its subsidiaries and a subsidiary of an MNC may not have been influenced by Buddhist philosophy to engage in SR to as great an extent as that of local listed and non-listed company managers. These companies may be focussing more on GRI guidelines when engaging in SR (which do not consider the impact of local religious and cultural concerns) due to their global exposure and subsidiaries of MNCs not publishing a separate report to local stakeholders. As a result, they may give less consideration to local values and beliefs that are inspired by Buddhist philosophy when engaging in SR.

Five Reflection Questions
1. Is Sri Lankan society influenced by Buddhist teachings such as 'kamma', rebirth, concern for the environment and society etc.?
2. Did Sri Lankan companies start to practise the concepts of CSR and sustainability well before the Western companies?
3. Are listed and non-listed company managers' beliefs and values to undertake SR influenced by Buddhist teachings?

4. Does Buddhist teaching influence SR practices of a large conglomerate and a subsidiary of an MNC?
5. Do GRI guidelines consider local impact such as religious/Buddhist influence on SR, which is a critical factor for developing countries like Sri Lanka?

References

ACCA. (2005). *A survey of environmental and social disclosures in the annual reports of the top 100 Sri Lankan companies*. Colombo: ACCA.

Abeydeera, S., Tregida, H., & Kearins, K. (2016). Sustainability reporting – more global than local? *Meditari Accountancy Research, 24*, 478–504.

Ajzen, I. (1991). The theory of planned behavior. *Organizational Behavior and Human Decision Processes, 50*(2), 179–211.

Akram, R. M. W., & Thilakarathne, P. M. C. (2016). Corporate sustainability reporting practices of financial service sector institutions in Sri Lanka. In *Undergraduates Research Conference*, Department of Accountancy, Faculty of Commerce and Management Studies, University of Kelaniya, Sri Lanka.

Alawattage, C., & Fernando, S. (2017). Postcoloniality in corporate social and environmental accountability. *Accounting, Organizations and Society, 60*, 1–20.

Beddewela, E., & Herzig, C. (2013). Corporate social reporting by MNCs' subsidiaries in Sri Lanka. *Accounting Forum, 37*(2), 135–149.

CBSL (Central Bank of Sri Lanka). (2019). *Economic and social statistics of Sri Lanka*. Retrieved from https://www.cbsl.gov.lk/sites/default/files/cbslweb_documents/statistics/otherpub/ess_2019_e.pdf

Cialdini, R. B., & Goldstein, N. J. (2004). Social influence: Compliance and conformity. *Annual Review of Psychology, 55*, 591–621.

Conroy, S. J., & Emerson, T. L. (2004). Business ethics and religion: Religiosity as a predictor of ethical awareness among students. *Journal of Business Ethics, 50*(4), 383–396.

De Silva, P. (1998). *Environmental philosophy and ethics in Buddhism*. New York: St. Martin's Press.

Dissanayake, D., Tilt, C., & Xydias-Lobo, M. (2016). Sustainability reporting by publicly listed companies in Sri Lanka. *Journal of Cleaner Production, 129*, 169–182.

Dissanayake, D., Tilt, C., & Wei, Q. (2019). Factors influencing sustainability reporting by Sri Lankan companies. *Pacific Accounting Review, 31*(1), 84–109.

Godakumbura, C. E. (1996). *Sinhalese literature*. Battaramulla: Department of Cultural Affairs.

GRI. (2020). *Global reporting initiatives*. Retrieved from https://www.globalreporting.org/information/sustainability-reporting

Gunn, A. S. (1998). Foreword. In P. De Silva (Ed.), *Environmental philosophy and ethics in Buddhism*. New York: St. Martin's Press.

Jariya, A. M. I. (2015). Environmental disclosures in annual reports of Sri Lankan Corporate: A content analysis. *Journal of Emerging Trends in Economics and Management Sciences, 6*, 350–357.

Kvale, S. (1996). *Interviews: An introduction to qualitative research interviews*. Thousand Oaks: Sage.

Quazi, A. M. (2003). Ïdentifying the determinants of corporate managers perceived social obligations. *Management Decision, 41*(9), 822–831.

Senaratne, S. (2009). Corporate social responsibility reporting in Sri Lanka. *Sri Lanka Journal of Humanities and Social Sciences, 1*, 1.

Senaratne, S., & Liyanagedara, K. (2009). Corporate sustainability reporting in Sri Lanka. In *Proceedings of the Sixth International Conference on Business Management*, Faculty of Management Studies and Commerce, University of Sri Jayewardenepura, p. 6.

SheConsults & Emagewise. (2015). *Sustainability reporting in Sri Lanka: The big picture.* Retrieved from http://she-consults.com/insights/Sustainability-Reporting-in-Sri-Lanka.pdf

Swan, B. (1987). *Sri Lankan mosaic: Environment, man, continuity and change.* Colombo: Marga Institute, Sri Lanka Centre for Development Studies, Ranco Printers and Publishers Limited.

Thoradeniya, P., Lee, J., Tan, R., & Ferreira, A. (2015). Sustainability reporting and the theory of planned behaviour. *Accounting, Auditing & Accountability Journal, 28*(7), 1099–1137.

Thoradeniya, P., Lee, J., Tan, R., & Ferreira, A. (2019). From intention to action on sustainability reporting: The role of individual, organizational and institutional factors during war and post-war periods. In *16th International Conference on Business Management (ICBM).* Melbourne: Monash University.

Ven. Narada. (1988). *The Buddha and his teachings.* Kuala Lumpur: The Buddhist Missionary Society.

Ven. Narada. (2010). *Buddhism in a nutshell.* Kandy: Buddhist publication society Inc.

Ven. Rahula, W. (1959). *What the Buddha taught.* Bedford: The Gordon Fraser Gallery Limited.

Ven. Sumangala, S. B. (1952). *The Mahavamsa XXXIII.* 3rd ed. Colombo.

Weathersby, R. (1993). Sri Lankan managers' leadership conceptualizations as a function of ego development. In J. Demick & P. M. Miller (Eds.), *Development in the workplace* (pp. 67–89). Hillsdale: Lawrence Erlbaum Associates Inc.

Wijayadasa, K. H. J. (2007). Buddhism and sustainable development. *The Island.*

Wijesekera, N. D. (1990). *The Sinhalese.* Colombo: M. D. Gunasena and Co. Ltd..

Dr. Prabanga Thoradeniya is a Lecturer in Management Accounting in the Department of Accounting at the Monash Business School. Her research interests are in the areas of environmental management accounting and environmental, social and sustainability accounting and reporting.

Correction to: Exploring Motivation for Listed Companies and Measures Taken Towards Managing Environmental Collision: Evidence from Sri Lanka

I. M. Withanawasam, G. Wickremasinghe, and M. Naidoo

Correction to:
Chapter 10 in: S. Dhiman, R. Samaratunge (eds.),
New Horizons in Management, Leadership and Sustainability,
Future of Business and Finance,
https://doi.org/10.1007/978-3-030-62171-1_10

Owing to an oversight, in the affiliation of the author G. Wickremasinghe M. Naidoo, "Victoria University" is missing after "Victoria University Business School". The corrected affiliation should read as below:

G. Wickremasinghe · M. Naidoo
Victoria University Business School, Victoria University
Melbourne, Australia

The updated version of this chapter can be found at
https://doi.org/10.1007/978-3-030-62171-1_10

C1

Index

573

9 783030 621735